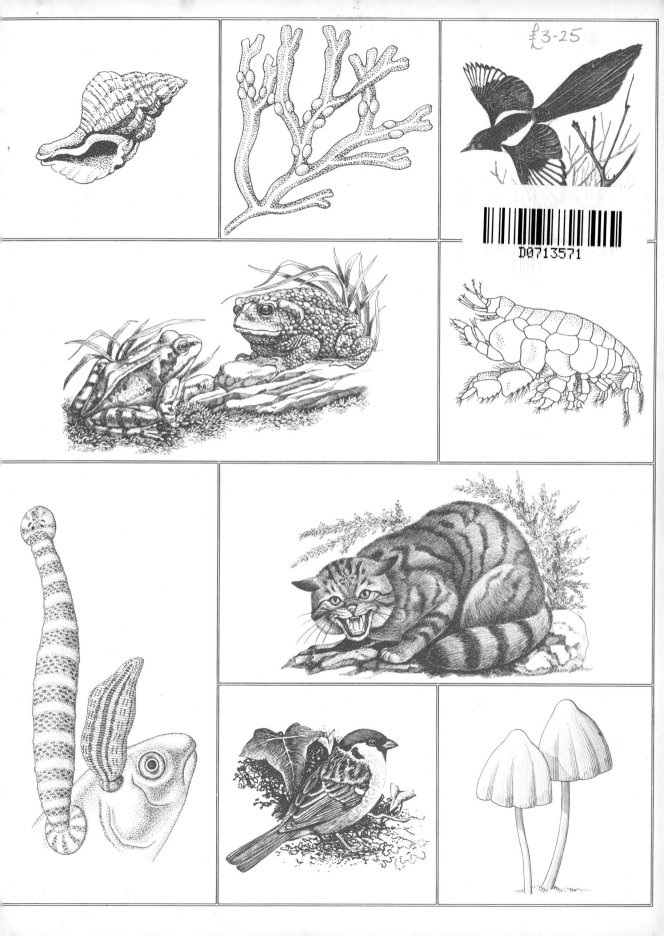

The Shell Natural History of Britain

The Shell Natural History of Britain

General Editor:
Maurice Burton DSc, FZS

Michael Joseph
in association with
Rainbird Reference Books

Designed and produced by
Rainbird Reference Books Ltd,
Marble Arch House
44 Edgware Road, London W2

7181 4033 8

Printed and bound by Jarrold & Sons Ltd, Norwich

Contents

List of colour plates

Introduction

From a natural history standpoint there is much to be said in favour of the British Isles. It is a point worth remembering in these days when expensive 'safaris' to distant continents are becoming fashionable. We can start with the ground on which we stand.

The continents are made up of layers of rock all of which have been named. The geological period during which these were laid down has been divided, if we exclude the vast era of the Pre-Cambrian, into thirteen periods. All except one are represented in Britain. Soil is formed from the breakdown of rocks, so there is a varied assortment of soils within the relatively small area represented by the British Isles. More immediately striking is it that four of the thirteen periods have names linked with British history. This may seem insignificant until we recall that only two of the other nine are named after places outside Britain, the rest having been given 'neutral' names such as Carboniferous for the coal-measures and Cretaceous for the chalk rocks.

The Permian Period is named after the province of Perm in the Ural Mountains and the Jurassic after the Jura Mountains on the border between France and Switzerland. Our four are the more romantic because they recall the history of our forbears. The oldest fossil-bearing rocks which take us back 600 million years belong to the Cambrian Period: the Roman name for Wales was Cambria. Slightly newer rocks, only 500 million years old, of the Ordovician Period, take their name from the Ordovices, a Celtic tribe that lived in part of Wales. The next in order, 400–440 million years old, the rocks of the Silurian Period, were first studied in another part of Wales where another Celtic tribe lived, the Silures.

So far the Principality has scooped that desirable return in modern international contests, a first, second and third in a row.

Even the fourth is not far removed. The Devonian Period, of 350–400 million years ago, is represented by rocks well developed in the name-county to the immediate south. The names are inevitably associated with that of William Smith, born in 1769 in the village of Churchill, in Oxfordshire, who quite literally put geology on the map. He has long been known as the Father of English Geology, which is unfair because he drew much of his inspiration and his information from Wales and also Scotland.

If there is any Father of international geology it should be the gifted Italian polymath Leonardo da Vinci (1452–1519), or possibly Martin Lister (1638–1711), house physician to Queen Anne. In any event, they were only among the first of a stream of able men who between them spelt out the meaning of the rocks. They included John Ray (1628–1705), a scholar of breadth and vision who all but anticipated the natural classification of living things in Linnaeus's *Systema Naturae* (1758).

It may be objected that so far this Introduction has been marred by the usual lamentable tinge of the insularity typical of our race. Yet the insularity of the British could be no more than an expression of our new-found freedom, for up to about 10,000 years ago these islands were part of Europe, physically joined to the Continent. The present-day wish to re-enter Europe is, therefore, only an attempt to turn the clock back economically to a time when physically the reverse took place, and with more profound effects.

Prior to that time there had been what is popularly called the 'Ice Age'. In fact there were four glacial and three inter-glacial periods during the million years before the final separation of the British Isles from the rest of Europe. During each glacial period, or ice age, the level of the sea was lowered and Britain joined the Continent. With each warming up – and the consequent melting of ice – the sea-level was raised again, even higher than it is today and our land was once more freed. The evidence for these changes consists of the raised beaches, the drowned valleys and the submerged forests, as well as the remains of moraines and scratchings on the rocks made by glaciers, a subject dealt with by Dr Rose in later pages.

Extremes of temperature of this magnitude could hardly fail to affect the plants and animals. It is usual to say of this that as the masses of ice moved south the animals retreated before it. Then, as the ice moved north again, during the inter-glacial period, the animals came back. After the last glacial period some species returned more quickly than others, and some started the return journey too late to cross the sea now surrounding our island home. This is one reason why there are species of non-flying animals in Europe that we lack. It also explains why so many of our resident animals are sub-species of those found in Europe. During those 10,000 years the populations of birds, mammals and insects, isolated on these off-shore islands of Europe have had time to change sufficiently to be that much different from their continental counterparts. The conscientious ornithologist distinguishes therefore between the British jay and the Continental jay, the British robin and the Continental robin, the British songthrush and the Continental songthrush. You or I might have difficulty in detecting the fine distinctions but would doubtless recognize that there are slight differences once they have been pointed out. A similar situation obtains in the reptiles but is more emphatic, and it brings us to another feature. Ireland became separated from Britain before Britain was separated from Europe. Reptiles of all kinds, including snakes, are less tolerant of low temperatures than most animals, which is one reason why we have so few species. It also explains why snakes and lizards grow less numerous as we go from Land's End to John O' Groats. After being pushed south by

the advancing ice in the four glacials or ice ages, they made a slow return. So slow, indeed, that they failed to reach Ireland before it was separated from Britain, as Mr Alfred Leutscher points out in his chapter on Reptiles. St Patrick may have had a hand in it, as tradition tells, contrary to what Mr Leutscher has remarked – who can say! – but his task would, to say the least, have been lightened by the geological sequence.

Now comes the question: What happened to the freshwater fishes? When the ice ages were at their height no fishes could have survived north of the line Thames-Severn. South of this line would have been barren tundra with only cold-adapted species able to keep alive, rather like the Alaska black-fish of today, erroneously reported to have been frozen at times in ice and yet lived. So our freshwater fishes must, in the main, have come from Europe. As the ice started to retreat, at the beginning of the last inter-glacial the Thames and other eastern rivers were tributaries of the Rhine which flowed northwards. Britain was joined to the Continent across the southern North Sea as far north as the Dogger Bank. By the time the North Sea had broken through to what is now the English Channel, the species of fishes we have today could have come down the Rhine. Accident must have played a part since species such as the wels and the bitter-ling, which are not native, have since been introduced successfully into Britain.

The coming and going of the ice-cap, the southernmost limit of which was never much further down than about the line of the River Thames, resulted in another feature, the relict faunas. Some deep lakes, Ennerdale Water in the Lake District is an example, contain small animals, such as shrimps that are physiologically adapted to cold water. They are believed to have been widespread over the country during the ice ages and were wiped out when a warmer climate returned, except in these pockets. There is still room for debate about how and when these relicts found themselves where they are today. It is, however, not possible to enter into such a discussion here for reasons of space. It must suffice to note there are such elements in our fauna.

Indeed, so far as this book is concerned, the lack of space has presented an acute problem, if only because a by-product of it is the lack of balance in dealing with the various groups. Because we have only six native amphibians in Britain and six reptiles they can be fairly adequately dealt with. The mammals, also, are not over-numerous so each can be given a fair mention. Once away from these it becomes very much a matter of squeezing more than a quart into a pint pot. There are, for example, over 500 species of birds most of which are residents or regular visitors, and this figure is small compared with the numbers of insects or wild plants, or the animals and plants found on the shore. The most the authors of these sections can do is to etch in a picture which to some extent informs but more especially might whet the appetite for more.

Had these islands not been severed from the European mainland the numbers of resident species to be included would have been greater. It would have robbed us, on the other hand, of many casual visitors which make the pursuit of British natural history exciting because we never know what may turn up. Having the sea moat all round us has given us a more equable climate. This may have its drawbacks in being too variable and highly unpredictable, but at least we do not have the extremes of a continental climate. The fact that we have the Dartford warbler, if only in favoured places in southern England, is because this bird is more a Mediterranean or southern European species. It is resident in Spain, southern Italy and up through the western third of France to have a toe-hold in southern England. It is much the same story for the cirl bunting except that it covers the southern half of England as well as Wales.

There are differences also in the plants some of which, in southern England especially, are at the extreme edges of their European range and are recognizable sub-species of their European counterparts.

We may have to thank our equable climate to some extent for the birds that come to us from Scandinavia and other parts of northern Europe for the winter. We are familiar with irruptions of crossbills and waxwings, and there are other birds that come to us from these same parts as regular winter visitors. Certainly, in many of these, the migrations are generally east to west, but it is conceivable that our milder climate plays some part in influencing them to make landfall here. There are even the occasional strays from North America, but their coming here may be due to no more than that the British Isles forms the nearest floating platform to the American seaboard. This is borne out by the records. Less than a dozen species have reached us this way, and their occurrences here are few and far between. The American bittern heads the list with a score of records, the American wigeon has clocked up a dozen. The others are less frequent. They have all been seen on the western side of Britain and especially in Devon and Cornwall.

Our west and south-west coasts sometimes receive other visitors from across the Atlantic but by another medium. Those shores more especially are washed by the waters of the North Atlantic Drift, or, as it is commonly called, the Gulf Stream. This sometimes brings stray fishes from the depths of the Atlantic. It also brings large seeds that have floated across from tropical America. Some years ago a strange colony of polyps was found growing in Lough Ine, on the southern coast of Ireland, and was presumed to have come from somewhere across the Atlantic. Indeed, it is said that the confidence of the early navigators that land lay to the west was founded on the finding of such things. Turtles that should be more at home in the tropics and subtropics sometimes are stranded on the south-west and western shores and there was the celebrated case of the sailfish, native of the western Atlantic and the Caribbean which was stranded in the Yealm River, in Devon, on 17 August 1928. It is the only sailfish that is known to have reached the coasts of Europe.

It is a feasible theory that the North Atlantic Drift and the visitors it brings here may underlie the readiness with which we accept stories of sea monsters, or even of other unusual beings. A few years ago, for example, there was an unprecedented rash of reports about pumas roaming the country-side of southern England, south of a line from the Wash to the Severn estuary, the most famous being the Surrey puma. People from Europe visiting England asked, with evident surprise, why Britain should have so many mystery animals. Some even asked why the British were so ready to believe such stories.

We have more than our fair share of sea-serpent stories, largely because decomposing and eroded carcasses of basking sharks are thrown up on our western shores and are mistaken for the remains of sea monsters. These huge beasts happen to be especially numerous off the north-western coasts of Britain. The Soay beast, twice reported at about the same spot off the Inner Hebrides, the last time in 1959, created something of a stir. In 1968, however, Professor L. D. Brongersma, of Leiden, showed beyond reasonable doubt, that it was nothing more than a leathery turtle.

The moral, if there is one at all, is that Britain is so situated that almost anything may turn up. It is a perplexing situation in which disbelief can be as hazardous as belief, the first bringing the risk of shutting one's eyes to an exciting discovery, the second leading to uncritical acceptance which is the handmaid of illusion.

Anyone who tries to take a realistic view of what has been called 'un-natural' natural history, such as the sea monsters already mentioned, is apt to be met with the reply that life is dull so such beliefs help add excitement to it. One can have sympathy with this point of view. It is always exciting to think there may be large, bizarre animals that still elude our searches. That is why the discovery of the coelacanth fish made such a stir. The very idea of an animal formerly thought to be extinct coming back, so to speak, from the grave, is enough to stir the pulse even of those who have no other interest in natural history. It was the same with the dawn redwood, *Metasequoia*, a tree believed to be extinct and then re-found. We cherish it to the extent that we try to get seedlings of it to plant in our gardens.

It is, however, not the naturalist who talks about life being dull because for him there is the daily prospect of new discovery, of some-thing turning up that may prove exciting. The discoveries may be of minor importance and they may add little to the sum total of knowledge. They may not be breath-taking but they engender in one the feeling of living in a world that is constantly beckoning us to adventure.

A small girl watching her goldfish re-marked in jubilant and excited tones: 'Daddy, a fish swims by wagging its tail!' Savants, after years of patient research, have come to the same conclusion. They may embellish their findings with abstruse mathematical formulae, and they take longer to say it, but basically they have made no greater dis-covery than the small girl.

Years ago an elderly jobbing gardener named Smith, who had been all his life a mole-catcher, told me about young tawny owls. He said that each tawny owl had its own territory, so that the countryside was more or less parcelled out between them. Each year, when young tawny owls left their parents they had to find a place to live. Each had to find a territory, but as it wandered from one point to another it found itself in one owl-occupied territory after another, and in each territory it was harassed by the owner. Only the fledgelings fortunate enough to find an unoccupied territory would sur-vive because a young inexperienced owl cannot feed itself properly when being continually harassed by adults. So is ex-plained the high mortality among young owls each year, so that the population as a whole remains constant.

Smith did not express it so briefly, but this was in essence what he told me. And he was very proud of his story, as well he might be for a few months later one of our leading zoologists published the results of several years patient research on tawny owls. There was little difference between what he said and what Smith had said except that it was supported by facts and figures, and therefore the more acceptable and convincing. Smith had used his eyes and his native common sense over the years, with no refined techniques to guide him such as the zoologist could command. My guess would be that the pursuit of truth and the ultimate discovery gave the mole-catcher and the zoologist an equal thrill.

Only a short while ago somebody asked me whether it was correct, as a gamekeeper had told him, that a rat's front teeth grow 5 inches in a year. We all know that a rat's incisors grow continually at the roots and that the rat must be continually gnawing something. We also know that if one of the upper incisors does not properly engage with its counterpart in the lower jaw, the two teeth unable to rub on each other grow enormously long, curve over the head or into the mouth, locking the jaws and starving the rat to death. But growth of 5 inches in a year seemed hard to believe.

I made a point of finding out from those who make a special study of rats. The gamekeeper was not quite correct. In fact, a rat's lower incisors grow slightly faster than the upper, at the rate of 0·33–0·42 mm. a day, which is 4·72–5·95 inches a year. So the gamekeeper was only slightly out, as is to be expected since he had to rely on his own eyes and native intelligence unaided by laboratory facilities. He also, quite obviously, had enjoyed the thrill of discovery, as has everyone else to whom I have told this story.

These may be relatively trivial events compared with such things as voyages to the moon, but they are often things we can see on our own doorsteps, and they can be seen almost any day. They are also peculiarly our own. There was an occasion, years ago when I found myself compelled to remain in a small garden for the afternoon. This irked me

and I began to feel bored. The thought then struck me that there *must* be something even in that garden which was of more than passing interest. I began to look around and in a short while found myself examining green-fly with a pocket-lens.

I had read how, during most of the summer, only female green-fly are around, how they produce young by parthenogenesis, or virgin birth, so that to all intents and purposes they bud off their young ones. But here I could see it happening before my eyes. I watched the tiny green 'bud' appear at the tip of the female's abdomen, saw it slowly grow larger, unfold its legs, kick about, finally drop off and plunge its proboscis into the leaf and begin to suck sap.

Before long I found myself timing the process of the birth, estimating how long between successive births, calculating how many offspring each female would produce each day, how long before each offspring matured and started herself to give birth to a succession of offspring. For the first time I really understood why one day your rose bush seems to have no green-fly on it and two days later it is infested with them. I have had people point to a rose bush and say 'Look at that blight. It came in with the east wind we had two days ago. Now all the leaves are shrivelled.' It may have come in with the east wind, or with the west, south or north wind. Green-fly are winged in spring. They do get carried on the wind. But the real cause of this annual population explosion is their incredible rate of reproduction.

That afternoon stands out in my memory as one of the most exciting and enjoyable I can recall. Many times since I have taken a hand-lens and initiated a friend, who has talked about blight striking his or her trees, into the mysteries of green-fly procreation. I have never known one to be bored.

History does not record how all the great men whose discoveries have revolutionized our ideas first became interested in their subjects. We know that Linnaeus started with very simple, if not humble beginnings, and Charles Darwin would have taken up an entirely different career if his attention had not been caught by some of the more trivial natural history phenomena. It may well have been the same with Leonardo da Vinci, Martin Lister, John Ray and a host of others that we have not the space to mention. We are, however, on very much firmer ground so far as William Smith is concerned. He was a farmer's son who first became interested as a boy in fossil sea-urchins he found on his father's land. These are the rounded lumps of flint about 2 inches across with rows of tiny pinholes on them. Some people call them 'shepherds' crowns'. Smith knew them as 'pundstones'. They have long attracted attention. There is some evidence that prehistoric man at times used them ritually in burials, placing a ring of them round a corpse at the time of interment. Smith was also attracted but they led him to mapping the geological structure of Britain. We may safely assume that all the great naturalists have followed a similar path. Gilbert White (1720–93), whose writings have given pleasure to millions, may not have achieved the same revolutionary results but he followed much the same road and the charm of his writings is in the trivialities he discusses.

The works of the great men listed above affect everybody. The writings of Gilbert White appeal more to those who use natural history as a hobby. In 1969 the British Naturalists' Association held a field week in Dorset. I asked one of its members what for him are the attractions of natural history as a leisure pursuit. He replied that it costs nothing, makes no great demands in effort, is of absorbing interest and is never-ending. It is the answer to the potential boredom of retirement as well as offering healthy recreation at all stages of one's life. His answer reflected no great ambitions about the acquisition of knowledge or the desire to make great discoveries. And I could understand his feelings without the need for further probing.

I can look back, and still enjoy in retrospect, finding the Lizard orchid on the Sussex Downs, a Water scorpion – which is not a true scorpion, only a large bug with a tail – in a pond on Hampstead Heath, seeing a Basking shark at close quarters off the Cornish coast and watching the play of dolphins in the bay below my cliff-top watch-point, and many other trivial events. Nothing except cerebral deterioration can rob me of the memory of these and so prevent my recalling them with pleasure. There are many things I have not yet seen but hope to see one day.

I, for one, therefore, have a vested interest in resisting change that may banish the things I have enjoyed or reduce my chances of seeing those things I have not yet seen. I also wish that other people may share these things, including generations yet to come. It is this last, purely altruistic consideration which makes me a conservationist, as it does the many thousands of others whose hobby lies in this same direction. Their ranks are swollen, also, by a far larger number whose interest is purely dilettante, or perhaps it is better described as desultory, and goes little further than the bird-table in the back-yard. Nevertheless, their sympathies go wider, so that they will readily support any movement for preserving the natural beauties and the amenities of the countryside.

Back in the 1920s a spiritualist congress was held in London. It so happened I found myself in conversation, quite fortuitously, with an American lady who was attending the congress. The only interest now in this event is to recall a remark she made, that we had learned all we could about this planet so it was time to explore other worlds. Fortunately, she has been proven a poor prophet by how much more we have learnt since then. If everything were known we should have been robbed of half the stimulus for living.

Perhaps here is the real point of division between the naturalist-conservationists and those who, usually unwittingly and certainly without malice, are opposed to them. The former recognize, perhaps often no more than intuitively, that every time a rare plant, butterfly or bird, or any other living thing is in danger of extinction, the chance of answering one more question in the future, or solving a problem, has been lost forever.

It is often said today that the countryside is fast disappearing under the spread of towns, roads, airports, power-stations and the like, so that soon there will be little to enjoy. There is a grain of truth in this yet it is surely an exaggeration. Anyone who drives about the countryside keeping this in mind, and especially those making long journeys, cannot but be aware that there are still vast stretches with at most isolated farmhouses well spaced out. Certainly much of this is arable land or pasture, not the most fruitful areas for the naturalist. Yet even in these there are pockets of a relatively wild terrain still worth exploring.

Perhaps the greater menace lies in another direction, and it may be this is what people have in mind when they deplore the rapid erosion of the countryside. It is not so much the actual area of land being buried under bricks, concrete and tarmac as the areas around that are being tidied up. We campaign, and rightly, against spreading litter around but often more damage is done from good intent. There is one place, for example, where a magnificent view of the country can be had from the top of a down. So that more people should have a greater opportunity of enjoying the view the local authority ordered the clearance of scrub – where nightingales have been regularly nesting for years past. Fortunately, as a result of early representations by local naturalists the clearance was reduced to a minimum and there is now less restriction of the view and there is still some scrub for the nightingales.

This single example epitomizes the present state of affairs. As the encroachment on green belts or open spaces grows, so does the number of those interested in preserving them increase. Even within local authorities there is a growing tendency to stay the woodman's axe – or its modern equivalent – and to meet half-way at least the requests from pressure groups, such as local preservation societies and the county trusts. It is a ding-dong battle, with gains and losses but with faintly increasing hopes. And the gains and the hopes stand a real chance of being increased the more knowledge of our flora and fauna is spread. This sums up one purpose of this book.

Maurice Burton, 1970

Plants

Green plants produce the organic food upon which all other forms of life. except certain kinds of bacteria, ultimately depend. They do this by the process of photosynthesis, which means 'building up by light'. in which the green chlorophyll contained in their cells serves as the essential seat for a chemical reaction. In this some of the energy of sunlight is absorbed and used to cause hydrogen from water, and carbon and oxygen from carbon dioxide in the air to combine to form sugars and other complex carbohydrates, which are then converted to starch, oils, etc. and stored by the plant. In the process of photosynthesis excess oxygen is produced; this is released into the atmosphere and can be used for respiration by animals, and by plants themselves. By further combination of carbohydrates with salts in solution in water. from the soil via the roots – salts containing elements such as nitrogen, phosphorus, sulphur and iron – the proteins and other complex organic compounds are produced. Animals can do none of these things themselves; they therefore depend for their organic food, and for the maintenance of sufficient oxygen in the atmosphere that they breathe, on green plants. One can see therefore that life, as we know it on this earth at any rate, would be impossible without the earth's green mantle.

Life probably arose in the primaeval oceans, perhaps 2,000 million years ago before the Cambrian geological period, so called because rocks of this age were first recognized in Wales – Cambria in Latin. How it happened is not certainly known, but it is believed that the light of the sun, in some way, induced chemical reactions which formed organic compounds in the water. Eventually some of these may have built up into very simple microscopic animals, which were able to feed upon the remaining organic compounds. to respire – to break

down or 'burn' – these foodstuffs to produce energy, and also to use them as 'bricks' for growth. Feeding. respiration and growth are the essentials of life. At some stage chlorophyll must, somehow, have been formed, and some simple organisms must have used it to carry out photosynthesis, thus becoming the first green plants. It is not known how this happened; but if it had not happened, the simple animals would in time have eaten up all the available food. There is no evidence that the supposed formation of organic substances by sunlight continued into later epochs of the world's history, possibly because the sun's radiation, and the earth's atmosphere, were very different at this early epoch.

The first recognizable plants were almost certainly microscopic one-celled algae. too small and delicate to have left any record as fossils. In later epochs, however. fossils of larger algae, the ancestors of our modern seaweeds, were formed. From the Silurian Period, about 400 million years ago, the first fossils of land-living plants are known. and in a later geological epoch, the Carboniferous Period, over 250 million years ago, there were certainly great forests of plants. We know a lot about the plants of this period, because the swampy forests of this time. which covered wide areas in what are now Europe. North America and parts of Asia, became converted, in the waterlogged, oxygen-poor soil, into peat, and then, by pressure of other sediments deposited on top through long ages of time, into coal. Because it is highly compressed, coal is a much better source of energy, or fuel, than fresh wood, although both have a similar origin, and is of great economic importance. Man has mined coal in vast quantities and this has given scientists the opportunity to make a full study of the abundant fossils it contains. It is true in fact that the flora of the Coal Measures of the

Upper Carboniferous Period is far better known than the modern flora of some remote parts of South America.

Typical land plants are rooted in soil and have aerial stems bearing leaves or leaf-like organs. They have roots which both anchor the plant and absorb water and mineral salts from the soil. They have stems which support the leaves, so that they can be well exposed to the available light; these stems contain strengthening tissues of woody fibres, also elongated tubular cells, or vessels, which carry water and salts to the leaves, the so-called vascular tissue; they have leaves which contain the chlorophyll essential for photosynthesis in their cells, and air spaces to permit the movement of gases within the leaf. The leaves, and the young stems, too, of land plants have a waterproof outer envelope of waxy material, known as the cuticle, over their skin which prevents uncontrolled loss of water, and this 'skin' or epidermis is pierced by special pores, known as *stomata*, from the Greek word for a mouth, which can open or close to control the entry of gases and water-vapour.

The plants of the Coal Measures had all these features. What is most interesting, however, is that they closely resembled certain living plants of today, particularly the horsetails, *Equisetum*, the club-mosses, *Lycopodium*, and the ferns, p. 17. Flowering plants were not present. There is one interesting difference, however. The modern horsetails and club-mosses are small plants, only from a few inches to a couple of feet in height at the most; the fossil horsetails, for example, *Calamites*, p. 17, and the fossil club-mosses, for example, *Lepidodendron*, p. 17, of the Coal Measures, were, for the most part though not entirely, great trees, up to 100 feet (30 m.) in height. Their great trunks are familiar to geologists studying coal deposits.

The illustration on p. 17 shows some of these early land plants and their modern relatives.

All these plants, horsetails, club-mosses and ferns, ancient and modern, reproduce by spores, not seeds. These spores, which are of

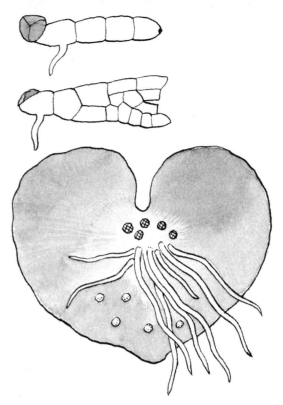

A fern prothallus viewed from below showing archegonia, antheridia below and rhizoids: *above*, the development of the prothallus from the spore

microscopic size, are produced in tiny capsules called sporangia. In the horsetails and club-mosses the sporangia are gathered into cones, superficially resembling those of conifers; in the ferns, the sporangia are borne in clusters on the edges or undersides of the fronds. A spore differs from a seed in that it consists of a single cell only, surrounded by a protective wall, and does not contain an embryo plant like a true seed. Also when a spore of one of these seedless land plants germinates, it does not develop directly into something resembling the parent plant, as is the case with a seed. Instead it forms a tiny plant known as a *prothallus*, which in ferns is green and scale-like, about $\frac{1}{4}$–$\frac{1}{2}$ inch (6–13 mm.) in diameter, and in club-mosses is usually a tiny tuber-like body. This prothallus bears minute sexual organs, sometimes of both sexes together, sometimes on separate plants. The male organs or antheridia produce sperms which, like the spermatozoa of animals, can swim in a film of liquid. In these early plants the liquid film is provided by rain water, and the sperms swim to the female organs, the tiny flask-shaped archegonia, where they enter and fertilize the eggs. Only when the egg is fertilized can an embryo form and grow into a plant like the original parent. This type of reproduction thus involves two different kinds of plants alternating with each other in time, a spore-bearing and a sexual generation and this phenomenon is known as alternation of generations. In the early types of land plants the conspicuous generation is the spore-bearing one, while the sexual generation. the gametophyte or prothallus. is tiny and inconspicuous. Hence these plants are called cryptogams from two Greek words meaning 'hidden marriage'.

Some of the giant club-mosses of the Coal Measures and earlier. such as *Lepidodendron*, and also certain fern-like plants, produced two different kinds of sporangia, one containing only a few large spores each, called megaspores; the other kind containing large numbers of small spores in each sporangium called microspores. The megaspores germinated to produce prothalli bearing only female organs or archegonia, some of which have actually been found preserved as fossils; the microspores germinated to produce very tiny prothalli within the spores themselves. bearing a single male organ or antheridium. Male sperms from the antheridia then apparently swam, in wet weather, to the archegonia and fertilized the eggs. Although the living genus *Lycopodium* has only one kind of spore, among living club-mosses we still see exactly the same phenomenon of two kinds of spores. known as heterospory. in the genus *Selaginella*. One species of this genus, *S. selaginoides*, is not uncommon in moist base-rich places on our mountains and in moist hollows of northern sand-dunes. It is a small superficially moss-like plant. with creeping stems bearing tiny pointed leaves; erect leafy stems 2–3 inches (5–7.5 cm.) high bear the $\frac{1}{2}$ inch (1.3 cm.) cones in which one can see with a lens that there

are two sorts of sporangia present, bearing few large and many small spores respectively. The development of heterospory (hetero = different) was of vital importance in the evolution of the seed.

Some plant fossils in the Coal Measures or Carboniferous Period have in fact been found to bear true seeds. In the evolution of a seed, what apparently happened was as follows. Some early plants bearing the two kinds of spores, probably both club-mosses and ferns, seem not to have shed their megaspores as soon as they were ripe. but to have retained them in the sporangia. Usually one of the spores then germinated to produce a prothallus inside it, while still remaining within the sporangium; the other spores apparently withered away. possibly because the first one took their food supply and so gained the upper hand. The prothallus in the first spore then produced archegonia or female organs as usual. The apex of the sporangium opened, making it possible for the wind or the rain to carry microspores from the same, or another plant, to lodge there. Around the sporangium. a bract grew up. protecting it but also leaving a narrow slit-like or tubular opening called the micropyle. In this opening. it was now possible for microspores from the same or another plant to lodge. carried there by the wind or the rain. The apex of the sporangium holding the megaspore with its contained prothallus. now opened. exposing the archegonia. The whole of this structure containing the megaspore now became an ovule. When the microspores germinated. they released their male sperms as usual. which then fertilized the eggs of one or more of the

Coal Measure flora and primitive land plants: *back left*, *Calamites*, a fossil tree related to the living horsetails with whorled branches: *back right*, *Lepidodendron*, a fossil tree related to the living club-mosses with spirally arranged leaves, forked branching and terminal cones; *front left*, a modern horsetail, *Equisetum sylvaticum*; *front centre*, the modern Male fern, *Dryopteris filix-mas*; *front right*, a modern club-moss with terminal cones on naked stalks, *Lycopodium clavatum*. The modern 'primitive' plants are quite small (2–3 feet, 61–91 cm., tall at most), while the Coal Measure trees reached 100 feet (30 m.) in height

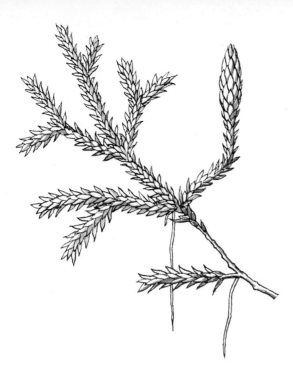

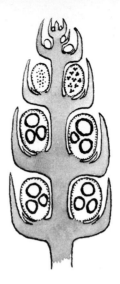

Selaginella, *left*, and a vertical section of cone showing mega- and microspores, *right*

female organs in the ovule, resulting in the development of one, or more, embryo plants. The structure now produced was a true seed.

A seed has the following features: (1) it contains an embryo plant. capable of growing when germinated directly into a replica of the parent plant. (2) it contains a food reserve tissue or endosperm. on which the seedling can feed until it can commence photosynthesis and manufacture its own food; in early types of seeds this tissue is provided by the female prothallus. (3) it has a protective coat or testa. formed by the bract. or bracts. which grow around the sporangium as explained above.

In the geological ages following the Carboniferous Period, the Permian, the Triassic and the Jurassic, the fossil record indicates that the cryptogamic or seedless plants became less and less important. while the

A mountain landscape in the Scottish Highlands. A glacial lake, dammed by a terminal moraine left by the melting ice at bottom right. The steep-sided valley has been gouged out by the movement of a former glacier. Note erratic boulders left by the glacier. In bottom left-hand corner are plants of acid mountain vegetation: Common heather with pink flowers, *left*; Dwarf birch, *centre*; Cowberry, *right*

bulk of the vegetation in what is now Britain. and indeed everywhere else. came to consist more and more of seed-bearing or phanerogamic plants – phanerogamic comes from two Greek words meaning 'visible marriage'. Indeed. the dominant vegetation by Jurassic times consisted largely of plants closely resembling the modern conifers. such as the pines and firs. together with certain palm-like seed-plants known as the Cycads. The sporangia of these plants were still borne in cones. but the cones were now of two distinct kinds as is the case in the living conifers. 'female' cones bearing sporangia each with a single large megaspore, and 'male' cones bearing sporangia each producing masses of tiny microspores or. as we may now call them. pollen-grains. As explained above. the 'female' cones eventually produced the seeds.

The development of the seed was clearly a great advance in the evolution of plants. The total disappearance of the great forests of giant seedless club-mosses and horsetails at the end of the Carboniferous Period. and their replacement in later ages by forests of seed-bearing trees, is a clear indication of the greater efficiency and adaptability to changing environments of seed-bearing plants. There is an interesting analogy here with the giant, cold-blooded, egg-laying reptiles of the Jurassic Period, which, when the climate changed, were unable to adapt to the new environment and became extinct, being replaced by the warm-blooded mammals and birds as the dominant fauna. A climatic change, towards cold and then to very dry conditions, occurred at the close of the Carboniferous Period; seed-bearing plants seem to have been the more flexible in adverse conditions than the seedless plants. So the seed-bearing habit must have conferred some advantage.

The three main features of a seed outlined above may give us the clues. The embryo plant is already well developed when the seed is shed and it is provided with a food reserve which keeps it going until its own leaves are expanded for photosynthesis. The seed coat protects it against excessive water loss and yet becomes porous enough to enable more water to be absorbed and so allow germination in the right conditions. Although spores may be dispersed by the wind even further than seeds, they have no food or water reserves, so will die rapidly once they have germinated unless there is moisture available externally for a fair length of time. The delicate prothallus is also very vulnerable to lack of sufficient moisture throughout its life. Fertilization depends on water being available at the right moment to carry the swimming sperms; the embryo plants resulting take time to develop, and until they have roots and leaves remain very vulnerable to lack of moisture, even with a very short period of drought, as there is no protective coat or food reserve. It is clear that reproduction by spores is much more of a hit-and-miss affair, and plants relying on reproducing this way have to use up valuable reserves in producing vast numbers of spores, thus ensuring that some at least reach favourable sites for establishment. Even the sturdy Bracken fern, which as an adult plant grows readily enough in dry heathlands, must have moist conditions for its spores to germinate successfully to produce prothalli and embryos, so enabling it to colonize new territory at a distance. The existence of moist,

shaded sites such as disused rabbit holes is a necessity for the bracken in successful colonization of new terrain in a dry, open countryside.

Another evolutionary advance which, it seems from the fossil record, came a little later than the evolution of the seed itself, was the development of the pollen-tube. Instead of the sperms needing water in which to swim down to the female organs, the pollen-grain developed a tube which grew down to the egg, and penetrated it, thus injecting the male nuclei, there to effect fertilization without the need for any external moisture. Fertilization thus became independent of wet weather. All living seed plants have pollen-tubes and perhaps this development, enabling fertilization in the most arid climates, was an advance nearly as important as the evolution of the seed itself.

Some time in the Jurassic Period, more than 100 million years ago, the flowering plants first appeared upon the scene. In the following Cretaceous Period, the time when the chalk rocks of England were being laid down, they became the dominant vegetation of much of the earth, except for the cooler parts of the north temperate zone, when the conifer forests remained dominant, and have continued to do so up to the present day. The features that the flowering plants have evolved which have led to their great success seem to have been two: the evolution of the *fruit*, and the evolution of the *flower*.

In the more primitive seed-bearing plants, such as the conifers, the ovules containing the female prothalli, and hence the archegonia and the eggs, are borne naked upon the scales of the female cones, protected by the cone scales when young, but at the time of pollination exposed. The resulting seeds are also exposed and so the more primitive seed-bearing plants are called Gymnosperms from the Greek for naked seeds. In the flowering plants the ovules are protected in structures of leaf-like nature, called carpels. These enfold and enclose them completely and the flowering plants are known as the Angiosperms from the Greek for enclosed seeds. When the seeds develop, the carpels remain enclosing them to form the seed-case or fruit.

Sometimes, as in buttercups, there is only one ovule per carpel; more often, as in Marsh marigold and Snapdragon, there are many ovules per carpel. The pollen grains, however, can now no longer fall directly, as in the Gymnosperms, on the pollination tube at the top of the ovule. To provide for this situation, evolution has produced a structure known as the stigma on the tip of the carpel. This is usually sticky so that pollen adheres to it, and it also produces a chemical secretion that causes the pollen-grains to germinate there. The stigma is usually borne on a stalk called the style. The pollen-tube grows out of the pollen-grain, and makes its way unerringly down the style, through the tissues of the carpel, to the ovule, where it releases its male nuclei.

The female prothallus in flowering plants is much reduced in structure and consists only of a little oval sac, the embryo sac. The flask-shaped archegonia of the seedless plants and the conifers are no longer produced – they are no longer needed. Instead, the embryo sac contains only a few cells or nuclei, one of which is the egg cell. One of the two male nuclei fuses with this as in the more primitive plants, and from this fertilized egg develops the embryo as before. Usually the other male nucleus fuses with two other nuclei in the embryo sac, and from the divisions of the resulting fusion-cell develops the endosperm, or seed food-reserve tissue, of the flowering plants. Unlike the conifers, the flowering plants do not produce enough prothallus tissue to act as a food reserve for the seed.

The carpels are separate from one another in those flowering plants that are regarded as more primitive, such as magnolias and buttercups. They are joined together in the flower in those flowering plants that are regarded as more advanced, such as campions, foxgloves, Honeysuckle and campanulas; but this question will be discussed more fully later on. After fertilization of the ovules, the carpel tissue changes in one of several ways to form the fruit. The fruit may become fleshy, as in berry-type fruits such as those of the Honeysuckle; such a fleshy fruit is usually coloured, evidently pleasant-tasting, and attractive to fruit-eating birds, though not necessarily edible to man. After being eaten by birds, the seeds inside the fruit usually remain undamaged and are excreted at a distance, so dispersing the species. The fruit may become woody and develop hooks, as in Goose-grass, *Galium aparine*, which may catch on the fur of animals, or the clothes of man, so again dispersal of the seeds can be achieved. Other fruits have developed a propeller-like wing as in Ash, *Fraxinus* and Maples, *Acer* species, or a feathery parachute-like structure on top, as in the Dandelion, *Taraxacum*; then wind is the dispersal agent. Dry capsules are a further form of fruit which open by slits or pores, as in poppies, *Papaver* species; the seeds are then shaken out as the fruit-stalk waves in the wind.

In a typical flower, the pollen-producing sporangia called anthers (a stamen is a group of two or more anthers with its stalk or filament) are grouped in whorls, or spirals, around the egg-producing structures or carpels which bear the ovules that develop into the seeds after they are fertilized. Around these reproductive organs there are usually two, sometimes only one, whorls of leaf-like structures. The inner whorl of floral leaves is composed of petals which collectively form the corolla. These are frequently coloured. The outer whorl of floral leaves is composed of sepals which collectively form the calyx; they are usually leaf-like and green and protect the flower when in bud as a rule. In addition glands may be present, producing perfume, and nectaries which secrete liquid nectar. All these features are attractive to certain types of insects.

In many cases these are bees; in others, they are flies, wasps, butterflies or moths. They are attracted to the flowers by their colour, their perfume or both. It has been shown that in some cases insects can detect

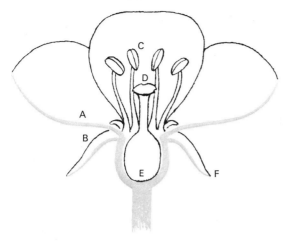

Vertical section of a flower showing, A corolla, of petals, B the nectary, C anthers, D stigma, E ovary, F calyx of sepals

perfumes that humans cannot smell and wavelengths of light radiation that we cannot see. The insects are seeking food either the nectar alone, or sometimes the pollen as well. In visiting the flowers, they quite accidentally, from their point of view, transfer pollen from the anthers to the receptive stigmas of the carpels, either in the same flower, or perhaps more often in another flower on a different plant, so effecting the pollination of the stigmas which of course must precede the actual process of fertilization of the ovules. Cross-pollination is more desirable from the genetic point of view, because it mixes genetic characters from different plants and avoids the bad effects that sometimes result from inbreeding. Cross-pollination is ensured in many flowers by a simple, but remarkable mechanism. The anthers of some species of flowers ripen and shed all their pollen before the stigmas of the same flowers are ripe and able to receive it. In these cases the pollen can only be effective if transferred to another flower in which the stigmas are ready to accept it and the anthers have withered. Such flowers are said to be protandrous. In other species, the stigmas ripen first, and the anthers later; such flowers are protogynous.

Although primitive insects, resembling dragonflies, are known as fossils from the Coal Measures, the more specialized types of insects, such as bees, flies, moths, etc., are unknown until the time when the flowering plants first appeared. They appear to have evolved simultaneously and both are mutually dependent upon one another. Neither, it seems, can survive without the other. This fact is perhaps one of the most fascinating in the whole story of evolution. Once different types and shapes of flowers began to evolve, it seems that the different types and species of flower-visiting and flower-dependent insects evolved at the same moment of time. Long-tongued insects, like moths and butterflies, are adapted to flowers with narrow tubular corollas, like buddleia and honeysuckle, too narrow for the head of a bee to enter and too long for the bee's short tongue to penetrate into. Some flowers are sweetly scented by day, less so by night and these attract day-flying bees and butterflies. Some flowers may even close at night, such as pinks. Other flowers, such as butterfly orchids, are scented strongly at night, and feebly scented by day; these are visited and pollinated by nocturnal moths. Some flowers even play 'confidence tricks' on insects by having attractive scents or colours, and even the appearance of nectar, simulated by shiny wax, but in fact produce no nectar at all.

The evolution of insect-attractive flowers meant that pollen did not need to be produced in the huge quantities that is the case with the conifers, to ensure pollination by the hit-and-miss agency of the wind. Tiny quantities of sufficiently sticky pollen would serve as well, once it could be guaranteed that insects would visit the flowers and transfer the pollen to other flowers. This resulted in great economy of plant material.

The evolution of the flowering plants was followed by the development of a great diversity of forms of flower. Some of this diversity was clearly an adaptation to pollination by different kinds of insects, but over and beyond this, great diversity of flower structure is a mark of the flowering plants, as compared with the earlier land plants. The flowering plants are indeed the most numerous group in species of all plants; there are several hundred thousand species known, of which about 2,000 only are native to the British Isles.

In order to identify and understand these great numbers, it has been necessary for botanists to devise schemes of classification and nomenclature. Linnaeus, the great Swedish naturalist of the eighteenth century, was the first to appreciate fully that plants show the greatest diversity in the structure of their flowers or sexual organs. He accordingly devised a sexual system of classification. This was based upon the numbers of carpels and the numbers of stamens, the plants being grouped into orders on this basis. As first produced by Linnaeus, this system, though a huge advance and a work of genius, was very artificial, and inevitably grouped together plants which were unlike in other features. For example, while most grasses have three stamens, one common British grass, the Sweet Vernal grass, *Anthoxanthum odoratum*, has only two and so in Linnaeus's system it had to go into a separate order from the rest of the grasses, although it was clearly very similar to them and different from plants which are not grasses. In attempts to overcome this problem, botanists later invented a 'Natural System' of classification, in which various other features of floral structure as well as numbers of parts, and also features of fruit, leaf, and even stem structure could be taken into account as well to group plants into 'natural orders'. They did their work so well that most of their 'natural orders' survive as the modern recognized families of flowering plants. However, today we have a more advanced 'natural system' which tries to arrange the plant families not only according to their actual flower, fruit and vegetative structures as we see them, but also according to what are believed, from various lines of evidence, to be their true evolutionary relationships. There is, however, much argument still over details of this latter question and so finality is at present impossible.

The flowering plants, however, break down into two great divisions recognized by all botanists: the Dicotyledons and the Monocotyledons. The dicotyledons are characterized by having, as the name tells us, a pair of first seedling leaves or *cotyledons*, which are formed within the seed, and on germination in most cases expand to form the first functional leaves of the seedling. In a minority of species these first two leaves act as part of the food store of the seed and may remain enclosed within it, as in the garden pea and bean. Dicotyledons normally have leaves with netted veining and floral parts in fives or fours or twos. In the woody species annual rings are formed each year and so thicken the stem. The monocotyledons are characterized by having a single cotyledon or seed-leaf of usually elongated form. They normally have narrow, elongated leaves with parallel veins and floral parts in threes. They do not produce tree- or shrub-like forms as a rule, but when the tree form is developed, as in the palms, wood is not produced in annual rings, but stem thickening is irregular and normally slight.

Most botanists think that the earliest flowering plants were woody and dicotyledonous like Magnolia and Tulip trees, which have large showy flowers, borne singly and not clustered in inflorescences. Such flowers have numerous parts with many sepals, petals, stamens and carpels. These parts are usually indefinite in number, more or less spirally arranged and not in whorls, on the axis of the flower, which is usually elongated like that of a cone. The parts are also usually all free from one another, like leaves on a stem, or cone scales, on a cone. This is believed by many to represent the primitive condition, and to show that early flowers were derived from shoot- or cone-like structures bearing modified leaves, as in the case of a palm-like naked-seeded fossil plant called *Bennettites*. This plant is found in Triassic rocks and thought by some to represent a type from which the flowering plants may have evolved.

As time went on, it is thought that evolution of the flowering plants proceeded in several ways. An attempt is first made below to indicate some of these ways which involved vegetative structures. rather than the floral organs themselves. Some of the features discussed seem to have evolved repeatedly in many different families, probably at different times and in different places. as responses to new environments. One evolutionary trend was the development of the deciduous habit. It is now generally believed that the early flowering plants were probably trees or shrubs with large, mostly undivided, evergreen leaves, which perhaps grew in a stable climatic environment, like

that of a tropical rain-forest today, where there is neither prolonged drought nor frost to worry about. Most tropical rain-forest trees today are evergreen. On the other hand, in a climate like that of Britain, most of the native trees are deciduous, and shed their leaves in autumn, so avoiding both frost damage to the delicate leaves themselves, and also excessive water loss through these leaves while the soil is frozen, or at least too cold for roots to function properly as water-absorbing organs. The deciduous habit is also seen in some trees of seasonally dry climates; the trees lose their leaves and become dormant in the season which is not too cold, but too dry, for active water uptake from a parched soil. The deciduous habit brings in its train such necessary concomi-

Side view of stamens and carpels of *Magnolia*. An example of a primitive flower with numerous free spirally arranged parts. The carpels are at the apex and stamens outside

tants as dormant buds with protective bud scales in the unfavourable season. and also the growth of cork over the scars where the leaves are shed; the occurrence of clear annual rings of wood. and of relatively thick bark. features not needed in tropical rain-forests. is also usual. Another instance is the development of the herbaceous habit. In herbaceous plants, the aerial stems die back in the season of the year unfavourable for growth, whether too cold or too dry, to buds either just above, or below, ground level, instead of producing permanent woody stems which increase in length (and thickness too in dicotyledons) indefinitely as in trees. This herbaceous habit is clearly an adaptation to climates of less uniform type. like the deciduous habit. A good example of the development of the herbaceous habit in plants of primitive floral structure is seen in the buttercup family. Ranunculaceae. which in floral features resembles the magnolia family, but is composed for the most part of herbs, while the Magnoliaceae are woody plants.

The herbaceous nature of most mono-cotyledons, such as lilies, orchids, rushes and grasses, is one feature that makes most botanists believe that they evolved from dicotyledons, and not the other way round. Bulbs, tubers, fleshy rhizomes and corms, such a feature of monocotyledons like lilies, orchids, irises and crocuses, are all adaptations for perennation, or survival through an unfavourable season, whether too cold, as in Britain, or too dry, as in the Mediterranean, where bulbous monocotyledons are so common. Then there is the further development by herbaceous forms of an annual, as opposed to a perennial, habit. In annuals, the whole life-cycle from seed to seed is normally accomplished in a single season. This can be an advantage in the colonization of new territory, such as ground bared by fire or some other natural disaster, or artificially and continually by man in his cultivations. Annuals have indeed become far commoner in most parts of the world in historic time due to man's activities in dis-

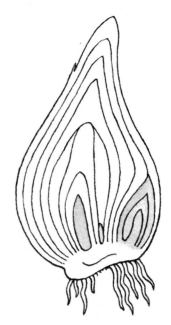

Section through tulip bulb showing food storage tissues developed from leaves which enable plant to perennate through an unfavourable season

turbing the previous continuous vegetation cover in various ways. Annual plants are also important in deserts, such as that of Nevada, where rain falls only every few years and the seeds lie dormant until wetted by heavy rain; a light shower is not sufficient to cause germination. They then quickly germinate. develop flower and produce seed while the moisture lasts. Annuals cannot compete well with other plants in dense closed vegetation; they are therefore rare in natural British plant communities such as wood-lands and old grasslands. but common in the loose open soil of such places as sand-dunes.

The most complex evolution of the flowering plants. however. has been in the development of floral structure, and, following Linnaeus' original ideas in a much modified form. it is on this basis in the main that they are classified into families. We can here again recognize several separate evolutionary tendencies. Firstly. the tendency for the floral parts to be in whorls. as in a campion or stitchwort. rather than in spirals. as in the stamens and carpels of a buttercup. which is relatively primitive. Secondly, the tendency for the floral parts to become of definite number – in whorls of fours, as in the petals of Shepherd's Purse and Cabbage; in threes, as in a lily or tulip; in fives, as in a stitchwort – instead of in indefinite numbers, as with all the parts of a magnolia, or with the stamens and carpels of a buttercup. Thirdly, there is the tendency for fusion of the floral parts. In magnolias and buttercups all are free; in poppies and stitchwort the carpels are fused to form an ovary which later forms a single fruit. In heaths, *Erica*, and primroses, *Primula*, the petals of the corolla have fused to form a corolla-tube. In the daisy family, Compositae, even the stamens are joined into a tube. Fourthly, there is the tendency for development of the ovary below the whorls of petals and sepals, as in bellflowers, *Campanula*, and the daisy family, producing an inferior ovary. Fifthly, the flower may become irregular, that is symmetrical only about one vertical axis, as opposed to regular, or radially symmetrical. Irregular flowers tend to be two-lipped, as in the pea family, Leguminosae, the snapdragon family, Scrophulariaceae, and the orchids. These are adaptations to insect pollination; the lower lip forms a landing platform for insects to alight on, the upper lip provides an umbrella which may keep rain out of the flower. Such flowers also force the insect to use some pressure in entering the flower, hence rubbing pollen on the stigma, or removing pollen from the stamens. With the development of irregular flowers, sometimes petals or stamens may be reduced in number. Sixthly and lastly, there is the tendency for the flowers to become smaller and aggregated together into showy clusters, umbels or heads, instead of having large single flowers as in magnolias and buttercups. We see this tendency developing in the umbrella-shaped but still fairly loose flower-heads of the carrot family, Umbelliferae, and reaching its ultimate conclusion in the tight heads of tiny aggregated flowers in the Daisy and Dandelion in the Compositae.

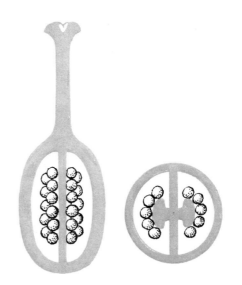

Vertical and cross-sections of a typical compound ovary, as in a Foxglove, showing two fused carpels

The use of all these characters, which are thought to indicate actual evolutionary tendencies, has led to the classification of the flowering plants into some hundreds of families, from the primitive Magnoliaceae, in which hardly any of these evolutionary tendencies are seen, to the very advanced Compositae. which display among their members examples of every one of them – indeed the common Dandelion, *Taraxacum officinale*, shows every one of these features in the one species.

There is, however, one more feature seen among the flowering plants which seems, at first sight, to be a backward step. This is the development of the wind-pollinated flower.

We have already seen how the rise of the flowering plants seems to have been associated with the development of insect-pollination – and simultaneously, it is believed, of insects able to pollinate flowers. The wind-pollinated conifers are seen as primitive, wasteful and relatively ineffective in comparison. However, at some stage in evolution, wind-pollinated flowering plants arose. There is controversy about when this happened. Some botanists believe that the common British wind-pollinated forest trees, like the oak, beech, birch, alder and hazel, are relatively primitive dicotyledonous flowering plants, more closely related to the conifers than other dicotyledons. Most botanists, however, would not any longer agree with this view. Be that as it may, nearly all botanists agree that the family which shows the most striking examples of wind-pollinated plants – the grass family, Gramineae, is of relatively late development. No fossil grasses are known until well into the Tertiary Period. It almost looks as if nature had second thoughts about the efficiency of wind-pollination.

In fact, the grasses form perhaps the most successful family of plants in the world at present. Being herbaceous, they can resist fires effectively: they can rapidly colonize, as perennials, ground previously disturbed, or as annuals, ground regularly cultivated. They tend everywhere to replace forests, which take decades to become re-established, when these are cleared by man, and they resist the nearly ubiquitous grazing of his animals. They do not need the presence of particular insects for pollination; granted dry weather while they are in flower, the

slightest breeze will effect pollination. The flowers are very reduced in structure. They have no need of showy petals or perfumes to attract insects, so they probably gain more from this reduction in flower structure than they lose on the need to produce rather large amounts of dry, dusty pollen. The stigmas are large, feathery and very sticky and hence trap pollen-grains efficiently. The slender inflorescence stalks, the long filaments of the stamens, and the flexible joints where the anthers are attached to the filaments, all are features that render wind-pollination more efficient. Many other families of both monocotyledons (the rushes, Juncaceae, and the sedges, Cyperaceae), and of dicotyledons (the goosefoot family, Chenopodiaceae, and the dock family, Polygonaceae), have also developed as

Flower forms, *top left*, Primrose showing petals fused into a corolla-tube; *bottom left*, Bellflower showing corolla-tube and inferior ovary; *top right*, part of daisy flower showing regular tubular disc florets and irregular strap-shaped ray or outer floret; *bottom right*, ray floret of Dandelion showing several advanced characters; *bottom centre*, Sweet pea showing irregular two-lipped flower

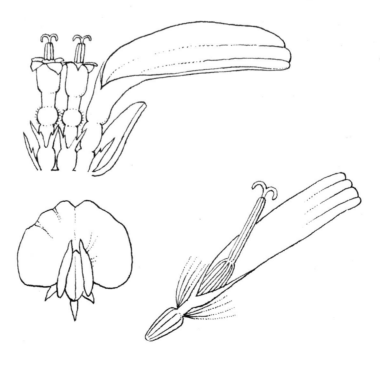

wind-pollinated groups – most of these families seem very successful today, and it may be that the evolution of modern man has to some extent tilted the balance against the insect-pollinated flowers.

Families are relatively large groups of plants with usually certain essential features of sexual structure in common, like the Ranunculaceae with all the parts of the flower free, or the Cruciferae (cabbage family) with their petals in fours and a two-carpelled fruit. Families are divided into the smaller groups called genera, in which the structure of the sexual parts and the form of the fruit is usually identical in all major respects. The genera usually consist of several species, which in any one genus tend to differ from one another in purely vegetative points, such as leaf shape, hairiness of leaves and stems, and exact shape of fruit as opposed to its basic structure. The species is really to be regarded as the ultimate unit, a population of individuals, like mankind, all of which are capable of breeding one with another, but normally cannot out-breed with other species. In some plants and animals, cross-breeding is possible but if the two species involved are 'good' species, then the hybrids will be sterile, as in the case of the mule, the hybrid between the horse and the donkey. The concept of breeding barriers of some kind is essential to the idea of the species. These breeding barriers may be genetic, resulting in sterile hybrids or none at all, but they may be equally barriers due to ecological, or geographical isolation of one species from another. Within the population of individuals that comprises any one species, the individuals are normally identical in structure and form, though they will vary in size. However, the species concept is in fact a very difficult one, and here we can only attempt a fairly simple explanation of it.

All plants have two scientific names in the binomial system invented by Linnaeus; the first is the name of the genus, the second the name of the species.

About 50 to 60 million years ago, at the start of the Tertiary Period, there was in southern England a vegetation consisting almost entirely of flowering plants. The London clay beds of the Eocene, in the Early Tertiary Period, are well exposed on the cliffs in the Isle of Sheppey on the Kent coast, and are quite rich in plant fossils. These fossils tell us that, in London clay times, the lower Thames valley was occupied by a vast forest of trees and other plants almost identical with the rain-forests of the Malay peninsula today. Besides great trees of the mahogany type, numerous palms occurred and it is clear that the climate was tropical in southern England at that time. It appears to have been cooler in Scotland, for conifers like the modern sequoias occurred there then. As time went on during the Tertiary Period, the fossil record informs us that the climate became cooler, until by the Mid-Pliocene Period, about 10 million years ago, it was evidently not dissimilar from today, though probably rather warmer. At this time great forests of many species of deciduous trees, with understoreys of shrubs and herbs, occupied the land area that is now Britain. A similar flora occurs today in the forests of the south-eastern United States, and in those of north-east China and Japan; besides oaks, elms, chestnuts, limes and other trees of genera still members of our native flora, it included conifers such as the great Wellingtonia, *Sequoiodendron*, now confined to California, as a native, the Tulip tree, *Liriodendron*, now confined to eastern North America and eastern temperate Asia, and other trees such as magnolias. As time passed, however, these plants seem to have disappeared, until about one million years ago, shortly before the great Ice Age began, the flora of Britain became apparently almost identical with that of today. This suggests that the Ice Age did not begin suddenly, but was preceded by long ages of very gradual cooling of climate.

The great Pleistocene Ice Age, as it is called to distinguish it from far earlier ice ages, was perhaps the most important event, geologically speaking, in the recent history of the British flora. At its start, about a million years ago, the flora was, as we have seen, very like that of Britain today. At its close the temperate flora appears to have been almost entirely destroyed by the ice sheets and their accompanying climate, and a flora of arctic tundra type had taken its place. Britain had then to be recolonized by a temperate flora once again, by gradual immigration from the southern parts of Europe unaffected by the great cold. The recent story of the British flora is thus the story of how, and from where, this re-immigration occurred.

It is not certain even now what caused the Ice Age; it may have been due to changes in the amount of heat reaching the earth from the sun, or it may have been due to changes in the pattern of land and sea, and consequent changes in the warm and cold currents of the oceans. However, it certainly happened, as the geologist Lyell was the first to show by pointing out the scratches made by the glaciers on the mountain rocks in Scotland and elsewhere. He also demonstrated that the great sheets of stony 'boulder clays' covering such areas as East Anglia and the Midlands contained rocks of varied sizes from tiny pebbles to large boulders, that could not have been deposited by water, because the stones were unsorted. He showed, too, that these 'boulder clays' resembled exactly some deposits known as moraines, laid down at the present by arctic and alpine glaciers. Many of the Scottish and Welsh mountain lakes today can be seen to have been formed by the ponding-up of their waters by end-moraines formed at the snouts of glaciers, p. 18. The Ice Age in fact consisted of at least four main periods of ice advance, separated by three interglacial periods of varied length when it became warm enough for the temperate forest flora to re-immigrate; but since even in the latest of the cold periods the fossil record tells us that the flora even in southern England, as for example in the Lea Valley close to London, was wholly arctic in character, the interglacial warm periods have not much significance to the question of the survival of temperate plants

through the Ice Age as a whole in Britain. In the most severe phase of glaciation, indeed, some hundred thousand or so years ago, vast sheets of ice, in places thousands of feet thick and resembling those of the Greenland ice-cap of today in scale, extended down to the Finchley and Epping areas in what are now the northern suburbs of London, and the arctic climate must have extended far south of that.

It is, incidentally, probable that the present Post-Glacial temperate period is in fact just part of another interglacial period. Only 12,000 years have elapsed since the close of the last ice phase in lowland Britain, and it has been calculated that one of the interglacial periods was probably some hundred thousand years in duration. However, if the ice comes again, and man has not destroyed himself by war or by pollution of his environment, perhaps he will be able to control its spread.

The flora in the last cold phase of the Ice Age was largely arctic in character. It consisted of plants which are characteristic of the tundra 'dwarf-shrub' heaths of places such as are found in the interior of Iceland, the coastal areas of Greenland, and such places as Baffin Land and Spitzbergen today, p. 35. Other plants are the arctic-alpines equally characteristic of the arctic and of the central European mountains such as the Alps. A mixing of the ancient floras of the Alps and the arctic occurred during the Ice Age, for the alpine flora descended into the plains at that time. However, the alpine plants today live in an environment of quite warm and sunny, though brief, summers, so that the true alpine element was probably never very important in the tundra of Britain.

Thus, besides a true arctic element including such plants as *Diapensia lapponica*, p. 35, and the Norwegian mugwort, *Artemisia norvegica*, the bulk of the tundra flora consisted of arctic-alpine species, such as listed below. In more calcareous well-drained sites, the beautiful Mountain avens, *Dryas octopetala*, p. 35, with white eight-petalled flowers and oak-shaped leaves $\frac{1}{2}$–1 inch

(1·3–2·5 cm.) long with white undersides was evidently common to judge by its abundant remains; as was Purple saxifrage, *Saxifraga oppositifolia*, p. 36, with thyme-like shoots and ½ inch (1·3 cm.) rose-purple five-petalled flowers. In more acid sites Dwarf birch, *Betula nana*, pp. 18, 35, a tiny shrub less than 1 foot (30 cm.) high with rounded, bluntly toothed leaves, was certainly common, with plants such as the Bearberry, *Arctostaphylos uva-ursi*, a low shrub with whitish pink bell-like flowers, glossy elliptical, deeply net-veined leaves and red berries. Boggy places, which must have been extensive on flatter ground, owing to the 'permafrost' layer of permanently frozen soil beneath the surface, would have had communities of true sedges, *Carex* species, and cotton-sedges, *Eriophorum* species, p. 137, with their cotton wool-tufted fruiting heads. Arctic and arctic-alpine willows, *Salix* species, abounded. Conditions for plants were particularly severe, not only because of the intense cold, the short summers, and the permafrost, but because of the slipping of soil on slopes after the spring thaw, over the surface of the permafrost, and the 'frost heaving' effects due to compression of mud between masses of ice. Patterns of 'stone stripes' and 'mud polygons' were thus common and must have produced very unstable conditions for roots.

As conditions became warmer at the close of the last glacial phase, which seems to have happened relatively rapidly, the arctic and arctic-alpine floras retreated up into the mountains, partly due to their need in some cases for colder conditions, but mostly due to competition from more temperate species which were now rapidly immigrating into the country from Europe. We can still see much of this flora today in the mountains of Scotland above 2,500 feet (*c.* 760 m.) and to a lesser degree on mountains of the north of England and of north Wales.

The richest sites today for these relic arctic-alpine floras are on the more calcareous mountain cliffs. There is always a greater variety of species in severe climatic environments on calcareous or at least base-rich rock, for the heavy rainfall of our hills tends to leach out the salts from the soil and promote the formation of raw humus, rendering the soil too acid for many of the more demanding mountain species except over rocks rich in bases. The hill tops are also often covered, owing to the high rainfall, with peat, due to the growth of bog, in which relatively few species can grow. Another factor which tends to limit the richest floras to cliffs is the sheep and deer grazing prevalent on many of our hills today. Many of these arctic-alpine plants are not well adapted to withstand constant nibbling, and so tend to survive best where sheep and, indeed, human collectors, cannot get at them very easily.

The strong, drying winds of the mountains of Britain to some extent cancel out the high rainfall of the exposed ridges, while on cliff ledges and gullies there is usually plenty of water seeping out of the rocks in springs and flushes; this is another factor which makes moist cliffs the richest habitats. Some of the 'cirques' or amphitheatres of cliffs found at the heads of ice-carved valleys in our hills are veritable gardens of arctic-alpine plants, particularly on the basic mica-schists of such places as Ben Lawers and Glen Clova. That these floras are truly relic from Late-Glacial times, and not relatively recent immigrants, has been proved in at least one case in Snowdonia, where Professor Godwin studied the fossil remains (including fossil pollens) in a peat bog below the famous plant-rich cliffs of the Devil's Kitchen. He was able to show continuity of remains of some of these arctic-alpine plants there, preserved in the peat, from Late-Glacial times to the present day. This type of vegetation is illustrated on p. 35.

Perhaps the nearest vegetation remaining in Britain today to the acid arctic tundra of Full- and Late-Glacial times, is to be seen on the high plateau of the Cairngorm mountains, which, at a height of over 4,000 feet (*c.* 1,220 m.), is too high for the development of *Sphagnum* bogs to have been able to occur since those times. On this bleak plateau remarkable communities of arctic-alpine mosses, lichens, rushes such as *Juncus trifidus*, Moss campion, *Silene acaulis* with its dense leafy cushions and short-stalked rose-pink five-petalled flowers, and sedges occur. A different community, mostly composed of mosses and liverworts, is found in places where the snow lies late, protecting the plants, but also shortening the growing season.

With the onset of a warmer climate, not without some oscillations back to a temporary colder one, great areas of the British lowlands became available relatively quickly for colonization by plants of more temperate type. The soils now available were relatively unweathered, poor in humus, but, since relatively freshly derived, either from glacial moraines left by the melting of the ice sheets, or by the exposure of almost unvegetated rocks, sands and clays, rich in plant nutrients and often alkaline, because as yet relatively unleached by rainfall. Hence many plants requiring calcareous or base-rich soils could find a favourable environment for explosive spread.

At this time, the sea-beds round the British Isles were almost entirely dry, because so much water was still locked up in the great ice sheets still existing further north and still covering Scandinavia and the Arctic. Hence it was relatively easier for plants to immigrate than it was later on, when much more northern ice had melted and 'filled up the moat', making the British Isles into true islands once again. This Early Post-Glacial Period seems to have been the time when most of the British flora of today came into these islands, though some more warmth loving, and slower moving species seem to have come in much later on.

When we look at the species of the present British flora in relation to their continental distributions, we find that they can be separated into a series of 'geographical elements' according to the position of the present main centres in Europe for the various species; centres which have probably not changed very much in Post-Glacial times,

and centres from which these species probably had to emigrate to reach the British Isles. We have already considered the arctic element, the arctic-alpine element which occurs both in the central European mountains and in the Arctic today, and the small true alpine element, which last is more characteristic of the limestones of northern England, as in Teesdale, than of the Scottish mountains. In addition, among the temperate plants, we can distinguish a boreal or northern-montane temperate element, coming from Scandinavia, a continental element coming from central and eastern Europe, a Mediterranean element coming from south Europe and the Mediterranean shores, and an oceanic element coming from south-west Europe – north Spain and Portugal.

The history of the immigration of these groups of plants after the Glacial Period, from their refuges, is the history of the British flora itself until man began to alter the landscape, for the British Isles have no true endemics, or species peculiar to themselves. The old flora, as we have seen, was destroyed *in situ* by the Ice Age, apart from the arctic-alpine plants, and there has not been time since for new species to evolve: plant evolution is a slow process. Among the only 'endemic' plants we can boast are the so-called 'micro-species' of brambles, *Rubus*, hawkweeds, *Hieracium*, and eyebrights, *Euphrasia*, forms on the way, perhaps, to evolving into new species, but hardly distinct enough to rank as such at present.

The first waves of plants to come into Britain with the warmer climate appear to have been mostly species of 'continental' type, herbs and dwarf shrubs of the kind that are most at home on the dry, alkaline soils and open habitats of the limestone hills of central Europe and the steppes of southern Russia. Their abundance in south Britain at this time, the Early Post-Glacial Period, has been established largely by the ingenious and invaluable technique of pollen analysis.

Invented by the Swedish botanist Von Post and so ably developed in Britain by Professor Godwin, this technique of pollen analysis depends on the following facts. Most plants produce pollen in considerable quantities, some of which gets carried, even with insect-pollinated flowers, for considerable distances. The pollen-grains of plants can be identified with the microscope in all cases to at least the family level, in nearly all cases to the genus level, and in many cases even to the actual species of plant, by means of the characteristic markings or sculpturing on their surfaces. The outer coats of pollen-grains which bear these markings are waxy in nature and almost indestructible by normal processes of decay if they fall into wet, poorly aerated habitats such as bogs and lakes. Bogs and lakes are sufficiently numerous, at least in most parts of the world, to preserve sufficient pollen-grains to identify the various levels of the growth of the peat or mud deposits, so that a bog, or a sequence of lake-floor muds, is like a history book, whose pages those who know the language can read. It is possible to date the various layers of sediments in deposits, either by the radioactive-carbon content, which declines with time, or from archaeological remains, or from calculations on rates of sedimentation, or from comparison with other deposits already dated. By counting relative numbers of different kinds of pollen-grains present one can form some picture of the relative amounts of the various species that occurred in the neighbourhood of the deposit.

Peat or mud deposits, of course, need careful preparation to remove other matter, so that the pollen-grains can be properly identified and counted. Pollen analysis has revealed the abundance, in the early post glacial period, of such plants as rock-roses, *Helianthemum* species, plantains, *Plantago* species, and mugworts, *Artemisia* species. Some of these plants are those typical of open, calcareous grasslands; some are more characteristic today as weeds of waysides, open waste ground, or cultivated land – what are known as ruderal plants.

Gradually, however, the pollen record tells us, trees appeared; at first birches, probably mostly *Betula pubescens*, but not the Dwarf arctic birch, *B. nana*, mentioned before which now largely disappeared from the record; then Scots pine, *Pinus sylvestris*; then Hazel, *Corylus avellana*, with still much pine. And so was ushered in the so-called Boreal Period (from Boreas, the north wind) of northern coniferous forest vegetation. This boreal forest, forced as far south as the Po valley in northern Italy, at the height of the Ice Age, gradually spread northward again over Britain and Ireland up to the hills to a tree-line at about 2,700 feet (820 m.) or even higher in places. It developed a characteristic soil beneath it, and acquired a characteristic flora and fauna. The valleys and lower mountain slopes of the Scottish Highlands still retain remains of this forest, and also something resembling the probable climate of the Boreal times in southern England. The highland climate is, however, probably now wetter and windier than it was in Boreal times. Britain was then still part of the continent as we have seen, and must have had, in the east at any rate, a more 'continental' climate than today, with more persistent high pressure, rather warmer summers, less violent and constant winds,

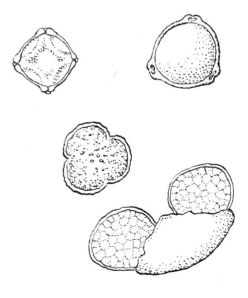

Examples of pollen grains ×500

and less rain, especially in winter, much as in north central Europe today.

The remaining natural pine forests of the Scottish Highlands thus probably resemble the forests of all Britain in the Boreal Period in many ways. It has been possible to show, again by pollen analysis, that some of them at least, for example the Coile-na-glas Leitire by Loch Maree in Wester Ross, which is now a nature reserve, are their direct successors without break in the continuity of the pine forest cover, except for occasional local fires.

Under such a Scottish pine forest, the soil parent material is usually a sandy rubble, derived from morainic debris left by the glaciers. The acid humus produced by the decay of pine needles when they fall, together with the cool climate, the relatively low evaporation, and the porous, often acid, nature of the soil parent material, tend to produce a net downward movement of water, and hence of salts, in the soil. The marked acidity which develops tends to leach out the iron salts, bleaching the upper layers, and depositing the iron oxide lower down as a 'hard pan' of reddish-brown colour. Such a soil is known as a *podsol*, and is characteristic beneath an evergreen plant cover of pines or heaths, in a cool, moist climate. On this poor acid soil, with its little-decomposed raw surface humus, a limited ground flora grows.

In the shade of the pines, Bilberry, *Vaccinium myrtillus*, p. 45, with winged stems, toothed deciduous leaves, pink urn-shaped flowers, and purple fruits, and Cowberry, *V. vitis-idaea*, p. 45, with round stems, untoothed box-like evergreen leaves, white bell-like flowers and red fruits, form a more or less continuous dwarf shrub layer under which many mosses grow. In the humus in between, one may find a number of interesting plants, most of which have green leaves and can hence carry on photosynthesis, but which have a fungus associated with their roots and seem at least in part, to live as saprophytes: plants feeding, via the fungus which they digest in their roots, on the organic humus on which the fungus in turn feeds. Such plants are the Chickweed winter-

Scots pine showing mature leaves, young leaves in spring, young female cone and one-year-old cone

green, *Trientalis europaea*, p. 45, a little plant of the primrose family with a delicate stem a few inches high, a whorl of elliptical leaves at its summit, and beautiful white seven-petalled flowers $\frac{1}{2}$ inch (13 mm.) across, in a small umbel. The true Wintergreens, *Pyrola* species, p. 45, with shiny dark green leathery rounded leaves on long stalks, and elegant, lily-of-the-valley-like spikes of globular white or pinkish flowers, are also frequent. The Twin flower, *Linnaea borealis*, is more local, and its trailing, delicate

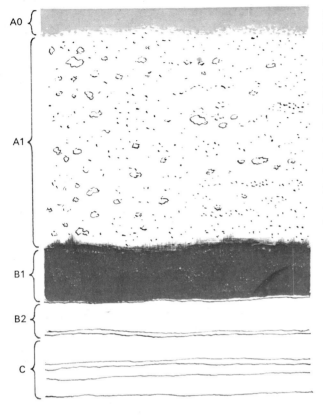

Podsol soil profile:
A0 Leaf-litter and raw humus with plant roots, black in colour
A1 Leached sandy soil, ash-grey in colour
B1 Zone of humus deposition, black
B2 Zone of iron deposition or iron pan, red-brown in colour
C The unaltered sandy subsoil, usually pale brown

stems bear pairs of tiny rounded leaves and erect stalks which carry small, pink, crimson-dotted bell-like flowers, hanging down in pairs.

Several orchids, such as Lesser Twayblade, *Listera cordata*, p. 45, with spikes of tiny pinkish flowers with hanging two-lobed lips and pairs of small ($\frac{1}{2}$–1 inch, 13–25 mm. long) shiny heart-shaped leaves, and Creeping ladies-tresses, *Goodyera repens*, p. 45, whose creeping stolons bear tufts of pointed leaves, and 6 inches to 1 foot (15–30 cm.) spikes of small downy white flowers, are quite frequent. In boggy hollows there occurs rarely the Coral-root orchid, *Corallorhiza*

trifida. This slender little orchid has brown leafless stems with little chlorophyll, and is a saprophyte, feeding on humus through the agency of the fungus associated with its roots. The flowers are few in a loose spike and have yellow-green sepals and white, pink-streaked lips 5 mm. across. More open parts of the forests are floored with heather, *Calluna vulgaris*, or with sphagnum moss and Cross-leaved heath, *Erica tetralix*, where the wetter depressions occur. A sort of open forest with much juniper, *Juniperus communis*, mixed with the heather, among more scattered pines, covers large areas.

The Scottish pine forests were once vastly more extensive than they are now, even until the eighteenth century. The Hanoverian regime destroyed great tracts of them by axe and by fire, to smoke out the Jacobites supporting the Old and Young Pretenders. Later vast areas were cut for timber. The best remaining areas, apart from the fragments near Loch Maree mentioned earlier, are in Strathspey near Aviemore – the Rothiemurchus, Abernethy and Glenmore forests; on Deeside – Glen Tanar and Ballochbuie forests; by Loch Rannoch – the Black Wood of Rannoch, and in Glen Affric. The forests that remain are, however, often of secondary growth after earlier fellings, and the natural tree-line is now only to be seen in a few places, felling having hindered regeneration up to this height elsewhere through causing exposure to the wind. The overstocking of the highlands with deer for sport in so-called 'forests' has undoubtedly also affected regeneration. Although the Red deer are true forest animals, when too numerous they damage and destroy the young trees.

The Boreal Period lasted from about 8000

Tundra vegetation typical of late-glacial times and of high mountains today (arctic or arctic-alpine species). The boulders bear flora of bryophytes and lichens only; the late snow-beds in the background with flora of bryophytes only. *Bottom left*, Dwarf birch, *Betula nana*, acid conditions; *left, above*, Reticulated willow, *Salix reticulata*, calcareous soils; *centre*, Mountain avens, *Dryas octopetala*, calcareous soils; *bottom right*, *Diapensia lapponica*, acid soils

to about 6000 B.C. Towards its close, the pollen record tells us that a mixed deciduous forest of oak began to develop in the extreme south of England, and after about 6000 B.C. this spread throughout lowland Britain and Ireland, and up into the lower slopes of the hills in the Scottish Highlands. There is still some debate as to whether the spread of this forest was only the natural succession of oak-forest following pine-hazel forest in a relatively uniform climate, or whether it represented the effect of a real improvement of climate. It has been argued that the pine-hazel forest may have built up the humus in the formerly humus-deficient soils of Early Post-Glacial times, and that slow-growing oak, with its heavy acorn fruits would in any case spread into Britain more slowly than the relatively fast-growing pine, with its light, winged seeds, capable of being blown in the wind. However, evidence from various sources suggests that at this time there was a 'climatic optimum', when the climate was warmer than at any other time before or since in the Post-Glacial Period in northern Europe. In Scandinavia at this time hazel and other trees spread further north than they occur today, and such warmth-loving animals as the Pond tortoise, *Emys orbicularis*, extended into parts of Germany and Poland from which they have since disappeared.

It was at about this time, too, that Britain became an island again. The North Sea and the English Channel became flooded as the great ice sheets of the Arctic finally melted away and retreated to their present limited area of the Greenland ice-cap. Evidence from the Dogger Bank area in the North Sea, of fresh-water peats and human settlements flooded by sea water at this time, dated by the radioactive-carbon technique, tells us when

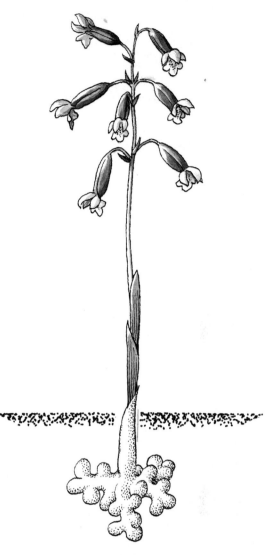

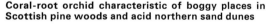

Coral-root orchid characteristic of boggy places in Scottish pine woods and acid northern sand dunes

Flora of base-rich mountain cliffs in a 'corrie' or amphitheatre formed by ice action: *left*, Sea Thrift, *Armeria maritima*, also found on sea cliffs; *back centre*, Globe flower, *Trollius europaeus*; *back right*, Rose-root, *Sedum rosea*; *bottom left*, Purple mountain saxifrage, *Saxifraga oppositifolia*; *bottom centre*, Yellow mountain saxifrage, *S. aizoides*; *bottom right*, Mossy saxifrage, *S. hypnoides*

this event took place. Ireland seems to have been separated rather earlier; many plants characteristic and widespread in the British flora, including the Small-leaved lime tree, *Tilia cordata*, never seem to have reached Ireland, yet they extend well north in Britain. Conversion of the British Isles into islands must have influenced the climate profoundly; a relatively continental type of climate with colder winters and warmer summers and less rainfall must have given way, as water spread around Britain, to a more oceanic or 'Atlantic' one with milder winters, more wind and rain, and perhaps slightly cooler summers.

The name of the new period of dominance of the mixed oak forest, the 'Atlantic' period, embodies this idea of more oceanic conditions.

What was this great primaeval forest like? It is difficult to imagine it now, as the British Isles and indeed most of north-western Europe, has been so thoroughly cleared of forests, and the fragments which remain have been so modified by man. But we know that it contained, in addition to the oaks, *Quercus robur* and *Q. petraea*, much alder, *Alnus glutinosa*, limes, *Tilia cordata* and some *T. platyphyllos*, the Large-leaved lime, as well, elm, mostly Wych elm, *Ulmus glabra*, as well as other trees and shrubs such as Yew, *Taxus baccata*, Holly, *Ilex aquifolium*, and Hazel, *Corylus avellana*, besides no doubt many others. The Beech, *Fagus sylvatica*, seems only to have become locally common and only in the south, much later on. It would have been an uneven-aged forest, unlike many woods today where all the trees have been planted simultaneously, and it would have regenerated itself naturally when gaps occurred through the fall of old trees. It would have contained many giant trees, because there were few human beings present to fell the mature trees; some of the trees may have been up to 100 feet (*c*. 30 m.) in height on the better soils, and because in places they grew close together, many trees would have reached a great height before branching, perhaps 60 or 70 feet (18–21 m.).

Also it was a forest rich in wild life, including many large mammals, predators such as the wolf, the brown bear, the wild cat and the polecat; and herbivores such as the red deer and the wild ox. The presence of these large animals must have ensured the existence of glades, open areas and trackways, especially those leading to waterholes; so the forest would not have been uniformly dense. Different plant communities would have occurred in the more shaded and less shaded areas, wetter and drier areas respectively. The period of human culture at this Atlantic period was the Mesolithic or Middle Stone Age. Man lived in Britain then, but only in small communities, mostly near water. With his small numbers and crude stone implements, he was incapable of clearing much forest, except perhaps very locally by fire after ringbarking the trees to kill them. Charcoal deposits associated with pollen of weeds of open ground have been found of this period. But man was essentially still only a subsidiary part of the great natural forest system of plants, animals and soil, the forest *ecosystem* as it is called. He lived by hunting, shooting with arrows, and fishing – activities still enshrined, perhaps by ancient folktradition, in the snobbish pursuits of the wealthy today – and was not a cultivator nor, it seems, a herdsman.

Although this great forest has gone, we can see some areas in Britain which still give us an idea of what it looked like. These are particularly in the older woodlands of the New Forest and in some of the ancient parklands of England, enclosed by the Crown or nobles as deer parks at, in some cases, a very early date, from what probably still approximated to the natural wilderness. These relics have undoubtedly been altered by some felling in the past, and the natural ecosystems have been upset by the extermination of the larger animals, both predators and herbivores. They still contain great trees, mostly beech and oak, partly in closed canopy, more often in open stands, and sometimes there is a range of ages of trees present. Most of these relic forest areas are on poor soils, for man has cleared or altered most of the forest on the better soils. The native trees which demand better soils, such as lime and elm, tend to be rare or absent though holly is usually common.

Because of the poor soils, often sands or gravels, the ground flora is often poor, and Bracken, *Pteridium aquilinum*, p. 48, or Bilberry, *Vaccinum myrtillus*, p. 45, may dominate, sometimes with the Great wood-rush, *Luzula sylvatica*, p. 48, which seems to be a good indicator of relics of old forest, together with, in the south of England, Butcher's broom, *Ruscus aculeatus*, p. 48, a low shrub with flattened spine-tipped, leaf-like twiglets. Strangely, in the New Forest, the Great wood-rush is lacking, possibly due to the centuries of grazing by deer in this Royal Forest, followed by the grazing of the New Forest ponies; but Butcher's broom is common enough there. Fine examples of old estates, mostly not open to the public without permission, where relics approximating to the old forest can be seen, include Eridge, Ashburnham and Parham Parks in Sussex; Savernake Forest in Wiltshire; Windsor Forest in Berkshire; Burnham Beeches in Buckinghamshire; Staverton Park in Suffolk; and Brampton Bryan and Moccas Parks in Herefordshire.

It is appropriate here to say a little about the ancient deciduous forest ecosystem. The deciduous trees shed their leaves in autumn on to the soil. These leaves are richer in mineral nutrients than those of conifers such as Scots pine. Deciduous trees take more from the soil than conifers, but they put more back into it as a result when their leaves fall. Hence earthworms and bacteria find these leaves acceptable food, but earthworms are very scarce in pine forests. The leaves are both well broken up mechanically as they pass through the earthworms, and well decomposed by the bacteria present and thus nutrient salts are released into the upper layers of the soil. The tendency to leaching down of the salts by the rain is to some extent counteracted by the earthworms, too, as they leave their 'worm casts' or excreted soil-food on the surface.

There is thus little tendency to the formation of a podsol type of soil with an iron-pan under a deciduous forest of oak. The oaks and other deciduous trees root more deeply than the shallow-rooted pines and produce a very efficient 'root-net' which picks up most of the nutrients coming out of the leaves, thus recycling them into the ecosystem. Very little is lost in the drainage water to great depths,

unless the soil is very light and porous; thus a typical deciduous forest, except in very wet climates, and on very porous poor sandy or gravelly soils, tends to maintain itself without deterioration. Where beech is dominant, conditions are less favourable; beech-leaf humus is more acid, intermediate in this respect between oak and pine, and beech is also shallow-rooted, and so has a less efficient 'root-net' to catch the salts in solution. Hence soil deterioration tends to be more marked under beech than under oak on light acid soils.

The animals of the forest ecosystem also show an interesting cycle. Herbivores of all sizes, from the caterpillars feeding on the leaves of the trees to the deer and oxen grazing the forest floor herbs, are preyed upon by predators – birds feed on the caterpillars, and mammals such as wolves and bears originally fed on the big herbivores. The predators breed more slowly and are thus less numerous than the herbivores. When they die in turn, they return the nutrients in their bodies to the soil, and so, together with the excreta of all the animals at all stages in the food chains, the cycles of nutrients are completed.

Some time after about 2500 B.C., a new factor arrived upon the British scene. This was Neolithic or New Stone Age man, the first real farmer. From now on, things would never be the same again. Man henceforward would no longer be a subsidiary part of the natural ecosystem; more and more he would dominate it, until no truly natural vegetation was left.

The Neolithic peoples came originally from the Near East, the cradle of civilization, where they had developed cultures long before this time. The British Isles were, however, very remote at this period and the New Stone Age arrived there very late. The Neolithic peoples had not developed the art of smelting metals to make tools, but they were far from being primitive savages. They used beautiful, delicately made implements of flint – axe heads, arrowheads, knives and scrapers for cleaning skins. These

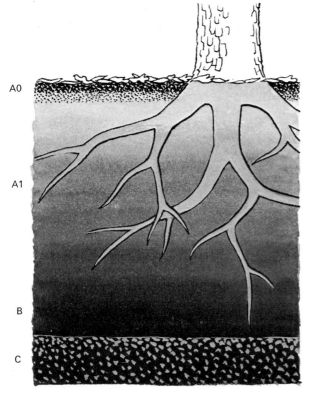

Brown forest soil profile as developed under deciduous forest of oak showing, by shading, fairly even distribution of iron and other salts in the soil
A0 leaf-litter layer and humus-rich zone
A1 Upper part of soil profile of paler brown, showing slight leaching of iron and other salts grading gradually into B
B Lower part of soil profile of deeper brown showing tendency for iron and other salts to accumulate
C Subsoil

the flints, and some of our ancient trackways, such as the Icknield Way, seem to date from this period.

Stone axes of the period were, perhaps, more efficient than one might suppose. A woman archaeologist showed this by fastening a Neolithic axe head to a modern wooden shaft. She found that she was able to fell small trees quite easily with this implement. However, clearance of dense forests of great trees would have been another matter. Such forests would have occurred on the heavier, more clayey soils, and there is little evidence of Neolithic occupation there. The main sites where evidence of Neolithic settlement have been found are entirely on the light soils of the chalk and oolitic limestone areas and on certain areas of sandy soils. The ancient trackways, too, nearly always follow the outcrops of the chalk and oolite. Because much of this type of country is open and free of forest today, and is known to have been similarly open in historic time, some people have believed that the chalk and limestone hills have always been naturally open country, primaevally grass-covered and incapable of bearing forest. One still sees statements in books to the effect that the Neolithic and other early peoples settled on the chalk lands because they were open and unforested areas. However, we now know that this was certainly not true in most cases, perhaps untrue in all.

In the open part of East Anglia known as the Breckland, a region till recent times of wide open stretches of chalky grassland, or of heathland on sandy deposits laid over the chalk in the Ice Age, there is a place called Hockham Mere. Until Tudor times this was a lake; now it has partially dried up and consists of an area of swampy woodland. Professor Godwin investigated this site and found deep peat deposits there which, he was able to show, commenced to form in Late Glacial times. He studied the pollen present in the peats and muds at the various levels from Late Glacial times to the present day, dating the levels by the radioactive-carbon method. He found that, in Atlantic

implements were made by skilled experts, apparently at a limited number of centres and for the first time a class of specialists arose in human culture. One of the great centres in England for making flint implements was Grimes Graves in Norfolk, where one can see the Neolithic flint mines, now re-excavated by the Ministry of Works, at the present day.

The bulk of the Neolithic people were apparently arable farmers; they kept some livestock but appear to have lived mainly by growing cereals of primitive types. As implement-making was largely centralized, trade routes were necessary for transport of

times, prior to the arrival of Neolithic man, the pollen 'rain' deposited at this site was wholly that characteristic of a closed forest of oak, alder, elm, lime and other woodland plants. At the levels corresponding to the Neolithic Period, a change occurred. The proportion of tree pollen decreased, to an extent suggesting clearance of perhaps a third of the forest in the district by the close of Neolithic times. At the same time, new types of pollen-grains appeared: those of wild grasses, suggesting the development of pastures on former forest sites; those of weeds or 'ruderal' plants, such as tend to invade cleared land – plants like plantain, *Plantago* species, Mugwort, *Artemisia* species, and Goosefoot, *Chenopodium* species; those of cereals, indicating arable farming; and finally, those of heath plants, such as the Ericaceae or heather family, perhaps indicating development of heath on abandoned cultivation sites.

This research gives us a remarkable picture of the changes wrought by Neolithic man on the light soils of one part of East Anglia. Since this research was carried out, much more information of a similar type has been produced from other areas, so that we can now be fairly certain that the Neolithic farmers settled in what was forest land, and progressively cleared it for farming. Such light lands probably bore less dense forest, of smaller oaks, than that on the heavier lands, and clearance, both by direct felling with stone axes of the smaller trees, and perhaps by ring-barking, followed by burning after the consequent death of the larger trees, would have been feasible. The lighter soils were attractive to early man for other reasons, too. The primitive wooden ploughs could cultivate the lighter soils but not the heavier, often waterlogged clays. Movement would have been easier, especially in winter, on the lighter lands; and since much of the chalk and limestone lands tend to be elevated above the clay lands, such sites would have been better from a defensive point of view, as the settlers could, after clearing the forest, get a good view of any

enemies before they arrived. Cultivation at first was probably of a 'shifting' type, moving from place to place as the primitive agricultural methods exhausted the soil, as in some parts of the tropics even today.

It looks very much, then, as if a large part of the chalk lands of East Anglia, the Wessex uplands, and the South Downs were cleared by the close of the Neolithic Period, together with much of the limestone country of the Cotswold Hills and the Pennines.

About 2000 B.C. the art of smelting metals was introduced into Britain. At first, this only concerned the smelting of copper ores and then the manufacture of bronze, which is a relatively soft metallic alloy of copper and tin, though tougher and harder than pure copper. Nevertheless, this was a great and significant advance, and it ushered in new waves of settlers – the peoples of the Bronze Age. Not only were these peoples equipped with superior weapons to the Neolithic people – men with bronze spears would readily overcome those equipped with only stone axes – but they were far better equipped for clearing the forest. Indeed, the evidence from Hockham Mere suggests that by the close of the Bronze Age, about 500 B.C., the East Anglian Breckland was almost entirely cleared of forest. By this date, hardly any tree pollen was being deposited at Hockham Mere.

For fuller information on the development of our flora in prehistoric times the reader should see Professor H. Godwin's great work, *The History of the British Flora* (Cambridge U.P.), 1956.

There were several successive waves of Bronze Age peoples, usually distinguished by archaeologists by their distinctive types of drinking or cooking vessels. Their effects on the vegetation seem, however, to have been very similar. They colonized not only the chalk and limestone uplands, where they built their distinctive round barrows or burial mounds, very different in shape from the long barrows of the Neolithic people, but also the sandy regions of such areas as the New Forest and east Dorset, the Lower

Greensand hills of the Weald, the Bagshot sand country south-west of London, and the uplands of north-east Yorkshire. These regions are, or were until recently, open heathlands, but Professor Dimbleby has produced evidence that these areas were forested with oak and other trees before the Bronze Age people colonized them. He studied the soil profiles both of the present surface soils, and of the buried soil profiles, beneath Bronze Age barrows, in certain present-day heathland areas, particularly in the North York moors, south of Whitby, and in the New Forest-east Dorset area. He found that the podsol soil profiles, as characteristic of heathland vegetation as of pine forests, were continuous over the present-day heathland surfaces and over the tops of the Bronze Age barrows. Buried beneath the barrows, however, he found in some cases very different soil profiles, which had been preserved and, in effect, fossilized.

Under these barrows known to be the oldest, soil profiles like those found in deciduous forests today were found in some cases – brown forest soils, without any definite iron-rich layer or 'pan' as in a podsol soil profile. He was able to extract pollen for analysis from some of these buried soils, and this pollen was largely of types characteristic of oak-forest. Some younger barrows had rather different soils beneath them, with a pollen and spore content characteristic of open scrubland with hazel, bracken, etc. In a few cases, some of the youngest barrows showed incipient development of podsol soil profiles beneath them, and contained pollen of heath plants. All this information suggested that the earliest barrows were built in land freshly cleared of its forest cover, that later ones were constructed on sites that had been cleared for some time, and that the latest barrows were built on land already cleared for such a long period that leaching by rain, together with the spread of heather, had led to the start of the process of podsolization.

It would appear, then, that by the close of the Bronze Age, most of the lighter lands on chalk, limestone, and sands and gravels in lowland Britain, together with great areas of the uplands up to the old tree-line, had been cleared of their primaeval forest cover. The Bronze Age peoples were pastoralists rather than arable farmers, and their herds of domestic animals must have helped in the destruction of forest, by preventing tree regeneration through trampling and nibbling of seedling trees. Hence the forest destruction in Bronze Age times was probably more widespread than in Neolithic times under a more largely arable farming regime of less widespread impact.

About 500 B.C., the Bronze Age came to an end with the invasion of Britain by people who had discovered the art of smelting ores containing iron. The people of the Iron Age were far better equipped for war than the Bronze Age peoples; bronze spears were probably no more a match for iron swords than were the stone weapons of the Neolithic people for the bronze spears of their successors. With the coming of the Iron Age, too, the superior axes now made it possible for forest clearance to begin on the lands of greatest forest density and of greatest agricultural potential: the deep rich loams of the river valleys and lowland plains. The heaviest clay lands, too stiff to cultivate easily, such as the Wealden clays and the Boulder clays of East Anglia, were still, however, left largely under forest: the still small population of Britain rendered their exploitation as yet unnecessary.

Now that it was possible to cultivate the best soils, much of the poorer sandy land occupied by the Bronze Age peoples seems to have gone out of cultivation and been abandoned, except perhaps for light and occasional grazing. At this time, about 500 B.C., there are clear indications of a deterioration in the climate of Britain. Bog surfaces, such as those at Shapwick Heath in Somerset, which had apparently been dry enough to be walked over freely by Late Bronze Age peoples, became much wetter, and trackways made of hazel faggots were built over them to maintain communications. These trackways in their turn were evidently flooded and smothered by the growth of Sphagnum moss. This increased wetness of climate may well have been responsible for great deterioration in the soils of the sandy lands, by leaching out the nutrient salts from the surface soils, and thus encouraging the formation of podsol soil types. It is likely that it was at this period – the Early Iron Age – that much of our heathland, both lowland and upland, was actually formed.

The chalk and limestone uplands, however, with their alkaline soils, would have resisted the leaching effects of the higher rainfall, and remained to a large extent in cultivation, or in use as grazing land, throughout the Iron Age and the succeeding Roman occupation period. Many of the Roman villas, or large farms, are concentrated on or near the chalk and oolite uplands. However, the increased rainfall after 500 B.C. may well have promoted serious erosion of the top soils over the chalk; many of our open chalk hills have remarkably shallow soils today, especially on the steeper slopes, while other hill slopes on chalk that still bear apparently ancient relic woodland have much deeper soils. Perhaps the original soils were largely lost at this time. Many Iron Age cultivation sites on chalk slopes show the remains of elaborate artificial terracing, the so called 'strip-lynchet' systems. This work may in part have been carried out in an effort to check soil erosion.

We can now see, by the time the Romans conquered southern Britain in the first century of the Christian era, that much of our original forest landscape had been profoundly modified. The apparently 'natural' lowland and upland heaths, and extensive chalk and limestone grasslands can now be seen to be, in great part, secondary plant associations, with secondary soils, too, establishing themselves on sites cleared by successive waves of earlier settlers. In the so-called 'Dark Ages' after the Romans left and before Anglo-Saxon civilization was fully established, the forests may have re-established themselves locally; but the medieval period, apart from the creation of royal hunting preserves in remnants of the old forests, was essentially a time of steady attrition of the remaining forests, until by the seventeenth century there was little more forest in the English lowlands than there is today. The great forests of the Weald lasted as long as any, but the late medieval iron (and glass) industries of Sussex and Kent destroyed most of the ancient woodlands there. In 1924, before the Forestry Commission began to make much impact in terms of reafforestation in Britain, only 5·3 per cent of the land area of Great Britain was under woodland or plantations. This meant that at this time the British Isles (Ireland had even less woodland than Great Britain) had a smaller proportion of their area occupied by woodland than any other country in Europe. In comparison, France had 18 per cent, Germany 24 per cent, Sweden 55 per cent and Finland 60 per cent.

We can see how Britain had changed from a land almost entirely covered with forest to one with the least amount of forest of any land in Europe in a few thousands of years. Economically, this situation was serious, as it meant that Britain was almost entirely dependent upon imported timber for her needs. The First World War brought home the gravity of this situation, and as a result the Forestry Commission was formed. However, the main timber need of this country in recent years has been for softwood (conifer) timber. It has a wide range of uses; it grows far more quickly than hardwood timber does, and most of the land available for reafforestation is poor 'marginal' land unsuitable both for agriculture and for good growth of hardwoods. Hence the Forestry Commission and more recently, since the Second World War, private estate owners, have tended to plant conifers rather than the native hardwoods, though this situation is now being modified to some extent.

From the point of view of the naturalist, these coniferous forests are rather dull, monotonous places, poor in flora and specialized in fauna. Nevertheless, though our remaining hardwood woodlands are now very limited in extent, a considerable number of them of diverse character still remain.

We have seen how, by 1924, only about five per cent of Britain was still under woodland of some kind. In England at that date, out of about one and a half million acres of woodland, about one third (485,000 acres or 196,000 hectares) was of the type known as coppice-with-standards woodland. Today there is probably far less of this type, as huge fellings have occurred, and continue to occur, but this type of woodland is still very much ꞏa part of the traditional lowland English scene in many counties in south, mid, and east England, particularly on the heavier soils, and it is remarkable for the beauty and interest of its flora, particularly in spring and early summer.

Coppice-with-standards woodland, pp. 46, 47, is far from being 'natural' in character, but it is very often the successor, without any real break in continuity, of the ancient forest cover. To understand its structure it is necessary to study the way this type of woodland arose.

The ancient primaeval forest was an uneven aged, self-regenerating forest. It was a 'high-canopy' forest, in which the standard trees formed a more or less continuous upper stratum, with occasional gaps, with a discontinuous stratum of subsidiary shrubs and young trees beneath this upper canopy. In medieval times, such woodlands as were not either cleared completely to create farmland, or protected as Royal Forests, tended to become more and more opened up. The tree layer tended to become sparser and sparser as more and more standard trees were removed. As a result of this, more light penetrated through the tree canopy to the shrub layer.

This stimulated the shrubs to more vigorous growth and led gradually to the formation of a more or less continuous shrub layer beneath the now very discontinuous tree canopy. It was then found that the shrub layer in the woods on the better soils, consisting largely of hazel, was of considerable value in itself as a source of small timber for various purposes. If cut back to the base, the hazel regenerated readily from the stumps or stools, and after some 12 to 15 years, produced poles of useful size. These poles could be used for fencing, for making charcoal, for firewood, for constructing hurdles, and in fruit and hop growing areas such as Kent and east Sussex, they were valuable as supports for hop-gardens or for peas or beans. Gradually cutting at regular intervals became the normal regime, and hence the coppice, as it was called, now gave a regular and useful return at relatively short intervals of time. Standard oaks, on the other hand, take about 100 years to produce timber of economic size. After a time, the density of the standard oaks themselves became standardized at from 12 to 20 trees to the acre. Under these conditions, the oaks grew in a different form from the trees in close-canopy high forest. Instead of producing long straight boles with few side branches below the high crown, they now, with much more space and light in which to expand, produced large lateral branches from a height of 12 to 15 feet (3·7–4·6 m.) above the ground, and relatively short boles. These lateral branches, in the case of the common English oak, *Quercus robur*, tended to be sinuous in form with many curves and zig-zags. Such branches were essential for the construction of wooden ships, and hence very desirable.

(*opposite*): Boreal pine forest of Scottish Highlands, Scots pine dominant: *left to right*, Cowberry, *Vaccinium vitis-idaea* with Bilberry, *V. myrtillus*; *above*, Chickweed wintergreen, *Trientalis europaea*; Medium wintergreen, *Pyrola media*; Lesser twayblade, *Listera cordata*; Creeping ladies-tresses, *Goodyera repens*

(*overleaf*): Lowland coppice with oak standards woodland. Coppiced shrubs including hazel and ash are seen growing up in the mid distance after having been cut a few years before; standard oaks are in open canopy. Flowers in foreground, on larger scale and not necessarily all to be seen at the same season, *from left to right*: Wood anemone, *Anemone nemorosa*; Primrose, *Primula vulgaris*; Bluebell, *Endymion non-scriptus*; Wood violet, *Viola riviniana*; Oxlip, *Primula elatior*; Early Purple orchid, *Orchis mascula*; Daffodil, *Narcissus pseudo-narcissus*; *behind*, Foxglove, *Digitalis purpurea*; *far right*, Wild cherry, *Prunus avium*

This type of woodland management therefore produced both valuable coppice or underwood, and trees of a form ideal for shipbuilding. Trees which in nature form standards, such as Ash, *Fraxinus excelsior*, and, in the south-east of England, Hornbeam, *Carpinus betulus*, were found to respond well to coppicing also, and many coppice-with-standard woodlands still contain these species as an important element in the underwood layer. From late Tudor times onwards, the alien tree, Sweet chestnut, *Castanea sativa*, was increasingly planted in the coppice woods of south-east England on the lighter more acid soils, as it was found to produce excellent straight poles of larger size and greater strength than those produced by other species. These poles are particularly valuable for constructing hop-gardens and, more recently, they have been used for splitting to manufacture spile-fencing. Sweet chestnut wood splits readily lengthwise in a way that other species will not do.

In earlier days, natural regeneration was apparently relied upon to replace the standard oaks when they were cut at intervals of 70 to 100 years, but later on, replanting became more usual. Many midland coppice-with-standard woodlands show the ridge-and-furrow pattern indicative of former cultivation, and hence must be wholly artificial in origin.

Many woods of this type became used for the rearing of pheasants for sport in the eighteenth and nineteenth centuries. With the object of protecting the pheasants, their young and their eggs, the gamekeepers tended more and more to kill as many of the natural carnivorous predators in these woods as they could, both birds such as hawks and owls, and mammals such as polecats, weasels and stoats, though foxes were tolerated to a

Primaeval deciduous forest of beech and oak, with holly understorey: Butcher's broom, *Ruscus aculeatus, bottom left*, with Bracken, *right*; Great woodrush, *Luzula sylvatica*, on bank of stream in *centre*. Trees are in high canopy and of varied ages from saplings to ancient giants, not even-aged as in planted woodland

certain degree for hunting. As a result, the populations of herbivores such as the small rodents and seed-eating birds greatly increased; the natural ecosystem was completely upset. These small herbivores prevented regeneration of the trees over wide areas, both by eating the seeds and the young seedling trees. The introduction of the Grey squirrel from North America made matters even worse, as this creature damaged or destroyed trees at all stages of their growth. Self-regenerating woodland has, as a result of these factors, become very rare.

In more recent years, since the First World War, the traditional coppice-with-standards type of woodland has become largely uneconomic as a means of timber production. Pure chestnut coppice is still of considerable economic value as a source of fencing material, but it grows better without the standard oaks, which tend more and more to be eliminated. Other types of coppice are of little value now; the hard wood of the hornbeam, for example, was formerly used for making wooden parts for machinery such as gear-wheels for mills, but such things are no longer made. The type of timber now in demand consists of tall, straight standard trees that can be made into planks, or into pit-props for coal mines. Hence increasingly we find replanting of coppice with standard trees in close canopy. On the chalky soils, where other trees do not grow well, the Beech, *Fagus sylvatica*, is usually planted; but on other types of soils conifers are now usually grown rather than deciduous hardwoods such as oak and ash. Conifers grow very much faster than most hardwoods and hence yield a return to the owner investing money in planting his land much more rapidly.

We must now take a look at the flora of our still extensive coppice-with-standards woodlands. The dominant oak is usually the Common oak, *Quercus robur*, which has leaves that are hairless below, almost unstalked and with ear-like lobes or auricles where the leaf joins the stem. The acorns of this species are borne on penduncles or

The Common oak with almost unstalked leaves but long stalked acorns

stalks about 2 inches (5 cm.) long, hence it is often called the Pedunculate oak. The Sessile or Durmast oak, *Q. petraea*, p. 73, is more characteristic of the woods on the lighter, more acid soils over sands and gravels, and on harder rocks in the west, south-west and north-west of Britain, described in the next chapter. It has, in contrast to *Q. robur*, leaves with tufts of star-shaped hairs in the side-vein axils below, as seen by a 10 × lens, long stalks, and no auricles; the leafblade tapers into the stalk gradually. The acorns, as the name suggests, are almost sessile or stalkless, and appear to spring directly from the twigs. In lowland Britain, however, both oaks are common,

and a great range of intermediates, probably hybrids, occur in many of our woodlands, though as a rule, *Q. robur* characters predominate on heavier soils in the lowlands, and *Q. petraea* characters on the sands and gravels. Professor Salisbury found *Q. petraea* to be the dominant oak, too, in association with hornbeam, on the rather clayey glacial gravels of south Hertfordshire.

Of the woody plants grown as coppice, the Hazel, *Corylus avellana*, is well enough known as regards its nuts with their leafy enclosing cups or cupules, but can also be readily distinguished by its leaves, which are 2–4 inches (5–10 cm.) in diameter, coarsely downy, and round in outline, apart from the long tapering point and marginal teeth. In early spring, the pale yellow 'lambs' tails' or male catkins are familiar to most people, but the female catkins, which produce the nuts after pollination, are far less well known; these look very like leaf-buds, except for the crimson-purple styles, a few millimetres long, which protrude from their apices. The Ash, *Fraxinus excelsior*, is very common as a coppice shrub on more base-rich soils, though of course it will form a fine tree if allowed to do so. The smooth grey bark and large grey-black buds are characteristic winter and spring recognition features, as are its opposite pairs of twigs (also described as decussate, or cross-like,

The Ash showing pinnate leaves and a cluster of fruits with their propeller-like wings which aid in wind dispersal

from the fact that successive pairs of branches are at right angles to one another when viewed from above, and hence give a cross-like appearance). The catkins which bear two stamens and two carpels in each flower, form attractive purple-brown clusters on the young twigs in spring as the leaves commence to expand. The leaves are pinnately compound, with several pairs of narrowly elliptical, feebly toothed side leaflets and one terminal leaflet.

The small-leaved Lime, *Tilia cordata*, with heart-shaped, almost hairless, leaves of thin texture, is only locally common in coppice woods today, probably because it has been deliberately eliminated in most areas as being of little value; it was abundant, as found from pollen-analysis evidence, in the English primaeval forests. In parts of Essex and Lincolnshire, however, it is still common enough in coppice on more fertile but well-drained soils. The Hornbeam, *Carpinus betulus*, is very local as a native, being confined to south-east England (the Weald, Hertfordshire, Essex and parts of East Anglia), but it is often the dominant coppiced shrub in these areas. If allowed to grow into a tree, it develops a form like that of beech, with a fairly smooth bark with an elliptical, not circular cross-section to the trunk. Then its greenish catkins in spring and its dense foliage of beech-like leaves (but more sharply toothed and deeper veined than in beech) render it readily recognizable.

In summer in the woodland the leaves of the trees and shrubs cast a dense shade. There is more opportunity even in mid-winter for the herbs of the woodland floor to receive light than in summer when the leaves are expanded; but then the days are short and sunshine is limited in amount, and temperatures are often too low for active growth and photosynthesis. The time of year when illumination of the ground is at its best is in March, April and early May, before the leaves of the trees unfold. Many herbs of deciduous woodlands take advantage of this season to carry out most of their photosynthesis. They expand their leaves in March,

or even, in mild seasons, in February, and flower towards the end of this 'light phase'. Hence the deciduous woodlands of western Europe are noted for their wonderful displays of spring flowers. Nowhere, perhaps, can these displays be seen to such advantage as in the woodlands of lowland Britain. In more continental Europe, the severer winters and later springs delay the flowering of many species; also many of the characteristic spring flowers of our woods are strongly 'Atlantic' species, which can expand their leaves even in mid winter in the relatively mild British climate, but cannot stand the harder winters of central Europe. Such plants are the Primrose, *Primula vulgaris*, and the Bluebell, *Endymion non-scriptus*, pp. 46, 47.

In mild winters, the Primrose retains some leaves right through the year, and is able to continue growth and photosynthesis even from December to February, producing a few flowers at this time. The Primrose, so common with us, hardly extends at all into continental Europe at the latitude of Kent and Sussex; even near the coast of the Pas de Calais it is rare, and in eastern France and Belgium it is unknown as a wild plant, though common enough in the milder climate of Normandy where the winters resemble those of southern England. In continental Europe, the place of the Primrose is taken in the woodlands on heavy base-rich soils by the Oxlip, *Primula elatior*, pp. 46, 47. The Oxlip is a very local plant in Britain, and interestingly enough is confined to that part of England with the most continental climate – the central part of East Anglia, where it is abundant enough in old coppice woods on the chalky boulder clay in the area from just west of Cambridge eastward towards Bury St Edmunds, Ipswich and Braintree. The Oxlip differs from the Primrose in bearing its flowers in loose heads or umbels on a common stalk 6–8 inches (15–20 cm.) high, like a garden polyanthus, instead of on single stems from the centre of the leaf rosette. The flowers of the Oxlip are smaller and less widely open than those of the Primrose, and of a deeper yellow; the throat of the flower is open and not contracted into a narrow tube by folds as in both the saucer-shaped Primrose flower and the cup-shaped flower of the Cowslip. Even the perfume of the Oxlip is different from that of the Primrose, being more peach-like in quality, though this character can usually only be detected on a warm sunny day. Where the Oxlip is abundant in East Anglia, the Primrose is normally absent, but around the edges of the well defined 'oxlip area' the two species meet and produce masses of sterile hybrids, which have large flowers rather like pale yellow garden polyanthuses.

The hybrid of the Primrose and the Cowslip is not uncommon at wood borders and in scrub where the more light-demanding Cowslip grows as well as the Primrose, and this is often mistaken for the Oxlip. Shakespeare's Oxlip – 'where oxlip and the nodding violet grow' – was almost certainly (in his own Warwickshire) the False oxlip, the hybrid of the Primrose and Cowslip. This hybrid has the contracted throat to the flower of its two parents, and usually wide open flowers like a Primrose, of a darker more Cowslip yellow, with the radiating orange streaks characteristic of the Cowslip flower present, unlike the Oxlip described above. The False oxlip has a scientific name – *Primula* × *variabilis*, the '×' indicating a hybrid. All these primulas have an interesting structural feature in common in their flowers. The plants are of two kinds, the 'thrum-eyed' and the 'pin-eyed' kinds. The 'thrum-eyed' plants have short styles and long stamens which are visible at the throat of the flower; the 'pin-eyed' plants have short stamens and long styles with a pin-head shaped stigma visible at the throat of the flower. This condition is known as heterostyly, and prevents self-pollination; an insect visitor to a pin-eyed flower gets pollen on the tip of its proboscis

The Hornbeam showing the leaves and female catkin at fruiting stage with the characteristic three-lobed bracts

or tongue, and this can only be transferred to the stigma of a thrum-eyed flower, deep in the throat of the corolla-tube. Conversely, an insect visiting a thrum-eyed flower picks up pollen at the base of its proboscis or even on its head, and this pollen can only be transferred to the long, emergent stigma of a pin-eyed flower.

Unlike the Primrose which flourishes on the heavier, base-rich soils, the Bluebell, p. 47, flourishes best on lighter, more loamy or even sandy soils, as long as these are not too leached out and acid, so, although they often grow together, good displays of both plants are rarely seen in one place. The Bluebell is not quite so strongly 'Atlantic' or oceanic as the Primrose, but even so it becomes rare in north-east France and does not extend into Germany. In the most oceanic parts of Britain, both Primrose and Bluebell are able to grow freely in the open fields and hedgebanks, as in Cornwall and in Pembrokeshire; but the presence of the Bluebell usually indicates former woodland. Unlike the Primrose, the Bluebell dies right down after fruiting in June, and remains dormant as a perennating bulb until early in the following spring.

Another plant which makes a brave show in the coppice woodlands in spring is the Wood anemone or Windflower, *Anemone nemorosa*, pp. 46, 47. This delightful member of the buttercup family, the Ranunculaceae, has a single perianth whorl of six or seven segments forming a white star-like flower which is frequently purple flushed beneath. Rarely, a pale blue variety is found, which must not be confused with the Blue anemone, *Anemone apennina*, which is an introduction from southern Europe with 10–15 very narrow perianth segments. Besides root-leaves, the Wood anemone bears a whorl of three stem leaves a little way below the flower; all the leaves are palmately lobed and divided. If the Wood anemone were rare, it would be much sought after for its beauty; but as it occurs plentifully in woods throughout the British Isles except in the outer Hebrides, Orkney and Shetland, its beauty is

perhaps less appreciated than it might be, like other common but lovely things. The root-leaves of the Wood anemone appear after the flower, and persist through much of the summer, like the leaves of the Primrose.

A very large number of our plant species are characteristic of our deciduous woodlands. It is not surprising that this is so when we remember that lowland Britain was once almost entirely covered with deciduous forest. It is impossible to mention more than a few more species of the spring coppice-woodland flora, but the common Wood violet, *Viola riviniana*, pp. 46, 47, with its scentless flowers, hairless heart-shaped leaves, and pale, curved notched spur must be mentioned, as also must the 'Daffodils, which come before the swallow dares, and take the winds of March with beauty'. The Daffodil, *Narcissus pseudo-narcissus*, pp. 46, 47, is now far more local than it seems to have been in earlier times, perhaps because it has been dug up so much to transfer to gardens, and perhaps because it is less happy in dense coppice woodlands than in more open types of high forest. Clusius, writing in 1601, said it was 'in such abundance in the meadows close to London that in that celebrated village [*sic*] of Ceapside the country women offer the flowers in profusion for sale in March, when all the taverns may be seen decked out with these blossoms'. What a delightful, nostalgic little picture of bygone London this brings to mind! But the March of Shakespeare and of Clusius was of course according to the old-style calendar – the Daffodil is usually found in flower in what is now the month of April. There are plenty of places still where Daffodils grow wild in abundance; very often, however, the plant seen is one of the cultivated daffodil hybrids that has been planted or has escaped from gardens. The true wild daffodil is a relatively tiny plant, rarely more than 8–9 inches (20–23 cm.) high, with small single flowers, with deep yellow, straight-sided, hardly bell-like trumpet and pale primrose-yellow perianth.

Moschatel, or Town Hall Clock, *Adoxa*

moschatellina, is characteristic of loamier or more base-rich areas; it has leaves rather like a Wood anemone, but with tiny spine-tips to each leaf segment, and of a more yellowish-green colour and fleshier texture. Like the anemone, it has a fleshy rhizome. In flower, however, it is unlike any other British plant; in fact it is usually put in a family of its own, the Adoxaceae. The inflorescence consists of five greenish-yellow flowers arranged, as its name indicates, like the faces of a town hall clock; four flowers face outwards, one faces upwards. The lateral flowers have a three-lobed calyx and a five-lobed corolla and five stamens; the terminal flower has a two-lobed calyx and a four-lobed corolla with four stamens, each stamen being split to the base and appearing as if a pair. This strange little plant is widespread, though somewhat local in Britain, and avoids heavy clay soils unless these are calcareous; it is equally at home on mountain cliffs up to 3,600 feet (1200 m.) as in lowland woods, and the one species of this strange family occurs throughout Europe, north and central Asia and in North America. It has no known close relatives and its evolutionary origin is obscure.

Speedwells of several species, genus *Veronica*, are common in our deciduous woodlands; perhaps the most characteristic woodland species is the Wood speedwell, *V. montana*, with trailing stems which are hairy all round, and which bear stalked, toothed leaves about 1 inch (2·5 cm.) long and short axillary racemes of pale mauve flowers about ¼ inch (6 mm.) across with four-lobed corollas. Commoner than this species, however, and extending on to open hedge-banks, is the lovely Germander speedwell, *V. chamaedrys*, with stems hairy on two opposite sides only, stalkless leaves, and rather larger, sky-blue flowers. The Yellow dead nettle or Yellow Archangel, *Galeobdolon luteum*, is a very common species of lowland

coppice oakwoods. Its trailing leafy stems persist in deep shade but after coppicing produce erect shoots to 1 foot (30 cm.) high with nettle-like but rather glossy leaves and attractive two-lipped bright yellow flowers in May.

The Cuckoo-pint or Wild arum, *Arum maculatum*, is another familiar flower of our coppice woods in spring, especially on bordering banks of the woods, though it hardly extends north into Scotland. It has shiny net-veined, sometimes black-blotched triangular leaves of dark green colour, about 6 inches (15 cm.) long, on long stalks, and a very peculiar inflorescence. This consists of a green sheathing hood, the spathe, some 6–10 inches (15–25 cm.) long, which encloses completely the actual flower spike in a rounded pouch; above this there projects

Germander speedwell, a very common plant of lowland woods and hedgebanks

Wood sedge, the commonest sedge of lowland woodlands

into the part of the spathe that is open a cylindrical tongue of purple colour about 2–4 inches (5–10 cm.) long, the spadix. Flies pollinate this plant; they enter the open part of the spathe, apparently attracted by the strange smell of the spadix, and crawl down to the spike of flowers enclosed in the lower, contracted part of the spathe. They reach first a whorl of sterile flowers, reduced to bristle-like structures. These they can push past downwards, but not upwards, so that they are temporarily trapped in the pouch. At the base of the spike there are female flowers which become ready for pollination first, and if these flies should be carrying pollen from another flower, this is transferred to the stigmas. Later, the whorls of male flowers, which are arranged above the whorls of female flowers, shed their pollen and the flies, in their efforts to escape, become dusted with this. Only now do the bristle-like sterile flowers which block their

escape wither, and the flies can at last escape from their vegetable 'lobster-basket', to fly away and get caught again in another *Arum* inflorescence, where they now pollinate the female flowers of this spike.

This very strange plant, related to the Arum lily and a member of the great Aroid family, Araceae, so widespread in the tropics, has long attracted the attention of country people. The spadix was thought to resemble the penis of a bird or animal, hence the old names of 'Cuckoo-pint' (the 'i' is short as in 'lint', not long as in 'pint') and 'Dog's Dibble', 'pint' being an old English word for the male organ. The other old English name of Lords-and-Ladies also has sexual connotations. It is therefore not surprising to learn that the plant was regarded as having valuable aphrodisiac properties; in fact it is quite poisonous. In late summer, when the spathe has withered away, a spike of bright scarlet berries is left, which are also poisonous.

Various grasses and sedges are found in our coppice woods, but most of them are not really so typical of this habitat as of others; but the Wood-sedge, *Carex sylvatica*, is quite common. This has large tufts of strongly keeled, deep green leaves, and long graceful spikes of inconspicuous green female flowers and male flowers with yellow stamens. The female flowers are grouped in separate, long-stalked drooping spikelets, and each flower consists of a tiny basal green scale or glume, and a flask-shaped green 'fruit' about $\frac{1}{4}$ inch (6 mm.) long from which protrude three white stigmas. The male flowers are in separate terminal spikelets and each consists of a glume and three stamens.

A very important ecological feature of coppice woodlands is the cutting of the coppice shrubs, or underwood as it is called, at intervals of 12 to 15 years. When this is done, in autumn or winter, there is a sudden great access of light to the woodland floor. Many perennial herbs which have passed into a semi-dormant vegetative state in the later years of the coppice cycle when shade is most intense are stimulated into activity the following spring. They produce extra leaves and photosynthesize much more actively than they have been able to do for many years. As a result, much food reserve is accumulated, and in the second year after coppicing, there is a great burst of flowering. Sometimes this occurs in the first year, if the winter has been mild and the spring early, but normally not enough food is accumulated until the second year for this effect of massive flower production. The resulting magnificent carpets of primroses, anemones, bluebells and other plants are a delightful and unique feature of our lowland British coppice woodlands at this stage of their cycle. Many people, who have seen this glorious phenomenon one year but not understood its cause, tend to take their families and friends to see 'that wood where the primroses – or bluebells – were so fine last year' (or more often, the year before that) – and they are puzzled to see a mediocre display among the now rapidly growing shrubs. After a year or two, brambles and other robust plants, in turn responding to the extra light, carpet the ground and commence to smother the herbs such as the bluebells and primroses. After a a few more years, the coppice shrubs themselves have grown enough to cast a dense shade around each coppice stool, and in seven or eight years their shoots meet overhead sufficiently to form a more or less continuous canopy. Beneath this, even the brambles are checked and shade-demanding plants, such as Dog's Mercury, *Mercurialis perennis*, with elliptical leaves and inconspicuous green flowers in spikes (common in Britain but extremely rare in Ireland), or Enchanter's nightshade, *Circaea lutetiana*, with thin, stalked, heart-shaped leaves and loose spikes of small two-petalled white flowers, may take over dominance of the herb layer on more base-rich soils. This state of affairs persists until the coppice is cut once again.

Besides perennial herbs, annuals and biennials may be prominent in the coppice cycle. In the first year after coppicing, many annual plants characteristic of open arable fields, such as the yellow crucifer, Charlock,

Sinapis arvensis, or Groundsel, *Senecio vulgaris*, may appear in quantity. It has been proved by experiments that such annuals do in fact remain as dormant seeds in the surface layers of the woodland soil during the 'dark phase' of the coppice cycle; their seeds can be germinated out of samples

Yellow dead nettle

of soil collected in the dark phase in the woodland if these soil samples are watered and exposed to light for some time. Biennial plants may also be important, such as Spear thistle, *Cirsium vulgare*; Foxglove, *Digitalis purpurea*, p. 47, may become abundant temporarily on sandy soils, and the yellow-flowered, furry-leaved Mullein, *Verbascum thapsus*, on calcareous soils. These biennial plants produce sterile leaf rosettes in the first year after cutting of the coppice, and flower in the second season when they have built up enough food supply for this purpose. Their seeds, when shed, remain dormant like those of the annuals until cutting takes place again.

The coppice woodlands of lowland Britain are a charming feature of our landscape which it would be tragic to lose entirely; unfortunately, as we have seen, the 'writing is on the wall' for the majority of them. Let us hope that some of them at least can be found useful, or interesting, enough to be conserved.

Coppice-with-standards has been the traditional method of management of the woodlands of much of lowland Britain. On the poorer, more acidic soils of western and northern 'highland' Britain, and also in certain hilly lowland southern areas, such as the sandy soils of the lower Greensand and of the High Weald in south-east England, a different type of management has long been the traditional practice. In these regions, the oak itself, usually *Quercus petraea*, has been usually coppiced as a source of charcoal, and of bark for tanning hides. Before the Industrial Revolution, many of the western oak woods were coppiced to provide fuel for local industries, as coal and other fuels were then too difficult and expensive to transport over long distances. In general, the coppicing of oak has long been an even more outdated practice than the coppicing of the underwood. Nevertheless, until quite recently, no other economic use was found for the former coppice oak woods. The woodlands were mostly on ground too steep and rocky, or on soils too poor, for any other type

of silvicultural use. In some, 'singling' of the coppice, the removal of all stems on the stool except one, was practised to create a kind of 'false high forest' of oak which in time came to have an almost natural appearance, though the tree boles produced in this way tended to fall over from their weak bases and rarely produced good timber. In other cases, the oak coppices were first left to grow unattended. Nowadays, land and timber production are too valuable for such neglect generally, and a large proportion of these woods have been converted to conifer-producing forests. Only conifers as a rule will grow well on these poor soils, sometimes degraded by centuries of cropping in a wet climate which tends to cause leaching of the limited nutrients available in the soils derived from the older siliceous rocks of highland Britain. Nevertheless, great areas of this type of woodland still remain. Some areas, by reason of their scenic beauty and biological interest, have been already preserved, by the active conservation and amenity movements of the present time. Associated with the oaks in such woods there often occur Birch, *Betula pubescens*, Holly, *Ilex aquifolium*, and Rowan, *Sorbus aucuparia*, with ash-like leaves and red berries.

The ground flora of many of our sessile oak woods is often very limited; in the most acid types, Bilberry, *Vaccinium myrtillus*, may be the dominant species. This is a dwarf shrub, already noticed in the flora of the boreal pine forests, which is deciduous but has its young shoots green: thus some photosynthesis can continue in winter. Ling or Common heather, *Calluna vulgaris*, may be locally common in the more open woods on the poorest soils; its abundance is usually a sign that the woods in which it occurs have degraded, often podsolized soils, and are degenerating towards heathland. The Cowwheat, *Melampyrum pratense*, so called from its large seeds like grains of wheat, is often common in sessile oak woods, though found also in other well drained habitats. It is a plant of the Figwort family, Scrophularia-

Rowan or Mountain ash, with foliage like Ash but more deeply toothed leaflets and umbel-like clusters of red fruits in autumn, common in dry acid woodlands

ceae, with unstalked narrow lanceolate leaves in opposite pairs which are often purplish-flushed, and bright to pale yellow flowers in the axils of the pairs of leaf-like bracts, forming loose spikes. The flowers have a long corolla-tube which is two-lipped and almost closed at its mouth, and long narrow calyx-teeth. This plant is interesting as it is a semi-parasite; although green, it obtains extra nutriment from woody plants such as the Bilberry and the Oak. If carefully dug up, the root connection may be found, but it is liable to break, so don't destroy many plants of Cow-wheat in a search for proof of its parasitism. In laboratory culture, it has been shown that the plant will grow vegeta-

tively on its own, but requires the extra nutriment from a host-plant in order to flower and set seed.

A great feature of many of our sessile oak woods, particularly in the wetter hilly western parts of Britain, is, however, the abundance of species of ferns. As mentioned earlier, ferns are 'flowerless' plants which exhibit the phenomenon of alternation of generations. Some ferns in their conspicuous spore-bearing generation, such as the Bracken, *Pteridium aquilinum*, do not need particularly humid conditions for growth. The Bracken indeed is not only common in the driest sessile oak woods, but is equally abundant on dry open heaths. However, the sexual generation, or prothallus, of all ferns is a delicate little plant, requiring high humidity for its development. Even in the case of the Bracken, this is true, and in order for a colony of bracken to start up, a damp spot, such as an old rabbit hole or a moist crevice in the shade of a rock, is necessary. Once the spore-bearing generation, or sporophyte, is established, however, it can spread vegetatively by means of its underground

Cow-wheat, a yellow-flowered semi-parasitic herb of sessile oak woods

east England, harbour a very rich fern flora of such species.

One of the commonest ferns of acid woodlands, which in the wetter areas of Britain may be quite plentiful in quite well-drained places in the oak woods, is the Hard fern, *Blechnum spicant*. This species is readily distinguished by its crowns of narrow lanceolate fronds which are only once-pinnate, with the narrow pinnae up to 1 inch (2·5 cm.) long in the centre of the fronds, and gradually lessening in length both above and below the centre to give the lance-shaped outline. This fern has two kinds of fronds. The outer ones are purely vegetative and arch outwards; they bear pinnae about $\frac{1}{4}$ inch (6 mm.) wide which are almost flat. The inner fronds are taller and are borne stiffly erect. These have narrower pinnae with strongly recurved margins, under which lie on either side of the midrib, continuous sori of narrow elongate form bearing the dark sporangia.

This fern does occur in eastern England but it is rather rare there, reaching a small size and being confined either to very sheltered places or boggy patches and ditches in the woodlands on acid soils: from the Weald westwards and along our western coastal regions northwards, it grows in dense masses on the sides of ravines, and in the Scottish and Welsh hills may occur right out in the open.

Our only other fern with once-pinnate fronds is the Common polypody, *Polypodium vulgare*. This fern sometimes grows on old walls or on shady hedgebanks, but it is seen in most characteristic abundance as an epiphyte on the boughs and in the forks at the apices of the trunks of oak trees in the western sessile oak woods. Unlike the Hard fern, its fronds are oblong to triangular in outline, and the pinnae, which may be up to $1\frac{1}{2}$ inches (4 cm.) long, do not become smaller to the base of the frond; there is always a long piece of leaf-stalk without pinnae at the base of the frond, which bears shaggy brown scales below. When the sori are present, this fern is unmistakable; the sori or sporangial clusters are rounded in form, about 1 mm. in

rhizomes into quite dry areas. The Bracken, which, for some reason, some people think quite erroneously is not a fern at all, is easily distinguished. It has very large, tall fronds, arising singly at intervals along the underground rhizomes, not in crowns from an erect stock as in many ferns. The almost scale-free (when mature) stalks or stipes bear large compound side lobes or pinnae alternately at intervals of several inches from each other. These pinnae may be up to 20 inches (51 cm.) long and are twice divided or bi-pinnate, the ultimate leaflets or pinnules being up to $\frac{1}{2}$ inch (13 mm.) long. Some of these bear spore-capsules or sporangia in dense rows or *sori* (singular, *sorus*) along their margins on the underside, protected by the reflexed edge of the pinnules themselves so that the sporangia are not at first visible.

Many of our woodland ferns, however, appear to require some degree of shelter and humidity even in the sporophyte generation, and some are confined strictly to constantly humid, often very shaded habitats; the rocky ravines of our western and northern sessile oak woods, and also of the Weald in south-

diameter, and borne naked on the undersides of the pinnae.

Common ferns of moist western oak woods which are also found in less abundance in woods and shady hedgebanks everywhere in Britain include the Buckler ferns, genus *Dryopteris*. In this genus, the rounded sori are borne on the undersides of the pinnae and are protected by kidney-shaped membranous scales, the *indusia* (singular, *indusium*). The kidney-shaped indusia were thought by some botanists to resemble shields (or 'bucklers' in old English), hence the name of Buckler fern. The Male fern, *D. filix-mas*, p. 17, is one of our commonest ferns after the Bracken; it has triangular-

Common polypody, with once-pinnate leaves, common as an epiphyte in damp oak woods but also seen on hedgebanks and old walls

lanceolate fronds from 2 to 3 feet (61–91 cm.) long, which are twice-pinnate with many narrow primary pinnae. The Broad Buckler fern, *D. dilatata*, is nearly as common; this has triangular bluish-green tri-pinnate fronds with long stalks or stipes which bear pointed light-brown shaggy scales, each of which has a dark brown strip down the centre. Much more local and confined to shady, sheltered ravines in west Britain and Ireland, with an outlying area of abundant occurrence in the Weald, is the Hay-scented fern, *D. aemula*, p. 73. This is one of our most beautiful ferns. It much resembles the Broad Buckler fern, which often grows with it, but it differs in the following points: the fronds are of a bright fresh grass-green, not blue-green; the pinnules are concave above, not convex as in the Broad Buckler fern, giving a crisp parsley-like look to the fronds; the lowest pinnae are much larger than the others; and the stalk of the frond bears numerous jaggedly cut scales which have no dark centre. The 'hay-scent' is only in evidence when fronds are being dried in a plant press, and the English name is misleading. Spiny Buckler fern, *D. carthusiana*, is a common and widespread fern of boggy places, both open and wooded, which must, however, be described to avoid confusion with the other *Dryopteris* species; it has tri-pinnate fronds like *D. dilatata*, but the fronds are erect, not arched back; oblong in form, not triangular; flat, not concave or convex, as regards their pinnules; and the scales of the stalk are wholly pale brown, but bluntly rounded.

The Lemon-scented fern, *Thelypteris limbosperma*, is an abundant feature of many sessile oak woods on moist acid soils, especially in the west and north; it much resembles a pale yellow-green Male fern, but the primary pinnae become progressively shorter both above and below the centre of the frond, giving it a lanceolate outline, and the secondary pinnae or pinnules are quite entire, that is untoothed unlike the toothed pinnules of the Male fern. When bruised, it emits a pleasant odour, somewhat lemon-like

. but also resinous in character. On our wetter hills, this plant grows out in the open.

More local and largely confined to ravines in the north and west are the Oak fern, *T. dryopteris*, and the Beech fern, *T. phegopteris*. Neither has any resemblance to, or special connection with, the trees whose names they bear, though both are usually found in oak woods.

The Oak fern has very delicate-looking fronds of a fresh green colour, borne on long slender, blackish stalks. At the summit of the stalk arise three slender branches, each bearing a bi-pinnate lobe. The Beech fern does not have this trefoil-like form; instead the fronds are triangular in outline, and twice-pinnate. The tip of the frond is drawn out into a long tapered point, and the lowest pinnae are longer than the rest and arch strongly upwards. Both species have creeping rhizomes bearing fronds at intervals and not erect rootstocks bearing crowns of leaves as in *T. limbosperma* and the Buckler ferns. Both are downy when young, and both are of peculiarly delicate texture. They may both occur together in great sheets in wooded gorges.

The sori in *Thelypteris* are rather like those of *Dryopteris* but smaller and with an indusium that soon withers. The Lady fern, *Athyrium filix-foemina*, is quite common fern of moist woods, rather like a pale, more delicate Male fern with more deeply cut pinnules to its lanceolate bi-pinnate fronds, but the indusial flaps protecting the sori are crescent-shaped and toothed, not kidney-shaped and entire.

The most extraordinary fern one may find in the moist shaded acid rock outcrops of our western sessile oak woods, however, is the Tunbridge Filmy fern, *Hymenophyllum tunbridgense*. Thos looks more like a moss than a fern, and behaves more like one ecologically. Its tiny oblong fronds are from 1 to 2 inches (2·5–5 cm.) in length, and apart from the dark veins are quite translucent, resembling dark green oiled silk in texture when moist; when dry they curl up as do most mosses on drying. The blades, or laminae, of the leaves are in fact only one cell thick, apart from the veins; one can see the cells with a ×10 lens. The fronds are sparingly bi-pinnate with tiny square-ended, spine-toothed pinnules. The sori are very peculiar: the sporangia are borne grouped on tiny cylindrical stalks at the tips of some of the pinnule veins and these stalks are enclosed in tiny, reversed-triangular pouches of two flaps which are toothed at the upper margins. This plant has very slender, almost horsehair-like, black rhizomes which creep about among mosses and liverworts in tangled masses on damp boulders. Its specific name of *tunbridgense* refers to the fact that it was first discovered, in the seventeenth century, near Tunbridge Wells. Like so many of our more humidity-demanding ferns, it still occurs in the Sussex High Weald near that town, in this case on moist sand-rocks in oak woods; westwards one seeks it in vain until the Quantock Hills of Somerset are reached.

One plant that is particularly abundant in the sessile oak woods is the Honeysuckle, *Lonicera periclymenium*. This is so common still, clambering over trees and bushes in

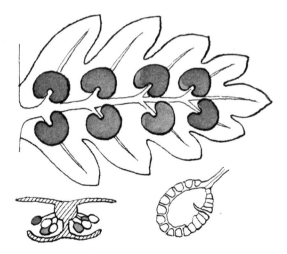

Pinnule or leaflet of Male fern viewed from below showing kidney-shaped indusium protecting the sori, *top*; section through sorus showing sporangia with umbrella-like indusium at bottom, *below left*; sporangium ×200, showing ring of thick-walled cells which contract on drying and so burst the capsule to shed the spores, *right*

Broad Buckler fern, one of our commonest woodland ferns, showing the scales on the leaf stalk with dark brown centres

Lemon-scented fern common in moist acid wood-lands throughout most of Britain and also on upland moors among boulders

well-lit hedges, that its clusters of trumpet-shaped creamy or golden flowers, with their unforgettably sweet scent, probably need little further description. What is less often realized is that this little shrub is an abundant component of the ground flora of dry acid oak woods, where, however, it never flowers, except where it is able to climb up a tree to the light. It can, however, be recognized in its flowerless state by its grey, elliptical or egg-shaped leaves, borne in opposite pairs along both the trailing stems and the erect branches.

It is one of the few examples of a liane, or woody climber, in our flora.

Another flower that is happily still common in our drier woodlands is the Wood-sorrel, *Oxalis acetosella*, p. 73. This has tri-foliate leaves rather like those of a clover, but far more delicate in texture, of a very fresh green colour, and with long pinkish-green stalks about 2 inches (5 cm.) long. The long-stalked solitary flowers are at first sight a little like small wood anemones; but the five white petals are pencil-streaked with lilac and more erect and translucent than those of the anemone.

Of the grasses characteristic of the sessile oak woods, space only allows mention of one, the Soft-grass, *Holcus mollis*. This plant forms continuous swards with its soft, greyish leaves about $\frac{1}{8}$ inch (3 mm.) wide, and its greyish-white Christmas-tree shaped inflorescences on slender stems about $1–1\frac{1}{2}$ feet (30–46 cm.) high. It can be distinguished throughout the summer by its tiny ruffs of white fur on the nodes or swellings of the otherwise hairless stems.

The Great wood-rush, *Luzula sylvatica*, p. 48, often forms great carpets, sometimes mingled with Hard fern (or in more humid spots, with Hay-scented fern) in this type of woodland. It bears strong clumps of strongly keeled glossy green leaves $\frac{1}{2}$–1 inch (13–25 mm.) wide and up to 1 foot (30 cm.) long, which bear scattered white cottony hairs. The inflorescence is up to 2 feet (61 cm.) tall and is much branched at the top, bearing clusters of brown flowers about 6–7 mm. wide,

each with three pinkish-white stigmas, six dark stamens bearing yellow anthers, and six brown perianth segments. Even commoner in our dry woods is the Hairy wood-rush, *L. pilosa*, which is much smaller than the Great wood-rush – up to about 8 inches (20 cm.) tall and the flowers instead of being borne in clusters are borne singly on long stalks about 1 inch (2·3 cm.) long, radiating stiffly from the top of the stem. The golden anthers contrast with the dark brown petal-like perianth segments.

In the boggy hollows and alongside stony rivulets of these woods, two charming little creeping plants of strongly south-western distribution may occur. One is the Ivy-leaved bellflower, *Wahlenbergia hederacea*, p. 73. This plant has delicate, almost thread-like, hairless pale green stems which creep about among the grasses and Sphagnum moss, bearing tiny thin whitish-green ivy-shaped leaves about $\frac{1}{2}$ inch (10–15 mm.) across, and beautiful pale sky-blue bell-shaped flowers also about $\frac{1}{2}$ inch (10–15 mm.) long with their ovaries below the corollas. The other is the Cornish Moneywort, *Sibthorpia europaea*. This plant is of similar delicacy and size, but its leaves are kidney-shaped, bluntly toothed and hairy, and it has very tiny pinkish-yellow five-lobed corollas to its flowers, which are only 1–2 mm. in diameter.

Ivy-leaved bellflower reaches north to Argyllshire, but Cornish Moneywort only to South Wales; both, however, occur in south-west Ireland, and also in the Weald, like so many oceanic plants. Both are members of the 'Lusitanian' element in our flora, whose headquarters is in north Spain and Portugal, where, in woodlands and on acid moist heaths, they find the mild, humid climate they require for optimum development. They are not plants of the dry, hot Mediterranean coasts of Spain beloved of sun-worshipping holidaymakers.

It will be seen that the moist, acid oak woods of south and west Britain and Ireland are rich in interesting flowering plants and ferns. Nevertheless, the total number of species is far less than in many of our lowland oak woods in central and eastern England, where the 'continental' element in our woodland flora is so richly developed on the more base-rich soils in a region of warmer summers, though colder winters. It is interesting to note that the Irish flora is singularly lacking in this continental element in its woodland flora. This may be partly due to the much more oceanic climate of Ireland, and perhaps partly due to the almost complete destruction of the natural woodlands of that island; but the main reason appears to be that many species migrating into the British Isles from central Europe after the Ice Age had ended did not manage to reach Ireland before the rising sea level cut it off from Britain.

The moss and liverwort (bryophyte) and lichen floras of the western sessile oak woods, however, are in complete contrast numerically to those of our eastern and midland woods; far more species of bryophytes occur in the wetter climates of the western woods than in the east. As in other respects, the woods of the Weald resemble those of the south-west far more in their bryophyte and lichen floras than those of East Anglia.

The Alder, *Alnus glutinosa*, has been an abundant tree in this country since 'Atlantic' times, as we know from pollen-analysis. It is characteristic, however, of soils with a water-table which is permanently high, and in such places, along with several species of willows, *Salix* species, it is the characteristic forest dominant. It is common along open streamsides, and probably alder forest always formerly occurred in these places, too.

The Alder can form a large tree, although it has often been coppiced in the past. It has characteristic glossy deeply veined dark green leaves of a very obtuse, rounded form, broader than long, and frequently shallowly notched at the apex, quite unlike those of our other forest trees. In winter and spring it can be recognized by its dark branches and twigs which appear in silhouette against the sky to be arranged in horizontal layers, rather like those of a deciduous conifer. The catkins

appear during the winter and open before the leaves unfold, and are characteristic. The male catkins are at first purplish brown and like small hanging cigars, but open, sometimes even in January, to resemble dark-speckled versions of the dangling 'lambs' tails' of the hazel, with dark bracts and yellow stamens. The female catkins are at first purplish, then green and egg-shaped and about $\frac{1}{2}$ inch (13 mm.) long, but these persist long after the seeds are shed as black

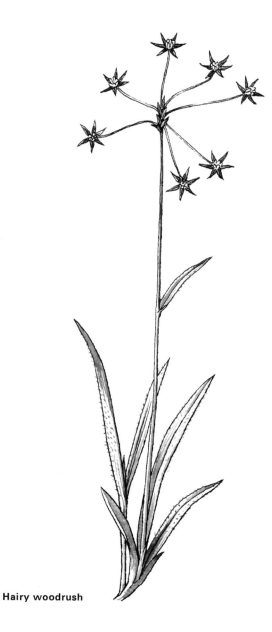

Hairy woodrush

woody structures like tiny pine-cones; they remain obvious still on the bare twigs the next winter, when the purple female catkins for the following spring are already developed.

The bark of the alder is glossy on young branches, but becomes very dark and fissured with age. Some of the roots of this tree are very shallow and bear peculiar reddish clusters of cylindrical coral-like outgrowths on them which are exposed on the surface of the soil. These may aid, like the so-called 'pneumatophores' of the mangroves of tropical tidal swamps, in the oxygen supply of the roots in a waterlogged soil; they certainly contain bacteria which 'fix' atmospheric nitrogen, thus rendering it available to the tree as a nutrient.

Extensive Alder woods occur in some of our fenland areas, as in the Broads district of Norfolk; such woods are perhaps the 'climax' or end-stage of succession on these waterlogged, alkaline peats. Because it is difficult to exploit them, they are often more 'natural' than many of our other types of woodland, and in high summer are often impenetrable jungles of brambles, wild hop, nettles and other plants.

Alder woods are, however, widespread throughout the British Isles, except Scotland, on waterlogged soils, particularly on springlines, where previous water-bearing strata overlie impervious rocks and the water emerges. Such sites are found in innumerable valleys, large and small, and at the foot of escarpments. The characteristic soils in such places are peats, or peaty muds, rich in vegetable remains which accumulate because there is not enough oxygen available in the waterlogged conditions for bacteria to decompose them as they do in better drained environments. Such Alder woods may have a nutrient-poor, usually acid oligotrophic water supply, or they may have a nutrient-rich eutrophic water supply of high, even alkaline, pH value, depending on the type of rock the water comes from.

The oligotrophic type of valley Alder wood is relatively poor in species. Sphagnum mosses may carpet the ground, studded with clumps of sedges such as the Greater tussock sedge, *Carex paniculata*, with almost pampas-grass-like foliage and oval spikes of brown flowers, or the slender *C. laevigata*, with long graceful inflorescences bearing widely separated drooping spikes of flowers, the green spikes of female flowers below and the yellow male spikes above. Where there is more movement of water, the Opposite-leaved Golden saxifrage, *Chrysosplenium oppositifolium*, p. 74, forms extensive carpets. This plant has a succulent, brittle texture, and its creeping mats bear erect flowering stems 3–4 inches (7–10 cm.) tall with rounded bristly leaves in opposite pairs and umbels of tiny flowers each with four golden-yellow sepals, eight tiny stamens, and two styles. These flowers, though small, are attractively massed in their umbels with surrounding whorls of glossy greenish-yellow bracts. In April in southern England, later in the north, this plant is a conspicuous feature of nearly all our springy Alderwoods, giving glowing masses of golden colour. One of our ancient plant genera, the Horsetail, *Equisetum*, is not uncommonly represented in north Britain in such places by the graceful Wood horsetail, *E. sylvaticum*, p. 17. This species, less common southwards, has the hollow stems, whorled branches and terminal cones of its genus, but may be recognized by its branches being themselves whorl-branched in a delightfully feathery manner, and by its bright green colour.

Those interested in bryophytes will find, in the springs and stony rill-sides of such woods, a rich harvest of moisture-loving species.

The more eutrophic valley Alder woods of southern and eastern England are, however, much more interesting places for flowering plants. They should, however, only be visited in spring, in late March or April, when they are carpeted with flowers. In high summer and early autumn they tend to be formidable tangles of rank nettles, etc., like the fen alder woods. In springtime, besides the Opposite-leaved Golden saxifrage, the much more local but far more beautiful Alternate-leaved species, *Chrysosplenium alternifolium*, p. 74, may be found. This species seems to require not only more calcareous water than the more ubiquitous *C. oppositifolium* demands, but water rich in iron as well, for it is absent from the calcareous but iron-free waters of the chalk-spring alder woods, though present in those deriving from more impure limestones. It is larger than *C. oppositifolium*, and has bluntly toothed kidney-shaped root-leaves on stalks 1–2 inches (2·5–5 cm.) long. The stem leaves are alternately arranged as the specific name suggests, and the flower-heads are larger with bigger, more deeply toothed bracts with a splendid golden, almost metallic, sheen.

Marsh Marigold or Kingcup, *Caltha palustris*, p. 74, like an enormous golden buttercup with flowers up to 2 inches (5 cm.) across, stout hollow, often sprawling, stems, and large glossy green, triangular to kidney-shaped leaves, reaches its best development in such woods. It differs from true buttercups, *Ranunculus*, in having a single perianth and bag-like carpels which contain several seeds each; in buttercups, there is a green calyx of five sepals and a yellow corolla of five petals, and the tiny carpels are one-seeded, indehiscent achenes or nutlets, not bag-like follicles which open at the top to release the several seeds as in *Caltha*.

In late April and in May, another attractive plant comes into flower in this type of Alder wood throughout most of Britain. It is Large-flowered bitter-cress, *Cardamine amara*, p. 74. It looks very like an erect-growing watercress except that its pinnately compound leaves are of a paler green colour and its much larger, $\frac{1}{2}$ inch (13 mm.) wide, white flowers have beautiful purple anthers. Many other plants may be found in such woodland; perhaps the Great horsetail, *Equisetum telmateia*, is one at least that should be mentioned. This is the largest British horsetail, reaching 3 feet (91 cm.) in height, and it tends to occur in dense stands on seepage areas. The stems are round and pale green and bear dense whorls of simple branches.

The cones are borne on unbranched stems in spring, and are up to 2 inches (5 cm.) long; the vegetative shoots, which bear no cones, arise later.

Those who wish to explore Alder woods are recommended to wear gumboots, and even then to tread warily.

Woodlands on calcareous soils developed over chalk or limestone tend to be very different in character from others and to have rich, rather specialized floras. The most familiar calcareous woodlands, to most people in southern England at least, are the beech hangers on the scarps and steep dry-valley sides of the chalk downs. The close stands of the smooth grey columnar stems of the Beech, the relatively bare floor, and the arching branches meeting overhead, suggest the interior of a Gothic cathedral, and there are those who believe that such forests provided the inspiration for the concept of Gothic architecture itself in some degree.

The Beech, *Fagas sylvatica*, is a familiar tree to most people, with its smooth grey bark and egg-shaped almost untoothed leaves which turn such a splendid bronze colour in autumn. The fruits or beech nuts, triangular in cross-section, and borne singly or in pairs inside woody cups or cupules which are shaggily scaly outside, are also fairly familiar edible objects of the autumn. The tassel-shaped male and cup-shaped female catkins borne in May are, however, less well known to most people. The Beech has, unlike the oaks, a relatively shallow root-system, as one can see when examples are blown over in a gale – a rare occurrence with the deep-rooted oaks.

In the typical calcareous beechwood of the chalk hills or of the Cotswold oolitic limestone, the trees are frequently close together and little ground flora is obvious at first. The soil is usually very shallow; in fact on the steeper slopes it consists of only a few inches of finely weathered chalk mixed with leaf-derived black humus over chalk rock; elsewhere a deeper blackish calcareous loam, also derived from the chalk itself, may be found.

It is known from records that many of the Chiltern beechwoods, at least, have been planted, probably to supply beech timber for the Chiltern furniture industry, either on former sheepwalk downland or on the sites of former mixed woodlands, and the naturally developed beechwoods studied by Watt on the south downs were shown by him to have occupied sites cultivated in Iron Age times, if not later. Thus it has been suggested that many of our calcareous beechwoods are secondary, not primaeval, in origin, and have colonized areas where erosion after felling and cultivation in the past, possibly in prehistoric times, have caused removal of older, deeper soils, and hence made it impossible for such trees as the oaks to recolonize, but no one knows for certain. What is certain is that the Beech is not a 'calcicole' species, that is one which requires a chalky alkaline soil. It grows best, in fact, on deep non-calcareous brown forest soils, developed on clay-with-flints parent material in such places as the Chiltern plateau. But nevertheless, as the shallow-rooted Beech is the only British tree that can form 'climax' forest on these chalk scarps, it has become dominant on most of those that have been allowed to develop woodland.

Within many calcareous beechwoods, there is little or no shrub layer, perhaps because of the dense shade the Beech casts. However, the Yew, *Taxus baccata*, may often form an understorey in older, perhaps more natural beechwoods of this type, probably because, being evergreen, it can carry on photosynthesis in our relatively mild winters, when the beech canopy is bare of leaves.

The Yew is a gymnosperm and a member of the conifer order, but it bears no female cones. Instead it bears solitary egg-shaped naked grey-green seeds, surrounded by coral-red fleshy cups, or arils, which are sickly sweet in taste and attractive to birds which eat and disperse the seeds. The arils are safe to eat, though all other parts of the Yew are very poisonous. The male cones of the Yew are tiny, about 3–4 mm. in diameter, globular bodies, borne on separate male trees, from the female trees which bear 'flowers' and seeds. The bows of our medieval archers were made from Yew, though much of the wood for these is said to have been imported in fact from Spain; the elastic qualities and great toughness of the wood are due to its being composed of close-set tracheids as they are correctly called, elongated cells with pitted walls and pointed ends, which differ from the tracheids of the softer, less-tough wood of pine and fir in having spiral thickenings inside them. Like the Beech, the Yew is not a true calcicole plant at all; it is not uncommon in old woodlands in south and west England and western Ireland on well-drained acid, even rocky soils; also like the Beech, it is able to colonize the shallow well-drained soils of the chalk where trees requiring deeper soil cannot compete successfully.

Pure woods of Yew occur on our southern chalk hills – a famous example is at Kingley Vale in Sussex. These woods are sombre, forbidding places, and due to the intense shade and toxic leaf-litter, have no ground flora at all.

The deep shade, and the rather toxic leaf-litter of a dense beechwood often preclude the growth of many herbs on the forest floor, but where the soil is rather deeper and more moisture-retaining, the Dog's Mercury, which tolerates much shade, may form a continuous carpet. On shallower soils, a small umbelliferous plant, the Sanicle, *Sanicula europaea*, is often dominant on the ground. It has basal rosettes of rather ivy-like leaves and stems about $1-1\frac{1}{2}$ feet (30–45 cm.) high, bearing loose umbels of pinkish-white flowers followed by rounded bur-like fruits with hooks on them which stick to passing animals – and the clothes of humans – so becoming dispersed. Also quite common is the Sweet woodruff, *Asperula odorata*, an elegant erect bedstraw-like plant with whorls of shiny narrow green leaves about 1 inch (2·5 cm.) long, and loose panicles of tiny bell-shaped four-petalled white flowers, also followed by bur-type fruits. This plant contains the aromatic chemical

Yew showing foliage and the fruits with their red enclosing cup, or aril, from which projects the tip of the seeds

coumarin, which gives it a delicious vanilla-like odour when bruised. Here and there one is likely to see a shrub of 2–3 feet (61–91 cm.) high with elliptical laurel-like evergreen leaves, the Spurge laurel, *Daphne laureola*, p. 91. In summer this bears black berries, but in early spring the clusters of inconspicuous four-sepalled green flowers with eight yellow stamens can be found below the terminal clusters of leaves. Some people find these flowers sweetly fragrant; others are quite unable, for reasons of genetics, to detect any perfume. Much more locally in such woods, and usually on chalk screes, one may find the Stinking hellebore, *Helleborus foetidus*, p. 91. This is actually a herb, but produces shrub-like over-wintering shoots, about 1 foot (30 cm.) tall. These bear distinctive dark green leaves which are divided into narrowly lance-shaped toothed segments, arranged like the ribs of a fan. The inflorescence, which is much branched, rises above the leaves, on a pale green stem and consists of very pale, almost yellowish-green cup-shaped flowers composed of five sepals, each with a purple margin, and numerous yellow stamens. Later the three free carpels of each flower develop into sack-shaped follicle-type fruits rather

like those of the Marsh Marigold; the Hellebores are members of the buttercup family. Close inspection of the flowers reveals trumpet-shaped nectaries within, full of viscous fluid. The 'stinking' epithet is misleading; the plant has a harsh acrid smell, but is hardly disgusting in odour.

Deadly nightshade, *Atropa belladonna*, a shrubby looking herb up to 3 feet (91 cm.) high with heart-shaped thin leaves, about 3 inches (8 cm.) long, and flowers like dull brownish-purple 1 inch (2·5 cm.) long Canterbury Bells, is occasionally found in open spots in chalky beechwoods. The fruits are the size and colour of black cherries, but these are deadly poisonous, as is the whole plant – so beware of it.

In early summer, various orchids may be found in chalky beechwoods. Very common and general in those from the Cotswolds and Cambridge southwards is the Large White helleborine or Egg orchid, *Cephalanthera damasonium*, p. 92. This plant has an erect simple stem up to about 15 inches (30–40 cm.) in height, bearing parallel-veined, dark green leaves, egg-shaped below, elliptical to shortly lanceolate above. The flowers are borne in a loose spike; they are about 1 inch

(2·5 cm.) long, egg-shaped, cream-coloured, and do not normally open widely. The lower petal or lip has a wrinkled surface the colour of egg yolk, so it is easy to discern the origin of the name. This orchid, in fact, normally pollinates its stigmas with its own pollen, so does not need to open widely. Such flowers are described as being cleistogamous. There are three outer perianth segments or sepals, and three alternating inner segments or petals, of which the lowest one is enlarged to form the lip. There is a single sessile anther, and a stigma which is also unstalked. The ovary is inferior and produces after fertilization a vast number of tiny seeds. These characters just outlined are characteristic of nearly all the orchids.

Much more rarely, one may find the Sword-leaved helleborine, *C. longifolia*. This differs from the Large White helleborine in its very long, narrow, almost grass-like, somewhat drooping leaves, and its pure white, smaller flowers which open widely and need to be cross-pollinated by bees if seed is to be set. This orchid is actually much more widespread than the Large White helleborine, being found almost throughout Great Britain and occurring in Ireland, too, but it is nowhere plentiful, except perhaps locally in the east Hampshire beech hangers.

Rarer still is the Red helleborine, *C. rubra*, very like the last but with rose-red flowers, downy stems, and shorter leaves; it is only known in a few beechwoods in the Cotswolds and one in the Chilterns.

Later in the year, in July and August, other types of orchid also called helleborines are found, members of another genus, *Epipactis*. The commonest is the Broad-leaved helleborine, *E. helleborine*. This plant has egg-shaped leaves rather like those of the Large White helleborine, but has many more flowers per spike, up to 50 or 60, and these are wide open, greenish to dull purple in colour, about 2 cm. wide, with lips that consist of a cup which appears to contain nectar, to which is attached a heart-shaped pinkish-white appendage about 4–5 mm. wide. This plant is pollinated only by wasps.

All these orchids, though they have green leaves, can grow in deep shade, and it is probable that they obtain at least some of their organic food, via the fungus always associated with orchid roots, from the decaying humus in the soil that this fungus breaks down. Such higher plant-fungus partnerships are called mycorrhizas; with orchids growing in better-illuminated places, the movement is probably the other way, with the fungus obtaining some organic food from the products of the photosynthesis of the green leaves of the orchid.

Some orchids, and certain other plants, however, have no green chlorophyll at all. Such plants must obtain their organic food entirely from decaying humus, through the intermediary of their fungus partner, and are called *saprophytes*. The commonest orchid of this type is the Bird's-nest orchid, *Neottia nidus-avis*, p. 92. This odd-looking plant is widespread in the British Isles, though commonest growing on the leaf-mould of our southern beechwoods. It is honey-brown in colour throughout, its leaves are reduced to brown scales, and it has a fleshy stem which is from 8 to 16 inches (20–40 cm.) high. It bears a cylindrical spike of flowers with hanging four-lobed lips. The name comes from the root system, which consists of a tangled mass of cylindrical bodies, which perhaps looks a little like an untidy bird's nest. Also occasional in similar habitats is the much shorter, 4–8 inches (10–20 cm.), yellow (not honey-coloured) Yellow Bird's-nest, *Monotropa hypophegea*. This is not an orchid, but a relative of the heath family, with tubular flowers and a pin-head shaped stigma in each flower. This is also a total saprophyte. Many other interesting orchids may be found in calcareous beechwoods; some of them are more characteristic of chalk scrub, and are described later.

The Beech, as noted earlier, is not a true calcicole; it flourishes also on the clay-with-flints covered plateaux of the downlands of south-east England, and occurs in ancient and undoubtedly (in many cases) natural forests on acid sands and gravels, such as in the New Forest, the Weald, and Burnham Beeches in Buckinghamshire. Locally in these areas it is even the dominant tree species of the forest, ousting the oak by its faster growth, and huge ancient individuals occur; sometimes these have been pollarded and have grown into grotesque shapes. Such trees may well be of early seventeenth-century origin, because pollarding became illegal, in the Royal forests at least, in 1698. The Beech, however, appears to have a very restricted distribution as a native in Britain; it probably is not native now north and west of a curved line from Epping Forest through Luton and the north Cotswolds to Breconshire, the Wye Valley, the Mendips and the Dorset-Hampshire border region. North and west of this line, old, apparently unplanted woodlands on limestone are dominated by other trees. Usually the Ash is the dominant tree today, but many of these woods appear to be of secondary origin; various lines of evidence suggest that the primaeval woodlands on limestone north and west of the natural limits of the Beech were dominated rather by Wych elm, *Ulmus glabra*, the two native limes, *Tilia cordata* and *T. platyphyllos*, Field maple, *Acer campestre*, and some oak, as well as various shrubs. Many of the pure ash woods on the Derbyshire limestone, for example, though with a well-illuminated floor and alkaline humus from the ash leaves, have relatively monotonous ground floras, while other woods, which contain in addition the other trees mentioned above, have far richer ground floras, possibly relic from the primaeval forest. Such 'relic' woodlands tend to occur on steep scarps or craggy places where they are more likely to have been left alone by man, and where organized silviculture would always have been difficult.

Wych elm, *Ulmus glabra*, forms a large tree with usually a branched main stem and a wide crown. It lacks the basal 'brushwood' of the English or Common elm of our lowland hedgerows, and has large, 4–5 inches (10–13 cm.) long, rhomboid or rounded diamond-shaped leaves with rough hairs and jagged teeth. Like other elms, it has oval winged fruits. It is usually confined as a native tree now to limestone scarps, though it was certainly widespread on the best soils in early times all over Britain up to the Scottish Highlands. The two native limes have heart-shaped leaves, fat blunt reddish buds, and hanging clusters of sweet-scented cream-coloured flowers in July. The Small-leaved lime, *Tilia cordata*, is still scattered about England in odd places such as ravines on the better soils, and as we have already seen, here and there in lowland coppice woods. The Large-leaved lime, *T. platyphyllos*, on the other hand, which has large, 4 inches (10 cm.) wide, long pointed leaves, downy below, and strongly ribbed fruits, in contrast to the small, 1½ inches (4 cm.) wide, glabrous, more orbicular leaves and smooth fruits of *T. cordata*, is a much more local plant, now almost confined to relic woods on a few limestone cliffs and ravines. The Common lime, *Tilia × europaea*, so commonly planted in our parks and gardens, is a hybrid of the two native species with intermediate characters; as a native tree it is very rare, but sometimes occurs with its two parents in the wild. The Field maple, *Acer campestre*, is a much more widespread species in Great Britain (but not apparently native in Ireland) where it is common as a hedgerow tree and shrub, and in pastures, as well as in old woodlands. It has palmately lobed leaves of typical maple shape but rarely more than 2 inches (5 cm.) wide.

The rich ground flora of the well-lit old mixed woods on limestone contains, besides plenty of Dog's Mercury and other plants common to other types of woodlands, more local and ecologically interesting species, such as Lily-of-the-valley, *Convallaria*

Western sessile oak wood with rocky ravine and waterfalls: foliage and acorns of Sessile oak, *Quercus petraea*, top right; foreground, left to right: Ivy-leaved bellflower, *Wahlenbergia hederacea*; Wood sorrel, *Oxalis acetosella*; Hay-scented fern, *Dryopteris aemula*. Boulders and oak trunks covered in lichens and bryophytes in this humid environment

majalis, which perhaps, with its racemes of cup-like white sweet-scented flowers and elliptical leaves, 4–6 inches (10–15 cm.) long, needs little more description. Herb Paris, *Paris quadrifolia*, is a feature in May and June of many such woods. It has an erect stem 6–8 inches (15–20 cm.) high which bears a single whorl of four, or sometimes five or even six, fresh green, elliptical leaves with net-veining, unusual in a monocotyledon, as *Paris* is in fact. Arising from the whorl of leaves is a single green flower about 2 inches (5 cm.) across of four narrow sepals and four narrow petals, eight narrow stamens, and a purple ovary of four carpels which develops into a black berry. *Paris* is also found in certain types of base-rich damp oak woods. It is often mingled with Dog's Mercury, whose leaves are of similar colour though narrower, and hence can be hard to spot unless in pure colonies. This is one of the woodland plants, frequent in Britain, that are unknown in Ireland. In more northern limestone ash-elm woods, many other species may occur, such as the lovely Wood cranes-bill, *Geranium sylvaticum*, with purple to lilac flowers up to 1 inch (2·5 cm.) wide with five notched petals and a prominent stylar column in the centre, and with hairy, palmate (open hand-shaped) leaves. The 'tall-herb' communities of these northern woods are among the loveliest associations to be seen in our woodland floras. Wild Garlic or Ramsons, *Allium ursinum*, with leaves like Lily of the valley in shape and umbels of white star-like flowers in May, is common on deep moist soils in limestone woods throughout Britain, but its garlic smell, though attractive to some, is repulsive to others.

We have seen already how low a percent-

Moist Alder wood: Alder, *Alnus glutinosa*, with leaves and male and female catkins shown in inset at top right, is the dominant tree. *From left to right*: Marsh marigold, *Caltha palustris*: Lesser celandine, *Ranunculus ficaria*; Large-flowered bitter-cress, *Cardamine amara*; Alternate-leaved Golden saxifrage, *Chrysosplenium alternifolium*; Opposite-leaved Golden saxifrage, *C. oppositifolium*

age, about 5 per cent, of woodland there is in Britain, how much of this is planted, and how little of the rest is truly natural. The landscape of the British lowlands is almost entirely man-made; yet it still has great beauty and a great abundance and variety of plant life, at least in some of its habitats. The great majority of our population lives in the British lowlands, and for most of us these man-made habitats are the most familiar, and most accessible, places in which to study plants. Therefore we shall take a look at some of them.

Before the Enclosure Acts of the eighteenth and early nineteenth centuries, the largely open landscape of lowland Britain had consisted mainly of huge open hedgeless arable fields and extensive common grazing lands, with only occasional woodlands and riverside meadows. After these Acts, it became largely the patchwork of small fields, some arable, some permanent pasture, all surrounded by thick hedges, that we see today. This is the landscape that still produces a nostalgic prickling in the throat of the returning traveller, who has been some time abroad, as his plane descends through the clouds and he sees the familiar 'patchwork quilt' of our countryside. Today, it is in the throes of a new agricultural revolution; fields are being made far larger to suit modern agricultural methods and machines, and in some areas, especially parts of East Anglia, hedges are being swept away on a huge scale. But much still remains for the naturalist to study in most districts of Britain.

The 'permanent pastures', so much a feature of our countryside since the Enclosures, are rapidly disappearing in favour of the more nutritious temporary 'leys', which are sown with mixtures of various plants, but above all with Rye grass, *Lolium perenne*, and Dutch White clover, *Trifolium repens*. After a few years, the ley sward tends to deteriorate, and it is usual then to plough and re-sow. The spread of leys means that the variety of wild flowers in our pastures has become greatly diminished, but this is one of the things that we must accept as a general

Wych elm showing leaves and winged fruits

rule in the interests of more efficient agricultural productivity. More stock can be fed
on a good ley than on the old type of permanent pasture. Nevertheless, there is still a
strong argument in many cases in favour of
the old mixed pasture swards, for the variety
of feed ensures that animals grazing there
obtain trace nutrients that they may not
get so readily from a pasture sown with only
a few species of plants. It has been noticed
that cattle grazed on a ley will often seek out
a variety of plants that have survived round

Small leaved lime showing leaves which are hairless
below, unlike Large leaved lime, and the characteristic fruits

Bulbous buttercup, still abundant in the drier permanent pastures and meadows

the edges of the ley, and eat them with evident relish.

The old type of permanent pasture is, however, still very widespread in most areas, and it will probably be a long time, if ever, before it disappears completely. In these old pastures, there is a very wide variety of species present, and many of these vary from district to district, or even from one field to the next according to differences in the soil. Grasses of various species form the bulk of the herbage as a rule, and these are best studied in June. Meadow Foxtail, *Alopecurus pratensis*, is very common on the heavier soils, and it is one of the earlier grasses to flower, often beginning in May. It has greyish-silvery inflorescences 2–3 inches (5–7·5 cm.) long, which as the name suggests are rather tail-like, though the resemblance is closer to the tail of a cat than that of a fox. The close-set spikelets, or units which build up the inflorescence, each consist of a pair of boat-shaped hairy glumes, 4–5 mm. long, which pair enclose one or two flowers. The flowers themselves consist of a pair of delicate scales called lemmas enclosing the three long stamens and the two feathery stigmas typical of grass flowers, but you will find it difficult to see the lemmas – the outer one, however, bears a long bristle, or awn, which projects from the enclosing glumes, giving the whole tail-like spike a silky hairy appearance. Rather later there flowers the rather similar-looking but more rigid Cats-tail grass, *Phleum pratense*, which has shorter, more bristly glumes of a more square-ended form, and short spines on the tips of each glume at the outer corners. The whole of each little spikelet looks like the end of a little ambulance stretcher 3–4 mm. long. This grass is usually in drier places than the foxtail.

Most of the other grasses in permanent pastures have much looser, more branched inflorescences, sometimes rather like a Christmas tree in form, in which the individual spikelets can be seen more easily on their longer stalks. Meadow fescue, *Festuca pratensis*, is typical of these. The loose inflorescence is about 2 feet (61 cm.) tall, pyramidal in form, with long stalked, shiny spikelets of flowers without bristles (awns), and the leaves are flat and about 5–6 mm. wide. Cock's-foot grass, *Dactylis glomerata*, is an abundant and nutritious pasture grass; it forms dense tufts of rough leaves which are strongly folded, or keeled, and up to 8 mm. wide and 10 inches (25 cm.) long. The pyramidal inflorescence, on a stalk from 1 to 3 feet (30–91 cm.) tall, has a few short branches which bear dense crowded clusters of grey-green, hairy flowers. Dog's-tail grass, *Cynosurus cristatus*, is equally common and has shorter stems, up to 2 feet (61 cm.) high, bearing spike-like narrow inflorescences, in which the spikelets all turn to one side, and have narrow, rigid, almost spine-like scales spreading like the fingers of open hands. Later on in the summer, Yorkshire Fog grass, *Holcus lanatus*, which has Christmas-tree shaped inflorescences on stems 1–2 feet (30–61 cm.) high, is often abundant, particularly on heavy land; it can be recognized from other similar-looking grasses because the whole plant – stems, leaves, leaf-sheaths and flowers – is wholly grey or pinkish grey downy.

Very conspicuous in permanent pastures in late May and in June are the buttercups, *Ranunculus* species. Most people do not, perhaps, realize that there are three, not one common species of buttercup in the pastures of this country. *Ranunculus bulbosus*, the Bulbous buttercup, is commonest in drier pastures (also on chalk downs and fixed sand dunes). It has an erect branched stem up to 16 inches (41 cm.) tall, with a corm-like tuber at the base. The lower leaves are three-lobed or ternate and rounded in outline, with toothed segments, the five-petalled flowers are of a clear bright yellow, and the five green sepals are strongly bent back on to the furrowed flower-stalk. *Ranunculus acris*, the Meadow buttercup, is the species most common in damper meadows and pastures; it is rather taller than *R. bulbosus* (up to 3 feet, 91 cm. high), and has flowers of similar colour. There is no corm at the stem-base, and the lower leaves are five-lobed. The sepals are not bent back or reflexed but are adpressed to the petals, and the flower-stalk is not grooved. *Ranunculus repens*, the Creeping buttercup, has a more sprawling habit, though it may reach a height of 2 feet (61 cm.), and it has creeping stolons, which the other two species lack; these are a dreadful nuisance in damp gardens. The leaves are three-lobed and sharply triangular in outline; the sepals, as in *R. acris*, are not bent back, but the flower-stalk is furrowed as in *R. bulbosus*. The flowers are of a deeper, more golden yellow than the other two species; and the plant grows mainly in the wettest parts of meadows, but is common on disturbed ground, as where cattle have trampled heavily, and also in damp woodland (where the other two buttercups rarely grow).

At one time, the Green-winged orchid, *Orchis morio*, with loose spikes of flowers which are usually deep mulberry colour, but may be pink or white, was very common in permanent pastures. This orchid resembles the tom-cat scented Early Purple orchid, *O. mascula*, pp. 46, 47, which may occur with it, but which is much commoner in our lowland coppice woods. It has tight hoods to the flowers with sepals that are striped with alternate green and purple lines, and green leaves, which lack the purple blotches usual in *O. mascula*. It is now becoming rare due to the conversion of the old pastures into leys.

The permanent pastures would all, at one time, have been oak forest, and still have not dissimilar soils, though with more black humus than in oak wood soils; their flora today, however, has little in common with woodland, owing to the selective effect of grazing. Where animals are allowed to graze open woodland, one observes that in a few years the woodland herbs disappear, to be replaced by the grazing-tolerant species typical of the pasturelands.

Meadowlands are typically wetter than ordinary permanent pastures, and occur mostly on the alluvial flood-plains of rivers and streams where probably damp alder woods once grew, but the term is sometimes used for any pastureland used for a hay crop

Snake's-head Fritillary, a local plant of
water meadows with strange chequer-
pattern flowers

rather than for grazing. This distinction is
unsatisfactory, as many water meadows are
used for a hay crop after the winter flooding,
then afterwards grazed during the drier
months of late summer and early autumn.

The flora of typical water meadows has
much in common with permanent pastures
generally, but extra species may appear, such
as the Meadow-sweet, *Filipendula ulmaria*.
This sweetly scented flower of late summer
has pinnately divided, toothed, dark green
basal leaves, 6–9 inches (15–23 cm.) long, and
tall, up to 3 feet (91 cm.), stems bearing loose
panicles of numerous cream-coloured five-
petalled flowers with 20–40 stamens in each.

Much more local is the lovely Snake's-
head Fritillary, *Fritillaria meleagris*. This
plant is still locally abundant in water
meadows in the upper Thames valley and in
a few other places in south England. It
resembles a narrow-leaved tulip with nod-

ding flowers, but the flowers are chequer-patterned with a soft pink and purple pattern, though occasionally white. The name *Fritillaria* means a dice-box, and the name *meleagris* a guinea fowl, in Latin; both refer to the strange but charmingly patterned flowers. This plant is so abundant in some of its limited habitats that its rarity in England as a whole is difficult to explain.

The hay-meadows of upland Britain tend to be very rich in flowers; woodland species often occur mixed with more typical meadow species. One species confined to the north of Britain which is very characteristic of this habitat is the 3 feet (91 cm.) tall, scarcely spiny, Melancholy thistle, *Cirsium hetero-phyllum*, with lance-shaped leaves white below and few large purple thistle heads.

The hedges of our lowland landscape are, as we have seen, for the most part of relatively recent origin. Nevertheless, they provide an immensely valuable reservoir of wild life, both of plants, birds and insects. Most of the herbs of our lowland hedges are woodland, or woodland edge, rather than pasture species. In some districts where there is little woodland they provide the main remaining habitat for plants that have already been mentioned, such as the Cuckoo-pint, Germander speedwell, and Dog's Mercury, and, in more humid districts, the Primrose. The Lesser celandine, *Ranunculus ficaria*, p. 74, with its 8–12 narrow petalled golden-yellow flowers is particularly characteristic of damp hedge bottoms, which are frequently bestarred with it in early spring before any other flowers are open. Red campion, *Silene dioica*, though a common woodland plant, is also particularly well developed in hedge-banks; this is a rather downy plant up to 3 feet (91 cm.) high with loosely branched inflorescences of bright rose-pink, five-petalled flowers and swollen ribbed calyx-tubes. The plants are dioecious, that is to say the sexes are separate. If one dissects the flowers one can see that some contain an ovary bearing five styles, while others instead bear ten stamens. Herb Robert, *Geranium robertianum*, with five-petalled

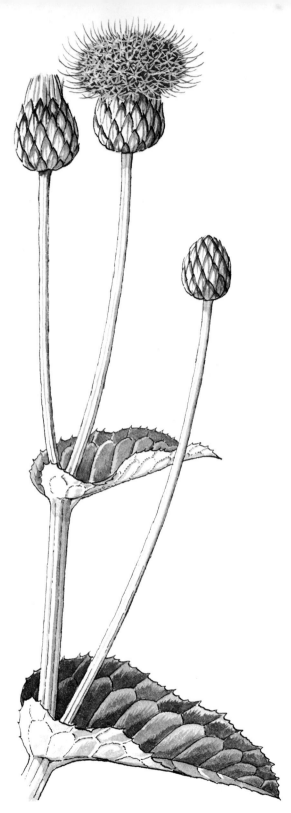

Melancholy thistle, common in the hay meadows and stony roadsides of northern and upland Britain

pink flowers veined with purple, and fern-like dissected triangular green leaves tinged with bright red, is common in shady hedges as well as in base-rich woodlands.

The modern tendency to grub up hedges wholesale is a serious threat to wild life – thousands of miles of them are now disappearing each year. To some extent this must be accepted, for many of our fields are too small for efficient cultivation by modern machinery. But hedges along roads, and around fields still have considerable value as nesting sites for useful birds, as habitats for predatory insects and as shelter from wind and snow for country roads. It has been discovered that the number of woody species in a hedge can be used to determine its age. Dr M. Hooper has found that, although most hedges were originally planted of one species, usually Hawthorn, *Crataegus monogyna*, on average one extra woody species appears in each hundred years of the life of the hedge. Study of old documents has shown, for example, that most hedges with five woody species in them are about five hundred years old. Though most hedges are far younger than this, some hedges on ancient boundary lines appear to date from Saxon times.

In lowland districts especially, trees are still a great feature of our hedgerows. On the heavier clay lands, oaks are still common in the hedges, as for example in parts of East Anglia, the Cheshire plain, and above all in the Kent and Sussex Weald. In such places the oaks have room to spread their branches and may achieve a fine development. It has been calculated that our hedgerows contain the main 'reservoir' of mature hardwood timber left in the highly cultivated districts of our lowlands. Foreign visitors are always very impressed by the splendid oaks of the Wealden roadside hedges; there are probably more fine oaks in the hedges of Sussex than in the whole of Holland and Belgium. Unfortunately, as these trees are felled, they are not often replaced, and any natural saplings tend to be beheaded in hedge-trimming operations.

On the alluvial soils of the great river valleys of the south, and over wide areas of the plains of the Midlands and east Somerset, elm species, however, predominate in the hedgerows. In general the principal species of elm in hedgerows is the English elm, *Ulmus procera*, with tall columnar trunk, few large heavy side branches, and a huge crown of branches which diverge at acute angles to one another at the apex. This elm has rounded, sub-orbicular to egg-shaped leaves 2–3 inches (5–8 cm.) long, which have their blades extending much lower down the stalks on one side than on the other. These leaves are very rough above and downy beneath. The trunk usually bears a dense brushwood of leafy twigs over part of its surface, and the tree reproduces largely, if not always, by vegetative suckers. It has been suggested that the English elm is an introduction, because it is little known except in artificial habitats such as hedges, and rarely if ever sets good seed. However, against this is the fact that this species is unknown outside England and is thus apparently endemic. Also, it has relatively recently been found to occur as the dominant tree in apparently natural woodland on the gravelly or sandy slopes of certain river-terraces bordering some of our southern river valleys.

The Smooth-leaved elm, *U. carpinifolia*, has a more spreading habit and hairless, shining leaves; this seems to replace the English elm in hedgerows in much of eastern England, in east Kent as well as Cornwall. The elms, however, are very difficult plants to classify, and some botanists consider that there are in fact quite a number of species differing in their growth habit, twigs and leaves. It is not, however, a subject upon which to enlarge further in a general work of this kind.

The ditches usually associated with hedges often carry interesting floras, and one can often get an idea of geological changes from the plants present. Moist clayey ditch banks in spring often are studded with the pale rosy-pink or white heads of the Cuckoo

Common hawthorn, the principal shrub of our lowland hedges, also important as an invader of ungrazed chalk grassland

flower or Ladies'-smock, *Cardamine pratensis*, with its pinnately compound leaves with rounded terminal leaflet and narrow side leaflets and four-petalled flowers. In midsummer such places have hairy Great willowherb, *Epilobium hirsutum*, a tall downy plant with spreading panicles of deep purple-pink four-petalled flowers with four fat creamy-white stigmas emerging from them. Sandy ditch banks are more likely to bear bluebells in spring and Bracken later on.

Roadside verges form another important man-made habitat; in May throughout lowland Britain they are normally a mass of the umbellifer, Cow parsley or Queen Anne's Lace, *Anthriscus sylvestris*. This has lacy fern-like foliage and frothy-looking umbels of white flowers. On limestone soils, in parts of central and northern England, the 1½ inch (4 cm.) wide, violet-blue flowers and deeply cut finger-lobed, digitate, leaves of the Meadow cranesbill, *Geranium pratense*,

Blackthorn or Sloe, common in hedges and in scrub especially on heavier soils. It has globular, 1-2 cm., plum-like fruits in summer and white flowers in early spring

are a glorious feature in June and July on the roadside verges. The need to control roadside herbage from the point of view of road visibility, however, and the expense of hand-cutting, has induced some local authorities to spray roadside verges with selective weed-killers. Fortunately, the invention of efficient power-driven mechanical cutters has checked this tendency.

Arable fields were formerly a rich botanical hunting ground, especially in chalky sandy cornfields. Cleaner seed, better cultivation, and the use of chemical herbicides have, however, enormously reduced the frequency and abundance of many of our arable weeds. The sky-blue Cornflower, *Centaurea cyanus*, the purple Corn-cockle, *Agrostemma githago*, and the Thorow-wax, *Bupleurum rotundifolium*, with its yellow umbels and rounded leaves surrounding the stems, are now all but extinct over most of Britain, and even the Field poppy, *Papaver rhoeas*, with its splendid scarlet crinkly petals, is becoming scarce except on disturbed ground. Unfortunately these changes, which impoverish the beauty and variety of our landscape, must be faced in the interests of more efficient food production for our huge population. Perhaps conservation bodies could set up 'weed museums' where old-fashioned agri-cultural methods could be maintained over small areas, without the use of weed-killers, and some of our disappearing rarer arable weeds could be introduced into such places. Most of these rarer weeds, especially those of chalky cornfields, would be safe enough to conserve in such places, as they do not show any tendency to explosive spread under any circumstances. The rarer fumitories, *Fumaria* species, and the Ground Pine, *Ajuga chamaepitys*, with its tiny narrow resinous-scented conifer-shaped leaves and pale yellow pendant lips to its flowers among these leaves might well be protected in this way.

After the forests on the chalk and limestone hills of south and east England were cleared by man from Neolithic times onwards and when arable farming ceased on much of this land, it became used for grazing. From the Middle Ages onwards, the principal grazing animal was the sheep and the production of wool for export, largely initiated by the Cistercian monasteries, was the foundation of the late medieval prosperity of England. Not for nothing does the Lord Chancellor sit upon a woolsack, for this began as a symbol

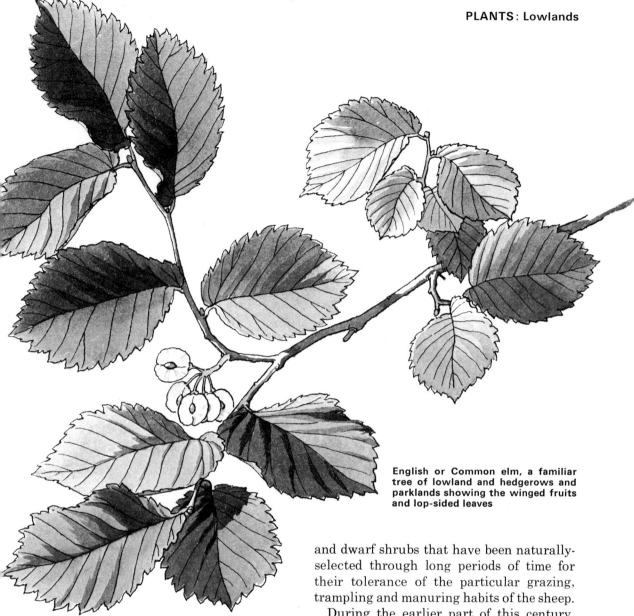

English or Common elm, a familiar
tree of lowland and hedgerows and
parklands showing the winged fruits
and lop-sided leaves

of the early roots of the kingdom's economic
prosperity through wool exports. Today,
however, the Woolsack is, I understand, no
longer stuffed with wool, and, moreover, the
sheep no longer roam over our downs in the
vast flocks that were once seen.

Nevertheless, it is the centuries of grazing
by sheep that have produced the downs as
we have known them until recent times:
sheep-adapted ecosystems of grasses, herbs

and dwarf shrubs that have been naturally-
selected through long periods of time for
their tolerance of the particular grazing,
trampling and manuring habits of the sheep.

During the earlier part of this century,
the grazing of sheep on the open downs under-
went a drastic decline. Various factors have
been responsible for this. The falls in the
prices available to the farmer for home-
produced mutton and wool, the difficulties of
obtaining men still willing to lead the hard
and lonely life of the shepherd, and, nearer
towns, an increase in sheep-worrying by an
inflating population of uncontrolled dogs,
were all in part responsible. For a time, the
huge expansion in the rabbit population
which occurred in later Victorian times kept

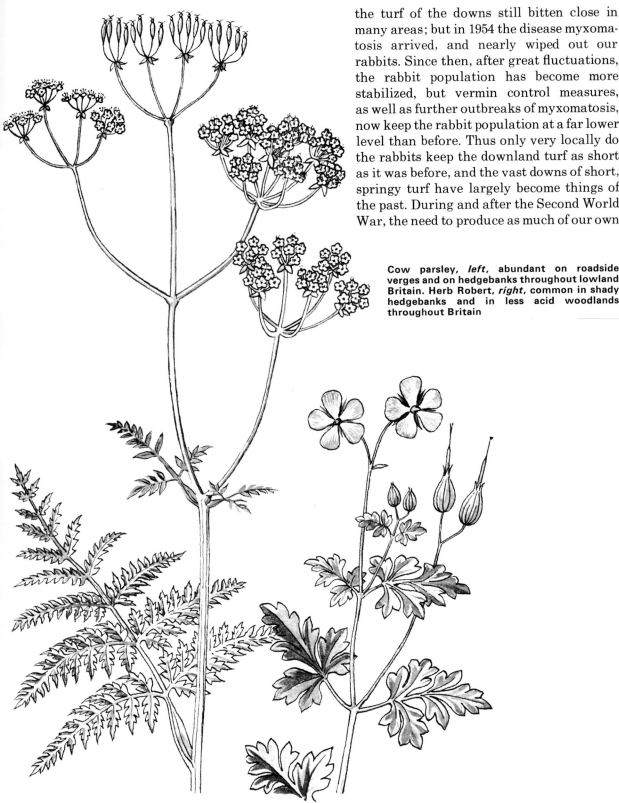

the turf of the downs still bitten close in many areas; but in 1954 the disease myxomatosis arrived, and nearly wiped out our rabbits. Since then, after great fluctuations, the rabbit population has become more stabilized, but vermin control measures, as well as further outbreaks of myxomatosis, now keep the rabbit population at a far lower level than before. Thus only very locally do the rabbits keep the downland turf as short as it was before, and the vast downs of short, springy turf have largely become things of the past. During and after the Second World War, the need to produce as much of our own

Cow parsley, *left*, abundant on roadside verges and on hedgebanks throughout lowland Britain. Herb Robert, *right*, common in shady hedgebanks and in less acid woodlands throughout Britain

food as possible led to extensive ploughing-up of former chalk grassland on the less steep slopes, and today our chalk landscape is perhaps nearly as fully one of arable farming as it has ever been in the past. Nevertheless, there remain many slopes too steep for arable cultivation even with modern tractors.

Some of these steeper downland slopes and escarpments are still grazed by sheep; others are grazed now by cattle, which have a different mode of grazing but nevertheless maintain chalk grassland of a kind. Other steep slopes, especially on steep south escarpments, are not grazed any more, but perhaps because of the very thin soil and the extreme dryness of such situations, still retain short open turf with much of its former character. Most unploughed areas on the chalk hills, however, have changed greatly in character since myxomatosis arrived, and invasion of coarse grasses and of woody scrub species is destroying their remarkable vegetation rapidly. Towards the end of this section, we shall look at these changes in more detail.

Such changes, however, bring home to us the fact that chalk grasslands are not natural 'climax' plant communities. They form what is known as a plagioclimax, that is vegetation held in a state of equilibrium by some arresting or deflecting factor – in this case grazing – and so prevented from proceeding by natural vegetational succession to the natural climax of forest. Once the deflecting factor of grazing is removed, the succession to forest, normally of beech, continues. If we study the natural invasion and succession of vegetation on bare chalk rock, as in a disused quarry, where there is no grazing, we shall see that first of all mosses appear, then a variety of herbs and some grasses, then woody shrubs, and finally trees. There is in these conditions no stage of open grassland. Thus chalk grassland as we know it does not form a stage in the 'primary' succession from bare chalk to forest. It is something created by the 'deflecting factor' of grazing – when grazing ceases, the vegetation proceeds, like a train returning to the main line from a loop siding, to take up its normal primary succession towards forest once more.

Fortunately quite a number of areas of rich chalk grassland remain in various parts of southern England, especially in Kent, Surrey and Sussex, in the Wessex chalklands from Hampshire and Dorset to Wiltshire and Berkshire, and here and there on the Chiltern Hills from the Thames across to Hertfordshire. In flat East Anglia, there is little left now except on roadside verges, or on some of the great chalk earthworks supposed to have been built in Saxon times as defensive works, such as the Fleam Dike and the Devil's Ditch in Cambridgeshire and the Suffolk Black Ditches. It is hard to believe now that, until the early nineteenth century enclosures, most of the wide chalk-lands of Cambridgeshire and from New-market to Bury St Edmunds in Suffolk were open sheep walks, covered with a carpet of downland flowers. Nearly all of this area is now arable land, except for such places as the horse-training area of Newmarket Heath and the occasional golf courses, where one may still find fragments of a chalk grassland flora.

Further north, on the Lincolnshire Wolds, there is almost no chalk grassland left now, except in a few old quarries and on roadside verges. On the east Yorkshire Wolds, there are still areas of excellent chalk grassland, but most are sadly overgrown or threatened by afforestation or ploughing-up. There are, however, still some fragments of good low-land limestone grassland on the Magnesian limestone along the west side of the Vale of York.

On the Jurassic limestone of the Cotswolds, grasslands similar in flora to those of the chalklands are still fairly widespread, especially around Stroud and Painswick; some of these still bear very rich floras. On the similar Lincolnshire limestone, also of Jurassic age, in south Lincolnshire, Rutland and the Soke of Peterborough, only a few fragments of limestone grasslands remain, mostly on roadside verges, prehistoric earth-works, and in old quarries, but some of these are still extremely rich in interesting plants. The grasslands of all of these lowland lime-stones are basically similar and all are considered here together as 'chalk grasslands'.

Everywhere, the County Naturalists' Trusts are doing their best to conserve the remaining areas of this wonderful plant community by purchase, lease, or 'gentle-men's agreement', but it is not only lack of funds that impedes this work; the problem of finding a farmer who will graze the land, and so hold back the succession to scrub and to forest, is perhaps the principal one. The Nature Conservancy has set up a number of valuable Nature Reserves on the chalklands, but they, too, have great problems over ensuring the continuance of grazing on their reserves, especially where the process of deterioration of the pasturage has already begun. The Conservancy, however, have now their own flock of sheep, which it is intended to move around from reserve to reserve to try to remedy the situation over as many areas as possible. Before sheep-grazing can be restarted, however, it is sometimes necessary to clear invading scrub laboriously by manual labour, or to get the coarser grasses under control by heavy initial grazing by such unselectively feeding animals as Belted Galloway heifers, combined with, in some cases, controlled burning.

The typical structure of sheep-grazed chalk grassland has a fairly short turf, composed of a great many species of plants. In fact, the large number of species to be found in any small area is one very characteristic feature of this type of plant community. A 'quadrat' or sample area, of as little as a square metre may in fact contain not infrequently as many as 30 species of flowering plants, and 20 or more species of bryophytes and lichens. Grasses of low, tufted form may predominate, but dicotyledonous herbs are most numerous in species, and in fact may often constitute the bulk of the vegetation. Most of the species are perennials; annual or biennial species occur, but are not numerous

and are clearly at some disadvantage, as it is difficult for annuals in general to enter such a dense, closed community of plants where there is intense competition for light above ground and for root space below it. Many of the plants are herbaceous, dying down to rosettes or over-wintering buds in autumn, or, as in the case, for example, of the orchids, to underground tubers or rhizomes. Many, however, such as Rock-rose, Thyme and Chalk milkwort, are in fact tiny shrubs an inch or two high (2·5–5 cm.) which have little creeping woody stems with evergreen leaves persisting in the low turf throughout the winter. The rosette-form is common among the herbs, as in Lambs-tongue plantain; leaves in a spreading rosette flat on the ground are clearly less likely to be eaten by animals than those which stand erect. Stemless thistle not only has its leaves in a rosette, but has them spiny as well, thus providing a double discouragement to grazing animals and also to picnickers when they happen to sit on it!

The soil beneath a chalk grassland is typically very shallow and ill developed. Chalk is a very pure limestone and may consist, apart from the bands of insoluble flints in the upper chalk, of as much as 98 or 99 per cent of calcium carbonate. This substance is soluble in rain water which, as it contains carbon dioxide washed out of the atmosphere, produces an acid solution, containing carbonic acid. The chalk dissolves in this acid water to give an alkaline solution, and hence chalk soils are normally alkaline throughout, with a pH value of 8·0 or even higher. Since there is almost no insoluble residue left on leaching of the surface by rain, normal soil development processes in a cool, moist climate such as ours do not occur, and the normal tendency for the soil to form a series of stratified 'horizons', such as we saw in podsols and brown forest soils, cannot take place. All that can happen is that the chalk rock particles become more and more broken down, as the surface of the soil is approached, by weathering by rain water, and by the action of tiny animals of the soil fauna. Humus from the leaves and roots of plants, and from animal excreta, becomes incorporated into the upper layers of the soil in a finely divided form, giving the upper layers a dark grey colour, while the lower layers remain the white colour of the chalk itself.

There is almost no silica present to form an inert soil 'skeleton'; hardly any clay minerals occur; and there is little iron oxide to form coloured horizons in the soil. Hence these chalk soils retain indefinitely an essentially immature, unstratified character. Immature soils without horizons are called rendzinas, and the chalk rendzinas are a special type of these which remain immature indefinitely, especially on slopes where humus cannot accumulate easily. In any case, vegetable matter is rapidly decomposed in these well-drained, relatively 'warm' alkaline soils. Only where there is some other residue of more insoluble material of different and later geological origin, as is sometimes the case on chalk ridges and plateaux, can more normal soil forming processes take place, with a tendency to the development of acid conditions.

The well-drained, alkaline soils of chalk grassland with their rich and varied floras, give a deceptive impression of richness. In fact they are, in their own way, nearly as poor as the podsolized soils of some heathlands. Apart from the abundant calcium which passes into solution and saturates the soil water films, the soluble mineral nutrients which plants need are in very short supply. Such vital elements as potassium, magnesium and iron, and salts such as sulphates, nitrates and phosphates, are in extremely low concentrations. What is even worse, the huge concentration of calcium in solution tends to 'inhibit' or prevent the uptake by plant roots of these other nutrients even when they are present in amounts that would normally be sufficient. This causes some crops or trees planted on chalk soils to develop symptoms of mineral deficiencies, sometimes shown, as in the Scots pine, *Pinus sylvestris*, by a yellowing or 'chlorosis'

of the leaves. The absence of certain clay minerals normally present in most good soils is also serious, because these clay minerals act as nuclei which can absorb certain important plant nutrients and retain them in the soil in a form in which they are available for the roots to take up. Only the black humus in the chalk soil can fulfil this function, and this is always being broken down.

Thus, in a sense, the shallow, immature soils of the chalk grasslands produce, not of course a climatic desert, but a soil – or edaphic – desert, rather as in a podsolized heathland. The leguminous plants common in chalk grassland mitigate this effect in one respect, because they have nodules on their roots in which live bacteria that can 'fix' atmospheric nitrogen, converting it into soluble compounds of nitrogen, such as nitrates, which the plant can use as food. When parts of leguminous plants decay, some of this nitrogenous material then becomes available for other plants: but under heavy grazing, the mineral nutrients are being constantly removed by the animals, and their wool, flesh and bones are removed by the farmer at intervals and not normally returned to re-enrich the soil.

Looking at the chalk grassland flora itself, it is best to take the principal grasses first. Sheep's fescue grass, *Festuca ovina*, is the most characteristic dominant of old sheepwalks, especially on the steeper slopes, the shallowest soils, and the more southerly, drier, aspects. This grass forms little tussocks of grey-green leaves, permanently rolled-up in such a way as to appear almost bristle-like, from 2–5 inches (5–13 cm.) long and less than 1 mm. wide. The inflorescences are borne on slender stalks up to 1 foot (30 cm.) high though usually less, and the stem-leaves are rolled up like the root-leaves. The inflorescence consists of a loose, more or less erect, branched panicle of spikelets, each 3–7 mm. long and composed of three to five florets each with a short awn on the end of the flowering glume. This grass is very palatable to sheep and was supposed to have

Chalk rendzina profile showing lack of stratification and gradual transition from chalk rock through finer and finer particles of chalk to the surface

given the Southdown mutton its flavour in the past, though the very mixed flora of the turf is more likely to have been responsible. Today, on overgrown ungrazed downlands, it is often confined to steep banks of old trackways. On rather deeper soils with more humus, on less steep slopes or in valley bottoms, or on north-facing slopes, one is more likely to find, in places still grazed, the Red fescue grass, *F. rubra*. This is not reddish coloured in chalk grasslands, though it sometimes is in salt marshes. It is a taller plant than Sheep's fescue, with longer basal leaves, 6–10 inches (15–25 cm.) long, and with stem-leaves which are flat when fresh and up to 3 mm. wide. It also produces creeping stolons, unlike Sheep's fescue. The inflorescence is similar to the last, but may be up to 16 inches (41 cm.) high in chalk grassland, and the spikelets are larger, 7–14 mm. long.

On dry downland on shallow soils, especially if grazing pressure is low, the Upright Brome-grass, *Bromus erectus*, may be dominant, often mixed with Sheep's fescue. This graceful tufted grass is up to 3 feet (91 cm.) high, with 2–3 mm. wide to 1 foot (30 cm.) long flat, or only slightly rolled, leaves, with scattered hairs along their edges, and with graceful, branched heads of stalked spikelets each $\frac{3}{4}$–$1\frac{1}{4}$ inches (20–32 mm.) long composed of narrow, pointed flowering glumes or lemmas.

Particularly in maritime districts, but now also increasing further inland, we shall find the Tor-grass, *Brachypodium pinnatum*. This grass has stiffly erect, yellow- or even orange-green leaves up to 10 mm. wide, though usually rather less than this, which are rough but scarcely hairy, and rather rigid stems up to 2 feet (61 cm.) high, bearing spikelets more or less than 1 inch (20–30 mm.) long in two alternating rows up the stem and edgeways on to it, in a close spike-like inflorescence up to 4 inches (10 cm.) long. This species not only forms dense tussocks; it reproduces both by seed and by vegetative spread from its rhizomes, forming dense swards in which both the tall, close, living foliage and the persistent litter of the previous year's dead leaves tend to smother all other chalk grassland plants. Many of our downlands, particularly near the south coast in east Kent, east Sussex and in Dorset, have in the absence of sufficient grazing, become ruined by the Tor-grass taking over complete dominance – ruined both as pasture and as habitats for interesting chalk floras.

The grasses so far named are those that can assume dominance in chalk grassland. In addition, many other species of grasses may occur quite commonly. One very distinctive species often associated with the fescues and Upright Brome-grass is the Quaking grass, *Briza media*. This has flat,

Calcareous beechwood in early spring: note bare floor with Spurge laurel, *Daphne laureola*, left, and Stinking hellebore, *Helleborus foetidus*, right

relatively short leaves 2–3 mm. wide, and loose panicles of flattish, heart-shaped, usually purplish-green spikelets which hang on stalks so long and fine that they quiver in the slightest breeze – hence the English name. The two Oat-grasses, *Helictotrichon pratense*, which is hairless and glaucous, and *H. pubescens*, which is downy, are quite common, too, and their 1–2 feet (30–61 cm.) tall inflorescences bear loose panicles of large silvery-looking spikelets $\frac{3}{8}$–$\frac{3}{4}$ inch (10–20 mm.) long, each containing two or three florets which have large, rigid awns up to 1 inch (2·5 cm.) long which arise from the middle of the flowering glumes and stand out stiffly, from a knee-like bend near the base.

There is one sedge which is well-nigh universal in chalk grassland, the Carnation-grass or Glaucous sedge, *Carex flacca*. This, as the name suggests, has leaves of a glaucous waxy texture rather like those of carnations. As in all sedges, these leaves are arranged in three vertical rows on the stems, so that when one looks down on the plant one sees three radiating sets of leaves. The inflorescence, up to about 1 foot (30 cm.) high in chalk grassland, bears two to three cylindrical drooping spikelets of female flowers with flattened-egg shaped fruits, and two or three dark purple-brown erect male spikes at the tip of the stem. Several other sedges may also occur, but the Glaucous sedge is the only one that is ubiquitous.

The vast number of plants, apart from the grasses and sedges, that occur in chalk grassland makes it very difficult to select a limited number for fuller description. Some are to be found on nearly every downland in England; at the other extreme, some, especially certain orchids, are so rare that they are known in only one or two restricted

spots in the whole country, and even there they may not always flower. In between there are those like the Round-headed rampion, *Phyteuma tenerum*, that are very common in certain areas, in this case in Sussex and parts of Hampshire and Surrey, but absent wholly north of the Thames. Our chalk grassland flora includes mostly species of the 'continental' element, species whose main home is in central Europe, but in addition there is a strong representation of species of the 'southern continental' element – species whose main home is in the hills of southern Europe; while a few, such as Bastard toadflax, Chalk milkwort and Fel-wort, are south-west European or 'southern oceanic' species in geographical origin.

Several of the common species of chalk grasslands are found equally in other types of dry grasslands or meadows that are non-calcareous but have soils that are not too acid. Such is the Bird's-foot trefoil, *Lotus corniculatus*. This leguminous plant has trefoil leaves each composed of three pointed egg-shaped leaflets, each about 1 cm. long, with pairs of similar shaped stipules where the leaf-stalks join the stems, and stalked inflorescences composed each of a single whorl of bright yellow flowers, 1–1·5 cm. long, of the pea- or bean-flower shape usual in leguminous plants. The buds are narrow and dark red in form and contrast with the inflated egg-yolk coloured opened flowers. This appearance of the two side by side has given rise to the other English name of the plant, Bacon-and-eggs, the buds being the rashers of bacon and the open flowers the eggs. Others of this group include the Bulbous buttercup, *Ranunculus bulbosus*, already considered in the section on perma-nent pastures, and the Ribwort plantain, *Plantago lanceolata*, a plant with strongly longitudinally ribbed lance-shaped leaves and spike-like inflorescences of wind-pollinated flowers each with a tiny chaffy four-lobed corolla and four long white stamens. It could be mistaken for a grass by those who do not know it. Lamb's-tongue plantain, *P. media*, with flat rosettes of

Plants of calcareous beechwood – early summer: *from left to right*, Fly orchid, *Ophrys insectifera* (×1½); Bird's-nest orchid, *Neottia nidus-avis* (×1); Large White helleborine, *Cephalanthera damasonium* (×¾); Yellow bird's-nest, *Monotropa hypophegea* (×1½); Greater butterfly orchid, *Platanthera chlo-rantha* (×1)

downy egg-shaped leaves and pink stamens, is, however, confined to chalky soils.

Most of the more local or more attractive flowers of chalk and limestone grasslands, however, are species that are more or less confined to calcareous soils in nature. Such plants are called calcicoles. Experiments have shown that some of these plants, while they can grow in soils without chalk if transplanted into them in the mature state, cannot establish themselves from seedlings unless the soil is alkaline in reaction. In others, such as the Yellow-wort, *Blackstonia perfoliata*, a slender erect annual plant up to 1 foot (30 cm.) high with waxy grey-green leaves which encircle the stem in pairs and flowers up to about $\frac{3}{4}$ inch (2 cm.) wide with six to eight lobed yellow corollas, competition seems to be the explanation of its calcicole behaviour. Without competition from other plants, it can grow quite well in weakly acid non-calcareous soils, but in nature more robust competitors crowd it out, except on chalky soils where these competitors cannot flourish.

The common dwarf shrubs of chalky grasslands include the common Rock-rose, *Helianthemum chamaecistus*, p. 109, a representative of the Cistaceae family so important in the Mediterranean scrublands or garigue. This has numerous creeping or ascending woody shoots which form dense mats, and bear opposite pairs of oblong grey-green leaves up to 2 cm. long which are woolly white beneath, and bright yellow flowers each with five rather crinkly petals, numerous yellow stamens, and five strongly veined sepals of which three are much larger than the other two. There are two species of wild thyme. *Thymus drucei* has stems hairy on two opposite sides, short dome-shaped inflorescences and only a faint scent and is widespread but less common in the east, while *T. pulegioides* has stems hairy on the four corners, cylindrical inflorescences and a strongly aromatic scent, and is only common in south-east England. Both have tiny rose-purple two-lipped flowers a few millimetres long and egg-shaped opposite sessile

leaves up to $\frac{3}{8}$ inch (1 cm.) in length. Much of the pleasant perfume of chalk turf is due to the bruising of their leaves as one walks over the plants. Chalk milkwort, *Polygala calcarea*, is one of our loveliest smaller flowers. It occurs locally in abundance in old short-turfed fescue grasslands in Wessex, the Cotswolds and in south-east England and, much more sparsely, north to Grantham on the Lincolnshire limestone. It has basal rosettes of glossy dark green leaves, $\frac{5}{8}-\frac{3}{4}$ inch (1·5–2 cm.) long, which are elliptical-obovate (wider above the middle). From these rosettes arise stems bearing scattered leaves of similar form, but shorter and narrower loose spikes of flowers each about $\frac{1}{4}$ inch (6–7 mm.) long of a glorious gentian-blue. Rarely the flowers are bluish white, pure white or even rose-pink. Each flower is enclosed in two large obovate petal-like lateral sepals which are the conspicuous parts of the flower; the three true petals, which are white and divided into finger-like lobes, are relatively inconspicuous and partly enclosed within the two large sepals. The Common milkwort, *Polygala vulgaris*, is a much commoner plant and it is herbaceous rather than shrubby. It has lanceolate leaves, widest at or below the middle, and similar sized flowers to *P. calcarea* which, however, have a more pointed pair of enclosing sepals of either a much duller blue or of a purple-blue, dull pink, or white colour. Common milkwort flowers all through the summer; Chalk milkwort normally only lasts from early May to mid-June.

Often associated with Rock-rose and Chalk milkwort in Sheep's fescue grassland, and flowering at the same time, is the Horseshoe vetch, *Hippocrepis comosa*, p. 109. This resembles a smaller-flowered Bird's-foot trefoil, but it has pinnate leaves with numerous side leaflets and a single terminal one, and is a much daintier and more lovely plant which produces masses of golden-yellow colour in the turf. The English name comes from the horseshoe-shaped segments into which the seed-pods break as they ripen.

One of the commonest of all herbs in

calcareous lowland grasslands is the Salad Burnet, *Poterium sanguisorba*. This plant has basal rosettes of rather rose-like leaves 1–3 inches (2·5–7·5 cm.) long with many pairs of rounded toothed leaflets and leafy 6–18 inch (15–46 cm.) stems which bear $\frac{3}{4}$ inch (1 cm.) diameter, globular inflorescences. In these the tiny male flowers with many pale yellow conspicuous stamens lie below the female flowers with feathery purple stigmas. Salad Burnet is one of the few members of the Rosaceae that are wind-pollinated.

Besides the tiny, erect, annual Fairy flax, *Linum catharticum*, with five-petalled white flowers about $\frac{1}{4}$ inch (5–6 mm.) across and egg-shaped opposite leaves 5–7 mm. long, there is another common, but perennial herb in chalk grassland with superficially similar flowers. This is Squinancy-wort or Quinsy-wort (once used for treating quinsy), *Asperula cynanchica*. It has a sprawling habit, whorls of very narrow leaves, $\frac{1}{4}$–1 inch (6–25 mm.) long, four to six in a whorl on the delicate stems, and loose panicles of tiny funnel-shaped white to pinkish flowers with four-lobed corollas. Bastard toadflax, *Thesium humifusum*, has five-lobed white star-like flowers 5–6 mm. across which superficially resemble those of Fairy flax; but it has only one perianth whorl and has a sprawling habit like Squinancy-wort. The stems and narrow lance-shaped leaves are both of a peculiar greenish-yellow colour and of a fleshy texture. This is a much more local plant with a range similar to that of Chalk milkwort, not extending north of Grantham in Lincolnshire. It is also unusual in that it is a partial parasite, its roots having attachments to various chalk grassland herbs. This is the only British representative of the important tropical family Santalaceae, to which the Sandal-wood tree belongs.

The earliest plants to flower in the chalk and oolitic limestone grasslands are the very common and scentless Hairy violet, *Viola hirta*, whose very downy leaves readily distinguish it from the common Wood violet, and the glorious Pasque flower, *Pulsatilla vulgaris*, p. 110. The latter appears in April,

often at Eastertime – hence the English name, derived from the French word for Easter. The Pasque flower has now far fewer localities than it used to have. Formerly it extended on the Magnesian limestone north to the Tees; now its northern limit is on the Jurassic limestone in north Lincolnshire. It has never been reliably recorded south of the Thames except in Berkshire. Its main strongholds now are in the Cotswolds and the eastern Chilterns from Tring to near Newmarket. It is closely related to the *Anemone* genus to which the windflower belongs, but there is little superficial resemblance. The erect stem, which is silkily hairy like all other parts of the plant, is covered at the time of flowering at the base with the remains of last year's basal leaves. The root-leaves of the current season expand during flowering and are ultimately long-stalked and bi-pinnately divided into narrow hairy segments. Higher up the stem is a whorl of three smaller sessile deeply-divided hairy stem-leaves which form a sort of cup below the solitary flower. The flower has a single perianth of six segments each up to $1\frac{1}{2}$ inches (4 cm.) long of a magnificent royal purple inside but paler and silky outside. At first the flower-stalk is short and the flower is erect, wide open and almost star-like in full sunshine, showing the mass of golden stamens, but soon the flower-stalk elongates, and the flower droops and becomes more bell-shaped. Later the silky styles elongate greatly up to a length of as much as 2 inches (5 cm.) and then spread out radially in a globose furry head in fruit. The nutlets, or achenes, depend on the plumed styles for wind dispersal.

This lovely plant is threatened by its very beauty; may I ask those who find by chance a downland empurpled with its flowers never to dig it up, but, if they are determined to cultivate it, to take only a few seeds instead? These will germinate fairly well if sown as soon as ripe in a chalky soil.

The Purple Milk-vetch, *Astragalus danicus,* is a leguminous herb, rather like a hairy purple-flowered Horseshoe vetch (but with less spreading flower-heads), which has a similar British distribution in chalk and limestone grassland to the Pasque flower. It extends right up the east side of Scotland, however, on calcareous sand dunes, and is interesting as a northern continental European species, which is one of the only two species of our chalk grasslands that do not occur in France. The other is the Field fleabane, *Senecio integrifolius*, p. 110, which resembles a small ragwort with egg-shaped very woolly leaves in a basal rosette. The stem-leaves are similar but narrower, and the attractive deep orange-yellow ragwort-like flower-heads occur several together in a loose umbel. This plant occurs throughout the southern chalklands, though it is rare or local in some areas such as the North Downs, so it is astonishing that it is unknown in France, though it occurs on the Swiss side of the Jura. The Round-headed rampion, *Phyteuma tenerum*, has globular, rather scabious-like heads, but of a deep Oxford-blue, on tall smooth stems that bear narrowly heart-shaped hairless leaves. It is so common on the Sussex Downs, where it varies in height from 2 inches (5 cm.) on the sea cliffs to 2 feet (61 cm.) inland, that it is surprising that it is unknown now on the Kent chalk and has never been found north of the Thames. The individual florets are tubular in form and the style pushes out the pollen from the stamens like a plunger as it elongates. Like the rampion a member of the Bellflower family, Campanulaceae, the Clustered bellflower, *Campanula glomerata*, p. 109, is much more widespread in calcareous grasslands, extending up the east Scottish coastal region almost as far as the Purple Milk-vetch. It has narrowly heart-shaped leaves like those of rampion in form, but they are downy, not glabrous, and the flowers, which are mostly grouped in a terminal cluster, are rich blue-purple in colour and form bells up to 1 inch (2·5 cm.) long with spreading lobes at the mouth.

Several thistles occur in chalk grasslands. Perhaps the most characteristic is the Stemless thistle, *Cirsium acaulon*, p. 109, with rosettes of spiny root-leaves and almost unstalked thistle-heads of a rich red-purple, which is abundant in short chalk and limestone turf as far north as south Yorkshire, but unknown north and west of a line from Tees-mouth to Swansea. Much more local, and far commoner on the oolitic grasslands than on the chalk, is the splendid Woolly thistle, *C. eriophorum*, p. 110. This stately biennial may reach a height of 4 feet (1·2 m.). It has deeply pinnately-cut grey-green stem-leaves up to 2 feet (61 cm.) long which have leaflets pointing both upwards and downwards and tipped with formidable spines; the unwinged stem bears similar but shorter leaves. The flower-heads, which are the largest of any among our thistles, are the size of small coffee-cups, up to $2\frac{3}{4}$ inches (7 cm.) wide. Each consists of a globular head of spine-like purple-tipped bracts cobwebbed together with white hairs from which arises a large stiff brush of red-purple tubular florets over 2 inches (5 cm.) long.

Several yellow dandelion-like composite flowers occur in chalk turf; the most characteristic is the Rough hawkbit, *Leontodon hispidus*, with 1 inch (2·5 cm.) wide discs of deep yellow strap-shaped florets borne singly on leafless roughly hairy stems 8–12 inches (20–30 cm.) high, and equally hairy, blunt-toothed lance-shaped leaves in a basal rosette. Another is the Mouse-ear hawkweed, *Hieracium pilosella*, now called *Pilosella vulgaris*, which is only 4–6 inches (10–15 cm.) tall, has heads of lemon-yellow florets on unbranched leafless white downy stems, and basal rosettes of oblong to ovate untoothed leaves which are downy white below and green above, with sparse long stiff white hairs on both sides. The Mouse-ear hawkweed also has conspicuous creeping stolons which bear tiny white woolly leaves.

In September, two gentians are found on our chalk downs. The common species is Felwort, *Gentianella amarella*, p. 109, a neat erect biennial herb normally 4–8 inches (10–20 cm.) tall, with lance-shaped untoothed leaves in opposite pairs and erect branches which bear tubular, bright purple flowers $\frac{3}{8}-\frac{3}{4}$ inch (10–20 mm.) long have four or five reflexed corolla-lobes, white-fringed at the throat. This species is almost universal in our calcareous grasslands. Almost confined to the Chilterns, but there locally common, is the German Gentian, *G. germanica*. This has flowers nearly twice the size of the Felwort, and of a brighter blue-purple colour, with transverse wrinkles conspicuous on the outside of the corolla-tube, but otherwise is similar.

The orchids, which form perhaps the most intriguing of all features of the chalk grassland flora, have been deliberately left till last of all in this account.

A large number of species, more than 20 all told, may occur in chalky turf, though only a few species are normally plentiful enough to be very conspicuous. The structures of the flowers in the Orchid family, Orchidaceae, are among the most remarkable, the most specialized and highly evolved of any flowers in the world. The majority of the peculiar modifications in structure seen in this family appear to be striking and often highly complex evolutionary adaptations towards cross-pollination of the flowers by particular insects. Perhaps the simplest way to explain the structure and mechanisms of the flowers of orchids is to select examples from our downland flora for more detailed description.

One of the commonest orchids of our chalky grasslands, which incidentally is quite common also in damp pastures, open woodlands, and grassy roadside verges on heavy base-rich soils, is the Common Spotted orchid, *Dactylorchis fuchsii*. In June, its pyramidal to cylindrical spikes of pink, purple-spotted and streaked flowers may locally be numerous and conspicuous among the grasses on stems from 10–16 inches (25–41 cm.) tall. The strap-shaped leaves are pointed at the tips; they are 3–6 inches (8–15 cm.) long, and are shiny and grey-green in colour with transversely elongated spots of normally a pale purple hue, unlike the longitudinally elongated or irregularly shaped deep purple blotches of the Early Purple orchid, pp. 46, 47, of our spring woodlands, described earlier.

Close examination of the flower of the Common Spotted orchid shows that it consists basically of a three-ridged inferior ovary, on top of which there are three outer petal-like sepals and three inner petals. The three sepals and two of the petals are all rather similar and arch loosely together over the top of the flower, not forming a close hood. The remaining petal, the lowest as one looks at the front of the flower, is, however, larger and modified into a three-lobed lip or labellum, which serves as a landing platform for insects which visit the flower. In this orchid there is an elongated conical to cylindrical pouch, or spur, at the rear of the lip and forming a part of its structure; this secretes and holds nectar.

Within the perianth, there is a single, erect, sessile anther with two anther-cells. The pollen-grains, instead of lying loose in the anther-cells as in most plants, are aggregated in each anther cell into a mass called a pollinium in orchids and in which the grains cohere in little packets. These, in turn, are bound together with elastic threads. In the Spotted orchid, the two pollinia are club-shaped bodies borne on little stalks within the anther-cells, which become partly exposed as the anther-cell walls split lengthwise in front. The stalks of the pollinia are attached to a sticky disc, known as a viscidium. The two viscidia, which are separate in *Dachtylorchis* and most other downland orchid genera, sit in a little hollow on the top of a small knob called the rostellum, or beak. This rostellum lies above the stigmatic surface of the flower, which in orchids is in a hollow on the top of a little column to which the single anther is attached on the upper side. When an insect visits the flower of the Spotted orchid, it lands on the labellum or lip and inserts its tongue into the spur behind to obtain the nectar present there. In the process of doing this, its head, or its antennae, cannot fail to strike the viscid discs, or viscidia, on the projecting beak or rostellum. These viscidia, sometimes one of them, sometimes both, stick to the insect, and as it withdraws from the flower and flies away it detaches one or both of the pollinia attached to the discs, carrying them off. Once withdrawn from the flower and exposed to the air, the stalks of the pollinia lose water and this causes the club-shaped pollen masses to bend forwards from their formerly erect position. Thus by the time the insect reaches the next flower, usually on another plant, the pollinia on its head, or on its antennae, are pointing forwards. Hence, as the insect forces its way into this next flower, the pollinia on it now strike against, not the anther of this flower, but the stigma, below the anther. Some of the sticky packets of pollen, or even the whole pollinium, will then adhere to the surface of the stigma, and so cross-pollination is effected.

One can demonstrate the whole of this process for oneself by using a pointed object such as a stout bristle, grass stem, or pencil to represent the insect's head; if gently thrust into a freshly opened orchid flower and then removed, it will be found that one or both of the pollinia have adhered to it. After waiting 10 or 20 seconds, one can see the pollinia bend forward slowly on their stalks, and on inserting the pointed object into another flower, one or both pollinia will be seen to strike the stigma, causing pollen-grains to adhere there.

Widespread and locally frequent, or even locally abundant on our downlands in June, is the Fragrant orchid, *Gymnadenia conopsea*. This delightful orchid has unspotted, strongly longitudinally folded or keeled leaves which are mostly at the base of the stem. These leaves are up to 1 inch (2·5 cm.) wide if flattened out, and up to 6 inches (15 cm.) long; they are of a deep glossy green colour and arranged mainly in two opposite ranks, one on each side of the stem. The flowering stem is normally about 1 foot (30 cm.) high, though occasionally it may be taller. It bears a dense, pointed-cylindrical spike 2–4 inches (5–10 cm.) long of very many reddish-lilac or rose-pink (occasionally white) flowers. The flowers, which have smaller

lips than those of the Spotted orchid (to 4 mm. long only, not 10 mm.) and are normally not more than 15 mm. across, have very narrow strap-shaped acute-tipped spreading sepals, shorter petals forming a tiny hood over the centre of the flower, and lips about as wide as long with three short rounded unspotted lobes. The flowers possess a strong sweetish fragrance which is responsible for the English name, but although very pleasant, this fragrance has a slightly acid rancid tinge for some people. The flowers have long narrow curved spurs up to 15 mm. long.

Flowering later, in late June and through July to early August, is the Pyramidal orchid, *Anacamptis pyramidalis*, p. 110. Many people tend to confuse this with the Fragrant orchid, but it differs in the following characteristics. The inflorescence is shortly pyramidal to dome-shaped, never elongated as in the Fragrant orchid. The flowers have longer lobes to the lip, of nearly $\frac{1}{4}$ inch (to 6 mm. long), and are of a bright deep rosy purple, not reddish lilac or rose-pink, and the spurs are rather shorter, usually to 10 mm. long. The scent of the flowers is hardly fragrant; it can best be described as 'foxy'. The leaves are of a more dull grey-green in colour and usually shorter than in the Fragrant orchid. Finally, if one removes the two pollinia in the manner described earlier, one will find that they are joined together on a sort of common 'saddle', and do not have separate viscid discs.

The Pyramidal orchid is one of our commonest late summer downland orchids, and it is very widespread in the British Isles, occurring also on calcareous fixed sand-dunes.

An orchid which is now much rarer than it used to be, though still very locally frequent on a few southern chalk downs, is the Dwarf or Burnt-tip orchid, *Orchis ustulata*, p. 110. This charming little plant is rarely more than 6 inches (15 cm.) high, and is usually only 3–4 inches (8–10 cm.) in height, so may be difficult to see among the herbage unless this is very short. It has unspotted grey-green leaves only 2–3 inches (5–8 cm.) long, and a dense spike, usually about 1 inch (2·5 cm.) long, of tiny flowers which have white lips with 'arms' and 'legs', bearing small round purple dots, and the sepals and petals form tight rounded hoods to the flowers. The individual flowers look like little clown-figures in traditional circus-costume. The flower hoods are very dark dull brownish-purple in bud and on first opening, so that the tip of the little spike appears as if scorched, hence its second English name of Burnt-tip orchid. When the flowers have been open a while, the hoods, however, fade to a pinkish white. The perfume is delicious and re-sembles that of boiled cherries or the garden plant Heliotrope. This plant is only known in our islands in England; though formerly found right up to the Scottish border counties. Today there is not much likelihood of finding it in any numbers except on the North and South Downs and the chalklands of Wessex, in May and June.

Those who explore the chalklands of Kent and Surrey are quite likely to come across the Man orchid, *Aceras anthropophora*. This plant has a basal rosette of unspotted yellow to grey-green leaves from 3–4 inches (8–10 cm.) long which are often transversely marked with tiny elongated blisters, and a stem from 6–18 inches (15–46 cm.) tall bearing a long dense spike of numerous flowers with tight globose green hoods and hanging lips of a dull yellow colour. The edges of both sepals and lips are frequently tinged with a reddish-maroon colour. The lips, which are half an inch or more (12–15 mm.) long, resemble little men, with two arms and two legs, hanging from the flowers. This orchid still occurs as far north as south Lincoln-shire, but it is only plentiful on the North Downs, where, particularly in mid-Kent, it is still quite common and sometimes abun-dant, both on open downland and in bushy scrub, hedgebanks, old chalk pits, and even in dense chalk woodland.

The Bee orchid, *Ophrys apifera*, p. 110. is one of the most remarkable species of this extraordinary family. It has relatively few large flowers (four to ten) borne in very loose spikes on stout fleshy stems 8–12 inches (20–30 cm.) tall. The flowers have three spreading strap-shaped pointed pink sepals about $\frac{1}{2}$–$\frac{3}{4}$ inch (12–20 mm.) long, two shorter square-ended greenish-brown downy petals, and extraordinary lips a half inch or more (12–15 mm.) long which look very like the bodies of Bumble bees. They are dark brown and very velvety, with small pointed furry side lobes, a yellow terminal tooth curled up behind so as to be at first out of sight, and a greenish-yellow U- or horseshoe-shaped loop on the upper part which encloses a patch which is dark greenish yellow and not furry. There has been much speculation among botanists as to how such extra-ordinary structures as the lips of the Bee orchid and other members of its *Ophrys* genus, evolved. It has been suggested that the development of this structure causes the bees (or wasps) which appear to pollinate the species of this genus to mistake the lip for a member of their own species; in particular for male bees to mistake it for a female bee, thus attempting copulation. Certainly cases have been recorded of male bees attempting to mate with the flowers of members of this genus *Ophrys*, and in such cases the head of the insect inevitably comes into contact with the viscid discs of the pollinia. But the whole subject is not well understood. Those who wish to study it further should read *The various contrivances by which Orchids are fertilised by Insects* by Charles Darwin, and also *Wild Orchids of Britain* by V. S. Summer-hayes.

In the case of the Bee orchid itself, the attraction of insects to the flowers to effect pollination is not necessary, as in this species the very long-stalked pollinia fall forward on to the stigma of their own accord, after a time, and this species almost invariably self-pollinates all its flowers. Darwin was unable to obtain any proof that the Bee orchid was ever, in fact, cross-pollinated by insects, but as Summerhayes points out, hybrids do occur between the Bee orchid and its rela-tives the Early and Late Spider orchids, p. 110, so the Bee orchid must sometimes be visited by insects which pollinate those other species. It looks, however, as though evolution has possibly gone one stage further than insect-attraction in the Bee orchid, with the development of automatic self-pollination, as in the Large White helleborine.

The Bee orchid flowers in June and early July; it is still quite frequent and locally common on the calcareous grasslands of southern England, and extends, much more rarely, up to southern Scotland and into Ireland. It also occurs in disturbed areas on other non-calcareous though base-rich soils and on calcareous dunes. It is, however, like several other orchids, often very erratic in its appearance, and even in well-known localities it may vary enormously in numbers. This may be connected with the fact that the individual plants take many years to mature from the germination of the seed to the flowering stage, and then, once sexually mature, may only flower once or perhaps twice. Good seeding years seem only to occur occasionally, and then a good flowering year may occur years later when all, or nearly all, the seedlings mature simultaneously.

Three other species of the genus *Ophrys* with its characteristic spurless insect-like flowers occur in Britain. The Early Spider orchid, *O. sphegodes*, p. 110, which is now very local and only found regularly in any quantity on the chalk downs of east Kent and east Sussex, and on the Jurassic limestone grasslands of east Dorset, flowers in April and May and resembles the Bee orchid fairly closely but has yellow-green sepals, and a shiny blue patch on the lip the shape of the Greek letter π. It has short-stalked pollinia, unlike the Bee orchid, and is thus dependent upon insects for pollination, being unable to cross-pollinate itself. Pollination in the Early Spider orchid is not, however, very effective, only a small proportion of the flowers (between 6 and 18 per cent according to different observers) setting seed in this country. The plant evidently, however, manages to achieve enough insect-pollination to set enough seed to maintain

its numbers in its strongholds, though not to spread to any extent.

The flowers of the Late Spider orchid, *O. fuciflora*, even more closely resemble those of the Bee orchid, but they are up to twice the size, and broader in form, and possess a more elaborate pattern of markings, consisting of two or three pale circles or horseshoe-loops on the labellum. The lip bears a little yellow heart-shaped terminal tooth as in the Bee orchid, but in the Late Spider this is bent upwards in front. The pink sepals resemble those of the Bee, but the petals are very short (3–5 mm. long), triangular, pink and furry. The Late Spider resembles the Early Spider in being wholly dependent upon insects for pollination. It is a very rare plant indeed, which is only known now in a limited stretch of the chalk downs of east Kent, and it is not common even there.

The Fly orchid, *O. insectifera*, p. 92, is more a plant of chalky woods and wood-borders, and of developing scrub, than of open downland, though it does often occur in the last habitat. It tends to be taller and slenderer than the other insect-like orchids. Its widely spaced flowers have lips that do really look very like flies sitting on green flowers. There are three green sepals, two narrow purple petals which look like the fly's antennae, and a lip about $\frac{3}{4}$ inch (2 cm.) long, of a reddish-brown colour with a shiny blue patch in the centre. It occurs north to Westmorland, and is known in Ireland in calcareous fens.

In the autumn, in September and early October, one orchid may still be found on the downs of southern England. This is the Autumn Ladies'-tresses, *Spiranthes spiralis*, which has slender, dense spikes 4–8 inches (10–20 cm.) tall of tiny white flowers veined with green. The ovaries of the flowers give the appearance, packed and twisted together, of a plait of green hair, hence the name.

On calcareous pastures that were regularly grazed by sheep, the spine-leaved coniferous shrub Juniper, *Juniperus communis*, was the only shrub that could normally invade and flourish, as the sheep tended to avoid it. The Juniper-studded, short turfed, downs of the past are now tending to be invaded more and more by other calcicole woody plants. Formerly these were mostly confined to the borders of woodlands and to hedgebanks. Some of these shrubs are, however, very interesting and beautiful plants.

Dogwood, *Cornus sanguinea*, is one of the commonest chalk shrubs apart from the ubiquitous Hawthorn. Dogwood has purple-tinted shoots which bear egg-shaped, pointed and untoothed leaves $2-2\frac{3}{4}$ inches (5–7 cm.) long, in opposite pairs, with side-veins that curve towards the leaf tip. The flowers, which are borne in attractive creamy umbels in late May and in June, have inferior ovaries, a minute calyx, four pointed petals and four stamens alternating with the petals, and later produce umbels of black berry-like fruits which, as the seeds are contained in 'stones' inside, are actually drupes like those of cherries and plums, but are not edible to humans. The purple stems account for the name *sanguinea*, which means bloody. Purging Buckthorn, *Rhamnus catharticus*, is rather similar in appearance but usually taller and is slightly spiny at the tips of the shoots. It has leaves of the same shape as Dogwood, with similar tipward-arching side-veins, but the leaves are distinctly toothed all round, not entire as in Dogwood, and the young twigs are green or grey-brown, never red as in Dogwood. The greenish flowers with four-lobed conspicuous calyx and four-lobed tiny corolla, have their four stamens opposite the petals, and their flowers are borne in small clusters, not in umbels, on short side shoots of the previous year's growth. The bark and berries were formerly used as a purgative.

White Beam, *Sorbus aria*, is a shrub (that may eventually grow into a large tree) with ovate sharp-toothed leaves 2–5 inches (5–13 cm.) long, which are glossy green above and white felted beneath. Its umbel-like heads of creamy white five-petalled flowers in summer give way to the bright red 'berries' of autumn.

Spindle, *Euonymus europaeus*, often grows taller than Dogwood; it has ovate to lance-shaped leaves in opposite pairs, and four parted flowers with oblong greenish petals and four stamens alternating with them. It is most distinctive in fruit; the lovely clusters of salmon-red capsules, each deeply four-lobed and 10–15 mm. across, are produced in

Common juniper showing its spine-like leaves in whorls of three and its purplish black berry-like cones which are used to flavour gin

Purging Buckthorn, a shrub frequent in calcareous scrubland and occasionally in fenland in southern England

the autumn. When these capsules open they reveal the seeds enclosed in bright orange cups or arils inside.

The Wayfaring tree, *Viburnum lantana*, has egg-shaped fine-toothed leaves, 3–4 inches (8–10 cm.) long and $2\frac{1}{2}$–3 inches (6–8 cm.) wide with indented veins above. The leaves, which are scurfily downy like the young shoots, are in opposite pairs. This shrub which, like most of the calcicole shrubs described here, has a southern distribution in Britain, is interesting in having no scales to protect its winter buds; these buds are composed only of the rolled-up leaves for the next season. The flowers are borne in May and June in dense, umbel-like heads, and have creamy five-lobed corollas with five creamy long-stalked protruding stamens. The inferior ovaries of the flowers give rise in late summer to oval flattened berry-like fruits, up to 1 cm. long, which are at first red but soon turn black, and form conspicuous flat-topped clusters on the bushes.

Wild Privet, *Ligustrum vulgare*, is like a narrow-leaved version of Garden Privet, *L. ovalifolium*. It is the only chalk shrub described here which tends to retain its leaves in winter, at least for a time. Its pyramidal panicles of creamy-white flowers with four-lobed corollas and two stamens in June and July give place to the black shiny berries in autumn. Like the Wayfaring tree it is not native north of Durham, and, like all the other shrubs mentioned, the fruits are not safe to eat.

Dogwood, one of the commonest shrubs of calcareous grassland and scrub in southern England.

Traveller's joy, *Clematis vitalba*, is another southern species; it is a woody climber, an anomalous member of the largely herbaceous Buttercup family Ranunculaceae. Its stems, with their fibrous peeling bark climb over other shrubs and trees on the edges of calcareous woodlands south of Yorkshire, and bear pinnately compound leaves with pointed, usually toothed, ovate glossy leaflets $1\frac{1}{4}$–4 inches (3–10 cm.) long in opposite pairs. The flowers produced in late summer are in

Spindle, a shrub of calcareous districts of southern England

loose panicles and have four, about 1 cm. long, greenish-creamy perianth segments and numerous creamy stamens. The flowers give way in autumn to fruiting heads of long white feathery-styled achenes or nutlets, which drape the trees and shrubs like wreaths of smoke.

As the chalk scrub closes in over the grassland, the typical small downland herbs disappear, to be replaced with other plants of more robust habit, such as the St John's worts and Marjoram. Common St John's wort, *Hypericum perforatum*, is a herb 1–2 feet (30–61 cm.) high whose stems bear hairless ovate leaves in opposite pairs about $\frac{3}{8}$–$\frac{3}{4}$ inch (1–2 cm.) long, dotted with translucent oil-glands and hence appearing 'perforated'. The flowers are borne in repeatedly branched flat-topped panicles, and are bright yellow, about $\frac{3}{4}$ inch (2 cm.) diameter, with

five petals and numerous stamens gathered into three bundles. Hairy St John's wort, *H. hirsutum*, is similar but has downy, longer, $\frac{3}{4}$–2 inch (2–5 cm.) leaves, and paler yellow, smaller flowers.

Marjoram, *Origanum vulgare*, is an aromatic herb of the Dead nettle family, Labiatae, 1–2 feet (30–61 cm.) high with broad pyramidal 2 inch (5 cm.) wide heads of small purple flowers individually like those of Wild thyme and with opposite, ovate 1 inch (2·5 cm.) long leaves.

When the shrub canopy is completely

closed, then the ground becomes much barer and shade-tolerant woodland herbs now take over more or less completely. At this stage in the Kent chalk scrublands, woodland orchids are often best developed, including the very local and stately Lady orchid, *Orchis purpurea*. This, one of our finest wild plants has large basal leaves up to 7 inches (18 cm.) long, rather like those of the Madonna lily and stems from 12 to 30 inches (30–75 cm.) tall which bear splendid spikes of flowers with four-lobed pink, crimson-spotted lips up to 1 inch (2·5 cm.) long and purple brown-green flecked hoods rather like giant flowers of the Dwarf orchid. Though almost confined to Kent, this magnificent orchid is still happily locally common there. Perhaps this is the best place to mention the two climbing herbs known as Bryony. Both have scarlet berries in glorious clusters in autumn, and are common in chalky scrubland in England north to Newcastle, though they occur in hedges and on wood-borders on other types of base-rich soils very commonly also. White Bryony, *Bryonia dioica*, has palmately lobed leaves and coiled tendrils which give it the aspect of a small grape-vine, though its yellowish green five-petalled flowers with net veining are more reminiscent of the vegetable marrow, to whose family, Cucurbitaceae, it belongs. The even commoner Black Bryony, *Tamus communis*, is quite unrelated; it is one of our few Monocotyledons with net-veined leaves. In Black Bryony these are dark glossy green, stalked, and heart-shaped. The tiny six-parted dioecious yellow-green flowers are borne in racemes. It belongs to the important and largely tropical Yam family, Dioscoreaceae.

We have seen already how immensely rich is the flora of our remaining open chalk grasslands. Since it is now almost certain that, until Neolithic times, practically the whole of our chalk downland of today was covered with forest of some sort, a question arises in the mind of the botanist. Where did this rich calcicole flora grow before there were any chalk grasslands for it to inhabit? To answer this question, we must turn back

once more in history to Late and Early Post-Glacial times. Then, pollen analysis tells us, many at least of the plants that we now find in our chalk grasslands probably occurred widely over our landscape – species of Rock rose, *Helianthemum*, for example. As the forest spread over the land, they seem inevitably to have disappeared in most areas, as they were shaded or crowded out. But there are areas in Britain, below the natural tree-line, where such plants could have continued to survive. These areas are the steep limestone or chalk cliffs, sometimes near the sea coast, but often by rivers far inland, where it has been impossible, for reasons of topography and failure of proper soil development, for trees ever to have formed closed forest.

Today, one can see very rich calcicole floras in areas of this type, particularly in certain restricted places. We can see such floras on the sea cliffs of hard Devonian limestone round Torbay in Devon. We can see them on the Carboniferous limestone sea cliffs near Western-super-Mare in Somerset, in the Gower of South Wales, at the Great Orme's Head near Llandudno in North Wales, and at Humphrey Head in north Lancashire. We can see exceptionally rich floras on the sea cliffs even of the relatively soft chalk about Dover in Kent, and about Beachy Head in Sussex.

Inland, almost equally rich concentrations of calcicole species demanding open conditions free of a continuous tree canopy, can be seen on the limestone of the Avon Gorge near Bristol, and on the limestone scars of north-west Yorkshire and of Westmorland. On the strange upland-plateau areas of Upper Teesdale, there are patches of 'sugar-limestone', limestone metamorphosed and recrystallized after contact with very hot volcanic rocks, which bear extraordinary concentrations of calcicole species. Even in the inland chalk country itself, there are places where rivers pass through gaps in the chalk hills and constantly undercut the chalk slopes, to maintain steep, unstable, 'river cliffs'. On these, even today, closed beech forest cannot establish itself, as, for example, on the west side of Boxhill in Surrey. It is thought that in earlier times, there may have been other places like this in the chalk river valleys, where later changes in river patterns have perhaps caused the steep cliffs to grade down into more gentle slopes, so that the former cliffs can no longer be seen today.

All these places have in common today extremely rich concentrations of calcicole 'open-habitat' plants. It is believed that they have acted as 'refuges' for the calcicole elements of the Late and Early Post-Glacial flora of the largely open landscape of those times. Many of the species of these cliff-habitats do not occur anywhere else, in lowland Britain at least, except in these places. Many other species of these cliffs, however, occur widely in chalk, and other lowland limestone, grasslands today. It is now believed by many botanists that these cliff-refuges acted as recolonization centres from which our lowland chalk grasslands were repopulated, with much of their present-day characteristic floras from Neolithic times onwards, as the forest was cleared by man and suitable grasslands created by grazing of animals or by the later abandonment of arable cultivations.

This theory, largely developed by Professor C. D. Pigott and Dr S. M. Walters in an interesting paper in the *Journal of Ecology* in 1954, would also help to explain some of the rather odd distributions of some of our chalk grassland plants. For example, the Dwarf sedge, *Carex humilis*, a small tufted grass-like sedge with low inconspicuous spikes of brownish flowers in spring, only occurs in chalk grassland as far east as western Hampshire in this country, though it is an essentially central European species abroad. It is, however, found also on limestone cliff-habitats of the type described in Somerset and in the Avon Gorge, but nowhere else on cliffs. Colonization of the chalklands by this plant may have only been able to take place from these centres, and the chalk of south-east England and elsewhere may be too far

Traveller's Joy, *left*, a woody climber or liane and Whitebeam, *right*, characteristic of calcareous scrub and woodlands of southern England

107

away for colonization to have been effective in the time available for spread until the grasslands became too closed for further extension of range. Similarly, as one moves away from the Dover cliffs, the Beachy Head cliffs, the Boxhill river cliff, and the steep slopes of the Medway river gap in the mid-Kent North Downs, one sees a progressive decline in the richness of the chalk grassland floras. The richness is at its maximum at, or close to, the places named; as one moves away, some species disappear at once from the chalk downs. Others are found still at various distances, but ultimately, at different distances in each case, the chalk grassland flora tends to become poorer and more monotonous in character and devoid of the rarer species centred on these above-mentioned sites.

The rich chalky areas of the Breckland and adjacent East Anglian chalk present a special problem. We have seen earlier how this area was almost undoubtedly forest-covered before Neolithic times; and here in this almost flat, heavily glaciated landscape, there are, at least today, no steep-sided river cliffs that might have remained as forest-free refuges from which colonization of the chalky parts of the Breckland heaths with calcicole plants might have taken place. Nevertheless, the East Anglian and Breckland chalk area is remarkable today for the rich assemblage of rare calcicole plants present there. Some of these are known in several other parts of our chalk lands. Others, such as the Spiked speedwell, *Veronica spicata*, with long spikes of rich violet-blue flowers; the Spotted Cat's-ear, *Hypochoeris maculata*, like a very large lemon-yellow flowered Dandelion with rigid stems and roughly hairy, purple-spotted leaves; and the Silvery heath sedge, *Carex ericetorum*, are not known elsewhere today on the chalk outside this East Anglian area, but are known far away on limestone-cliff habitats. The Spiked speedwell, for example, is in the Avon Gorge, on the Gower Cliffs, on the Great Orme's Head, and in north-west Yorkshire, in Westmorland and north Lanca-

shire; the Spotted Cat's-ear is on the Great Orme's Head, in north Lancashire, at the Lizard in Cornwall, and on the Lincolnshire limestone. It is very difficult to believe that these plants could have reached the East Anglian chalk from such places as these northern or western cliff sites by long-range dispersal.

There seem to be three possible explanations of the strange distribution patterns. The first is that small areas of the Breckland heaths always remained open; the second is that there were suitable 'cliff-refuges' in East Anglia in the past which have now been eroded away; the third is that early man brought them accidentally to East Anglia along his migration – or later trade – routes, from somewhere else, either in Britain or abroad. There is some support for the third possibility from what is known of Neolithic man and his movements. It is now considered by some that Neolithic man may have reached East Anglia from the north-east of England, probably by following the Magnesian limestone outcrop down to the north of Derbyshire; then across east to the Lincolnshire limestone and down this to the edge of the Fens, then across the fenland (then dry land as yet unflooded) to East Anglia. If he did take this route, it is very interesting; for the Silvery heath sedge occurs today in Teesdale and Westmorland on the Carboni-ferous limestone, all down the Magnesian limestone through Yorkshire to north Derby-shire, on the Lincolnshire limestone, and on the chalk and chalky Breckland of East Anglia, and nowhere else in these islands. This and other plants, such as Horseshoe vetch and the purplish-red flowered Bloody cranesbill, *Geranium sanguineum*, p. 127, could have taken this route from the north-country limestone cliffs to East Anglia in the

Chalk grassland plants with scrub Beech and White-beam invading from top left. In the foreground are, *from left to right*: Felwort, *Gentianella amarella*; Rock-rose, *Helianthemum chamaecistus*; Stemless thistle, *Cirsium acaulon*; Clustered bellflower, *Campanula glomerata*; Horseshoe vetch, *Hippocrepis comosa* (×2)

wake, as it were, of early human migration; but we shall probably never know for certain. A few plants of the Breckland chalk-heath areas, such as Spanish catchfly, *Silene otites*, with viscous 1–1½ foot (30–45 cm.) high stems with whorls of small greenish-yellow flowers, and narrow-obovate basal leaves, and the Breckland mugwort, *Artemisia campestris*, are known nowhere else in Britain though widespread in Europe. Such plants may have arrived in England more directly as weeds with early man immigrating from the continent.

The Upper Teesdale limestone area, to which we have already referred, contains in addition many other rare calcicole plants, some of which, such as *Dryas octopetala*, p. 35, the Mountain avens, and the purple Alpine bartsia, *Bartsia alpina*, are arctic-alpine species still frequent in some of our other mountain areas. Another is the lovely alpine plant Spring gentian, *Gentiana verna*, p. 127, with ¾ inch (2 cm.) wide flowers of rich sky-blue, which is locally frequent in and near the Teesdale area, but only known otherwise in these islands in western Ireland in the limestone area of the Burren. Yet another species whose British distribution is confined to open stony ground in Upper

Right:
Breckland flora, Spring speedwell, *Veronica verna*, *left*, an annual plant of loose sandy calcareous soil; Spanish catchfly, *Silene otites, centre,* a sticky perennial herb resembling a small creamy flowered campion of calcareous grasslands; both confined to the Breckland; Silvery heath sedge, *Carex ericetorum, right*, a small sedge of about 10-15 cm. high with downy fruits in globular heads. The solitary terminal spikes of male flowers have blunt blackish-brown glumes and silvery margins. It is characteristic also of the chalky Breckland grasslands but has a wider distribution

Left:
Chalk grassland plants with Juniper scrub at top. The dominant grass is Sheep's fescue, *Festuca ovina*, and the taller Upright brome, *Bromus erectus*. Flowering plants, *from left to right:* Pasque flower, *Pulsatilla vulgaris*; Field fleabane, *Senecio integrifolius*; Dwarf orchid, *Orchis ustulata* (×2); Early Spider orchid, *Ophrys sphegodes*; Pyramidal orchid, *Anacamptis pyramidalis*; Bee orchid, *Ophrys apifera* and, *behind*, Woolly thistle, *Cirsium eriophorum* (×$\frac{1}{10}$)

Teesdale, the nearby Lake District and the Irish Burren, is Shrubby cinquefoil, *Potentilla fruticosa*. This is a low shrub 1–2 feet (30–61 cm.) tall with masses of glorious yellow flowers about 1 inch (2·5 cm.) across like small single roses, and palmately cut leaves about 1 inch (2·5 cm.) long. Teesdale also contains a few species, such as the Teesdale violet, *Viola rupestris*, like a tiny Dog violet with kidney-shaped leaves and downy leaf-stalks and fruits, and Teesdale sandwort, *Minuartia stricta*, that are confined in the British Isles to Upper Teesdale (the sandwort) or to its immediate region (the violet). Clearly Upper Teesdale has had an interesting ecological history, for nowhere else in England at least does such a strange and rich assemblage of plant species occur.

As was mentioned earlier, some of our western and northern limestone cliff habitats provide sites for some calcicole plants which grow in no other places in this country. Such

are the White rock-rose, *Helianthemum apenninum*, p. 127, like a white-flowered Common rock-rose with grey-white downy leaves, confined to Torbay and the Weston-super-Mare limestones; Hoary rock-rose, *H. canum*, found only on limestone cliffs at the Gower, the Great Orme, Westmorland, and north Lancashire, on sugar limestone, Upper Teesdale, and in western Ireland; and the Goldilocks, *Aster (Crinitaria) linosyris*, known only at Torbay, near Weston, in the Gower, at the Great Orme. and at Humphrey Head in north Lancashire. It is strange that this last species, of central to south-eastern distribution in Europe, should in Britain be confined to our west coast, until one starts to consider this question of possible refuges from the spread of the forest for open-habitat plants.

The cliffs of the Lizard peninsula in Cornwall, composed partly of the unusual magnesium-rich rock serpentine, have another strange and unique assemblage of species, which, besides some of the species we have already discussed, like the Spotted Cat's-ear, contains three species of clovers

Shrubby cinquefoil, a low shrub common on a stony ground by the River Tees in Upper Teesdale, also found on limestone in Ireland

Alpine bartsia, a herb with purple bracts and flowers found in Upper Teesdale and the Scottish Highlands in moist calcareous habitats

on the exposed coastlines of north-west Europe, including western Britain. Soil-pollen studies by Professor Géhu in Brittany have shown that a narrow belt of heathland has existed along the top of the coastal cliffs there since the Early Post-Glacial Period, while the heathlands more than a few hundred yards inland lie on the sites of former deciduous forest. Similar, but less detailed evidence indicates the same pattern may well have occurred in parts of Cornwall and even as far east as the Wareham area in Dorset. In exposed coastal sites, presumably trees were never able to establish themselves.

Through the Middle Ages and until this century, most of our lowland heaths were used as common grazing by those with commoner's rights. Heather was cut at one time for such purposes as thatching and floor covering, while furze was used as fuel or as kindling material. Grazing of lowland heathland still occurs extensively in such places as the New Forest and in parts of Devon and Cornwall, but elsewhere, particularly in east and south-east England, such grazing has now largely ceased. Where common rights did not exist, and in many cases where they did, extensive enclosures of heaths took place during the nineteenth century. In some cases the land was cultivated, in others it was too poor for this and was planted extensively with conifers. Many of these enclosed former heaths lie in what is now the 'stockbroker belt' to the south-west of London in Surrey, north-east Hampshire and east Berkshire, and many of them have now been developed with low-density, high-class, housing. Others have remained as unenclosed open land, in many cases jealously guarded by boards of conservators or by the National Trust as amenity areas, while many in the Aldershot region and in east Dorset are used as army training grounds. However, with the absence of the former grazing and cutting, and with the presence of numerous plantations of Scots pine in their neighbourhood since the mid-nineteenth century, a great many of these heaths that are still unenclosed are tending to become colonized by

known nowhere else in Britain, and also the Cornish heath, *Erica vagans*, a large and shrubby heather whose centre is in south-west Europe. This is an area well worth a visit in early June, when most of its special plants are at their best and before most of the holiday-makers arrive.

We have already seen earlier how it is considered most of the dry lowland heaths of Britain came into existence as a result of the clearances by early man, and we have also seen something of the features of their characteristic soil type, the podsol. Now we shall look at the more recent history of our lowland heaths and at their present flora and usage.

While most of our lowland heaths appear almost certainly to have originated on land once forested as a result of events set in train by man, there is now evidence that there is such a thing as primitive, natural heathland

pine and to develop gradually into pine forest. Such areas, however, are subject to increasing public pressure from those seeking recreation in the fresh air, and fires get started very easily among the inflammable heather and pines, especially in spring when the vegetation is dry and there is often much dead bracken foliage present. Such fires tend to hold back the succession to pine forest and to keep these heaths open. Often one can distinguish a mosaic of areas covering heath, each burned at a different date and with recolonizing heather seedlings, and pines, of different ages. A severe fire often seems to bring in birch. The bed of ash left by such a fire is relatively rich in plant nutrients – it contains most of the 'nutrient capital' of the heathland ecosystem – and produces an ideal seed-bed in which birch can establish itself on soils that otherwise might be too poor for effective colonization.

In a typical lowland dry heath today in south-east England, Ling or Heather, *Calluna vulgaris*, is usually the dominant dwarf shrub. Associated with it in the better-drained areas is Purple Bell-heather, *Erica cinerea*, p. 128. Ling has very short sessile leaves, 1–2 mm. long, which are densely packed on and adpressed to the younger shoots, and small flowers of which the 3–4 mm. long, petaloid and four-lobed pink calyx, which persists on drying and largely encloses and hides the corolla, is the most conspicuous part. Bell-heather has much longer, 5–7 mm., linear leaves with tiny stalks that stand out from the stem in whorls of three. The margins of the leaves of all the heaths, *Erica*, are strongly rolled back underneath or revolute. The flowers of Bell-heather have urn-shaped crimson-purple corollas 5–6 mm. long borne in elongated racemes. In damper areas, where the soil is more peaty, the Cross-leaved heath, *E. tetralix*, occurs. This differs from Bell-heather in the following features. The leaves are borne in whorls of four, not of three, and are grey-downy with many long gland-tipped hairs, while the flowers, which are rose-pink, are borne in short umbel-like heads rather than in elongated spikes or racemes. In dry heathland, the flora of higher plants is limited, except in more open grassy areas or along pathways, but two spiny leguminous shrubs are frequent and characteristic. The commoner is the Dwarf gorse, or Dwarf furze, *Ulex minor*, p. 128. This has a low spreading habit, and rarely exceeds 2 feet (61 cm.) in height. Its branches are all spine-tipped but green; in the mature plant they bear no leaves, though these are present in the seedlings. It bears, in late summer and autumn, deep yellow pea-type flowers of elongated form (about 15 mm. long) with a hairy calyx nearly as long as the corolla. Needle whin, *Genista anglica*, is a much slenderer, more straggly plant which has strong brown spine-tipped twigs $\frac{3}{8}$–$\frac{3}{4}$ inch (1–2 cm.) long, which bear small egg-shaped pointed hairless leaves when young. The yellow flowers are smaller than those of Dwarf gorse (to 8 mm. long), are more inflated, and are borne in May and June in looser, shorter heads. It never shows the abundance displayed by the Dwarf gorse, which may, in certain areas, such as parts of Ashdown Forest, cover a high proportion (up to over 50 per cent) of the ground. Common gorse or Furze, *Ulex europaeus*, is a much larger shrub which flowers mostly in early spring and has deeply furrowed spines. Though found in disturbed areas on heaths, it is of much wider distribution in all types of rough open ground throughout the British Isles.

In more open spots the Wavy hair-grass, *Deschampsia flexuosa*, p. 128, also found in dry oak woods, may be common. This has dark green bristle-like leaves rather like those of Red fescue (but not grooved above as in that grass) and tall stems to 2 feet (61 cm.), which bear loose pyramidal panicles of long stalked spikelets of silvery-looking awned florets. Tormentil, *Potentilla erecta*, p. 128, is often quite common; the fine trailing stems of this little rosaceous herb bear ternate, or occasionally palmate – five-lobed, compound leaves a few centimetres long with toothed leaflets, and loose inflorescences of flowers each with four yellow petals, rarely three or five. The petals are notched at the tips. Heath bedstraw, *Galium saxatile*, is common, especially where the heath is grassy; it has the six-whorled pointed-tipped leaves characteristic of most bedstraws but is smaller and more prostrate than the common Hedge bedstraw, *G. mollugo*, of our roadsides, and has smaller clusters of white flowers.

All the plants mentioned above are calcifuge or lime-hating plants which avoid chalky or base-rich soils.

Beneath the canopy of dwarf shrubs, mosses are sometimes plentiful, such as the Common fork-moss, *Dicranum scoparium*, with erect shoots in turfs or cushions and long pointed green shining translucent leaves all turned to one side or secund. The Heath feather-moss, *Hypnum cupressiforme* var. *ericetorum*, forms mats of shoots like silvery green feathers in which the fine leaf-points are all hooked over at the tips. More open patches usually bear communities of lichens of the genus *Cladonia*. These may be white and intricately branched like small bushes as in *C. impexa*, or may have greygreen basal squamules or scales which bear stalked grey or yellowish grey cups. One beautiful species with yellow-grey cups has fruiting bodies like drops of scarlet sealingwax on their edges; this is *C. coccifera*. Those who wish to know more of mosses or lichens might start by reading the *Observer's Books* on these groups of plants.

Often Bracken, *Pteridium aquilinum*, is abundant, tending to smother and then to replace the heathers; Bracken seems to be helped by repeated heath fires, which destroy the Ling, which then has to start again from seed, while not damaging the underground rhizomes of the Bracken at all.

Further west, the heathland flora tends to be richer. This is probably because the primitive heathlands were all in that region, and because most heathland species tend to be 'oceanic' species anyway, with their centres of origin, or of maximum abundance, in south-west Europe: such are members of the so-called 'Lusitanian' element in our flora.

West of a line from Dorchester northwards through Bath, Birmingham and Nottingham, and in north-west England, south Scotland and in Ireland, Dwarf gorse is replaced by Western gorse, *Ulex gallii*, on heaths. This is a rather larger plant with much stouter and stiffer spines than Dwarf gorse; like it, it flowers in late summer and autumn. The side petals or wings of the flowers are longer than the lower two petals, or keel, not shorter as in Dwarf gorse, and its calyx-teeth are pressed to the corolla instead of spreading outwards. Strangely, Western gorse also appears in the extreme east in Kent and near the coast of East Anglia.

In east Dorset, and in parts of Devon and Cornwall, one may find the lovely Dorset heath, *Erica ciliaris*. This is a relatively tall heath, of Lusitanian distribution, 1–2 feet (30–61 cm.) high, with rather wide ovate leaves bearing long gland tipped hairs but otherwise hairless above, and white beneath, borne in whorls of three. It has long one-sided racemes of large urn-like curved flowers 8–10 mm. long of a deep rich pink colour. In damper heath areas in east Dorset it may be very abundant, but is more local further west.

In western Ireland there is a small heath, *E. mackaiana*. The deep pink flowers are borne in umbel-like terminal heads as in Cross-leaved heath, but the leaves are widely ovate-lance-shaped, hairless except for scattered long gland tipped hairs, and white below. The calyx is shiny brown and hairless except for a few gland-tipped hairs and not shaggily hairy as in Cross-leaved heath. This very rare plant is mentioned because of its extraordinary geographical distribution. Apart from two limited areas of Irish blanket bog, one in Connemara and one in Donegal, it is only known elsewhere in the world in a limited area of north-west Spain. Its distribution is thus the most 'disjunct' of any of our Lusitanian plants, and poses the problem of how it ever reached Ireland. Possibly its distribution was more continuous between the two areas during times of lower sea level in Early Post-Glacial times or even earlier, on land now under the sea.

Where the water table, or water level in the soil, is nearer the surface, the plant community known as wet-heath occurs. Usually this community forms a zone of vegetation between the permanently 'dry heath' and the permanently wet 'valley bog' community that tends to occur in the larger valleys on our heaths. In wet-heaths, the water table is usually high, often near or even at the surface, in winter but far lower in summer. Wet-heath areas are usually dominated by the Cross-leaved heath, with varying amounts of Purple moor-grass, *Molinia coerulea*. This grass tends to form dense tussocks of leafy shoots up to 2 feet (61 cm.) high from which protrude the inflorescences on long stalks. The leaves are grey-green, (straw-coloured in winter) lance-shaped, up to 1 cm. wide and sparingly hairy. Where they join the stem there is no flap or ligule, as in most grasses, but only a row of hairs. The erect narrow much-branched panicles bear clusters of grey green, narrow purple flushed spikelets.

In this community of the wet-heath one may find many species of the bogs discussed on the following pages. A few species are, however, very characteristic of this community. In southern England on the bare moist peaty soil one may find Bog club-moss, *Lycopodium inundatum*, with bright green creeping stems 2–4 inches (5–10 cm.) long covered in spirally arranged tiny pointed leaves, and erect leafy cone-stalks up to 2 inches (5 cm.) tall bearing cylindrical cones with green cone-scales 10–15 mm. long, in whose axils lie the sporangia which all contain identical tiny spores.

The loveliest plant of the wet-heath, however, is the ill-named Marsh gentian, *Gentiana pneumonanthe*, p. 128, ill-named because the places where it grows are usually quite dry in the late summer when it flowers.

This gentian is from 6–12 inches (15–30 cm.) tall, and has erect, un-branched stems bearing linear leaves, about 5 mm. wide and

up to 1½ inches (4 cm.) long in opposite pairs. At the apex, either singly or several together are borne the flowers – narrowly conical trumpets which are deep sky-blue, with five green-streaks on the outside, blue with paler dots within. The corolla tube is five-lobed at the top, with five extra tiny lobes between the large ones. The Marsh gentian is far less common than it was even 100 years ago; many of its former haunts have been drained or cultivated. It still has a few strongholds, however, from Dorset to east Sussex, and there still exist scattered localities up into northern England, and north Wales.

We may also find in damp or wet heathland throughout the British Isles an attractive orchid with spotted leaves, the Heath Spotted orchid, *Dactylorchis ericetorum*. This differs from the Common Spotted orchid in possessing 10–12 mm. wide pink or white lips which are not deeply divided into three equal parts, but form a single skirt-shaped lobe, bearing three small teeth at the lower margin. The lip tends to be more heavily marked with crimson-purple streaks and spots than in the Common Spotted orchid, and the plant is usually shorter, rarely more than 10 inches (25 cm.) tall.

In association with it we may find Sawwort, *Serratula tinctoria*; this is a plant 1½–2 feet (46–61 cm.) tall like a slender spineless thistle with pinnately cut leaves and several narrow thistle-like flower heads. Strangely enough, this species may also be found in chalk and limestone grasslands in south-west England especially; perhaps we have here a different ecological race, or ecotype, adapted to calcareous soils.

Over much of the hilly country of west and north Britain, usually over old, acid rocks of Palaeozoic age, we may find plant communities containing acid-loving, or calcifuge plants, and dominated by the Ling or Common heather. These communities, which occupy vast areas, are mostly developed in the zone up to about 2,000 feet (610 m.) above sea level, in other words, below the original natural upper limit of the forest, though they extend in many places above this. They are, therefore, like the lowland heaths, plant communities which have resulted largely from the clearance of former forest by man. They differ from the lowland heaths in their generally even poorer flora and the much greater tendency to the development of a thick peat layer beneath the heather. These characteristics are probably a result of the much more severe, and much wetter, climate of the zone in which upland heaths occur. The usual name for the upland heaths is heather-moors, and while most of them are used for sheep-grazing or as deer-forests in parts of Scotland, many others are preserved primarily as grouse-moors. Signs of early human activity and even of settlement are frequently widespread and stumps of the former forest trees (usually of oak at lower levels, and of pine and birch higher up) may be occasionally found in the peat.

Our heather-moors are fine places for healthy exercise, but are not as a rule botanically rewarding. Besides the Ling, the Bilberry, the Purple moor-grass and several other moorland grasses, the main plant of some interest to the lowland botanist is likely to be the Crowberry, *Empetrum nigrum*. This looks like a large-leaved sprawling green heath. Its leaves are shiny dark green with strongly rolled-back edges, and are 4–8 mm. long and 2 mm. wide, and rather blunt. Its flowers, however, are quite un-heathlike: they are six-parted, green, wide open, and only 1–2 mm. across, and the three-stamened male flowers and female flowers with six stigmas are borne on separate plants. Later the female shrubs bear black berry-like drupes about 5 mm. across, the Crowberries themselves, which are not fit for humans to eat. The little Lesser twayblade, probably a relic of former pine forests, is not uncommon on heather moors in Scotland, and occurs as far south as Exmoor in such habitats, but is very rare south of the far north of England. The high plateaux of our moorlands are usually occupied by the blanket bogs described later under Bogs. In both upland heather moors and in blanket bogs in north England and Scotland one is likely

to find the Cloudberry, *Rubus chamaemorus*. This is really a very small, arctic, creeping herbaceous Bramble with glossy ternate or five to seven lobed leaves with leaflets about 2 inches (5 cm.) long, 1 inch (2·5 cm.) wide and white solitary flowers and large fruits like hard orange-coloured raspberries in shape.

The Bracken may be quite common on the lower parts of our upland heather-moors, but it rapidly fades out above about 1,500 feet (450 m.) above sea level, due apparently to the fact that above this altitude its highly frost-sensitive fronds are too regularly destroyed by the severer frosts and stronger winds on the higher ground.

It will probably help the reader if the distribution of heath communities in the British Isles is summarized at this stage. Lowland heaths are characteristic of the sandy and gravelly soils up to about 1,000 feet (300 m.). (1) on the Tertiary sand formations of the south of England, such as the Bagshot sand areas of north-west Surrey, south-east Berkshire, north-east Hampshire, and the New Forest–east Dorset country; (2) on the Lower Greensand areas around the Weald and in Bedfordshire, Norfolk, and in west Dorset and south-east Devon; (3) on the Ashdown and Tunbridge Wells sands of the central Weald of Sussex; (4) on the Glacial sands of east Suffolk, north-east Norfolk, north Lincolnshire, and, now much reduced in extent, of the Vale of York; (5) on the drift covered plateau of the Jurassic rocks of the north-east York moors; and (6) on the Bunter Sandstones of Cannock Chase in Staffordshire. Fragments of lowland heaths occur in many other areas in England and Wales, but they are usually small and ill-developed today, and many of these fragments have been whittled away gradually by building or cultivation. In eastern central Scotland, however, lowland heaths are still quite extensive on Glacial and other sands formerly occupied by pine forests. Valley bog communities, described further on, are to be found in most of the larger valleys and low-lying basins of all these lowland heath areas.

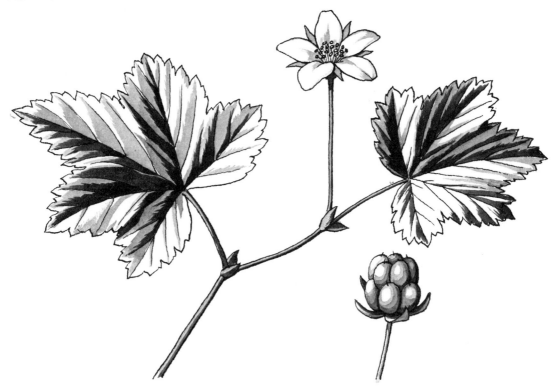

Upland heaths of the 'heather moor' type are characteristic of the higher parts of Bodmin Moor, Dartmoor and Exmoor, etc. in south-west England; of some sandstone areas of the Welsh uplands; of the Pennine and Cheviot Hills; and all over the Scottish Highlands up to the altitude of about 2,000–2,500 feet (610–760 m.), at which more arctic-alpine types of vegetation commence. They are common on the Irish hills too.

Fire, and grazing, are perhaps the dominant factors in maintaining all these heath communities in their present form. Our upland heather-moors are mostly regularly burnt, or 'swaled', to maintain a fresh growth of young shoots of heather for either sheep or grouse, or both, to feed upon, and to prevent the heather becoming 'leggy' and eventually dying off. This practice of regular burning, however, has been shown to lead to loss of nutrients both by leaching and by wind-blow of the ash. Most of this upland heather-moor is now probably best used, from the point of view of the national economy, as timber-producing land, under conifers, rather than as grazing land, as its fertility is now desperately low. Our heath communities can, in the main, be regarded as 'nutrient deserts', and this remark applies above all to our high-level heaths on severely leached-out poor soils in the very wet, cool, sunshine-deficient upland climate.

Much of our upland country below the former tree-line, however, is neither heather-moor nor bog, but consists of grassland. These 'hill grazings', occupied usually by sheep at necessarily low densities, bear various communities. The better drained areas on the more fertile soils still carry fescue-bent grasslands, with some Sheep's fescue, and much more Common bent-grass, *Agrostis tenuis*, a tufted or creeping grass with narrow lance-shaped leaves and Christmas-tree shaped inflorescences of tiny, 2–3·5 mm. long, translucent brown or purplish pointed one-flowered spikelets. This type of grassland is still worth retaining as pasture. Poorly drained areas are often dominated by Purple moor-grass; overgrazed leached-out areas, which are often the most extensive type, may carry grassland dominated by Mat-grass, *Nardus stricta*, p. 128, associated often with Bilberry, *Sphagnum* mosses and other heath or bog plants. Mat-grass which occurs also sparsely on some lowland heaths, has very tough, wiry and unpalatable foliage in dense rosettes or tussocks. The individual leaves are hard, rough and bristle-like, and are bent back at right angles to their basal sheaths; they are whitish and long persistent when dead, and are rejected as far as possible by sheep. The inflorescences, 4–12 inches (10–30 cm.) in height, are slender and bear narrow spine-like spikelets, often purple tinged, in a row along one side of the upper part of the stem, rather like a little comb with very oblique teeth.

These *Nardus* dominated hill-grazings are characteristic of the more clayey glacial drift soils and of rocks which yield a high but infertile clay fraction on weathering; they cover particularly large areas of the Welsh uplands and of much of the northern English, southern Scottish and Irish hills. Where possible they are being reafforested with conifers, as in the great Kielder Forest of the Border Country.

Bogs may be defined as plant associations developed on more or less permanently wet, acid nutrient-poor peat, usually more or less dominated by a cover of *Sphagnum* mosses. Several different types of bogs occur in the British Isles, distinguished more by their mode of development and by their structure, than by their actual floras, so bog structure and development will be considered first, and most details of their flora will be looked at afterwards.

As mentioned earlier, valley and hollows of lowland heath areas tend to bear valley-bogs. These develop wherever some impediment to drainage occurs such as where a layer of more impervious clay material beneath the sand or gravel throws out acid water draining from the surrounding heath, along a spring-line. They may also develop where a stream in a valley, draining off heathland, has been blocked, sometimes by an artificial dam such as a causeway carrying a track. If of sufficient size, they usually show a clear zonation of plant communities. If there is a central stream, conditions along this are usually favourable for the growth of shrubs or even trees, as by the running water, the supply of nutrient salts per unit time is better than elsewhere, although the water itself may contain only low concentrations of plant nutrients. Also the movement of the water ensures a better supply of oxygen for root respiration. In a large valley-bog, the sides of the central stream may even bear a narrow belt of Alder carr. Where the stream is smaller or less rapidly flowing, carr of Birch, or of Sallow, *Salix atrocinerea*, a willow with obovate leaves that produces the well-known 'palm' or 'pussy willow' catkins of spring, with silky female and golden male catkins, may occur instead.

Outside this zone of carr, on both sides of it, communities of sedges and rushes may occur. These include the Greater Tussock sedge, mentioned under Alder woods, the Bottle sedge, *Carex rostrata*, with long narrow to 2 feet (61 cm.) leaves and slender inflorescences whose cylindrical $1\frac{1}{4}$–$2\frac{3}{8}$ inch (3–6 cm.) female spikelets are composed of dense packed tiny (5–6 mm.) fruits shaped like Italian wine bottles, and the Acute-flowered rush, *Juncus acutiflorus*, with about 2 foot (61 cm.) high stems bearing narrow cylindrical hollow pointed leaves with cross-partitions inside, like miniature bamboo shoots, and dense much branched heads of brown six-parted flowers which produce narrow pointed red-brown fruits 4–6 mm. long.

Outside this zone, often on both sides of it, one finds the *Sphagnum* bog community

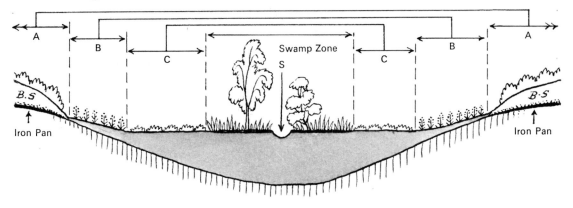

Valley bog profile, A dry heath, B wet heath, C sphagnum zone, BS bleached sand beneath dry heath of podsol and in swamp zone note carr along the stream, S with open swamp on either side

itself, p. 137. Here there is little oxygenation and little movement of the water. Water supply here is mostly derived, not from the central stream, but laterally from off the acid, podsolized heathland itself on the upper slopes, and is extremely poor in nutrients. The combination of permanent waterlogging of the ground, negligible oxygen supply, and nutrient-poor water is ideal for both the growth of *Sphagnum* moss and for the accumulation of peat. Under these conditions the bacteria which normally break down vegetable matter cannot operate and so plant remains build up. In the peat so formed one can usually recognize, either with the naked eye or with the microscope if necessary, the actual species of higher plants and mosses that have built up this peat in the past, and one may thus have, in a deep, old bog, a chronological record of the flora, which can be dated by the means discussed earlier. Most valley bogs, however, are relatively recent in origin, and they appear also often to have been cut for peat in past times. The peat one finds also is often soup-like and uncompressed. Thus such bogs are not usually useful as records of past vegetational history and climatic changes. The surface vegetation of such bogs, however, is often very typical of actively growing *Sphagnum* bogs in general.

It is indeed usually in a more vigorous state today than that of the other older types of *Sphagnum* bogs to be described, which have been and are still subject as a rule to much more interference by man than the valley bogs on our heaths, both by burning and by cutting of the deeper, more compacted and more valuable peat.

At this point, some account of the structure of the *Sphagnum* moss genus in general, appears desirable.

Sphagnum differs from other mosses in several ways. It has weak, slender stems which cannot support themselves, but either rely on the support of their neighbouring stems in the close dense turfs or cushions in which the plants characteristically grow, or else, in the case of a few aquatic species, in pools of water. These stems bear branches which arise in whorls at intervals up the stem like the spokes of a wheel, forming conspicuous rosettes 1–2 cm. across at the surface of the cushions or turfs. Other branches hang down the stems and help to draw up water like the wicks of oil lamps. The branches are thickly covered with over-lapping branch leaves, and there are also stem-leaves, usually of different form, on the main stem. If the individual branch leaves are examined under the microscope, one can see that each is composed of two sorts of cells, disposed in a layer one cell thick. There is a trellis-like lattice of narrow living cells, containing chlorophyll: in between these there are much larger empty dead cells with pointed ends, and with holes or pores in them. These dead cells absorb water through their pores to a remarkable degree.

The whole mass of shoots in a *Sphagnum* cushion is wonderfully adapted, both to draw up water by capillarity from below, and to hold rain-water falling on it from above. If we take up a tuft of fresh wet *Sphagnum* from the surface of a bog in the hand and squeeze it hard, an amazing amount of water comes out of it. The effect is similar to squeezing a bath sponge. Some species of *Sphagnum* can, in fact, hold 20 times their own dry weight of water when fully wetted. This extraordinary property explains how *Sphagnum* can build up bogs in a valley or basin, or even on flat ground in a wet climate, well above the original water level until a convex mass or 'lens' of peat, often miles across, is formed. At the same time, the living *Sphagnum* actually creates acidity by removing cations, or positively charged atoms of metals, that it requires for its food from the water, and replacing these with ions of hydrogen, thus acidifying the water. In this way an alkaline, nutrient-rich fen may be converted into an acid, nutrient-poor bog.

The different species of *Sphagnum* are mostly distinguished by the shape of their branch and stem leaves. In the field, to some extent, they may be also distinguished by their colour, which ranges in different species from yellow through grass-green to dark brown, rich red and even purple-black.

Let us now return to our valley bog.

Bordering the permanently wet *Sphagnum* bog zone on the sides of the valley, there is always the zone of wet-heath vegetation described earlier, in which the water table fluctuates between summer and winter. This variation does not encourage the healthy growth of most species of *Sphagnum*, and it promotes some decomposition of peat during the drier summer period, so that only a shallow peat layer a few inches thick is usually found here. There are two *Sphagnum* species, however, which appear to be favoured by the intermittent drying out and these together usually dominate the surface

of the ground in wet-heath. These are *S. tenellum* and *S. compactum. S. tenellum* is our smallest British species and its rosettes of branches, bearing egg-shaped branch-leaves only 1–2 mm. long are of a pale- to orange-yellow colour. *S. compactum*, which is almost confined to wet-heaths and very rare on deep peat bogs, has its whorled branches all curved upwards so that the rosette-appearance is lost, and in habit it looks more like the grey-green woodland moss *Leucobryum glaucum*, which also has water-absorbing properties but is quite unrelated to *Sphagnum. S. compactum* is deep yellow-green to rich orange-brown in colour and has blunt parallel sided leaves about 2 mm. long.

In former times, the most important type of lowland bog in these islands, except in the most oceanic districts of the west and far north-west, was the raised or domed bog. This takes the form of a convex lens of peat, normally developed in a basin over an initial marsh or lake. Because of its elevated central part, it is known to ecologists as the *Hochmoor*, from the German for 'high moor'. Formerly, such bogs, often many square miles in extent, though sometimes of only a few hundred acres, occurred all over the glaciated plains of northern England and central Scotland, and in estuarine regions. In the latter they have been shown to have developed on sites that were initially salt-marsh, especially in the Solway Firth and Morecambe Bay areas and along the central Welsh coast. In the central Irish plain, such bogs are still abundant, and occupy a large part of certain counties such as Leix, Offaly and Westmeath. They were apparently always less common in the southern unglaciated parts of England where suitable shallow basins for their initiation, dammed by glacial morainic materials, are generally absent, but they did occur on the Somerset levels at Shapwick Heath, at Amberley in Sussex, and bordering the East Anglian fenland as around Whittlesey Mere.

Today, however, few raised bogs remain in anything like their original condition;

Raised bog profile, *from bottom to top*, lake mud with shells, fen peat, brushwood peat and sphagnum peat. On either side are shown the zones of marginal lagg, fen or fen woodland, with drainage stream S

most have been drained and extensively cut for their compacted peat which was formerly so valuable as fuel before coal was readily obtainable, and is still valuable as horticultural peat. Even the few whose central areas remain more or less intact are mostly nibbled away round the edges. The best remaining examples left in Britain are Glasson Moss in Cumberland and Borth Bog in Cardiganshire, both of which are now nature reserves. In Ireland, many remain relatively intact, but this type of bog is rapidly disappearing in Ireland too, as the peat is being used as fuel by specially-designed electric power stations. Conservation of good examples of this type of bog in Ireland is a matter of desperate urgency. Already the largest and best ones have been completely destroyed. On the continent of Europe, such bogs are still numerous, and sometimes still quite intact as in Scandinavia, especially in Sweden. Fine examples exist in the north German and Polish plains and also in the south German tableland in Bavaria and Württemberg.

A raised bog is initiated normally by succession commencing in an aquatic environment, the so-called hydrosere. Vegetation, either on the edge of an estuary or in a fresh-water lake, builds up until a fen stage is reached. A fen, as we saw earlier, is a peat building plant association in a water-logged but relatively nutrient-rich environment and it is often, though not always, alkaline. As in a bog, peat accumulates from the plants growing on it due to the lack of the oxygen necessary for decomposing bacteria to do their work. However, since at this stage nutrient salts are plentiful and con-

stantly replenished by seepage or flooding over the flat fen surface, especially during the winter when the water level is high, such a fen is dominated at first, not by *Sphagnum*, but by various monocotyledonous plants such as species of sedges, rushes and grasses, together with various dicotyledonous herbs that can tolerate waterlogging of their root systems.

Eventually, the fen in the raised bog hydrosere became invaded by woody plants, and usually willow and birch, then pine, form a wet woodland or 'carr' on its surface. The surface of the peat is now built up to a critical stage, just at the limit to which the highest winter flooding by nutrient-rich ground-water could reach. At this point, certain species of *Sphagnum*, particularly those, like *S. squarrosum* and *S. plumulosum*, which can tolerate base-rich water of high pH, begin to colonize. After a time, the whole centre of the bog becomes carpeted with *Sphagnum*. Along one or both side margins, there normally remains a belt of fen – the *lagg*, from the Swedish word for this – where more base-rich water from higher ground prevents *Sphagnum* growth, and through which the drainage stream through the basin, if any, becomes diverted. In the centre of the *Sphagnum* carpet, conditions for growth of this genus are now better than at the edges; the *Sphagnum* here is protected from both flushing by less acid, nutrient-rich water and from the risk of drying-out periodically by the protective 'sponge' of the *Sphagnum* nearer the edges of the bog. Hence species of *Sphagnum* intolerant of nutrient-rich water are now able to invade and to grow more rapidly in the centre of the bog than near the edges. Thus after a time the bog assumes a convex, lens-shaped form. *S. imbricatum*, a large, robust species with branch leaves each shaped like a half egg-shell about 4 mm. long and bearing 'combs' of long fibrils projecting into their empty cells from their walls, visible with the microscope, now became dominant in most cases in British bogs at this stage of their history. One can follow the whole of this story, in the peat profiles of cut raised bogs, or with the peat-borer in uncut bogs, with eye and microscope.

Even in the raised bogs that remain more or less intact, *S. imbricatum* is now often absent, on the living surface, and only rarely does it remain abundant. This species seems to have been particularly sensitive to human interference, though the full reasons for its great decline from general dominance to great scarcity in our bogs are still not completely clear. Drier phases of climate may have played their part.

The development of raised bogs does not appear, as has often been suggested, to depend on a particularly high rainfall. On the continent of Europe, actively growing raised bogs exist in places where the rainfall today is only 25 inches (63 cm.) per annum.

In the wettest parts of the British Isles, however, particularly in western Ireland near sea level in Connemara, Mayo and Donegal, and widely at various heights on our hills up to about 2,700 feet (820 m.), another type of bog occupies vast tracts of flat or gently sloping terrain. This is the blanket bog. Many of the blanket bogs of the north Pennines and the Scottish hill plateaux are really only versions of the raised bog; the vegetation is similar, and sometimes a convexity can be distinguished on the surface. Near sea level in western Ireland, however, the surface is more broken up by pools, and *Sphagnum* is often less important;

a more fen-like vegetation of sedges such as *Schoenus nigricans*, and grasses such as *Molinia coerulea* may replace it locally. Possibly this is partly due to extra salts coming in to the habitat with sea spray. Possibly it is the very mild oceanic climate that is important. Or possibly the more depressed parts of these bogs receive mineral salts from the rocky outcrops that project everywhere through the surface; and really we have here conditions more like those of a valley bog. Research data provide conflicting suggestions for answers to these problems. It is clear, however, that in the sufficiently wet climates of parts of Britain, *Sphagnum* bog, once initiated, has been able to spread over solid ground and even to cover slopes of up to five degrees or more steep, and to dominate hundreds of square miles of our landscapes.

Blanket bogs in many remote areas have remained relatively intact, even until today; their very remoteness has preserved them from such things as drainage and peat-cutting. Drainage and afforestation, however, are now altering many of these areas, particularly in the north Pennines, but enlightened co-operation between the Forestry Commission and conservation bodies means that active steps are being taken to preserve some of the best examples of these magnificent, awe-inspiring relics of primaeval Britain.

In the south Pennines, the extensive blanket bogs have undergone great changes in the last century or so. *Sphagnum* mosses have become almost extinct over wide areas, and with them most of the delightful bog flora. Instead, one component of the original flora has taken over complete dominance to the exclusion sometimes of all other species bar one or two true mosses over vast areas. This is the Hare's-tail cotton-sedge, *Eriophorum vaginatum*, p. 137. This change has been ascribed to burning and overgrazing of the bogs, and these factors have no doubt played their part; but Dr Tallis has now produced good evidence to suggest that severe air pollution from the

Manchester, Sheffield and Leeds-Bradford conurbations is the main factor in this change.

Gullying and erosion of the peat is another phenomenon which is very prominent in many blanket bogs, and it has been thought to be due in part at least to human interference. This may well be so: the formation of 'peat-haggs', where the original vegetation remains poised in patches on broad sloping-sided pillars of peat some yards across, while elsewhere a raw peat surface, gullied and eroded in places even down to the mineral soil beneath, is very much a feature of the much burned, highly polluted bogs of the south Pennine plateaux. However, this phenomenon is in fact widespread all over our upland blanket bogs, and evidence of healing and regrowth of erosion channels is not infrequent. So it is now thought by many that blanket-peat erosion is a largely natural phenomenon in our wet hill climate, perhaps especially after the peat reaches a certain thickness and degree of instability. So-called 'bog flows' or 'bog bursts' are known even in large lowland raised bogs, especially in Ireland; it appears that peat built up to a certain height in a raised bog, or in a sloping blanket bog, can become unstable if oversaturated by excessive rain, and can commence to flow rather like treacle or porridge.

Earlier writers on bogs described a so-called 'regeneration complex' phenomenon by which bogs were supposed to be built up by the initiation of a series of hummocks alternating laterally with pools. As the pools in turn filled with *Sphagnum* peat, they now became the new hummocks, and the tops of the former hummocks were now flooded to become the new pools and so on. It now appears that this is not a normal phenomenon; level, intact bog surfaces tend to be smooth; but on a slope, lateral peat flow, on a smaller scale than that described in the last paragraph, may cause ridging and furrowing of the peat to occur, causing lines of pools or wet hollows and lines of 'hummocks' at right angles to the slope.

At the present day, most of our actively growing *Sphagnum* bog surfaces, whether they be of the valley-, raised-, or blanket-bog types, show a sequence of *Sphagnum* species, which may sometimes be a succession in time, from the pools to the driest parts of the surface. The aquatic *S. cuspidatum* tends to be the species in the wettest places. It is usually light yellow-green in colour and has narrow linear, almost grass-shaped branch-leaves up to 5 mm. in length, and is normally found floating in the bog pools. When removed in a tuft, it has something of the appearance of a drowned, greenish mouse. Forming 'lawns' with the rosettes an inch or two (2·5–5 cm.) above the water level is found *S. recurvum*, with an erect turf-forming habit and lanceolate close-set usually orange-green branch leaves. At a higher level still and forming low hummocks or platforms there is the main peat-builder of our bogs today, *S. papillosum*. This large species has dense packed rosettes of fat-looking, ochre-yellow or buff branches, whose leaves are convex externally, egg-shaped and hooded at the apex. The name refers to the microscopic papillae or warts on the walls of the empty cells. In a similar habitat we may find hummocks of *S. magellanicum*, which is of identical external form to *S. papillosum*, but is beautifully flushed with a wine-red colour, as if someone had emptied a bottle of red wine over *S. papillosum*. Forming the highest and most conical hummocks we will find *S. rubellum*, which has delicate branches in small 1 cm. wide rosettes, with lanceolate, 2 mm. long branch leaves; the whole plant is normally of a rich dark red, but may sometimes be partly greenish.

The *Sphagnum* mosses are both ecologically important in their roles and aesthetically pleasing in their appearance. Though they are difficult to study deeply, the amateur should have no problem over identifying the few species mentioned here when they are growing in well lit situations, if these descriptive notes are used. He will then be aquainted with the majority of our important peat-builders of today.

The flowering plant flora of our *Sphagnum* bogs is not as numerous as that of our woodland or chalk grassland habitats, but it is numerous enough. It contains however a number of plants of great interest and, sometimes, beauty. Perhaps best known are the Sundews, the species of *Drosera*. These little plants have green leaves in basal rosettes, which bear red gland-tipped hairs on the edges and the surface. The glands secrete mucilage to which insects are attracted and on which they become trapped as on a fly-paper. When an insect has become stuck, the longer hairs on the edges of the leaves are stimulated to bend inwards slowly, enclosing the insect eventually as in the clasped fingers of two hands. The glands now secrete digestive enzymes which break down and dissolve the proteins present in the body of the insect, and the shorter stalked glands on the leaf surface then absorb the 'soup' so produced. It is possible to 'feed' these plants artificially in cultivation with small pieces of meat, but most of those who attempt this overdo it, and the plant usually dies after a time.

The Sundews have slender leafless stems a few inches high which bear one-sided, forked inflorescences of tiny 5 mm. wide white, star-like, six-petalled flowers, but these only open for a short time each day, usually about noon, and are not familiar to many people.

The commonest species is *Drosera rotundifolia*, p. 137, the Round-leaved sundew; this has almost circular spreading leaves up to $\frac{3}{8}$ inch (1 cm.) across on stalks up to 1 inch (2·5 cm.) long. This species is still very general wherever *Sphagnum* bogs still exist and on bare moist peat on wet-heaths. More local and largely southern and western is *Drosera intermedia*, the Long-leaved sundew; this species has narrow spoon-shaped leaf blades, less than 1 cm. long, which stand more or less erect on stalks to over 1 inch (3 cm.) long. It is characteristic of wet-heaths and acid peaty lake shores rather than of bogs, but sometimes occurs in bog pools which dry out partly in the summer. It has

far shorter inflorescences than *D. rotundifolia*, little longer than the leaves.

Common in Scotland and in much of Ireland, but very local now in mid and southern England, where it is to be found mainly in east Dorset, the New Forest and in Norfolk fens and bogs, is the Great sundew, *D. anglica*, p. 137. This species has leaves up to 4 inches (10 cm.) in length, including the stalks into which the blades narrow gradually and almost imperceptibly, unlike those of *D. intermedia*. It has inflorescences about twice as long as the leaves, up to about 8 inches (20 cm.) tall. Unlike the other two sundews, this species grows also in calcareous fens, but is always in very wet hollows or pools.

It has been suggested that the insectivorous habit of these plants, and of others like Bladderworts and Butterworts, is an adaptation to habitats poor in nitrogenous salts. Pale butterwort, *Pinguicula lusitanica*, occurs in acid bogs more or less throughout south-west and western Britain from Cornwall and the New Forest northwards, and throughout Ireland. It has basal rosettes of oblong, pinkish-grey leaves $\frac{3}{8}$–$\frac{3}{4}$ inch (1–2 cm.) long with inrolled edges from which arise leafless stems usually over $2\frac{1}{4}$ inches (6 cm.) tall, bearing solitary pink-lilac flowers like tiny 6–7 mm. long snapdragons but with spurs 2–4 mm. long which bend downwards. The Common butterwort, *P. vulgaris*, has larger $\frac{3}{4}$–$3\frac{1}{8}$ inches (2–8 cm.) long bright yellow-green more pointed leaves, taller, nearly 6 inch (to 15 cm.) flower stalks with larger violet coloured flowers. It sometimes occurs in bogs, but it is more characteristic of small hummocks in calcareous fens, and also of wet dripping rocks where illumination is good; when growing adpressed on rocks the leaf rosettes resemble green starfishes. It is common throughout the hilly parts of the British Isles, and in the Norfolk valley fens, but is very rare, and largely absent, throughout most of mid and southeast England.

Many species of the sedge family are found in acid bogs, but most of the species of true sedge (*Carex*) are confined to the more flushed or less acid areas. The Beak-sedges, *Rhynchospora*, are, however, true bog plants. *R. alba*, p. 137, the White beak-sedge, is common in wet hollows and round pools in bogs and on wet-heaths in most of the British Isles except in the midlands and eastern England, where it is rare, or even absent now due to drainage or to lack of bogs anyway, except in Norfolk. It has bright green grass-like keeled leaves 2–3 mm. wide, borne in basal tufts, from which arise in July stems up to 1 foot (30 cm.) high, which bear both terminally and in the axils of short bracts pure white V-shaped clusters of spikelets. It is a very pretty plant when plentiful, as it is still on some of our southern wet-heaths. Brown beak-sedge, *R. fusca*, is much rarer and found, usually with *R. alba*, in only a few very scattered places from Devon, the New Forest and Surrey to west Scotland, but it is frequent in the central Irish bogs. It has a creeping habit, larger dark-red brown spikelets in more ovoid clusters, and the bracts overtop the flowering spike, unlike those of *R. alba*. It is particularly common locally in south-east Dorset on bare moist peat on wet-heaths. Two of the Cotton-sedges, or Cotton-grasses, as they are often misleadingly called, *Eriophorum*, are very important species of our bogs. *E. vaginatum*, the Hare's-tail cotton-sedge, has already been mentioned. It has dense tussocks of bristle-like dark green leaves, from which arise many stems up to 2 feet (61 cm.) tall, each bearing short straw-coloured stem leaves with inflated sheathing bases. Its solitary terminal spikes of bisexual flowers, which each bear three white stigmas and three bright yellow anthers, in April and May, later develop the conspicuous 1–1½ inch (2·5–4 cm.) diameter globular white cottony heads of bristles, which arise from the bases of the fruits and make this plant so conspicuous in early summer. It is abundant in raised and blanket bogs throughout the British Isles except in the midlands, east and south-east of England, where however it still occurs in some areas, such as west Surrey and west Sussex, in some

quantity locally on wet-heaths. Common cotton-sedge, *E. angustifolium*, is common throughout most of the British Isles, even in the valley-bogs of the lowlands of south-east England; it is more characteristic of wetter places than *E. vaginatum* and is also found, unlike that species, in less acid swamps and fens. Each stem bears 3–7 cottony heads.

A true sedge characteristic of bog pools in north Britain and in Ireland and also found in a few places in the south, such as the New Forest, is the so-called Mud sedge, *Carex limosa*. This has rhizomes which creep under the water in very wet bog-pools, and produce tufts of narrow greyish-green leaves, and slender inflorescences in June or July with two or three drooping ovoid female spikelets about 1 inch (2·5 cm.) long with oval pale brown glumes and blunt flat egg-shaped grey-green fruits, and one or two erect narrow male spikelets. In primitive bogs, it seems to be an important primary colonist of the open pools.

The Deer-sedge or Deer-grass, *Scirpus caespitosus*, is common on the drier parts of raised and blanket bogs, and is usually also to be found scattered on our lowland wet-heaths. It has dense tussocks superficially like those of Hare's-tail cotton-sedge, but these are in fact of fine ridged pale green stems, not of leaves. The true leaves are minute sheathing flaps at the bases of the stems. Each stem bears in May a tiny brown spike of bisexual flowers with a larger bract-like glume at the base of the spike.

Bog asphodel, *Narthecium ossifragum*, is one of our loveliest bog plants, and is common enough wherever bogs are still found, except in the midlands of England. It has flattened leafy shoots like those of a miniature garden iris a few inches tall, from some of which arise 6 inch–1 foot (15–30 cm.) stems bearing spikes of splendid golden yellow

Plants of limestone cliff habitats, *from left to right*: Spring gentian, *Gentiana verna* (×2); Dover catch-fly, *Silene nutans* (×1); Jacob's ladder, *Polemonium coeruleum* (×½); Bloody cranesbill, *Geranium sanguineum* (×2); White rock-rose, *Helianthemum apenninum* (×1)

flowers, each 12–16 mm. across, like tiny lilies, with six perianth segments, and six orange anthers which have deep orange fur on their filaments or stalks. Its flowers may colour the bog surface golden in July, and in September its richly coloured fruits may paint the bog orange-red.

Still frequent in raised and blanket bogs among *Sphagnum* from mid-England and Wales to mid-Scotland, and in central Ireland, is a charming shrub of the heath family, the Bog rosemary, *Andromeda polifolia*. This little shrub, only a few inches high, has lance-shaped evergreen leaves up to 1 inch (2·5 cm.) long, which are smooth grey-green above, and pure white beneath with thickly recurved margins. Its flowers which are borne only a few together, are delightful little globular bright rose-pink bells with narrowed mouths, about 5–7 mm. long. Often associated with the *Andromeda* within that plant's range but occurring further north in Scotland and also, though very locally, in south-east and south-west England and in Norfolk, is the Cranberry, *Vaccinium oxycoccos*, p. 137. This is an even tinier, creeping shrub, with tangled masses of trailing stems which bear elliptical evergreen leaves up to 1 cm. long, and, in June, flowers on stalks about 1 inch (2·5 cm.) high that look at first glance like minute pink cyclamens 4–6 mm. across, but have in fact four corolla-lobes, not five. Later on appear the spherical or pear-shaped 6–8 mm. diameter fruits; these are spotted with red or brown and are edible; they make an excellent jelly if one can find enough of them.

The fresh water aquatic habitat presents special problems for plants, due largely to the fact that oxygen is not very soluble in water. Hence many water and swamp plants have had to evolve special tissues, which contain air, and, in the case of plants which are only partly submerged, to provide passages by which air can circulate from the aerial parts down to the roots. Plants in running water have less of a problem than those in stagnant water, for clearly they can obtain more oxygen for respiration from the water that flows over them than can those where there is no flow, which need to store the oxygen they produce in photosynthesis. In other respects, however, the aquatic habitat can be very advantageous to plants. Plants of this medium have no worry about excess water-loss leading to wilting; they require no waterproof cuticle, nor stomata, hence can carry out gas exchange, and absorption of nutrient salts and water, freely over their whole surface. Since uptake of water and salts occurs in this way, little is needed by way of vascular tissue to conduct inorganic solutions, or for that matter synthesized food, through the plant, and vascular tissue is often largely lacking in submerged aquatics.

Since the water itself provides support, little mechanical support tissue is needed either. Extremes of temperatures are absent in deep water; beneath an ice cover in winter there is good insulation from frost damage. Thus, though most water plants, submerged or floating, tend to perennate as buds on the bottom of the pond or river in winter, they are less affected in their geographical distributions by climatic differences than are land plants, and some of them are remarkably cosmopolitan. The aquatic habitat tends to encourage, too, wide seed dispersal by the many wading birds who frequent ponds and lakes.

Aquatic flowering plants are all considered to be derived from terrestrial ancestors. We can distinguish two main types, those that are partly floating or even emergent, and those that are wholly submerged. Even the latter, in most cases, project their flowers above water for pollination either by wind or insects; this has been taken as one indication of their origin from land plants.

A good example of a floating aquatic is the

Lowland heath vegetation. Scots pines and Ling in background and in front, *from left to right*: Marsh gentian, *Gentiana pneumonanthe* (×1) ; Wavy hair-grass, *Deschampsia flexuosa* (×¼) ; *behind*, Mat grass, *Nardus stricta* (×½) ; *front*, Dwarf gorse, *Ulex minor* (×½) ; Tormentil, *Potentilla erecta* (×1) ; Bell-heather, *Erica cinerea* (×1)

White water-lily, *Nymphaea alba*, p. 139. Often cultivated, especially in its coloured varieties, this is a very familiar plant in rivers, ditches and lakes. The floating leaves have an unwettable waxy cuticle on the upper surface which bears stomata, like those of a land plant; on the lower side there is however no cuticle or stomata, only soft spongy tissue which can store, as in so many water plants, oxygen produced in photosynthesis for later use in respiration. The petioles or leaf-stalks are long, flexible and rubbery in texture, with air canals leading to the short stout stem which is attached by its roots to the mud at the bottom. The Yellow water-lily, *Nuphar lutea*, is even commoner than the White one; it has much smaller cup-like flowers with less numerous, yellow petals. Both genera belong, not to the lily family, but to the Nymphaeaceae, which is composed of aquatic herbs with numerous free sepals, petals and stamens, and an ovary of many carpels joined together into a fruit of characteristic form. The Yellow water-lily has another name of Brandy bottle – the flask-shaped fruit often smells rather alcoholic when old, due to fermentation of sugars present in it, hence the name.

A good example of a submerged aquatic is the Hornwort, *Ceratophyllum demersum*. This is attached at first, but later may become free-floating; submerged water plants need no roots to absorb water and salts, only to hold them down. Sometimes the attachments break without much harm resulting to the detached portion, unless it gets carried away, in a river, to tidal salt water. The Hornwort has a brittle translucent stem which bears whorls of once or twice forked, leaves with toothed, narrow segments. Divided leaves with narrow segments are common in submerged aquatics, particularly those that grow in rivers, where the divisions permit the current to flow through the mass of foliage without damaging the plants. The inconspicuous separate male and female flowers are not easy to find and pollination in this plant normally takes place under water, which is unusual. The fruits take the form of oval, 4 mm. long, nuts with a pair of spines or horns at the base.

Spiked water-milfoil, *Myriophyllum spicatum*, is a rather similar looking plant also with leaves in whorls. Here the leaves are usually four to a whorl in this species, five to a whorl in the related *M. verticillatum*, and are pinnately divided into many bristle-like parallel segments. In *M. spicatum* the flowering spikes, which are modified shoots with smaller leaf-like bracts, emerge from the water, and the tiny flowers are pollinated by wind. The uppermost flowers are male and have each four tiny but quite obvious dull red petals.

In swiftly running water, the River crowfoot, *Ranunculus fluitans*, is locally quite common; there are several related species too difficult to attempt to distinguish here. This is really a white flowered aquatic buttercup with very long, up to 1 foot (30 cm.), submerged leaves with tassel-like segments. In stagnant water, other water Crowfoots occur; one, *R. peltatus*, p. 139, has finely dissected submerged leaves of shorter and more rounded general outine than in *R. fluitans*, and kidney-shaped floating leaves with unwettable cuticles on their upper surfaces.

Acid waters, poor in nutrients, are characteristic of our uplands, and in such places relatively few plants grow. One interesting plant of such places, however, is the Quillwort, *Isoetes lacustris*, which bears tufts of hollow translucent pointed cylindrical to conical leaves, and grows between the stones on the floors of mountain lakes. It is actually a flowerless plant, related to the Clubmosses, with sporangia, bearing spores of two kinds as in *Selaginella*, that are almost immersed in the swollen bases of the leaves where they join the stem.

We have earlier on considered the later stages of a succession beginning in freshwater, or hydrosere, which may culminate in a raised bog, or, in some circumstances, as one can see today in the Norfolk Broads region, apparently in a damp oakwood. The earlier stages of such a hydrosere consist of

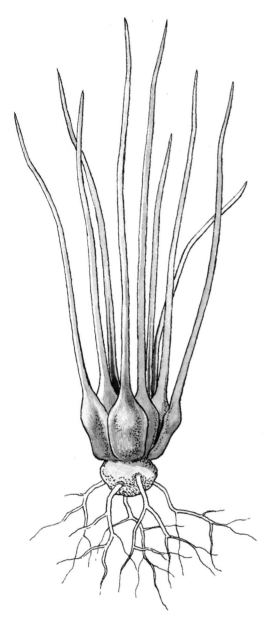

Quillwort, a strange aquatic cryptogamic plant of mountain lakes; the swollen bases of the leaves enclose the sporangia

Butomus umbellatus, and the Arrow-head, *Sagittaria sagittifolia*, p. 138. The first has long, sedge-like leaves, triangular in cross-section, which rise out of the water. Among these one will see the flowering stem which may be up to 5 feet (150 cm.) tall. It bears at its apex an umbel of splendid pink flowers on individual stalks up to 4 inches (10 cm.) long. The flowers which are up to $1\frac{1}{4}$ inches (3 cm.) across, have six perianth segments, six to nine stamens, and six to nine reddish carpels which form follicles, like those of the Marsh marigold.

The Arrow-head has arrow-head shaped leaves, as its name suggests, up to 8 inches (20 cm.) long, which stand out of the water on long stalks; lanceolate floating leaves and ribbon-like translucent submerged leaves are also present. The flowers are borne in whorled spikes and each has three large $\frac{3}{8}$ inch (1 cm.) long petals with purple blotches at the base. The lower flowers are female, and produce numerous free nutlets or achenes rather as in buttercups. The male flowers each bear many stamens.

As plant remains build up, the swamp becomes a fen. The Common reed, *Phragmites communis*, is often an important agent in this process. This great almost bamboo-like grass, up to 10 feet (3 m.) in height, has $\frac{3}{8}-\frac{3}{4}$ inch (1–2 cm.) wide, lanceolate leaves that are arranged all the way up the stem. They have no basal ligule where the blade joins the leaf sheath, but only a ring of hairs. The much-branched tassel-like inflorescence at the top of the stem is dark, dull purple in colour.

The Reed mace, *Typha latifolia*, often wrongly called the bullrush, with linear leaves several feet long and cylindrical chocolate-coloured inflorescences, may also be important at this stage, especially on inorganic muds.

If deposition of inorganic silt predominates over that of organic peat, as in some kinds of alluvial water meadows that flood in winter, or along the banks of rivers, especially tidal ones, then freshwater marsh is formed, rather than fen.

plants of the sort just described. Then swamp species, or erect emergent semi-aquatic plants, come in. Their roots and lower parts are in water, but the leaves and flowering stems stand out of the water. Two lovely examples of these are the Flowering rush,

Normally, however, in most more stagnant fresh water environments, peat build up predominates over that of silt, and eventually the peat fills up the lake basin until its surface, at least in summer, is level with or even above the water level. In the fen thus formed, of which fine examples can be seen in the Broads region of Norfolk, the bulk of the vegetation is composed of sedges, rushes and grasses with, at the same time, a good many species of dicotyledonous herbs. Fen vegetation is only one stage in a succession; things do not stop that way for long. Around many of the Norfolk Broads (which, by the way, are now known to be artificial lakes and due to later flooding of medieval peat-cuttings made in peat with vegetation at a later stage of succession, perhaps even at the raised bog stage) we can see quite a rapid advance of swamp vegetation into the shallow, silted water. This is followed by a brief fen stage which, in the absence of interference, rapidly becomes invaded by bushes and develops into carr. Formerly, however, large areas of fen in East Anglia were maintained at this stage of succession by cutting of the vegetation for thatching and other purposes. Hence the fen stage can only normally be prolonged by the presence of a deflecting factor, in this case mowing. Fen is therefore really a plagioclimax community, like chalk grassland, which as we saw needs grazing to maintain it, and as a truly natural phenomenon is only an evanescent stage.

When fen is mown every four years or less, it tends in East Anglia to become totally dominated by the Saw sedge, *Cladium mariscus*. This tall and formidable plant forms great stands of evergreen, sharply saw-tooth edged leaves up to 4 feet (1·3 m.) long, and to over $\frac{3}{4}$ inch (2 cm.) wide, which are borne in dense ranks on the stems. The stems themselves may be up to 10 feet (3 m.) tall and bear much-branched loose panicles of clustered milk-chocolate coloured spikelets each up to 4 mm. long and each of which bears one to three bisexual flowers. To try to push with bare legs through the great stands of this plant that are still found in the Norfolk fens, or at Wicken Fen in Cambridgeshire, and in other more scattered places throughout these islands, is to ask for multiple lacerations of the skin. If it is cut at intervals of less than four years, however, *Cladium*, being evergreen, suffers badly and ceases to remain the dominant. Other species, such as *Molinia coerulea* at Wicken, or *Schoenus nigricans*, the Black bog-rush, with wiry grey-green narrow leaves to 2 feet (61 cm.) long with black basal sheaths and blackish $\frac{1}{2}$–1 inch (13–25 mm.) long V-shaped heads of flowers on stems up to 3 feet (91 cm.) tall, tend to come in. *Phragmites* may also become prominent again. In this way, through regular cutting for thatch and other purposes, the 'mixed fen' communities of East Anglia, and of scattered localities elsewhere, have been formed. We have only space to mention a few species of their rich and varied floras.

Perhaps the various orchids characteristic of calcareous fens are among the most interesting subsidiary species. Several Marsh orchids, of the genus *Dactylorchis*, or *Dactylorhiza* of the latest floras, are frequent. Perhaps the commonest is Common Marsh orchid, *D. praetermissa*. This has in June and July spikes of flowers rather like those of *D. fuchsii*, the Common Spotted orchid, but the stems are stout and hollow, not solid, the leaves are unspotted, and the flowers are of a rich purple-pink colour with a pattern of fine dots on the feebly three-lobed lips. This fine plant, up to 1 foot (30 cm.) tall, also occurs in rich, moist meadows as well as in fens. Rather more local and more exclusively a fen species is the Early Marsh orchid, *D. incarnata*, which flowers in May and early June. This has more strongly folded and unspotted leaves, normally flesh-pink, though sometimes white or purple, flowers with both the sides of the lips and the lateral sepals arched back, so as to produce much narrower looking flowers. The lips bear a pattern of two fine loop-shaped crimson lines, one on each side of the centre of the lip, enclosing a pattern of fine dots.

In July, the fine Marsh Fragrant orchid, *Gymnadenia conopsea* var. *densiflora*, occurs. This resembles giant, up to 3 feet (1 m.) tall, specimens of the Common Fragrant orchid of our chalk downs. Apart from its size, it differs in its later flowering, much sweeter carnation-like scent and its wider, darker purple-pink flowers with broader lips and more square-cut tips to the lateral sepals. With it one may find quite common locally the lovely Marsh helleborine, *Epipactis palustris*, p. 138. This orchid, which is also found in the slacks, or wet hollows, between the ridges, of calcareous sand-dunes, is from 1 to 2 feet (30–61 cm.) tall, with a few deeply veined elliptical leaves up the stem, and a loose spike of flowers at the apex. The flower has a frilly white distal lobe to its lip about 6 mm. long, which is attached to a white cup with crimson veins, the proximal part of the lip joining it to the flower. The whole effect is rather like an eighteenth-century clergyman's cravat in miniature. The sepals and the two other petals are of a delicate brownish or purplish green and hairy outside, and paler within.

The Grass of Parnassus, *Parnassia palustris*, is not uncommon in fens where the vegetation is short. This has fine cup-like five-petalled flowers 1 inch or more (2·5–3 cm.) across which are white with green veins at the base of the petals inside, borne on slender stems up to 1 foot (30 cm.) tall with a single sessile heart-shaped leaf on each near the base; there are several long-stalked root-leaves. Bladderworts, *Utricularia* species, are aquatic plants found mainly in fen ditches and pools. They catch tiny insects in little bladder-like sacs on their finely-divided, submerged or partially floating leaves. They have yellow flowers rather like Snapdragon or Toad-flax in form, with a spurred two-lipped corolla. Lesser bladderwort, *U. minor*, is only 3–4 inches (7–10 cm.) tall with flowers only about 1 cm. long, of a pale creamy yellow; this may also occur in less acid bog pools as well. Common bladderwort, *U. vulgaris*, is up to 1 foot (30 cm.) tall with flowers of deep yellow

up to 2 cm. long, much larger underwater leaves to 1 foot (30 cm.) long, and bladders up to 5 mm. in diameter (2 mm. in *U. minor*).

Of the rushes of calcareous mowing-fens or grazed fen-meadows, perhaps Blunt-fruited rush, *Juncus subnodulosus*, is most characteristic. This 2–3 feet (61–91 cm.) tall rush is, like *J. acutiflorus*, of acid valley-bogs, a plant with dense much branched terminal inflorescences, and leaves with cross-partitions inside them. It differs from *J. acutiflorus* in its pale brown, blunt fruits and perianth segments, and in the leaves having longitudinal, as well as cross wise, partitions inside.

As the fen invades with bushes, so conditions become more suitable for the far creeping rhizomes of the fresh green, bipinnate fronded Marsh fern, *Thelypteris palustris*, which often occurs in dense pure stands. The shrubs that invade the fen may be of various species: Birch, *Betula pubescens*, with downy twigs and various willows, *Salix* spp., are usual, but at Wicken Fen and elsewhere, Purging buckthorn, *Rhamnus catharticus*, already mentioned under chalk scrub, is common, together with Breaking buckthorn or Berry-bearing alder, *Frangula alnus*, which has pale green untoothed bluntly obovate leaves and red berries.

We can distinguish four types of habitat in which land plants occur under the influence of the sea. These are the salt-marshes, the shingle-beaches, the sand-dunes and the sea cliffs.

Maritime vegetation, as distinct from the truly marine zone occupied mostly by seaweeds or algae, is largely dominated by flowering plants.

The salt-marsh zone is, of course, tidal, and in that sense comes under direct marine influence; but the true salt-marshes of our coast only occupy at most the upper third of the intertidal zone. The only flowering plant that can live lower down, where it is immersed for longer periods, is the strange ribbon-leaved grass-wrack, *Zostera*; this has peculiar strap-shaped, partly enclosed inflorescences which are pollinated under sea water. Most salt-marsh plants have to endure immersion in sea-water for far less than one third of the time.

Salt-marshes do not occur on exposed coastlines. One finds them either along the sides of sheltered estuaries or tidal creeks, or else built up behind the shelter of a shingle-spit or sand-dune system. On the mud flats at the base of most of our salt-marshes one now finds Townsend's Cord-grass, *Spartina × townsendii.* Until the middle of the last century this grass did not exist and until much more recently, most mud flats were bare or bore only Grass-wrack in open associations. Then an American grass of salt-marshes, *S. alterniflora,* was accidentally introduced into Southampton Water, possibly with ballast. It hybridized with a small inconspicuous and now uncommon species of Cord-grass, *S. maritima*, which grew there at that time higher up the salt-marsh, and produced several hybrid strains. One of these was a vigorous plant, fertile unlike most hybrids, which proved to be a successful colonist of mud-flats. It spread considerably by natural means; it was then realized that it had economic value as a mud binder which could help in reclaiming mud flats, and it became widely planted by coastal protection authorities. This hybrid is now widespread in suitable places round much of our coastline and unfortunately has developed the habit of invading, and to some extent destroying by its aggressiveness, many closed upper salt marsh communities as well, with all their interesting vegetation.

It is a tufted and rhizome producing grass with stiffly erect aerial shoots up to about 3 feet (91 cm.) tall. Its stout stems bear rigid, horizontally arranged acutely tapering leaves, and branched yellowish inflorescences composed of several erect spikes of spikelets.

The salt-marsh zone proper shows, where there is an even gradient to the mud flats, a clear zonation of plant communities. This zonation is largely based upon the tolerance of the different species present to different periods of immersion in, or exposure from, sea-water, according to the rise and fall of the tides. Salt-marsh plants are land plants rather than aquatics; they are rooted in the mud, and, although they absorb some water through their aerial parts when immersed, most of their absorption of water and salts is via the roots. Ordinary land-plants, however, with normally dilute cell-sap, would lose water if immersed in salt water, by the process known as osmosis, rather than gain it by absorption. Water always tends to pass through semi-permeable membranes such as a plant's cytoplasmic cell-envelopes from weaker to stronger solutions. It is, therefore, not surprising to find that most if not all salt-marsh plants, at least in the lower levels of the marsh, have concentrated cell-sap, containing a salt solution, with osmotic pressures equal to 100 atmospheres or more. This enables them to adsorb sea-water immersing them at high tide, or at least not to lose water. Many salt-marsh plants, too, are succulent, like some desert plants; this feature conserves water when the tide is out and the weather is warm and dry. There are several features in common between salt-marshes and salt deserts.

In many of our south and east coast salt-marshes, the coastline is sinking slowly, rather than remaining level, so that the natural tendency of salt-marsh plants to build up the level of the mud or silt by 'straining' the muddy tidal water through their network of stems and leaves is counteracted, and succession does not take place as it does on western and northern marshes. One tends to find in the east and south-east as a result rather flat, unsloping salt-marshes, with an irregular mosaic of vegetation, rather than bands or zones of plant associations parallel to the shoreline at successive levels as in the west of Britain. Even in the south-east, however, one can distinguish the uppermost marsh communities, and those of the lower mud-flats, from those of the 'general salt-marsh' associations of the middle, main part of the marsh. On the north Norfolk coast, although the coastline is slowly sinking there too, salt-marshes have grown up behind protecting sand-dunes which have built up on shingle-spit 'islands' offshore, and here the supply of sand, blown off the dunes, helps to maintain a clearer zonation of associations with a tendency to build up of surface and of plant succession.

Let us look now at a typical south-east coast salt-marsh, on an estuary such as that of the Thames or Medway or in such a place as Chichester harbour. It is a dreary forbidding scene in winter, especially in dull weather, though even then it has a sombre charm, heightened for the naturalist by the great flocks of waders and other winter migrant birds. But in July and August, especially in sunshine, it is a carpet of many colours, some subtle, some more brilliant, like the pale lavender blue of the Sea-lavender, and the gold of the Golden samphire.

At the outer edge of the general salt-marsh, there is often a low eroded cliff, beyond which there will be great swards of Townsend's cord-grass. Among this, just below the low cliff, may be found open colonies of one of the several species of annual Glassworts, probably in this situation *Salicornia europaea*. The Glassworts are strange succulent plants without obvious leaves. They have cylindrical branches jointed into segments and these branches, which are in opposite pairs, are rather like miniature sausages. Sunken into the segments and scarcely visible at this season are the tiny flowers, usually in groups of three; in September and October, the stamens, usually one per flower, and the styles will emerge from tiny pores, and pollination will be affected by wind. *S. europaea* is of erect habit, of grey-green colour, and has smooth cylindrical branches.

A little higher up, in the general salt-marsh community, will be found other Glassworts of varied colours, some reddish, some brown, and some dark green, with more knobbly branches than *S. europaea*. At this level, the annual forms, though so diverse in appearance are all grouped under one species, *S. ramosissima*. The creeping Perennial Glasswort, *S. perennis*, may also be seen

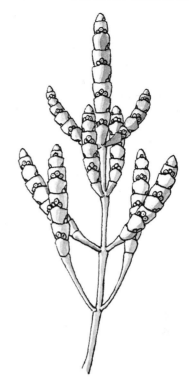

Annual Glasswort, a characteristic fleshy plant of salt marshes

on firmer mud or sand rather higher up. With the Glassworts will be another fleshy rather similar-looking plant, but this time there are cylindrical fleshy leaves, of either red or green colour, and tiny rounded green flowers are visible. This is the Annual Sea-blite, *Suaeda maritima.*

The general salt-marsh bears a sward composed mostly of a spreading grey-green grass with rather stiff grey spreading stems and openly-branched inflorescences. This is the Sea Poa or Sea Manna-grass, *Puccinellia maritima:* where stock are allowed to graze the salt-marshes, they feed upon it eagerly. Among it we shall see clumps of the elliptical lanceolate leaves, with a tiny curved spine at the tip of each, of the Common Sea-lavender, *Limonium vulgare*; with its approximately 1 foot (30 cm.) tall panicles, sometimes very lax, sometimes dense and pyramidal, of pale lavender flowers. Lower, more muddy places may bear swards or

Common Sea-lavender, frequently in salt marshes in south and east England

stands of the Sea aster, *Aster tripolium*, which looks very like a fleshy-leaved pale violet-flowered garden Michaelmas daisy. More elevated areas will bear swards of the Sea Thrift, *Armeria maritima*, p. 36, with its cushions of short narrow dark green leaves and inflorescences like pink buttons on stems 4–8 inches (10–20 cm.) high, and in the region under consideration, south-east England, large bushy clumps of the Golden samphire, *Inula crithmoides*, may stud the marsh. This plant has dark green, fleshy strap-like leaves about 2 inches (5 cm.) long on its stems, and numerous flower-heads like golden daisies an inch or more (2–3 cm.) across.

The surface of the marsh is diversified with shallow depressions called pans, in which often nothing at all grows, though some of them may still contain the now rare little Cord-grass, *Spartina maritima*, only about 6–8 inches (15–20 cm.) tall with brownish green narrow erect leaves, not stiffly spreading like its hybrid offspring, *Spartina* × *townsendii*. Also there, if the marsh is large enough, will be deep drainage channels or creeks, which can be dangerous to cross as, if one falls in, it is very difficult to extract oneself from the tenacious mud.

(*opposite*): Bog plants, top, Hare's-tail cotton-sedge, *Eriophorum vaginatum*; *Sphagnum* mosses, mostly *S. papillosum*, forming hummocks in middle distance, and in the foreground, *from left to right*: White beak-sedge, *Rhynchospora alba*; Cranberry, *Vaccinium oxycoccos*; Round-leaved sundew, *Drosera rotundifolia*; Bog violet, *Viola palustris*; Great sundew, *Drosera anglica* and below, *Sphagnum subsecundum*

(*overleaf, left*): Fen and fresh-water aquatic plants of stream and ditch margins; *left to right*: Marsh helleborine, *Epipactis palustris*; Flowering rush, *Butomus umbellatus*; Arrow-head, *Sagittaria sagittifolia*

(*overleaf, right*): Fresh-water aquatic plants, background, White water-lily, *Nymphaea alba*; foreground, *left to right*: Water violet, *Holtonia palustris*; Water crowfoot, *Ranunculus peltatus*; Water crowfoot, *R. aquatilis*

These creeks will be bordered with a thick fringe of a strange-looking shrubby plant with ovate grey-mealy leaves, the Sea purslane, *Halimione portulacoides*. It bears panicles of insignificant looking flowers, golden anther-bearing male ones, and grey female ones, and is characteristic of well-drained sites such as creek edges. In the uppermost parts of the marsh, just below the sea-wall which protects the drainage pastures or arable land behind, may be found the rigid 2–3 feet (61–91 cm.) tall Sea rush, *Juncus maritimus*. This has dark green leaves ending in sharp spines and panicles of pale brown, six-parted flowers.

On the sea-wall itself, Sea couch-grass, *Agropyron pungens*, a rigid grey-green grass with stiff flower spikes up to 3 feet (91 cm.) tall, is likely to be dominant. At the top level of the marsh, tidal immersion may be only a few hours per month.

Many salt-marshes are protected from the sea by shingle beaches, deposited in long spits by wave action. In south-east England, these are composed mostly of flint pebbles; elsewhere, the local rock forms the shingle. The low-lying south and east coasts of England are frequently fringed with shingle beaches; sometimes, as at Chesil Beach in Dorset or Orford Beach in Suffolk, great bars, miles in length, parallel with the coast but separated from it by a tidal channel, are formed. At Dungeness in Kent there occurs a vast headland of shingle, about 12 square miles (31 sq. km.) in extent; this, which has been built up over thousands of years from hundreds of individual and successive 'storm ridges', is the largest area of its kind in Europe. Shingle beaches are not favourable places for the growth of most plants; the drainage is excessive, and soil formation

Sand-dune vegetation, nearest sea, fore-dunes with Sand couch-grass, *Agropyron junceiforme*, dominant mid-foreground, *left to right*: Sea holly, *Eryngium maritimum*; Sea spurge, *Euphorbia paralias*; Marram grass, *Ammophila arenaria*, receding into background as dominant on the main dune ridge; nearest foreground, Sea bindweed, *Calystegia soldanella*. Salt marsh with creek visible on extreme right

Golden samphire, locally common in drier salt marshes and also on sea cliffs in the west

Sea pea, local on shingle beaches in south and east England

slow and difficult. Nevertheless, with time and increasing distance from the sea, first bryophytes and lichens, then grasses and other herbs, and finally a low scrub of the yellow-flowered Broom, *Sarothamnus scoparius*, has been able to establish itself on the more inland parts of Dungeness Beach. Along the seaward margin of shingle areas, but few species can grow. These few are deep-rooted perennials that mostly reach down to more water retentive substrata beneath the shingle. One such is Sea-kale, *Crambe maritima*, which forms great cabbage-like masses, up to 1 yard (91 cm.) across of fleshy, wavy-edged grey leaves, from whose centres spring huge rounded panicles of white crucifer flowers up to 1·5 cm. across, giving way to strange little fruits like hard yellowish peas. Another is the mat-forming Sea pea, *Lathyrus maritimus*, like a fleshy leaved creeping garden pea in foliage, but with lovely heads of rich purple-pink flowers each 1–1·5 cm. long. These are followed by pods like miniature garden peas, whose contents are pleasantly edible even when raw. The Sea pea and the Sea-kale are now very local plants, but the Yellow horned-poppy, *Glaucium flavum*, is far more general. This lovely plant bears its yellow four-petalled poppy-flowers on branched leafy stems 2–3 feet (61–91 cm.) tall, whose leaves are grey-green, very waxy and somewhat hairy, with wavy-toothed margins to their oblong outlines. It has narrow sickle-shaped pods 1 foot (30 cm.) or more long. Curled dock, *Rumex crispus*, is very common on shingle beaches; the stems, 2–3 feet (61–91 cm.) tall, bear thin textured, very wavy-edged oblong green leaves and dense erect panicles of green flowers each with three rounded green inner perianth segments up to 5 mm. long, each of which bears a large central corky brown wart. This dock, like several others, is also common on waste ground inland.

Sand-dunes often develop on a basis of wave borne shingle, though they themselves are created by the wind. Dunes are best developed on coastlines where the prevailing winds are onshore, and where the currents bring a good supply of sand, to be exposed at low tide on the foreshore. As this sand dries out, the wind blows it on to the shoreline above high-tide mark. If it meets no obstacle, it will just go on blowing inland: but if there is some object on the beach, such as an old boot or a piece of driftwood, sand will tend to collect *behind* this because of the eddy currents carrying it into the 'dead' air behind the obstacle. If the obstacle is a living plant, such as the rigid, glaucous-grey, Sand couch-grass, *Agropyron junceiforme*, p. 140, then, as sand accumulates around the foliage the rhizomes and roots of the plant can grow into the sand and 'fix' it. As more sand accumulates, so further growth occurs, and low 'fore-dunes' are built up by this salt-tolerant grass. It has stiff but rather sprawling spike-like inflorescences which bear fan-shaped to diamond-shaped several flowered waxy-grey spikelets up to about ¾ inch (2 cm.) long, broadside on to the stem, and alternating along it, first one side then the other, their own length or nearly so apart. Sea couch-grass, *Agropyron pungens*, mentioned earlier in the salt-marsh section, differs in its erect inflorescences with much more overlapping, shorter spikelets.

Growing along the driftline of the shore a little below where one finds the Sand couch-grass, there may be, if they have not been trampled out of existence, several annual plants. Besides the frosted-leaved green-flowered, Frosted orache, *Atriplex laciniata*, the charming cruciferous Sea rocket, *Cakile maritima*, with spikes of 1 cm. wide pink flowers and glossy, toothed leaves, is likely to be seen. Further back, out of reach of salt water in the soil, the Marram grass, *Ammophila arenaria*, p. 140, is able to colonize the low dunes built by the Sand couch-grass. Marram grass has great tufts of leaves up to 1 yard (91 cm.) long, which roll up in dry weather, and tall greyish-white foxtail-like panicles of flowers. It is able to spread not only horizontally like Sand couch-grass, but also to grow up vertically through a fresh cover of sand and then produce a new layer or 'storey' of horizontal rhizomes and accompanying roots in the new sand. Thus it can build up dunes of more or less indefinite height – 50 feet (15 m.) high dunes are usual, but dunes up to 100 feet (30 m.) high are known in this country.

After a rank of dunes has built up, frequently the process starts again, further towards the sea, especially if a storm has produced a new 'storm-ridge' of shingle in front of the existing line of dunes. In this way, where conditions and supply of sand are favourable, as in the big west coast dune systems at Braunton in Devon, Harlech, Kenfig and Newborough in Wales and Southport in south Lancashire, a number of parallel lines of dunes may be formed.

The dune ridges are porous, and hold water rather like sponges. This causes the

Coastal sand dune profile, section of younger part of dune system. HW highwater line, DL drift line with Sea rocket and other plants, FD fore dune with Sand couch-grass, WD white dune with Marram grass, WDS wet dune slack, CD fixed dune with a variety of plants

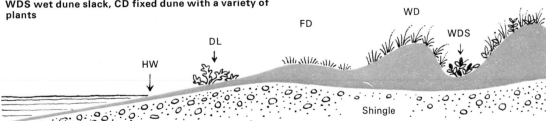

hollow depressions between the ridges to become wet, forming dune-slacks. Where, as is usual, the dunes are calcareous, due to broken up fragments of mollusc shells, the slacks have calcareous water and develop fen-like floras. The flora includes such plants as Marsh helleborine, mentioned earlier under Fresh-water and fenland, and also the Creeping willow, *Salix repens*, a low shrub with elliptical silvery-grey leaves 1–2 cm. long. In the great west coast dunes mentioned a little earlier, the slacks may bear large stands of our largest true rush, Great Sharp rush, *Juncus acutus*. This resembles a huge Sea rush with leaves up to 4 feet (122 cm.) long, but it has chestnut-brown globular fruits up to 6 mm. in diameter. Its cylindrical leaves are so rigid and tipped with such sharp spines as to be dangerous to the hands, and especially to the eyes, if approached closely.

As time passes, humus from the decayed Marram leaves builds up in the surface of the dunes. But the main agency in initiating soil formation is probably a small moss, *Tortula ruraliformis*. This moss forms low turfs on the sand, composed of rosettes of yellow-green leaves only about 4 mm. long with silvery hair-points. When dry, the leaf-rosettes curl up in corkscrew like fashion, and dry sand may blow over them; but immediately on moistening, the leaves open out again into rosettes, pushing the sand aside. Gradually this moss, and others, build up a humus layer, and after a time various herbs and grasses, particularly forms of the Red fescue grass, can establish themselves in the soil formed by the mosses.

The 'fixed dune' stage is now reached, and the flora tends to resemble somewhat that of chalk grassland. Further fixation by the grey mealy-leaved, spiny, orange-fruited shrub, Sea buckthorn, *Hippophae rhamnoides*, occurs on the east and south-east coasts where it is native. Elsewhere on our shores, there seems to be no native scrub former of importance, but conifers are often planted on fixed dunes to stabilise them further and to give some hope of commercial profit. Excessive use of sand-dunes by holiday makers can be disastrous. 'Blow-outs', scoured out by the wind, may develop where the vegetational carpet is broken by excessive trampling and large parts of a dune system can become mobile once again.

Other very attractive plants of our sand-dunes besides those mentioned already are the delightful Sea holly, *Eryngium maritimum*, p. 140, with its waxy grey-blue spiny leaves and ovoid heads of bright blue flowers with spiny calyx teeth, and the Sea spurge, *Euphorbia paralias*, p. 140, with fleshy grey-green oblong 1 inch (2·5 cm.) long pointed leaves on stems that are reddish below, and umbel-like heads of tiny flowers with yellow-green bracts. Both unfortunately are decreasing.

The upper parts of sea cliffs bear vegetation which tends to be related to the type of rock, rather than to its maritime position; but lower down, in the zone affected by spray, salt-tolerant vegetation is characteristic. It has been shown that some plants that are normally found inland, become fleshy and develop high concentrations of salt in their cell-sap when growing on spray-exposed sea cliffs. Many of the plants of this zone are those, like Sea Thrift and Golden samphire, which also grow in the drier parts of salt-marshes; but the yellow flowered four-petalled Wild cabbage, *Brassica oleracea*, the ancestor of our garden cabbages, is particularly characteristic of this habitat. So are a yellow-flowered fleshy-leaved umbelliferous plant, the Samphire, *Crithmum maritimum*, and the little Rock Sea-lavender, *Limonium binervosum*. The latter differs from Common sea-lavender not only in being much smaller but also in its tiny leaves with three strong, more or less parallel main veins, not with one main vein and faint pinnate side veins as in Common Sea-lavender.

The plants that are believed to be the most ancient, the algae, form a very diverse series of groups with little in common with one another, though showing parallel lines of evolution in each of the main groups.

Wild cabbage, the ancestor of our garden cabbage,
native to calcareous sea cliffs

The land plants are believed to have descended from the grass-green algae or Chlorophyceae. This group, besides possessing chlorophyll, and the associated yellow pigments of carotin and xanthophyll that one finds in all the higher plants, has cell walls of cellulose, and most of the members of the group store their reserve-sugars as starch, again like the higher plants. In structure and reproduction, however, the Chlorophyceae are most varied and diverse. Some, such as the one-celled microscopic *Chlamydomonas*, are unicellular plants, which though green and possessing a cell-wall of cellulose, swim about in water by means of whip-like flagella. Others, such as *Volvox*, are composed of colonies of hundreds, or even thousands of chlamydomonas-like cells aggregated together in a gelatinous hollow spherical matrix. Both of these can be found fairly commonly in fresh-water ponds, but a microscope is needed to see their characteristic features. Some unicellular green algae, like the *Protococcus* that forms a green powdery covering to tree trunks in shady places, have no means of locomotion. Many others, such as *Spirogyra*, the 'Blanket weed' scum common in ponds, have a filamentous structure, and are composed of chains of cells. Others, such as *Ulva lactuca*, the Sea lettuce, form thin sheets of tissue like green translucent plastic sheeting, and have a marine habitat.

Some of these algae reproduce sexually by means of equal-sized sex cells or gametes; others have large female gametes and numerous tiny male sperms, as in higher cryptogamic plants. In all cases the male gametes swim to the female egg-cells in water.

The other groups of algae, considered in the section on the sea shore, are represented particularly among marine habitats by the seaweeds. They differ from the green algae basically in the presence of various accessory pigments, besides chlorophyll and its usual associated pigments mentioned above, in the presence of different types of food reserve materials, and of different chemical substances present in their cell walls. They are classified, according to the colours of their accessory pigments, into such important groups as the Brown algae or Phaeophyceae, the Red algae or Rhodophyceae, the Blue-green algae or Cyanophyceae, and several others as well. There are many thousands of species of algae in the fresh-waters of this country and in the seas around it, far more than the 1,800 or so

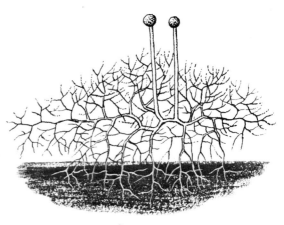

Mucor, a simple fungus which forms the characteristic mould found on such things as stale bread. The stalked globular bodies produce spores

clearly-defined species of flowering plants and vascular cryptograms, ferns. The fungi are even more numerous; it has been estimated that there are over 10,000 species of these in the British Isles alone, but the exact number is not known, and undoubtedly more remain to be discovered.

The fungi, besides the familiar toadstools, include a vast number of tiny forms, including the various moulds, such as *Mucor*, the white pin-mould which produces wefts of white filaments on bread bearing minute pin-head shaped fruiting bodies, and also the yeasts, so important in fermentation.

Fungi of course all lack chlorophyll, but otherwise must be classed as true plants. They are all either saprophytes, living on dead organic materials, and playing an important role as decomposers of leaf litter, dead wood, and even animal remains, or parasites, feeding either upon living plants, or even upon animals. Some human diseases, such as athlete's foot, are caused by parasitic fungi.

Many of the saprophytic fungi play a vital role in forests as members of mycorrhizal associations with the roots of forest trees. Others are associated with the roots of herbs such as orchids, and most orchid seeds are unable to germinate under natural con-

The Orange cup fungus, an example of the group of fungi known as the Ascomycetes

ditions unless infected by the right mycorrhizal fungus. When this happens and symbiosis is set up – this word means 'living together' – then the orchid seed can start to feed on the organic food supplied by the fungus, and so develop to the stage where it can produce its own green leaves.

The classification of the fungi is complex, but apart from the simplest forms composed of filaments, or *hyphae* without cross-walls, the Phycomycetes, there are two great groups of 'higher' fungi. The first group is the Ascomycetes, which fruit, after a sexual nuclear fusion, by means of sporangia, normally of a club shaped form, which contain spores, usually eight in number, inside them. These sporangia are called asci, and the cup-fungi, such as *Peziza*, with orange fruit-cups, belong to this great group. The second great group is the Basidiomycetes, which fruit, after a sexual nuclear fusion, by means of basidia – structures which produce spores externally, usually four per basidium,

on projecting stalks. These basidia line the walls of gills in enormous numbers in the fruiting bodies or toadstools, of typical agaricaceous fungi. In the polyphores, the basidia line the walls of pores, and there are many other arrangements of the fruiting bodies. The rust and smut fungi which parasitize cereal crops are special groups of Basidiomycetes. The most familiar fungal objects to most people are, of course, toadstools, of which the Common mushroom, *Psalliota campestris*, is only one out of thousands of species. Most of them are in fact harmless enough to eat, though no one should experiment with eating fungi unless he has the botanical knowledge to be quite certain of what he is eating.

Many of our woodland toadstools are in fact only the fruiting bodies, formed of packed-together hyphae or fungal threads, of mycorrhizal fungi associated with the roots of the forest trees. The beautiful but poisonous Fly agaric, *Amanita muscaria*, for example, with its white gills, ring round the stem, cup or volva at the base, and bright orange-red white spotted cap, is a saprophyte, associated in a mycorrhiza with the roots of birch. The bracket fungus, *Polyphorus betulinus*, with honeycomb-like pores that one sees on birch trees, is on the other hand a parasite on birch.

The Common mushroom, an example of the fruiting body of the Basidiomycete fungi

PLANTS : Lichens

The lichens are a numerous group in this country, comprising some 1,300 species. They are not actually a major group or class of plants on their own, but are in fact fungi – nearly all Ascomycetes – which are living in symbiosis with algae. The fungus determines the species and produces the framework of tissue within which the algal cells live. The fruiting bodies of the lichen are fungal ascocarps. The true nature of lichens was discovered about a century ago, but only within the last few years has it been found possible to synthesize them in the laboratory from fungus and alga. Although it is the fungus that determines the species of lichen, and the same fungus species can form in some cases very similar plants with two different sorts of algae, nevertheless the fungus partner, grown in test-tube culture on an organic medium on its own, is unable to form the typical lichen morphology until it is inoculated with a suitable alga. The fungus provides shelter and moisture and the alga

The lichen, *Parmelia physodes*, a common foliose lichen found on tree bark, *left*; *Polystictis versicolor*, a Basidiomycete bracket fungus, *right*

Psathyocela gracilis, a further example of the fruiting bodies of a Basidiomycete fungus

responds by manufacturing sugars and other organic food from the water, gases and salts provided through the fungus, using the chlorophyll in its cells. Lichens grow in a variety of habitats; some, such as the *Cladonia* species already mentioned, are characteristically saxicolous, growing on rocks, such as the bright orange *Xanthoria aureola* that one often sees on tiled roofs, walls or tombstones in country districts. A large number are corticolous, that is to say, they grow epiphytically on the bark of trees. Examples of these are the shrubby, filamentous Beard-lichens of the genus *Usnea*; and the large foliose or leafy lichens of genera such as *Parmelia* and *Lobaria*. Lichens are particularly sensitive to air pollution, especially those species that grow on trees. They have a great facility for rapid absorption of gases from the atmosphere when in the wetted, turgid state, and if these gases are poisonous ones, such as the sulphur dioxide produced in such vast quantities today by the combustion of fossil fuels such as coal and certain types of crude oils, then severe damage, or death, due mainly to the destruction of the chlorophyll in the algal cells, eventually takes place. Hence lichens

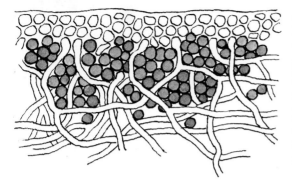

The lichen, *Xanthoria aureola*, section through upper surface of thallus showing framework of fungal hyphae which enclose cells of an alga, shown dark

in general, and in particular corticolous species, are now rare or absent both from large conurbations and often from huge areas around them.

The Bryophyta, or mosses and liverworts, are the last group of lower cryptogams we have to consider. There are about 1,000 species in this country – some 700 mosses and nearly 300 liverworts, or hepatics, as they are sometimes called. We have already had a look at the *Sphagnum* genus which forms a class on its own. The Bryales, or true mosses, such as the common woodland mosses, *Mnium hornum*, *Polytrichum formosum*, are small plants in which the sexual or gametophyte generation is the conspicuous one, and the spore bearing or sporophyte generation is permanently attached to, and largely parasitic on the gametophyte, as in all the other bryophytes. The moss plant consists of a very simple stem with little or no true vascular tissue, which bears simple leaves that are normally only one cell thick, but often have a thickened midrib and sometimes a thickened border. There are no true roots, but the base of the stem in erect growing species bears multicellular branched filaments known as rhizoids, which have some of the functions of root-hairs in higher plants. In species with prostrate or creeping stems, the rhizoids may be borne at any point along the stem.

Growth is from an apical growing point,

as in the higher plants; in mosses and in liverworts there is a single apical cell, which forms new tissue by its divisions. In fungi and in most of the algae, except certain brown seaweeds, growth is accomplished quite differently by the mere aggregating or packing together of filaments. Only the Bryophyta, of the plants considered here, show true parenchymatous tissue growth from the divisions of an apical cell.

In the mosses the male organs, or antheridia, and the female organs, or archegonia, are borne in heads at the tips of shoots, normally protected by rosettes of leaves around them, and sometimes also by hairs mixed in with them. The inflorescences may be unisexual, or the male and female organs may be mixed in one inflorescence. After fertilization, which requires external moisture for the sperms to swim in to reach the necks of the archegonia, the fertilized egg develops into a cylindrical embryo. At the

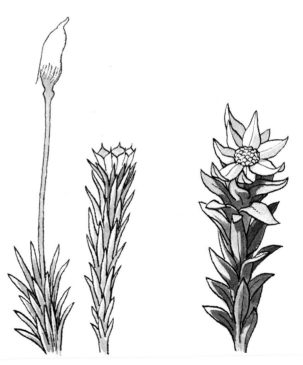

Mosses, *Polytrichum formosum, left*, showing capsule and male inflorescence; *Mnium hornum, right*, showing male inflorescence

base there develops an absorbing organ or foot; then there is a stalk, or seta, which elongates by growth of an apical cell; later a capsule develops on the top. This remains covered for a time, in the true mosses, by the enlarged remains of the archegonial wall, which forms a protective cap, or calyptra. Underneath it on top of the capsule there normally develops a lid or operculum which falls off in due course when the capsule is

A common leafy liverwort, *Scapania nemorea*, showing the two-lobed toothed leaves in two opposite and alternate rows around the stem and the gemmae; the green granules which can grow into new plants, at the apex of the stem

ripe, to expose the peculiar mechanism, known as the peristome which controls spore dispersal. This structure consists of sixteen, sometimes more, sometimes fewer, radially arranged teeth, attached round the periphery of the top of the capsule. These teeth are hygroscopic and in dry weather lose water and curl back, exposing the spores within the capsule, while in wet weather they absorb

water and close together in the centre. This ensures that spores are only shed from the capsule under dry conditions – conditions in which dispersal to a distance is most likely to occur. The capsule wall contains some chlorophyll when young, and even has in most mosses, a few stomata; but these appear not to open and shut as they do in higher plants, and it is clear that the sporophyte is essentially parasitic on the sexual moss plant or gametophyte. The spores on germination form at first a mass of green branched filaments, known as the protonema; soon however buds appear on this, and typical moss shoots develop from these.

The liverworts or *Hepaticae* are closely similar to the true mosses or Bryales, but are in general simpler plants. Most of them have their gametophyte differentiated into stem and leaves, but the leaves are without midribs and are often variously lobed and divided, as in *Scapania*. In true mosses, the leaves are always simple, though they may be toothed round the margins. In leafy liverworts, too, the normal leaves are usually in only two rows, not three or more as in most mosses.

Some liverworts have thallose gametophytes, in which there is no distinction into stem and leaves at all, but instead a prostrate, forking ribbon-like plant body, as in *Pellia*; this has some resemblance in form to one of the larger seaweeds, such as *Fucus*. The rhizoids of liverworts are unbranched and are not divided up by cross walls, but are unicellular. The inflorescences of liverworts are essentially similar to those of mosses, but the sporophytes are much simpler. The seta or stalk elongates largely by increase in size of its cells after early initial growth, not by means of an apical cell. Instead of the elaborate moss capsule with calyptra, operculum, and peristome, the liverwort capsule is normally just a simple spherical body which splits into four lobes or valves to release the spores. Their discharge is aided by hygroscopic fibres inside the capsule, which jerk about in drying, called elaters, not present in mosses. The bryophyta are all small plants;

as they have no vascular tissue and no cuticle, hence effective means or regulating water loss, they either live in very humid environments, or else are adapted to survive quite drastic drying-out for periods of time. They are mostly able to absorb water as vapour over their whole surface in a saturated atmosphere, as one can easily demonstrate by placing a stem of a freshly-dried moss inside one end of a closed tin, with a large piece of saturated cotton wool inside the other end. If the lid is left closed for an hour or so at the most, the dried-up moss will absorb water vapour from the moist atmosphere inside the tin and become fully turgid once more.

Bryophyta, since they grow in close contact with the surface of the soil, are often excellent indicators of the ecological environment in which they live. Like the lichens, many of the epiphytic bryophytes are highly sensitive to air pollution. Since many species can only survive in very humid places they tend to occur only in the western or hilly parts of the British Isles, where the rainfall is high, or, when occurring in drier districts, to be confined to very sheltered places such as moist rocks or springy places in sheltered, wooded ravines. Certain western districts of the British Isles are extremely rich in species of bryophytes; richer in fact than most parts of Europe. Such areas are the Highlands of Scotland, North Wales and South West Ireland.

★　　★　　★

Those who have read these pages will have certainly become aware that natural plant communities in this country, and still more partly artificial ones like hedges, are threatened as never before by the huge and ever increasing pace of 'development' of all kinds. Development for residential, transportation, industrial and agricultural purposes, must go on; it cannot be stopped in a small, over-crowded country with an ever-increasing population. But in the interests of man's own happiness and even his own survival, at least as a sane and integrated being,

development must be controlled so that the minimum of unnecessary damage is done to our environment.

One of the greatest environmental problems today is that of pollution. Although pollution of the air by solid particles of smoke is well on the way to control as a result of the official policy of encouraging the use of smokeless fuels and by formation of smokeless zones.

Air pollution by sulphur dioxide and other products of the combustion of fossil fuels is still increasing, particularly in the London area and over southern Britain generally. Freshwater pollution is gradually being brought under control, and here the outlook is brighter but even highly purified sewage effluents, when in large quantity, may overwhelm small rivers with an excess of nitrate and phosphate salts, upsetting the fresh water ecosystems, and producing vast growths of certain algae which smother the plants on which small invertebrates feed. These small animals are essential links in the food chains of many fishes. We hear a lot about coastal and marine pollution, and much is being done to combat this, but accidents are increasingly likely to occur.

Environmental damage through the ignorant misuse of herbicides and pesticides is still serious. Many harmless and attractive plants are destroyed or damaged needlessly, and what is worse, poisons get into the food chains and become progressively concentrated, resulting in the sterility or even death of the predator birds or animals at the summits of the food chains. The manufacturers of these agricultural chemicals are largely extremely responsible in their attitude to these problems and greatly concerned about them. They are carrying out much research on these matters and in time it appears likely that these problems will be fully solved, as long as the public who use these chemicals cooperate fully and also understand the implications of misuse. Here programmes of education are of vital importance.

Today, the conservation movement in this

country is more active and stronger than it ever has been. Unfortunately, awareness of the problems confronting us took time to develop, and we are faced with situations of extreme urgency in every direction.

Conservation does not mean mere preservation of nature reserves, or countrysides, as museum pieces. It means a constructive and integrated approach to the whole question of the use of all the resources, physical and biological, of our planet, much of which must be on a world scale. If man is to survive, it must not merely be in a non-toxic environment in which he has enough food; the world must continue to be a place in which man can enjoy life; and for this to be possible in the future, the remaining natural ecosystems must be conserved as far as is possible along with the artificial ecosystems man has to construct for his own purposes.

Invertebrates

The earliest known animal fossils are somewhat problematic. They include marks that look like worm-tracks in a solidified mud and a remarkable impression in stone that has all the appearance of a flattened jellyfish. There is another, known as *Xenusion*, little better than a rusty stain in a piece of sandstone, that has all the features of an animal that was half-worm, half-insect. All these are invertebrates – animals without backbones – all are in excess of 600 million years old, and they belong to the Pre-Cambrian Era. For nearly another 300 million years the only animals on the earth were invertebrates, living mainly in the sea. Then the first fish-like vertebrates appeared and in a few million years after this came the first invasion of the land-masses, and these also were invertebrates. They had these land surfaces to themselves, except for the plants.

Among the first land-living invertebrates, possibly aquatic or semi-aquatic, were some very small crustaceans looking like our present-day woodlice and some wingless insects. They are preserved in the Rhynie chert of Aberdeenshire, together with grass-like primitive plants. In some way not easy to explain they were overwhelmed and preserved in silica, a glass-like mineral. And now, 300 million years later, chunks of it can be removed containing the low-growing flora and fauna of those times, as if in a block of ice. By placing thin slices cut from these blocks under the microscope the crustaceans and insects can be seen in almost perfect detail.

This is unusual because the best invertebrate fossils are of animals with hard skeletons, like corals and molluscs. In various parts of the country these abound. Corals in the limestone laid down in the Coal Age tell us that then the climate of what we now call Britain was tropical. They are only one of the fossils to indicate the changes of climate that have taken place, from warm to cold and to warm again. They also tell of the sea-bed being upheaved and submerged again, time after time, of changes also from deserts to luxuriant vegetation, from marsh to forest. The changes also resulted in the wiping out of whole groups of animals, like the trilobites, the primitive crustaceans, whose living representatives today are the king crabs or horseshoe crabs now found only off the Atlantic coast of North America and the western Pacific. One of these, in the Silurian rocks of Worcestershire, could roll up like a woodlouse and its fossils have been named the Dudley locust by the quarrymen. In Shropshire, in the coal-measures, are found the fossils of king crabs, part of the evidence that these were once widespread in the earth's seas.

The Dudley locust is not the only fossil to have been noted and given a nickname. In various rock formations all over the country the shells of bivalve molluscs abound. One of peculiar shape, the *Trigonia* of the Inferior Oolite of Dorset, has been called the Devil's Toenail. Then there are the familiar 'thunderbolts', like large rifle-bullets. People finding these in the days before geology had been reduced to a science, could only guess at their origin, and the name they gave these common fossils was, for that time, a reasonable assumption. They were not to know they were fossilized 'shells', all that was preserved of large squids that swam in the seas that once covered the whole of Britain.

Related to them are the attractive coiled ammonites, the shells of animals related to the present-day argonaut of the tropical Pacific. These may be as small as a shirt-button or as large as cartwheels, a yard (91 cm.) across. Ammonites can be found in large numbers in the cliffs between Lyme Regis and Charmouth, in Dorset. These are 150 million years old, but even as recently as

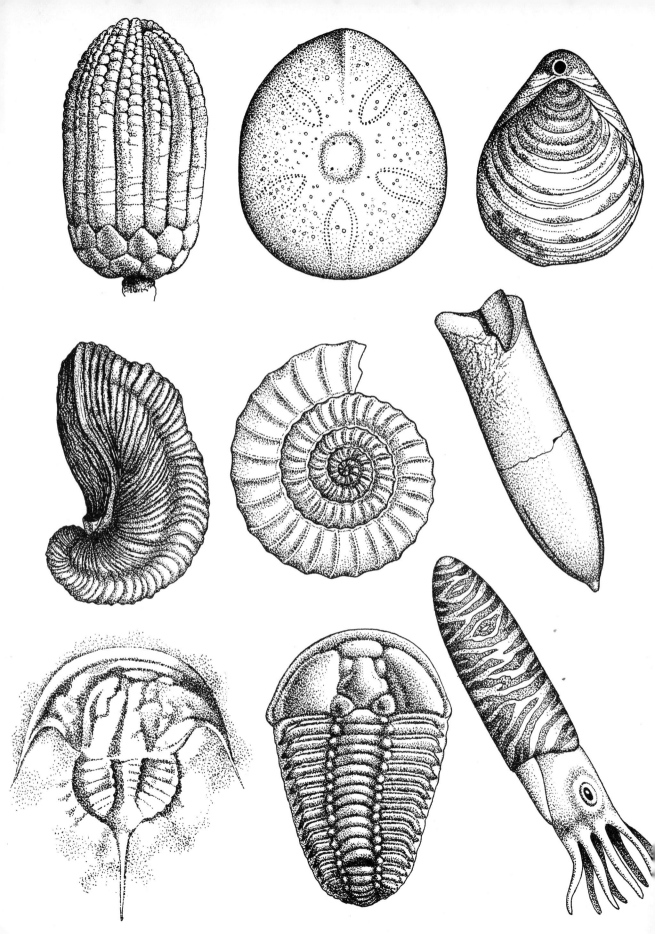

the Eocene, a mere 50 million years ago, there were tropical marine animals over the sea-bed, the future British Isles. In the Bracklesham Beds in the New Forest is found the shell *Fusinus*, whose relatives today still live in tropical seas. And in the crumbling cliffs of the north-west corner of the Isle of Wight, also of Eocene age, the dilettante geologist can fill his pockets with the small bony plates from the disintegrated shells of marine turtles of 50 million years ago.

Some rock formations are bare of fossils. Others contain large numbers either of one kind mainly or of great diversity. Some rocks are almost exclusively made of the remains of dead animals, often of one kind only. Lampshells (Brachiopoda) especially were rock-builders. These look like bivalve molluscs but are unrelated. They are named for their resemblance to a Roman lamp, with a spout where the two halves of the shell join. Through this ran a fleshy stalk by which the animal fixed itself to the sea-bed. Lampshells were so numerous in shallow seas in former times, although today they are rare, that their dead shells formed beaches, now converted into solid rock by the process of time.

Lampshells are found mainly in the deep sea today, and so are sea-lilies, the stalked relatives of starfishes and sea-urchins. Their long stalks and arms were supported by chalky 'bones' and these at times form a high percentage of the matrix of the rocks in which they occur.

The shepherd's crowns of the chalk areas of southern and eastern England are the flint casts of the shells of sea-urchins that lived in the warm seas of Cretaceous times. Attractive to look at because of their five-rayed design, they have furnished the geo-logist with valuable information on the evolution of species. The English Chalk is in places a thousand feet (305 m.) thick, accumulated at a rate of a foot (30 cm.) per 30,000 years. It is made up of pure calcium carbonate largely precipitated by single-celled algae in warm seas. It also contains the shells of microscopic single-celled animals, the siliceous remains of numerous deep-sea sponges, many bivalve shells, fragments of crabs and multitudes of shepherd's crowns.

Through the patience, largely of one man, C. T. Rowe, these remains of sea-urchins were collected in the early years of this century, from the bottom to the top of the Chalk. In this highly valuable series of specimens can be traced the evolution, over a period of 30 million years, of several kinds of sea-urchins. As we follow these series through we see the almost imperceptible changes by which sea-urchins are converted from one species at the base of the Chalk to a totally different one at the top. It is the most complete evolutionary series so far collected anywhere in the world.

The traditional method of dealing with the animal kingdom is to divide it into two sections – those animals which have backbones (the vertebrates) and those which do not have backbones (the invertebrates). This is a convenient rather than a scientific division, the two groups being of markedly unequal value. The vertebrates form a part only of one phylum or branch, albeit the major part, whereas the invertebrates include a score of phyla of very diverse character. Nevertheless, the vertebrates include the larger and, except for insects and spiders, those more familiar to us. The invertebrates, on the other hand, account for some 98 per cent of the million or more species in the animal kingdom. Most of them are small or very small, even microscopic, but they make up for this by their vast numbers: up to 20 million nematode worms and 200,000 mites per square yard (0·8 sq. m.) of grassland soil for example. A few are, however, very large. The giant squid may

Examples of some fossil invertebrates which have helped in the understanding of animal evolution

from left to right, top row: A sea-lily or crinoid, a sea-urchin, a brachiopod; *centre row:* an oyster-like bivalve, *Gryphaea;* an ammonite, a belemnite guard; *bottom row:* an arachnid king crab, a trilobite, a belemnite reconstruction

reach a length of 50 feet (15 m.) including the long tentacles, while the giant clam of Southeast Asia may be 4 feet (122 cm.) across and weigh 500 lb. (227 kg.), both being much bigger than the majority of vertebrate animals.

Scientifically the animal kingdom falls into three well-defined groups or subkingdoms: the Protozoa, the Parazoa, and the Metazoa. The Protozoa, mainly of microscopic size, consist of animals in which the body is composed of a single cell, exceptionally of a few cells. The two other groups contain animals made up of many cells. The sponges are so unlike the other many-celled animals that they are placed in a subkingdom by themselves, the Parazoa. The Metazoa contains all the other invertebrates, the worms, insects, crabs, snails, and so on as well as the vertebrates. There is no proof that the three subkingdoms are in direct line of descent. More probably the Metazoa and the Parazoa as well as the Protozoa living today have been derived from ancestral protozoans along three distinct evolutionary lines.

The protozoans consist of a single cell, all minute creatures, rarely visible without a

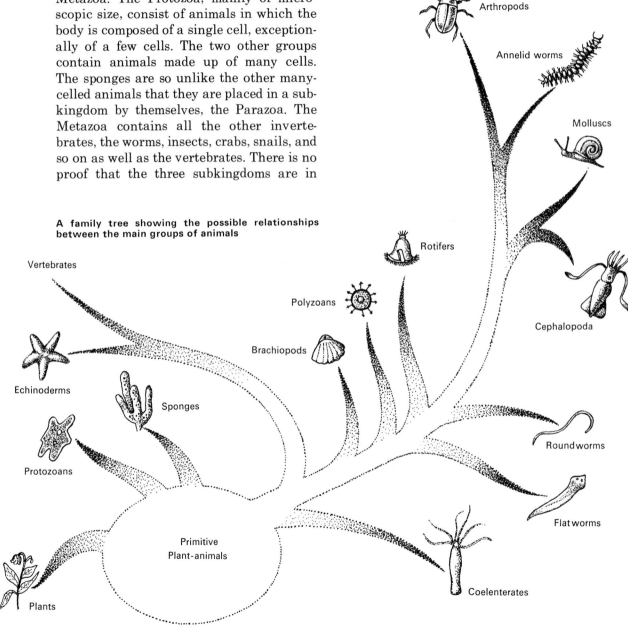

A family tree showing the possible relationships between the main groups of animals

Arthropods

Annelid worms

Molluscs

Rotifers

Cephalopoda

Vertebrates

Polyzoans

Brachiopods

Echinoderms

Sponges

Roundworms

Protozoans

Flatworms

Primitive Plant-animals

Coelenterates

Plants

microscope. Most people have heard of the Amoeba, however, which is popularly regarded as the lowest form of life. It is certainly very simple when compared with the higher animal but is still a very efficient animal with a sophisticated structure.

Several related species can be found in ponds and ditches, most of them barely visible with the naked eye. Under the microscope an Amoeba looks little more than a blob of jelly with a darker nucleus near the centre. This apparently almost featureless jelly can move, feed, reproduce itself, and do all the other things that characterize living organisms. It moves along simply by flowing over a solid surface, pushing out finger-like projections of protoplasm, known as pseudopodia, in any direction. Should they encounter a food-particle, they simply flow round it and engulf it. Once inside the Amoeba's body, digestive juices are poured on to the food which is then absorbed into the Amoeba's protoplasm. Breathing is no problem: Amoeba is very small and has such a thin skin that enough oxygen diffuses in without special breathing apparatus. Excretion is simple. Waste matter is extruded and left behind as the animal flows on. Amoeba normally reproduces itself by what is called asexual reproduction: by dividing into two halves. Each half then lives an independent life and divides, division again taking place when it has grown sufficiently large. These divisions as well as all the other life processes are under the control of the nucleus. Each division is, in fact, preceded by a division of the nucleus in to two, one half going to each of the new amoebae.

The majority of protozoans live in water, fresh or salt, and many different kinds await the enthusiast with a microscope. Some, like *Paramecium*, are clothed with tiny protoplasmic hairs, called 'cilia'. Others have a relatively few but longer hairs called 'flagella' and are known as 'flagellate' protozoans. They are often regarded as being very like the ancestral types of living organisms from which all animals and plants other than bacteria and other micro-organisms, have

been derived. Some flagellates, like the minute *Chlamydomonas*, which makes pond water green in summer, are clearly plants. Others, like *Euglena*, combine both plant and animal characteristics and are often referred to as plant-animals because it is hard to say whether they are plant or animal. It is reasonable to suppose that the early ancestors of forms like *Euglena* gave rise to the plant kingdom, on the one hand, and the animal kingdom on the other.

The protozoans play important roles in nature. Those that live in water form the food for many insects, crustaceans and worms which are in turn food for fishes and other larger animals. Many live inside other animals and are beneficial. Goats are a good example; they have a population of protozoans in their food-canals which break down the otherwise indigestible plant cellulose they eat.

Finally, there are protozoans, especially in the sea, that have shells of carbonate of lime and when they die these shells sink to the bottom to accumulate as oozes, covering wide areas of the ocean-bed. These accumulations have in past ages been upheaved to form dry land. The chalk downs and the white cliffs of Dover are largely composed of these microscopic shells.

There are two species of freshwater sponges common in Britain, the Pond sponge, *Spongilla lacustris*, and the River sponge, *Ephydatia fluviatilis*. The first lives mainly in lakes and large ponds, but may be found in rivers, encrusting plant stems, tree roots and submerged posts. The second lives in slow-flowing rivers but may be found in lakes, forming long fingers up to a foot (30 cm.) in length. It is often found growing on lock-gates. Their normal colour is greyish to cream-coloured but they are often green when growing in well-lit situations. The green colour is due to the presence in their tissues of small green algae, *Chlorella*, less than $\frac{1}{500}$ inch (0·05 mm.) across. The shapes of these sponges, together with the fact that they are green in the light and yellow when light is excluded, caused the early

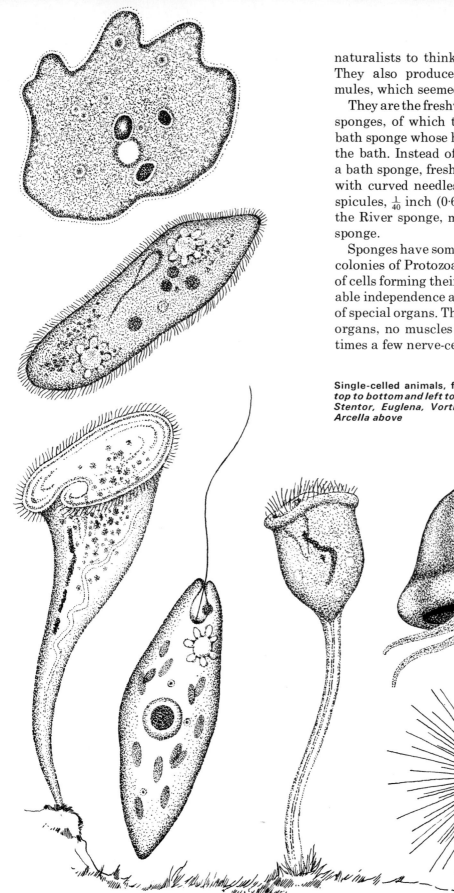

naturalists to think that they were plants. They also produce brown seed-like gemmules, which seemed to support this belief.

They are the freshwater relatives of marine sponges, of which the most familiar is the bath sponge whose horny skeleton we use in the bath. Instead of the fibrous skeleton of a bath sponge, freshwater sponges are filled with curved needles of silica, the so-called spicules, $\frac{1}{40}$ inch (0·64 mm.) long, smooth in the River sponge, microspined in the Pond sponge.

Sponges have sometimes been described as colonies of Protozoa because the thousands of cells forming their tissues retain considerable independence and form little in the way of special organs. There are no special sense-organs, no muscles or nerves except sometimes a few nerve-cells, and no set digestive

Single-celled animals, freshwater protozoans, *from top to bottom and left to right: Amoeba, Paramecium, Stentor, Euglena, Vorticella, Actinophrys sol* with *Arcella* above

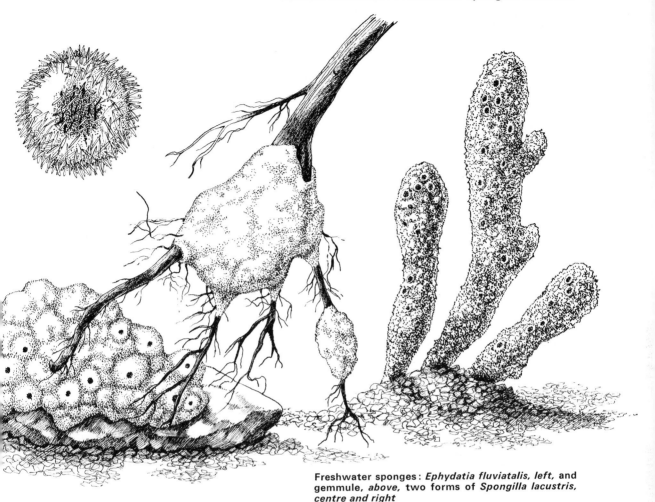

Freshwater sponges: *Ephydatia fluviatalis, left,* and gemmule, *above,* two forms of *Spongilla lacustris, centre and right*

system. On the surface is a skin, one or two cells thick, perforated by numerous microscopic pores, with here and there larger openings up to a $\frac{1}{4}$ inch (6 mm.) across. Inside is a network of star-shaped cells, with jelly filling its interstices, traversed by a labyrinth of tubes which are dilated in places. These dilations are lined by collared cells, each with a rounded body bearing a protoplasmic collar from the internal base of which springs a whip-like flagellum. The concerted beating of the flagella sets up a current drawing water in through the pores and driving it out through the larger openings or vents, which used to be called, erroneously, oscules or little mouths.

The incoming current brings water carrying oxygen and food-particles, microscopic fragments of dead plants and animals, possibly bacteria. The outgoing current takes away carbon dioxide and body wastes.

Sponges are both male and female and in the summer, when they reproduce sexually, sperms are liberated into the surrounding water and sucked in by a neighbouring sponge to fertilize its ova. The fertilized ovum develops into a larva covered with cilia, the beating of which drive the larva through the water after it is carried from the parent body by the outgoing current. After a few hours the cilia on its surface start to withdraw, the larva loses momentum, sinks

159

to the bottom and grows into a tiny sponge. In the early stages a sponge can creep slowly about – at the rate of about an inch (25 mm.) a week – but later it remains fixed to one spot.

Towards autumn the asexual gemmules, the size of a pin's head, begin to appear scattered through the sponge body. Each gemmule is a hollow sphere with a double wall of a tough material strengthened by even smaller spicules. Each gemmule contains a small mass of cells and at one point on its surface is an opening through which, next spring, the mass of cells can creep out to grow into a new sponge. Gemmules are reproductive bodies capable of surviving drying up and other adverse conditions such as low temperatures.

Sponges usually pass unnoticed because they look like green slime or else like water-plants. They have been known to grow in and block water-pipes or to foul reservoirs. Otherwise they do not affect man's affairs. When dried a freshwater sponge readily crumbles to a powder filled with minute sharp-ended glassy spicules.

Rubbed on the cheeks the spicules cause a fine laceration of the skin, producing a maidenly blush. Years ago in parts of Europe it was used by peasant women, as a face powder, to to be rubbed on afflicted joints, as a cure for rheumatism, or as a substitute for capsicum in an embrocation for cholera. At one time it was sold in this country as 'Russian fleas', small boys putting the irritant powder under the collars of their playmates.

The Metazoa includes all the multi-cellular animals apart from the sponges. They are arranged in about 20 groups called phyla, of which the major ones are listed below.

Some of these phyla appear to have little connection with each other, but one can detect certain similarities. For example, it is not too difficult to see a connection between the bristle-worms and the millipedes. Both are long-bodied with the body divided into segments or rings, and the internal anatomy of the two is similar. The millipedes lead on to the crustaceans and insects in which the body although shorter is also segmented and usually there is a distinct head, thorax and abdomen. The basic plan is, however, similar.

The relationship between a worm and a

Phylum	Examples
Coelenterata	Jellyfishes, Sea-anemones, Corals
Platyhelminthes	Planarians, Liver flukes, Tapeworms
Nematoda	Round-worms
Endoprocta	Moss animals*
Annelida	Bristle-worms, Earthworms, Leeches
Arthropoda	Crabs, Woodlice, Insects, Spiders, Scorpions, Millipedes, Centipedes
Mollusca	Slugs, Snails, Bivalves, Squids
Ectoprocta	Moss animals*
Brachiopoda	Brachiopods (marine shelled animals)
Echinodermata	Starfishes, Sea-urchins
Chordata	Lancelets, Sea-squirts, Acorn-worms, and all backboned animals

* These two groups are superficially very similar and they are commonly lumped together under the title Polyzoa or Bryozoa.

snail is less obvious, but many marine snails have larvae just like those of the bristle-worms, and there are other features in common, such as the structure of the nervous system. It seems that annelids, arthropods and molluscs are related through some remote ancestor common to all three groups.

The echinoderms appear to be quite unrelated to any other phylum if only the adult animals are studied, but their young stages reveal affinities with the vertebrates. The link here is the Acorn-worm (*Balanoglossus*). This marine burrowing animal, which looks so like a worm, has a larva just like that of certain echinoderms. On the other hand, the adult Acorn-worm, although it has no backbone, is related to the vertebrates through its internal anatomy. To go further into this here would not be practical since it would

involve details belonging to the province of the specialist zoologist. It is sufficient to say that there appears to have been at least two main lines of evolution within the Metazoa. One takes us from the annelids to the arthropods and molluscs, the other is through the echinoderms to the chordates (including the vertebrates). These two lines might well have arisen independently from separate protozoan ancestors, but at this level in the animal scale we do not really know enough to trace the lines of evolution with certainty. Whatever happened took place during that early part of the earth's history from which no fossils have been preserved.

The members of the Coelenterates are nearly all marine and they include the jellyfishes, sea-anemones and corals. They differ from the more familiar animals in being radially symmetrical. That is, they are built on the radial plan. Their bodies are little more than hollow bags with a mouth at the upper end, surrounded by tentacles, the interior of

A group of hydra with a budding hydra in the centre and on the right drawings to show the hydra's somersaulting movement

the bag forming the digestive cavity. The word 'coelenterate' means 'hollow stomach'.

Although most coelenterates live in the sea, a few have taken to living in fresh water. If you collect duckweed or other floating leaves from a pond in summer and put these into a jar of water you will probably find the well-known little animal called hydra. After the leaves have been left undisturbed for a while the hydra will show itself. Its body is a slender green or brown tube, up to about an inch (25 mm.) long when fully expanded. One end is attached to the vegetation and the free end carries a ring of usually five or six hollow tentacles. The mouth, being the only opening to the body, also has to act as the anus and is at the centre of the ring of tentacles. The body-wall and the tentacles are composed of two layers of cells – ectoderm on the outside and endoderm on the inside – separated by a thin layer of jelly. Nearly all the cells have muscular 'tails' embedded in the jelly. In the outside layer of cells these tails run lengthways along the body, while those of the inner layer run round the body. Contraction of the outer ones shortens the body, while contraction of the inner layer makes the body long and slender. These actions are controlled by a simple network of nerves. When disturbed, as when the leaves are removed from the water, hydra contracts to a pinhead, withdrawing its tentacles at the same time, so that it is almost impossible to see except with a lens. Only when all has been still for a while will it stretch out again to the full length of the body and tentacles. The hydra is more or less colourless but minute green or brown algae live in many of the outer cells and give the animal its colour. This relationship between plant and animal, known as symbiosis, is one of mutual benefit. In this example the algae get

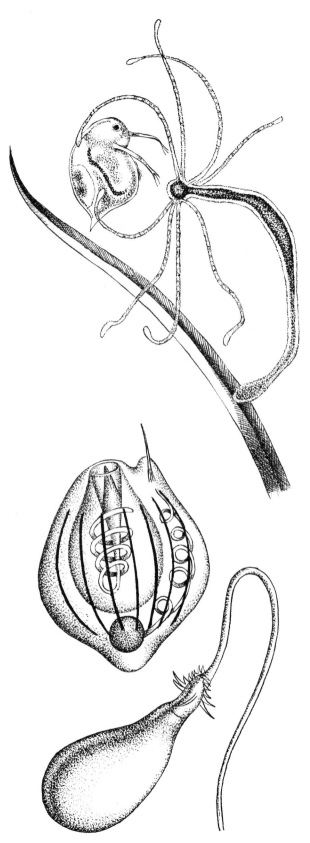

top: A hydra with water-flea. The hydra's body expands to accommodate its prey.

centre: A hydra's stinging-cell and *bottom* discharged from its capsule

shelter and a supply of nitrogenous food material, while the hydra benefits by having its waste nitrogenous material removed. Hydra also obtain a certain amount of oxygen absorbed through the skin from the surrounding water. There are three species in the British Isles, Green hydra, *Chlorohydra viridissima*, formerly known as *Hydra viridis*, Brown hydra, *Hydra oligactis*, and Slender hydra, *H. attennuta*, the last two are both greyish brown in colour.

The Slender hydra, however, is only about $\frac{2}{5}$ inch (10 mm.) long and its tentacles are proportionately shorter than those of the Green and the Brown hydras. Its body, also, is clearly divided into a stomach region and a narrower stalk.

Although small and delicate, the hydras are deadly enemies of water-fleas and other small pond-dwellers. The tentacles are armed with batteries of stinging-cells or cnidoblasts, each of which contains a little capsule called a nematocyst. The cnidoblast also has a little 'trigger' protruding from its surface. When a water-flea brushes against the tentacles the trigger causes the nematocyst to fire out a tiny thread. Lots of these threads are fired out together and they combine to trap the prey. Two main types of thread are involved: penetrating hollow threads which pierce the prey and inject poison, and coiling threads which wrap themselves round the hairs of the prey. The cnidoblast-cells are self-contained and the firing process is independent of the nervous system. Once the prey has been trapped, however, the nervous system comes into play causing the arm which has trapped the prey to bend towards the mouth which takes the food into the body. The tentacles will go through these movements without solid food on them. For example, the juice from a crushed water-flea alone will make them go through the motions of cramming food into the mouth. A single chemical, glutathione, is responsible.

A third type of nematocyst is defensive, only shot out when a larger animal approaches. A fourth type, used to fasten the tentacles to the surface on which the hydra is somersaulting or 'walking', has no sting. It merely shoots out a sticky thread.

Digestion takes place partly inside the gastric cavity and partly inside the endoderm-cells. There are several kinds of these: some secrete digestive juices which start to break up the food while it is still in the gastric cavity, others have tiny hairs or cilia which wave about and keep the fluid in the cavity on the move, while others act rather like amoebae and engulf small food-particles to complete their digestion. Undigested material passes out again through the mouth.

The stinging-cells can be used only once and they are replaced by new ones within about 48 hours of firing. The fired capsules remain attached to the food and the cnidoblast-cells left behind degenerate. Reserve cells migrate through the body and quickly develop into cnidoblast-cells to take the places of those that have been used. One of the puzzles is how these reserve cells 'know' where to go and how do they orientate themselves so that the nematocyst always fires outwards?

The reserve cells, or interstitial cells to give them their proper name, are located throughout the body, scattered between the cells of the ectoderm and endoderm. As well as producing new stinging-cells, they play an important part in reproduction. The reproductive organs usually appear in late summer. The male organs or testes are little swellings which appear just below the ring of tentacles in the ectoderm, while the ovaries are larger swellings near the base of the body. Male and female organs are usually on different individuals, but they may be on the same individual. Both start as groups of interstitial cells which gradually take shape. Each ovary contains only one egg-cell, but a testis releases many flagellated sperms into the water, the sperms being attracted to the egg-cells by chemical means, fertilizing the egg-cell while it is still inside the ovary.

A tough coat then forms round the egg

which is later released from the ovary directly into the water by rupture of the ectoderm. Under warm conditions the egg will develop into a small hydra, but it may well rest in its protective coat throughout the winter and not hatch until the following spring. The tough-coated eggs are very resistant to cold and drought and they can be carried long distances by the wind, or stuck to the feet of water-birds. So it is easy for hydra to colonize new ponds.

Hydra can also reproduce by budding. When food is plentiful, as in early summer, it will produce buds which grow out to form new hydras. The buds also are formed initially from interstitial cells. For a time they remain attached to the parent, but they break away sooner or later to lead an independent life.

Perhaps the most striking feature of hydra is its ability to regenerate lost parts. For example, a lost tentacle can be rapidly regrown. The interstitial cells are involved in this also. They accumulate round the injury and by their division form new body-cells. Regeneration does not proceed so quickly, if at all, when buds or reproductive organs are developing. The tendency of the interstitial cells to migrate to an injured part is overruled by the presence of developing buds or reproductive organs. Regeneration does not stop at replacing lost tentacles. Cut a hydra in half and both halves will grow into complete individuals. Even very small pieces can regenerate into complete animals as long as both ectoderm- and endoderm-cells are present in the original piece. Although the cells of these two layers look so alike, they are not interchangeable. This was shown by experiments in which hydras were turned inside out. Both sets of body-cells migrated until they reached their normal positions again. They merely swap places. Most coelenterates, sea-anemones and corals are notable exceptions, have two distinct stages in their life-histories, known as the polyp and the medusa. The polyp is fixed and looks rather like hydra. The medusae are free-swimming jellyfishes,

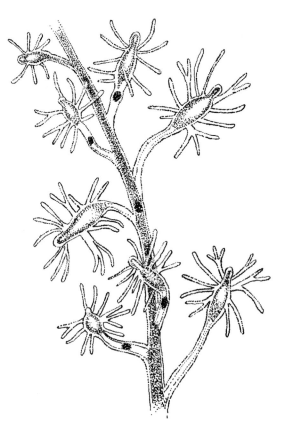

A *Cordylophora* colony

carrying the sex organs, that develop from buds on the polyp. Each fertilized egg develops into an oval larva which, after swimming around for a while, settles on the bottom and becomes a new polyp. The medusae are carried about by currents, effectively dispersing the species. Hydra, with its resistant capsules being carried on water-birds' feet or blown by wind, is as effectively dispersed. There is, however, another freshwater coelenterate in which the main stage of the history is a medusa. This is *Craspedacusta sowerbii*, a freshwater jellyfish up to $\frac{3}{4}$ inch (19 mm.) diameter with up to 400 tentacles around the edge of its umbrella. It is not common and, since its initial discovery in a lily pond at Regent's Park in 1880, it has been found only in a few botanical gardens and reservoirs, the latter mainly in the south-west of England where temperatures are generally a little higher than elsewhere. It may be seen in late summer, usually basking near the surface. It is an active swimmer and, like hydra, it feeds mainly on water-fleas. Its polyp stage is very small and has no tentacles. Until its connection with the jellyfish stage was proved it was called *Microhydra*. The polyp survives the winter surrounded by a horny covering, in which it could probably be carried like the hydra capsules to new places. During the spring and summer the polyp produces buds, some of which grow into new polyps and some of which become detached and grow into a new generation of jellyfishes.

The only other non-marine coelenterate in the British Isles is *Cordylophora lacustris* found in some of the Norfolk Broads and other brackish waters. It would appear to be gradually making the transition from the sea to fresh water. *Cordylophora* forms colonies in which many polyps are joined together. The colony arises by continual budding with the buds not separating as they do in hydra. It consists of a 'root' or stolon which creeps over stones and logs and throws up polyp-bearing branches at regular intervals and giving the colony the appearance of a miniature forest. There is no free-swimming stage in *Cordylophora*, but there are medusa-like buds which remain attached to the colony and which release the reproductive cells into the water.

From the earliest times the name 'worm' has been used for anything that crawled. So we have Slow-worm, a legless lizard, Wireworm and Mealworm, both beetle larvae, and a number of other animals known simply as 'worms'. The biologist, however, tries to look beyond superficial similarities when classifying animals. Nevertheless, anything long and slender that crawls is apt to be given the name. The flatworms, the first of these, and the most primitive of the Platyhelminthes, show several advances over the coelenterates. One of the most fundamental differences is that the flatworms, like all the higher animals, have

three body-layers whereas the coelenterates have only two. Flatworms also have definite front and back ends, a feature not seen in the more or less circular polyps and jellyfishes.

Although the body is always more or less flattened, there is a wide range of shapes among the flatworms, which are divided into three classes. Two, the flukes and the tapeworms, are completely parasitic. Members of the third class, the turbellarians, are free living in salt and fresh water and in damp soil.

If mud is taken from the bottom of a pond or stream and allowed to settle in a dish of water, some small grey or black creatures will soon be seen gliding about on the surface of the mud or on the sides of the container. These are planarians and belong to a group of turbellarians in which the gut is divided into three lobes, one reaching forward and two reaching backward. The mouth is near the centre of the body. They resemble small leeches at first sight but a lens will soon show that their bodies are not divided up into rings like those of the leeches.

Our freshwater planarians, of which there are about a dozen species, range from about 1 to 4 cm. in length and from very pale grey to black in colour. *Dendrocoelum lacteum* is very pale and the three-branched gut can be clearly seen through the body.

A planarian is covered with minute protoplasmic hairs, or cilia. These, beating rhythmically, enable the animal to glide smoothly over almost any surface. It can even glide along the underside of the surface film. Movement is aided by slime given out by certain cells just under the skin which lubricates the surface and is especially important for those planarians that live on land. Faster movement can be produced by waves of muscular contractions along the body, but the animals cannot swim: they must always have a surface on which to creep. Although the cilia themselves are too small to see with the naked eye, a lens will reveal the tiny currents they set up in the water. The name *Turbellaria* in fact refers to this turbulence.

Planarians are generally to be found in dark places, under stones or on the undersides of water-plants. The freshwater species live mainly in slow-moving streams or ponds although *Polycelis cornuta* is found in the swifter streams.

Planarians feed on insects, water-fleas, and other small animals. They are sometimes a nuisance in fish-hatcheries, where they destroy large numbers of small fishes. The mouth is at the end of a muscular tube, the pharynx, which can be pushed out to catch food. This food is then covered with slime and eaten; very small animals are swallowed whole, larger animals are broken up by digestive juices and then the pieces are sucked into the mouth. The branches of the gut carry the food to nearly every part of the body. There is no anus and any undigested material is passed out through the mouth.

Planarians have a nervous system considerably in advance of that found in coelenterates and there is a simple sort of brain at the head end and simple eyes are present in all the British planarians. They find their food by chemical means, detecting 'smells' in the water and then moving towards them.

Like most other flatworms, they are hermaphrodite – both male and female organs being present in each animal. There are elaborate arrangements to prevent self-

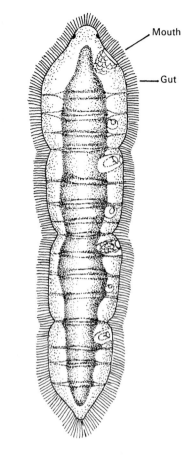

The flatworm, *Microstomum,* with four individuals in a chain

The flatworm, *Polycelis nigra,* feeding

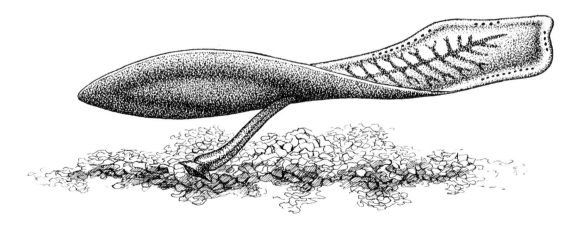

fertilization and the animals must pair before they can lay their egg-cocoons.

Regeneration in the planarians is on a par with that found in hydra. Minute pieces of the body can grow into complete individuals after separation and each piece seems to have some 'memory' of its original position in the body: the new head will always develop at the original front end of a separated piece. In addition to the power of regeneration, a planarian can go without food for long periods – several months if necessary. The animal keeps itself going by gradually digesting its own body: the eggs and the reproductive organs are used up first, then the packing tissue in the body, then the muscles and the gut begin to disappear. Only the nervous system is safe from this process and the starved animal may shrink to a quarter of its original size, although the head does not shrink to the same extent. When food is available again,

provided part of the gut still remains, the animal will regenerate all the lost parts.

As well as the freshwater planarians, we also have a number of marine forms, generally much smaller than the freshwater ones, and a few terrestrial species. One of the commonest of our land planarians is *Rhynchodemus terrestris*. It is less than 1 cm. long and lives in decaying tree-stumps. Some terrestrial planarians in the tropics are very large, up to 1 foot (30 cm.) long, and often colourful. One species, *Bipalium kewense*, sometimes comes in with tropical plants and turns up from time to time in hothouses.

Britain's other group of turbellarians consists of the rhabdocoels. They resemble the planarians in shape but are rarely more than 5 mm. long and they do not have the three-branched gut. Rhabdocoels are generally more or less transparent, although often brightly coloured. They live in salt and fresh, usually still, water. Many reproduce by budding and the new individuals often remain attached to each other so that they form loose chains. One of the most interesting is *Microstomum lineare*. This and other species of the genus feed on hydra. Far from being deterred by the stinging-cells, the

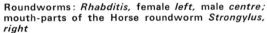

Roundworms: *Rhabditis,* female *left,* male *centre;* mouth-parts of the Horse roundworm *Strongylus, right*

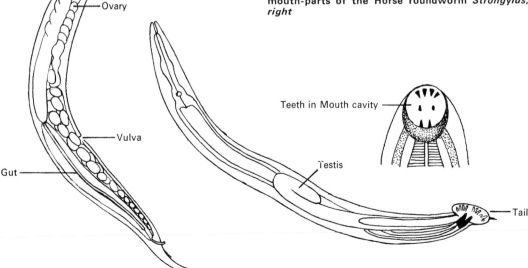

Mouth

Lip

Pharynx

Ovary

Vulva

Gut

Testis

Teeth in Mouth cavity

Tail

flatworms use them for their own protection. Somehow the unused stinging-cells from the hydras are not digested but are carried to the surface of the flatworm where they are orientated correctly for the defence of their new owner.

The tapeworms and most of the flukes are internal parasites in other animals and they often cause a great deal of damage. They are, however, outside the scope of a work of this kind not only because their complicated life-histories would take so long to explain, but because they are mainly of interest to the specialist. A few flukes are external parasites on fishes. *Gyrodactylus* can be found from time to time on the gills of various fishes. It resembles a planarian but is distinguished by the large sucker at the hind end.

Gardeners are sometimes troubled with what they call the potato eelworm, which sometimes gets on to their tomatoes as well. This is only one of 10,000 species of roundworms, known to the scientist as Nematoda. Although we rarely see them they are all around us in extremely large numbers. Best known are the parasites, which attack plants and other animals, but there are huge numbers living free in the soil and in fresh and salt water, and to give an idea how they penetrate everywhere, one species, *Turbatrix aceti*, even lives in vinegar sediment. Indeed, roundworms are just about the most numerous of the multi-cellular animals. There may, for example, be up to 20 million per square yard of grassland soil, while a single rotting apple has been known to yield 90,000 assorted roundworms. The free-living nematodes are generally very small, extremely thin and rarely more than $\frac{1}{16}$ inch (1·6 mm.) long, more or less colourless and almost invisible to the naked eye. One of the easiest ways of getting hold of them, for anyone wishing to study them, is to leave a piece of meat, or even a dead earthworm, in the soil for a few days. The nematodes will soon congregate to feed on the bacteria attacking the meat. They can then be scraped off and examined under the microscope. Most of them will be species of *Rhabditis*, but identification of roundworms is very difficult even for the expert. What the microscope does reveal is that they have a surprisingly detailed structure for such small animals. Compared with the flatworms, there is a more complex digestive system and a notable improvement in the nervous system, including further development of the 'brain'.

They are no less complex in matters of reproduction. Usually the sexes are separate. The males are identifiable by the fan-shaped bursa at the hind end which acts as a sucker for clinging to the female during pairing. Usually males and females are equally numerous but the males in some species are very rare or even absent altogether. In these the species is perpetuated by parthenogenesis, or virgin birth, or else by a strange form of hermaphroditism in which the sex organs are first male and then female. In the parthenogenesis the eggs develop without being fertilized. In the hermaphrodites the young adults produce and store sperm and then, as they get older, they start to produce eggs. These are fertilized by their own sperm but develop normally from then on. Usually the eggs are laid before they hatch, but in some species they hatch inside the female's body.

Young roundworms normally moult four times before reaching maturity and they often pass through a resting stage after the second moult, the skin of the second stage remaining around the young worm and protecting it against drought and cold. At this stage they can be blown over a wide area by wind or carried on the feet of animals.

While the majority of roundworms in the soil feed on bacteria and various microscopic animals, a few feed by nibbling plant roots. They do little damage unless present in very large numbers, but it is a small step from nibbling roots to burrowing into them, which is what a number of them have done. The potato eelworm, *Heterodera rostochiensis*, is one of them. This is a native of Peru and has been with us for little more than 50 years, but it has spread to most of the potato-growing regions of western Europe. It is most destructive in the lighter soils. The juvenile worms, usually misnamed larvae, penetrate the small roots and interfere with the flow of water and sap. A plant can carry several thousand of them without injury but a heavier infestation soon weakens the plants and causes a substantial drop in the potato yield. This is one of the species with males as well as females. They mature in a few weeks and the males then leave the roots. The females remain behind, their bodies swollen with eggs, and later they push through the root tissues to the outside where their eggs are fertilized. After fertilization the female's body forms a tough skin round the egg and she then dies. The bag of eggs, known as the cyst, drops off into the soil.

Each cyst contains up to 600 eggs and they can remain alive for as long as 10 years. They will eventually hatch spontaneously, but chemicals produced by the potato roots themselves cause them to hatch early. The only effective way of controlling the potato eelworm is to have a long cycle of crop rotation so that most of the eggs hatch and the young worms die before a new potato crop is grown.

Many animals, man included, are subject to attack by roundworm parasites. Most of the parasites live in the food-canal. Some feed on the digested food of the host. Others feed on blood and tissue from the gut-wall and have rings of teeth round the mouth to hold on and rasp away their food. One of the largest nematodes, *Ascaris lumbricoides*, reaching up to 16 inches (41 cm.) long, lives free in the intestines of man and pigs. In Britain, where sanitation is efficient, people are rarely infected but it is a different story in regions where human excrement is allowed to contaminate drinking-water. Like all parasites, nematodes have a high reproductive rate to ensure that at least some offspring will find suitable hosts. The female *Ascaris* may lay as many as 200,000 eggs every day. All domestic animals have

roundworms, but unless the infection is severe these have little effect and farm livestock are generally dosed at regular intervals to keep the infestation at a low level.

Hair-worms resemble roundworms in several ways although they are not closely related to them. There are only four British species but *Gordius villoti* is quite common in stagnant water during the colder months of the year. A foot (30 cm.) or more long, it looks rather like a coarse hair moving about by whip-like contortions of the body. Adult hair-worms do not feed but the larvae, hatching from strings of eggs attached to water-plants, are parasitic inside arthropods, especially insects living in or near water. The worm may pass through two hosts during its development. It may, for example, start off in a midge larva and continue its existence in the beetle that eats the midge larva. The worms are mature in the late summer and it is said that parasitized hosts actually make their way back to the water for the emergence of the adult parasites.

A true nematode, very like the hair-worm in its ways, is the thunderworm, *Mermis*. It lives in grasshoppers and other insects when young, feeding on their internal organs. Then in summer we sometimes find the adult, thread-like and up to 20 inches (51 cm.) long, coiled up in the top-soil looking like a tangle of cotton. More often people see the worm climbing over rose bushes after rain, especially after a thunderstorm.

The true worm may be distinguished from the roundworms and others like them by the body being divided into numerous rings or segments. The zoologist speaks of earthworms and others related to them as ringed worms or *Annelida*.

There are three main groups of annelids: the polychaetes (meaning many bristles) or bristle worms, which are all marine; the oligochaetes (oligo=few), which include the earthworms and various freshwater worms; and the leeches, which live mainly in fresh water.

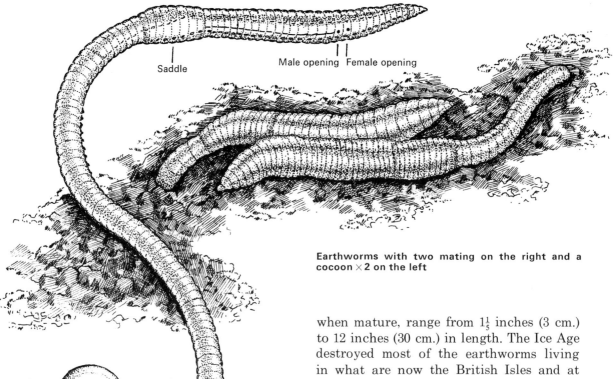

Saddle   Male opening Female opening

Earthworms with two mating on the right and a cocoon × 2 on the left

Oligochaete worms vary in length from about $\frac{1}{5}$ inch (5 mm.) to more than 3 yards (3 m.), although the British species do not even approach this upper limit. *Lumbricus terrestris*, our largest earthworm, rarely exceeds 12 inches (30 cm.) in length. Each segment carries a few short bristles, very short and hard to see in earthworms although they may be much longer on some of the aquatic species.

The British earthworms all belong to the family Lumbricidae, and there are 25 species. They are all purple or bluish brown and,

when mature, range from $1\frac{1}{5}$ inches (3 cm.) to 12 inches (30 cm.) in length. The Ice Age destroyed most of the earthworms living in what are now the British Isles and at least 17 of our present species are immigrants, brought in by various agencies during the last few thousand years.

Earthworms are very uniform in structure and a brief description of *L. terrestris* will serve for them all. The body is more or less cylindrical, tapering to a point in front and usually flattened a little at the rear. The number of segments varies – usually more than 100 – and each is similar to the next except that certain segments in the front half of the worm bear the openings of the reproductive organs.

Each segment carries four pairs of tiny bristles on the lower side, difficult to see but easily felt if a worm is rubbed with a finger. They are the worm's equivalent of legs. The worm has two sets of muscles in its body-wall, one set running lengthways and the other running round the body. Rhythmic contraction of these muscles, combined with the action of the bristles, produces movement. The circular muscles of the front region contract, this part becoming long and thin and nosing forward.

The bristles of the front part are then put out to hold the worm while contraction of the longitudinal muscles then draws the next region forward. These waves of contraction pass rhythmically down the body and the whole worm moves forward. Earthworms are helpless on a perfectly smooth surface into which they cannot dig their bristles. The bristles are also used to hold the worms securely in their burrows and they do this very well as you will know if you have watched a thrush trying to pull a worm from the ground: the thrush does not always win.

Earthworms are scavengers, tunnelling through the ground partly by squeezing between the particles and partly by swallowing soil as they go and digesting the decaying material and bacteria in it. *L. terrestris* and a few other species will, however, come to the surface at night and drag dead leaves into their burrows. The indigestible residue is later passed out through the anus and is used as a sort of lining plaster to the burrow by most species, but two, *Allolobophora nocturna* and *A. longa*, deposit it as wormcasts on the surface.

When fully mature the worms develop the familiar clitellum or saddle, a swollen, glandular region occupying several segments round about segment 32, the exact position varying from species to species. Its function is to produce the egg-cocoon. Almost all earthworms pair underground but *L. terrestris* pairs on the surface on warm, damp nights. Earthworms are hermaphrodite and as well as testes and ovaries, each has two pairs of spermathecae which receive sperm from the other worm. During pairing the two come together each with its saddle closely pressed against the spermathecae openings of the other. They dig their bristles in and the two become surrounded by a sheath of mucus. Sperms are released and travel along to the saddle of the same worm, from where they are passed into the spermathecae of the partner. The worms then separate and, after some days, a cylinder of skin breaks away from the saddle. The worm

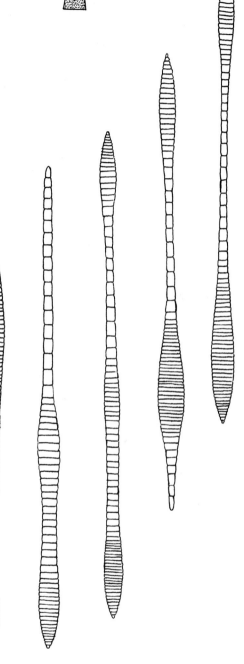

A simplified diagram to show how an earthworm moves, by stretching out the front end, anchoring it with bristles, and then drawing the rest of the body along stage by stage

backs out of the cylinder and, while doing so, discharges into it eggs and sperm from the spermathecae. The ends of the skin cylinder close up to form the cocoon, pea-sized and dark brown, and the eggs (as a rule only one develops in a cocoon of *L. terrestris*) hatch in a few weeks. The breeding-season extends from the spring to the late autumn and, during this time, each worm will mate several times, each mating resulting in a dozen or more cocoons. Little is known of the natural life span of worms, but several species have lived for 10 years or more in captivity.

There are tremendous numbers of earth-worms in the soil and they play a vital part in maintaining soil fertility. Worm popula-tions are generally highest on permanent pastures, where animal dung and abundant plant roots provide an inexhaustible food-supply. When a pasture is ploughed up the worm population gradually falls. Estimates of worm populations in pasture-land go as high as 3 million per acre, although 500,000 is probably a truer figure for most pastures. These open up the soil, improving drainage and allowing air to penetrate. They also act as natural ploughs, churning the soil over and over. Most of the undigested soil is deposited at or near the surface and, as they cannot swallow particles more than about $\frac{1}{12}$ inch (2 mm.) in diameter, they are sifting the soil all the time, producing a fine stone-less surface layer. By bringing soil to the surface they help to replenish the top-soil with minerals lost by leaching. They also perform a natural liming because they absorb a lot of lime when swallowing soil and special glands secrete excess calcium car-bonate which passes out with the residue. It is worth remembering these valuable functions when cursing the worm-casts on a lawn. Many a fine lawn has become water-logged through the wholesale poisoning of its worm population.

Earthworms also play a part in burying objects, even buildings. The stones of Stone-henge appear to be sinking at a rate of about 6 inches (15 cm.) per century. Charles

Darwin was the first really to appreciate the importance of earthworms and his book, *The Formation of Vegetable Mould Through the Action of Worms*, gives a fascinating account of their activities.

Although the members of the Lumbricidae are all called earthworms, not all of them live in the soil. Many live in dunghills and rubbish-heaps or in mud-banks round lakes and rivers. The Brandling, *Eisenia foetida*, recognizable by its orange banding, is a well-known inhabitant of the compost-heap and also a constant member of the angler's bait-tin. Of the worms that do live in the soil, the common ones include *L. terrestris* (brownish red, up to 12 inches/30 cm.), *L. rubellus* (red, 8 inches/20 cm.), *L. castaneus* (dark red, $1\frac{1}{5}$ inches/3 cm.), *Allolobophora longa* (grey, 10 inches/25 cm.), *A. nocturna* (brownish grey, 10 inches/25 cm.), *A. cali-ginosa* (pale pinkish, $3\frac{3}{5}$ inches/9 cm.), and *Octolasium lacteum* (bluish white, $7\frac{1}{5}$ inches/ 18 cm.).

Most worms, especially the young ones, remain in the top few inches of the soil,

(*opposite*) Waterside insects, *from left to right and top to bottom*: Alder fly, *Sialis* sp.; dragonfly, *Libellula depressa*; a stone fly; two damselflies, the Banded agrion, *Agrion splendens* and *Lestes sponsa*; a lacewing, *Sisyra* sp.; Gold ringed dragonfly, *Cordulegaster boltoni*; a mayfly, *Ephemera danica*; China marks moth, *Nymphula nymphaeata*; caddis-fly, *Phryganea grandis*; a caddis-fly, *Leptocerus* sp.

(*overleaf, left*) Hedgerow insects, all ×2, *from left to right and top to bottom*: Hawthorn shield bug, *Acanthosoma haemorrhoidale*; Green lacewing, *Chrysopa* sp.; Scorpion-fly, *Panorpa* sp. and insert to show beak; Cuckoo spit with adult frog-hopper below and Linceine plant bug; Dark bush-cricket, *Pholidoptera griseoaptera*; *Capsus ater*; Pied shield bug, *Sehirus bicolor*; Common field grasshopper, *Chorthippus brunneus*; Great green bush-cricket, *Tettigonia viridissima*; House cricket, *Acheta domes-tica*; Field cricket, *Gryllus campestris*

(*overleaf, right*) Butterflies, *from left to right and top to bottom*: Large blue, *Maculinea arion*, male and caterpillar, with *below*, Chalkhill blues, *Lysandra coridon*, female and male with wings closed; Clouded yellow, *Colias croceus*, female; Mountain ringlet, *Erebia epiphron*, male with below, Large skipper, *Ochlodes venata*, male; Green hairstreaks, *Callophrys rubi*, female and male; Swallowtail, *Papilio machaon*, male; Brimstone, *Gonepteryx rhamni*, males, and a Small copper, *Lycaena phlaeas*, male; Orange tips, *Anthocaris cardamines*, males and caterpillar; Scotch argus, *Erebia aethiops*

though *L. terrestris* can go as deep as $4\frac{1}{2}$ feet (135 cm.) in cold or dry weather. Some species will come out of the ground at night, but although they have no eyes, they withdraw into their burrows at the first sign of light. They soon die if left exposed to sunlight: ultra-violet appears to be lethal to them. The two cast-making worms, *A. longa* and *A. nocturna*, regularly go into a diapause (inactive state) during the summer months and hide away deep in their burrows.

Worms are most numerous on the light alkaline and neutral soils. Acid, sandy soils do not support many worms and this is one factor contributing to the coarse vegetation on these soils. A good population of earthworms will drag down dead leaves and prevent the build up of a mat of undecayed vegetation on the surface: fine grasses can then flourish.

Also living in the soil, especially where it is damp and contains plenty of humus, are small, white, almost transparent worms known as 'pot worms'. Mostly in the region of $\frac{1}{5}$ inch (5 mm.) long, these are very like earthworms but are placed in a separate family, the Enchytraeidae.

We often see worms on pavements in big cities or squashed by cars, or even merely dried up, as they were crossing the roads. People often ask why this should be, but there is no simple answer to the question except that probably the worms had come to the surface during the night through cracks in the pavement, had lost their way and had failed to find an easy way back into the soil. More important, the sight of these is an indication of how many worms are living under pavements and roads. They remind us that in a ditch at Verulam sealed over by floors of successive buildings during the

first four centuries A.D. have been found during excavations populations of mudworms, *Eophila oculata*. These were incarcerated and being able to live with little oxygen, and having presumably sufficient food there, have continued to live permanently imprisoned.

Another 'worm phenomenon' on our doorsteps is the heaps of pebbles often found on gravel paths, as if torrential rains had swirled the gravel. These hillocks have been made by worms. Each may consist of 200 pebbles weighing about an ounce (28 gm.) or more. And at the centre of the hillock a worm is living. After dark, especially when a light rain is falling, one can watch the worms – using a red lamp – picking up pebbles using the mouth as a sucker, to add to the heap. By listening intently one can even hear the chink of pebbles.

Several families of oligochaetes live in water, including some members of the earthworm family Lumbricidae. The water worms are mostly under an inch (25 mm.) long but are similar to the earthworms in structure. Many are transparent and their internal anatomy can easily be seen under a low-power microscope. They also are scavengers and live burrowing among the mud and vegetable rubbish at the bottoms of ponds and streams, some making little tubes of mud, or among the water-plants.

Mostly they live in shallow water, rarely below 3 feet (91 cm.) depth, although some *Tubifex* species can live at much greater depths. *Tubifex* can be seen on the filthy mud exposed at low tide in the freshwater stretches of tidal rivers such as the Thames. They may sometimes be found in mud bordering cattle ponds or even in drinking-troughs. There is often little oxygen in such situations and many water worms have haemoglobin in their blood which helps them absorb what oxygen there is.

These aquatic oligochaetes breed in the same way as earthworms except that some use an asexual method more often than they lay eggs. The worm, by reorganization of its tissues in certain regions becomes two worms

Butterflies, *from left to right and top to bottom*: Comma, *Polygonia c-album*, males, with wings spread and *below* closed to show comma mark; Purple emperor, *Apatura iris*, male; Silver-washed fritillary, *Argynnis paphia*; White admiral, *Limenitis camilla*, female; Small tortoiseshell, *Aglais urticae*, male; Ringlet, *Aphantopus hyperanthus*, male; Peacock, *Nymphalis io*, male; Marbled white, *Melanargia galathea*, female; Red admiral, *Vanessa atalantica*, males and caterpillar

which then separate. Very often, before they themselves have separated, the new individuals begin to divide again and so chains of several worms may be found. The common green and red *Lumbriculus variegatus* apparently never lays eggs but reproduces solely by breaking into pieces, each of which grows into a new worm.

One of the best-known aquatic worms is *Tubifex*, of which there are several species.

This is the little red worm used for feeding aquarium fishes. It lives in the mud of lakes and ponds, in little tubes that stick up into the water. It lives head down in the tube and by waving its hind end about sets up currents that bring oxygen for breathing. The lower the oxygen content of the water, the more the worm projects from its tube and the more it waves its tail. A sudden vibration sends the *Tubifex* into its burrow.

A common pond-dwelling worm, *Stylaria*, that crawls about on water-plants can be recognized by its sharp proboscis and the long bristles on its sides. *Haplotaxus*, found in shallow streams and ditches, may be mistaken at first for a hair-worm. It is very slender and up to 1 foot (30 cm.) long, but its segmentation shows it to be a true worm. *Eiseniella*, a member of the Lumbricidae, looks like a typical earthworm but is pink,

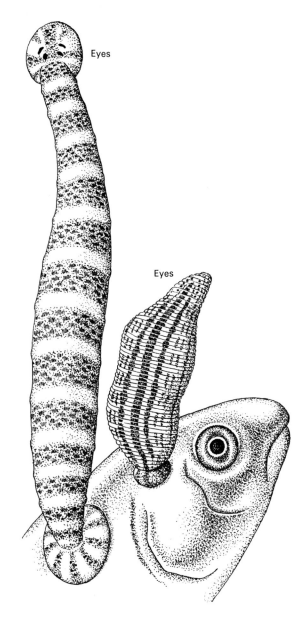
Eyes

Eyes

Leeches ×6: *left,* an extended leech, *Pisicola geometra* and a contracted Medicinal leech, *Hirudo medicinalis*; *right,* the heads of four species; *top left, Glossiphonia complanata* and *right, Hemiclepsis marginata*; *bottom left,* the Horse leech, *Haemopis sanguisuga* and *right, Trocheta subviridis*

about 2 inches (5 cm.) long and has a square-ended tail. It lives in the mud of ponds and streams.

Blood-worms are not worms at all. We find these in water-butts and other standing water, $\frac{1}{2}$ inch (13 mm.) long, blood-red, and swimming by jerky S-shaped contortions of the body. They are the larvae of the midge *Chironomus*, and unlike true worms they have antennae and biting jaws.

Leeches, belonging to the class Hirudinea, are distinguished from other annelids by their flattened shape, the sucker at each end and the lack of bristles. Some live in the sea, others in damp soil, but the majority live in ponds and sluggish streams. All are carnivorous, feeding on the blood of other animals, even devouring the smaller ones completely. There are 11 freshwater species in Britain differing mainly in the shape of the head and the arrangement of the simple eyes. Mature leeches are never less than $\frac{2}{5}$ inch (10 mm.) long and most of our species range from $\frac{4}{5}$ inch (20 mm.) to $2\frac{1}{5}$ inches (51 mm.) when at rest and therefore contracted. They can, however, treble their length when fully extended. They range from pale grey to deep greenish black but this is a poor guide to species because they can alter their colours to some extent to match their background.

Leeches spend most of their time resting under leaves and stones in the water. When disturbed they will seek shelter again, moving about by stretching forward, anchoring by the front sucker, and then contracting the body to draw the hind end forward. Some species will swim away if the disturbance continues, with the body stretched long and slender and swimming with a graceful undulating movement.

Like earthworms, leeches are hermaphrodite and each mature animal has a saddle or clitellum. Pairing is less complicated than in the earthworms but the behaviour of the sperm is unusual. Each leech deposits a packet of sperm on its partner and the sperms then burrow through the skin to reach the ovaries. The fertilized eggs are then laid in a cocoon formed from the clitel-

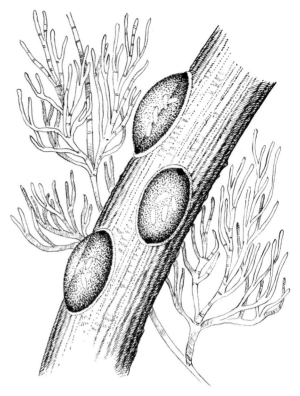

Leech eggs in their cocoons

lum as in earthworms. The cocoons are often flat and horny and attached to stones and water-plants. Some leeches carry their cocoons around attached to their lower surfaces. Others leave the water and deposit them in damp soil. There is no asexual reproduction.

There are two main groups of leeches: those with a piercing beak or proboscis, and those with jaws. The beaked leeches are all blood-suckers: they hold on to the victim with the front sucker and thrust in the beak to draw blood. Water-birds, fishes, snails, as well as other worms are among their victims. The jawed leeches include both flesh-eaters and blood-suckers. The jaws are armed with teeth which cut into the victim, although the Medicinal leech, *Hirudo medicinalis*, is the only one in Britain capable of penetrating human skin. Huge numbers of these were once used in blood-letting, which was believed to cure sick people by getting rid of their 'bad blood'. The Medicinal leech is not a native animal, however, and those released into our ponds are fast dying out.

The Horse leech, *Haemopis sanguisuga*, similar to the Medicinal leech but much more common, is usually a rusty brown and just over an inch (3 cm.) long when at rest. It lives in muddy ponds and streams, feeding on snails, insects and other worms. One of the flesh-eating leeches, it uses its teeth to chop up its victims. The teeth are, however, quite blunt and incapable of cutting human skin, let alone the skin of a horse. It may occasionally have fastened on to the noses and mouths of horses drinking from leech-infested waters, but 'horse' here means large. Horse leeches lay their cocoons in damp soil round the water's edge. *Herpobdella* is another common leech, similar in size and colour to the Horse leech, although somewhat more slender. Its brown, oval cocoons abound on the undersides of water-lily leaves.

Our largest leech is the brownish-green *Trocheta subviridis*, up to 4 inches (10 cm.) when at rest, and more cylindrical than the other leeches. It is a flesh-eater and often leaves the water in search of earthworms and insects.

Flesh-eating leeches feed frequently, usually at night, but the blood-suckers often go many months without a meal. When they do feed they may take two or three times their own weight of blood and store it in special pouches of the gut. Bacterial activity in the gut seems to prevent the blood from decaying – an interesting reversal of the usual – while an anticoagulant called 'hirudin' keeps it in a liquid state. The leech then digests a little at a time. The leech also pumps hirudin into the wound while it is feeding and its anti-clotting action means that a wound will continue to bleed for some time after the leech has dropped off. Some leeches also inject an anaesthetic or pain-killing substance, enabling them to feed unnoticed by their victims.

At first sight there seems little to connect the annelids with insects, yet there are fossils as well as a few living species to bridge the gap and suggest how the ancestors of our present-day earthworms, hundreds of millions of years ago, probably gave rise to the earliest insects. It would have been logical, therefore, to go next to the Arthropoda, the jointed-legged animals that include the insects. For the sake of completeness, however, we need to step aside and deal with a group of animals that have no obvious relationship with either of these. They are the moss animals, so called because those living in the sea often coat the surfaces of rocks much as moss covers boulders on land. They are colonies of small animals formerly known as polypides because each has a superficial resemblance to coral polyps. Most of them live in the sea but there are a few in fresh water. They were for a long time thought to be related to the coelenterates because they look so like tiny sea-anemones, but they are a good deal more complex than these. They form two distinct groups known as the Endoprocta and the Ectoprocta, now generally regarded as separate phyla. They are, however, so alike in general appearance and habits that most naturalists continue to treat the two groups under one name, the Polyzoa, literally 'many animals', or Bryozoa, moss animals. All our freshwater polyzoans belong to the Ectoprocta.

Each individual in the colony is called a zooid – 'polypide' is now obsolete – and is like a transparent cup, through which runs a U-shaped food-canal. Around the mouth of the zooid is a retractable crown of tentacles with which it obtains its food. The tentacles are clothed with tiny cilia which vibrate rhythmically and draw currents of water over the tentacles. Bacteria, protozoans, and other morsels are trapped by the cilia and used as food. Each polyzoan colony starts life as a single zooid, which buds off fresh zooids and each of these in turn buds off other zooids until a little colony is built up, all connected by a horny or jelly-like matrix secreted by the animals themselves.

Three species are quite common in ponds

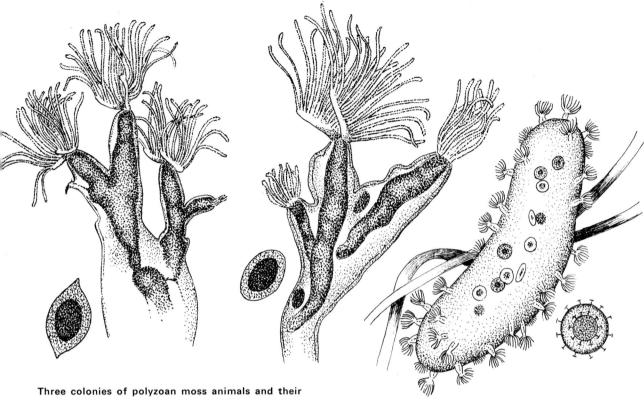

Three colonies of polyzoan moss animals and their statoblasts, *from left to right*, **Lophopus** ×15, **Plumatella** ×15, **Cristatella** ×1½. The statoblasts are ×30

and streams, although they are not very easy to find. The animals quickly withdraw their tentacles when disturbed and, in that state, the colonies are easily passed over as lifeless objects. Late summer is the best time to look for polyzoans and the best procedure is to collect water-plants, especially duckweed and lily leaves, and put them into aquarium tanks for later examination. If left undisturbed for a while the zooids expand and show themselves.

The one most frequently found, *Lophopus cristallinus*, lives on the rootlets of duckweed. Incidentally, it was the first polyzoan ever to be described. Each colony of *Lophopus* is about ⅖ inch (10 mm.) in diameter and is embedded in a jelly-like matrix. Its zooids are among the largest of all polyzoan zooids but there are only about a dozen in each colony. *Cristatella mucedo* also has a matrix

of jelly but the colony is much larger than *Lophopus*, because it is made up of many more zooids. It is about 2 inches (5 cm.) long and can be found on a variety of water-plants. When all the tentacles are out the colony looks rather like a pale green furry caterpillar. Most polyzoans are found on the undersides of leaves and stones, but *Cristatella* is one of the few that seeks the light. It can actually creep slowly over the vegetation in search of a favourable site. The only other common polyzoan in British fresh water is *Plumatella repens*. The zooids of this species live in horny tubes attached to stones and river-banks and a colony looks like small branching plant roots. This species and some others occasionally get into water-pipes and block the flow.

At the approach of winter the zooids die off and the matrix breaks down, although

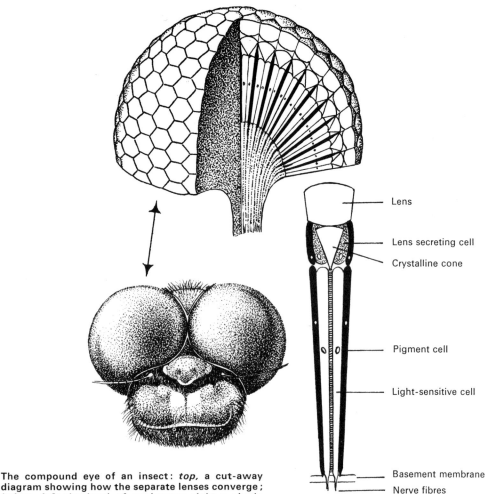

Lens

Lens secreting cell

Crystalline cone

Pigment cell

Light-sensitive cell

Basement membrane

Nerve fibres

The compound eye of an insect: *top,* a cut-away diagram showing how the separate lenses converge; *below, left* the head of an insect; *right* a single ommatidium to show structure

the horny tubes of *Plumatella* may remain for some months after the death of the animals. They leave behind numerous tiny buds called statoblasts. These are formed during the summer inside the zooids and each consists of a group of cells enclosed by two horny plates. The statoblasts are generally oval or spherical and about $\frac{1}{25}$ inch (1 mm.) across, those of each species having its characteristic pattern. When the adults die the statoblasts are released and float in the water until the spring. Many of them are washed on to the banks and from there they may be transported to new areas by the wind or on the feet of animals. The statoblasts of

Cristatella are provided with minute hooks which presumably catch into other animals and so aid dispersal.

The two plates of the statoblast separate in the spring and a young polyzoan creeps out. After a short period of drifting in the water it settles down and begins to form a new colony by budding.

Although asexual reproduction, through the formation of statoblasts, is the most important as far as the freshwater polyzoans are concerned, sexual reproduction does take place from time to time. The zooids are hermaphrodite and produce both eggs and sperm. The fertilized egg develops into a free-swimming larva very like the larvae of annelids and molluscs.

The Arthropoda, by far the largest phylum in the animal kingdom, includes crustaceans, insects, spiders, millipedes, centipedes and other animals accounting for more than 80 per cent of the known animal species. The arthropods are segmented animals like the annelid worms and there can be little doubt that the arthropods have descended from the annelids. Two of the most noticeable advances are the development of limbs and of a definite head.

The limbs, or appendages to give them their proper name, occur in pairs and each is made up of several segments or joints, which gives the phylum its name, the word arthropod meaning simply 'jointed foot'. In the ancestral arthropods the appendages were probably all more or less alike and probably occurred on almost all the segments, but today's arthropods bear many types of dissimilar appendages. Some retain the ancestral function of moving the animal from place to place. Others are concerned with catching and eating food, for arthropods have no jaws inside the mouth and some of the appendages of the head have taken on the job of cutting and chewing the food before passing it into the mouth. Some appendages have been converted into sense-organs – the antennae – while others are involved in the reproductive activities of the animals. Many segments bear no appendages at all.

Although the earthworm has a definite front end, it has no real head. Some of the more active marine bristle-worms have a distinct head region, but there is nothing as pronounced as the arthropod head. This development is associated with a much greater development of the nervous system and a more active way of life. The head contains an elaborate brain and bears a number of sense-organs. The antennae or feelers, when present, are specially modified limbs acting as organs of taste, smell and touch. Almost all arthropods have eyes of some sort and, in most crustaceans and insects, there are very complex organs known as compound eyes.

The compound eye is made up of a number of cone-shaped units called ommatidia, packed tightly together and each having a tiny lens at the surface of the eye. This construction gives the eye a latticed appearance when seen through a lens. Each ommatidium transmits light rays along to the optic nerve and the arthropod builds up a mosaic picture from all the units. Such a picture is not very clear but the animal does not need to see detail. Movement in the surroundings is the important thing and this is easily detected by the compound eye because a moving object affects different units in turn as it moves across the field of view. The number of ommatidia in a compound eye varies from species to species. It is highest in certain dragonflies, which rely entirely on sight to catch their food. Some of them have 30,000 units in each eye. On the other hand, some ants, which find their way about by the senses of smell and touch, have only half a dozen ommatidia. Some arthropods have no compound eyes at all and rely on simple eyes which do little more than detect light and darkness.

Less obvious than the limbs and the head, but still very important, is the tough waterproof cuticle of most arthropods. It is made of a horny material called chitin. It is flexible at the joints, to allow movement, but harder elsewhere and often impregnated with calcium carbonate and other materials which give it extra strength. It is this waterproof cuticle that has enabled so many arthropods to divorce themselves from a watery environment and spread over the surface of the earth. A hard outer covering of this kind does, however, have one big disadvantage: it does not grow with the animal. The arthropods, therefore, have to moult periodically and grow larger coats to accommodate their increasing bulk. The new coverings are soft at first and the animals are easy prey for their enemies at such times.

Reproduction in arthropods is normally sexual, with separate males and females.

Males are rare in certain species, though, and virgin birth (parthenogenesis) is quite common, especially at certain times of the year. There is usually some kind of metamorphosis during the life-cycle, the young animal differing somewhat in appearance from the adult. This is especially so in many insects and crustaceans.

The arthropods are arranged in a number of classes whose relationship to each other is not always very clear. There are fairly clear links between the myriapods (millipedes and centipedes) and the insects, but the crustaceans do not fit into this picture. The spiders and their relatives are even further removed because, unlike all other arthropods, they have no antennae. The predominantly aquatic crustaceans, the millipedes, centipedes and insects, and the spiders and their relatives may well represent three distinct groups that have arisen independently from the ancestral annelids.

Crustaceans are mainly aquatic arthropods and the feature which immediately distinguishes them from all other arthropods is that they have two pairs of antennae, although in some species one of the two pairs of antennae may be small and inconspicuous. The cuticle is frequently of a stony texture, as in crabs, due to impregnation with calcium carbonate, but although this saves them from drying, all but the smallest crustaceans have gills which absorb oxygen from the water, so they are tied to a watery environment. The majority, including nearly all the large species, live in the sea. Freshwater species are numerous, however, and a few live on land. Our only terrestrial crustaceans are the woodlice, although even these have not completely broken away from their aquatic origins and cannot live in really dry places.

One of the simplest crustaceans is the Fairy shrimp, *Chirocephalus diaphanus*, transparent, up to nearly $1\frac{1}{4}$ inches (3 cm.) long and, apart from a reddish tinge on its extremities, almost completely colourless. Its main habitat is small temporary pools

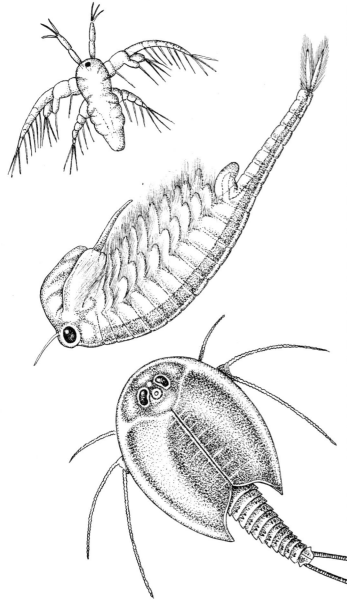

The Fairy shrimp, *Chirocephalus diaphanus, centre* with its larva *above* and Triops, *Apus cancriformis, below*

that fill up in winter and disappear again before summer is finished. Even very small pools, such as water-filled cart-tracks, may support it. The Fairy shrimp belongs to the group of crustaceans known as the Branchiopoda (or gill-footed) because their limbs act as gills as well as organs of locomotion. The Fairy shrimp has 11 pairs of trunk limbs which are broad and fringed with bristles, and they are constantly moving. The shrimp swims on its back and the rhythmic beating of the limbs sets up water currents which drive it forward. At the same time the fringes of bristles strain particles from the water which are conveyed to the mouth where they are sorted, the edible particles being chewed and swallowed, the rest being rejected. These limbs are well supplied with blood and, as well as propelling the animal and collecting its food, they take up oxygen from the water as it flows over them.

During mating, the male holds the female with specially modified, clasping antennae. The eggs have tough shells and are very resistant to cold and drought. They are unharmed by the pools drying up. Provided they remain wet they hatch the following spring but where pools dry up many eggs are carried by the wind or on the feet of animals especially and transported to new homes. So Fairy shrimps can suddenly appear in a new pool.

The closely related Brine shrimp, *Artemia salina*, lives in salt-marshes but it appears to be extinct in the British Isles now. In Triops, *Apus cancriformis*, another relative, the head and trunk regions are covered over with a shield or carapace, so it looks a miniature of the marine living fossil, the Horseshoe crab. This is another of those extraordinary animals in which males are rare and the race is carried on largely through parthenogenesis, or what is often called virgin birth. Triops is not often seen but it can turn up anywhere, in small pools, at any time and quite unexpectedly.

The best known of freshwater crustaceans are the water fleas, the little pinkish creatures that can be seen bobbing up and down in almost any standing water. There are many species. *Daphnia pulex*, daphney to the aquarist, about 2 mm. long, is one of the most common. Those who keep aquarium fishes – the real enthusiasts – go out

Water fleas: *Simocephalus, left,* Daphney, *Daphnia pulex, right;* both carrying eggs

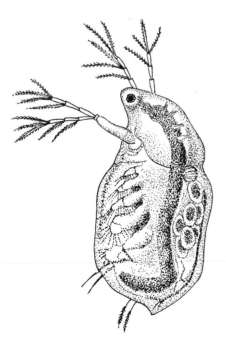
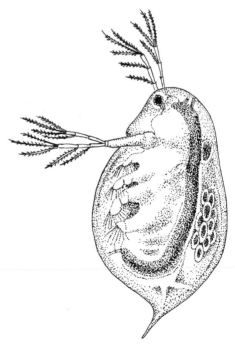

with their dip-nets and collect these and related species, and they are frequently sold, both living and dead, in pets' stores. Like the Fairy shrimps, they belong to the Branchiopoda, but they are very different in shape. They have fewer legs and the whole body behind the head is enclosed in a transparent carapace, an outgrowth of cuticle, attached to the back of the animal and curving round on both sides, enclosing the body and limbs like a stiff cloak. The body is more or less transparent and, under even a low-power microscope, one can see not only the limbs moving inside the carapace, but the action of the heart and digestive system as well.

The first pair of antennae are generally small and are sense-organs. The second pair are large and branched and used for swimming. 'Daphney' stands head up in the water and beats its antennae up and down. Each beat jerks the animal upwards and as soon as the antennae stop beating the animal starts to sink. This jerking motion is responsible for the name water flea.

Inside the carapace are the trunk limbs. These play no part in movement and are concerned solely with feeding and breathing. The five pairs differ in shape but all are fringed with long bristles. The beating of these limbs draws a current of water in through the carapace opening and the bristles strain out algae, bacteria and other particles which are then passed to the mouth.

For most of the year only female water fleas can be found and they reproduce parthenogenetically. Their eggs are laid into a brood-pouch just under the carapace, between it and the animal's back and they remain there until they hatch. This takes only a day or two but the young water fleas, which are just like their parent, remain in the pouch for a further day or two before venturing into the water. There may be as many as 20 youngsters in the pouch at one time. They are normally all female, but towards autumn male water fleas are hatched. At the same time the females start to produce eggs that need fertilization. They are ferti-

lized within the brood-pouch but they develop very slowly and, next time the water flea moults, they are deposited in a hardened piece of the carapace cuticle called the ephippium. Protected in this way, they are very resistant to cold and drought and can survive the winter with no difficulty. These 'winter eggs', of which there are only two or three in each ephippium, all give rise to females which begin breeding in the spring. It appears that falling water temperatures in autumn stimulate the development of the males and the sexual eggs (i.e. those needing to be fertilized). Males may, however, appear at other times, at the beginning of summer for example. The stimulus here is either overcrowding or a shortage of food and, although asexual reproduction still continues, the appearance of the males and the resistant eggs at this time acts also as an insurance in case the pond should dry up.

Water fleas are most abundant in ponds with a high organic content; that is, ponds with plenty of rotting leaves or other such materials. They often exist in such numbers as to make the water almost red. Their numbers build up very rapidly in spring as a result of asexual reproduction and an abundance of food. The water fleas are not evenly distributed through the water, however, and a pond may be swarming with them at one end while the other end has hardly any. Water fleas are very sensitive to light and will always congregate in the most favourable areas, where it is not too light and not too dark. So sensitive are they that they alter their level in the water according to whether the day is bright or dull; in bright sunlight they go down, in dimmer light they swim nearer the surface.

Two other kinds of small crustaceans are commonly found in ponds with the water-fleas. These are the ostracods and the copepods. Ostracods look like minute shellfish, the whole body being enclosed in a tiny hinged shell. They are extremely common but, because they are usually less than 2 mm. long, they are seen only when pond-water is examined closely. At rest the animal

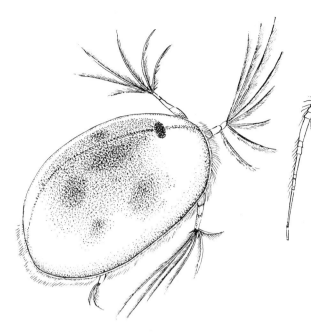
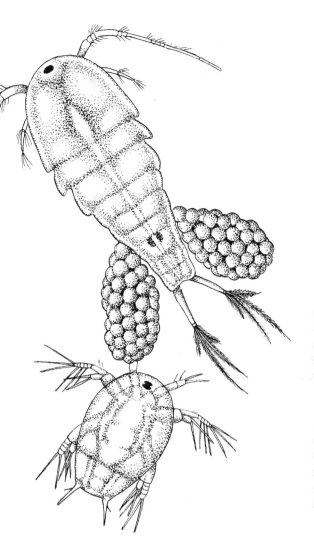

An ostracod, *left* and a copepod, *Cyclops* with egg-sacs, *right* and first-stage larva *below*

closes the shell tightly but when active it opens the shell and pushes out two pairs of antennae which it uses to row itself through the water. It can also creep over solid surfaces by walking on the second pair of antennae and one pair of legs. Ostracods take a variety of foods, including other small animals. Small particles are drawn into the shell by movement of the limbs inside it, but larger pieces are shovelled in by the antennae and the jaws. As in the water fleas, oxygen is extracted from the water flowing through the shell.

Males are unknown in some ostracod species and reproduction is entirely by parthenogenesis. Other species have males and females in more or less equal numbers and the females lay their eggs in little rusty-coloured clusters on water-plants. The eggs normally hatch in a month or two but they are not harmed if the pond dries up during the summer. In fact they are so resistant that some have been known to hatch after being kept in dried mud for 30 years. These resistant eggs can easily be carried from pond to

pond by wind or by animals. The young ostracods hatching from the eggs are not quite like their parents but the brownish opaque shell hides most of the differences.

The copepods are small, rather pear-shaped, abundant in nearly all stretches of fresh water. The British species are rarely more than $\frac{1}{10}$ inch (3 mm.) long but they are easily spotted in a dish of pond-water by their shape, the relatively long first antennae, and the egg-sacs carried by the females. Best known of our copepods are species of the genus *Cyclops*, named after the one-eyed giants of Greek mythology which, like the copepods, had one eye at the centre of the head. This feature is also shared by the water-fleas and the ostracods, but the eye of the copepod is not a compound eye like that of the water-flea.

The first pair of antennae are quite long but the second pair are short and often unseen. Behind them, on the underside of the animal, are several pairs of appendages concerned with movement. These swimming limbs produce a rapid, jerky movement which makes an individual *Cyclops* difficult to catch, even when in a small container. *Cyclops* can also swim, more leisurely, by beating its antennae.

Although some of the smaller and more primitive copepods feed by filtering particles from the water, *Cyclops* appears to capture individual food-particles with its mouthparts. It feeds mainly on microscopic algae but it can also nibble at larger pieces, such as dead worms and other animals. The limbs do not play much of a role in breathing

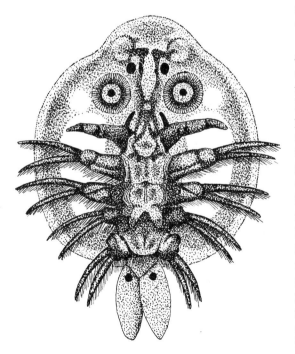

A fish louse, *Argulus,* drawn from below to show suckers

either, much of the oxygen needed by *Cyclops* diffusing in through the body surface.

Male and female *Cyclops* occur in more or less equal numbers and, after fertilization, the female cements her eggs into little clusters called 'egg-sacs' which she carries about attached to her body. The female *Cyclops* always has two of these egg-sacs, but some copepods have only one. The eggs of *Cyclops* all hatch within about 10 days, depending on temperature, and produce larvae which take about a month to change into the adult form. Some copepods, however, can produce resting eggs rather like those of the Fairy shrimps and water-fleas.

Copepods exist in enormous numbers in the sea as well as in fresh water and in both habitats they form a most important item in the diet of fishes. A few copepods have reversed the role, however, and live as parasites on fishes. The young stages are free living but the adults – sometimes only the females – attach themselves to fishes, usually round the gills, and feed by sucking blood. Most of these parasitic copepods live in the sea but there are a few species in our fresh waters.

The fish lice, of which *Argulus foliaceus* is a typical example, are parasitic crustaceans similar in some ways to the copepods but usually placed in a separate group called the Branchiura. They are blood-sucking external parasites attacking various fish species, including trout, pike, perch, dace, and even the little stickleback. The parasites most frequently attack the gill region but they will attach themselves to any part of the body and a single fish may carry many of them. Infested fishes can sometimes be seen hurling themselves at rocks in the water, trying to dislodge the parasites, but they are rarely successful. The lice hold on with two powerful suckers carried on the mouthparts, and their extremely flattened shape means that they can withstand the strongest currents without being washed off. A piercing beak draws blood from the host but the parasites do not remain permanently attached to the fishes: from time to time they

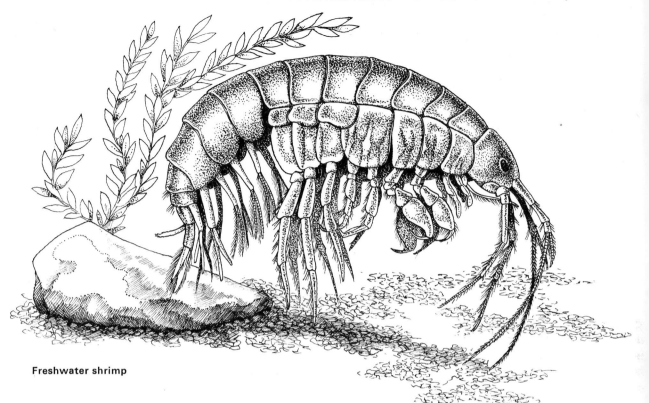

Freshwater shrimp

drop off and swim freely by means of their four pairs of feathery, oar-like legs.

The females, which are larger than the males and about $\frac{1}{4}$ inch (6 mm.) long, lay their eggs in little clusters attached to stones and the young fish lice are just like their parents except in size.

Moving on from the small, mainly planktonic crustaceans, we come to the most advanced group, the Malacostraca. This group contains all the well-known crustaceans such as crabs, shrimps and lobsters, as well as the only truly terrestrial crustaceans, the woodlice. Members of the Malacostraca vary a great deal but almost all of them have 20 segments in the body: six in the head, eight in the thorax, and six in the abdomen, although it is not always easy to make the segments out. The thorax is usually protected by a thick shield or carapace which extends down the sides and usually extends forwards to cover part of the head as well. The compound eyes are usually at the ends of movable stalks, and every segment but the first has a pair of appendages.

The majority of the Malacostraca are marine but there are a few freshwater species. Few of our streams or rivers are without the little Freshwater shrimp, *Gammarus pulex*, in their shallow regions. This lives among the gravel and water-plants and is easily captured with a dip-net, although its need for well-oxygenated water makes it unsuited for aquarium life.

Although not true shrimps, the Freshwater shrimps resemble them in general appearance, being flattened from side to side and strongly curved. It has, however, no carapace and its eyes are not stalked. It is brownish and about $\frac{3}{4}$ inch (19 mm.) long, the females being a little smaller than the males. Its head carries the usual mouthparts and there are five pairs of thoracic legs. The first two of these are strongly clawed and they help to pick up food, which is dead and decaying matter, both vegetable and animal. The next three pairs are used for crawling about on the stream-bed or over the vegetation. These are turned back over the body when not in use. The Freshwater shrimp swims with the first three pairs of abdominal limbs, the shrimp swimming quite fast by straightening the body and vibrating these legs. When it comes to rest the body at once becomes curved again but the abdominal legs continue to vibrate for they ventilate the gills, which are feathery outgrowths from their bases. The last three pairs of abdominal limbs are relatively stout and are used for jumping, propelling the animal up from the stream-bed when it starts to swim. The shrimps will also jump quite well if stranded out of water, a habit even better known to us by their relatives the sand-hoppers of the sea-shore.

Freshwater shrimps breed all the year round although the rate is higher in summer than in winter. Pairing begins with the male clasping the female up underneath his body. The two swim about like this and usually continue to do so for some time after the eggs are laid. The several hundred eggs are attached to the legs of the female and remain there until they hatch. The young are tiny replicas of their parents and, after a short period of attachment to the mother, they swim off to start life on their own.

Water fleas and Freshwater shrimps are not very obvious except to those who dabble in ponds. Nor indeed, but for other reasons, are our largest freshwater crustaceans the crayfishes, which are like small lobsters. We have two species, *Astacus pallipes* and *A. fluviatilis*, although only the former is actually a native of the British Isles. *A. fluviatilis* was introduced from France, where it is reared in large numbers as food, and is now found in a few rivers of southern England. Usually a little longer than the 4 inches (10 cm.) attained by our native species, it can be further distinguished from them by the red colour on the underside of its pincers.

Gills

A crayfish with a detached leg to show gills

Crayfishes need well-aerated waters, which usually means fast-flowing streams. Children sometimes find crayfish in a stream, take them home and put them in an aquarium and are disappointed to find they die within 12 hours. The aquarium must be aerated. Crayfish also require plenty of lime for their skeletons, so they are confined largely to streams in chalk and limestone districts. Their numbers seem to be decreasing rapidly, probably the result of pollution and collecting them for school and laboratory use.

They are largely nocturnal, spending most of their time hiding under stones or in holes in the stream-bank, which is why we seldom see them. They dart away if their hideout is disturbed and their speed, together with their sombre brown or greenish colouring, makes it very difficult for the eye to follow them. The traditional way of catching them is to dangle a small piece of meat into the water on the end of a string. The crayfish grabs the meat with its pincers and can then be hauled out; but children, who do not mind paddling and stooping, can find them without such aids.

Their food consists of any small animals they can catch, including worms, tadpoles, insects and fishes. Prey is carried by the large pincers to the mouth. Behind the pincers come four pairs of legs on which the crayfish walks slowly about the stream-bed in search of prey, but it can also swim slowly by means of the paddle-shaped swimmerets on the abdominal segments. The last pair of limbs form part of the fan-like tail fan which, when the animal is disturbed, is spread as the abdomen is whipped forward with force, shooting the crayfish backwards out of harm's way.

A continuous current of water is maintained over the feathery gills, hidden within the carapace, by the constant vibration of some of the mouth-parts.

Pairing takes place in late autumn. The male, usually slightly larger than the female, turns his mate upside down with his pincers and then, using his specially modified front pair of swimmerets, he sprays sperm on to her swimmerets. The female then lays her eggs and glues them to the swimmerets where they are fertilized. She carries the pinkish eggs around with her for several months, during which time she is said to be 'in berry'. The eggs hatch late in the spring and, after a short period of attachment to the mother, the young crayfishes swim away. They take four years to mature but the youngsters are readily devoured by other creatures and only a few of the hundreds produced by each female will ever reach maturity.

Among the few crustaceans that live wholly out of water are the woodlice, known by an assortment of local names such as 'shoe-laces', 'coffin-cutters', and 'sow-bugs'. Even they are relative newcomers to the land and they have not all completed the transition from water to land. The Shore slater, *Ligia oceanica*, $1\frac{1}{5}$ inches (3 cm.) long, is in an evolutionary sense still in the process of leaving the sea, while some have remained in, or returned to fresh water. A typical

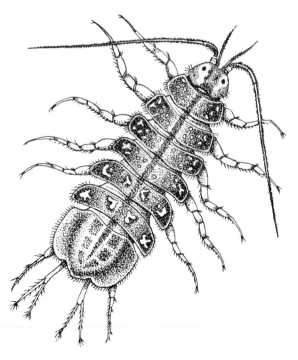

The **Water hog louse,** *Asellus*

example is the Hog louse, *Asellus aquaticus*, extremely common in ponds and streams, which occasionally invades public water-supplies.

Although terrestrial woodlice can breathe out of water, they do not have a waterproof cuticle and so are still more or less confined to damp places. Moreover, they are active mainly at night, when the humidity of the air is greater. Their oval bodies are clearly segmented, usually greyish and less than $\frac{3}{4}$ inch (2 cm.) long. The first pair of antennae are very small and invisible from above, but the second pair are large and, when the animal is on the move, they are constantly in motion, feeling and 'sniffing' the surroundings. The compound eyes, if present, are not on stalks. The head is fused with the first thoracic segment and together they nestle neatly in the second thoracic segment. There is no carapace.

The first pair of thoracic limbs assist the mouth-parts but the other seven pairs are walking legs. They are all alike and they have given the name Isopoda (=similar feet) to the woodlouse group. The abdomen, which makes up the rear third only of the woodlouse, bears six pairs of flat, leaf-like limbs which form 'gills'. The last pair of limbs, the uropods, project from the rear of the animal like little horns. The gills are branched. Oxygen diffuses into the bloodstream through the thin walls of the inner branch, the thicker outer branch acting as a protective cover which also helps to keep in moisture.

Woodlice feed on dead and decaying plants and animals. They are, in fact, our number one composters. They will occasionally nibble at young plants but the damage they do is negligible when compared with their useful role in breaking down waste and returning the goodness to the soil. Most species live in and around the soil and leaf litter. One species, *Platyarthrus hoffmann-seggi*, a tiny blind, white woodlouse, lives as a scavenger in the nests of various ants.

Although no woodlouse is able to live in really dry surroundings, some species have

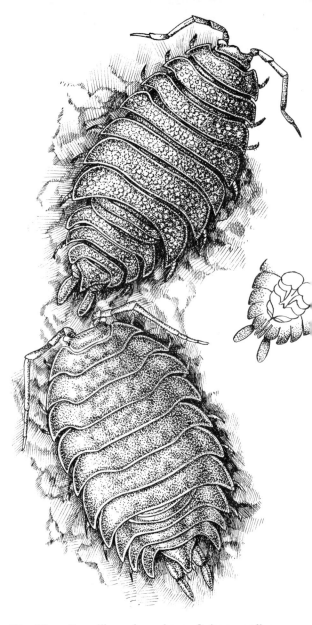

Woodlice: *Porcellio scaber, above*; *Oniscus asellus, below*; *centre, right*, section of underside to show position of 'gills'

a greater tolerance of dryness than others, because they have the beginnings of a breathing system approaching that of insects. The outer branches or plates of some of the abdominal limbs bear tiny pores which lead to tufts of minute tubes known as pseudotracheae, penetrating into the limb. Air can diffuse into these tubes and the animals can get at least some of their oxygen in this way, without the need for a permanently moist surface.

Woodlice without pseudotracheae are normally found in damp woodlands or under logs and stones. One is *Oniscus asellus*, our commonest woodlouse, rather flat, mottled grey, and about ⅗ inch (15 mm.) long when adult. It can often be found in large numbers under stones in the garden. *Porcellio scaber*, similar but distinguished by the rows of tubercles on its back, is found in the same places as *Oniscus* but it can tolerate slightly drier conditions because it has pseudotracheae. It is often found under the bark of standing trees. Another well-known species is the Pill-bug, *Armadillidium vulgare*. It and its close relatives can roll up into a neat ball when disturbed and the rolled-up ani-

mals were actually used as medicine at one time in the belief that they helped the digestion. *Armadillidium* has well-developed pseudotracheae and it also has a particularly thick cuticle so can live quite well in open grassland. The Pill-bug is easily confused with the Pill millipede, *Glomeris marginata*, which can also roll up into a neat ball. *Glomeris*, however, is generally much more shiny and, even when rolled up, it can be identified by the broad 'shield' at the end of the body. When the animals are unrolled, the many legs of the millipede immediately identify it.

Most woodlice have one or two broods each year and, at the beginning of the breeding-cycle, the female develops an egg-pouch under her thorax, formed by ingrowths from the thoracic legs. Up to 200 eggs are laid directly into the pouch and are fertilized there. The female carries her eggs about with her until they hatch and an egg-carrying female can often be recognized by her humped posture and slow movement. The young animals may stay in the pouch for some time after hatching but then they gradually disperse. They take about two years to mature, after moulting several times. Moulting takes place in two stages. The hind part of the body sheds its skin first, and not until the new skin is hardened, in about three days, does the front part moult. This is why we sometimes see woodlice half black and half white, although usually when moulting they hide away for protection.

The centipedes and millipedes are all slender, segmented animals with many pairs of legs. It is not difficult to imagine how these animals could have arisen from some ancestral annelid and there are, in the warmer parts of the world, caterpillar-like animals called onychophorans which show many features intermediate between those of annelids and millipedes. For many years the centipedes and millipedes were grouped together in a class known as the Myriapoda (=many footed), but there are several differences between them and they are now placed in separate classes known as the

The Pill millipede *Glomeris marginata, above;* the Pill-bug, *Armadillidium vulgare, below*

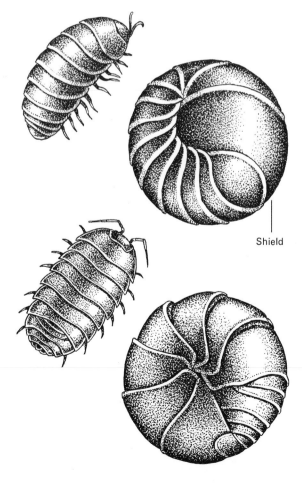

Shield

Chilopoda (centipedes) and the Diplopoda (millipedes). These are clearly related to each other and also to the insects, but there is no obvious connection with the other arthropods.

Centipedes are rather long, flattened animals with a leathery cuticle. The latter lacks a waterproof covering and so the animals can live only in damp places. Many of them live in the soil and leaf litter but they can also be found under bark. Their instinct is to have both surfaces of the body in contact with a solid object when at rest, so they creep under logs and stones. They are averse to light and soon scuttle away when exposed. The head is not unlike that of an insect and it carries a pair of long, bristly antennae which are the main sense-organs. None of the British centipedes have compound eyes but many have a number of simple eyes called ocelli. These probably do no more than tell the centipede whether it is in light or darkness. Some centipedes have no eyes at all and detect light simply through the general body surface.

There are three pairs of mouth-parts on the lower surface of the head but food is actually caught with a pair of poison claws carried on the segment just behind the head. When not in use these claws arch round the sides of the head. Behind the claws are numerous pairs of walking legs, one to each segment except that the last two or three segments have none. Not all centipedes have 100 legs, as the name centipede would suggest: British species have from 15 to 101 pairs according to the species. A last pair of legs are always directed backwards and play no part in walking. They seem to be sensory, rather like a pair of antennae for the hind end.

All centipedes are carnivorous, feeding at night on slugs, insects and other small animals. They occasionally take a little plant food but are definitely on the side of the gardener in his war against pests. They are very agile and their multi-articulated body enables them to make quick turns when after food. The prey is caught with the poison claws and carried to the mouth-parts which break it up for swallowing. The British centipedes are quite harmless to man, although some tropical species can inflict a painful bite.

Breathing is by a system of branching tubes or tracheae, as in insects. The tubes run from openings on various segments of the body and conduct air to all parts. We saw the beginning of a tracheal system in the woodlice but this does not mean that the two groups are related. The two groups live in similar situations and it is not surprising that they develop similar features because they are subjected to similar evolutionary pressures. This phenomenon is known as parallel evolution.

Breeding goes on through spring and summer but females fertilized in the autumn do not lay until the following spring. The mating behaviour is highly unusual. The male first spins a silken pad and then deposits a packet of sperm on it. His role is then over and the female picks up the sperm with her tail end. She lays her eggs sometime later. The amount of care and protection given to their eggs varies from one species to another.

There are about 45 species of centipede in the British Isles, most of them centred in southern England. Only about 32 are native and one of these, *Lithobius variegatus*, is found nowhere else in the world. Our centipedes fall into three main groups: the geophilids (more than 35 pairs of legs), the scolopendrids (21 pairs of legs) and the lithobiids (15 pairs of legs).

Geophilid centipedes are mainly soil-dwellers and many of them can be dug up in gardens and grassland. They are often wrongly called wire-worms. They are very slender and have up to 101 pairs of short legs. The horny plates of each segment are divided into two halves. Such an arrangement gives the animals much greater flexibility and they can bend back on themselves with ease. They are also able to move backwards – a great advantage to animals that tunnel through the soil – and the last pair of

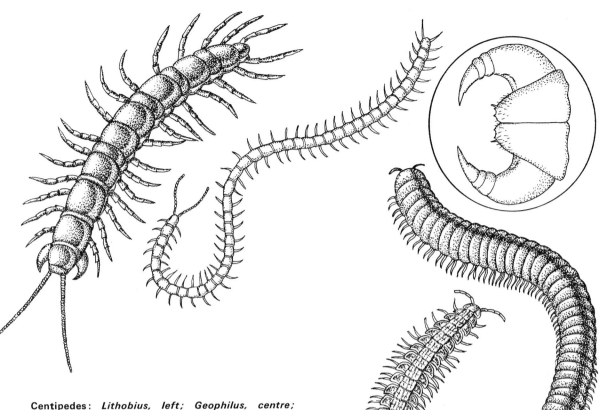

Centipedes: *Lithobius, left; Geophilus, centre;* poison fangs of a centipede, much enlarged

Millipedes: a flat-backed millipede, *Polydesmus, lower centre;* a snake millipede, *Iulus, lower right*

legs are well supplied with sense-organs to guide the backward movement. These animals are totally blind.

The reddish-brown *Geophilus carpophagus* is typical. It grows to a little over 2 inches (6 cm.) in length and is sometimes called a 'glow worm' because, in common with some other members of the genus, it produces a faint luminous glow when disturbed. The glow can be seen only at night but the pungent odour given off by these animals can be detected by handling them at any time. Female geophilids, which are generally a little larger than the males, lay their eggs in cavities in the soil and then guard them. The young geophilids are relatively undeveloped when they hatch, although they have the full number of legs, and the mother continues to guard them until they are able

to fend for themselves. They take about three years to mature.

Our commonest centipede is the lithobiid *Lithobius forficatus,* chestnut-brown and up to over an inch (3 cm.) long. It is very easy to find under stones or loose bark and the only species with which it could be confused is *L. variegatus.* The latter, however, can be distinguished by its banded legs. All our other lithobiid centipedes are much smaller, although all of them have 15 pairs of legs when adult. *Lithobius* lays its eggs singly in the soil, the female camouflaging them by first covering them with mucus and then rolling them around in the soil. The soil-

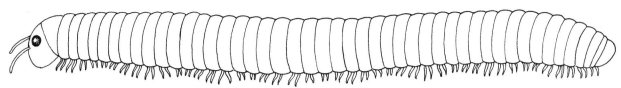

A snake millipede showing the waved walking movements of the legs

particles stick to the mucus which then hardens into a protective coat. The young *Lithobius* can look after itself as soon as it hatches but it does not have the full 15 pairs of legs for some time.

Millipedes resemble centipedes in many ways, but their bodies are generally more cylindrical. The most important difference, and certainly the most obvious, is that they have two short pairs of legs on nearly every segment where centipedes have one. Their cuticle is harder than that of the centipedes, because it is impregnated with lime salts, yet are still liable to dry up as they lack a waterproof covering. Consequently they are found in the same damp and dark places as centipedes.

On the millipede's head are simple eyes or ocelli and a pair of short antennae. Their mouth-parts are less well developed than those of centipedes and they have no poison claws, being vegetarians and scavengers. A large part of their diet is dead and decaying vegetation, especially rotten wood, but several species have a liking for living plants and they can be a nuisance in the garden.

The number of body segments varies in the different millipedes from 11 to more than 100. The four segments immediately behind the head have only three pairs of legs between them and this region is sometimes called the thorax. The rest of the body, known as the abdomen, bears two pairs of legs on each segment and, although millipedes vary in shape this feature will always distinguish them from any other 'creepy-crawly'.

When a millipede walks a series of waves travels forwards along the sides of the body. Starting from the back, the legs on each side move forward one by one. The effect is like the ripples across a field of corn, as each ear in turn bends before the wind. Before the wave gets far along the millipede's body, however, the hind legs are on the back-stroke and they soon start a new wave. Several waves, each composed of several legs, are in process before the first one reaches the animal's head. The waves carry the millipede along in a smooth glide and also provide the power needed to push the animal into crevices. Most millipedes move slowly and rely for protection on an offensive oily secretion from glands situated all along the body. Many species are able to coil up or roll into a ball for protection, and this habit also enables them to survive temporary drought, by reducing the amount of evaporation from the skin.

Millipedes, like centipedes, breath by tracheae, but theirs do not branch inside the body.

Some millipedes lay their eggs singly, coat them with excrement and soil, and leave them loose in the earth. Others build simple nests of soil cemented with excrement in which to lay. The female often stands guard over her nest for a while but does not stay once the eggs hatch. Young millipedes have only three pairs of legs at first and look like tiny insects, but at each moult they add more segments and more legs.

The most common millipedes are the so-called snake millipedes, long and slender with remarkably cylindrical bodies. They can be found under stones and bark and when disturbed they normally coil up into a tight spiral. The flat-backed millipedes, typified by *Polydesmus* species, are rather flattened and the segments are very distinct. Without looking at the legs, one might well mistake them for centipedes. They are found mainly in leaf litter. Mention has already been made of the Pill millipede (p. 193), for its similarity to certain woodlice. It occurs in a variety of habitats, including open grassland, tree-stumps, and woodland leaf litter, but seems to require a certain percentage of lime in the soil.

Anyone who searches soil and leaf litter for centipedes and millipedes is almost certain to come across some small white centipede-like creatures with 12 pairs of legs but without the poison claws of the centipede. These, ranging from $\frac{2}{25}$ to $\frac{2}{5}$ inches (2–10 mm.), are symphylans and they are of particular interest because, although clearly related to centipedes, they have mouth-parts and other features resembling those of insects. Indeed, it is believed that insects evolved from some early type of symphylan.

There are a million known species of insects, by far the largest group of animals, and they probably account for a greater weight of living material than the rest of the animal kingdom put together. Well over 20,000 species are known in the British Isles and, through their numbers alone, they force themselves on our notice. As well as being numerous, insects are extremely varied, catching our attention directly by their bright colours or irritating bites, or indirectly through the vast amount of damage done by grain weevils, timber beetles and other pests. Yet, although something like 10 per cent of the world's food-supply is destroyed each year by insects, the number of injurious species is relatively small. The majority are harmless and some, such as the honeybee and the ladybird, are extremely beneficial to man's interests. Their phenomenal success is due to a waterproof cuticle enabling them to escape from damp habitats and find new niches in which to live, the development of wings by which they spread far and wide, and their small size enabling them to colonize habitats not available to larger animals. Some of these habitats are incredibly restricted, such as the space between the upper and lower surface of a leaf. In addition insects have evolved a very wide range of structure and behaviour,

especially with regard to food so that they avoid too much competition. Moreover the young insects usually have a different diet from that of the adults, so reducing competition among themselves.

Insects are often confused with other terrestrial arthropods, but this need not be. The clearly segmented body of an insect is made up of three parts: head, thorax and abdomen. The head, composed of six segments fused together, carries a pair of antennae and usually a pair of compound eyes. The mouth-parts, which are subject to great variation, are on the underside of the head. Three segments make up the thorax and, in the adult, each normally bears a pair of legs – hence the alternative name of Hexapoda (=six legs) for the insects. Insects are the only invertebrates with wings and so any winged invertebrate must be an insect. The converse is not true, however, for there are many insects without wings. The wings are usually carried on the last two thoracic segments of the adult insect but the two pairs are not necessarily alike. There are no walking legs on the abdomen in the adult insect, although there may be a number of appendages at the hind end.

Along each side of an insect's body, like the portholes of a ship, is a line of holes, the spiracles. Each leads into a tube or trachea which carries the air into the body. Oxygen will not diffuse efficiently over a long distance. In large animals it is carried all over the body by the blood. The tracheal system of breathing limits the size to which the animal using it can grow. The largest insects are certain tropical butterflies and moths, with wing-spans of about 1 foot (30 cm.), but these still have quite slender bodies. The bulkiest insect, the Goliath beetle, *Goliathus regius*, of Africa, weighs only about 4 ounces (112 gm.). Large or very active insects increase the effectiveness of their tracheal breathing by using their body-muscles to pump air in and out of the tubes. This ventilating movement can be seen in wasps or hover-flies when they settle.

Although wings are characteristic of most

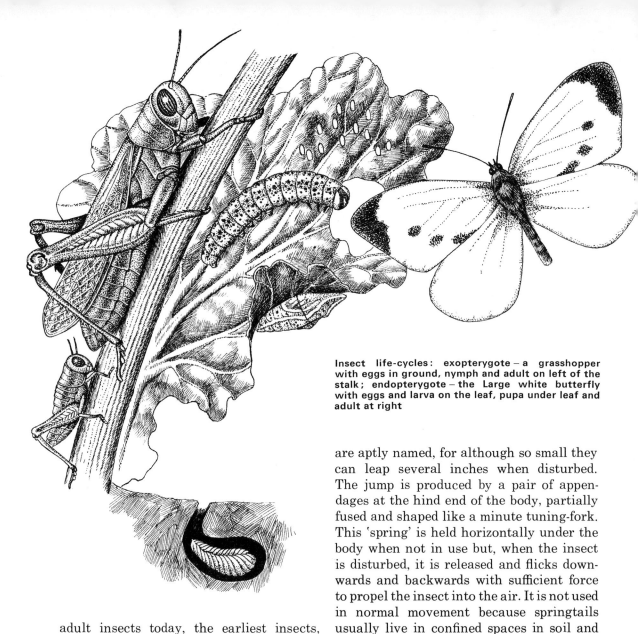

Insect life-cycles: exopterygote – a grasshopper with eggs in ground, nymph and adult on left of the stalk; endopterygote – the Large white butterfly with eggs and larva on the leaf, pupa under leaf and adult at right

are aptly named, for although so small they can leap several inches when disturbed. The jump is produced by a pair of appendages at the hind end of the body, partially fused and shaped like a minute tuning-fork. This 'spring' is held horizontally under the body when not in use but, when the insect is disturbed, it is released and flicks downwards and backwards with sufficient force to propel the insect into the air. It is not used in normal movement because springtails usually live in confined spaces in soil and leaf litter. There is virtually no metamorphosis in these primitive insects and the young ones look just like their parents except for size.

Fleas, lice and several other insects lack wings but are not primitive. Their ancestors had wings – proved by the structure of the thorax – but the wings have been lost since the insects adopted parasitic life where wings would be a hindrance rather than an advantage.

The winged insects, including those that have lost their wings secondarily, are known

adult insects today, the earliest insects, evolved from some centipede-like ancestor, were wingless. Some of these primitive wingless insects are alive today and are known collectively as apterygotes (=without wings). One of the most familiar is the household Silver fish *Lepisma saccharina*, a shiny little insect inhabiting dark corners. It feeds on starchy materials and is most likely to turn up in a food cupboard, where it thrives on spilt flour or breadcrumbs.

Most abundant of the apterygotes are the springtails, hordes of which can be scooped up in a handful of leaf litter or moss. They

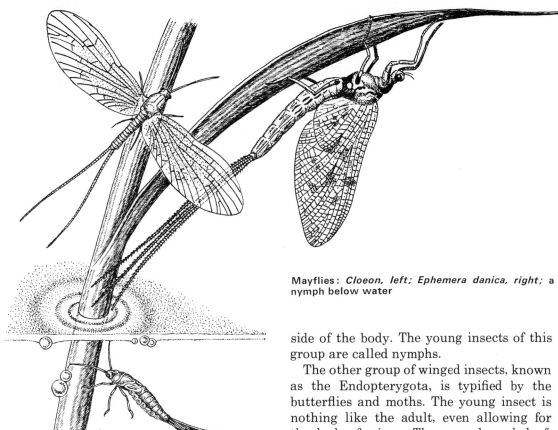

Mayflies: *Cloeon, left; Ephemera danica, right;* a nymph below water

as the pterygote insects and they can be divided into two main groups, according to their life-histories. With a few exceptions, all insects lay eggs. The creature that emerges from the egg, however, is usually unlike the adult. Not only is it smaller, it also lacks wings. In one group, typified by the grasshoppers, the young animal looks something like the adult and the resemblance increases with each moult. The wings first appear as little buds on the back and they grow larger at each moult, although they do not appear as true wings until the animal is fully grown. When once the fully developed wings appear the insects do not grow any more and, except for the mayflies, will not shed their skins any more. This group, which also includes the dragonflies, earwigs, and bugs, is called the Exopterygota because the wings develop on the out-side of the body. The young insects of this group are called nymphs.

The other group of winged insects, known as the Endopterygota, is typified by the butterflies and moths. The young insect is nothing like the adult, even allowing for the lack of wings. The many-legged, leaf-chewing caterpillar is a far cry from the winged, nectar-sipping butterfly. Young insects of this kind, very different from the adults, are called larvae. As the larva grows it changes its skin in the normal way but it does not change its form as the nymph does: it merely becomes a bigger larva. Instead of taking place gradually during the young insect's life, the change to adult form takes place in one big step. When the larva is fully grown, it splits its skin once again to reveal the pupa or chrysalis. This stage, which is missing from the life-history of the exopterygote insects, is often stated to be a resting stage but, although it does not feed and only rarely moves, the most wonderful changes are taking place inside. The whole larval body is liquefied and re-built into the body of the winged adult.

Within these two main groups, the insects are classified into Orders, based mainly on the structure of the wings. The names of most of the Orders end in *-ptera*, which means 'wings', and so we have Lepidoptera (scale wings), Orthoptera (straight wings), Hymenoptera (membrane wings), and so on. There are 29 Orders altogether, including four apterygote Orders, and 24 of them occur in the British Isles.

The mayflies are very delicate insects belonging to the Order Ephemeroptera, a name which means 'short-lived wings' and refers to the relatively short life of the adult insect. The name 'mayfly' is a little misleading because one species or another can be found throughout the summer.

Mayflies spend their early lives in ponds and streams and the adults are rarely found far from water. Most of our 46 species are less than $\frac{1}{2}$ inch (12·5 mm.) across and they are easily mistaken for midges as they flutter over the water. Close to, however, they are readily recognized by the two or three slender 'tails' at the hind end as in *Cloeon* and *Ephemera*, p. 173. The wings are extremely thin and the front ones are always much larger than the hind ones which are minute or may be absent altogether in some species such as *Cloeon*.

The adult life is very brief and may last no longer than a single evening, although some species live for a few days. When they emerge from the water the males congregate in swarms and dance up and down over the water. Females are attracted to these swarms and the insects pair up. Eggs are laid soon after mating and the female either scatters them over the water or else, in some species, she goes down into the water and deposits her eggs on water-plants.

Each species has its own particular habitat, some living in fast streams, some in slow streams, and others in still water. The nymphs feed mainly upon plant debris and they are extremely well adapted to their own habitats. Those living in fast streams, for example, are flattened and cling tightly to stones to avoid being swept away by the current. The nymphs breathe by means of a set of gills, which are fine, leaf-like outgrowths from the sides of the body. The gills contain tracheae, continuous with those inside the body, and oxygen diffuses into them from the surrounding water. Most species spend about a year in the nymphal stage and they undergo many moults.

When fully grown the nymph comes to the surface and its skin splits down the back. The mayfly comes out and flies off right away to some convenient support – an overhanging tree for example. This insect is not yet fully adult and is known as the sub-imago. It is rather dull in colour and fishermen call it the dun, but it soon moults again and out comes the much brighter imago. This is the true adult and fishermen call this one the spinner. The mayflies are unique in that they are the only insects that moult after getting their fully developed wings.

The adult mayflies have no functional mouths and they cannot feed. After a short aerial existence, during which time they ensure the continuance of the species, they die. The dying insects fall into the water and are greedily snapped up by a variety of fishes. Fishermen have put this fact to good use and many of their artificial flies are modelled on various mayfly species. It is probably true to say that fishermen know more about the habits of mayflies than many entomologists.

The dragonflies belong to the Order Odonata and, like the mayflies, they spend their early lives in water. Many dragonflies are strong fliers, however, and they are frequently found far from the nearest pond or stream. They include some of our largest insects – up to 4 inches (10 cm.) in wing-span – and also some of our most attractive ones. The gauzy wings are generally colourless but they glitter in the sun and, together

Moths, *from left to right and top to bottom*: Eyed hawk, *Smerinthus ocellatus*, caterpillar and imago: Narrow-bordered bee hawk, *Hemaris tityus*; Buff tip, *Phalera bucephala*; Garden tiger, *Arctia caja*, female; Small elephant hawk, *Deilephila porcellus*; Cinnabar, *Callimorpha jacobaea*, male ×2; Emperor, *Saturnia pavonia*, female with caterpillar below; Oak eggar, *Lasiocampa quercus*, female

with the bright body colours, they produce a most pleasant effect. The body colours include reds, greens, blues and browns and they are produced by combinations of pigments and iridescence. In addition, many of the older individuals develop a pale blue powdery deposit or pruinescence on certain parts of the body.

We have about 45 species of dragonfly in the British Isles but several of them have not been seen for years and may well be extinct in these islands. Within the Odonata there are two distinct groups: the slender, fragile damselflies in which all the four wings are the same size and shape, and the more robust true dragonflies in which the hind wings are somewhat broader than the front ones. As well as these structural differences, the two groups differ in their behaviour. The damselflies spend most of their time resting on reeds by the water and fly very slowly when disturbed, whereas the true dragonflies fly very strongly, hawking up and down their chosen territory for hours on end and resting only occasionally.

The dragonfly's food consists entirely of midges and other small insects which it catches in full flight. The spiky legs are held forward under the head and scoop the prey from the air. It is then chewed up by the strongly toothed jaws, which are responsible for the name of the Order – Odonata means 'toothed'. The huge compound eyes, occupying nearly all of the head and containing up to 30,000 lenses, enable the dragonfly to locate the smallest insect flying near it. Locating the prey is only half the battle, however, and must be backed up by a very high degree of manœuvrability, especially in the faster-flying species. This manœuvrability is provided by a well-orga-

nized nervous system linking the eyes and the flight-muscles and one has only to watch a dragonfly to appreciate the speed with which it can change direction to scoop up a fly. Dragonflies can hover and even fly backwards.

The male dragonfly has a pair of claspers at the tip of his body and he uses these to grip his mate behind the head. The two then fly together in the 'tandem position'. Before taking his mate in tow, however, the male transfers sperm from the reproductive organs near the tail end to special structures near the front of his abdomen. When held by the neck, the female simply curves her body round to receive sperm from the front end of the male's abdomen. In many species, especially among the damselflies, the male continues to hold the female while she lays her eggs. The female damselfly normally descends partially into the water and lays her eggs on water-plants, but other dragonflies scatter their eggs over the water or else just dip the tips of their bodies into the water to wash off the eggs.

The nymphs all live in ponds and streams and they are fiercely carnivorous, prowling about on the bottom in search of worms and insects. The food is caught with a clever device called the mask, which is formed from a pair of mouth-parts. It is long and slender and acts rather like the tongue of a frog: when food is spotted the mask shoots out and traps it with two powerful claws. There is a hinge about half-way along the mask and, when not in use, it is folded back under the head.

Damselfly nymphs are much more slender than those of the true dragonflies but the most obvious difference lies at the hind end. The damselfly nymph has three blade-like projections from the end and these are the gills. They contain tracheae and, like the gills of the mayflies, they absorb oxygen from the water. The nymphs of the true dragonflies also have gills but theirs are hidden inside the hind end of the food-canal. Water is pumped in and out of the anus to serve these gills.

Moths, *from left to right and top to bottom*: Dark crimson underwing, *Catocala sponsa*; Yellow underwing, *Noctua pronuba*; Magpie, *Abraxus grossulariata*; Angle shades, *Phlogophora meticulosa*; Peppered, *Biston betularia,* with melanic form, var. *carbonaria, right*; Small magpie, *Eurrhypara hortulata*; Ghost Swift, *Hepialus humuli,* female and *below*, male; Six-spot burnet, *Zygaena filipendula*; *Nemotois degeerela*, male ×3

When fully grown – usually after about a year – the nymph climbs up a reed or some other plant and emerges into the air. The skin then splits and out comes the adult. Emergence usually occurs early in the morning and by the time the air warms up the wings are fully hardened and ready for flight, but the full colours take several days to develop.

Among the damselflies, most striking is the Banded agrion *Agrion splendens*, p. 173. The body is metallic blue and the wings of the male bear deep bluish patches. *Lestes sponsa*, p. 173, has a metallic green body. Many other damselflies have black and blue patterns. The true dragonflies include long-bodied forms, such as the brown *Aeshna grandis* and the Gold ringed dragonfly, *Cordulegaster boltoni*, p. 173, and shorter species such as *Libellula depressa*, p. 173. The swift, darting flight of the latter group has earned them the name of 'darters'. They are also known as 'horse stingers', although they are quite harmless and without any kind of sting.

The stoneflies, Order Plecoptera, are another group of insects with aquatic nymphs. They are quite common around running water but they do not fly much and they are not often seen. Anglers probably know them best and they have given some of the commoner species English names, such as Yellow Sally, *Isoperla grammatica*. Most of our 34 species are brown or yellow and some are used as models for artificial flies.

Stoneflies are very delicate, soft-bodied insects with long antennae and a pair of 'tails' at the hind end. Most stoneflies can be recognized by the ladder-like arrange-

A dragonfly with wings outspread

ment of veins in the middle of the fore-wings, p. 173.

Dragonflies and damselflies pair up when the male grips the female by her neck. They then fly in tandem, *top,* and settle on a plant where sperm transfer takes place, *centre.* After this the male may continue to hold the female while she lays her eggs, *bottom*

Mating takes place on the ground or in vegetation and the female flies or swims over the water, dropping batches of eggs as she goes. The nymphs are rather flattened and they crawl about on the bottom of the stream, feeding on algae and on the young of other insects. They resemble mayfly nymphs but they have no gill-plates and they have only two 'tails'. Some stonefly nymphs have tufts of 'hairs' which act as gills, but others get their oxygen through the general body surface. Almost all of them live in running water, where there is plenty of oxygen.

Most stoneflies take one year to mature, although some of our larger species take three years. The nymphs crawl out of the water and the adults emerge from the nymphal skin on land. The adults feed a little by scraping algae from stones and trees but they spend most of their time just sitting on the waterside vegetation.

Nearly everyone will know the 'song' of the grasshopper, but fewer people will know the insect itself. It is usually brown or green in colour, with a blunt head, well-developed 'shield' over the thorax, and straight wings held tightly back along the body. In addition, the hind legs are very long and used for jumping. The Order name, Orthoptera, means 'straight wings' but there is an increasing tendency to use the name Saltatoria, meaning 'leapers', for the grasshoppers and their relatives.

There are two groups of grasshoppers

A dragonfly nymph casting off skin which has become too tight

A dragonfly nymph using its mask to attack a damsel-fly nymph. These carnivorous creatures often eat their own kind

the short-horned grasshoppers, with short antennae, and the long-horned grass-hoppers, in which the antennae are longer than the body. The latter group are more correctly called bush-crickets. The Order also includes true crickets and mole crickets.

The short-horned grasshoppers, family Acrididae, live mainly in open country, such as grassland and heathland, and feed almost entirely on grass which they chew up with their strong biting jaws. We have eleven species in Britain concentrated in the south and only five reach the Humber.

Except for the Meadow grasshopper, *Chorthippus parallelus*, in which the hind wings are vestigial and the front ones re-duced, all our species have two pairs of wings. The front ones are relatively tough but the hind wings are broad and membra-neous. All the winged species can fly, although they rarely fly far. They leap or fly a short distance when disturbed and then drop down into the grass where their colora-tion hides them from all but the sharpest eyes. The grasshoppers are extremely vari-able in colour and the Common field grass-hopper, *Chorthippus brunneus*, p. 174, has at least 13 colour forms, from green, through red and brown, to black. The colours are under genetic control and natural selection favours greens in grassland, browns on heathland, and so on. Because of this colour variation it is not easy to identify grass-hoppers on sight. The surest method is by the 'songs' which are not difficult to learn.

The grasshopper 'sings' by rubbing the

hind legs against the wings. The femur of the hind leg carries a row of tiny pegs and, as the leg is moved rapidly up and down, the pegs strike a wing-vein and set up vibrations which we hear as the chirp. This method of producing sound is called 'stridulation' and it is usually only the male who performs, although the females of some species do make a rather soft chirp. Each species has its own frequency and a characteristic song pattern made up of chirps and pauses of various duration. Many species actually have two songs, one of which is the 'courtship' song produced only in the presence of a female. Grasshoppers are strictly diurnal animals and sing only when the weather is warm and the sun is shining.

Eggs are laid in little groups round the bases of tufts of grass. They are covered with a liquid that hardens into a protective 'pod' in which they pass the winter. Nymphs emerge in spring and mature from June onwards. None of our species survives the winter in the adult state and only the eggs carry the species on from year to year.

Closely related to the grasshoppers are the groundhoppers, family Tetrigidae, but they can be distinguished readily because the 'shield' of the groundhopper extends right back along the body. Groundhoppers live in woods and heathland, feeding on mosses and other lowly vegetation. Two species are quite common but they are dark brown in colour and are active only in very warm weather. They do not advertise their presence by chirping.

The bush-crickets belong to the family Tettigoniidae and are superficially similar to grasshoppers but they are generally rather stouter. They are easily identified by their long, slender antennae and in addition, the female possesses a large blade-like ovipositor which gives her a somewhat fearsome appearance. Male bush-crickets all possess wings, although these may be very small and incapable of flight, but several species have wingless females.

Bush-crickets are very much insects of the south and only two of our 10 species

reach Scotland. They live mainly in hedgerows, nettle-beds, and so on. They will eat a variety of plant food but also take a considerable proportion of aphids and other insects in their diet. Whereas grasshoppers are diurnal insects, active only in sunlight, the bush-crickets tend to be nocturnal: they start to sing in the afternoon and go on well into the night. Singing does not involve the legs in bush-crickets and the sound is produced by rubbing the bases of the wings together. The song is generally shriller than that of the grasshoppers and goes on usually for indefinite periods, without the characteristic pauses of the grasshopper songs. Only the

A stonefly, adult *above*, nymph, *below*

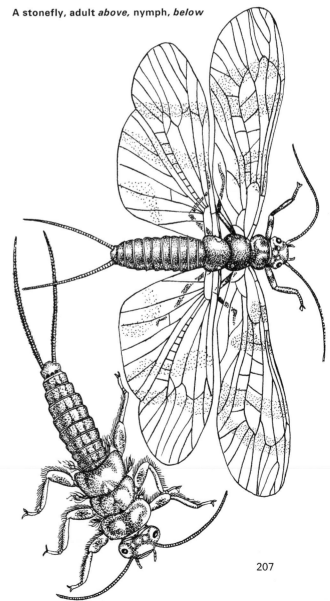

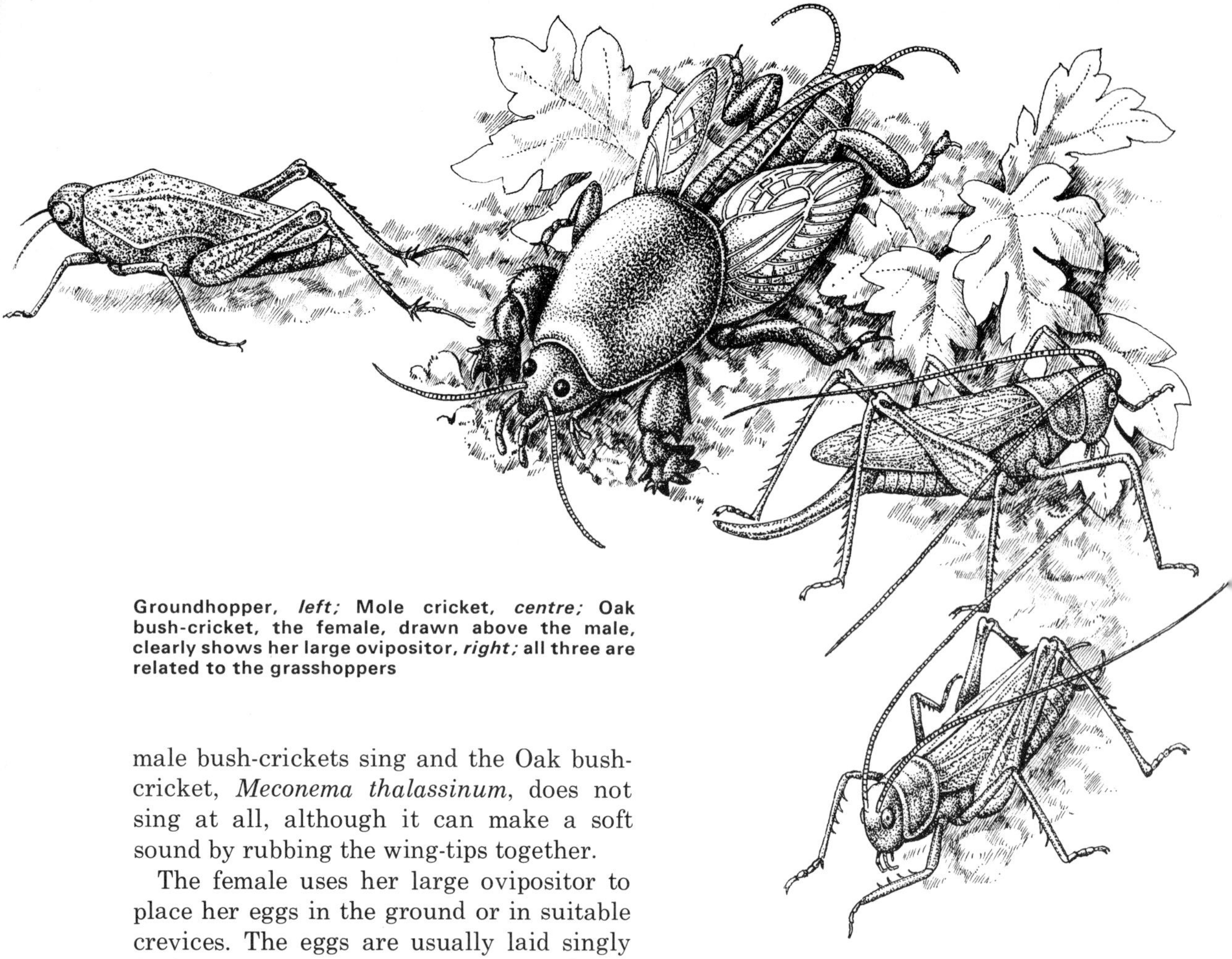

Groundhopper, *left;* Mole cricket, *centre;* Oak bush-cricket, the female, drawn above the male, clearly shows her large ovipositor, *right;* all three are related to the grasshoppers

male bush-crickets sing and the Oak bush-cricket, *Meconema thalassinum*, does not sing at all, although it can make a soft sound by rubbing the wing-tips together.

The female uses her large ovipositor to place her eggs in the ground or in suitable crevices. The eggs are usually laid singly during early autumn and they do not hatch until the late spring. Bush-crickets remain active until late autumn and then die, leaving only their eggs to survive the winter.

Our largest bush-cricket is the Great green bush-cricket, *Tettigonia viridissima*, p. 174, approaching 2 inches (5 cm.) in length. It is most frequently found on the south coast and its loud song fills the air on summer evenings. The commonest species is probably the Dark bush-cricket, *Pholidoptera griseoaptera*, whose staccato bursts come from many a hedgerow. The insect is not often seen, however, and the most familiar species is undoubtedly the pale green Oak bush-cricket which lives in a variety of trees and frequently flies into houses at night.

Both grasshoppers and bush-crickets are easy to keep in captivity. A large jar with damp sand in the bottom will serve as a cage

and, if stood in a warm place, the males will oblige with a song. Care must be taken, however, to avoid overcrowding with the bush-crickets because they are quite likely to devour each other.

Apart from the House cricket, *Acheta domesticus*, p. 174, which is not really British, crickets, family Gryllidae, are not common in these islands. They resemble bush-crickets but are somewhat flatter and both sexes possess two long 'tails' or cerci. The female's ovipositor is needle-like, not blade-like.

The House cricket, a brownish insect about 15 mm. long, came to us from the Middle East and lives here in kitchens and warehouses where the temperature remains fairly high. It also lives on rubbish-dumps where fermentation produces warmth. It is a scavenger, eating any organic material. The male sings, like the bush-crickets, by rubbing his wings together. The House cricket flies well but is not a very good jumper.

The Field cricket, *Gryllus campestris*, p. 174, is about 20 mm. long. It is much rarer than it was but still occurs here and there on well-drained grassland. The males sing loudly near their burrows but retreat quickly when disturbed.

The Mole cricket, *Gryllotalpa gryllotalpa*, belongs to the family Gryllotalpidae and is one of our largest insects, about 4 cm. long. It lives underground in alluvial soil around water-courses but it is extremely rare now.

Cockroaches, Order Dictyoptera, are flattened insects with long, slender antennae and rather spiky legs. There are usually two pairs of wings and the front pair are rather leathery in texture. Many species can fly but are most likely to scuttle away.

Most of the cockroaches seen in Britain are immigrants that have come in on ships. There are two well-established species: the Oriental cockroach or 'Black beetle', *Blatta orientalis*, and the German cockroach, *Blattella germanica*. There are also a number of others, notably the American cockroach, *Periplaneta americana*, that are established in dockland areas. These immigrant species all come from warm regions and can establish themselves only in kitchens, warehouses, and places where temperatures are high. They cause a lot of damage by chewing food and other materials.

Besides these imported species, we do have three native cockroaches. All are less than 12 mm. long and all are confined to the southern counties, where they live in woods and on heathland. Like the larger species, they are all omnivorous and feed on a variety of plant and animal material.

Cockroaches lay their eggs in little purse-like cases called 'oothecae', which are sometimes carried around by the females until the eggs hatch.

The earwigs, Order Dermaptera, are readily recognized by the forceps or pincers at the tail end. They are often feared on account of these pincers, but these are quite harmless and certainly incapable of piercing human skin. One of the commonest myths is that the earwig will crawl into a human ear and bite through the eardrum. An earwig certainly will crawl into one's ear if it has the chance, and this is undoubtedly how the idea originated, but it would regard the ear-passage as nothing more than a resting-place. Earwigs are nocturnal creatures and they hide away by day in crevices: the ear-passage is probably just as acceptable as a piece of loose bark.

Earwigs are scavengers, feeding largely on fallen fruit and carrion. They will, however, take living insects and, as every gardener knows, they are quite partial to flower-petals – especially those of prize blooms. Although these are not very obvious, most species of earwig do have wings. The

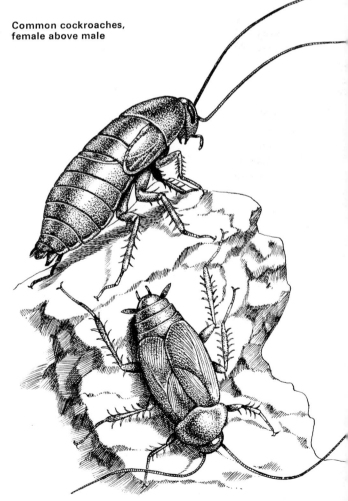

Common cockroaches, female above male

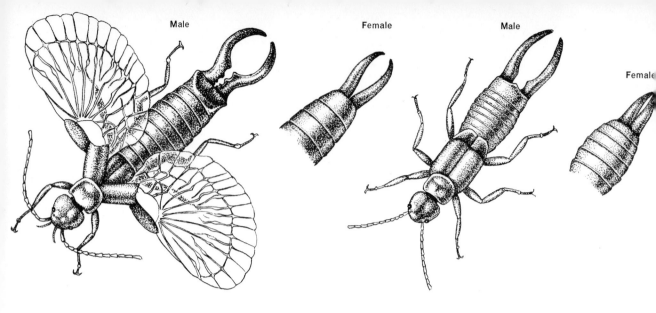

Male   Female   Male   Female

Earwigs, *Forficula auricularia*, *left*, and *Labia minor*, *right*, showing how the forceps differ in the two sexes

front pair are short and leathery but they conceal a much larger pair, elaborately folded away. These hind wings are extremely thin, Dermaptera means 'skin wings', and in general, earwigs fly very little. The pincers, which are strongly curved in the male and straighter in the female, are mainly weapons of defence, although they are said to be used for folding the wings away and for catching food.

There are only two earwig species that are at all common in this country, the Common earwig, *Forficula auricularia*, and the Small earwig, *Labia minor*. The former is a rich brown insect about 12 mm. long and it is the earwig that most of us see under loose bark and in flowers. The Small earwig is a pale yellowish colour and only half the length of the Common earwig. It is fond of compost-heaps and, unlike other earwigs, it flies readily. Two other species occur locally along the south coast and this is the sum total of our native earwigs.

The life-history of the Common earwig is known fairly well but little is known of the other species. The Common earwig pairs up in late summer and hibernates in the soil. Eggs are laid in winter or early

spring and the female guards them zealously. She will even gather them all up again if they become scattered. The young nymphs are cared for by their mother for some time and one can often find family groups in spring. Gradually they disperse and go their separate ways, becoming mature in late summer.

Many insects have taken up a parasitic life, either inside or outside their host animals. The lice are well-known external parasites of birds and mammals and they feed by sucking blood or by chewing skin and feathers. They are wingless, although they are descended from winged ancestors,

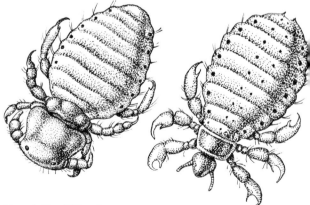

Lice: *left*, a biting louse; *right*, a sucking louse

The head of an aphid showing its piercing and sucking 'beak' and section, *left; right,* examples of the two main groups of bugs, a Cicada and Shield bug, *right*

and, like many parasites, their senses are poorly developed. Most species, however, have strong claws with which they maintain a firm grip on the host's hair or feathers.

There are two main groups, biting lice and sucking lice, which differ mainly in the construction of the mouth-parts. Those of the sucking lice, which are found only on mammals, are adapted for piercing the host and withdrawing blood.

Eggs are normally glued to the hairs or feathers of the host and the young nymphs soon mature. They will move from one host to another if two animals come into contact, but otherwise they do not leave the host

animal until it dies. A small infestation of lice may not harm the host but large populations cause severe irritation and loss of condition. In addition, lice can also carry diseases, including typhus in man.

The largest order of exopterygote insects, that is without a pupal stage, is the Hemiptera. Its members are the bugs and they range from tiny aphids to large carnivorous waterbugs. Just about the only feature common to all members of the Order is the 'beak' which is used to suck the juices of plants or other animals. It is made from specially modified mouth-parts which are like grooved needles and which fit together to pierce tissues and form a channel for imbibing the juices.

The name of the Order means half wings, because many of its species have front wings which are partly leathery, partly membranous. These are placed in the suborder Heteroptera. There are others with wings

211

wholly leathery or wholly membranous, and these are placed in a separate suborder, the Homoptera. In both suborders, however, there are species that have secondarily lost their wings altogether.

Heteropteran bugs include both blood-sucking and plant-feeding species and many of the carnivorous forms live in fresh water. Well-known examples are the backswimmers, *Notonecta* species, which are found in nearly all ponds and streams. These insects are so named because they swim on their backs, 'rowing' themselves along with their long black legs. They have a silvery appearance, due to a film of air trapped around the body by a coat of fine hairs. Backswimmers feed on a variety of aquatic life, including fishes, and they will give an unwary finger a nasty prick with the sharp beak. Other aquatic bugs include the weird Water scorpion, *Nepa cinerea*, which creeps along the bottom of the pond and uses a long 'tail' to obtain air from the surface. Unlike the backswimmers, which have to come to the surface every now and then to renew their air-supply, the Water scorpion can remain fully submerged all the time. Despite its sinister name, the insect is quite harmless.

Part way between the aquatic and terrestrial bugs there are a number of interesting species that live on the surface of ponds and streams. Most familiar of these are the pond-skaters, *Gerris*. The insects 'row' across the surface with their very long middle legs and use their hind legs as rudders. Water-repellent hairs at the tips of the legs keep them on the surface. Pond-skaters feed on other insects, which they catch with their short front legs.

The majority of the terrestrial Heteroptera are plant-feeding bugs, often brightly coloured and commonly confused with beetles, although the beak and the membranous tip of the wing will always distinguish them. Some heteropteran bugs are predatory and feed on other insects, and some take the blood of larger animals. The Bed bug, *Cimex lectularius*, feeds on man,

Water bugs: *top,* a Pond-skater; *below, left,* a Water scorpion and *right,* a backswimmer

Winged and wingless aphids and young on a stem with, *below*, a purse gall on poplar, caused by an aphid

'song' of the cicadas. The males produce this sound by vibrating two tiny membranes on the abdomen. There is only one cicada in Britain and that is a rather rare insect, *Cicadetta montana*, found only in the New Forest. There are many smaller hoppers, and they can be beaten from almost any vegetation during the summer. Most of them are less than 5 mm. long and they soon jump away when disturbed. Leaf-hoppers of this type are serious pests in some countries but do little harm in the British Isles.

One group of hoppers are known as 'spittle bugs' because the nymphs cover themselves with froth. They exude a rather viscous fluid from the anus and then pump air into it to froth it up. The froth prevents the nymphs from drying up and also helps to protect them from their enemies, although certain solitary wasps regularly pluck them from their retreats. Adult spittle bugs are also called froghoppers from their some-what frog-like appearance.

The aphids – greenfly and blackfly – are only too well known as a result of their attacks on roses, beans and many other plants. Aphids are rarely more than about

although it does not remain permanently attached. It is interesting to note that the Bed bug's nearest relatives are parasites of bats, pigeons and house martins – three groups of animals which have been associated with man since his cave-dwelling days. It may well have been a single parasite attacked all three in 'cave-man' times and then broke up into several races, each with a preferred host, that have now evolved into distinct species.

The homopteran bugs are all plant-feeders and they include many serious pests, such as aphids, leafhoppers and scale insects. Readers who have visited the Continent will know only too well the shrill, monotonous

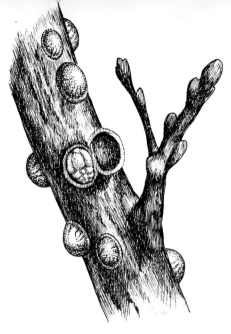

Terrapin scale insects, *Parthenolecanium corni,*
with one scale opened to show the insect

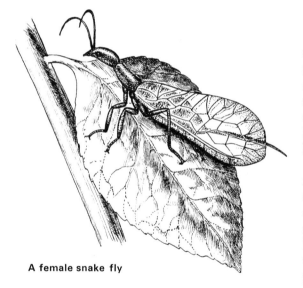

A female snake fly

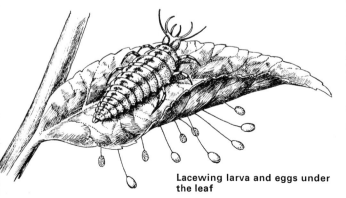

Lacewing larva and eggs under
the leaf

3 mm. long but they exist in enormous numbers and do much damage, both by injuring the plant tissues with their beaks and by spreading virus diseases of plants. The dense populations that build up on plants in the summer result from rapid parthenogenetic reproduction. The aphids do not lay eggs at this time but bring forth several live young each day. Most of these are wingless and they quickly mature and reproduce. Winged generations occur from time to time and move off to other plants where the build-up starts again, but not until the autumn are males produced. They mate with the females and the latter lay cold-resistant eggs which survive the winter. Several species, including the Black bean aphid, *Aphis fabae*, lay their winter eggs on trees and shrubs and migrate back to the herbaceous plants in spring.

It is well known that certain species of ant 'farm' aphids and 'milk' them for the sweet secretion known as honeydew. This sugary liquid, derived from the plant sap, is exuded from the anus of the aphids (and some other small bugs) and one can often see it falling like fine rain from the trees, especially oaks and limes. It makes the lower leaves very sticky and is later attacked by a fungus which turns everything black.

Scale insects are strange creatures, the females of which are generally motionless and cling to the host plants under a horny or waxy covering called the 'scale'. Because they are difficult to detect, they have been carried inadvertently to all parts of the world and many have become serious pests, especially of fruit trees. They are difficult to control because the scale protects them from insecticides. Male scale insects are rather like small midges but they are rarely seen.

We now move on to the endopterygote insects, those which have a pupal stage in their life-history and whose young are known as larvae.

The Order Neuroptera includes the lacewing flies, the snake flies, and the alder flies, although the latter two groups are often put in a separate order known as Megaloptera. These insects have a complex network of wing-veins, hence Neuroptera, which means 'nerve wings', which usually fork just before reaching the wing-margins.

Snake flies, so called from the long 'neck' between the head and the wings, are mainly woodland insects and their larvae generally live under the bark of trees. Like all members of this Order, these larvae are carnivorous. Alder flies, p. 173, are stouter than the other neuropterans and their wing-veins do not fork at the tips. Their larvae live in ponds and streams and the rather sluggish adults can be found sitting on waterside vegetation in early summer.

The lacewing flies, of which we have five families, are usually green or brown. Green lacewings, p. 174, of the family Chrysopidae are the best known, for they often enter lighted windows on summer evenings. Some hibernating species also come in during the autumn in search of suitable winter quarters. These insects are true friends of the gardener because both adults and larvae are avid hunters of greenfly. The larvae have long, curved jaws, each of which encloses a narrow canal. The jaws are plunged into a victim and the lacewing larva then sucks up the body fluids through the tubes. Some lacewing larvae then use the drained skins of their victims to cover their own bodies and camouflage them. When fully grown the larvae spin flimsy silken cocoons among the herbage and enter the pupal stage. During the summer the adults emerge within a few weeks, but insects spinning up in the autumn will spend the whole winter in the pupal stage.

Osmylus fulvicephalus, with a 2-inch (50 mm.) wing-span, is our largest lacewing. The larva lives among moss and damp stones and the insect is most likely to be seen around woodland streams. *Sisyra fuscata*, p. 173, and two near relatives spend their early days feeding inside freshwater sponges and the larvae, like those of the alder-flies, are provided with feathery gills on the abdomen. Most of our brown lacewings, however, belong to a different family and their larvae

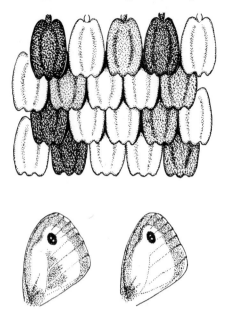

The scales of a butterfly wing. Some male butterflies, notably the Gatekeeper, have patches of special scent-scales; the male wing is to the left of the female

are terrestrial like those of the green lacewings.

The scorpion flies (Order Mecoptera) are quite common hedgerow insects, recognizable at once by the broad beak-like extension of the head, p. 173. The jaws are carried at the tip of this extension. The common name is a reference to the swollen tip of the male abdomen which is reflexed over the body rather like the sting of a scorpion. Scorpion flies are quite harmless, however, and feed on decaying matter, both animal and vegetable. There are three species of *Panorpa* in the British Isles, all with mottled wings, and all very similar.

Scorpion flies lay their eggs in the soil and the caterpillar-like larvae scavenge there for some months before turning into pupae. Adults can be found throughout the summer.

A fourth species, *Boreus hiemalis*, is wingless and less than 3 mm. long. It jumps about and, as it is active in winter, it is called the Snow flea. The male lacks the turned-up abdomen but the 'beak' is clearly seen.

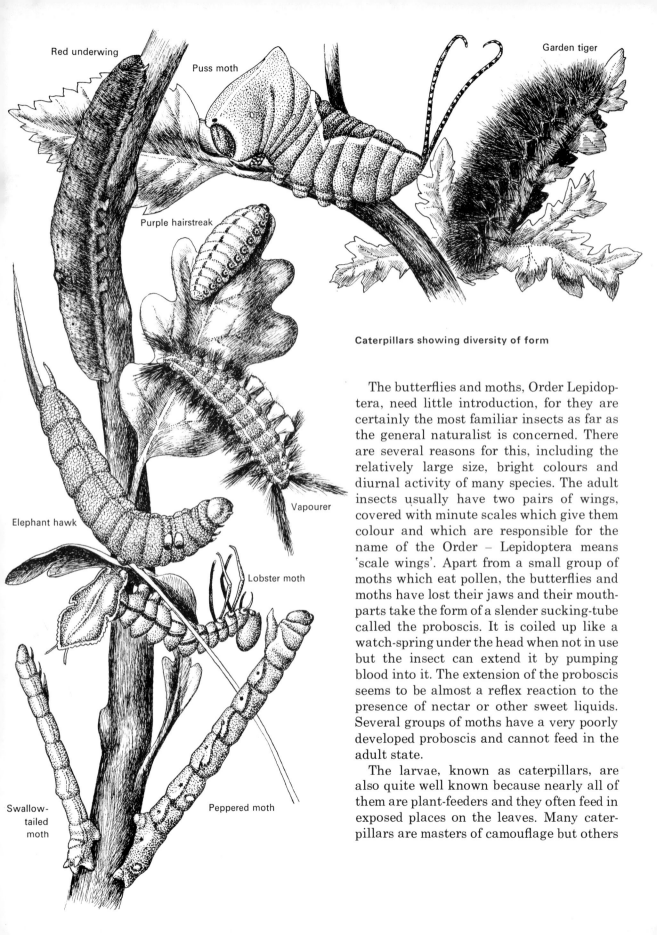

Red underwing

Puss moth

Garden tiger

Purple hairstreak

Vapourer

Elephant hawk

Lobster moth

Swallow-
tailed
moth

Peppered moth

Caterpillars showing diversity of form

The butterflies and moths, Order Lepidoptera, need little introduction, for they are certainly the most familiar insects as far as the general naturalist is concerned. There are several reasons for this, including the relatively large size, bright colours and diurnal activity of many species. The adult insects usually have two pairs of wings, covered with minute scales which give them colour and which are responsible for the name of the Order – Lepidoptera means 'scale wings'. Apart from a small group of moths which eat pollen, the butterflies and moths have lost their jaws and their mouthparts take the form of a slender sucking-tube called the proboscis. It is coiled up like a watch-spring under the head when not in use but the insect can extend it by pumping blood into it. The extension of the proboscis seems to be almost a reflex reaction to the presence of nectar or other sweet liquids. Several groups of moths have a very poorly developed proboscis and cannot feed in the adult state.

The larvae, known as caterpillars, are also quite well known because nearly all of them are plant-feeders and they often feed in exposed places on the leaves. Many caterpillars are masters of camouflage but others

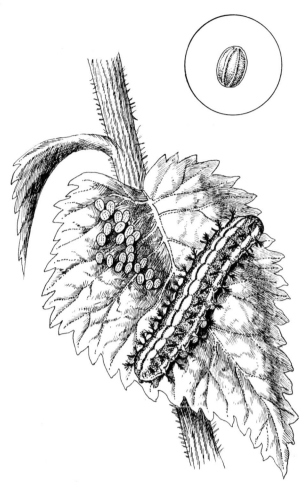

rely for protection on hairy coats or unpleasant tastes, advertising their unpleasantness with bold warning colours. Quite a number of species are pests: the Large white butterfly, *Pieris brassicae*, is a well-known destroyer of brassica crops, while a family of Buff-tip moths, *Phalera bucephala*, p. 201, can make short work of the foliage of a small fruit tree. It is, of course, the larvae that do the damage: the adults, if they feed at all, take only nectar and other liquids.

The pupa, or chrysalis, is usually protected in a silken cocoon and is often under

The eggs and caterpillar of a Small tortoiseshell butterfly with an enlarged egg above

The proboscis of a butterfly: in the diagram the outer channels contain blood and muscles and the nectar is sucked up through the centre; the butterflies on the right show one sucking nectar and the other with proboscis coiled

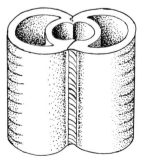

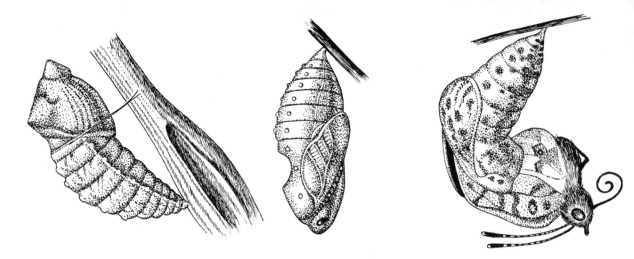

Butterfly pupae: Swallowtail suspended by a girdle of silk, *left;* Red admiral hanging by the tail end, *centre;* Heath fritillary emerging from its chrysalis, *right*

the ground, although certain butterflies pupate out in the open, hanging naked from a suitable support.

The division into butterflies and moths is rather like the division of animals into vertebrates and invertebrates – there are several superfamilies within the Lepidoptera and the butterflies belong to just one of these. The moths are, therefore, a much more numerous and varied assemblage than the butterflies. There are only about 70 kinds of butterfly in Britain, including rare immi-

grants such as the Bath white, *Pontia daplidice,* but there are about 2,000 species of moths. As far as the British species are concerned, it is very easy to distinguish between butterflies and moths: all butterflies have clubbed antennae but none of our moths has a real club. A few, such as the burnet moths, have thickened antennae but these can be separated from butterflies by looking at the wings. All Lepidoptera link the front and hind wings in some way so that they work together. Butterflies and some moths do it by having a big overlap, but some moths, including all those with thickened antennae, possess a device called a 'frenulum'. This is a stout bristle projecting from the hind wing and passing forwards under the front wing, where it is held in place by a little hook. There is a popular idea that butterflies are all brightly coloured and fly by day, whereas all moths are drab and fly by

The wing-coupling frenulum of a moth

Flies, *from left to right and top to bottom:* Hoverfly, *Xylota lenta;* Bee-fly, *Bombylius major;* Snipefly, *Rhagio scolopacea;* Hoverfly, *Chrysotoxum festivum;* Clusterfly, *Pollenia rudis;* Crane-fly, *Tipula maxima,* with Thistle gall, *Euribia cardui, below;* Dung fly, *Scopeuma stercorarium;* two forms of the Hoverfly, *Volucella bombylans;* Warble-fly, *Hypoderma* sp.; Horse-fly, *Tabanus bovinus;* Robber fly, *Asilus crabroniformis;* Green bottle, *Lucilia caesar*

night. This is not completely true, however, for many moths fly during the day and are extremely attractive insects.

Compared with even the nearest parts of the Continent our butterfly fauna is very meagre. We have only 60 permanently resident species and another dozen reach us in greater or lesser numbers each year from elsewhere. Even some of our permanent residents, such as the Peacock, *Nymphalis io*, p. 176, are reinforced each year by immigrants. As with many of our insects, the majority of butterflies are concentrated in the southern counties, and relatively few reach Scotland. There are, however, two species which live in Scotland and northern England only – the Mountain ringlet, *Erebia epiphron*, p. 175, and the Scotch argus, *E. aethiops*, p. 175, two alpine butterflies which probably reached us during the Ice Age and then withdrew to isolated strongholds as the ice retreated. Many other species are extremely local in their distribution, occurring in very restricted areas although quite common within those areas. One of the best examples is the Glanville fritillary, *Melitaea cinxia*, whose only British home is on the Isle of Wight, although it is widespread on the Continent. Climatic factors can explain this perhaps, while the occurrence of the food plant may limit other species such as the Chalkhill blue, *Lysandra coridon*, p. 175, but these factors cannot explain the restriction of the sloe-feeding Black hair-streak, *Strymonidia pruni*, to a handful of woods in the Midlands. Perhaps some of the mysteries of distribution will be solved by a new Nature Conservancy scheme to map all the British butterflies and moths.

The largest family of British butterflies is the Nymphalidae, which contains all the fritillaries, the Peacock, the tortoiseshells, and the 'king' of them all the Purple emperor, *Apatura iris*, p. 176. These butterflies vary a great deal in appearance and habits and one of the few features they have in common is the reduction of the front legs to little 'brushes'. The majority of our butterfly species pass the winter as eggs or pupae, but a number of the nymphalids hibernate as adult butterflies. They seek out barns, hollow trees and any suitable dry crevices and remain there during the winter. It is significant that these hibernating species, which include the Peacock, tortoiseshells, and the Comma, *Polygonia c-album*, p. 176, have very dull undersides, well suited to concealing the resting butterfly.

The 'Browns', family Satyridae, also have reduced front legs, but they are nearly all brown butterflies, decorated with various small 'eye-spots'. The butterflies are quite well camouflaged and the eye-spots are believed to be decoys for birds and other predators such as lizards in case the insects are attacked. The eye-spots are in non-vital places near the wing-margins and would tend to lead a predator's attention away from the vital parts. Many butterflies are seen with beak marks round the eye-spots and so the method presumably works quite well. The larger eye-spots carried by some other insects work by 'frightening' attackers into believing that the insect is really part of a much larger animal.

The larvae of the browns feed mainly on grass and these insects are found in grassy places nearly everywhere, although each species has its preferred habitat. The Gatekeeper, *Maniola tithonus*, for example, frequents hedgerows, whereas its cousin the Meadow brown, *M. jurtina*, is much more an insect of open meadows. Butterflies usually find their mates by sight at first, but scent plays an important part in courtship. It is the male butterfly who emits the scent, giving it

Sawflies and parasites, *from left to right and top to bottom*: Marble galls of oak and insect, *Andricus kollari*; ×4 Willow galls and sawfly, *Pontania vesicator* ×3; Apple sawfly, *Allantus cinctus*; ichneumon fly, *Rhyssa persuasoria*, laying eggs in a larva of the Wood wasp: chalcid *on leaf, Torymus* sp. ×3; chalcid, *Habrocytus bedeguaris* ×3; Gall wasp, *Diplolepis nervosa* ×3; Wood wasp, *Urocerus gigas*; sawfly, *Allantus arcuatus*; Robins' pincushion gall, gall wasp *Diplolepis rosae* ×4, and two pea galls of *D. nervosa*: Ruby-tailed wasp, *Chrysis ignita*; ichneumon fly, *Ophion luteus*, with Cabbage white caterpillar, *below*, surrounded by cocoons of *Apanteles glomeratus*; *Ichneumon suspiciosus*

off through special scales on the wings. These scales are often scattered all over the wings but in male satyrids and some others they are collected into patches on the front wings. The pupae of the browns, like those of the nymphalids, normally hang upside down from the food plant.

The 'Blues', family Lycaenidae, are nearly all small butterflies, in which the males are usually some shade of blue. The females are usually brown, although there may be some blue scales here and there. The insects feed on various low-growing plants and they are essentially insects of open fields and hillsides. The larvae are rather flattened and somewhat reminiscent of woodlice. They all possess a honey-secreting gland on the abdomen and they are frequently attended by ants, which find the 'honey' most attractive. This association with ants benefits the larvae as well because the ants appear to keep parasites away from the larvae. The association goes even further with the Large blue, *Maculinea arion*, p. 175, whose caterpillars are taken into the ants' nests and actually fed on the ants' own offspring. This carnivorous diet is less surprising when one realizes that many of the 'blue' caterpillars are cannibals, but the Large blue's life-history is nevertheless remarkable.

As well as the blues, the Lycaenidae includes the coppers and the hairstreaks. The latter are mainly woodland butterflies which, like the browns, have prominent scent-patches in the male.

The 'Whites', family Pieridae, are mainly white or yellow butterflies, including the Brimstone, *Gonepteryx rhamni*, p. 175, the Clouded yellow, *Colias croceus*, p. 175, and the Orange-tip, *Anthocharis cardamines*, p. 175, as well as the 'cabbage whites'. The latter comprise three species; the Large white, *Pieris brassicae*, the Small white, *P. rapae* and the Green-veined white, *P. napi*. The first two are serious pests in the garden and they are our only economically important butterflies. Both species are augmented by immigrants from the Continent. The pupae of this family are attached to stems and other upright sup-

ports by means of a silken pad at the tail end and a girdle round the middle.

The Swallowtail, *Papilio machaon*, p. 175, is our largest butterfly and our sole member of the family Papilionidae. This handsome insect now lives only on some of the Norfolk Broads, although some continental butterflies reach the south coast from time to time. The continental form is a different subspecies and is by no means confined to watery habitats.

Skipper butterflies, family Hesperidae, are all small and they show certain moth-like features. The antennae, for example, have a less abrupt club than those of other butterflies, while the pupae, unlike those of most butterflies, are enclosed in cocoons. The skippers have a quick, darting flight and a characteristic resting attitude p. 175, with the front wings half open. In cold weather, however, they will close the wings like other butterflies.

Turning now to the moths, the families are less easy to identify than those of the butterflies because the distinctions are based mainly on differences in the wing-veins. The traditional treatment is to split the moths into macros and micros, the big ones and little ones, but this is a very artificial division: those families with mainly large members are known as macros, while those families with mainly small members are known as micros. As a result, some relatively large moths, such as the Mother-of-Pearl, *Sylepta ruralis*, are grouped with the micros, while many smaller species, including the pugs, are officially macros.

Among the well-known micros are the Small magpie, *Eurrhypara hortulata*, p. 202, which feeds on stinging-nettles, and the plume-moths. The clothes-moths also belong to this division and their larvae are among the few non-plant feeding caterpillars. The original homes of these insects were the nests of birds and rodents, where they fed on feathers, hair and other debris. Smallest of all the moths are the pigmy-moths, shiny little creatures about 5 mm. in wing-span. Most of their larvae live as leaf-miners, carving out tunnels for themselves between the upper and lower surfaces of leaves. The tunnels show up as pale patches on the surface. One of the commonest of these moths is *Nepticula aurella*, whose tunnels twist and turn through bramble leaves. Related to the pigmy-moths, although rather larger, are the 'longhorns' of the genus *Nemotois* p. 202. The antennae of these insects may be several times as long as the body. These 'longhorn' moths fly by day and the males 'dance' in swarms, presumably to attract the females. In most moths, however, the female attracts the male, by emitting scent. The male picks up the scent with his antennae and makes his way to the female. In some moths there is no other way for the sexes to meet because the females are wingless. A well-known example is the Mottled umber, *Erannis defoliaria*.

Although many moths can be attracted to light, especially to the entomologist's mercury vapour lamp, they are basically insects of the dark and they hide away during the hours of daylight. They rest on tree-trunks or among the herbage and they are usually well camouflaged: the Buff-tip, for example, looks just like a broken twig when it wraps its wings round the body, while the Angle shades, *Phlogophora meticulosa*, p. 202, looks like a dead leaf. Many other moths resemble bark and 'disappear' when they settle. Some species, however, advertise their presence with bold colours which deter predators. Well-known examples include the Garden tiger, *Arctia caja*, p. 201, and the Cinnabar, *Callimorpha jacobaeae*, p. 201. Yet other moths combine camouflage with bright colours by having bright hind wings. These are covered by the more sombre front wings when the insect is at rest but, if it is disturbed, the bright colours flash as the insect flies away and this is believed to distract the predator and allow the insect to escape. This 'flash coloration' is well shown by the Dark crimson underwing, *Catocala sponsa*, p. 202, and the Yellow underwing, *Noctua pronuba*, p. 202.

Day-flying moths are usually more brightly coloured and they rely for protection on hairy coats or unpleasant tastes, coupled with warning colours. Examples are burnet moths, p. 202, the Oak eggar, *Lasiocampa quercus*, p. 201, and the Emperor moth, *Saturnia pavonia*, p. 201. The males of the latter species fly mainly by day, the females are more nocturnal. The male Emperor is remarkable for its ability to 'smell out' a female more than a mile away and a fresh female, put out in a muslin cage, will attract dozens of males with her scent. This moth gains a good deal of protection from the large eye-spots which warn predators away.

Eye-spots are also used with effect by the Eyed hawk-moth, *Smerinthus ocellata*, p. 201. The resting moth is concealed by its sombre front wings but, if disturbed, it opens its wings and displays the large 'eyes', giving the impression of a much larger creature. Hawk-moths, family Sphingidae, include some of our largest moths, with stout bodies and relatively narrow wings. They fly very fast and often come to lights at night. Some hawk-

Mottled umber, *Erannis defoliaria*, wingless female moth, *top;* 'looper' caterpillar, *below*

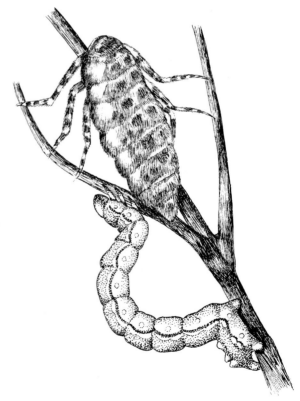

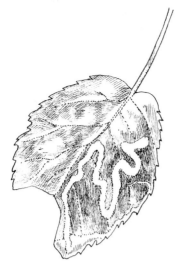

The mine of the leaf-miner, *Nepticula aurella*

moths are diurnal, however, and our two bee hawk-moths, *Hemaris fuciformis* and *H. tityus*, p. 201, mimic bumble-bees. The wings of these moths are covered with scales when they leave the pupae, but the scales nearly all fall during the first flight and only a brown border remains round the transparent wings. Hawk-moth larvae are generally green, with diagonal stripes which help to camouflage them among the leaves. They can be recognized as hawk-moth larvae by the little horn at the tail end. The larvae of the Elephant hawk-moth, *Deilephila elpenor*, and the Small Elephant hawk-moth, *D. porcellus*, p. 201, are brown in colour and can be quite frightening because the head can be retracted into the thorax and the latter bears eye-spots which give it a snake-like appearance.

The family Geometridae contains a wide assortment of rather slender and fragile-looking moths whose larvae have lost the first three pairs of abdominal legs. The larvae are known as 'loopers' because they move about by stretching forwards and then looping the body upwards as they draw the hind legs up to meet the front ones. Many of these loopers are remarkably like the twigs on which they live, even down to little 'warts' which resemble the buds. Notable examples include the larvae of the Swallow-tailed moth, *Ourapteryx sambucaria*, and the Pep-

pered moth, *Biston betularia*, p. 202. The latter species is also of great interest because it illustrates evolution in action. Two main forms of the moth exist – the 'normal' form, which is basically white but heavily mottled with black, and the melanic form, which is completely black. One hundred years ago the melanic form was very rare but then it started to increase rapidly until today it is generally more common than the 'normal' form. The spread of the melanic form started in industrial regions and the explanation for this 'industrial melanism' is relatively simple. With the coming of the Industrial Revolution tree-trunks, walls and so on became blackened with soot and grime and the occasional melanic moth was, therefore, protected by its camouflage. 'Normal' moths were easily picked off by predators and the melanics survived to breed. They increased gradually and today the 'normal' form is the rarity in industrial regions. Until fairly recently country areas, with clean, lichen-clad tree-trunks, favoured the 'normal' form, but the melanic moths are now spreading even into rural regions and so there must be other factors at work besides straightforward selection by predators. The most likely explanation is that the melanic moths are generally hardier than the 'normal' forms and that their hardiness is an advantage in an environment being increasingly poisoned by smoke and diesel fumes. Industrial and rural melanism is not confined to the Peppered moth and has been discovered in about 20 other species so far.

The most primitive of our macro-lepidoptera are the Swift moths of the family Hepialidae. They can be recognized by their very short antennae and by the wings which, unlike those of other large moths, are all the same shape. The Ghost Swift, *Hepialus humili*, p. 202, displays an interesting sexual difference, the male having a pure white upper side, while the female is yellowish brown. The males come out soon after dusk and hover about over the grass, rather like marionettes bobbing up and down on strings. As they 'dance' their white upper sides flash regularly and attract the freshly emerged females. Whereas most female moths lay their eggs carefully on the correct food plant, the Swift moths simply scatter their eggs as they fly about. The larvae, however, are not very fussy about their food and they feed underground on a variety of plant roots.

Caddis flies resemble moths in many ways, but their wings are covered with hairs instead of scales and they never have the coiled proboscis possessed by most moths. The most fundamental difference between the caddis flies and the moths, however, is in the life-story: the caddis larvae are aquatic. Caddis flies are, therefore, placed in a separate Order known as Trichoptera (=hairy wings). The adult insects are generally rather dull in colour, predominantly grey or brown, and they are nearly all nocturnal. During the day-time they hide among the vegetation, assuming a characteristic

resting attitude, p. 173, with the long antennae projecting forward. They do not necessarily stay close to the water and often come to lighted windows far from the nearest stream. They are very common visitors to the entomologist's moth-trap. The association of the caddis flies with water makes them well known to the angler, who usually calls them sedge flies and uses them, like the mayflies and stone flies, as models for artificial flies.

Caddis fly and larva without case, *right;* larval cases: *Anabolia nervosa*, *below; from left to right bottom, Setodes, Limnophilus* using pieces of plant, *Oligotricha* and *Limnophilus* using small shells

The caddis larvae, often called caddis-worms or stick-worms are of special interest because many of them build portable homes. These are known as 'caddis cases' and are usually open-ended tubes composed of various materials such as sand-grains, leaf fragments, twigs and even tiny mollusc shells. The particles are built up on a silken envelope which the larva spins round itself before starting to build. The figure shows how neatly the caddis-worm fits the particles together and also how the pattern varies from species to species.

Most of the caddis body is very soft, but the head and legs have a tough cuticle and they protrude from the front of the case, allowing the insect to move about in search of food. Caddis-worms are largely omnivorous and will eat both plant and animal material. They maintain a constant stream of water through their cases and extract oxygen from it with feathery gills along the sides of the body.

Inside their cases the caddis-worms are protected from many enemies, but fishes and water-birds will swallow the cases as well. *Anabolia nervosa*, however, has evolved the habit of attaching small sticks to its case and this prevents it from being eaten, at least by fishes. Many species living in swift streams attach stones to their cases, thereby reducing the risk of being swept away.

Some of the caddis larvae living in running water make no cases, but spin silken shelters among the vegetation. The edges of the shelters are often extended to form snares and the insects feed on small plants and animals that get trapped there. A few caddis larvae live quite freely on the stream-bed.

Pupation takes place in the case and even those species that do not normally live in cases make special ones for this purpose. The pupa is quite unlike that of most moths and all its appendages are movable. When the adult is fully developed, the pupa bites its way out of the case and swims to the surface. There its wings expand extremely rapidly, allowing it to fly away almost immediately.

Eggs are laid in or around the water and the life cycle begins again.

Most winged insects have two pairs of wings, but the House-fly and its relatives have only one pair. These insects, known collectively as 'two-winged flies' or simply as 'flies', are placed in the Order Diptera (=two wings). This is a very large Order, with well over 5,000 species in Britain, and its members vary from tiny midges to long, slender crane-flies and stout hover-flies.

Although there are some wingless species, the flies normally have fully developed front wings and they are no mean aeronauts. The hind wings are like tiny pins and are known as 'halteres' or 'balancers'. They vibrate rapidly when the insect is in flight and their gyroscopic action helps the fly to maintain its balance. The halteres are very clearly seen in crane-flies, but they are often concealed under flaps of tissue in other flies.

The fly's head is usually fairly large in relation to the body and it carries a pair of prominent compound eyes. The antennae vary from long and slender in some of the midges to very short and bristle-like in the house-flies. Mouth-parts vary considerably among the flies but are always adapted for sucking up liquid food. The majority of flies feed by mopping up fluids, especially from decaying matter, but a number of species, including horse-flies and mosquitoes, feed on blood and have mouth-parts capable of piercing the skin of other animals. Blood-feeding is usually, but not always confined to the females. The figure illustrates two very different types of fly mouth-parts.

Fly larvae are always legless, although some of them possess stumpy outgrowths here and there. The larvae of crane-flies, mosquitoes and certain others have fairly well-developed heads, but there is considerable reduction of the head in other flies, until one gets to the carrot-shaped maggots of house-flies and blow-flies in which there is virtually no head. The majority of larvae feed on liquid or semi-liquid decaying material and they occupy a wide range of habitats, many of them aquatic. Some species feed on

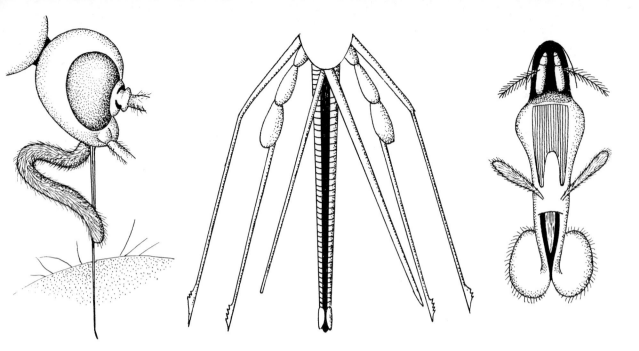

The mouth-parts of the House-fly, *right*, and the mosquito, *left,* represent two extremes. The House-fly mouth-parts form a spongy pad which mops up fluids. The mosquito has needle-like mouth-parts which fit together to pierce the host and form a channel for imbibing blood. They are shown separated in the centre picture but they all fit neatly into a sheath which is drawn back as the insect feeds, *left*

plants and among these there are many gall-causers, including *Euribia cardui*, p. 219, which causes swellings in the stems of thistles. Many other fly larvae are parasitic, living inside the bodies of animals which range from other insects to cattle and horses.

Economically, the flies are extremely important and, because of their varied habits, they affect man in many different ways. Mosquitoes and other blood-feeders affect us directly, not only by their annoying bites but also by transmitting several serious diseases such as malaria and yellow fever. House-flies and blue-bottles spread diseases such as polio and dysentery by contaminating our food. Many flies, including the Warble-fly, *Hypoderma bovis*, p. 219, affect our domestic animals, while others affect our growing crops. Hoverflies, however, are beneficial because many of their larvae feed on aphids while the adults, in common with many other flies, play some part in pollinating flowers and crops.

The crane-flies, of which we have some 300 species in the British Isles, are rather long, leggy insects and the larger species, many of which come into houses in late summer, are known as 'Daddy-Long-Legs', p. 219. Although they are disliked by many people, these insects are quite harmless in the adult stage. Most of the larvae, too, are harmless and spend their days in decaying wood or the detritus at the bottom of a pond. A few larvae, however, prefer to feed on the roots of plants and they do considerable damage to fields and gardens. These destructive larvae are called 'leather-jackets' and they are particularly common in grassland. One of the commonest species is *Tipula paludosa*, the adults of which are greyish brown.

Mosquitoes or gnats look rather like small crane-flies but are readily distinguished by the scales that clothe the wing-veins. The eggs are laid on still or slow-moving water and the larvae are aquatic, feeding on micro-organisms which they filter from the water with an elaborate series of bristles round the mouth. Although they live under the water, the larvae breathe air and they spend much of their time hanging from the surface with the breathing-tubes at the hind end just breaking through into the air. Mosquito pupae are comma-shaped, with very large heads. They spend most of the time hanging from the surface, with their thoracic breathing-tubes in contact with the air, but they are remarkably active for pupae and they will swim vigorously away when disturbed. The adults emerge at the water surface and soon fly away.

Only the female mosquitoes are blood-suckers and most of them seem to need a meal of blood before they can lay fertile eggs. Their mouth-parts consist of several needle-like blades which pierce the skins of their victims and form channels for withdrawing blood. The male mosquitoes, easily distinguished by their feathery antennae, feed mainly on nectar and they lack the piercing mouth-parts.

Mosquitoes are best known for their ability to transmit malaria, but not every mosquito is a carrier. The malaria parasite has to undergo various changes in the mosquito body and reach the insect's salivary glands before it can infect another human, and these changes can take place only in certain mosquitoes known as anophelines. We do have some of these mosquitoes in Britain, but drainage of marshland has reduced their numbers and malaria occurs only occasionally in this country. Most of our mosquitoes are of species known as culicines and, although some of them have painful and irritating bites, they rarely carry diseases in this country. Anophelines

can be distinguished from culicines quite easily by their resting attitudes.

Among the most attractive of our flies are the hoverflies, family Syrphidae. They vary enormously in shape and colour but they all have large eyes and the most characteristic

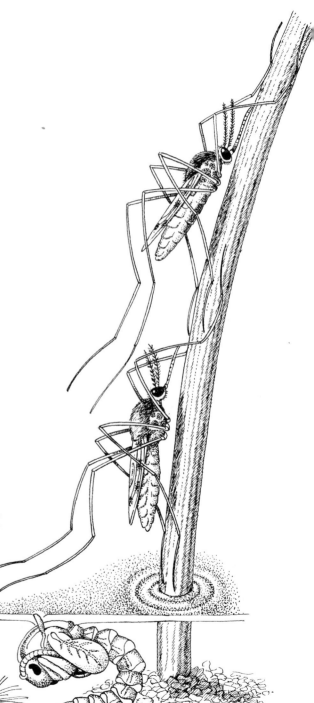

Mosquitoes, the life-cycle: *left to right,* of a culicine – eggs, larva, pupa and adult above water; the mosquito at the top is an anopheline

228

feature is the 'false margin' of the wing, formed by a vein running parallel to the edge but a little way in from it. We have about 250 species and they can be found on and around flowers from March until late autumn. The hovering flight is very noticeable but probably the most striking thing about the hoverflies is the marked resemblance of many species to bees and wasps. All of us must at some time or other have drawn back from the yellow and black *Syrphus ribesii* in the belief that it was a wasp, and this resemblance surely protects the hoverfly from many birds and other predators. Some hoverflies, such as *Volucella bombylans*, p. 219, exist in two or more forms, each mimicking a different species of bee or wasp. More will be said about this mimicry later.

Another fly that hovers, although not related to the hoverflies, is the Bee-fly, *Bombylius major*. This stout, furry fly can be seen at flowers in early spring and is easily recognized by its long proboscis, p. 219. Some of the horse-flies may also be confused with hoverflies, but their wing-veins are very different. Female horse-flies, p. 219, are blood-suckers and they possess stout, dagger-like mouthparts which they sink deeply into the skin of their victims.

The House-fly, *Musca domestica*, once the commonest fly found in houses but now rare, is by no means confined to houses, the larvae feed on all kinds of decaying matter and the fly finds suitable conditions in rubbish-dumps and farmyard manure-heaps, as well as in and around houses. It is one of the many insects that have followed man around the world, taking advantage of the conditions he has created and thereby becoming a pest. The House-fly cannot bite and does not damage us directly, but its liking for garbage and excrement makes it a serious carrier of germs, including those causing dysentery and other intestinal troubles.

The Cluster-fly, *Pollenia rudis*, p. 219, is quite similar to the House-fly but can be distinguished by the rather golden hairs on the thorax. Cluster-flies enter houses only in the autumn and they hibernate in dense clusters in attics and other dark places. The larvae of these flies live as parasites inside earth-worms.

Blow-flies or blue-bottles are large, noisy flies which often come into houses during the summer. They are similar to the house-flies in their habits but prefer animal matter in which to lay their eggs. These are the flies that most often lay their eggs on an uncovered joint or fillet of fish and they are serious pests around slaughter-houses. Green-bottles, of which there are several different kinds, do not often come indoors and are most often seen on and around dead animals. *Lucilia caesar*, p. 219, and *L. sericata* lay their eggs in sores and scratches on sheep and the maggots burrow into the flesh, causing much damage to the animals.

Fleas, like lice, are external parasites of warm-blooded animals and cat-owners probably know them better than anyone. They are little brown insects, flattened from side to side, and extremely difficult to catch as they scuttle through the host's hair or feathers. Fleas have a remarkable jumping ability and often jump from one host to another. They are blood-suckers and, although each species has its own particular

House-fly life-cycle: eggs, larva, pupa and adult

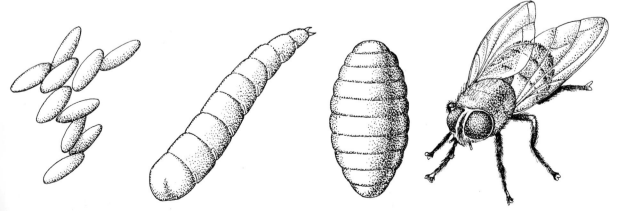

host, they will bite more or less any warm-blooded animal that passes, including man. The bite itself is not harmful but, like lice, fleas can transmit diseases and they should always be controlled.

Unlike the lice, fleas are not parasitic throughout life. The young flea is a maggot-like larva that lives on debris in the host's nest. It will also live quite happily under carpets frequented by cats or other domestic animals.

The flea larvae pupate in little cocoons in the host's nest and the pupae can remain dormant in the cocoons for many months. Emergence of the adults is stimulated by vibrations – a neat arrangement ensuring that the fleas come out only when the host is in or around the nest.

Fleas are quite unlike any other insect and are placed in their own Order, the Siphonaptera (=wingless suckers). They have long been considered as related to the two-winged flies but they are now thought to be more closely related to the scorpion-flies.

The Order Hymenoptera is another extremely large one, with well over 6,000 species in the British Isles. These include bees, wasps, ants, sawflies, ichneumon flies, and a host of smaller, less familiar insects. Their sizes range from the large, hairy bumble bees, down to the minute fairy-flies which spend their early lives inside the eggs of other insects. This variation in size is matched by a variety of habits unequalled in any other Order of insects. There are straightforward plant-eating sawflies, various gall-causers, predatory wasps, numerous parasites, and the various social insects which are perhaps the most fascinating of all the Hymenoptera.

The wings, when present, are membranous (Hymenoptera means 'membrane wings') and they are linked together by a row of tiny hooks on the front margin of the hind wing. Apart from this, there is little to suggest that all these insects belong to a single Order. There are actually two well-defined sub-orders: the Symphyta, sawflies, in which the abdomen is broadly joined to the thorax, and the 'wasp-waisted' Apocrita.

The sawflies, of which there are over 400 species in Britain, take their name from the egg-laying apparatus or ovipositor of the female, which is usually composed of two saw-edged blades used for splitting plants stems and depositing the eggs. Most of the sawflies are dark in colour and they are often to be seen sunning themselves, wings folded, on leaves and flowers. They do not fly a great deal and, when disturbed, they are more likely to scuttle away, waving their antennae as they go. Sawflies have biting mouths and the adults feed on pollen and also on small insect life. The eggs are usually laid in slits in leaves, but some species bore into stems and lay their eggs there. The larvae are all plant-feeders, many of them feeding freely on the leaves and looking very much like moth caterpillars. Sawfly larvae can be distinguished, however, because they have at least six pairs of stumpy abdominal legs, whereas the moth caterpillar never has more than five pairs. The larvae are certainly more often seen than the adults, although the first indication of their presence is usually a

Flea life-cycle: eggs, larva, pupa and adult

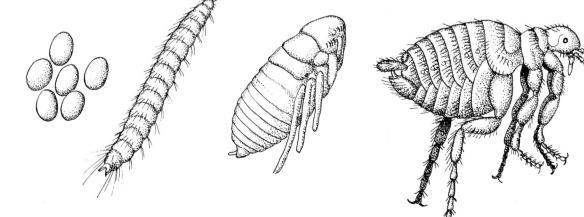

duced and the abdominal legs are absent. They take up to three years to complete their growth, during which time the tree may well be felled. It is not unusual for the larvae to survive the saw-mill, however, and for the adults to emerge in new buildings, much to the consternation of their occupants. One might expect the Wood wasp grub to be safe from attack in its woody retreat, but the ichneumon *Rhyssa persuasoria*, p. 220, is able to detect it and drill down to lay an egg beside it. On hatching the *Rhyssa* larva then proceeds to consume the Wood wasp grub at leisure.

The suborder Apocrita is by far the larger of the two groups and its members can be recognized by the 'wasp-waist'. This group is further split into two subdivisions: the Parasitica, which are nearly all parasitic insects,

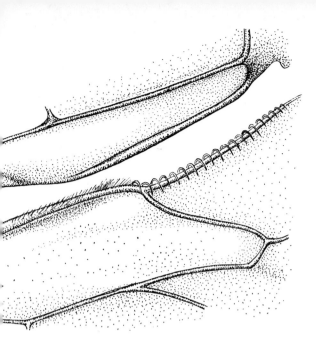

The hooks of a bee's wing, used to link the wings together

partly defoliated plant. The Gooseberry sawfly, *Nematus ribesii*, is a very common and troublesome pest in gardens. Another very common sawfly, although the insect itself is not often seen, is *Pontania proxima*. This is one insect responsible for the red 'bean galls' so common on willow leaves, p. 220. Unlike most galls, this one starts to develop as soon as the sawfly has laid its egg in the leaf and, by the time the egg hatches, it affords a plentiful supply of food for the larva. When fully grown the larva leaves the gall and pupates in the soil or in a suitable crevice of bark.

One of the most frightening insects in our islands is undoubtedly the female Wood wasp, *Urocerus gigas*. This sawfly is a yellow and black insect, a little more than an inch (25 mm.) long and possessing a very prominent ovipositor, p. 220, which most people take to be a powerful sting. In fact, it is nothing of the kind and the insect is quite harmless. It uses its ovipositor to drill into pine and spruce trunks and lay its eggs deep in the wood. The larvae feed on the wood and, being surrounded by food, have little need to move far. Their legs are, therefore, considerably re-

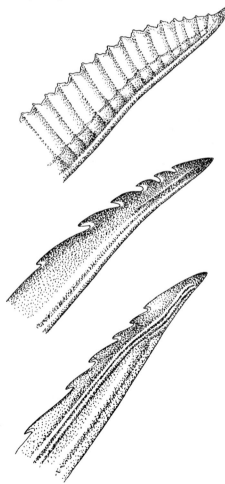

Blades of a sawfly ovipositor, *top;* bee sting, *centre;* wasp sting, *bottom*

and the Aculeata, which includes the bees, wasps and ants. In many of the Aculeata, the ovipositor is modified as a sting. All members of the Apocrita provide food for their larvae in one way or another and the larvae need move very little. Consequently, they are legless and generally poorly developed.

The ichneumon flies constitute a very large group of parasites, most of which attack the young stages of other insects. One of the commonest species is *Ophion luteus*, p. 220, a yellowish-brown insect which frequently comes into lighted rooms at night and whose larvae parasitize various moth caterpillars. The female ichneumon relies mainly on scent to find a victim and she runs about on the herbage, tapping her long antennae here and there to locate a suitable caterpillar. Having done so, she uses her needle-like ovipositor to pierce the host and lay one or more eggs inside it. Not all ichneumons actually lay their eggs inside the host: some deposit their eggs close to the host and the young ichneumons either tunnel into the host themselves or, as with *Rhyssa*, they attach themselves to the outside of the host. The ichneumon larvae do not kill their hosts right away but feed on non-essential organs so that the hosts just about stay alive. Only when the parasites are fully grown do they finally kill their hosts.

The parasites then pupate in little cocoons, inside or outside the host body.

Another common ichneumon is *Apanteles glomeratus*, p. 220, which parasitizes caterpillars of the Large white butterfly. A single caterpillar may support over 100 parasites and their bright yellow cocoons are very often seen clustered round dead larvae or pupae of the host. *Apanteles* plays an important role in controlling the numbers of the Large white, but it is kept in check itself by another ichneumon known as *Hemiteles fulvipes*. This insect is a parasite of a parasite and is therefore called a hyperparasite. It detects the *Apanteles* larvae within the host caterpillar and proceeds to lay its eggs inside them, drilling right through the caterpillar's skin to reach them. But this is not the end of

the story: *Hemiteles* itself has a parasite, a minute chalcid which somehow manages to find its host deep in the caterpillar's body.

The chalcids are all tiny insects and almost all of them are parasites or hyperparasites. Many of them spend their larval life inside the eggs of other insects. Some of the chalcids that parasitize gall wasps have enormous ovipositors, several times the length of the body, which reach right down into the gall to lay the eggs beside the host insect.

Gall wasps are small ant-like insects, although they usually have wings. The insects themselves are not often seen, but many of their galls are common objects in the countryside. One of the most conspicuous is the 'robin's pincushion' or bedeguar gall, a fluffy red ball found on the wild rose. It is caused by a little black and red insect called *Diplolepis rosae*, p. 220, which lays its eggs in the rose stem or leaf in the spring and the developing larvae cause the plant tissue to grow abnormally and produce the gall. It is green at first but soon becomes reddish. The red hairs conceal a hard, woody swelling with several chambers, each containing a gall wasp larva. The larvae feed on the tissues within the gall and are usually fully grown by the end of the autumn. After resting through the winter, they pupate and the adult insects emerge in the spring. Males are extremely rare in this species and the insects reproduce almost entirely by virgin birth or parthenogenesis. Several other species of gall wasp attack the wild rose, but by far the greatest number of species are found on the oak.

One of the most abundant galls on the oak is the marble gall, p. 220, often wrongly called the oak-apple (another gall). It is a round swelling about the size of a marble, green at first but becoming brown as it matures. It is caused by *Andricus kollari*, which lays its eggs in the twigs of the oak in late spring. Each larva causes the oak tissues to swell up round it and provide it with nutritious food. By late summer the larva is fully grown and it pupates, the adult emerging a few weeks later through a neat hole in the gall. The insects emerging in the autumn are all females and they fly off in search of the Turkey oak, *Quercus cerris*. They lay their parthenogenetic eggs in the buds and the new larvae cause small galls to develop in the buds in the early spring. Adult insects emerge from these buds during the spring but they are not quite like the autumn insects and both males and females are present. After mating, the females fly back to the common oaks and lay their eggs in the twigs, starting the cycle again. This alternation between a sexual generation and a parthenogenetic generation is typical of gall-wasps affecting the oak, although *Andricus kollari* is unusual in affecting two different host plants. Most gall wasps have both generations on one host.

Gall wasps are quite easy to obtain if the mature galls are collected, but the insects are subject to heavy parasitism and many of the insects emerging from the galls are likely to be chalcids and ichneumon flies. There are also a number of gall wasps which do not induce gall formation themselves but which invade the galls of other species and live there as inquilines or lodgers. Although they do no direct harm to the rightful occupant, these lodgers take a large amount of food from the gall and the original occupant usually dies of malnutrition.

The division between the Parasitica and the Aculeata is not clear-cut and there are several small groups of insects that show affinities with both sections. One such group contains the ruby-tailed wasps, brilliant metallic-coloured insects with maroon abdomens. They parasitize various species of bees and wasps and during the spring they can be seen running about over tree-stumps in search of their host's nests.

In the Aculeata the ovipositor is usually modified into a sting. It is composed of three

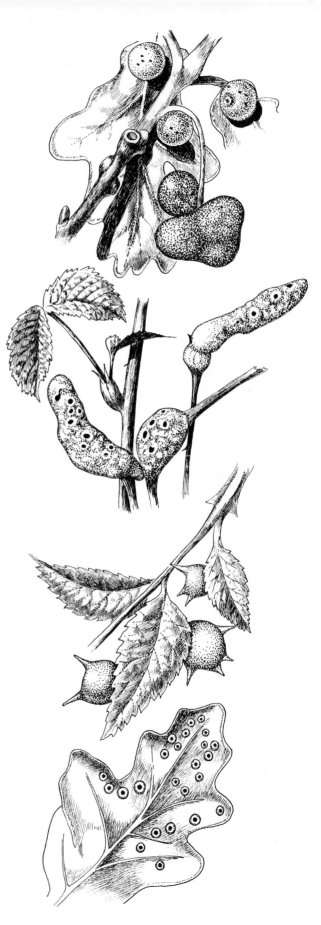

Plant galls caused by gall wasps, *from top to bottom:* Currant gall, *Neuroterus quercusbaccarum;* Blackberry gall, *Diastrophus rubi;* Spiked pea gall, *Diplolepis nervosa,* on rose ; Silk button spangle gall, *Neuroterus numismatis,* on oak

needle-like blades connected to a poison gland. It is used primarily for defence and, among the wasps, for paralysing prey. Because this sting is derived from the egg-laying apparatus, only female insects are able to sting.

To the layman, there are probably only two kinds of bees – bumble bees and honey bees – but there are actually some 250 different kinds of bees in the British Isles, including 25 species of bumble bees. Most of them lead solitary lives, without any sign of colony formation, but they all provide their off-spring with food in the form of pollen and nectar obtained from flowers. This is one of the main differences between bees and wasps, because all wasps feed their young on animal material.

Most of our solitary bees are spring insects and they play an important role in pollinating the spring flowers. Typical examples of these bees are the members of the genus *Andrena*, p. 237, rather flattened but not unlike small honey bees. They are often called 'mining bees' because each female digs a small burrow in which she lays her eggs. The burrows are usually in sandy soil and are often so close together that one might be forgiven for thinking they are social insects. This is not so, however, and each burrow is quite separate. The female bee makes about six chambers in each burrow and, having provisioned them with a mixture of pollen and nectar, she lays an egg in each. She then closes the burrow and pays no more attention to it. Some species develop quickly and produce a summer brood, but others take a whole year to mature and the adults are found only in the spring.

Many of the mining bees' nests are invaded by little wasp-like bees of the genus *Nomada*, p. 237. They have no pollen-collecting equipment of their own and they provide their larvae with food by laying their eggs in the nests of other bees. They are often called cuckoo bees.

Bumble bees, p. 237, are large, hairy bees with long tongues. They are all social insects with elaborate colony formation and co-operation between individuals. The colony is usually underground, often in an old mouse-hole, and it is an annual affair with only mated females or queens living through the winter. The queens emerge from their hibernation in the spring and look around for suitable nesting-sites. Having found a site, a queen will make a rough nest with grass, and then deposit a lump of 'bee bread' in it. This is a mixture of pollen and honey and the bee then lays about a dozen eggs on it. She surrounds them with wax and sits on them until they hatch. The grubs feed on the bee bread, which the queen replenishes as necessary, and become adult after two or three weeks. These new adults are all sterile females and they are called workers. Workers are found only in social insects and their job is to build up the nest and feed their younger sisters and later their younger brothers, the drones. This co-operation between individuals is the basis of all social life. When once the first brood of workers has emerged, the queen bumble bee gradually retires from food-gathering and remains inside the nest. She spends much of her time laying eggs but she does do some of the domestic chores, such as feeding the young grubs. Workers continue to be produced for much of the summer but then males and fully developed females appear. After mating these new females or queens seek winter quarters but, with the first frosts, the rest of the colony perishes.

The single mating of the queen provides her with enough sperm for the whole year and her eggs are fertilized as they develop. She is able to control fertilization, however, and she lays a certain number of unfertilized, parthenogenetic eggs. It is these unfertilized eggs that develop into males or drones. The appearance of fully developed females which become new queens appears to depend upon the ratio of workers to larvae. Towards the end of summer egg-laying falls off a little but there are a large number of existing workers. The young larvae, therefore, get more food and attention and they develop into fertile females.

Like the mining bees, the bumble bees have their 'cuckoos'. These are the large bees of the genus *Psithyrus* and they closely resemble the bumble bees themselves, except that they have no pollen-collecting equipment. Female *Psithyrus* bees enter the nests of bumble bees in late spring and, if they survive an initial attack by the workers, they settle down to lay their eggs. *Psithyrus* has no worker caste and it relies entirely on the bumble-bee workers to bring up its young. When once the cuckoo bee is established the nest will produce no more bumble bees, for *Psithyrus* either kills the bumble bee queen or eats all her eggs.

The Honey bee, *Apis mellifera*, p. 237, is not a native and, apart from the occasional swarm which escapes the bee-keeper and builds its combs in a hollow tree, the insect does not live wild in this country.

The name 'wasp' is, unfortunately, given to several widely separated groups of Hymenoptera and we have already mentioned wood wasps, gall wasps, and ruby-tailed wasps. Now, in the Aculeata, we meet three more groups, including those more familiar to the layman. All of them feed their young on other small animals which are paralysed by the sting. The adults, however, are not carnivorous and they exist on a diet of nectar and fruit juice.

Bees: the hind legs of a pollen-gathering bumble bee, *left*; a cuckoo bee, *Psithyrus, centre*; the feathery hairs of a bumble bee used for gathering pollen, *right*

The true wasps, which include the 'domestic' species, belong to the family Vespidae and can be recognized by their habit of folding the wings lengthwise when at rest. This family includes both social and solitary species and among the latter is the famous Potter wasp, *Eumenes coarctata*, p. 237. This little insect lives on heathland and the female builds a number of small 'flasks' from sand-grains cemented together with saliva. She stocks each one with small caterpillars and lays an egg in each. The caterpillars are paralysed but not dead and they provide a regular supply of fresh food for the developing wasp larva until it pupates some months later. Similar insects, called mason wasps, build little nests in old walls and cliff-faces.

We have seven species of social wasp, of which the commonest are the Common wasp, *Vespa vulgaris*, and the German wasp, *Vespa germanica*. These are the ones that annoy us in late summer when they buzz around our fruit and jam. The wasp's life-story is very much like that of the bumble bee, with only the mated queen surviving the winter. Nesting and feeding habits are very different from those of the bumble bee, however.

The queen wasp comes out of hibernation in the spring and soon begins to look for a nesting-site. The two common species usually nest under the ground, but the Tree wasp, *V. sylvestris*, p. 237, hangs its nest in a tree or bush. Wasp nests are made from paper which the wasps manufacture themselves. They select a suitable tree-stump or fence-post and begin to scrape the wood off with their strong

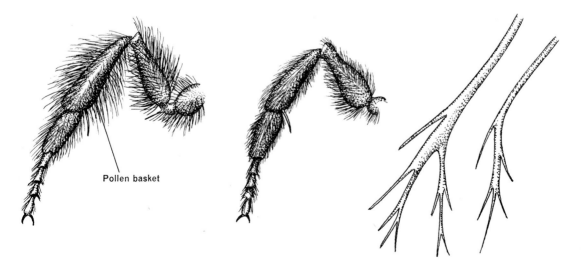

Pollen basket

jaws. The sound of scraping is quite audible and, once you have located a scraping wasp, you will be able to watch it at leisure because it will return time and time again to the same spot. When the wood has been removed it is pulped up with the wasp's saliva and converted into a rough sort of paper which is used to build the nest. The queen starts off the nest by building a little hanging dome and she then constructs neat six-sided cells on its undersurface. She fixes an egg in each cell and feeds the larvae on chewed-up caterpillars and other insects. Within a few weeks these larvae turn into worker wasps and they begin to build up the nest by adding more layers of cells. More workers are produced and the queen gradually retires from work, devoting herself from then on to laying eggs.

The workers complete the nest, which is finally ball-shaped and covered with a thin and very fragile layer of paper, and continue to rear the young larvae for most of the summer. Huge numbers of insect pests are consumed by the wasp larvae during the summer and so the wasps are really useful insects. Egg production falls off towards the end of the summer and male and female wasps are then reared. When these have matured the workers have no more household duties and this is when they turn their attention to the tea-table. The colony gradually breaks up and the wasps die as autumn comes in, leaving only the mated queens to survive until the following spring.

The Hornet, *Vespa crabro*, p. 237, is our largest wasp. It usually makes its nest in hollow trees, but its life-story is just the same as that of the Common wasp. Among our 7 species we also have the Cuckoo wasp, *Vespa austriaca*, which has no workers and lays its eggs in the nests of other wasps.

Our 230 members of the family Sphecidae are all solitary wasps and they are commonly called digger wasps because many of the species construct underground nests. Many species are black or black and yellow, but others, such as the long slender sand wasps, *Ammophila* species, are far from the popular idea of a wasp, p. 237. The digger wasps may construct one or more chambers in each nest and they provision them with a wide variety of insects, although each species keeps to a particular diet. *Gorytes*, p. 237, for example, provide their larvae with nothing but froghopper nymphs.

The spider-hunting wasps, family Pompilidae, p. 237, have a similar life to that of the digger wasps, the main difference being that they provide spiders for their larvae instead of insects. The males of all these solitary wasps are relatively lazy insects, sipping nectar all day while the females alone construct the nests and provide for the young.

Many bees and wasps sport bold patterns of black with red or yellow. One might think that such conspicuous insects would soon be snapped up by birds but observations show that this is not so. Young birds do try to eat bees and wasps but they quickly reject them because of the stings and the bitter taste of these insects. Before long the young birds avoid them altogether. Experiments have shown that the bold colours actually protect the insects because the birds soon learn to associate bold colours with unpleasantness and they leave the insects alone. The bold colours, therefore, act as a warning.

The lessons learned with bees and wasps extend to all black and yellow or black and red insects and even we have come to think twice before approaching any insect showing warning coloration. The same thing happens with birds, and many edible insects are saved simply because they resemble wasps. This phenomenon is known as 'mimicry'. The unpleasant insect which is copied is known as the model and the harmless one that copies it is the mimic, not that there is any conscious action by the mimic – it just happens

Bees and wasps, *from left to right and top to bottom*: Honey bees, drone, worker and queen; Tree wasp *Vespa sylvestris*, male, female and queen above nest; Hornet, *Vespa crabo*; Potter wasp, *Eumenes coarctata*, and nest 'pots'; Spider-hunting wasp, *Pompilus fuscus*; Red-tailed bumble bee, *Bombus* sp., with the Digger wasp, *Gorytes mystaceus*, *below*; the wasp-like Nomad bee, *Nomada* sp.; Sand wasp, *Ammophila* sp.; Mining bee, *Andrena* sp.

to resemble the model. Any degree of resemblance, however small, will benefit the mimic species but the system will work only if the model is more common than the mimic. If the mimic were the commoner of the two, young predators would get more of the edible insects and would associate the bold pattern with good food.

Some of the best mimics are the hoverflies mentioned earlier and they mimic a wide range of bees and wasps. Some hoverflies exist in two or more forms, each form mimicking a different species of bee or wasp. In this way the mimic can increase its numbers considerably without danger of exceeding the total number of models. *Volucella bombylans* is a well-known mimic which imitates several species of bumble bee, p. 219. Another excellent mimic is the Wasp beetle, *Clytus arietus*, p. 238. Although it does not look much like a wasp when examined closely, it runs over the tree-trunks and herbage waving its antennae in a very wasp-like fashion and it is very easily mistaken for a solitary wasp. Mimics are also found among the Lepidoptera with the bee hawk-moths and other Hymenoptera with the wood-wasps.

Ants are among the most advanced of all insects and all ant species are social. Their nests are usually under the ground and, except when we disturb a nest in the garden or inadvertently picnic near one, we do not see much of the occupants. Once a year, however, the ants go on their marriage-flights and all the ant nests in the neighbourhood seem to erupt at the same time,

providing a feast for birds and sending the housewife scurrying to the shop for ant-killer. These flying ants are the males and fully developed females but they represent only a small proportion of the ant community, most of which are wingless workers.

Soon after the marriage-flight the males die but the females are only just beginning the useful part of their lives. Their first act on returning to earth is to remove their wings, for these will be of no further use in the confines of the nest. The new queens then either enter an existing nest, perhaps the one from which they came, or they hole up in some crevice while their eggs develop. Nourishment during this period is provided by their degenerating flight-muscles. Eggs are laid in spring and the young queen feeds her larvae on her own saliva. These larvae

A typical wasp with wings folded lengthwise and a typical bumble bee with wings laid flat

Beetles, *from left to right and top to bottom*: Leaf beetle, *Melosoma populi*; Seven-spot ladybird, *Coccinella septempunctata*, with larva *above*; Nut weevil, *Curculio nucum*; Cockchafer, *Melolontha melolontha* $\times \frac{1}{2}$; Green tiger beetle, *Cicindela campestris*; Elmbark beetle, *Scolytes destructor*, and tunnels; Soldier beetle, *Cantharis livida*; Wasp beetle, *Clytus arietus*; Stag beetle, *Lucanus cervus*, male and *below* head of female; Glow worm, *Lampyris noctiluca*, larva, male and female; Cardinal beetle, *Pyrochroa coccinea*; Devil's coach horse, *Ocypus olens*; Click beetle, *Agriotes lineatus*, and larval wireworm; Violet ground beetle, *Carabus violaceus*; Burying beetle, *Necrophorus investigator*

become workers and they begin construction of the nest, which consists of a number of chambers and corridors excavated in the soil. The queen retires to her 'royal chamber' and, constantly tended by workers, she devotes herself to laying more eggs. These are carried away by the workers and placed in incubation-chambers. When they have hatched the larvae are taken to larval quarters where the workers feed them on honey and insect grubs. The pupae, too, have their own quarters – usually near the surface where they get some warmth from the sun. If the surface of the nest is disturbed one can often see the workers hurriedly carrying the pupae to safety. A mature nest will contain several thousand ants. Males and females are produced during the summer and, when climatic conditions are suitable, they emerge for their marriage-flight. Each nest seems to produce mainly males or mainly females and so there is little risk of in-breeding. Whereas the mating-flight marks the end of the colony for wasps and bumble-bees, the ant colony goes on from year to year. Food is stored up for the winter and life continues. The individual workers do not live very long but the queen lives for several years and the colony is remarkably stable. Quite often there will be two or more queens in one nest and, by accepting new queens every now and then, the workers can ensure that the colony goes on for many years.

It is well known that ants have a liking for sweet things and this is the reason for their association with aphids. The aphids produce a sweet secretion called honeydew and the ants 'milk' them by gently stroking them. Some of our ant species actually collect aphids and carry them to the nest, where they attach them to plant roots. The aphids are protected from enemies and the ants benefit from a handy supply of honey-dew. The workers consume some of the honeydew themselves and give the rest to the larvae. Other items in the ants' diet include oil-containing seeds, nectar and other insects.

Quite a number of other creatures can be found in an ant nest and mention has already been made of the Large blue caterpillar earlier. Many of these 'guests' are simply scavengers and they help to clean the nest. They are more or less ignored by the ants. A good example is the little blind woodlouse *Platyarthrus hoffmannseggi*. Some 'guests', however, are unwelcome and these include various beetles and their larvae which prey upon the ant larvae.

Not all ant species possess a sting, although some make up for it by being able to squirt formic acid at their enemies. The strong jaws are also used as weapons and some foreign species possess, in addition to the normal worker caste, a soldier caste whose job is to defend the nest with extra-large jaws.

The beetles make up the largest of all

Ant castes, *from top to bottom*, female worker, male, queen

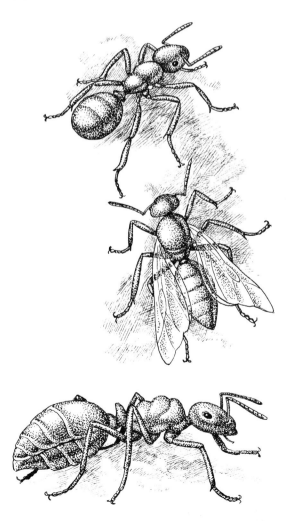

insect Orders, the Coleoptera, with more than 250,000 different species in the world and nearly 4,000 of these are found in Britain. As one would expect with such a large Order, its members are extremely varied and they include the largest insects as well as some of the smallest. All beetles have biting jaws and their front wings form tough, horny covers (Coleoptera means 'sheath wings'). These covers are called elytra and they usually completely conceal the abdomen when the beetle is at rest, although the rove-beetles and certain other groups have short elytra. The hind wings, when present, are membranous and they are the ones used for flying. In flight, the elytra stick out rigidly from the body and probably provide some lift although they do not flap. Beetles are basically ground-living insects, however, and many of them have lost their hind wings. Elytra are almost always present and there can be no doubt that these tough covers have contributed to the success of the beetles. In many of the flightless beetles the elytra are fused tightly together and give even more protection.

Another factor in the beetles' success has been their adaptability. They have retained the basic biting jaws with little specialization and they have, therefore, been able to use a very wide variety of food materials. Among the foods taken by the beetles and their larvae are dung, carrion, wood, woollen fabrics, fresh plant tissues and other animals. The beetles' habitats vary enormously as well and one or more species can be found almost everywhere. Many species are aquatic.

The life-history of beetles is generally quite typical of endopterygote insects, with egg, larva, pupa and adult stages. There is much variation among the larvae, from the active predatory ones such as the ground-beetle larvae to the legless grubs of weevils and some others which live surrounded by plant food and never need to move. In between there is a whole range of intermediate forms. The pupae are rather pale and soft and, unlike the pupae of butterflies and moths, the legs and other appendages are usually free. Some species spin cocoons before pupating but more usually the pupa is simply fixed to a plant or it lies naked in a little chamber in the soil.

Our largest beetle is the male Stag beetle, *Lucanus cervus*, p. 238, with a length of over 3 inches (60 mm.) including its 'antlers'. These antlers, which are missing in the female, are really overgrown jaws but they are too clumsy to be of much use and they seem to be mainly ornamental. Stag beetles breed in old tree-stumps and, because of better forest management perhaps, they are becoming rare. Related to the Stag beetle are the dung-burying scarabs and the cockchafers. These are generally quite large insects and both have antennae of which the last few segments have leaf-like outgrowths. They are best seen in the Cockchafer, *Melolontha melolontha*, p. 238, in which they can be drawn together to form a 'club'. The larvae of all these beetles are soft and fat and permanently curved into a C-shape. They are always surrounded by food – wood, dung or plant roots – and they move very little. Cockchafer grubs do a great deal of damage to cereal and grass roots, while the adults feed on leaves and flowers.

Another large beetle is the Bloody-nose beetle, *Timarcha tenebricosa*. This black, rounded insect is very common in grassy places during the summer and it is one of those species in which the elytra are fused together. It belongs to a large family of leaf-feeding beetles which also includes the infamous Colorado beetle, *Leptinotarsa decemlineata*, and many other pests. The insect owes its common name to its habit of exuding a drop of bright red blood from its mouth when disturbed. This 'reflex bleeding' is believed to scare away any enemy.

The Wasp beetle, p. 238, whose mimicry has been described earlier, belongs to a group known as longhorns because of their relatively long antennae. Their larvae all feed in wood and the adults are most likely to be found sitting on tree-trunks or on leaves and flowers.

Weevils make up one of the largest groups

of beetles and they are readily identified by the long 'beak' or 'rostrum' which extends forwards from the head and carries the jaws at its tip. The antennae spring from half-way along the rostrum and are sharply bent near the middle. Weevils are all small beetles and they are all plant-feeders. The larvae usually feed inside the plant tissues – root, stem or seed as a rule – and they are completely without legs. Several species attack cereal grain, both in the field and in the granary. The Grain weevil, *Sitophilus granarius*, is a well-known example and one which causes enormous losses in stored grain. The female Nut weevil, *Curculio nucum*, p. 238, uses her snout to drill into young hazel nuts. She then lays her eggs inside and her larvae mature there, nourished and protected by the developing nuts.

Closely related to the weevils are the bark-beetles, typified by *Scolytes destructor*. The bark-beetles themselves are small and in-conspicuous but their larvae tunnel just under the bark of trees and make charac-teristic patterns which are exposed when the bark falls. *S. destructor* attacks damaged and unhealthy elm trees but its relatives cause much damage in coniferous forests. The adult beetles pair up and each pair then burrows down into the bark of an elm

tree. Somewhere in this burrow the beetles mate and the female then begins to tunnel vertically just under the bark. This vertical tunnel is called the 'mother gallery' and the female lays eggs along each side of it. The larvae hatch and they then tunnel at right angles to the mother gallery and the whole tunnel system looks something like a centi-pede, p. 238. The larval tunnels increase in width as the larvae grow and get further from the mother gallery. The larvae then pupate and the adults bore straight out of the bark, leaving neat little holes rather larger than that of a woodworm. There are usually several tunnel systems close together and the bark soon separates from the wood, revealing the tunnels in the bark itself and, less deeply, in the wood. Other species of bark-beetle all have their own characteristic tunnelling patterns.

Moving now from the plant-feeders to the carnivorous beetles we can look first at the ground beetles – the long-legged, swift-running species that commonly scuttle away

Beetle larvae: *top row,* Violet ground beetle, *left;* Cockchafer, *centre;* a leaf beetle, *Melasoma populi, right; bottom row,* Cardinal beetle, *left;* a longhorn beetle, *Rhagium mordax, centre;* Spruce weevil, *right*

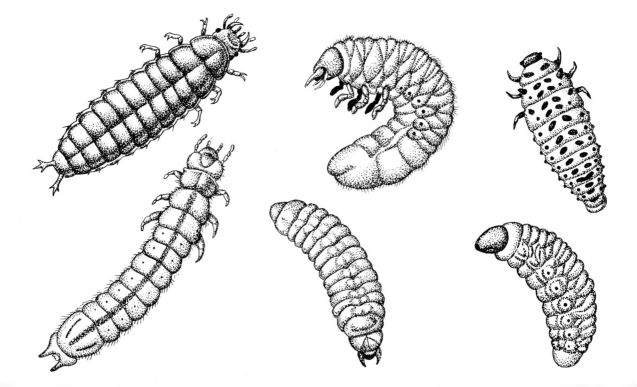

when a stone is overturned. Most of them are black but many, notably the Violet Ground beetle, *Carabus violaceus*, p. 238, have a metallic sheen. The elytra are usually decorated with a number of ridges and grooves. These insects are generally nocturnal and both adults and larvae are active predators. Worms, slugs and other insects all figure in their diet. The tiger beetles are closely related to the ground beetles but they are active during the day and they are fond of sunning themselves on the ground. Unlike the ground beetles, many of which cannot fly at all, the tiger beetles readily take to the air. Tiger beetle larvae dig little pits and lie in wait for their prey, in contrast to the hunting behaviour of the ground beetle larvae.

Another well-known group of predatory beetles are the ladybirds, p. 238. There are 45 species in Britain. They are extremely useful allies of the farmer and gardener because adults and larvae destroy huge numbers of green-fly and other insect pests. The ladybirds' bright colours are of a warning nature and advertise the insect's bitter taste. When handled, they often emit a pungent liquid which stains the hand.

Nearly everyone will have heard of the Glow worm, but probably very few people can say what sort of animal it is. It is, in fact, a beetle, *Lampyris noctiluca*, p. 238. All stages of the insect give out some light but the adult female glows the most brightly and it is she who has provided the common name, for she is completely wingless (even her elytra are missing) and she looks not unlike a woodlouse. The 'lamp' is on the underside of her abdomen and it produces a bluish-green light by a chemical process. The insects 'light up' soon after dusk on July evenings and the fully winged males fly to the females as they sit in the grass. Eggs are laid and soon hatch into larvae which are very much like the adult females. The larvae feed on small slugs and snails but the adults do not feed at all. Grassy slopes and verges are the places to look for glow worms, but they are rather local in distribution and found mainly in the southern counties.

The rove beetles, of which we have about 1,000 species in Britain, are nearly all predators or scavengers. Most of them are only a few millimetres long, although the Devil's Coach horse, *Ocypus olens*, p. 238, grows to an inch (25 mm.) in length. The majority of rove beetles, also called 'staphs' by entomologists from the family name of Staphylinidae, have very short elytra and they look rather like pincer-less earwigs. The hind wings, however, are relatively large and most of the insects fly well. The greatest numbers of rove beetles can be found on compost-heaps, in leaf litter and around animal dung. Many of them take decaying matter as food, but the majority are probably feeding on fly larvae and other insects which themselves feed on the decaying material. Several species live as scavengers in ants' nests.

It is not very often that one comes across a small carcass in nature, but when this does happen the carcass is frequently attended by a pair of black or black and orange beetles of the genus *Necrophorus*, p. 238. These insects, which range from under $\frac{1}{2}$ inch to over 1 inch (about 13 mm. to 25 mm.) in length, are called Burying beetles or Sexton beetles for they have taken upon themselves the job of burying the dead. The efficiency with which they work is borne out by the few carcasses we see lying about. The beetles are attracted to the carcasses by the smell and the first beetle to arrive seems to repel later arrivals unless they happen to be of the opposite sex. When once they have paired up and mated the beetles begin to bury the carcass by removing the soil from under it. Jaws and legs are used in this operation and the carcass disappears remarkably rapidly if the soil is reasonably light. If the soil is heavier the beetles may take a little longer or they may even drag the corpse to a better burial-ground. This behaviour is not altruistic of course and has been evolved simply as a way of providing the beetles' own family with food. The female lays her eggs in a small chamber close to the carcass and then she begins to feed. Like the rove beetles, she

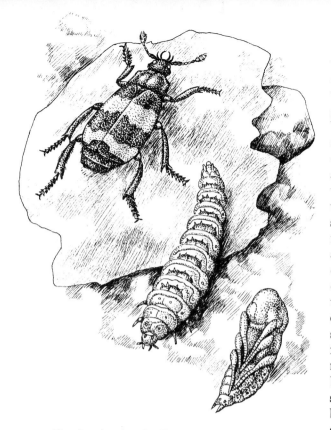

The Burying beetle, *Necrophorus:* adult, larva and pupa

probably feeds partly on the decaying matter itself and partly on the other scavenging creatures such as fly maggots. The male may also remain and feed for a short time but he usually makes off before the eggs hatch. The young larvae are quite active and they make their way from the egg-chamber to the carcass, but they do not feed themselves to start with: the female provides them with drops of regurgitated liquid for the first few hours of their lives. Having reached their feeding-ground, the larvae do not need to be particularly active and at each moult they become less mobile, ending up as almost legless grubs. The existence of more than one larval form during the life-cycle is known as hypermetamorphosis and such a state of affairs is also known in some other species. The fully grown Burying beetle grubs bore their way out of the carcass and pupate close by in the soil.

Of those species that live in fresh water, as

with the bugs, there are surface-dwelling species and fully aquatic ones. Best known of the surface-dwelling beetles are the whirligigs, such as *Gyrinus marinus*. This small black beetle lives on ponds and slow-moving streams, especially where there is plenty of emergent vegetation, and it skates round and round picking up insects that fall on to the surface. Whirligigs are extremely sensitive to vibration and they dart away at great speed if disturbed. They can also dive down into the water. Their eyes are admirably adapted for life on the surface because each eye is completely divided so that there are in effect four eyes. The upper ones look out over the water surface, while the lower ones look down into the water. Eggs are laid in the spring and the larvae live under the surface, feeding on a variety of other insects. They mature in July and August and huge numbers of adult whirligigs can then be seen swarming on the water. Like many water beetles, they fly well and many will fly to other ponds before hibernating in the mud.

The aquatic beetles cannot obtain their oxygen directly from the water and they all carry a bubble of air around with them, tucked under their elytra or trapped by a coat of fine hairs on the body. The tracheae open into this air-bubble. A few of the smaller beetles can stay submerged, because the oxygen in the air bubble is replenished as fast as it is used by diffusion into the bubble of oxygen dissolved in the surrounding waters, but most beetles need to surface every now and then to renew their air-supply.

Our largest family of water beetles is the Dytiscidae, which includes the Great diving beetle, *Dytiscus marginalis*, as well as a host of much smaller beetles. They all swim well, using the broad hind legs as paddles. Dytiscids are all carnivorous and the larger species will attack frogs and fishes without hesitation. The larvae are carnivorous as well and they feed in a rather similar fashion to the lacewing larvae, by sucking up their victim's juices through a narrow canal in each jaw. These beetles all renew their air-supply by coming tail first to the surface. Water-repellent hairs at the tip of the abdomen break the surface and form a channel along which air can reach the elytra.

The other major family of water beetles is the Hydrophilidae, although not all its members are aquatic. They are almost entirely vegetarian and they are generally poor swimmers, spending much of their time crawling about on the water-weeds. Most of the species are small but the Silver water beetle, *Hydrous piceus*, reaches nearly 2 inches (50 mm.) in length and is one of our largest beetles. Although a vegetarian, it can inflict a nasty wound through a sharp spine on its under-surface. When seen in a pond the hydrophilid beetles can always be recognized because they come up for air head first. The antennae are short and hairy and these break the surface and conduct air down to the elytra. The sensory role of the antennae has been taken over in these insects by enlarged palps springing from the mouth-parts.

The Arachnida include the spiders, scorpions, mites and several other smaller groups of animals. They are all arthropods but they differ from the other arthropod classes in having no antennae: the first pair of appendages of an arachnid are known as chelicerae and they are always claws or pincers.

The second pair of appendages, often very large, are called palps or pedipalps and they function either as sensory organs or as grasping organs. Behind them there are generally four pairs of walking legs. The arachnids have no jaws and the food is broken up by the chelicerae, aided by outgrowths from the bases of the limbs. Only liquid food can be taken in through the narrow mouth, but the arachnids deal with solid food by digesting it outside the body. They are nearly all carnivorous, feeding mainly on insects.

The spiders, Order Araneida, are the major group among the arachnids and most people can recognize one when they see it. Few people bother to take a close look, however, because there seems to be a very strong and a widespread aversion to spiders. It is difficult to see why this should be so, for very few spiders are harmful to man. In fact, they are positively useful because they destroy untold numbers of flies and other insect

Water beetles: Great diving beetle, *left*;
Silver water beetle, *centre*;
Whirligig beetles, *right*, on the surface
and larva below

pests. It is interesting that, side by side with the general dislike of spiders, there is an equally widespread idea that it is unlucky to kill a spider.

As in all the arachnids, the head and thorax are fused together to form the cephalothorax. This region is separated from the abdomen by a narrow waist. The front of the cephalothorax carries six or eight simple eyes, the arrangement of which is of great value in identifying the species. The chelicerae, under the 'face' of the spider, consist of sharp fangs, each of which is pierced by a narrow canal connected to a poison gland. These fangs are used to capture and kill the prey. The poison is strong and the spider's victim quickly dies. Some of the larger spiders found abroad can inflict a painful bite on humans, but the British species are harmless because they cannot usually pierce our skins.

The spider's palps function as sense-organs, rather like the antennae of insects.

The female's palps are slender and rather like short legs, but the male has distinctly clubbed palps which play a vital role in courtship and mating. Behind the palps there are four pairs of walking legs.

Spiders breathe by means of tracheae and unusual organs called lung hooks. The tracheae are similar to those of insects, although they do not spread to all parts of the body, and they open through one or two spiracles on the underside of the abdomen. The lung books, of which there is usually one pair, are situated near the front of the abdomen. Each consists of a small chamber packed with fine blood-filled leaflets. The chamber is connected to the outside by a narrow slit and the spider is able to pump air in and out. Oxygen is then taken up by the blood in the leaflets. The position of the lung books is marked externally by the narrow slit and by pale patches on the underside of the abdomen.

All spiders produce silk. It is formed in abdominal glands and is extruded through two or three pairs of spinnerets near the hind end of the abdomen. Several kinds of silk are produced and the spider uses them for different purposes. The best-known use is for making a web. The spider's web is a trap or snare for insects, and spiders share with man and certain caddis larvae the distinction of being the only animals that make traps of any kind. Each species has its own web pattern and the most attractive are the circular orb webs made by the Garden spider, *Araneus diadematus*, p. 255, and others of the family Argiopidae. These webs abound in every hedgerow and they are a most pleasant sight when laden with jewels of dew or frost on autumn mornings. It is at this time that one realizes just how many spiders there are. The orb web is a master-

Spiders differ from insects in four important respects: they have four pairs of legs compared with the insects' three, and spiders also have only two body divisions compared with three. They never have wings nor antennae though their palps may look like antennae

piece of design and construction and it is incredible that the spider manages to produce it in an hour or less, guided only by instinct.

Some of the stages involved in the construction of an orb web are illustrated and these stages may be observed by anyone with an hour or so to spare in the autumn. Mornings seem to be the best time, especially after rain. The first thread to be put in place is the bridge thread. This is the thread that forms the top of the frame and its initial position is determined very much by the wind. The spider extrudes a thread of silk and allows the wind to carry it. If it should anchor itself on a near-by support, the spider has formed its bridge thread. Details of the succeeding stages depend on the species: some complete the frame first, others construct the major radii before completing the frame. The shape of the frame varies according to the availability of the supports, and the number of radii may vary according to the age of the spider, but otherwise the construction of the web is remarkably constant for each species. When all the radii are complete, it can be seen that they do not all meet neatly in the centre. They meet at an irregular hub which is usually above the centre and traversed by a number of distorted threads. The spider's next task is to surround the hub with a few closely spaced turns known as the strengthening spiral. Having done this, it moves out a little way and starts to lay down a fairly open spiral of thread which extends nearly to the frame. This spiral is the temporary spiral or dry spiral. After a short rest near the outside of the web, the spider begins the last stage – the construction of the viscid spiral which actually traps the prey. The viscid spiral starts from the outside and it is made from a different kind of silk, this time coated with gum. The turns of the viscid spiral are much closer together than those of the dry spiral and the spider uses its legs as 'rulers' to ensure that the turns are correctly spaced. Because the hub is not central, the spiral is not a true spiral and there are more turns on one side than on the other. The viscid spiral is taken nearly to the strengthening spiral, but the spider always leaves a little gap – the free zone – between the two. The web is then complete and the spider retires to await its prey.

The spider's retreat may be on the strengthening spiral at the hub of the web, or it may be some distance away in a rolled-up leaf. The spider will always maintain contact with the web, however, and will rush out as soon as vibrations indicate that food has arrived. An acceptable morsel will be

Spiders: a typical spider, *Linyphia*, *left*, its fangs enlarged, *centre* and the palp of a male, *right*

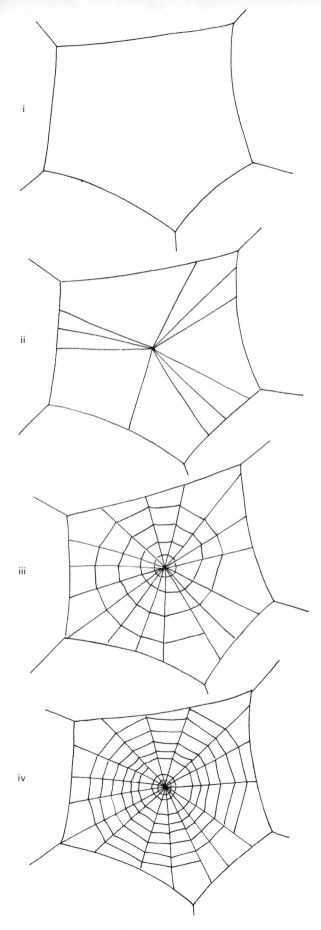

subdued by poison, shrouded with silk, and then consumed at the spider's leisure. Dead objects or unacceptable insects are cut from the web and released. Although the viscid spiral forms a death-trap for insects, the spider itself is able to run over it without trouble because its feet are covered with an oily secretion.

Although the orb web is fairly strong and flexible, it is always being damaged by wind, rain or large insects. The spider has to repair it almost daily. Minor damage is made good by patching but a badly damaged web is completely rebuilt, although the spider will not necessarily make a new frame each time.

There are, of course, many webs apart from the orb webs. Most of us are familiar with the web of the bath-frequenting House spider, *Tegenaria atrica* – a triangular sheet set in an out-of-the-way corner and leading into a tunnel-like retreat. These webs are not rebuilt regularly like the orb webs but are added to every now and then. The result is a thick and rather dusty 'cob-web'. The threads are not sticky and the prey is trapped by an elaborate system of 'trip-wires' overlaying the net surface.

Another very common type of web is the sheet or hammock, which is spread horizontally on bushes and low-growing herbage. This type of web is characteristic of the small 'money spiders' of the family Linyphiidae, which outnumber all other spiders in Britain. Whole lawns and fields may be covered with these webs and turned into sheets of silver by the autumn frosts. The spider usually hangs underneath the hammock, waiting for prey to fall on to it from above. The snaring of prey is often aided by a tangle of threads constructed above the sheet, but the threads are not sticky.

The most unusual web is certainly that of the Purse web spider, *Atypus affinis*. This

Stages in the construction of a spider's orb web within a pre-existing frame, i frame, ii with radii, iii with the dry spiral, iv completed

species is our only representative of the mygalomorph spiders, which include the large, hairy 'bird-eating' species and the trap-door spiders. It is a chestnut-brown animal and the female reaches about $\frac{1}{2}$ inch (13 mm.) in length. The male is somewhat darker and smaller than the female but both have huge, forward-pointing chelicerae. *Atypus* lives in various places in the southern half of England, usually on dry, sunny slopes with light soil. Its web is a closed silken tube, about 8 inches (20 cm.) long and a little thicker than a pencil. Most of this tube is buried in a shaft which the spider excavates with its chelicerae, but a careful search will reveal the upper 2 or 3 inches lying on the surface among the herbage. The spider sits at the bottom of the tube and waits for a meal to walk on the exposed portion. Beetles, woodlice, earwigs and many other crawling arthropods are accepted readily. The spider detects movements on the upper part of the tube and rushes up to investigate. The large fangs pierce the prey through the walls of the tube and then little saw-like teeth on the basal part of the fangs cut slits in the tube so that the spider can draw in its prey. The food is taken to the bottom of the tube for consumption, but the spider returns to the top to repair the tube before getting on with its meal.

Male Purse web spiders live just like the females until their last moult. Then, during the autumn, they leave their tubes and search for mates. Having found a female's tube, the male must carry out an elaborate series of tapping signals to indicate that he is a male and not the female's next meal. He can then enter the tube and, after more signals, mating can take place. Eggs are not laid until the following summer, however, and it may be a further nine months before the young spiders emerge from their mother's tube.

Many spiders make no webs at all and they actively hunt their prey or merely sit in wait and pounce when something comes along. Best known of the hunters are the Wolf spiders, *Lycosa* species, which run down their prey and overpower it. Most of these spiders have no home or territory and they spend their whole lives wandering over the

The sheet web of a spider, *Linyphia*, with the spider underneath at the centre ground. The females even carry their eggs with them in a neat ball of silk attached to the spinnerets. The female Wolf spider is a good mother and she will search diligently for her egg-ball if it becomes dislodged. She also carries her offspring around for some time on her back.

The Crab spiders, so called because they walk sideways with a crab-like motion, are among those spiders that lie in ambush for their prey. They are usually well camouflaged and they conceal themselves in flowers or among leaves, just waiting for an insect to come within range. Some of these spiders will leap out on to their prey, but others will wait until the insect comes near enough to be drawn in by the strong front legs and stabbed with their fangs. Crab spiders include the beautiful green *Micrommata virescens* and the pink or yellow *Thomisus onustus*, p. 255.

As one last example of spiders that make no webs, we can look at the Spitting spider, *Scytodes thoracica*, p. 255, a domestic species rarely found away from houses in this country. It is found only in the southern counties but it has increased its range considerably in the last few decades. *Scytodes* has rather weak, spindly legs and it captures its food by a remarkable method. It stalks slowly up to its prey and then squirts a quick-setting gum from its fangs. During the firing, the fangs are oscillated rapidly from side to side and the effect is that the prey is stuck down by two zigzag threads of gum. *Scytodes* then bites its victim to kill it and, having dragged it clear of the sticky threads, proceeds to suck it dry. The gum can be fired very accurately from about a $\frac{1}{4}$ inch (6 mm.) and it is used to repel enemies as well as to capture food.

Although many groups of spiders do not make food-catching webs, they do all make and use silk – for wrapping their eggs and as life-lines. Many of them leave silken threads wherever they go and it is not difficult to imagine how such behaviour could have evolved into web-making behaviour in some groups.

After his last moult a male spider does not pay much attention to food and he focuses all his efforts on finding one or more females. Before setting out on his search, however, he must charge his palps with sperm, for it is the palps which actually deliver the sperm into the female's body. Soon after moulting the male spider constructs a little silken platform and deposits some sperm on it. The sperm is then taken up by the swollen tips of the palps and the spider is ready to go courting.

Purse web spider: the purse web, *top*; catching prey, in this case a woodlouse, *centre*; the spider, *bottom*

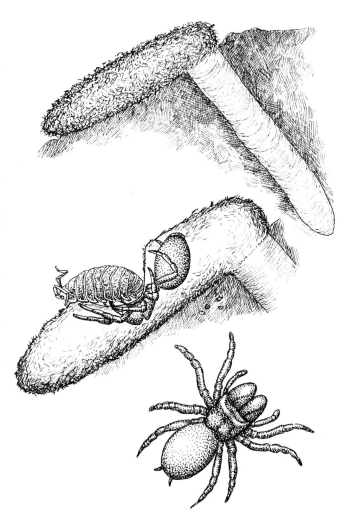

Web-spinning spiders rely very largely on vibrations to tell them of a meal trapped in the web. When these vibrations are received the spider usually rushes out and attacks the victim right away. A courting male has therefore to be very careful to signify to the female that he is not her next meal. He does this by a complex sequence of web-tapping which triggers off the female's mating behaviour and subdues her aggression. The male can then approach the female, displaying continuously the instinctive courtship behaviour. Should the female not be receptive, or should the male make a mistake, he will probably be killed and eaten. Hunting spiders have a similar problem when courting, but here the male gives a display of visual signals by waving his palps and legs.

If the male successfully completes the ritual and reaches the female, he will usually stroke her a little with his palps and then insert them into her spermathecae where the sperm is released. Soon after this the male takes his leave and goes off to recharge his palps and start courting again. It is popularly believed that the female kills the male after mating but this happens only rarely. It is true that dead males are often found in and around the female's web but, with their life's work complete, these have probably died a natural death.

The eggs are laid in batches and covered with silk. Some species carry the eggs around with them, others conceal the cocoon and abandon it. The majority of species lay their eggs in the autumn but the young spiders do not emerge from the cocoons until the spring. For a while, until they have exhausted their yolk reserves, the young spiders may cluster together, but then they will begin to disperse. They either crawl slowly away from each other or, in some families, they extrude fine threads and use them as kites to carry them to distant pastures. The length of life depends on the species: many argiopids and linyphiids survive for only one year, while *Atypus* may live for four or five years.

Although the spiders, and arachnids in

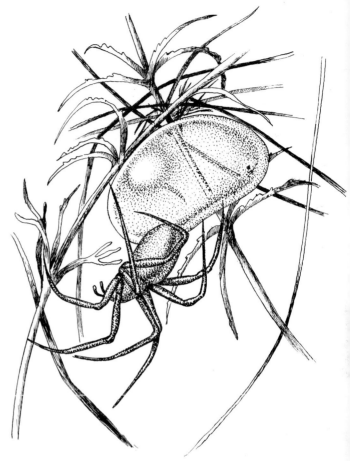

The Water spider with its air-bubble

general, are essentially terrestrial animals, one of our species has taken to living permanently under the water. This is the Water spider, *Argyroneta aquatica*, quite common in ponds and other still waters throughout the country. The spider still has to breathe air and it constructs a silken 'diving bell' which it fills with air-bubbles brought down from the surface trapped by the hairy back legs. As long as the surrounding water has a fairly good oxygen-supply, oxygen will continue to diffuse into the bell and the spider needs to make only occasional visits to the surface to replenish its air-supply. The Water spider is a hunter and is active mainly at night, although it will always dart out of its bell during the day-time to capture a passing insect or crustacean. The prey is then always taken back to the bell to be eaten, or occasionally taken on to dry land.

Frequently confused with the spiders, although only distantly related to them, are the Harvestmen, also called Harvest-spiders, of the Order Opiliones. They are similar to the spiders in having four pairs of walking legs and a pair of slender palps, but their bodies are not divided into two parts. Another characteristic feature of the Harvestmen is the eye-turret or ocularium which carries the two eyes up above the surface of the body. Harvestmen spin no silk and they have no venom: their chelicerae are in the form of small pincers instead of fangs. They are basically carnivorous but, unlike the spiders, they will eat an assortment of dead material. The palps are mainly sensory and they help to find food which is then torn up by the chelicerae. The second pair of legs, which are always longer than the others, also have a sensory function and are often carried out in front of the animal, feeling the ground as it goes.

The common name for these animals comes from the fact that the majority of our 21 species mature and become apparent at harvest-time. Most of them live on the ground and low vegetation, although some species, notably the long-legged *Leiobunum rotundum*, p. 255, are found on walls and tree-trunks. Large numbers of individuals can often be found under pinks and other low-growing plants. Many of these will be *Odiellus spinosus*, recognizable by its squat body and short legs as well as by the horizontal trident of spines at the front.

Harvestmen mate without any of the ritual associated with spider courtship and eggs are usually laid in the soil in the autumn. These eggs hatch in the spring and the animals mature by late summer. A few species mature in the spring, having over-wintered as young animals, while those that normally live amongst leaf litter have no definite breeding-season, young and adults being found throughout the year.

The examination of leaf litter is a very good way of finding small arthropods and none of these animals is more fascinating than the false scorpions. These little arachnids – the largest British species is less than 4 mm. long – are generally grey and they carry a relatively huge pair of pinkish claws or pedipalps. These claws are covered with sensitive bristles and they are used to catch the minute insects on which the false scorpions feed. The claws of most species are provided with poison glands, but the claws are much too weak to hurt man.

There are 26 known British species, most of which live in leaf litter and moss. Some species live in ants' nests, while a few live in stored products where they feed on mites and other small creatures. The false scorpions move about in a very slow and dignified manner, with the claws held out in front. When disturbed, however, the claws are drawn back and the animal moves rapidly backwards.

While searching for false scorpions, one will certainly come across large numbers of rounded, spiky creatures only a millimetre or two across. These are mites and they

A Harvestman

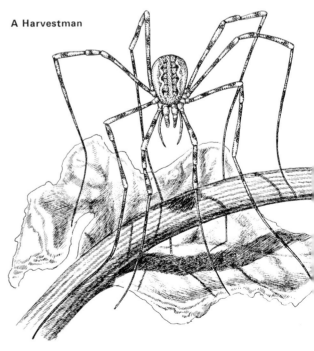

False scorpions, moving forward, *left,* and retreating, *right*

belong to the order Acarina, which they share with the ticks. Soil-dwelling mites are exceedingly abundant, especially in forest soils, and they feed mainly on fungi. Several species feed on mouldy bread and cheese, while quite a number infest food-stuffs stored under damp conditions. Other mites feed more openly on plants, well-known examples being the red spider mites of the family Tetranychidae. Some of these species cause serious damage to ornamental and crop plants by feeding on the leaves, and several of them disturb householders by entering houses in their thousands for hibernation. Another important group of mites are the gall mites of the family Eriophyidae. These minute mites are not like the free-living species because they are rather worm-like and they have lost their two posterior pairs of legs. The bright red pustules on maple and sycamore leaves, the spiky nail galls of lime, and the damaging big-bud of black currant are among the galls caused by this group of mites.

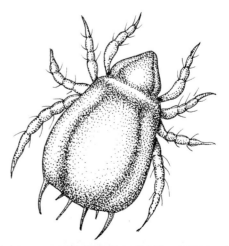

Mites: a gall mite, *top,* with a lime leaf showing its nail galls *below;* a soil mite, for comparison, *right*

Many animal species, including man, suffer from parasitic mites which get under the skin and cause great irritation known as mange or scab. Sheep scab is a very serious menace in many countries, although compulsory sheep-dipping has eradicated it from Britain.

As well as invading a vast number of terrestrial habitats, the mites have also made themselves at home in the water. We have about 200 species of water mites, little rounded creatures averaging about 2 mm. in diameter and often brightly coloured. They exist in ponds and streams in large numbers and swim smoothly around by means of their hair-fringed legs. Most of them pass through a parasitic stage in their life-histories, the larvae attaching themselves to aquatic insects, molluscs or fishes and sucking the body tissues.

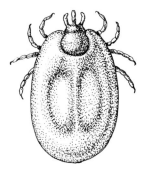

A sheep tick showing the mouth-parts which distinguish ticks from mites

Ticks are all blood-sucking arachnids which parasitize vertebrate animals. In the warmer parts of the world they cause enormous losses among cattle but they are of little importance in this country. The Sheep tick, *Ixodes reduvius*, is the commonest species, occurring in damp pastures and attaching itself to cattle and horses as well as to sheep.

The molluscs, with over 100,000 different species, constitute the second largest phylum of the animal kingdom and they include slugs, snails, mussels and squids. Although widely different in appearance, these animals all agree in having a soft, unsegmented body and the majority of them have a conspicuous outer skeleton or shell which gives them protection.

There are five main groups or classes: the Amphineura (coat-of-mail shells), the Scaphopoda (tusk shells), the Gastropoda (slugs and snails), the Lamellibranchiata (bivalves such as cockles and mussels) and the Cephalopoda (squids and octopuses). The great majority of these animals live in the sea. Only some gastropods and bivalves have been able to escape from the marine environment and only the gastropods have mastered life on the land. Although the molluscs are basically aquatic animals, more species live on land than in fresh water. This suggests that the land was conquered via the seashore, with the animals gradually moving up the shore and becoming less and less dependent on the sea. Several species of mollusc, notably the periwinkles *Littorina neritoides* and *L. rudis*, seem to be making this transition at the present day. Having left the shore, the original land snails gradually spread over the land and some of them later entered fresh water to become watersnails, although it is probable that some water-snails arrived by the more difficult estuarine route. The bivalves are completely aquatic and they must have reached fresh water through the brackish waters of the estuaries.

The gastropods are by far the largest class of molluscs and they include all the land-living species and all the water-snails. Apart from the marine species there are about 140 species native to the British Isles: 80 land snails, 40 water-snails and 20 slugs. Rela-

Spiders and harvestmen, *from left to right and top to bottom*: *Micrommata virescens*, female; the harvestman, *Leiobunum rotundum*; *Argiope bruennichi*; Spitting spider, *Scytodes thoracica*; Cross spider, *Araneus diadematus*; Crab spider, *Thomisus onustus*; Wolf spider, *Pisaura* sp.; the harvestman, *Lacinius ephippiatus*; House spider and web

tively few come to notice, however, because many are very small, the Dwarf snail, *Punctum pygmaeum*, is only 1·5 mm. across, and, unlike most marine molluscs, they are rather drab in colour.

The name gastropod literally means 'stomach-foot' and refers to the way in which the animals creep along on the belly surface. This highly muscular region is called the 'foot' and it makes up a large part of the gastropod body. The animal is propelled along by rhythmic contractions of the under-surface and these waves are quite easy to see if a slug or a snail is made to glide over a sheet of glass. The nature of the surface makes very little difference to a gastropod because it paves its own way with a layer of mucus secreted by a gland at the front of the foot. The animal then almost swims in the mucus. Some slugs produce a very thick glue-like mucus which is very difficult to remove from the hands after touching these animals. The slugs use this tough slime as a 'climbing rope' to drop from one level to another; they attach strands to an over-hanging ledge and then descend slowly, paying out more mucus as they go. The slugs also climb back up the 'rope' if they do not reach suitable territory below. The Great grey slug, *Limax maximus*, p. 256, mates in mid-air, the partners suspended by thick strands of mucus. This must surely be one of the strangest forms of animal behaviour.

The general appearance of land snails, typified by the Garden snail, *Helix aspersa*, p. 256, is known to most people. The most obvious feature is the shell, always coiled but varying in shape from almost flat in some species to almost cylindrical. Emerging from the shell aperture is the rather long, narrow foot which merges, at the front, into the

ill-defined head. The latter bears two pairs of tentacles, the longer pair having eyes at their tips. Most of the snail's internal organs are arranged in the visceral hump, a long bag-like structure coiled up within the shell.

The shell, which is made mainly of lime, is rather like a hollow cone which has been coiled round a central column. This column is known as the columella and it is hollow. Its opening, known as the umbilicus, is clearly seen in some snails but it is often concealed by the thickened lip of the shell. The whole shell is secreted by the mantle which is a thick, cloak-like flap of skin surrounding the visceral hump. The outer, horny layer of the shell is called the periostracum and it is this layer that gives the shell its colour. Under this there is the prismatic layer, or shell proper, formed of calcite crystals, and on the inside a thin layer of 'mother-of-pearl'. As the snail grows the mantle periodically adds more to the edge of the shell so that it keeps pace with the growth of the body. This periodic addition produces the little ridges on the shell.

The mother-of-pearl layer is secreted by the whole of the mantle, but the two outer layers are secreted only at the edge of the mantle. A damaged shell cannot, therefore, be completely repaired: it can only be patched up with pearly material and such 'patched-up' shells are quite common, especially among marine snails.

The shape and size of snail-shells vary a great deal and the classification of these animals depends very much on shell form. The direction of coiling, however, is nearly always the same: if you hold a shell upright with the opening facing you, it will nearly always be on the right of the shell. Such shells are said to be dextral or right-handed. The only common sinistral – left-handed – snails we have are the little door-snails, such as *Clausilia bidentata*, which are commonly found on moss-covered walls and tree-trunks. Species which normally have dextral shells occasionally throw up a left-handed specimen and these are real prizes for the shell-collector.

Slugs and snails, *from left to right and top to bottom*: Snails – Round-mouthed, *Pomatias elegans*; two shell colours of the White-lipped; *Cepaea hortensis*; Roman, *Helix pomatia,* with the rare sinistral spiral; Garden, *Helix aspersa.* Slugs – Great grey, *Limax maximus*; Shelled, *Testacella haliotidea*; Red, *Arion ater rufus*; Large black, *Arion ater*

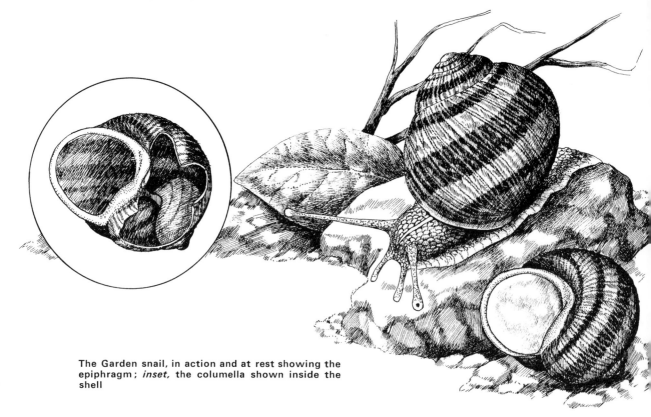

The Garden snail, in action and at rest showing the epiphragm; *inset,* the columella shown inside the shell

Because the shells need lime for their formation, snails are far more abundant on lime-rich soils than on sandy soils. Some species, including the large Roman or Edible snail, *Helix pomatia*, p. 256, cannot live away from calcareous soils. Most soils, however, contain some lime and as long as temperatures are high enough the snails will be there. Calcium is more easily absorbed at higher temperatures and snails which demand lime-rich soils in cool regions can make do with ordinary soils under warmer conditions. Species such as the glass-snails of the family Vitrinidae, which live in sandy regions, usually have very thin, almost transparent shells.

When the snail is at rest its head and foot are concealed within the large outer whorl of the shell, pulled in by strong muscles. Two of our land snails, the Round-mouthed, *Pomatias elegans*, p. 256, and the tiny Point snail, *Acme fusca*, have the added protection of a horny disc called the 'operculum' which closes the entrance to the shell when they have retreated. These operculate snails, however, belong to a different group, the majority of which are aquatic.

The snail extends its body again by pumping blood into the head and foot: the body gradually swells out and finally the tentacles extend. The tentacles serve largely as organs of touch and smell and the snail uses them to feel its way, very much as an insect uses its antennae. The eyes are at the tips of the larger tentacles but they are not very efficient. The whole body surface is sensitive to light in fact and this helps the snail to avoid bright light. Snails have not completely mastered life on land and they need to keep to relatively damp places. They tend, therefore, to be nocturnal because the humidity is always greater at night. Many species, however, will come out in numbers after warm summer rains. The purplish-brown

Wrinkled snail, *Helicella caperata*, swarms on roadside verges, especially after the grass has been cut, where it feeds on the decaying plant material.

The food of snails consists mainly of fungi, mosses and decaying vegetation in general, although some species exhibit carnivorous tendencies when the opportunity arises. Flowering plants are rarely eaten in the wild, although some of the more tender cultivated ones are readily consumed, especially when they are in the seedling stage. Only the Garden snail and the little Strawberry snail, *Hygromia striolata*, however, can really be considered garden pests. The snail's mouth is bordered by soft lobes or lips which act as taste and smell receptors and find suitable food. Inside the mouth there is a horny upper jaw and a file-like 'tongue' called the 'radula'. This is a thin, horny ribbon studded with thousands of tiny teeth – about 15,000 in the Garden snail – and it is used to rasp away particles of food. As the front part of the radula is worn away with use it is progressively renewed from behind, so that the snail is assured of a continuous succession of teeth throughout its life.

The food passes from the mouth into a capacious crop, rather like that of grain-eating birds, so that the snail can feed in haste and then digest at leisure in the security of its hideout. Snails, like snakes, can go without food for long periods and some species have lived for several years without a meal.

If you look at the right-hand side of an extended snail, just by the lip of the shell, you will see a small hole open and close every minute or so. This is the entrance to the mantle cavity, the space between the mantle and the tissues of the visceral hump. In the marine snails the cavity contains gills, but during the evolution of the land snails the gills have been lost and the lining of the cavity has become richly supplied with blood-vessels to extract oxygen from the air. The cavity has, in fact, become a lung and these snails are known as 'pulmonates' from the Latin *pulmo* meaning 'a lung'. Even those snails that later entered fresh water have retained the lung and they generally come to the surface periodically to breathe. Some freshwater snails, however – those which reached fresh water via the estuaries without a terrestrial stage – retain the gills and do not need to surface. These snails can be recognized by the fact that they also have opercula.

Apart from the two operculate species, all our land snails are hermaphrodite, with male and female organs in each individual. This arrangement has a definite survival value for these slow-moving animals because it doubles the chances of meeting a suitable partner; a similar state of affairs to that in the earthworms. The courting snails wrap

Roman snails mating; inset, a love dart

themselves round each other and, during the course of this amorous activity, each one fires a 'love dart' into its partner. This dart, composed mainly of calcium carbonate, penetrates deeply into the tissues of the snail and seems to trigger off the climax of the mating behaviour – the exchange of sperm. The genital organs are situated in a little pit just behind the head and copulation occurs with these regions in contact. Sperm received from the partner is stored in spermathecae and one mating provides enough sperm for several batches of round, whitish eggs. Batches are laid in the soil, especially under stones or logs, and they take about three weeks to hatch.

Most of our snails become mature about a year after they hatch and, although some of the larger species can live for several years, most of them die before they are two. Snails are generally active only during the warmer weather and most species spend the winter in hibernation. Snails hibernate in sheltered crevices, under logs and stones, among leaf litter or buried in the soil. The Garden snail usually congregates in crevices and large numbers can be found stuck to each other by dried mucus. The snails use the mucus to seal up the shells and the layer of hardened slime is called an epiphragm. Several epiphragms may be formed across the shell in very cold weather, but there is always a little breathing-hole. Snails will also shut themselves away during hot, dry weather because their soft bodies are very susceptible to water loss. This summer rest is called aestivation.

Our water-snails belong to two distinct groups – the lung-breathing pulmonates and the operculate, gill-breathing species. The aquatic pulmonates are closely related to the land snails but they differ in having only one pair of tentacles, with eyes at the base instead of at the tip. In this respect the aquatic pulmonates resemble the operculate snails.

Like the land snails, the water-snails require a certain amount of calcium for their shells. Soft waters are therefore rather poor

in molluscs and the greatest numbers are to be found in shallow, well-aerated lakes and rivers in calcareous regions. Snail-collecting at various points along the course of a river will reveal marked changes as one proceeds from headstream to estuary. The swiftly flowing waters of the headstream support few molluscs but they do contain the River limpet, *Ancylus fluviatilis*. This little creature, no relation of the marine limpets, has a hood-shaped shell with a hooked apex. It clings tightly to the stones and feeds by scraping algae from them. It is a pulmonate snail but it has lost the lung and part of the mantle acts as a gill. A similar species, known as the Lake limpet, *Acroloxus lacustris*, lives attached to plants in still and slow-moving water.

Further downstream, in the troutbeck regions, one finds the Valve snails, *Valvata* species, the sinistral Bladder snail, *Physa fontinalis*, and the thick-shelled Nerite, *Theodoxus fluviatilis*. The meandering lowland reaches, however, are the richest stretches, with many species of Pond snail, *Limnaea*, and flat Ram's-horns, *Planorbis* species. Numbers decline again as the river reaches the estuarine regions, for not many species can survive the ever-changing salinity of estuarine waters.

The gill-breathing snails are generally found in running water where the oxygen content is relatively high. Lung-breathing species, however, not dependent upon the oxygen content of the water, can survive in stagnant waters. Not all the pulmonate water-snails actually breathe air: some of the smaller ones fill their mantle cavities with water and absorb oxygen directly from the water. All water-snails get some oxygen through the general body surface and the Ram's-horns have evolved a 'false gill' – an expanded lobe of the mantle – which helps them to obtain more oxygen. Oxygen uptake in these snails is increased even further by the presence of haemoglobin in their blood and the Ram's-horns can make do with only infrequent visits to the surface. For example, the Great ram's-horn, *Planorbarius corneus*,

Freshwater snails: *Nerite, left;* Great pond snail, *top left;* Jenkins' spire, *top right;* River limpet, *right;* Valve snail, *bottom, left;* Ram's-horn, *bottom, right*

surfaces only two or three times an hour, whereas the Great pond snail, *Limnaea stagnalis*, comes up every five minutes. All water-snails can live for some time out of the water as long as they are kept damp.

Reproduction in the water-snails is similar to that in the land-living species, except that in most of the operculate snails the sexes are separate. The eggs are normally laid in long strings of jelly, attached to stones and water-plants. Some species, however, bring forth active young, the eggs having hatched before leaving the parent's body. Examples include the River snails, *Viviparus* species, and Jenkins' spire shell, *Potamopyrgus jenkinsi*. The latter species has a remarkable history

in the British Isles. About 100 years ago it was known only in brackish estuaries but it has now spread throughout our rivers and canals. Only one male has ever been found and the species reproduces entirely by parthenogenesis.

Slugs are pulmonate gastropods which, during the course of their evolution, have almost or quite lost their shells. Apart from this reduction of the shell and the flattening of the visceral hump, their structure and biology is very much like that of the land snails. Slugs are generally more of a nuisance in the garden than snails and there are about nine species which cause trouble. Oddly enough, these are usually the small ones

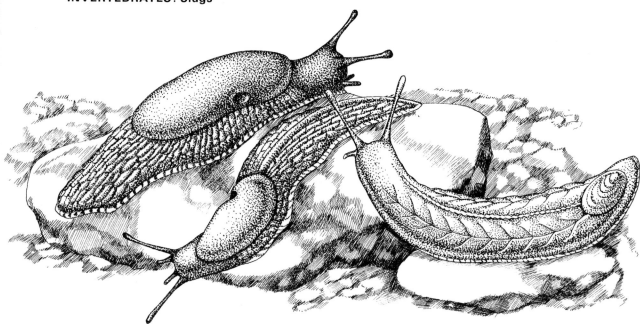

because the larger species prefer decaying material and rarely feed on growing plants other than fungi.

Our three families of slugs have evolved independently from distinct groups of snails and they form a rather heterogeneous assortment, more closely related to various snails than to each other. The similarities between the three groups are due to convergent evolution and not to a common ancestry.

The family Testacellidae contains three British species. The Shelled slug, *Testacella haliotidea*, p. 256, is the most common. All three species possess a small shell right at the hind end and the body gradually gets thicker from front to back. These slugs feed almost entirely on earthworms which they catch on the surface at night. As *Testacella* approaches its prey it shoots out its long radula and the barbed teeth impale the worm which is then rapidly swallowed. The Shelled slug hides under the ground by day and it is found mainly in gardens and other cultivated places.

The family Arionidae contains the round-back slugs, in which the upper surface of the body is gently rounded. The mantle sits on the anterior region of the body and the

Slugs, representatives of the three British families: Round-backed, *left*; Keeled slug, *centre*; Shelled slug, *right*

breathing-pore opens on its right-hand side, well before the middle of the mantle. Apart from the Kerry spotted slug, *Geomalacus maculosus*, whose only British home is in Ireland, all our roundback slugs belong to the genus *Arion*. In these slugs the shell is reduced to a few chalky granules embedded in the mantle. Other diagnostic features include the elongated tubercles on the dorsal surface and the fringe round the sole of the foot. The Large black slug, p. 256, common in gardens and hedgerows, is *Arion ater*. The tubercles are very prominent in this species and it grows to a length of about 6 inches (15 cm.) When disturbed, the animal contracts into a hemispherical lump and sways from side to side in a rather sinister fashion. It eats pretty well anything that is decaying but rarely attacks growing plants. *Arion ater* is not always black and one can find all shades from black to the chestnut form, *Arion ater rufus*, p. 256. The Garden slug, *Arion hortensis*, is one of the serious garden pests, feeding on both leaves and roots. It is a slender, black slug reaching about 3 cm. in length and it can be recognized by its yellowish or orange sole.

The third family of slugs is the Limacidae or keeled slugs, so called because the back carries a marked ridge or keel. The mantle is near the front, as it is in the roundback slugs, but the breathing-pore is more than half-way back along the mantle. The mantle conceals a thin, flat shell. The pale, mottled Netted slug, *Agriolimax reticulatus*, is the worst of all the garden slugs because, whereas most species remain at ground-level or below, this one will crawl up and chew the leaves of taller plants. This is the slug that is most often found in lettuces and cabbages. The other members of this family do not often feed on green plants. The Great grey slug, *Limax maximus*, whose strange mating habits have been described earlier, is one of our largest slugs, reaching up to 8 inches (20 cm.) when extended. It is common in gardens and it often finds its way into old houses, especially damp ones. It is a most handsome slug p. 256 and, feeding entirely on fungi and decaying matter, it does not deserve the harsh treatment usually accorded to it. The Ash black slug, *Limax cinereoniger*, is our largest species, occasionally reaching a length of about 15 inches (38 cm.). Its habits are much like those of the Great grey slug but it lives in woods and other undisturbed places and does not come into cultivated land.

The lamellibranchs or bivalves are those molluscs in which the shell consists of two valves, hinged along one edge by an elastic ligament and usually connected with interlocking teeth as well. These animals filter food-particles from the water and they are entirely aquatic. The majority of them are marine but we have about 30 freshwater species, ranging from the Swan mussel, *Anodonta cygnea*, which may reach a length of 6 inches (15 cm.), down to the little Pea cockles, *Pisidium* species, no more than 10 mm. long. Most of these bivalves live in still or slow-moving water where there is a muddy, but firm bottom. Canals are usually very rich in bivalves, as shown by the heaps of shells hauled out during dredging operations.

The larger species live half-buried in the mud and they can plough their way slowly through it by means of the tongue-shaped foot. This organ is pushed out through the lower front end of the shell and it can be considerably distended by blood-pressure. This action ploughs out a furrow in the mud and the tip then swells up and grips the sides of the furrow. Strong muscles then pull the rest of the animal along.

The bivalves have no head and the bulk of the body consists of the large gills, which hang inside the thick flaps of the mantle. Gills and mantle are covered with tiny cilia and the hind edge of the mantle is drawn out to form two short tubes or siphons (only one in the Pea cockles).

When the shell valves are open the cilia draw a current of water in through the lower siphon. Oxygen is extracted from this water current by the gills and the mantle, while the gills also strain out suspended algae and other food-particles. These are conveyed in a stream of mucus to the mouth and the water then flows out through the upper siphon. Some of the larger mussels filter several pints of water every hour and this is why they are commonly used to keep aquarium water clear.

When necessary the mussel can withdraw completely into the shell and close the valves by means of two powerful muscles, whose attachment scars can be clearly seen inside empty shells. When the muscles relax the elastic ligament pulls the valves open again, although they never open very wide.

The larger species, typified by the Swan mussel, have separate sexes. The females lay their eggs into brood-pouches in the gills. The males liberate their sperms into the water and the sperms are taken in through the siphons of other mussels. Any eggs in the brood-pouches will thus be fertilized. They remain in the brood-pouches for several months and gradually develop into tiny larvae called 'glochidia'. Each glochidium has a bivalve shell, although it is only half a millimetre across when released from the brood-pouch. The glochidia float about in the water for a time but no further development occurs unless they come into contact with a fish, for the larvae now embark on a parasitic life. When a fish comes near a glochidium the latter shoots out a tacky thread which sticks fast to the fish. The glochidium then uses the tiny teeth round the edge of its shell to anchor itself to the host, usually on the fins or the gills. The fish's tissues swell up round the larva and the young mussel remains there for up to three months, nourished by the body fluids of the fish. Then, having grown a new shell, the young mussel drops from the host to start an independent life which may last for several years. The Pea cockles and the slightly larger Orb cockles, *Sphaerium* species, are hermaphrodite animals and they do not pass through a parasitic phase. The Zebra mussel, *Dreissena polymorpha*, also has no parasitic phase, but it is thought to be a relative newcomer to fresh water and it is more closely related to the marine mussels than the other freshwater species.

If a piece of sand or other irritant gets inside a mollusc shell, the animal will often deal with the irritation by secreting a smooth layer of mother-of-pearl round it. Pearl formation is well known in certain marine oysters, but it is not confined to those animals. Our Pearl mussel, *Margaritifer margaritifer*, sometimes produces good quality pearls and these have been exploited commercially at various times. The Pearl mussel is unusual in that it inhabits the swifter, clearer streams of the north and west. The water in these streams is soft and it is difficult to explain the abnormally thick shell of this species.

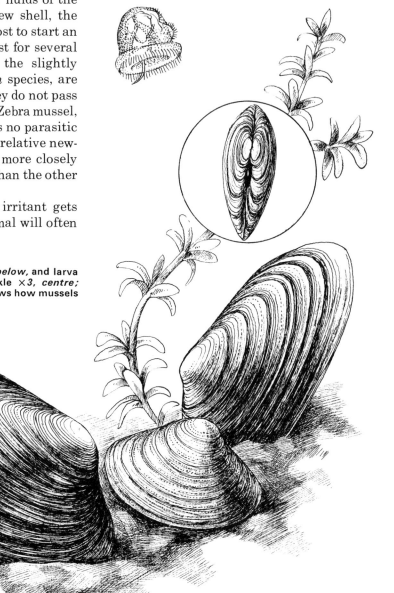

Freshwater mussels: Swan mussel, *below*, and larva (glochidium) *above, left;* Pea cockle ×3, *centre;* Painter's mussel, *right;* the inset shows how mussels are hinged

The Sea Shore

The sea-shore lies between sea and land but belongs to neither, although the bulk of its population derives very largely from the sea. Many of its inhabitants occur nowhere else; so they are truly shore-living animals and plants. The shore is thus unique but it also affords us a glimpse of that unfamiliar world below sea-level.

The coast has a charm all its own. Suddenly the varied pattern of the land ends and we are confronted with a wide expanse of water bounded by a distant sharp horizon. The land behind us is green, the sea before us is usually blue, but not with life; indeed, the most lifeless seas are the bluest because the richness of colour is an indication of the depth to which light penetrates and that penetration is greatest where there is least life in the water. Nevertheless, even such sea teems with life which is very broadly divisible into the pelagic, swimming, life of open waters and the benthic, life on the bottom. It is also divisible into plants and animals. The seaweeds, including the massive brown weeds that may rise and fall in the swell at low tide immediately offshore, are the most obvious of the seas' plant life; although of very minor importance in the economy of the sea. They represent the merest fringe round the margin of the land. As the light on which they depend rapidly diminishes with increasing depth so do the seaweeds, petering out altogether at depths of around 90–100 feet (27–30 m.).

The oceans cover some two-thirds of the globe and in the top layers there is an infinite abundance of microscopic plant life made up of diatoms as well as naked green or brown peridinians, or dinoflagellates, often of bizarre form but each with two whip-like flagella, one encircling the body, the other projecting from one end. In their countless millions these plants represent the primary production of the ocean, the equivalent of grass and green herbage on land, and they are of profound significance to shore animals also, many of which feed directly upon them.

These microscopic plants form the phytoplankton. The animal or zooplankton consists in the main of extremely small animals, transparent and almost of the consistency of water, although some of its members, such as the jellyfish, may be large. In it are representatives of almost every group of animals living in the sea, from single-celled protozoans to the early, larval stages of fishes. It is of the greatest significance to the inhabitants of the shore. Many of them spend some part of their lives as temporary members of the plankton. To others it is a source of food.

The sea is the home also of a host of actively moving creatures which inhabit all depths. These, the nekton, include the majority of the fishes and also seals, as well as whales and porpoises. Finally, there is the bottom life, the benthos, including many shore inhabitants. They have extended upwards on to the shore having developed powers to withstand the force of the waves, the effects of desiccation and exposure to wide ranges of temperature and salinity. They include representatives of almost every group in the animal kingdom apart from insects, spiders and vertebrates, although a few of these forage on the shore. The shore is in process of long-term change but our present shores are, roughly, divisible into rocky, sandy and muddy. A point to note is that the shore is a region of altogether exceptional abundance of food constantly being renewed.

A matter of prime importance round British coasts is tidal movement. Tides are set in motion by the pull of the moon and of the sun. And although the moon is infinitely the smaller it is also much the nearer and so exerts the greater effect. When the two forces act together they produce spring tides – which means the lowest as well as the highest extremes – and when in opposition they cause neap tides. Tidal movements are essentially oscillations (such as one can set up in a bath) within the great oceanic basins and the size of the Atlantic Basin is such that we have two tides daily. Owing to frictional effects they are, on average, some

low tide but this varies from place to place although it is always about the same time at any particular locality, influenced some-what by winds and barometric pressure. The lowest low tides are always a little after the day of full or new moon and the lowest of these at the equinoxes, around 21 March and 21 September, when forces from sun and moon are exactly in the same line. These

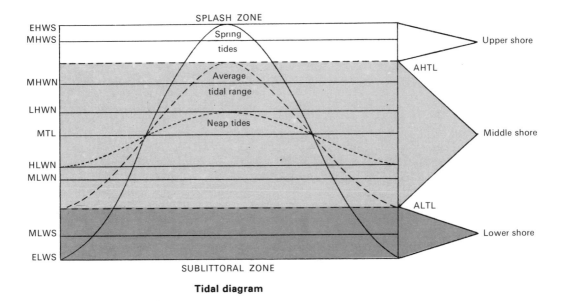

Tidal diagram

50 minutes later each day. In other words, our tides are diurnal which is not neces-sarily true in other parts of the world. Moon and sun act in unison at the times of full and new moon and this is when the low tides allow us to see the greatest extent of un-covered shore. In the up-and-down tidal movements speed slackens over the periods of highest and lowest water as indicated by the slope of the curve in the figure; the steeper this is the more rapid the tidal movements up or down the shore.

In the open sea tidal movements are small but round continents they become exag-gerated particularly in narrowing inlets such as the Bristol Channel where tidal extremes may be over 40 feet (12 m.) apart. The best view of the shore is clearly around

may be inconvenient times for exploration if the time of lowest tide comes in early morning and again in the evening but from the standpoint of the shore inhabitants this is an advantage. If the shores are exposed around midday they will suffer the full effects of summer heat and winter cold which they avoid if the water, colder than the air in summer and warmer in winter, covers them during the middle of the day.

The result of widely differing powers of adaptation to shore conditions is zonation. One sees on the shore, sometimes within a few dozen yards if the shore is steep, different bands of seaweed and different types of animals as one moves from one extremity of the uncovered shore to the other. The tidal diagram shows how the shore may be subdivided from extreme high water of spring tides (EHWS), by way of the lowest high water of neap tides (LHWN) – the whole range of high-tide levels – to the highest low water of neaps (HLWN) to the ultimate exposure of extreme low water of springs (ELWS), i.e. the full range of low tidal levels. The two curves of spring and neap tidal movements have inserted between them a curve based on the average tidal range which extends between the average high- and the average low-tide levels (AHTL, ALTL on the right side of the figure). In the middle where all three curves ideally cross is the mean tidal level (MTL). In a very arbitrary fashion one may consider the region above AHTL as the 'upper shore', that region which is only normally covered by sea-water during the period of spring tides, and the lowest region below ALTL may be termed the 'lower shore', uncovered for correspondingly infrequent periods. Between these is the 'middle shore' which, in most places, is covered and uncovered twice daily. Above the upper shore comes the 'splash zone', an area of very varying extent where shore animals and plants can survive solely by virtue of the spray, the force of which conditions the area over which it operates. Below the lowest tidal levels comes the 'sublittoral fringe', a region of shallow water with characteristic seaweeds that may spread up the shore where there are permanent deep pools.

Rocky shores, which give the best opportunities for study, vary greatly in character. Some consist of flat platforms with frequent pools backed by sheer cliffs, or the rocks may be lower with a more gradual, sometimes very tumbled, rise from low to high tidal levels. According to the nature of the rocks they weather differently, providing greater or less shelter. The various rock-borers can only penetrate into the softer sedimentary rocks.

But whatever the particular nature of the rocky shore it will, given not absolutely extreme exposure, carry a zoned population of seaweeds which must be our first concern.

Some flowering plants extend to the strand-line and there may be grey or yellow lichens on the rocks high on the shore, but beyond this there is only one kind of plant that is not a seaweed. It is the Eel grasses with long, strap-like leaves and inconspicuous flowers occurring the world over but restricted in the British Isles to two species of *Zostera*. All other marine plants are algae, flowerless and reproducing mainly by spores. They are divisible into the three groups of green, brown and red weeds – and by characters more significant than colour which is occasionally misleading.

Very broadly speaking we shall find the seaweeds in three colour groups arranged in zones from high-tide mark downwards: green – brown – red, due to the differing properties of the photosynthetic pigments, the greens being most efficient in bright light and the reds, some of which extend to considerable depths in clear water, capable of functioning in dim light, with the browns coming between. Moreover, the greens are not averse to the presence of fresh water and where a rivulet of green runs down the shore through the brown weeds this is sure indication of the presence of a stream of fresh water. The two most obvious green weeds are the broad-fronded Sea-lettuce, *Ulva lactuca*, which usually grows in bunches together, and the appropriately named *Enteromorpha intestinalis* which consists of long tubular fronds, up to a foot (30 cm.) long but usually constricted from place to place. When fully grown the fronds may become detached. Both of these weeds are associated with fresh water and occur in estuaries, *Enteromorpha* being most abundant in spring and early summer while *Ulva* reaches its maximum growth in July and August. The other green weeds, with one exception, are delicate. There are the dark green tufts of *Cladophora*, of which there are several species, with branched filaments and found in damp places under brown weeds or else in pools. *Brysopsis plumosa* is unmistakable, a beautiful little weed with each branch subdivided and feather-like. Both are widely

THE SEA-SHORE: Seaweeds

Green algae: *from left to right*, Sea-lettuce, *Ulva lactuca*; *Enteromorpha intestinalis*; *Codium tormentosa*; *Cladophora rupestris*

distributed and grow to heights of 3–4 inches (7–10 cm.). The Hog's bristle, *Chaetomorpha melagonium*, which grows a little longer, consists of stiff unbranched threads, and though widespread is not quite so common. It is usually found in pools. Finally there is the much larger *Codium tormentosum*, dark green with rounded branches of an unmistakable spongy texture which grows to a length of a foot (30 cm.), branching dichotomously. It occurs usually in deep pools low on the shore and is most abundant in winter.

The brown weeds are far more abundant and important. We start with the fucoids or sea-wracks which on any typical rocky shore form a draped covering when the tide is out.

Each plant is attached firmly to the rock by a disc-shaped holdfast which enables it to withstand the pounding of the sea. The species occur in zoned series down the shore. Highest is the Channelled wrack, *Pelvetia canaliculata*, p. 281, which occurs in tufted bunches some 6 inches (15 cm.) long, each frond inrolled and ending in a forked tip. This would appear almost a land plant because it is exposed far more than it is covered, in some places for 90 per cent of the year. It turns hard and black with prolonged exposure but regains normal texture and the typical olive-brown colour when again washed by the sea. Immediately below it, still on the upper shore, comes a second narrow zone, that of the Flat wrack, *Fucus spiralis*, p. 281. Here the broader frond grows up to a foot (30 cm.) or more in length and, like all species of *Fucus*, has a conspicuous midrib. When ripe the tips of the fronds become swollen with granular fruiting bodies. This weed is exposed for, on average, around 70 per cent of the year.

Next in level, and covering much of the middle, and most extensive, area of the shore occur two other wracks, occasionally together but more often the presence of the one excludes that of the other. There is the Knotted wrack, *Ascophyllum nodosum*, p. 281, and the Bladder wrack, *Fucus vesiculosus*. The latter has bladder-like swellings occurring in pairs over the surfaces of the fronds. The former also has bladders but they occur singly extending the full width of the frond which has no midrib. There are other differences but these are fully adequate to separate them. Both are much longer weeds, as befits the greater depth of the water which more frequently covers them, floating well clear of the bottom buoyed by the gas-bladders and swaying with the water currents. Of the two, the Knotted wrack is less capable of withstanding violent seas; its fronds are both longer and thinner, without the tensile strength of the Bladder wrack where the fronds are thicker and have the strengthening midrib. However, they may occur together, sometimes mixed and

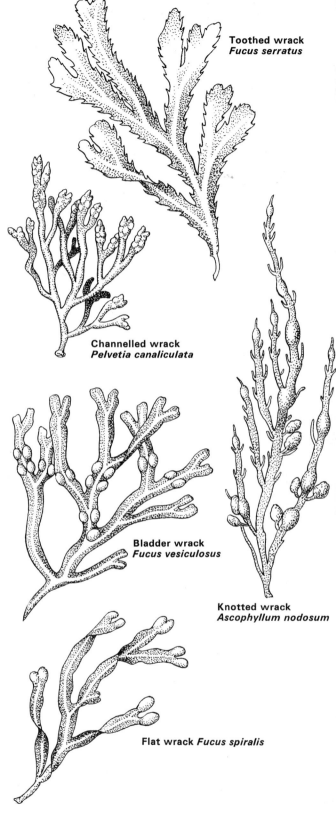

Toothed wrack
Fucus serratus

Channelled wrack
Pelvetia canaliculata

Bladder wrack
Fucus vesiculosus

Knotted wrack
Ascophyllum nodosum

Flat wrack *Fucus spiralis*

sometimes in distinct zones. Below them, the lower shore is occupied by a distinct band of the Serrated or Toothed wrack, *Fucus serratus*, p. 281, with marginally serrated flat fronds and no bladders. Finally, there is *F. ceranoides* which occurs often on stones in the middle shore in the brackish waters of estuaries or opposite the mouths of streams. This has no bladders and most resembles the Flat wrack but it grows to lengths of 3 feet (91 cm.) and has a more wavy margin to the fronds. The Knotted wrack may occur in rounded, unattached masses at the heads of west coast inlets on the coasts of Scotland and Ireland where the bottom is of gravel or even mud. This is known as *Ascophyllum nodosum* variety *Mackaii*.

The zonation of these brown weeds is due to their varying powers of withstanding exposure to the air and the mechanical force of the sea. Reproductive cells are discharged into the sea which eventually disperses them over the full extent of the shore. Those

Brown algae: *from left to right,* Peacock's tail, *Padina pavonia*; Rainbow bladder-weed, *Cystoseira ericoides*; Thong-weed, *Himanthalia lorea*; Pod-weed, *Halidrys siliquosa*

that settle in unsuitable places simply die.

There is a wide diversity of other brown algae, many too small for description, but keeping first to the middle and lower shores, the following should easily be recognized. Forming compact bushes in pools is the Pod-weed, *Halidrys siliquosa*, much branched with oval and subdivided gas-bladders and usually around 18 inches (46 cm.) tall. This is commonest in the north with the somewhat smaller *Bifurcaria rotunda* with a few small bladders on its branches taking its place in the south. Also exclusively on southern shores is the beautifully fan-shaped Peacock's tail, *Padina pavonia*, more yellowish green than brown, some 6 inches (15 cm.) high and the surface covered with concentric lines of iridescent hairs and whitish patches of lime. Also along the west coast, though never in the north, is the so-called Rainbow bladder-weed, *Cystoseira ericoides*, which has numerous branches with many small bladders and terminating with fine bristles. Particularly when viewed under water when it is iridescent it is unmistakable. It grows to heights of up to 2 feet (61 cm.), is yellowish olive and the home of many minute animals. Weeds with unbranched hollow fronds are *Scytosiphon lomentaria*, about a foot (30 cm.) tall and each frond frequently constricted, and the smaller green *Asperococcus fistulosus*. Both are widely distributed. The various species of *Desmarestia*, again confined to the south and west, are easily distinguished by their delicately fern-like growth; they may be up to 6 feet (183 cm.) long. On the lowest levels, often fully exposed at low tide, is the unmistakable Thong-weed, *Himanthalia lorea*. This consists of a rounded stalked button about 1½ inches (38 mm.) high from the centre of which during the winter grows an elongated branched thong, 4 feet (122 cm.) or more long, bearing the reproductive organs which ripen in the summer.

Belonging to the sublittoral fringe but with their broad fronds visible at any good low tide, and to some extent completely uncovered at the lowest springs, are the massive tangle-weeds or oar-weeds. Below the broad frond is a stipe, a stout stalk attached to the rocks by an elaborately branching holdfast which provides a secure home for a variety of small animals and for that reason is well worth examination. Under the right conditions of rocky substratum and often violent seas, these impressive weeds dominate depths down to about 15 fathoms (27 m.) where, presumably, the light becomes too feeble. The principal species are easy to determine. Highest up is usually the smooth-surfaced *Laminaria digitata*, the specific name indicating the digitate or finger-like character of the fronds. Distinguished from it by the stouter, rounder and more roughened stipe is *L. hyperborea* (*cloustoni*). Both may be up to 6 feet (183 cm.) long. Growth, which is very rapid, occurs at the tip of the stipe, a new frond being produced annually and pushing off the old one. *L. saccharina* occurs somewhat further out but may be found in deep pools. Here the frond is undivided, with crinkled surface and wavy margins, p. 281. It may reach a length of 20 feet (6 m.).

The presence offshore of *Sacchorhiza polyschides* (*bulbosa*) is revealed by the appearance, washed-up, of their remarkable holdfasts, large hollow masses covered with warty protrusions and up to a foot (30 cm.) across. They also are safe retreats for small invertebrates. The fronds are subdivided, like those of *Laminaria digitata* but more completely and the flattened stipe has wavy margins. The last of these large weeds is the Murlins, *Alaria esculenta*, with undivided frond but with a well-developed midrib distinguishing it from *Laminaria saccharina*. This is a weed of the most exposed shores where it may replace *L. digitata*.

The red weeds are the most numerous in species but often difficult to distinguish and identify, so attention must be restricted to the commoner and more obvious species. Widely spread over the shore, often where there are stones with some sand with which they tend to become covered, are species of *Porphyra*, p. 282, in form rather like the green *Ulva* but purplish red or brown. This is the edible laver, fried after being rolled in oatmeal. Other common edible weeds are the Dulse, *Rhodymenia palmata*, with flattened fronds arising without stalk from the hold-fast, dark red to purplish and growing in bunches up to a foot (30 cm.) in height, and the Irish moss or Carageen, *Chondrus crispus*, p. 282, much branched and very variable in colour but strikingly iridescent under water. Closely resembling it and also very common on flat expanses of rock low on the shore is *Gigartina stellata*, p. 282, really only distinguished from Carageen by the somewhat greater extent of branching. Both form a kind of thick felting. During the war *Gigartina* proved a valuable source of agar-agar. A particularly beautiful weed, the deep red fronds having a pronounced midrib with

Tangle-weeds: *Laminaria digitata*, *left*, with an oval stem is similar to *L. hyperborea* with a round stem; *Sacchorhiza polyschides*, *centre*; the Murlins, *Alaria esculenta*, *right*

lateral veins like the leaf of a tree, is *Delesseria sanguinea*, p. 282. It is usually confined to deep pools low on the shore. The Pepper-dulse, *Laurencia obtusa*, is finely divided with stiff opposite branches. It is generally common on the middle and lower shores but only during the summer months.

These are the most obvious of the larger red weeds but there are many very fine ones such as the easily distinguished *Polysiphonia fastigiata*, extremely common, growing as little reddish tufts on the fronds of *Ascophyllum*. Together with species of the brown *Ectocarpus*, of very similar habit, it merely grows on the larger plant, i.e. is epiphytic, not parasitic. A notable section of the red weeds incorporate calcium carbonate in their tissues and the sides of rock pools are frequently covered with a pinkish encrustation due to the spreading growth of one of these, *Lithophyllum incrustans*. Another, more obviously plant-like growth, consists of stiff little tufts of pink branches, divided into short sections and growing to a height of a few inches. This is the Coralline alga, *Corallina officinalis*, almost universally present in pools and on sheltered damp surfaces of rock. There are a variety of smaller coralline algae or seaweeds, all brittle and turning white on death.

There are some general remarks to make about shore seaweeds before passing on to the animals. As indicated above, there is annual renewal in some cases, the wracks live two or three years only but young plants are there in abundance to take over every vacant site so that the rocks are perpetually clothed. Turnover in other weeds is great enough to permit seasonal movements up and down the shore. Some of the filamentous red weeds move upshore in the winter as does the brown *Scytosiphon*, but the commoner green algae which live in profusion in marginal high pools in the summer occur mid tidally in the winter. The covering of wracks in particular has a major effect. It blankets the rocks and the cliffs behind from the force of the waves and is an even greater protection to the animals so common beneath and within it, sheltering these not only from mechanical shock but also from the effects of desiccation and of extremes of temperature and salinity. Their fronds, and those of the broader tangles lower down, provide extensive attaching surface for many small animals that collect food from the surrounding water and for a smaller number that actually feed upon the seaweed itself. But its major value as food comes mainly after it dies and is broken down by mechanical and bacterial action to form much of the organic detritus on which so many shore animals find a somewhat nondescript but obviously adequate diet.

Zonation of animals on a rocky shore is less obvious because it is largely obscured by that of the plants. However, on the most exposed shores wracks may be absent or very sparse, the young plants being either unable to attach themselves or to maintain themselves after attachment. Then a simple, but universal, pattern becomes apparent. Highest of all, and extending beyond the confines of the true shore, is the zone characterized by the presence of the periwinkles *Littorina neritoides* and *L. saxatalis*, below that comes a broad *Balanoid* zone composed of species of sessile barnacles, that is, barnacles without stalks. Below that again is a *Laminaria* zone. This general pattern has been found to be universal on rocky shores throughout the world, although the superimposed patterns vary widely, being greatly influenced by the local distribution of seaweeds.

By and large it is the gastropod molluscs, the sea-snails such as periwinkles and top-shells, as well as the limpets and the barnacles, which best exhibit zonation. These are all extremely common which implies complete adaptation for shore life. There are four species of periwinkle, the Small periwinkle, *L. neritoides*, and the Rough periwinkle, *L. saxatilis*, both true inhabitants of the upper shore and above, the Common periwinkle, *L. littorea*, on the middle shore and top of the lower shore and the Round periwinkle, *L. littoralis* (*obtusata*), which is dependent on algae, being confined to the fronds of the Bladder wrack and Knotted wrack, indeed bearing some resemblance to their bladders. The Small periwinkle, with its blue-black rounded shell about $\frac{1}{5}$ inch (5 mm.) high, with the rounded opening typical of the periwinkles, is usually packed in such numbers in crevices that they cannot be missed. It feeds by scraping encrusting vegetation with its horny toothed tongue or radula, the characteristic feeding-organ of all molluscs. Its gill is reduced and its respiratory cavity forms a lung. But this independence of the sea does not extend to reproduction. Small periwinkles spawn fortnightly over the winter months, at each spring tide, which are the only times the sea reaches them. Development takes place in the sea and the young eventually settle among the barnacles, gradually making their way up to the splash zone. The Rough periwinkle, with its rounded shell up to $\frac{1}{2}$ inch (13 mm.) high, varies in colour from red to black. In comparison with the Common periwinkle the upper lip of the shell opening meets the last whorl of the shell at right angles instead of tangentially. This periwinkle, however, is very variable in form, no less than six subspecies and twelve varieties having recently been distinguished.

With little doubt this variability is due to the fact that this animal bears living young that settle down straight away with their parents and are not carried about by currents, so local populations tend to inbreed. This cannot happen when the young are planktonic and develop as free-swimming larvae in the sea, so are likely to be carried to regions remote from where they were spawned.

The Rough periwinkle does not occur below mid-tidal levels where it slightly overlaps with the larger Common periwinkle. Here the shell, usually grey-black or red and always with concentric darker lines, is up to 1 inch (25 mm.) high. This is an enormously successful animal (no matter how many are collected the supply seems undiminished) living on any bottom from bare rocks to stones, gravel and even on mud. It appears to live equally well fully exposed to the surf or sheltered from it, or in the protection, with their lowered salinity and pollution, of estuaries. It spawns into the sea and the young settle below tide levels and then move up the beach, as does the Rough periwinkle, although starting from a different level – to the region of its final distribution which it reaches when about one year old. There it maintains itself by a behaviour pattern which involves appropriate reactions to both light and gravity. When artificially displaced all these periwinkles slowly

Periwinkles: Small, *Littorina neritoides*, life-size, *top left*; Rough, *L. saxatilis* ×$\frac{1}{2}$, *top right*; Common *L. littorea* ×$\frac{4}{5}$, *bottom left*; Round, *L. littoralis*, life-size, *bottom right*

move back to their appropriate zone. The Round periwinkle is smaller and almost globular with only a tiny shell-spire. It is unlikely to be confused with the others, especially as it is largely confined to the surface of the bladder weeds. It has a wide range of shell colour, from bright yellow to olive-green, brown, purple or streaked. It lays its eggs in gelatinous masses on the surface of the weed and from these the shelled young eventually emerge. There is no free-swimming larva so the young have no need to search for their proper habitat or their food.

The topshells are less rounded than the periwinkles with straighter sides rising to a sharp spire. There are several British species not all as widely distributed as the periwinkles but very characteristically zoned. The large Painted topshell, *Calliostoma zizyphinum*, is one of our most handsome shells, flat based and straight sided and up to 1 inch (25 mm.) high, pink or yellow with red streaks, occasionally white. When moving this topshell puts out four pairs of lateral tentacles as well as the pair on the head. It lives on the lower shore on our south and west coasts but keeps below tidal levels on the colder east coast. The almost equally large *Gibbula* (*Monodonta* or *Osilinus*) *lineata*, the Thick topshell, is similarly restricted geographically, but it inhabits the middle shore. The shell is a mottled grey. The smaller Flat and Grey topshells, *Gibbula umbilicalis* and *G. cineraria*, both about $\frac{1}{2}$ inch (13 mm.) high, occur on the lower half of the shore, the former also being restricted to southern and western shores, the latter more widely distributed. The Flat topshell is distinguished by having an opening, the umbilicus, in the centre of the under-surface of the shell. All topshells feed on seaweeds and are found only on rocky shores.

Limpets are also sea-snails but the final coil of their shell is so enlarged that it houses the entire animal and the initial coiling of the shell disappears. The foot on which all snails move is rounded and sucker-like, enabling the limpets to grip the surface and

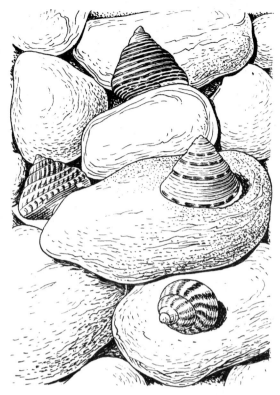

Topshells : *top*, Thick topshell, *Gibbula lineata* ; *centre left*, Grey topshell, *G. cineraria* and *right*, Painted topshell, *Calliostoma zizyphinum* ; *bottom*, Flat topshell, *G. umbilicalis*

pull the shell-margins tightly down for protection. Periwinkles and topshells close the much smaller aperture with a rounded lid or operculum carried on the back of the foot. In the Common periwinkle this is black and known popularly as the 'winkle head'. The limpet form, and the habit which goes with it, is enormously successful, and has been independently evolved some ten times. The limpets that colonize our rocky shores are probably the most successful of all. The Common limpet is *Patella vulgata*, a species found on every rocky shore. Even when the tide is out it will continue to graze, very slowly moving about while the rock is wet. But the moment there is any danger of its being dislodged or drying up it grips firmly and pulls its shell down and so it remains until the tide returns. You can knock a limpet off with a sudden blow, but give it the warning of an initial tap and it grips so firmly that the shell will be broken before it can be moved. Some shells are higher than others and these usually occur where the animal lives on exposed rocks involving frequent contraction of the muscle connecting foot and shell. Limpets that live in pools have no such needs so the margins of the shell tend to grow further outward. The Common limpet is found widely over the middle and lower shores. There are two further species, *P. intermedia* and *P. aspera*, the former confined to the south-west coasts and the latter to the west and extreme

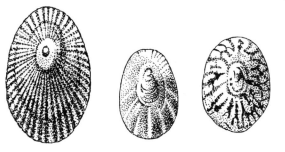

Three uncommon limpets: the Keyhole limpet, *Diodora apertura*, *left*; the Blue-rayed limpet, *Patina pellucida*, *centre*; the Tortoiseshell limpet, *Acmaea tessulata*, *right*

north-east. Both live on exposed shores, and lower down than the Common limpet. Both are flatter than that species and there are differences in the interior of the shell which is marginally rayed in *P. intermedia* and paler in *P. aspera* than in the Common limpet. The colour of the foot also differs, being darker in *P. intermedia* than in the Common limpet, and orange in *P. aspera*. These limpets graze the young algae in an area round a 'home', which in soft rocks may be a scar, with the surface of which the shell margins make perfect contact. It is unknown how they find their way back. Development is by free-swimming larvae. In the Common limpet the majority of young begin as males suggesting that, as in a variety of other sea-snails, there is a later sex change.

There are other types of rock-dwelling limpets. The more flattened Tortoiseshell limpet, *Acmaea tessulata*, about 1 inch (25 mm.) long with smooth characteristically patterned shell is a northern species; the smaller white *A. virginea* is widely distributed. Both occur on the lower shore where may also be found, but never openly exposed, two more primitive species, the Keyhole limpet, *Diodora (Fissurella) apertura*, with a 'keyhole' opening on the apex of the shell, occurs on the south and west coasts, the smaller Slit limpet *Emarginula reticulata*, with a marginal slit in front, is more widely found. These limpets have a more primitive respiratory system: they draw in water on either side of the head and expel it through the aperture or slit.

Chitons, or Coat-of-mail shells, have the habits of limpets. They are flattened, oval and have a shell of eight plates lying along the upper surface. The commonest, *Lepidochitona cinereus*, ½ inch (13 mm.) long, is often found clinging to rocks. About the same length are the cowries, *Trivia arctica*, but they can be found living only at extreme low-water springs.

Acorn barnacles are everywhere on the surfaces of rocks. No animals are more common, none better adapted for shore life and yet none more utterly dependent on the sea. The calcareous shell consists of an outer wall of plates closed above by four horizontally disposed plates. These open to permit the emergence of six pairs of feathered – obviously crustacean – limbs which, disposed like the bent fingers of a hand, make repeated casting movements. They can be seen doing this when barnacles on the side of a rock pool are submerged and even occasionally, when it is damp, when they are exposed. They are feeding, not on the products of the shore but on plankton.

Barnacles are hermaphrodite, the numerous eggs being fertilized by sperm conveyed by the long penis of another individual which is inserted within the opercular plates. Thus barnacles must be closely packed; isolated ones are invariably sterile. Only

Cowrie, *Trivia arctica*, left; Chiton, *Lepidochitona cinereus*, right

Three types of Acorn barnacle

Balanus balanoides

Chthamalus stellatus

Elminius modestus

after some months of development are the larvae released into the sea to become free swimming. There they grow further and change into a 'cypris' stage with a bivalved shell and three pairs of legs. It is then they are cast on the shore to search briefly for a sheltered place to settle in; they then cement themselves, grow protective plates and proceed, as aptly observed 'to kick food into their mouth' with their former legs.

Two native species, *Balanus balanoides* and *Chthamalus stellatus*, inhabit the barnacle zone. The former is a northern species occurring round the shores of Great Britain, except in the extreme south-west; the latter is a southern species which extends north along the coast of Wales, the Atlantic coast of Ireland and along the west of Scotland to the far north. It does not occur along the east coast. It has extended further north and *B. balanoides* has somewhat retreated over the past generation with the gradual warming of the sea, a condition which may now be changing. The two species may be distinguished by the shape of the plates as shown in the figure, but the differences are not always easy to make out in practice. They have somewhat different preferences. When the two occur together *Chthamalus* extends the higher up the shore. An interesting competitor to both, the Southern Hemisphere barnacle, *Elminius modestus*, was brought in on ships' bottoms into Southampton Water from Australia early in the Second World War. It has since spread widely round our coasts, a process shown to be controlled by local water movements carrying the larvae, passing further up the west than the east coast. It has four outer plates instead of the six found in the other two species. It occurs in much the same regions but can withstand higher temperatures and more varied salinities and, with a longer breeding-season, is liable to be the first to settle on any available space, so depriving our native species of living space. Two larger acorn barnacles, *B. perforatus* and *B. crenatus*, occur at lower levels, the latter only exposed at very low water.

The Saddle oyster,
Anomia ephippium
×⅔

Common mussel,
Mytilus edulis
×⅔

Horse mussel,
Modiolus modiolus
×⅔

Bearded horse mussel,
Modiolus barbatus ×⅔

The Common mussel, *Mytilus edulis*, is another inhabitant of rocky shores although it is versatile and can also establish itself on stones, even in estuaries. It attaches most effectively to a hard surface by means of the horny threads, or byssus, which are produced by a gland at the base of the foot and then directed, while still fluid, along a groove on the underside of that organ. So attached, as by the guy-ropes of a tent, the animal can withstand water movements in all directions – and if the threads are broken it can re-attach elsewhere. Mussels are bivalves but with the posterior end enlarged, the better to draw in water for feeding and respiration while attached by the flattened under-surface. It is a very effective shape arrived at from the primitive symmetrical form (like that of a cockle) while the byssus probably represents the retention into adult life of a mechanism widely present in bivalves for the temporary attachment of the newly settled young. Like all bivalves, mussels feed, with enormous success, on plant plankton and, under suitable conditions, form great colo-

nies. At very low tide, or perhaps washed up after storms, the larger Horse mussel, *Modiolus modiolus*, may be found, while the Bearded horse mussel, *M. barbatus*, with the brown outer shell-layer forming threads at the wide, hind end, is not uncommon on the lower shore. There are also a number of smaller mussels, the Bean horse mussel, *M. phaseolinus*, the Marbled crenella, *Musculus marmoratus*, and the Green crenella, *M. discors*, which may be encountered. Before leaving rock-living bivalves, the Saddle oyster, *Anomia ephippium*, should be mentioned. It looks like a small oyster but is attached by a byssus. It lies on one side with the threads emerging through a deep embayment in the under, actually right, valve. Although old oyster-shells, which are long lasting, are common on some shores this species, the common Flat or Native oyster, *Ostrea edulis*, is now all too rare and normally lives offshore.

One of the most obvious of all intertidal sea-snails, and one present in great numbers amongst barnacles and mussels, is the Dog-whelk, *Nucella (Purpura) lapillus*. This has a stouter shell than the Common periwinkle, which it resembles in size and it lives more exposed. The mouth of its shell is prolonged into a groove through which a tubular siphon can be protruded for taking water into the gills. The Dogwhelk is carnivorous. It is armed with a proboscis usually infolded but having the mouth with its powerful radula at the tip. When feeding this is everted, the animal apparently forcing apart the opercular plates in the barnacles, a process possibly assisted by poison. The radula then proceeds to tear out and swallow the flesh. Only when the barnacle population has been seriously reduced do the Dog-whelks normally turn attention to the mussels, forcing apart the valves of young individuals but actually boring through those of larger ones. This is a highly successful species, never limited by lack of food for which it has few competitors. The danger comes from violent storms but the stout shell, with operculum firmly in place, can be rolled without sustaining damage, and if washed away the Dogwhelk will find its way back to the zones occupied by its food. There is much colour variation in the shell. White is commonest, but shells may be yellow, mauve, pink or brown. The brown is said to be due to feeding on mussels. Male and female Dogwhelks gather in numbers for spawning (they also collect in hollows during storms or over the winter). The eggs are laid in conspicuous capsules, each having the size and appearance of a grain of wheat. They are attached to rock surfaces, upright in groups, usually in some sheltered spot. Anything up to 30 may be laid at any one time, the process for each occupying about one hour. Although many eggs, not all fertile, are in each capsule, only some dozen young, shelled miniatures of the adult, emerge.

The molluscs and barnacles so far mentioned are the commonest shore animals to be fully exposed on intertidal rock surfaces. Others live while the tide is out in damp shelter under weeds and rocks or in pools or attached to the surface of weeds or to the damp underhang of rocks low on the shore.

Shelter is a matter of prime concern to all but the most adapted of intertidal animals. If we part the curtains of weed or turn over rocks all manner of animals will be found on or in the sand and gravel beneath, among

them a variety of worms. Anything very long, obviously without segments and projecting tentacles and lateral bristle-bearing flaps or parapodia, as they are called, will be a nemertine. There are several kinds of these, notably the Red-line-worm, *Lineus ruber*, p. 284, up to 6 inches (15 cm.) long and reddish brown. Closely related is the surprisingly long Bootlace worm, *L. longissimus*, up to 5 yards (4·6 m.) if fully extended but usually tied into an intricate knotted tangle. This is our largest, but by no means our most impressive, worm. Another lengthy nemertine is the reddish, patterned *Tubulanus annulatus* which inhabits mucus tubes. All live at low levels of the shore. Bristle-worms are more numerous. The ragworms of the very common genus *Nereis* are bound to be seen. They are very obviously segmented, with projecting parapodia on every body segment and an array of tentacles and eye-spots on a head which carries quite impressive jaws. 'Parapodium' means 'like a foot' and the parapodia are fleshy flaps used by ragworms as a kind of paddle for swimming. The largest ragworm is the really magnificent *N. virens*, p. 284, green and up to 18 inches (46 cm.) long. It emerges in numbers for spawning in spring and should be handled with care – it bites. There are too many different ragworms to deal with them all. They are of many colours from purplish red to bronze

The Dogwhelk, *Nucella lapillus*, and egg-cases

and to greyish green. Many live in simple tubes. In some of these worms the parapodia are obviously more leaf-like. These are the more actively swimming species, notably the large, bluish or green Paddle-worm, *Phyllodoce lamelligera*, with the smaller *P. maculata* which is usually found under rocks embedded in sand. But although the common ragworms spend their lives hidden away under rocks, feeding on almost any plant or animal food they can find, some come out into the water above for breeding. Certain of their parapodia then become even more paddle-like and the sense-organs needed for more active life become enlarged. Meanwhile, the sexual products multiply and at spawning individuals of both sexes just burst, shedding eggs and sperms into the sea with a resultant mass fertilization and the formation of larvae which, with those of barnacles and mussels and so many other shore animals, augment the temporary planktonic population. But some ragworms, such as the common, usually yellowish-brown, little, *N. dumerilii*, do all this more domestically. It lives in a mucus tube and it retains the developing eggs within this tube.

Leaving this obscure habitat for the moment for that of rock surfaces, we shall find the unmistakable scale-worms. They are short, flattened worms, none more than 8 inches (up to 20 cm.) long, covered by a series of flat scales or elytra. There are several species including the small *Harmothoë impar*, $\frac{1}{2}$ inch (13 mm.) long, that lives under stones usually beneath weeds, the common *H. imbricata*, of similar size, which crawls freely on upper rock-faces, and *Halosydna gelatinosa*, 4 inches (10 cm.) long, translucent purple or brown, which is commonest under stones amongst *Laminaria*, and the Sea mouse, *Aphrodite aculeata*, p. 284, of similar size which lives below the extreme low-tide mark but is sometimes washed up in hundreds by storms.

On the lower levels of the shore we sometimes see scarlet, orange, or sometimes yellow, threads, perpetually writhing. These are the tentacles of the redthreads, *Cirra-*

tulus cirratus, common in the north. The larger *Audouinia tentaculata* occurs in the south. Both are thin-bodied worms, 4 inches (10 cm.) long. The threads are food-collectors, the animals usually inhabiting somewhat odorous areas of organic decay. These worms emerge, sometimes in great and unexpected numbers, on to the upper surfaces of the rocks for spawning in the early

(*opposite*): A sandy shore at low tide showing the upper strand-line and a rocky shore showing the zonation of the seaweeds figured below. *from top to bottom*, the Channelled wrack *Pelvetia canaliculata*; Flat wrack *Fucus spiralis*; Knotted wrack *Ascophyllum nodosum*; Toothed wrack *Fucus serratus* and a tangle-weed *Laminaria*

(*overleaf, left*): Red seaweeds: *top left*, Irish moss *Chondrus crispus*; *right*, *Gigartina stellata*; *bottom left*, *Porphyra umbilicalis*; *right*, *Delesseria sanguinea*

(*overleaf, right*): Sea-anemones and a sponge; *top left*, the Beadlet *Actinia equina*; *right*, the Dahlia anemone *Tealia felina*; *centre left*, the Snakelocks anemone *Anemonia sulcata*; *right*, the Plumose anemone *Metridium senile* and *bottom right*, *Sagartia elegans* with, *left*, the Crumb-of-bread sponge *Halichondria panicea*

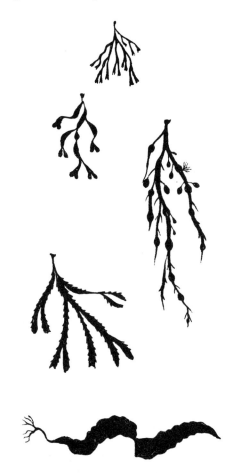

months of the year. Other beautiful but obscurely dwelling worms are the long red *Marphysa sanguinea*, p. 284, and the shorter brown *Eunice harassii*, both often in mucus tubes.

This habit of temporary tube formation may well have been the forerunner of the habit of making more permanent tubes. A surprisingly wide range of marine bristle-worms do this. Some we shall not meet until we reach sandy shores. As the worms have developed the permanent tubes so they have grown at the head end increasing numbers of tentacles, for respiration and for feeding, as in the handsome *Amphitrite johnstoni*, p. 284. This has a swollen yellow to brownish body surmounted with a mass of orange to pink tentacles and is generally common in simple, mucus-lined tubes under boulders. It is, however, a true tube-worm with the now unnecessary parapodia reduced to bristles that grip the sides of the tube. In rock pools, unfortunately on southern and western shores only, lives the really magnificent *Bispira volutacornis*. It has a flexible tough tube of mixed mucus and mud usually sunk in a crack but, when the animal is expanded, it pushes out a double crown of spirally wound tentacles, 48–50 in each crown. These are pale in colour and while serving for respiration are more directly concerned with collection of fine particles and plankton, strained from the water and conveyed by the action of vibratile cilia to the mouth which lies at the base of the double crown. The commonest tube-worms on rocky shores are the serpulids which form strong calcareous tubes firmly cemented to a solid surface. The large and very common *Pomatoceros triqueter*, with a sharp keel on the upper surface of the tube, can hardly be overlooked. Few animals are so common

Worms: *top*, a ragworm *Nereis virens*; *centre left*, *Marphysa sanguinea*; *centre*, the Peacock-worm *Sabella pavonina*; *right*, *Amphitrite johnstoni*; *above* with the Sea-mouse *Aphrodite aculeata below*; *bottom left*, the Red-line-worm *Lineus ruber*; *right*, the Lugworm *Arenicola marina*

except the much smaller species of *Spirorbis*, rolled in clockwise coils no more than $\frac{1}{5}$ inch (5 mm.) across, which cover every available surface, rocks, shells, and the fronds of wracks and tangle-weeds. Usually these are *S. borealis* but there are other species including the deeper water *S. spirillum* which coils in the opposite direction. Then there is the colonial bristle-worm *Filograna implexa* with interlacing cylindrical tubes up to 6 inches (15 cm.) long which forms masses on the sides of rocks, among *Laminaria* holdfasts and elsewhere on the lower shore. These serpulids, as may be seen by watching *Pomatoceros* under water, protrude their tentacles for feeding but on withdrawal the opening of the tube is neatly plugged by one tentacle the end of which is plate-like, forming an operculum.

Almost every stone we turn over and every corner in a rock pool will have its crab. The

Tubes of the serpulid worm, *Pomatoceros triqueter*

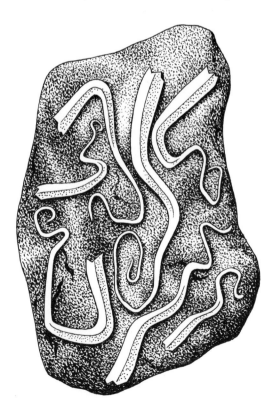

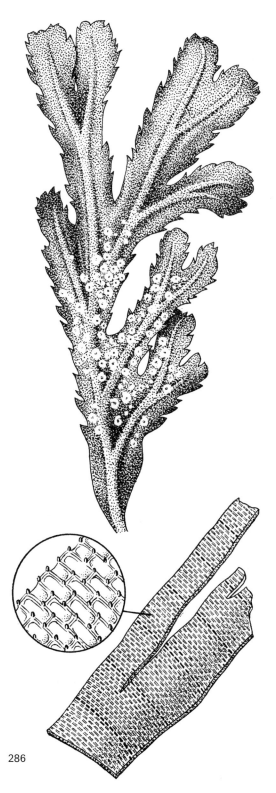

The coils of the tube-worm, *Spirorbis borealis,* on a fucoid seaweed, *top,* a piece of the sea-mat, *Membranipora membranacea* ×2, *bottom,* with an enlargement to show its cellular formation ×20

commonest is the ubiquitous Shore crab, *Carcinus maenas,* p. 293, which ranges over all but the higher shore on any kind of shore, rocky, sandy or muddy. It varies widely in colour and is an indiscriminate scavenger. The well-known Edible crab, *Cancer pagurus,* may be encountered at low levels sometimes in pools; and perhaps it may be large enough to be worth taking home. But this will only be in summer: it moves offshore in the winter. A rarer crab, found only in certain areas in the west as far apart as Cornwall and the Hebrides, is *Xantho incisus,* like a smaller, more rounded version of an Edible crab. The large Velvet swimming crab, *Portunus puber,* p. 293, is not infrequent in low pools. It has the last pair of legs flattened at the ends and these serve as paddles. Its shell has a thick covering of fine hairs. Crab-like and yet more related to the hermit crabs are the small hairy porcelain crabs, *Porcellana platycheles* and *P. longicornis,* to be found on the lower shore, often under stones. The asymmetry of the undertucked abdomen recalls that of the hermit crabs and is the key to their nature. Then there are the spider crabs all easily identifiable as such. The smallest and commonest, *Macropodia rostrata,* is typical with its extremely fine legs and body only some $\frac{1}{2}$ inch (13 mm.) across. *Inachus dorsettensis* and *Hyas araneus,* p. 293, are larger, their bodies four times as wide. All are rock-pool inhabitants but they may also be found under weeds between rocks.

Great numbers of snail shells, from periwinkles and Dogwhelks to those of the Large whelk, *Buccinum,* will frequently be found congregated under or at the bases of boulders. A significant proportion will be found to start moving when we disturb them. They are inhabited by what must be just about the most successful inhabitants of any such shore the world over, namely hermit crabs. On the shore these are almost always the larger *Eupagurus bernhardus,* the smaller *E. prideauxi* being usually offshore and confined to the south and west. It is, however, only the younger *E. bernhardus* that are found between tide marks. As they get larger they tend to move into the sublittoral areas.

The easiest way to induce a hermit crab to leave its acquired home is to heat the tip of the shell with a lighted match. The hermit crab quickly leaves the shell. It can then be seen how asymmetrical the body of this crustacean has become to fit itself for occupancy of a coiled home. It secures itself inside by means of a roughened, sickle-shaped appendage on the last body segment which grips the central pillar of the shell, the columella, so securely that the hermit can draw itself firmly inside. At the same time it blocks the opening of the shell with its large pincer, or chela, of the right side, the pincer on the left being very much smaller. As the crab moults successively and grows progressively larger it must change its house. Finding a suitably larger shell, it carefully probes within and without using the long antennae on its head. Then with a sudden flip, while holding the edge of the shell with its pincers, it inserts its highly vulnerable abdomen into the new shell. Hermits are amongst the major scavengers of the shore, poking into every crack, but they are also capable of filtering food out of sea-water, like their relatives the porcelain crabs.

Hermits in deeper water just offshore not infrequently share occupancy of their shell with a ragworm, *Nereis fucata*, which is capable also of living independently. The habits of the two have been studied by keeping them in transparent glass or plastic 'shells'. It appears that the worm lies on the upper side of the hermit and on its right side where the respiratory water current created by the crab enters. The worm may also put out its head when the hermit is feeding and doubtless gets pickings. However, it is not the only, or even the more usual, companion to do so. Certainly all of the larger hermits carry on their shells a Sea-anemone, *Calliactis parasitica*, the tentacles of which collect fragments of the hermit's food. This is a two-sided partner-

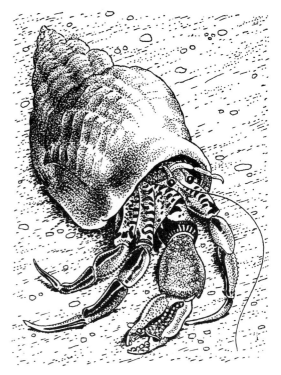

A hermit crab, *Eupagurus bernhardus*, in the shell of a whelk, *Buccinum*

ship because the stinging-cells with which these tentacles are profusely armed are a real protection against the attacks of enemies, largely fish some of which would otherwise crunch up shell, hermit and all. A rather moss-like pinkish growth which also is common on the shells occupied by larger hermits, consists of colonies of a small sea-fir, *Hydractinia echinata*, beautiful to observe under suitable magnification because it consists of three kinds of individuals, some for feeding (which look like miniature stalked anemones), some for protection and some for reproduction.

The charming little Squat lobsters, *Galathea squamifera*, p. 293, and *G. strigosa*, move up onto the lower shore during spring and summer, into rock pools. The former, greenish brown and about 3 inches (7·6 cm.) long is the more common. The other is amongst the handsomest of shore creatures, largely red with blue markings. Both keep the abdomen (the 'tail' of a true lobster) tucked under the body but, unlike that of a crab, it is fully formed and mobile so that the animals can swim rapidly backwards by sudden extensions and bendings of this broad under portion of the body. But this is only an occasional 'escape reaction', normally these animals walk, searching for food with the long claws extending forward.

The commonest starfish is the Red or Common starfish, *Asterias rubens*, p. 311, although like most of its kind, it is variable in colour and usually it is more yellowish than red. Like most, although by no means all, starfish it has five arms each with a groove on the underside from which a double series of 'tube feet' project. Operated by hydraulic pressure, these are a very slow but quite effective means of locomotion. The body is firm and its surface is spiny. It is naturally commonest where its food is most abundant, such as mussel-beds. Starfish are carnivorous with the capacity to protrude the stomach over the prey, digesting this outside the body; they are thus able to digest far larger animals than they could possibly swallow. The much larger *Marthasterias glacialis*, grey and more spiny, occurs in the south and west. On the east coast, as well as elsewhere, should be found the so-called Scarlet starfish, *Henricia sanguinolenta*, also five-armed but very variable in colour and still more variable in distribution. It is a shore animal which also occurs at great depths.

Our other shore starfishes are the small *Asterina gibbosa*, sometimes called Starlet or Cushion star, up to about 1 inch (25 mm.) across, but with the areas between the arms largely filled in. It is inconspicuous but unmistakable, and it too is only found in the south and west. Only on these shores also, may occasionally be encountered the very handsome Common sunstar, *Solastar papposus*, p. 311, with a variable number of arms, up to 13. It is very much an inhabitant of the lower shore. Its northern representative is the Purple sunstar, *S. endeca*,

an extremely striking animal usually of a violet colour and with a particularly granular texture. This occurs, though less commonly, everywhere except in the south. All these animals have planktonic larvae totally unlike the adults.

Sea-urchins, nearly related to starfishes, have their internal organs inside a globular test or box made up of close-fitting limy plates. These empty tests are often thrown up on the shore, dried and often broken. Our largest species, up to 6 inches (15 cm.) across, is the reddish Common sea-urchin, *Echinus esculentus*, p. 311, which is most commonly found on shores where the low water of spring tides does not occur over midday. There is no more handsome marine animal with its covering of hinged spines, with between them fine pincers needing a lens for their examination, and the five meridional rows of transparent tube feet best observed under water when they may extend for $\frac{1}{2}$ inch (13 mm.) or more. The mouth, on the underside; has five teeth carried in a complex skeletal framework, known as 'Aristotle's lantern', with muscles which force them together to crop the encrusting plant and animal life. Although often confined to the sublittoral, this urchin is widely distributed as is the much smaller green, *Psammechinus miliaris*, about 2 inches (5 cm.) in diameter, often found low on the shore at the base of boulders in suitable damp shade. It frequently covers itself with pieces of weed and other debris. The somewhat larger but very similarly coloured and more flattened *Strongylocentrotus drobachiensis* (it has, alas, no common name) is a northern animal which comes down our east coast where alone it occurs in Great Britain. Finally, of about the same size but more rounded, there is the truly southern, typically Mediterranean, *Paracentrotus lividus*, with purplish spines, which often occupies rounded cavities in rocks. This is commonest off the west of Ireland but may be encountered on the shores of Devon and Cornwall and, very occasionally, on those of the Hebrides. It is yet another example of a southern species spreading up our western shores.

Brittle-stars will also be encountered insinuated in complicated fashion under stones. Their arms are sinuous and they, not the tube feet, are the agents of sometimes very rapid movement. Always sober in colour pattern, they are also distinguished from starfish because their arms are sharply delimited from the central disc, the two merging in the starfish. The commonest species, pretty well confined to the lower shore like most such animals, is *Ophiothrix fragilis*, with its central disc around ½ inch (13 mm.) across the arms five times that length. The same is true for the larger and dark-centred *Ophiocomina nigra*, p. 311, in the south and west and *Ophiopholis aculeata*, with a five-pointed rather than a rounded disc, commoner in the north. Brittle-stars can be amazingly abundant and are a very successful group, carnivorous but not everting the stomach as do starfish.

The final group of echinoderms, as the starfishes and their relatives are called, are the elongated tough-bodied holothurians or Sea-cucumbers. They are represented on our rocky shores by *Cucumaria lactea*, about 1 inch (25 mm.) long and usually attached to stones or shells, and *C. normani*, p. 311, and *C. saxicola*, both 2–4 inches (5–10 cm.) long, confined to the south and south-west coasts respectively and living in narrow crevices or holes drilled by molluscan rock-borers.

The damp underhangs of rocks protected by weed often show a rich display of colour made up of encrusting sponges, sea-squirts (ascidians), moss animals (bryozoans), sea-firs (hydroids) and some of the smaller sea-weeds, together with a variety of grazing or predating animals. Prominent among them are the green or yellow relatively thin masses of the Crumb-of-bread sponge, *Halichondria panicea*, p. 283, with the tan-coloured *Hymeniacidon perlevis*, if anything even more common. A dull red sponge, with a more even surface, is *Ophlitaspongia seriata*. In places far more abundant than either of these is the Purse-sponge, *Grantia compressa*, white and flattened, 1 inch (25 mm.) or more long. Growing with it very often is the cylindrical *Scypha ciliata*, better known as *Sycon coronatum* and the lace-like colonies of *Leucosolenia*.

Some sea-squirts are solitary but others form colonies and are called 'compound' ascidians. They form beautiful patterns like the well-named Golden stars sea-squirt, *Botryllus schlosseri*, p. 312, which is common everywhere except on sandy shores. The individuals are grouped in coloured stars within the gelatinous matrix of the colony. In others, such as *Botrylloides leachi*, the individuals are grouped in long ovals, and its colonies may be orange and yellow or a more sombre grey. Grey is indeed the prevailing colour of the less striking *Didemnum gelatinosum* with the individuals forming white dots. Some ascidians form colonies of a different kind, in which individuals are joined at their bases but otherwise free. They include the suitably named Gooseberry sea-squirt, *Dendrodoa grossularia*, p. 312, in which each 'berry' has two small projections marking the positions of the inhalant and exhalant openings. The very beautiful translucent orange *Clavelina lepadiformis* is another. The commonest solitary sea-squirts are the elongated *Ciona intestinalis*, semi-translucent and yellowish or pale green, which projects from rock surfaces, and the larger *Ascidiella aspersa*, p. 312, a southern species with a tougher test. If in doubt about its identity squeeze the bag-like body of the sea-squirt and a resultant jet of water will show how it got its name.

Another common encrusting animal is the polyzoan Sea-mat, *Umbonula verrucosa*, which forms large lace-like mats on rock surfaces. Its skeleton is calcareous and therefore rough to the touch.

Sponges are eaten by few animals apart from species of sea-slugs, notably the Sea-lemon, *Archidoris pseudoargus*, p. 294, which feeds largely, if not exclusively, on the Crumb-of-bread sponge which it closely resembles both in texture and in coloration, yellow blotched with pink, green or brown.

Its frilled coils of white spawn are very common. This is a sea-slug without shell and with a ring of plume-like gills round the anus, in the mid-line near the hind end of the back, and with two pairs of head-tentacles. A more striking sea-slug, *Rostanga rufescens*, only about ½ inch (13 mm.) long but red with the hinder pair of tentacles yellow, is difficult to find because it feeds on, and so merges with, areas of red sponge. These beautiful little animals, so strikingly different from land slugs with which they are only remotely connected, are the most specialized of feeders. Search of the barnacle zone may have revealed the brown and white *Onchidoris fusca* which feeds on these animals, while yet another, *Goniodoris nodosa*, often pink speckled with white but actually very variable in colour, eats sea-mats and sea-squirts. These last two are about 1 inch (25 mm.) long. The plant-sucking *Elysia viridis*, p. 294, occurs on the green weed *Codium*. It is worth looking at the sparse insect fauna. On the surface of very sheltered pools, often small and always high on the shore, groups of minute bluish insects are frequently to be seen on the surface film – and on the adjacent rock surface on to which they must move when the tide rises. *Lipura (Anurida) maritima*, one of the primitive springtail insects which, together with a large animal of the same type, *Petrobius maritimus*, and the midge, *Clunio marinus* – the female wingless and the male using his pair of wings for sculling over the water surface – represent the extent of our truly shore-adapted insects.

Parting the covering weeds of a rock pool will reveal, through the clearest of water, a scene of great beauty and one which also, when quiet is restored, is full of life. Apart from many animals already described here will be sea-anemones, fully expanded and their rounded columns crowned with a ring of tentacles. Much the commonest, in rock pools and on exposed rocks where it will be found contracted to a shapeless blob when the tide is out, is the Beadlet, *Actinia equina* var. *mesembryanthemum*, p. 283,

usually dark red with blue spots at the bases of the tentacles but it is sometimes green or red speckled with green, the so-called 'strawberry variety'. On this, which is the commonest of all anemones, careful search may reveal the closely adhering body of the little eight-legged sea-spider, *Pycnogonium littorale*. Then there are the delicately beautiful sea-anemones *Sagartia elegans*, p. 283, and *S. troglodytes* of most varied colour patterns, both to be seen expanded in pools, the latter, as its specific name indicates, in cracks or little cave-like depressions. The Daisy anemone, *Cereus pedunculatus*, usually patterned grey or brown, can be distinguished by its longer column. It may also be found elsewhere, sometimes between stones and among gravel.

The handsome Dahlia anemone, *Tealia felina*, p. 283, our largest species, is unmistakable with its broad base and blunt tentacles. It will readily take anything of animal nature, a periwinkle, limpet, small crab or fish, any empty shell being later discarded. No less obvious is the Plumose anemone, *Metridium senile*, p. 283, with its subdivided tentacles forming a feathery mass. It may be pure white, brown or orange and occurs very low on the shore but may often be viewed in full glory on the surfaces of pier-piles, fully expanded under water. The Snakelocks anemone, *Anemonia sulcata*, p. 283, yet another animal confined to the south and west, is brown or dull green and seeks light owing to the needs of the population of unicellular plants which it harbours, symbiotically, in its tissues. The Gemmed anemone, *Bunodactes verrucosa*, distinguished by the conspicuous white 'gems' on a green background has a similarly restricted distribution.

On the shores of Devon and Cornwall careful search at the lowest tides could possibly reveal a true coral – looking exactly like an anemone from above. The Devonshire Cup coral, *Caryophyllia smithii*, is pure white or pinkish and the much rarer scarlet Gold star coral, *Balanophyllia regia*, may both be found. When touched, they retreat into the shelter of a cup-shaped skeleton with radial partitions. But do not attempt to collect them; they will soon die and are all too rare. Under the same conditions of lowest exposure in the extreme south-west may be found the Jewel anemone, *Corynactis viridis*, which is colonial and somewhat intermediate in character between anemones and corals. The polyps are small, vary greatly in colour and have short tentacles swollen at the tips.

Much less conspicuous coelenterate inhabitants of pools, particularly on the weeds, will be hydroids or sea-firs. These little plant-like growths need careful examination under magnification for adequate identification. They are broadly divisible into those in which the polyp heads arise usually each on a separate stalk which does not enlarge terminally into a protective cup, and those where the subdivided plant-like skeleton carries many minute polyp heads for each of which there is a protective cup. Perhaps the commonest of the former are the little pinkish blobs on the surface of fucoids – put these under water and their true character will be revealed – and the much larger *Tubularia*, one species with stalk up to 6 inches (15 cm.) long, with conspicuous polyps each crowned with a double ring of tentacles, which occurs not uncommonly in pools and on the sides of rocks and on pier-piles. The branching 'cupped' hydroids are very common and of many types, and they are certain to be found in pools and on weed. Some form compact tufts. The commonest, certainly the most easy to identify by eye, are species of the Sea-oak, *Sertularia* or *Dynamena*. Another well-known sea-fir is *Obelia geniculata*. The majority of these hydroids bud off medusoids, minute jellyfish which are the sexual individuals, the product of whose fertilized eggs are new, attached hydroid colonies.

A widely distributed sea-slug which feeds exclusively on sea-anemones is the handsome brownish-grey or greenish *Aeolidia papillosa*, the common Grey sea-slug. p. 294. It grows up to 3 inches (7·6 cm.) long with the

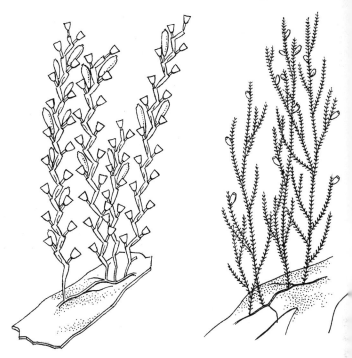

Sea-firs: *left, Obelia geniculata*; *right*, the Sea-oak, *Sertularia operculata*

back covered with a soft fur of tissue projections called 'cerata'. There are various similar kinds of sea-slugs, all feeding on coelenterates. There is the smaller *Facelina auriculata* again restricted to the south and west, with pale body and red cerata while even smaller slugs prey on hydroids, notably the little *Doto coronata*, p. 294, its red-spotted cerata shaped like the most minute fir-cones.

Certain to be found in pools are prawns, the most delicate of crustaceans, walking gently on the three last pairs of 'walking' legs with the two first, equipped with terminal nippers, held out in front. The eyes, mounted on movable stalks, and the branches of the two pairs of feelers explore what lies ahead. These animals, resembling in this their relatives the crabs and hermits, are omnivorous searching delicately for anything that may be edible. Our largest prawns are *Leander serratus*, yet again in the south and west, and the somewhat smaller but widely distributed *L. squilla*,

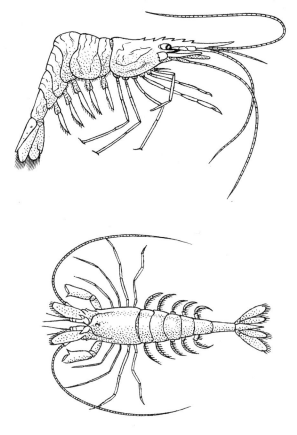

The Common prawn, *top, Leander serratus* and a shrimp, *below, Crangon vulgaris*

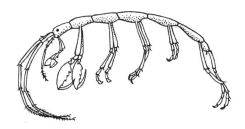

A Skeleton-shrimp, *Phtisica marina*

becomes opaque. More difficult to find will be the smaller Chameleon-prawn, *Hippolyte varians*, less than 1 inch (25 mm.) long with arched body and the capacity for altering colour to conform with a background of green, brown or red weeds. This is achieved by appropriate extension of colouring matter within the branches of the pigment-containing cells or chromatophores which are numerous under the transparent shell. All prawns are summer visitors, moving into warmer offshore waters in winter. When alarmed they escape backwards by a sudden bending of the segmented, abdominal region, just like a squat lobster. They also swim forwards by means of the paddle-like swimming appendages on the underside of the abdomen. And it is to these appendages that the eggs are attached after they are laid and where they develop for some time before being released. In the female crab, this 'berry' is carried in a mass beneath the permanently undertucked abdomen which is notably broader in the female than in the male.

It is in the recesses of a deep pool round the lowest tidal levels that, during the summer months, the large relative of the prawns, the impressive Blue lobster, *Homarus vulgaris*, can possibly be encountered. Also here perhaps may be found the most impressive member of our molluscan fauna, either the Common octopus, *Octopus vulgaris* (actually confined to the English Channel where in odd years it may be abundant), which has a double row of suckers on each tentacle, or the more widely distributed, indeed primarily northern, *Eledone cirrhosa*, which has a single row.

Careful examination of the fine weeds, especially the corallines, or the hydroid stems can reveal the very engaging Skeleton-shrimps, species of the odd amphipod family Caprellidae, such as *Phtisica marina*,

the former up to 4 inches (10 cm.) long, the other only half this length. In life they are so transparent that only the pigment-spots, the eyes and the digestive system are really visible, but on death the body immediately

Crabs and a lobster: *top right,* the Shore crab, *Carcinus maenas*; *right, Hyas araneus*; *bottom left,* the Velvet swimming crab *Portunus puber* and *right,* a squat lobster *Galathea squamifera*

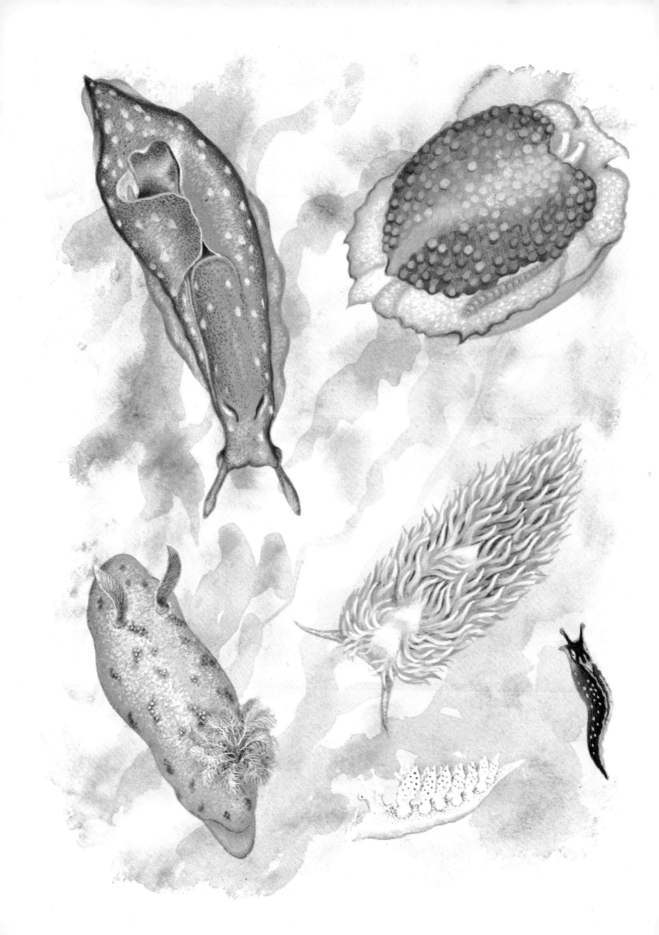

with few appendages on the slender body, less than ½ inch (12·7 mm.) long. Simulating the weed, it holds on by the hind appendages, the anterior claws free, not unlike a Praying mantis. It moves with the slow looping deliberation of a stick insect.

A beautifully delicate lattice-work that spreads over the surface of the fronds of laminarians consists of the rectangular compartments of the most easily recognized of the sea-mats, *Membranipora membranacea*. *Bugula turbinata* hangs in 2 inch (5 cm.) tufts, sandy with orange tints, from rock overhangs. Other such colonies occur widely on brown and red weeds, notably the more spiny, whitish *Flustrella hispida* and the fleshy lobes of the grey *Alcyonidium hirsutum*. The hollow holdfasts of the tangle-weeds are the invariable home of the easily recognizable little Blue-rayed limpet, *Patina pellucida*, which eats its way into the hold-fast or the stipe sinking into the depressions so created. Rocky shores present innumerable possibilities for life nowhere more so than in wave-created or weathered crevices which provide not only temporary protection but also contain a characteristic 'nestling' population often strikingly zoned. Some idea of this may readily be conveyed by picturing, in section, the profile of an oblique outcrop of slate on the coast.

The smooth southern surface bears, at highest levels, orange patches of the lichen *Xanothoria*, below that down to the level of extreme high water of spring tides, the extensive tarry black areas of *Verrucaria maura*, and lower comes the uppermost level of the southern barnacle, *Chthamalus*.

The northern face is very different, here the parallel thicknesses of the slate have been cut into a series of deep crevices. At lowest levels there is a carpet of fucoids

Gastropods: *top left*, the Sea-hare *Aplysia punctata*; *right*, *Pleurobranchus membranaceus*; *centre right*, the Grey sea-slug *Aeolidia papillosa*; *bottom left*, the Sea-lemon *Archidoris pseudoargus*; *centre*, *Doto coronata*; *right*, *Elysia viridis*

and above that in each successive crevice a characteristic population of surprising diversity. Under these conditions, particularly of enduring dampness, animals can live surprisingly high on the shore although there is a gradual diminution in variety the higher we go as, for one species after another, the effects of increasing exposure become insupportable. Finally, little more than the Small periwinkle, *Littorina neritoides*, is left. Many animal groups are well represented,

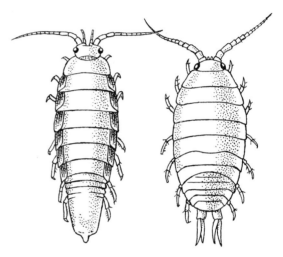

Sea-slaters: *Idotea baltica, left; Ligia oceanica, right*

the most conspicuous of many bristle-worms being the thin green *Eulalia viridis*, which can also be seen elsewhere on the shore. There are many minute univalve and bivalve molluscs and a most interesting assortment of usually purely terrestrial types of animals, the two bristle-tail insects already mentioned, several mites and the solitary Marine (actually shore) centipede, *Scolioplanes maritimus*. This feeds at night on periwinkles and barnacles, with a miscellaneous assortment of crustaceans including the notable shore-dweller, the Sea-slater, *Ligia oceanica*. This slater can be up to 1 inch (25 mm.) long and is very flattened; the head bears a pair of conspicuous antennae. This, a relation of the familiar wood-

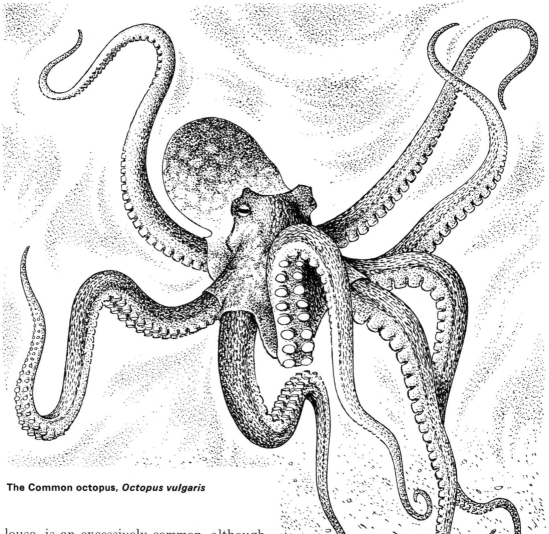

The Common octopus, *Octopus vulgaris*

louse, is an excessively common, although also an excessively retiring, animal living always around high-tide level. It spends the daytime sheltering in deep crevices to emerge at night when it is damp and enemies easier to elude, scavenging widely amongst the dead seaweed and other litter around high-tide level. A shore seemingly bare of them will be found after nightfall thickly populated when illuminated by a torch. The fertilized eggs are incubated under the body of the female, the young emerging as miniatures of the parent. The Sea-slater has almost parted company with the sea. Its near relative *Idotea baltica*, about the same size, lives lower down the shore.

In an evolutionary sense, the habit of nestling in an uneven rock surface may lead to the animal enlarging the cavity in which it is cradled and so to actually burrowing in rock. This certainly is true of our commonest bivalve rock-borer, the so-called Red-nose, *Hiatella (Saxicava) arctica*. Like the Common mussel, this attaches itself to rocks by its beard of byssal threads, and while some individuals live permanently in this manner others grind their way, rather crudely but most efficiently, into limestone or sandstone, so that only the red tip of the siphon finally projects. Perfect protection has been achieved while water, for feeding and respiration, is drawn in through the siphons as in the sand-burrowers. Indeed, from the sand-burrowers, operating in increasingly dense materials, have evolved other rock-borers, the piddocks. Their shell is beautifully constructed for this mode of life, that of the large *Pholas dactylus*, up to 3 inches (7·6 cm.) long and white, has some 50 rows of spines. Although surprisingly delicate, it is very hard and forms an admirable drill. The shell is cut away on the lower side in front allowing protrusion of a sucker-like foot which holds the shell against the head of the boring while the piddock turns and scrapes first in one direction, then in the other, to wear away the rock. There are several southern species but the Oval piddock, *Zirphaea crispata* occurs widely; all live in the softer rocks, sandstones through shales to thick clay and even peat. Their bivalve shell possesses additional plates on the upper side in front of the hinge. Around the Thames Estuary, in limestone and thick clay, lives the imported American species, *Petricola pholadiformis*, superficially resembling a piddock but not cut away below and without accessory plates. It was accidentally introduced with American oysters, relaid near Whitstable, and with it came two major oyster pests, the boring Oyster drill, *Urosalpinx cinerea*, and the smothering masses of the Slipper limpet, *Crepidula fornicata*, both all too abundant on east coast oyster-beds. Final mention of rock-borers should include the little bristle-worm, *Polydora*, and the yellow Boring sponge, *Cliona celata*, both common in calcareous shells or rocks. *Polydora* burrows appear as pairs of nicks in stones, as if someone had jabbed with the point of a penknife. *Cliona* works its way through the rock or shell, every now and then pushing a yellow papilla through to the surface.

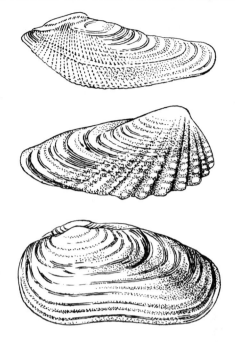

Bivalve rock-borers: *top, Pholas dactylus; centre, Petricola pholadiformis; bottom,* the Red-nose, *Hiatella arctica*

From the piddocks and related rock-borers have probably been evolved the more specialized wood-borers, the shipworms, most usually *Teredo norvegica*, which occur in driftwood and sometimes in unprotected pier-piles. The animal has become worm-like with the shell-valves, purely cutting tools, very small and confined to the front end. There is the same sucker-like foot as in the piddock. In driftwood their former presence is indicated by the long, usually very straight borings which eventually become lined, when the animal ceases boring, with a calcareous casing. The presence of shipworms within intact timber is most difficult to determine; exposed wood shows no more than minute, calcareous-lined dumb-bell-shaped openings from which, when submerged, two fine siphonal tubes project. Much more obvious attacks on timber, which cannot fail to be observed both on driftwood and pilings, is due to the small crustacean known as the Gribble, *Limnoria lignorum*, an isopod which burrows just

The Oyster drill, *Urosalpinx cinerea*

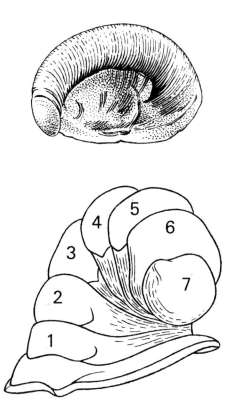

The Slipper limpet, *Crepidula fornicata*, and a diagram showing how they cluster together

below the surface, gradually working in lower and lower levels. It bores by means of a well-adapted pair of mandibles. Associated with it, although not itself contributing to the boring process, is the larger amphipod, *Chelura terebrans*.

A final word on pier-pilings, of iron or concrete as well as of wood, which are often richly covered with intertidal animals and plants. Anemones, especially the plumose

Metridium, may be numerous. So also may the dead white, yellow or orange lobulate masses of our solitary 'soft coral', *Alcyonium digitatum* or Dead men's fingers. When under water its surface is covered with a delicate fur of polyps each bearing eight plumose tentacles. These are withdrawn when the animal is out of water. The matrix of the colony is strengthened with limy spicules. Also on the piles are likely to be dense zones of mussels, adhering to the piles and to one another by their byssus threads and forming a mass in which numerous nereid bristle-worms live. And of course there will be barnacles and serpulid tube-worms. Indeed, provided they are not in a badly polluted harbour, piles provide a graphic demonstration of the kind of vertical zonation we see on the shore between the extremes of tidal action.

The fascinations of rocky shores are endless contrasting strongly with other shores of sand and then of mud, which are superficially so apparently empty of life. This is an illusion since both kinds of shore harbour many animals burrowing into the soft substrate. The sand may be in restricted patches between closely adjacent masses of rock or in the form of long sandy beaches backed by dunes. The sand is composed of fragments, largely of the hardest, siliceous, rocks, partly derived from erosion of rocks by the sea, partly from silt brought down by rivers. Such materials often tend to be carried alongshore and so to collect on one side of piers or groins. Shingle beaches are unstable and effectively without life, but sand-particles are small enough to cohere because of the water held between the grains by capillarity. Even when the sea retreats from a sandy beach water is largely retained between the sand-particles and animals living within the sand can easily, by going deeper, keep pace with the slow fall in the water-table, which is always higher than that of the falling tide. So there is neither danger of drying out nor of exposure to extremes of temperature, the water held in the sand being effectively uninfluenced

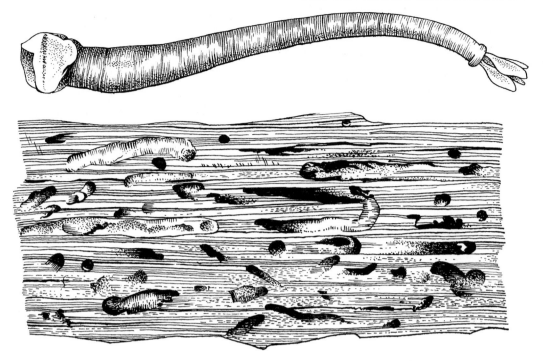

A bivalve shipworm, *Teredo norvegica*, and bored wood

by temporary increase in heat or cold on the surface or even by the flow of fresh water over this. Occasionally during major storms the sand will be disturbed to such depths that the occupants may be displaced. But unless thrown up high and dry they may often regain shelter.

The prime qualifications for life in sand is the capacity to burrow. Some groups such as sponges, coelenterates, sea-mats and sea-squirts, are largely or completely absent from sand shores and the main populations are of bristle-worms, crustaceans, univalve and bivalve molluscs and echinoderms. Basically these animals depend on the suspended plant life in the sea but they feed increasingly on particles of organic debris as sand merges into the different medium of mud.

The Gribble, *Limnoria lignorum*, and a diagram of its burrow

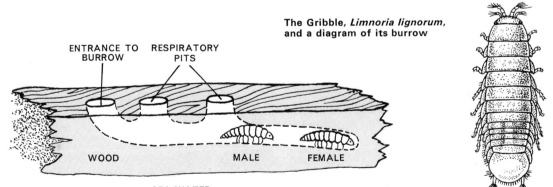

ENTRANCE TO BURROW   RESPIRATORY PITS

WOOD   MALE   FEMALE

SEA-WATER

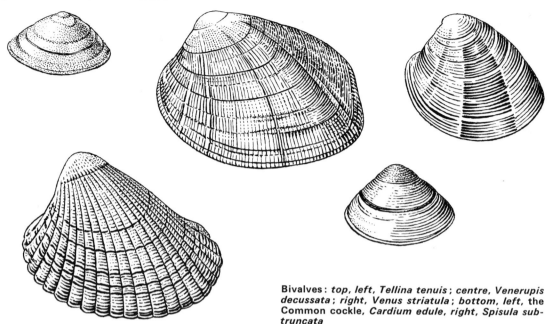

Bivalves: *top, left, Tellina tenuis*; *centre, Venerupis decussata*; *right, Venus striatula*; *bottom, left*, the Common cockle, *Cardium edule*, *right, Spisula subtruncata*

And on these largely suspension-feeding herbivores prey a group of carnivores that move actively through the sand.

The bivalve molluscs are the most numerous and successful of burrowers. So far we have encountered them in a highly successful and yet secondary role, either attached by a byssus to rocks or boring into them, but bivalves are basically adapted for insinuating themselves through a soft substrate. The body is compressed between the two hinged valves and so is the muscular foot. Dilated by an inflow of blood, this is pushed out forwards or downwards; the tip then dilates even more so gripping the sand while the muscles running to the shell contract pulling it forward. This process continues until a satisfactory position is attained when movement stops and contact is made with the water above by way of the siphons. These consist of paired tubes through the lower of which water, drawn by a current created by the beating of cilia on the gills, enters the mantle cavity and leaves again through the upper siphon. While in the mantle cavity the water passes through the gills which strain off the particles and other

cilia pass these to the mouth. Excess material is expelled from time to time through the inflowing siphon by sudden contractions of the adductor muscles running between the valves. Waste products and, at the appropriate time, reproductive products pass out of the exhalant siphon.

The commonest shore bivalve is probably the Common cockle, *Cardium edule*, easily distinguished by its globular ridged shell. It lives near the surface and when exposed quickly reburies itself by means of the powerful foot which is bent double when withdrawn. The larger Spiny cockle, *Cardium echinatum*, may actually leap 6–8 inches (15–20 cm.) clear of the surface by suddenly straightening its foot. Other species of cockles occur offshore. A variety of other short-siphoned bivalves with rather thick shells are likely to be species of *Venus* or *Spisula*. The larger rounded *Dosinia* and the more oblong species of *Venerupis* (*Paphia* or *Tapes*), both related to *Venus*, may all be found in the sand. Easier to describe but demanding active digging if they are to be examined are the deep-burrowing gapers and the well-known razor-shells.

Taking the razor-shell first, the largest is the straight Pod razor-shell, *Ensis siliqua*, of up to 8 inches (20 cm.) long and with the curved valves of its tubular shell about 1 inch (25 mm.) deep. There are two smaller species not too easy to distinguish but *E. arcuatus* has a slightly curved shell some 6 inches (15 cm.) long while *E. ensis* is more curved and somewhat shorter. All occur in the lower reaches of sandy beaches and are very widely distributed. The smaller, very straight and very cylindrical, Grooved razor-shell, *Solen marginatus*, occurs only in the south and in muddy conditions. Razor-shells are wonderfully adapted for up and down movement in sand. The hinge and ligament of the shell are very close to the front end and from this the foot extends, with the short siphons projecting from the other. Any razor-shell dug out and replaced in a shallow sandy pool will proceed to re-bury itself. The foot is pushed out and bent down, groping into the sand. As soon as the foot is well into the sand it swells at the end, so taking hold, and the muscles start to pull the shell and body first obliquely upward and then, with successive

further extensions and dilations of the foot, vertically downwards. The process is assisted by downward expulsion of water each time the foot is extended; this makes the sand easier to penetrate. For protection, or when the tide ebbs, the razor-shells just move deeper. When the tide returns they move up, the short siphons extend from the upper (actually hind) end and the animals proceed to feed and respire. All movement is vertical. There is no need to move horizontally because the source of food is in the sea and so is constantly being renewed.

The deep burrowers or gapers have large oval shells, up to 5 inches (12·7 cm.) long, with massive siphons up to twice this length. There are several species which, despite great superficial similarities, belong to two distinct groups of bivalves. It is an instance of 'convergence' of form and so of habit. There are three species of Otter shells of which *Lutraria lutraria* is the most widely distributed; the other two, *L. angustior* and *L. magna*, being confined to the south, the second largely in mud. Confining description to *L. lutraria*, the oval valves are olive-brown and the horny covering of

Bivalves: *top, left,* **Wedge shell,** *Donax vittalus*; *right,* a razor-shell, *Ensis ensis*; *centre,* the Pod razor-shell, *E. siliqua*; *bottom, left,* Sand gaper, *Mya arenaria*; *right,* Otter shell, *Lutraria lutraria*

the long siphons is usually transparent. The two species of *Mya* are both common. The larger Sand gaper, *Mya arenaria* (the American 'soft shell clam' and there greatly appreciated as food) has a browner shell than *L. lutraria* and the covering of the siphons is also much darker. It is larger than the Blunt gaper, *M. truncata* in which the posterior end of the shell is obviously truncated. However, if in any real doubt about the nature of the bivalve open the shell and examine the dark ligament in the hinge region. In *Lutraria* this is attached to a similar spoon-shaped area of shell on each valve, in *Mya* this extension occurs only in the left valve curling round under the margin of the shell on the right valve.

These animals are known as 'gapers' because the empty valves do not meet, but gape, at the hind end. In life this is the region into which the massive trunk-like siphons are withdrawn. Unlike the razor-shells, these bivalves cannot move up and down in the sand. As they grow larger so do they burrow more deeply; the foot is relatively small and if left exposed on the surface they can only very slowly re-enter the sand. Indeed, were this to happen naturally the gaper would be eaten by some predator long before it could reach safety. But they are not in life likely to be exposed, at any rate after they have attained adult size. It is the siphons which reach up, perhaps 8 inches (20 cm.), to the surface where they take in and expel water. Even if bitten off, as by a plaice, as may often happen, the cut end regenerates a new tip with its surrounding fringe of tentacles. It is by means of these tentacles aided by minute eyes when these are present, as in cockles, that bivalves have most contact with their environment. The head, so conspicuous in sea-snails, has in the bivalves been enclosed by the valves and disappeared, its former sensory functions transferred to the margins of the siphons.

Another highly characteristic group of shore bivalves are the tellinids with delicate shell-valves which flatten out, like the wings of a butterfly, when the animal dies and before the ligament disintegrates and breaks. The commonest species is *Tellina tenuis* which may occur in enormous numbers starting about the level of high water of neap tides, increasing in numbers down to the lowest tidal levels and finally disappearing at depths of about 15 feet (4·6 m.). It is a truly intertidal animal. The delicate translucent shell is frequently coloured pink, orange or yellow. These animals feed in a somewhat different way from the razor-shells. Their two siphons are separate and capable of great elongation; the one through which the water current enters moves actively around the surface of the sand taking in fine particles like the tube of a vacuum-cleaner. In other words these bivalves are deposit-, not suspension-feeders although they do of course also take in suspended matter.

Occasional specimens of the larger oval-shaped *Gari depressa*, 1 inch (25 mm.) or more in length with rays of pink running from the hinge region to the edge of the shell, may be found on our southern shores. On the most exposed shores the very beautiful Wedge shell, *Donax vittatus*, with polished variously coloured valves, usually blotched with violet internally, is a characteristic inhabitant. Forced out of the sand by violent seas, the polished shell slides back, with the aid of the quickly protruded flattened foot, into protection before it can be carried away. The separate siphonal tubes are short and this bivalve is a suspension-feeder, there being no organic deposits on such exposed beaches.

Of the animals that prey upon the bivalves probably the commonest are our two species of Necklace shells, the smaller and commoner *Natica alderi* and the larger, more locally distributed *N. catena*. These are quite characteristically globular, the larger some 1½ inches (3·8 cm.) in diameter, the smaller half of this. If dug out of sand they should be examined in water, when the literally enormous foot will emerge and dilate itself with water so that it covers all but the upper regions of the shell. So equipped it progresses under the surface of the sand to prey on small species of *Tellina* or *Venus*. It grips these with the foot and then extrudes a proboscis which carries a disc-shaped gland at the tip. With the combined action of acid produced by this organ and by the rasping of the radula an opening is most neatly made through the shell, almost always in the region near the hinge. The flesh is then eaten out. The local presence of *Natica* is usually indicated by its collar-like egg-capsules, the matrix of jelly being strengthened by a thick admixture of sand-grains.

Another predator is the Sand-burrowing starfish, *Astropecten irregularis*, p. 311, which may be dug out around low-water level of spring tides. It has the usual five arms but is very flattened and its arms are bordered by projecting spines. The tube feet are pointed, not sucker-like, as in the majority of other starfish. Their action enables the starfish to penetrate and move through sand. The Sand-burrowing starfish swallows its prey intact and the empty shell, of mollusc or crustacean, is later extruded.

The other notable echinoderms of the mid and lower levels of sandy shores are the burrowing urchins. One is the Sea-potato, *Echinocardium cordatum*, 2–3 inches (5–7·5 cm.) long, somewhat elongate and more flattened than the free urchins. Another is the Purple heart urchin, *Spatangus purpureus*, p. 311, 4 inches (10 cm.) long. The first burrows in fine sand, the second in coarse sand. Both need to be dug out, and their presence in a given locality may be

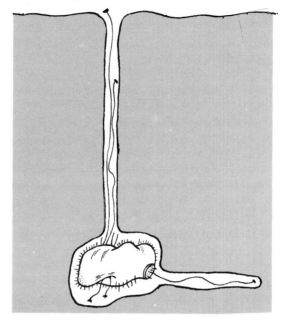

Diagram showing the burrow of the Sea-potato, *Echinocardium cordatum*

indicated by the fragile, almost papery, tests which collect along the strand-line. When dug out the test of the commoner Sea-potato is seen to be covered with backwardly directed spines with the aid of which the animal moves in the one direction, the mouth, although still on the under-surface, being at that end. Contact is maintained with the surface, some 6 inches (15 cm.) above, by way of a respiratory funnel formed by elongate tube feet, other tube feet round the mouth collect sand-grains from which any adhering organic matter is scraped off. Waste is deposited in a 'sanitary tube' in the sand behind the urchin. These urchins slowly move into new feeding-areas, a fresh respiratory funnel being formed about every 20 minutes.

The one spectacular sand-dwelling crustacean is the Masked crab, *Corystes cassivelaunus*, which may be dug out on southern beaches at very low water. It has a pair of upwardly directed spinose antennae which when held together form a tube down which water is drawn for respiration. Placed on the

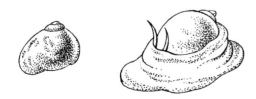

The Necklace shell, *Natica alderi*, enclosed *left* and expanded *right*

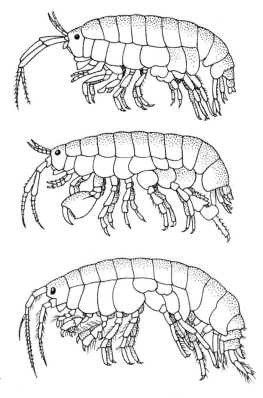

Sand-hoppers: *top, Talitrus saltator; centre, Orchestia gammarella; bottom, Gammarus locusta*

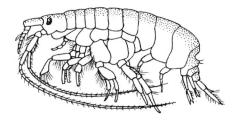

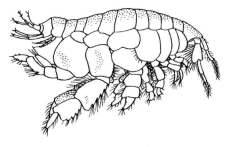

Sand-burrowers: *top, Bathyporeia pelagica; bottom, Haustorius arenarius*

surface this crab quite literally sinks straight down into it by digging with its legs. A better known shore crustacean is the Common shrimp, *Crangon vulgaris*, which lives just buried in sand during the day, coming out to feed at night. It has a more flattened body than a prawn while only its first pair of appendages carry pincers. It also lacks the toothed sabre-like beak going forward from the head. There are also a variety of sand-dwelling amphipods and one isopod which burrow in sand. These animals inhabit zones within the sand as do also certain small bristle-worms, species of *Ophelia*. By digging at various levels and then sieving the sand differing populations will be revealed. Highest on the shore, in the dry sand often amongst rotting seaweed, lives the amphipod Sand-hopper, *Talitrus saltator*, with related species of *Orchestia*, although the latter also occur on rocky shores. *T. saltator* is almost terrestrial. It burrows by day but emerges in the damper air of evening when it fully justifies its name, progressing in a series of high jumps due to sudden contractions of the laterally flattened body.

Other related crustaceans are the common *Gammarus locusta*, usually living in pairs, the smaller male held within the curved body of the 1 inch (25 mm.) long female. the very tiny *Bathyporeia pelagica*. $\frac{1}{5}$ inch (5 mm.) long and *Haustorius arenarius*, double its size, both of which burrow in sand, and both swim, the first with its body vertical, the second on its back.

The worm population of sand is largely buried but the sandy tubes of the Sand-mason, *Lanice conchilega*, are frequently seen projecting about 1 inch (25 mm.) above the surface. their openings frilled with sandy threads. This worm. which is easily dug out. is up to 10 inches (25 cm.) long with a crown of mingled pink feeding-tentacles and red gills. Its flexible tube is made of sand-grains mixed with mucus and is easily repaired, or even replaced, when damaged. The beautifully constructed, tapering sand-cases of *Pectinaria belgica*, over 1 inch (25 mm.) long, rigid but fragile, are often washed up. Remarkable aggregations of the Honeycomb-worm, *Sabellaria alveolata*, may be encountered where sand meets rock in some sheltered places, where water movements are sufficient to bring it food but not too rough to damage its tubes. There must be enough disturbance of the water to hold sand-grains in suspension for the construction of the ramifying mass of sandy tubes and yet not so much that the worms cannot settle. Each has a ciliated feeding-crown for collecting suspended food-particles and a beautiful operculum composed of yellow spines arranged in a circular pattern. The reefs of the Honeycomb-worm may be over 3 feet (1 m.) across, and they also provide shelter for many other small animals.

Finally, there are the carnivorous bristle-worms, the rounded and very active Cat-worm, *Nephthys hombergi*, about 4 inches (10 cm.) long, and the rather smaller species of *Glycera*. They are readily dug and easily recognized; when squeezed – and often without this stimulus – the rounded muscular proboscis with powerful terminal jaws will be violently extruded.

Description of one of the commonest of all shore animals, the Lugworm, *Arenicola*

Bristle-worms: *left to right*, tube of the Peacock-worm, *Sabella pavonina*; *Lanice conchilega*; the tube of *Pectinaria*; reefs of the tubes of *Sabellaria alveolata*

marina, p. 284, so frequently dug for bait, involves reference to a changing environment, namely to the increasing presence amongst the larger sand-grains of the smaller constituents of mud, a significant proportion of which consists of organic matter. This occurs when water movements diminish so that progressively finer particles drop out of suspension in the water. And, with the increase in organic matter, so does the medium in which the animals live become a source of food as well as of protection. The presence of the characteristic castings of the Lugworm, not unlike those of an earthworm, is an indication of an adequate content of deposited food material within the sand.

A short distance from each pile of castings a small rounded depression will be noted. This denotes the position of the head. The worm inhabits a U-shaped burrow, with a horizontal gallery, and vertical head and tail shafts. From time to time the head is pushed up the head shaft to swallow sand from the food-rich surface layer. This passes through the gut where the edible part is digested, the great bulk of the material being ejected through the anus which projects upwards in the tail shaft causing the castings to appear above the surface. Water is also drawn in by way of the tail shaft and passes along the outside of the body so that oxygen may be extracted by the red plume-like gills which project from the middle regions. There are alternating periods of feeding, when sand at the head of the shaft is kept loose and open, and of irrigation for respiratory purposes. As its vast numbers frequently indicate, this is a highly successful animal.

In muddy areas, which may be bordered by rocks, are the meadows of Eel grass, *Zostera marina*, in sheltered creeks or round the mouths of estuaries. The smaller *Z. nana* may be exposed at the lowest tides but the larger, and much the more important, species is effectively never uncovered. The most interesting animals found upon them are the beautiful little lucernarians, little jellyfish attached by a basal sucker, the margins of the bell decorated with eight bunches of little tentacles. There are several British species, all difficult to find and most of them confined to the south-west. Hydroids and

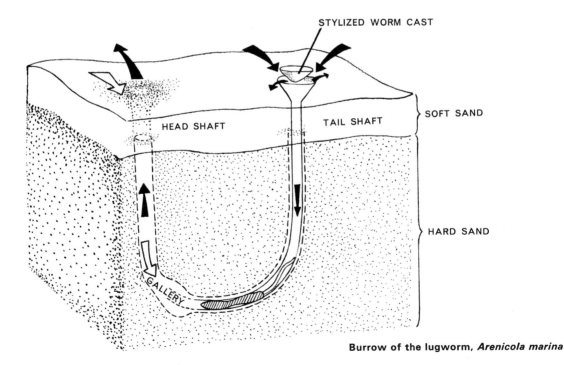

Burrow of the lugworm, *Arenicola marina*

sea-mats in abundance will be attached, also, during the summer months, the flat egg-capsules, unmistakable because laid in rows, of the very common little mud-snails, the Thick-lipped dogwhelk, *Nassarius* (*Nassa*) *reticulatus* and the Netted dogwhelk, *N. incrassatus*. It is in such an environment that the largest of our sea-slugs, although it does have a delicate largely internal, shell, the Sea-hare, *Aplysia punctata*, p. 294, may be encountered often with its purplish-coloured twining masses of spawn. This is a striking animal, reddish brown to olive-green, up to 6 inches (15 cm.) long and with the foot upwardly extended at each side forming parapodia which, on occasion, may be used for swimming. Like all its kind, this animal is an annual, coming inshore when near maturity to spawn and to feed with its well-developed jaws on the Sea-lettuce, *Ulva*. A related animal, not much smaller, is the massive reddish-brown *Pleurobranchus* (*Oscanius*) *membranaceus*, p. 294, with no up-rising parapodia but with a dome-shaped warty back and a conspicuous plume-like gill on the right side. It feeds on large simple ascidians, usually on muddy gravel but it may be found among Eel grass. Another related but rather smaller, yellow animal with a smooth back, *Berthella plumula*, is more likely to have been encountered on the lowest levels of rocky shores, under stones or perhaps within a shell.

On muddy shores, with occasional boulders and gravel, we find again the Common periwinkle and the no less ubiquitous Shore crab. On gravelly areas and around rocks are probably as likely places as any to encounter at low tide, the Large whelk, *Buccinum undatum*, perhaps up to 5 inches (12·7 cm.) although it grows larger offshore where indeed it is commonest. The shell is divided by deep sutures between successive whorls and there is an obvious siphonal canal at the lower end of the shell opening. This animal is a carnivorous scavenger, usually unable to tackle living prey, but insinuating its long proboscis into the shells of dead or dying molluscs, usually bivalves,

and other intertidal carrion and then tearing out the flesh with a radula bearing few large, curved teeth. The similarly sized *Neptunea* (*Fusus*) *antiqua*, spindle-shaped and with smooth, white surface and prominently ridged whorls, occurs in the north although most often found as dead shells.

The mud surface is the home of the two smaller mud-snails of the genus *Nassarius*. Both have brownish high-spired shells, much narrower than those of the ordinary dogwhelk. They have a prominent siphon. The larger species is some 1½ inches (3·8 cm.) long, the other half that. The minute snail, *Hydrobia ulvae*, which is only ⅓ inch (8·5 mm.) long appears as a granular covering over the mud where it has been reported in

A mud-snail, *Hydrobia ulvae*, left; the Netted dogwhelk, *Nassarius incrassatus*, right

populations of up to 60,000 per square yard (0·84 sq. m.), feeding on minute fragments of organic debris on the surface mud. It has a definite tidal cycle. During the lowest tidal withdrawal it burrows just below the surface to reappear as the tide rises when, on a raft of mucus from its pedal glands, it becomes attached to the surface film and so is carried some distance upshore at the same time collecting some food in the mucus. Eventually it comes to rest higher up, later spending the initial period of low tide browsing on the surface before again burrowing. It is impressive in terms of its numbers and because of its dependence on the organic content of the mud-flats.

Another common animal on mud-flats is the small amphipod crustacean, *Corophium volutator*, in its little U-shaped burrow from which it emerges when the tide is in, to forage for edible fragments on the mud. To

Jellyfish: *top, Aurelia aurita; centre, Chrysaora; bottom, Cyanea*

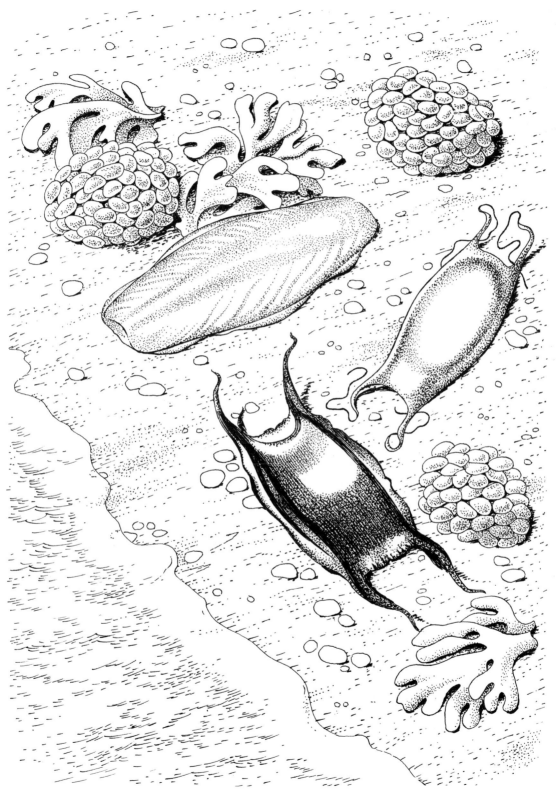

Jetsam on the strand-line showing the egg-cases of the whelk *Buccinum*; *top*, Cuttlefish bone, Mermaid's purses of Dogfish, *right*, and Skate, *left*, with a frond of the Hornwrack *Flustra foliacea*, *below*

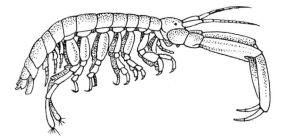

Corophium volutator

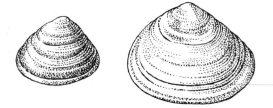

Tellinid bivalves: *left, Macoma balthica; right, Scorbicularia plana*

this category of pure deposit-feeders may be added two tellinid bivalves. The first is *Macoma balthica*, less than 1 inch (25 mm.) long and thicker than the Tellinas, which inhabits sea-shores. The second, larger and very flattened, with almost circular shell, is *Scrobicularia plana*. Of the tube-worms the one most commonly seen is the Peacock-worm, *Sabella pavonina*, p. 284. Even when retracted this worm catches the eye because of its parchment-like tubes rising some 4 inches (10 cm.) clear of the muddy bottom. When fully expanded its crown of tentacles rises from two semicircular lobes and is variously coloured from brown to violet with darker bands. The animal is 4 to 10 inches (10–25 cm.) long but its tube is about twice that length.

Digging in such areas where there is evidence of burrowing may well produce specimens of the so-called 'mud-shrimps' or 'burrowing prawns', including *Callianassa subterranea* and species of *Upogebia*. The first is a southern species but the others occur more widely. They have a distinctive appearance with an enlarged abdominal region primarily concerned with creating an effective current of water through the burrow, and a relatively small front end in which head and thorax are fused. The two are interestingly different in habits, *Callianassa* being a deposit-feeder and digging for food as well as for protection, while *Upogebia* burrows for protection only and strains tiny particles from the inflowing water through its hairy mouth-parts in a very similar manner to that used by hermit and porcelain crabs to which they are related.

Of the animals often washed up much the commonest is the jellyfish, *Aurelia aurita*, from up to a foot (30 cm.) across. It is whitish

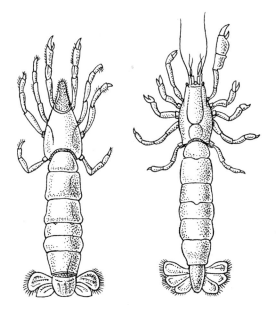

Burrowing prawns: *Upogebia; left, Callianassa subterranea, right*

Echinoderms: *top left*, a sunstar *Solaster papposus*; *right*, the Red starfish *Asterias rubens*; *centre left*, the Sand-burrowing starfish *Astropecten irregularis*; *right*, the Purple heart urchin *Spatangus purpureus*; *bottom left*, a sea-cucumber *Cucumaria normani*; *centre*, the Common sea-urchin *Echinus esculentus* and *right*, a brittle-star *Ophiocomina nigra*

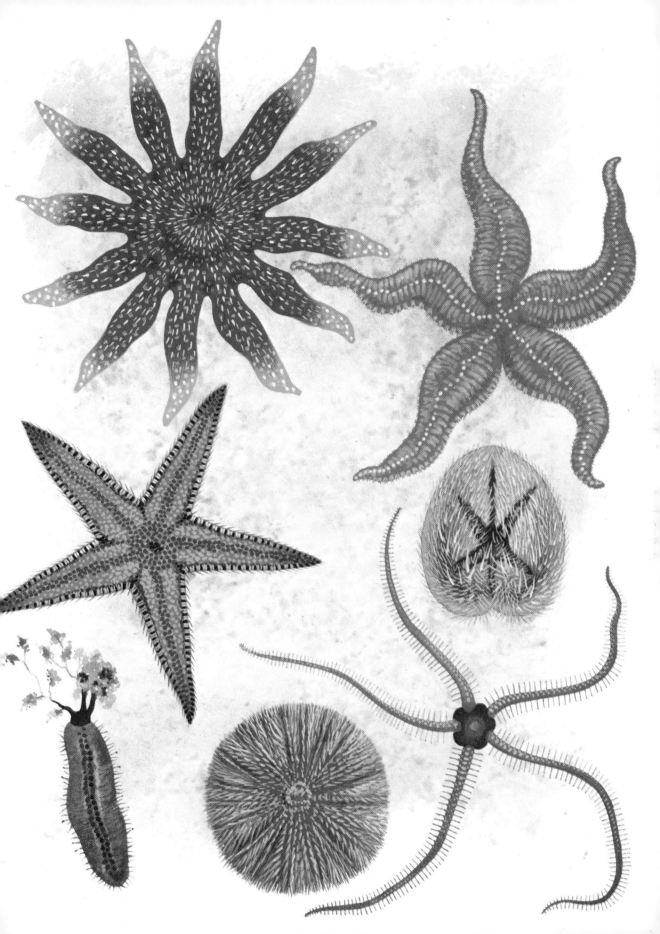

Jellyfish and sea-squirts: *top left*, the Portuguese man-o'-war *Physalia physalis*; *right*, the By-the-wind-sailor *Velella spirans*; *centre top*, the Golden stars sea-squirt *Botryllus schlosseri*; *right*, the Gooseberry sea-squirt *Dendrodoa grossularia*; *below* *Ascidiella aspersa*

The Cuttlefish, *Sepia officinalis*

with four pale violet crescents – the reproductive organs – on the underside grouped round the mouth.

The spectacular *Chrysaora isosceles*, up to 8 inches (20 cm.) across, is more massive, mostly white but with rich brown streaks and patches. It has numerous marginal tentacles and four trailing brown tentacles from the mouth, and it can inflict a severe sting. There are also the blue *Cyanea lamarcki* and the yellow *C. capillata* with the bell margin deeply lobed and bordered with eight trailing tufts of long tentacles.

On the strand-line appear all manner of marine objects, the broad bone of the Cuttle-fish, *Sepia officinalis*, which lives on sandy bottoms close to the shore, the horny egg-cases of dogfish and skates, the so-called 'Mermaid's purses', the former slender with terminal tendrils, the latter broader with terminal projections, the sponge-like empty egg-cases of the whelk, *Buccinum*, up to the size of a fist, and the branched, plant-like masses of the polyzoan Hornwrack, *Flustra foliacea*. During long calm spells south-westerly winds may blow on to our western shores two remarkable floating coelenterates, the Portuguese man-o'-war, *Physalia physalis* and the smaller By-the-wind-sailor, *Velella spirans*, both illustrated on p. 312. The first of these consists of a 6 inch (15 cm.) long, pale blue, gas-filled float with a complexity of mouths, tentacles and reproductive organs beneath it – it can catch and kill a fish yards below the surface, its tentacles delivering a most virulent sting. The second is a flat disc with a triangular sail and, underneath the disc, a central mouth ringed with concentric rows of tentacles and reproductive organs. This also is blue.

Fishes

The earliest fish-like fossil, *Jamoytius*, so far found is from the Silurian shale of Lanarkshire. It is about a foot (30 cm.) long with a fish-like tail, a fin running nearly the length of the back and a long fin along each flank. It had no jaws and almost certainly no backbone, and lived over 400 million years ago. Contemporary with it are other fish-like animals, the ostracoderms, which had bony-plated bodies, but they also lacked jaws and are called the Agnatha, or jawless ones. Also in rocks of this same age are found occasional remains of true fishes. By the next geological period, the Devonian, there are abundant fossils, of Agnatha, lungfishes with leg-like fins apparently able to crawl out on to land and, in the sea, sharks and true fishes. The Devonian Period has been called the Age of Fishes, because they were so numerous; and they were divided into three main groups: the jawless Agnatha, the sharks with skeletons wholly of cartilage, or gristle, and the true fishes with bony skeletons. During the succeeding 200 million years the sharks, with their relatives the skates and rays, reached their maximum development and then to an extent stood still. Many of the descendants living today are little changed to what they were, say, 150 million years ago. The bony fishes made, in geological terms, a slower start, but went on to proliferate a wide variety of species, which account for the great majority of the 30,000 species of fishes living today.

In the following pages those fishes living in and around Britain are dealt with in the order in which they are scientifically classified. In the colour plates we see some of them portrayed, grouped ecologically under freshwater, shore and deep-water marine fishes.

The Agnatha, which formed the dominant fish group during the Devonian Period, 350–400 million years ago, are represented now by the Hagfish and the lampreys. The Hagfish is a rare marine scavenger or parasite which buries its head in the body of dead or dying fish, eating the flesh and often leaving only an empty skin. The lampreys are much more common, although their feeding habits are rather similar. The mouth of a lamprey is surrounded by a strong sucker, armed with sharp teeth. There are also teeth on the tongue. The animal attaches itself to its victim with the sucker and rasps away the skin and flesh with its tongue.

The interest of the lampreys to the zoologist is that they show some features which it is thought were possessed by all the fossil Agnatha. They have no lower jaws, and they have seven separate gill openings which are not connected with the mouth. Most fish take in mouthfuls of water which pass over the gills and out through an opening on each side of the head. The gills of lampreys are in blind sacs supported on a framework of gristle. Water is squeezed out by the contraction of muscles and sucked in again through the elasticity of the gristle. The rapid pumping of water into the gills is very characteristic of live lampreys. Other primitive features are seen in the kidneys and nervous system. However, their breeding and feeding are very specialized.

There are three species of lampreys in Britain. The largest, reaching 3 feet (91 cm.) in length, is the Sea lamprey, *Petromyzon marinus*. It is reddish brown with mottled markings and blotches. Sea lampreys migrate, ascending the rivers in spring, and pairs begin to make nests by moving stones from a gravelly area 2 to 3 feet (61–91·4 cm.) in diameter with their suckers. After the eggs have been laid and fertilized in the nest, the stones are replaced. The adults are so emaciated and exhausted that they then die. Each egg hatches to give a small worm-like creature which was once thought to be a different animal and was called *Ammocoetes*

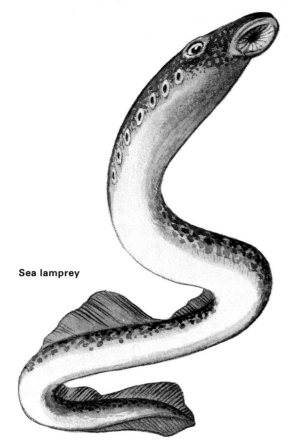

Sea lamprey

branchialis. These larval lampreys are blind and they move from the gravel to deep muddy pools where they feed on minute animals and plant fragments. After three to five years they change to the adult form and migrate to the sea.

Sea lampreys cannot stand much pollution, so they are prevented from entering such rivers as the Thames and Mersey. They are commonest in the southern half of England and are rarer in Ireland, Scotland and northern England.

The River lamprey, *Lampetra fluviatilis,* is like the Sea lamprey but only 20 inches (51 cm.) long and is a uniform grey without any marbling. Most River lampreys live much of their time in the sea. They enter fresh water in the autumn and spawn in the spring. During this time they do not feed and the gut atrophies and becomes impassable to

food. It is little wonder that like the Sea lamprey they die after spawning. The spawning of River lampreys is similar to that of the Sea lamprey, but the nests are farther upstream in shallower water among pebbles.

The Brook lamprey, *Lampetra planeri,* at about 8 inches (20 cm.), is the smallest of the three species, and is very common in streams. The Brook lamprey spends most of its life as an ammocoete larva, and only changes to the adult form a few months before spawning. Whereas the ammocoete of the River lamprey is always immature, and the adult only becomes mature some time after metamorphosis, in this species the ripening of the roes commences during the larval ammocoete stage. Spawning is a communal affair with four to eight individuals using the same nest. The Brook lamprey is the commonest British species, perhaps because it lives permanently above the sources of pollution. It is found throughout England, Ireland and Wales, and in Scotland south of the Caledonian Canal.

The cartilaginous fishes or Chondrichthyes include not only the many fossil fishes already mentioned, but also the sharks, dogfish and skates of the present-day fish fauna. They are distinguished from the Agnatha on the one hand in having proper jaws and from the Osteichthyes (the bony fishes) on the other, in having separate gill openings, an exception being the rare Rabbit fish, *Chimaera monstrosa.* They are also distinguished from the bony fishes by having a skeleton of cartilage only. The Rabbit fish lives in deep water. It is an extraordinary fish for which the specific name *monstrosa* is very suitable.

The name 'shark' always conjures up the image of an evil, dangerous and cunning fish that may come up from the depths to attack some unlucky swimmer. In tropical seas sharks are very dangerous, but round Britain they are rare and the most frequent damage they do is to fishing-nets. In recent years shark fishing, based on Looe in Cornwall, has become a very popular sport. The Blue shark, *Prionace glauca,* the Porbeagle,

Basking shark

is probably the commonest of the large sharks. It grows to over 35 feet (10·6 m.) and migrates up the west coast in early summer to become very common off western Scotland. Sometimes dead specimens get washed ashore and give rise to stories of dead sea-monsters, particularly since the long backbone, together with some gristle, is often all that remains. The Basking shark has fine comb-like bristles on its gill supports, and these filter out the minute animals on which this shark feeds. The Basking shark sieves out its food as it swims along with mouth and gill slits wide open. In spite of its great size, it has minute teeth and is quite harmless.

Very much more common than large sharks are the smaller dogfish. The two commonest are the Spurdog, *Squalus acanthias*, up to 4 feet (1·2 m.) long, and the Lesser Spotted dogfish, *Scyliorhinus caniculus*, p. 351, of about 20–28 inches (51–71 cm.). These two are very important commercially and the latter particularly is marketed as rock salmon.

Some of the sharks and dogfish, for example the Porbeagle, Mako, Basking shark, Tope and Spurdog, give birth to live young, but others, notably the Spotted dogfish, lay eggs in rectangular horny cases which have long 'tendrils' at each corner. These are the

Lamna nasus, the Mako, *Isurus oxyrinchus*, and the Thresher, *Alopias vulpinus*, are caught by anglers. Another species, very commonly caught is the Tope, *Galeorhinus galeus*. This is the fish that provides the main ingredient of Chinese shark-fin soup.

The Basking shark, *Cetorhinus maximus*,

mermaids' purses which are very often found washed up on the beach.

Also belonging to the Chondrichthyes are the skates and rays, adapted to living on the bottom. They have very flattened bodies, with large 'wings' on each side and a thin, usually spiny, tail. Their flattened appearance is quite unmistakable and is very different from that of the plaice or other flatfish which will be described later.

The eyes are always on the upper side and the mouth, which usually has many rows of teeth suitable for crushing food, is always on the underside. Skates breathe by taking water in through the first visible gill slit (called the spiracle) situated on the upper surface behind the eye, and out through five gill slits on the underside.

Some of the species, such as the Common skate, *Raja batis*, which may be up to 7 feet (213 cm.) across have smooth slimy skins and others, for example the Thornback ray, *Raja clavata*, p. 351, have a rough prickly covering with sharp spines, particularly down the centre of the tail.

All skates lay eggs in mermaids' purses, like those of the Spotted dogfish, but more square in shape.

The food of the adult includes not only bottom-living shrimps and other animals, but also a surprising number of fish which they catch by wrapping their wings round them. The Electric ray, *Torpedo nobiliana*, up to 3 feet (91 cm.) or more long and 2 feet (61 cm.) across, which has a rounder body than the skates, stuns its victims with a severe shock from large electric organs in the wings. Live specimens should be handled with care! The Sting ray, *Dasyatis pastinaca*, of up to 3½ feet (107 cm.) long, has a spine on

Tope

its tail with poison glands, and this species can cause intensely painful wounds and inflammation.

The Osteichthyes, or bony fishes, form, as mentioned before, the dominant group of present-day fishes. There is, however, one section that is best known from its fossils of the Carboniferous Period, 300–350 million years old, but it has a few species that survive today. They are, therefore, in the nature of living fossils. They also provide a link

Mermaid's purse, the egg case of a dogfish

Sturgeon

between the sharks and the bony fishes, for although in most respects they are true fishes they still have a skeleton of cartilage with bone only in the skull. One of these is the Sturgeon, *Acipenser sturio*, widespread through North America and Asia, with a few stragglers reaching our coasts each year and very occasionally migrating into fresh water. By an Act of Parliament of Edward III, all Sturgeons belong to the Crown, and any that are caught have to be offered to the Queen.

One primitive feature of the Sturgeon, reminiscent of the sharks, is that the body tapers into the upper lobe of the tail, whereas with other bony fish the tail skeleton is composed of fin rays only. Another distinctive character of the Sturgeon is the five rows of bony tubercles along the length of the body.

Sturgeons are delicious to eat and are perhaps best known for their eggs which are made into the Russian delicacy caviare. Sturgeon grow to over 10 feet (3 m.) in length, and live to an age of 30 years. With fish of this size and longevity it is easy for them to be overfished almost to extinction, and this has happened with some populations. Those surviving at the mouth of the Gironde in France, and the Guadalquivir in Spain, and the populations in Russia, are very carefully regulated.

The Herring, *Clupea harengus*, p. 334, which grows up to 1 foot (30·5 cm.), is one of the more primitive, or more generalized, of the bony fishes. It is by far the most important member of the family and a great deal of research has been carried out by fishery scientists into its feeding, spawning and other aspects of its life history. Not only are the nutritious Herrings eaten fresh, as well as smoked as kippers and bloaters, but also in recent years they have been caught, along with other fish, in ever increasing quantities for processing into fish meal and cattle cake.

The Herring family is at once distinguished by having a single dorsal fin midway along the back, and by not having a lateral line – the line that can be seen running from head to tail along the flanks of most fish and which is associated with special sense organs beneath. Herrings are completely covered with scales that are rather easily detached and are predominantly silvery in colour with a dark blue or greenish-blue back.

There are several different races of Herrings which spawn in different places and at different times. Some are autumn spawners and others breed in the spring. Some spawn in shallow water and others on the edge of oceanic banks. One of the main objects of herring fishery research has been to identify these various groups and discover the degree of their intermingling, so that if one population is exploited too heavily, the extent of the damage will be known. Partly as a result of the different water temperatures at which the eggs and larvae of the different herrings grow, the races have different characteristics, particularly in such things as the number of vertebrae in the backbone and the number of scales and fin rays. Other racial characters are found in the bones, gill rakers and number of eggs laid each year.

Herrings spawn in enormous shoals. The fertilized eggs sink to the bottom and stick to sand, gravel and broken shells, often in a huge carpet several eggs thick. The eggs hatch in a few weeks and the newly hatched larvae are about a quarter of an inch long (6 mm.) each with a small yolk-sac on which it subsists until it is ready to start feeding. These young Herring drift in the currents and usually get carried inshore with the surface water. Here they live and grow in bays and estuaries, and even penetrate quite far into fresh water. When they have reached 1 or 2 inches (25–51 mm.) in length they are sometimes caught and sold as 'white bait'. Later the adolescent Herrings move to deeper water and when mature migrate to their traditional spawning grounds.

The food of Herrings is almost entirely plankton – the small animals which live in the main mass of sea water and drift wherever the currents take them. Herrings have some long spine-like projections on the gill supports and it was once thought that these act as a sieve, the Herring feeding while swimming along with its mouth open, sieving out its food, rather in the manner of the basking shark. However, the function of these gill rakers, as they are called, is actually to prevent food escaping via the gills, and the Herring snaps up and swallows each minute bit of plankton individually.

The planktonic food is composed of hundreds of different types of animals, some of which live all their lives in the plankton and others like crab larvae, which spend only one phase of the life cycle in the plankton. However, nearly all planktonic animals are very nutritious and it is from this rich food supply that the herrings get their oily character.

Herrings are found all round Britain, but the main fishing grounds are on the east coast with Yarmouth, Lowestoft, Whitby and North Shields as the principal ports in England; and Peterhead, Fraserburgh, Wick,

Freshwater fish (*opposite, from top to bottom*): Brown trout; Grayling; Atlantic salmon – adult with egg, alevin, parr and smolt; Char

(*overleaf left, from top to bottom*): Minnow; Common carp; Roach; Dace; Gudgeon

(*overleaf right, from top to bottom*): Three-spined stickleback; Perch; Stone loach; Bullhead or Miller's Thumb; Pike; Common eel

Stronsay and Lerwick in Scotland. On the west coast there are thriving populations of Herrings in the Minch, fished from Stornoway, Ullapool, Mallaig and Castlebay, in the Firth of Clyde, round the Isle of Man, and off Dunmore and Killibegs in Ireland.

It used to be thought there were vast shoals of Herrings migrating from north to south in the North Sea, with fishing fleets putting out from successive ports to catch them. Herrings do best in temperatures of 43–59 °F. (6–15 °C.). Each year the Gulf Stream moves north-east to reach first the coasts of France, then the British Isles, the Low Countries, Scandinavia and Iceland. When, in summer, the warm waters withdraw first from Shetland then successively down our east coast, to Brittany in January, the shoals from the different local populations come up from deep water, one after the other, to spawn.

The Sprat, *Sprattus sprattus*, is very like the Herring, but it is smaller at 6½ inches (16·5 cm.) and has keeled scales along the belly. It is a more coastal species than the Herring and even when adult often enters estuaries. Young Sprats are canned in large numbers by the Norwegians as 'brisling'. 'Sardines' are the young of the Pilchard, *Sardina pilchardus*, when canned. It grows to 9 inches (23 cm.) and is a more southern species than the Sprat and is only plentiful off Cornwall and in the English Channel. The Anchovy, *Engraulis encrasicolus*, 8 inches (20 cm.) long, is another southern species, whose main fishery is in the Mediterranean, which occasionally visits our shores, more particularly in the south-west.

There are two other members of the Herring family which have very different spawning habits from those considered so far. These are the shads which enter fresh water and spawn in rivers.

The Allis shad, *Alosa alosa*, up to 2 feet

(61 cm.) long, is like a deep-bodied herring and it has a greenish-blue back and silvery sides with a brassy sheen. Now a rare fish which has suffered from pollution, it used to spawn very plentifully in the Shannon and Severn.

The Allis shad enters fresh water from the estuaries in shoals in spring and spawns in fast-flowing water. After spawning the adults return to the sea and disperse. The eggs settle among boulders and the young go to the sea after a year or more.

The Twaite shad, *Alosa fallax*, is a smaller species of the same colour as the Allis shad, but with a row of five black spots down each side behind the head. It spawns in rivers at or just above the high tide limit. There is a smaller race of land-locked Twaite shad permanently resident in the lakes of Killarney.

The Herring and the Shads are marine fishes that sometimes enter fresh water. The Salmon spawns in fresh water and regularly goes down to the sea to feed and grow. Even the first sight of an Atlantic salmon, *Salmo salar*, p. 321, either lying quietly in a pool or leaping a waterfall, is enough to convince anyone that here is the finest of all our fishes. It grows 3–4 feet (91–122 cm.) long and exceptionally may weigh 100 lb (45 kg.) or more. Not only is it a fine-looking and powerful fish, but there is so much mystery surrounding its life history that no one with a spark of imagination can fail to be enthralled and intrigued by it.

The story starts when the Salmon come up from the sea to spawn in the head-waters of the rivers. They may enter the rivers in almost any month of the year though some rivers habitually have spring fish whereas in others the Salmon mainly run in the summer or autumn. During their stay in fresh water they migrate up to the spawning grounds and this often involves a long journey with weirs and waterfalls to be surmounted. It is well worth visiting a waterfall in autumn to see the Salmon leaping. No matter when the fish have come, by mid-October they are lying in pools near gravelly stretches where the water is about 2 feet (61 cm.) deep. When

Shore marine fish (*from top to bottom*):
Fifteen-spined stickleback; Short-spined sea scorpion; Common blenny; Butterfish; Lesser weever; Sand goby

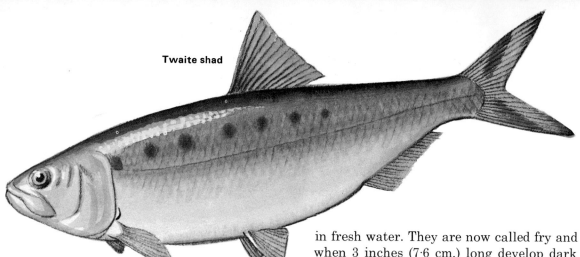

Twaite shad

spawning first starts the females move to the gravel beds and begin to make a nest or redd by lifting the stones with an upward flick of the tail. Eventually a depression about 8 inches (20 cm.) deep is made and here the female is joined by the cockfish and her eggs are shed and fertilized. She then moves slightly farther upstream and in digging a new redd covers the eggs with more sand and gravel. When spawning is finished the salmon are exhausted and so emaciated that many do not survive the journey back to the sea. These spent fish are called kelts and they may also have picked up fungal infections and parasites which further lower their condition. During their time in fresh water the Salmon do not feed, yet they have the arduous journey upstream, their roes have to mature, and they have to face the rigours of spawning. It is little wonder that the kelts are in poor condition, but those that do reach the sea survive. The salt water kills their freshwater parasites and the salmon begin to feed again, soon recovering their former plump condition.

The eggs develop slowly in the gravel and after about 100 days (depending on the water temperature) they hatch and the little salmon, called alevins, emerge. They are only about half an inch (12·7 mm.) long and still retain a large amount of yolk on which they live while in the gravel. When they have absorbed the remaining yolk they are large enough to feed themselves and grow slowly in fresh water. They are now called fry and when 3 inches (7·6 cm.) long develop dark vertical bands along the sides of the body and are then called parr. After two to five years they become silvery and are called smolts and they then migrate to the sea.

Once they have gone to the sea very little is known about them. Some come back to spawn after one year, in which case they are called grilse, but others remain four years or more and return as fully grown salmon. The length of time spent at sea varies considerably, and where they go is quite unknown. A feeding ground of British and other salmon has recently been discovered off western Greenland, but grilse have not been caught there. How the salmon find their way over these vast distances of ocean, and how they so often manage to return to the same river which they themselves left as smolts, are questions that can only be partially answered. More study has been made of Pacific salmon and the picture now emerging is that, at the right season, they make their way back to the coast using celestial navigation, guided by the sun by day and the stars by night. On reaching coastal waters they pick up the taste (or the smell?) of the water brought down to the sea by the river in which they were hatched, and they follow this up to its source.

In Britain the Atlantic salmon is less widespread than it used to be. At one time the Thames and many other rivers had good runs of salmon, but they have now been ruined by pollution.

The Atlantic salmon we have considered here must not be confused with the Pacific salmon of which there are several species. These are only found in Britain imported in tins, apart from one or two stragglers which come from a Russian experimental introduction in the Arctic White Sea area.

The trout, *Salmo trutta*, p. 321, the second of the salmon family, is the most variable of all British fishes, not only in its size and colouration, but also in its general natural history.

The two extremes of this variation are seen in the small Brown trout resident in moorland streams on the one hand, and the large migratory Sea trout on the other. Modern scientific opinion is that these, together with all the other varieties that have been described, belong to the same species. This opinion is based on the observations that there are all intermediates between the different types, that they can all interbreed and produce fertile offspring, that to some extent the different characteristics depend on the environment in which the trout live, and they that are thought to be pure strains of one variety, can produce fish of another.

The colour of trout varies from the beautiful fish with a greenish-brown back, silvery yellow sides and covered with brown speckles and red and blue spots, to the entirely silvery Sea trout with only black spots. Even the Brown trout exhibit great variation in colour from one water to another, and the red colouration depends on the diet of the fish including some crustacea with red carotenoid pigments.

The life history of Sea trout is similar to that of salmon. The fish run up the rivers in late September and October to spawn in the smaller tributaries particularly when the rivers are swollen after rain. Unlike the salmon, trout feed during their stay in fresh water. The making of redds 3–4 inches (7·6–10 cm.) deep and the shedding of eggs is also similar, but the spawning beds have less coarse gravel and are in shallower water. The eggs hatch to give alevins but the trout fry are more territorial than salmon fry, and each tends to keep to its own little area 8 inches (20·3 cm.) square. The fry grow into

a parr stage and after this comes the difference in behaviour, when the Sea trout become silvery and migrate as smolts, back to the sea, and the resident Brown trout get left behind and gradually take on the adult colouration.

The size trout grow to is also very variable. In the poor upland becks they may never grow much beyond 8 inches (20 cm.) whereas the trout of lakes can reach over 2 feet (61 cm.) in length. The rates of growth are also remarkably variable, in a northern acid beck a five-year-old trout may be 8 inches (20 cm.) long, whereas in a southern chalk stream they may be over double the size at that age.

Their food also varies, but trout are opportunists and will take advantage of whatever animal life is available. When young they feed mainly on the small insects that drift in the current into their territories. Later they take to feeding on bottom insects, snails, pea mussels, caddis larvae, freshwater shrimps and others, as well as worms, beetles and other insects of terrestrial origin. With trout in ponds and lakes larval insects form an important part of the diet and with the larger trout minnows, small perch and other fish are eaten.

After spawning the adult Sea trout return to the sea. Perhaps because they continue to feed in fresh water, there is not the same mortality among the spent fish as there is with salmon. The river trout tend to drop downstream after spawning, and lake trout return to their usual haunts.

The variability of trout is the result of their adaptability to different conditions, and they are found widespread through Britain in upland becks, rivers, canals, ponds and lakes. They prefer clear, well-oxygenated water and are less common in the slow-flowing weedy rivers of lowland Britain.

The Rainbow trout, *Salmo gairdneri*, is another variable member of the salmon family, but it is mainly imported into Britain from America for raising in commercial fish ponds, though some are also liberated for sport.

The Char, *Salvelinus alpinus*, p. 321, is one of the most beautiful salmonid fish and grows to about 1 foot (30·5 cm.) long. In Britain it is a lake fish and is found in the Lake District, numerous Scottish Lochs, Llym Tegid (North Wales) and many Irish Loughs. All Char have dark upper parts and lighter bellies, with a white leading edge to the paired fins and buff-coloured spots on a darker background. During the breeding season the males take on a brilliant crimson or brick-red belly. The Char are probably land-locked remnants of Char that ran to the sea during the Ice Age, and farther north Char still have this habit. Since they have been isolated, with each population in its own lake for so long, the Char from different lakes are distinguishable.

The Brook char, *Salvelinus fontinalis*, is another introduction from America. It has become naturalized only in a very few localities in the Lake District and Scotland.

Several species, related to the Char, are known collectively as whitefish. Firstly the Houting, *Coregonus oxyrinchus*, which grows to 16 inches (41 cm.), is a very rare marine fish which migrates into fresh water to spawn. Then there is the Vendace, *C. albula*, smaller at 9 inches (23 cm.), which comprises fish living in Derwentwater, and Bassen-thwaite Lake in Cumberland, and some lochs round Lochmaben in southern Scotland. As the Pollan, they are found in Lough Neagh, Lough Erne and in some Shannon lakes in Ireland. Each form differs slightly from the others. Another group, *C. lavaretus*, is made up of the Powan in Loch Lomond and Loch Eck, the Schelly in the Lake District and the Gwyniad in Wales. These are thought to be relics, like the Char, of more widespread, migrating species at the time of the last Ice Age. They grow to about 18 inches (46 cm.) long.

The Grayling *Thymallus thymallus*, p. 321, which grows to about 10 inches (25 cm.), is found in widely scattered, locally very abundant populations in various parts of Britain. It is at once seen to be a relative of the salmon by its small dorsal adipose fin in front of the tail and is recognizable by its very large dorsal fin. The body is a leaden silvery colour darker above and with hori-zontal purple stripes. It is a fish of clear, well-oxygenated rivers where the gradient is becoming a little less steep than the usual trout zone. There has been much controversy about whether Grayling compete with trout. The spawning time of Grayling is in the spring when the trout alevins have left the gravel, and where trout and Grayling are together the former tend to keep to the riffles and areas of broken water, while the Grayling keep to the deeper pools.

The Smelt, *Osmerus eperlanus*, of 7–12 inches (18–30 cm.) long, is another fish of the salmon family, with an adipose fin. It is commonest inshore on the continental coasts of the North Sea, and also on the English east coast and south-west Ireland. It is very silvery and spawns in estuaries in spring.

The Argentine, *Argentina sphyraena*, grows to about 1 foot (30 cm.) and is always fully marine, living over a muddy bottom. It is long and thin with a silver strip down each side, and a small adipose fin near the tail.

Perhaps the most easily recognized of our freshwater fish, certainly the most voracious, and a popular sport fish is the Pike, *Esox lucius*, p. 323. Its upper parts are olive-green with cream blotches on the flanks often arranged in diagonal stripes. The belly is whitish cream. Its mouth is very large with numerous backward-pointing teeth. The dorsal fin is small and set far back near the tail over the anal fin.

Pike usually live in still or slowly flowing canals, ponds, lakes and other weedy places where they lie motionless in wait for their prey, which they catch after a sudden dash. Their diet is almost entirely of fish swallowed head first. Young Pike eat larval fish, stickle-backs and minnows. The adults take what-ever is available, and perch, eels, roach, rudd, gudgeon, bream, trout and salmon are all eaten, as well as frogs, newts, water birds and aquatic mammals.

Pike are found all over England and Wales but not in Scotland north of the Caledonian

Canal, and they are absent from some parts of western Ireland. They breed in April and May. The eggs and milt are shed over weeds in shallow water. The eggs, which are sticky and adhere to the weeds, hatch to give small larvae, each of which hangs on the undersides of leaves and occasionally makes excursions to capture water fleas and other plankton. After one year they have grown to about 3 inches (7·6 cm.) and at two years old they are about 7 inches (18 cm.) long; the females grow faster than the males. They live to at least 17 years of age by which time they have grown to over 3 feet (91 cm.). They are regularly caught at over 30 lb (13·6 kg.).

The carps, family Cyprinidae, also well known, are all freshwater species. The cyprinids all have only one dorsal fin and they have two rather special internal characters. They have no teeth in the mouth, but two bones in the floor of the throat, called pharyngeal bones, have tooth-like projections that bite against two horny pads on the base of the skull. Carp, p. 322, swallow their food whole and chew it up in their throats. The other characteristic is a series of bones, the Weberian apparatus, linking the swim bladder and the organ of hearing. These probably act as an accessory to the inner ear by accentuating sound waves, but in what way is not fully understood.

There are more species in this family than in any other. They are found in many types of habitat and are able to exploit several different sources of food. In the upper reaches of our streams, that are the head-waters of the large lowland rivers, the gradient is steep and the current fast. This is the domain of the trout and the cyprinids are not usually represented, but sometimes there are Minnows, *Phoxinus phoxinus*, p. 322, in these streams, although they are more characteristic of the region lower down where the gradient is less steep and the current less rapid. They are also found round the margins of lakes and the smaller lowland rivers, where the water is well oxygenated, clear and cool. Minnows rarely grow to more than 4 inches (10·2 cm.) and they have a golden sheen with a stripe or blotches on the flanks, the back being an olive-greenish brown. They spawn in the spring in gravelly places where they congregate in large numbers. Some of those that live in lakes and tarns spawn on the shore; others migrate into the inflowing streams. The small eggs, which stick to the gravel after falling between the stones, hatch in a few days. After one year the Minnows may have reached 1½ inches (3·8 cm.) long and in six years they will have grown to about 4½ inches (11·4 cm.). Some mature after one year but others do not spawn until their second year.

Minnows feed mostly on water fleas and other crustaceans, as well as on insect larvae. They are in turn preyed upon by pike, eels, fish-eating birds, and large perch and trout, as well as by aquatic mammals. They form an important link in the food chain from invertebrates to higher animals.

Another cyprinid of fast-running water is the Barbel, *Barbus barbus*, but it is only locally common in a few British rivers, including some tributaries of the Thames, the Severn, the Trent and the Hampshire Avon and Stour. It grows to a large size and fish of about 30 inches (76 cm.) in length are often caught. The British rod-caught record weighed 11 lb 6 oz (5·1 kg.). Barbel are muddy coloured on the back with a yellowish glint on the sides. The long pointed head has four barbels, one at each corner of the mouth and a pair at the tip of the snout. The dorsal fin is short and the tail fin has a longer upper lobe and more rounded lower lobe.

A more common cyprinid of clear running water is the Dace, *Leuciscus leuciscus*, p. 322. It is a lively shoaling fish of up to 10 inches (25·4 cm.) in length that is most often noticed suddenly as a flash of silver as the shoal turns, or a fish breaks the surface. Its back is greenish blue and the rest of the slim body silvery. The mouth is small. Dace are found through most of England outside Cornwall. They are absent from Wales and Scotland, and are only present in the Blackwater River in Ireland.

Dace eat a considerable amount of vegetable matter, as well as snails, freshwater shrimps and drifting insects. They spawn from March to May, after a short upstream migration. The young grow fast and by two years old average 6 inches (15 cm.) in length. They are a popular fish for angling.

The Chub, Bleak and Gudgeon are other cyprinids of running water. Chub, *Leuciscus cephalus*, grow to 2 feet (61 cm.) in length, are gregarious when young, but solitary when older. At this later stage they may sometimes be seen from the bank or a bridge lying motionless by an obstruction or tree root. They are found throughout England, other than Cornwall, but not in Wales, Scotland or Ireland. Chub can be recognized by their powerful body, grey or dark green back shading to silvery sides with a metallic sheen.

The Bleak, *Alburnus alburnus*, is very silvery and grows to 8 inches (20 cm.). It is found throughout England but not in Cornwall. The silvery material of the scales is used in making artificial pearls. The Bleak, slim of body, greenish blue above and silvery below, feeds mainly on water fleas and insect larvae. It lives in enormous shoals near the surface.

The Gudgeon, *Gobio gobio*, p. 322, is a small version of the Barbel growing to 6 inches (15 cm.), but with a row of spots on each flank and only two barbels. It is bottom living. Large shoals keep to stony and gravelly places and deep pools. The sticky eggs adhere to the gravel after they have been spawned in May or June. Gudgeon, found in central and eastern England and scattered in Ireland, eat some vegetable matter, but mainly the larvae of mayflies, caddis and midges as well as freshwater shrimps and other bottom-living animals.

As the rivers grow larger and descend to the lowlands, the gradient is more gentle and the current becomes less. In these situations, and in slowly flowing ditches and canals, as well as in ponds and weedy lakes, are found two other cyprinids, the Roach, *Rutilus rutilus*, p. 322, and the Rudd, *Scardinius erythrophthalmus*, often associated with Perch, Pike and Eels.

The Roach is common in central and eastern England, but is not found in Cornwall, Wales or western Scotland. In Ireland it is at present restricted to the rivers Blackwater and Foyle, but may be expected to spread. It is olive-green above, shading to cream on the belly, and the whole fish has a metallic bronze sheen. The fins are pinkish and the eyes are red.

Roach spawn in April or May among vegetation, with considerable commotion. The straw-coloured eggs are sticky and get caught on the leaves of the vegetation, hatching about ten days later. The small larvae hang from the leaves of water plants for a few days. The growth is very variable. In some waters Roach reach $5\frac{1}{2}$ inches (14 cm.) in three years whereas in other localities they take five years to grow to this size. The females sometimes mature at three years, more usually at four, the males maturing earlier. The food includes vegetable matter as well as the larvae of midges, caddis, water beetles and other insects, freshwater shrimps, slaters and snails. Roach are much sought after by anglers.

The Rudd is very similar to the roach but has two rows of pharyngeal teeth instead of one and the dorsal fin is behind the vertical line above the pelvic fins. Rudd are restricted to south and east England and part of the Midlands, but are much commoner than Roach in Ireland.

Finally, the rivers reach the flat lowlands where they are very slow flowing and meander with many ox-bow lakes and backwaters. Here the cyprinids are the Tench, Carp, Crucian carp, Common bream and White bream. These are also found in still and stagnant ponds, lakes and canals, particularly where there is much weed and little oxygen.

In the upland streams the riffles and continuous flow keep the water well oxygenated. In these fast-flowing Trout waters the fat and lethargic Tench and Carp would get washed away, but in the lowland rivers and ponds which are inhabited by these cyprinids, Trout would succumb from lack of oxygen. They begin to suffer if there is less than about 7 mg. of oxygen per litre of water, whereas Tench and Carp often make temporary visits to feed on a bottom where there may be a complete deficiency of oxygen. They can live continuously in water containing ten times less oxygen than Trout can. These are the conditions often met with at the bottoms of very rich stagnant ponds and rivers, and here the hump-backed shape of these fish is not the disadvantage it would be in a highland stream.

The Tench, *Tinca tinca*, grows up to 2 feet (61 cm.) and is very thick set, with a dark olive-green back and lighter sides with a slight golden glint. The rounded fins are dark, and there is a short barbel on each corner of the mouth. The scales are small and the skin is very slimy. Shoals of Tench spawn in early summer from May to July and the eggs are small and stick to aquatic plants. The small larvae remain in the vegetation for some time and at this stage they eat algae. Later the Tench move to deeper water and feed on insect larvae, crustaceans and snails which they get by rooting about on the bottom. They are widespread through eastern England but scattered through the south and Midlands, and also in Ireland. They are absent from northern England, Cornwall, Wales and Scotland.

Common carp, *Cyprinus carpio*, p. 322, have four barbels, two at each corner of the mouth. Their upper parts are muddy green and their flanks have a bronze sheen. The dorsal fin is long and concave. They root about on the bottom for midge larvae, snails and crustaceans, as well as bits of vegetable matter and they take in a good deal of indigestible mud.

Sticky eggs are spawned on to submerged plants in May or June. The wild fish grow to about 20 inches (51 cm.) and live to 15 years of age, but pond fishes are said to live to 40 or more.

Carp can withstand stagnant conditions better than any other of our fish. They are found in slow-running rivers, lakes, ponds and backwaters where the water is relatively warm and there is plenty of weed. They have been naturalized since their introduction at least as far back as the mid-thirteenth century. On the Continent carp have been domesticated and cultivated for the table. As in other domesticated animals, special breeds have been selected and with carp these have become more hump-backed and almost free of scales. The different varieties are called Mirror and Leather carp. The former have one or two rows of large scales along the flanks and small scales at the bases of the fins, the rest of the skin being naked. Leather carp have a thick roughened skin and no scales.

The Crucian carp, *Carassius carassius*, is

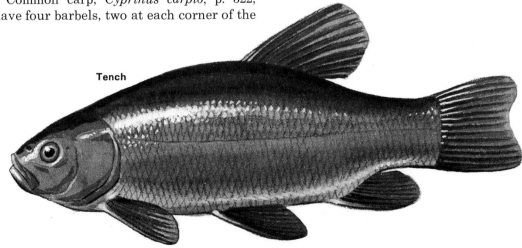

Tench

much smaller than the common species and is usually found at about 10 inches (25 cm.). It can be distinguished from the Common carp by its convex dorsal fin. The back is a brownish green and there is a brassy sheen on the sides. In eastern Europe it is extensively kept in fish ponds for food. Although it has been widely introduced into Britain, from the Continent, it is found mainly in the southern and eastern counties.

Both the Bream and Silver bream have

Common bream

shorter dorsal fins than the carps. The Bream, *Abramis brama*, is found in slowly flowing or stagnant waters throughout most of England, Ireland and southern Scotland, but is absent from Cornwall and Wales. It has a flattened hump-backed body and grows to 20 inches (51 cm.) and 7 lb (3·2 kg.) or more weight. It is a very popular sport fish.

The Silver bream, *Blicca bjoerkna*, is very much smaller. It averages 9 inches (23 cm.) in length and 1 lb (0·45 kg.) weight. It is found mainly in East Anglia, Lincolnshire and south Yorkshire in slowly flowing water, lakes, ponds and canals.

Lastly there are three species of cyprinids which were originally introduced to Britain as aquarium or ornamental pond fish.

The Goldfish, *Carassius auratus*, is known

to everyone. It originated in China, Formosa and Japan and was brought to Britain in about 1691. The highly coloured strains are unlikely to survive in the wild, but some have reverted to their natural brownish-green colours.

The Ide or Silver Orfe, *Leuciscus idus*, is another ornamental pond fish which has escaped and often causes considerable confusion when it is caught. Another continental introduction it is generally silvery with a greyish back and red fins, but there is also a golden orange variety. They may grow up to 30 inches (76 cm.) but are usually much smaller.

The Bitterling, *Rhodeus sericeus*, introduced from Europe, which has become naturalized in a few ponds in Lancashire and Cheshire, has a most remarkable life history. The female grows a long thin tube which is generally believed to be the ovipositor

through which she lays her eggs, but this has recently been disputed. However, it is universally agreed that the eggs are laid into the gill cavity of a freshwater mussel. The male sheds his sperm near the mussel's ingoing respiratory current and the eggs are fertilized, grow and hatch inside the mussel. The young do not leave their shelter until they are able to fend for themselves.

The loaches belong to a different family, the Cobitidae. The Stone loach, *Noemacheilus*

Shore marine fish (*from top to bottom*):
Lesser sandeel; Ballan wrasse; Three-bearded rockling; Dragonet; Lumpsucker

barbatulus, p. 323, is common in running water throughout England – other than Cornwall, Wales, Ireland and southern Scotland. It grows to 5 inches (12·7 cm.) in length and has four barbels round the mouth. The Spined loach, *Cobitis taenia*, is about the same length but has six very small barbels, 10 to 20 round blotches on the flanks and a short spine beneath each eye. It is only found in eastern England from the Thames to Yorkshire.

The European Wels, *Silurus glanis*, has been introduced into some lakes and grows over 16 feet (5 m.) in length in some countries. It is a voracious predator and could become a terrible pest.

The Common eel, *Anguilla anguilla*, p. 323, has a very widespread distribution on rocky sea-shores and throughout the British Isles in fresh water, and is able to withstand an amazing amount of pollution. It probably lives in situations more uncongenial to fish than any other species can tolerate.

Eels first appear off our coasts as long thin creatures that are completely transparent except for their eyes. These are called 'glass eels' and they move inshore where they become pigmented and are known as elvers. Some remain living on the rocky shores but most migrate up rivers and streams in April and May, to take up life in fresh water. Small eels inhabit ditches and streams and larger ones are found in ponds, rivers, canals and lakes. Their length of stay in fresh water is variable; the males are about eight to ten, and the females 10 to 18 years old when they migrate back to sea. There are also differences between the sexes in the size of mature eels. The males are from 14 to 17 inches (36–43 cm.) long and the females from 18 to 36 inches (46–91 cm.). The maximum size of an eel is around 54 inches (137 cm.).

While they are in fresh water eels are a muddy olive-green above, and a yellowish-cream colour below, but during the summer before they migrate their backs become black

Deep-water marine fish (*from top to bottom*): Herring; Mackerel; Cod; Haddock; John Dory

and the yellow is replaced by a silvery sheen. These colour differences are accompanied by internal changes. The intestines begin to atrophy, the roes begin to develop and the eyes enlarge. In late summer and autumn they migrate down to the sea and are never seen again. It is presumed that they migrate 3,000 or 4,000 miles (4,800–6,400 km.) across the Atlantic to south of Bermuda, spawn and die. Here the floating eggs appear and the movement of the larvae that hatch out has been followed in the North Atlantic Drift across to Europe. The larval eel is a very thin leaf-like creature called a leptocephalus larva and it takes two or three years to reach the European shores, by which time it is 3 inches (7·5 cm) long. When it changes into a glass eel it actually shrinks, not only in weight but also slightly in length.

The eel larva was first found in 1856. It was believed to be a distinct species and was given the name *Leptocephalus brevirostris*. Forty years later, two Italian scientists kept some of these larvae in an aquarium and saw them change into glass eels. Only then was their true nature revealed. The original generic name, by now familiar to all who have studied fish, became anglicized. Leptocephalus larvae have very large teeth which are shed at metamorphosis and they feed on various kinds of zooplankton. Eels living on the shore are reported as having eaten crustaceans. The food of freshwater eels has been much better studied and found to consist of bottom-living invertebrates such as insect larvae and molluscs. Large eels eat dead and dying fish and also bullheads, stone loach and other bottom-living fish.

The Conger eel, *Conger conger*, is a wholly marine species which grows to a maximum of 15 feet (4·6 m.) but usually only to 5 feet (1·5 m.). It is found all round the British Isles on rocky shores and the large specimens are found on rough ground farther offshore. The conger has a shorter lower jaw than the common eel and is muddy brown above and cream on the belly. Congers spawn near the Azores and the young are leptocephali very similar to those of the common eel.

The pipefishes and related Sea horse have a unique breeding behaviour. The eggs from the female pass down a tube to the male for safe keeping. In the Oceanic pipefish, *Entelurus aequoreus*, 8 inches (20 cm.) long, the Straight-nosed pipefish, *Nerophis ophidion*, 11 inches (28 cm.) long, and the much commoner Worm pipefish, *N. lumbriciformis*, 5 inches (13 cm.) long, the eggs are kept by the male on the underside of the body in a shallow groove. In the *Syngnathus* species, a foot to 18 inches (30–46 cm.) long, the Broad-nosed pipefish, *S. typhle*, the Lesser pipefish, *S. rostellatus*, and the much commoner Great pipefish, *S. acus*, the eggs are passed into a special pouch on the belly of the male. They are incubated and hatch in this pouch and the young sometimes return to it when danger threatens.

The *Syngnathus* species have pectoral and anal fins; these are absent in *Nerophis*. Pipefishes are commonest in eel grass (*Zostera*) and among seaweed on rocky shores. The *Syngnathus* pipefishes have marked rings and ridges on the body but these are less conspicuous on *Nerophis*.

The well-known Sea horse, *Hippocampus ramulosus*, is a rare visitor to our southwestern and south coasts, coming up from the Bay of Biscay. It swims with the body vertical, and is 3–4 inches (7·5–10 cm.) long, half this being a prehensile tail with which the fish can anchor itself among seaweeds. It looks like an animated chessman, has its eyes on turrets and can move them independently like a chameleon and has the further peculiarity that the male bears the young. In the breeding season the female places her eggs, using a long ovipositor, inside the pouch on the belly of the male. There they are fertilized and hatched. The baby fishes which are miniatures of their parents are born one or two at a time, the male ejecting them from the pouch by convulsive movements of his body.

The cod family includes many of the economically most important sea fish landed at British ports. It is a very large family and embraces some rare British fish as well as

Great pipefish (*left*)

Sea horse (*right*)

some of the commonest. The different species have come to exploit different niches in the marine environment; for example Whiting and Hake feed in mid-water; Cod and Haddock feed on the bottom, and among the rocklings some live in deep water and others are shore fish. One British member of the family lives in fresh water. One group of fish in this family has three dorsal and two anal fins, and the well-known Cod is an example.

The Cod, *Gadus morhua*, p. 334, is very variable in colour. Most individuals are brownish green or yellow, but others, usually small ones from inshore, are distinctly red. The back and sides have reddish-brown spots and the lateral line is light. There is a small barbel on the chin.

In the North Sea Cod breed from February to April, particularly in the northern area of the Great Fisher Bank. Other spawning areas are scattered widely over the Continental Shelf and the floating eggs are often found in the plankton. Cod eggs are spherical, 1·1 to 1·6 mm. in diameter, and have a small oil globule. They hatch in 10 to 14 days depending on the water temperature. For three weeks the larvae subsist on the food in their yolk-sacs. After that they feed on small planktonic crustaceans. Young Cod are very often abundant inshore where they feed on amphipods, small shore crabs, hermit crabs and other crustaceans. Large Cod are mainly fish-eaters, and consume haddock, cod, and various small members of the cod family as well as sandeels and herring, but they also eat whelks and *Nephrops* ('Scampi'). The rate of growth is variable from one locality to another, and a Cod 2 feet (61 cm.) in length is often four years old, but may be six or seven. They grow to a large size, but they do not often exceed 50 lb (22·7 kg.).

Cod are found all round Britain and are very often caught by sea anglers, particularly on rocky coasts. They are the most important British fish caught commercially and most of those landed come from the North Sea and off Iceland. The catches from commercial trawlers are over 350,000 tons (356,000 tonnes) annually, and this is well over a third of the total weight of all species in the commercial catches landed in Britain.

The Haddock, *Melanogrammus aeglefinus*, p. 334, is another important commercial species, but whereas the cod is mainly landed in England, the Scottish landings of haddock make up more than half the United Kingdom total.

The colour of the Haddock is dark purplish brown above and silvery grey below with a paler belly. The lateral line is black, and there is a black patch on each shoulder just above the pectoral fin. Haddock are smaller than Cod, and most range up to about 25 inches (64 cm.) but the largest caught off Iceland, was 44 inches (112 cm.) long.

Haddock are found all round Britain, but are not plentiful in the south. They spawn over much of the northern North Sea, and the eggs are very slightly larger than those of the Cod. The early life histories are very similar. Young Haddock when inshore are found more on sand and mud than on rocky ground. Their food consists mainly of marine worms and other bottom-living creatures such as brittlestars and crustaceans. The mouth of the Haddock is small compared with that of other members of the family and they cannot eat large prey.

The growth of this species is fairly fast; they reach about 12 inches (30 cm.) at two years of age, 18 inches (46 cm.) at four, and about 30 inches (76 cm.) when ten years old. The age of Haddock can be told from the scales which lay down 'sclerites' at the margins. The sclerite is the hard outer layer. Those sclerites laid down in winter are close together, and those laid down in summer farther apart, very much like the annual rings in a tree.

The Haddock is one of the most delicious sea fish and is often smoked and eaten as finnan haddock.

The Whiting, *Merlangius merlangus*, is another important species commercially, with a slightly more southern distribution than the previous two species. It inhabits more inshore waters than Cod or Haddock and so is regularly caught by anglers and the small inshore fishing boats. Its upper parts are a muddy green, the sides and belly silvery white with a brassy sheen. There is a black spot at the base of the pectoral fin.

The Whiting has a more stream-lined body than have Cod or Haddock, and this is connected with living more in mid-water than near the bottom. Young Whiting eat plankton and even when larger they continue to feed on mid-water organisms such as euphausid shrimps, sprats, sandeels and small members of the cod family. Whiting, which feed mostly in daylight, also eat some prawns and crabs.

Spawning takes place mainly in March and April. The young Whiting are very often seen close inshore round piers and they associate with the stinging jellyfish *Cyanea*. They swim around and under the jellyfish in small shoals and take shelter among the tentacles. It is possible that they have some immunity from its stings.

Whiting are smaller than Cod or Haddock and very rarely exceed 24 inches (61 cm.) in length. They have a delicate flavour and are often filleted and marinaded.

The Pollack or Lythe, *Pollachius pollachius*, and the Saithe or Coal fish, *P. virens*, are often confused. The Pollack has a more protruding jaw, larger eye, and the lateral line is arched over the pectoral fin. Small Saithe have a minute barbel which is absent in large specimens. The Pollack does not have a barbel at any stage of its life. The upper parts of the Pollack are browner than those of the Saithe which tend to be greenish. The Pollack has yellower sides and a dark lateral line; the Saithe has dull silvery grey flanks and a light lateral line.

The Pollack is found all round the British Isles but is commonest in the south and west where it inhabits rocky inshore waters. It grows to a size of 30 to 40 inches (76–102 cm.), but specimens of this size are rare. Small Pollack eat plankton and as they grow larger they begin to turn for food to small fish, and then larger fish. They eat sandeels, sprats, herrings, small members of the cod family and small shore-living wrasses and blennies.

The Saithe is also found all round Britain but is commonest in the north and west. Very large numbers are present throughout the summer among the weeds on rocky shores, and round the piers of most Scottish islands and the mainland. In the past they formed a very important item in the diet of the crofters and were salted down for winter. The commercial importance of Saithe is not great in Britain now though they are sometimes seen for sale in the north.

The food of the Saithe is very similar to that of the Pollack. Saithe grow fast and reach 2 feet (61 cm.) in length in four or five years. Very large specimens approach 4 feet (122 cm.) in length.

The fish in the second group of the cod family have one short dorsal fin and a second longer one, and a single long anal fin. The best known is the Hake, *Merluccius merluccius*, which may grow to a large size and specimens of over 3 feet (91 cm.) in length are often caught. The colour of the upper parts is slate-grey and the rest of the fish is silvery. The Hake has a large head, and the big mouth is black inside and has large teeth.

Hake spawn in about July, mostly in deep water off the west coasts of Ireland and Scotland. The floating eggs and small larvae drift with the prevailing currents to inshore nursery grounds where the young feed first on small drifting crustaceans, and then on krill (euphausids). Large Hake feed by night only, in mid-water, on herrings and mackerel, whiting and other members of the cod family. By day the Hake are near the bottom and they are therefore caught on long lines set in mid-water for the night as well as by trawlers working on the bottom by day.

Hake are a prime fish of considerable economic value and the chief ports where they are landed are Fleetwood and Milford Haven.

Another deep-water fish of moderate economic importance is the Ling, *Molva molva*. It has a barbel on the chin and is a more northern species than the Hake and is larger, growing 4–6 feet (122–183 cm.) long.

Another fish in this group of the cod

Hake

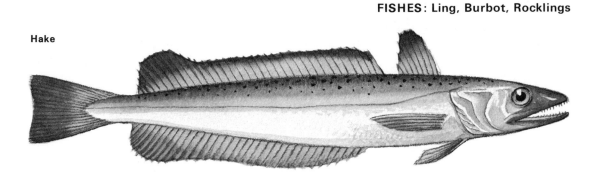

family is the only freshwater representative found in Britain, the Burbot, *Lota lota*. This has a relatively smaller head and smaller eye than the Hake and it has a small barbel on the chin. The sides and upper parts are brown with marbled patterns in the smaller fish, the marblings disappearing later in life. The underparts are paler. Burbot do not grow larger than about 2 feet (61 cm.)

Spawning takes place in winter in shallow water over stones among which the eggs sink. The young fish feed on water slaters and insect larvae and the larger individuals eat perch, ruffe, gudgeon and bullheads.

Burbot used to be found in eastern England in clear rivers from Essex to Yorkshire, but it is now a very rare fish and may possibly be extinct in Britain.

The last group in the cod family is made up of the rocklings. Most of the species so far described are those which either are most commonly seen on the fishmonger's slab, or are regularly caught by sea anglers. The

rocklings that live in deep water are too small to be of any economic importance and those that live on the shore tend to skulk among boulders and seaweed, as well as being too small to interest the angler. However, they are very likely to be found by the inquiring naturalist who looks beneath boulders at low tide.

The Shore rockling, *Gaidropsarus mediterraneus*, has three barbels, two on the snout and one on the chin, and the Five-bearded rockling, *Ciliata mustela*, has two on the upper lip and one on the chin. Both these species are commonly found on rocky shores and in rock pools. The Shore rockling is mostly found in south-western England, Wales and the Irish Sea and only occasionally in northern Scotland. The Five-bearded rockling is a more northern species and is also found on the English east coast.

Both these rocklings are a uniform brown colour, which may sometimes be almost black and sometimes almost red, depending on the fish's background. They eat small shore crabs, gammarids and isopods as well as other invertebrates and small fish.

Ling

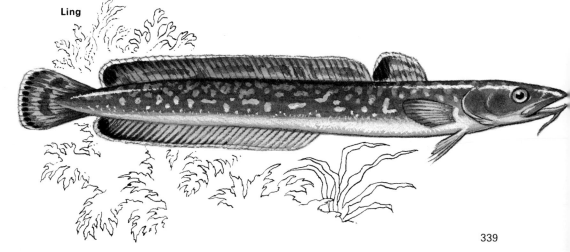

Both these species, and the other rocklings, have the rays of the first dorsal fin (other than the first ray) reduced to a small fringe set in a groove. This fringe keeps up a continuous wave-like motion and draws water along the groove and over taste buds which sense chemical substances in the water ahead.

The Shore and Five-bearded rocklings both breed in winter offshore and the young do not come into the littoral zone until the summer when they are a little over an inch (2·5 mm.) in length.

The two commonest offshore species are the Three-bearded rockling, *Gaidropsarus vulgaris*, p. 333, which is beautifully coloured with brown blotches, and the Four-bearded rockling, *Rhinonemus cimbrius*, which is a sandy brown northern species. These two fish can be identified by their colour and number of barbels.

The Three-bearded species is the largest of the rocklings; it reaches 20 inches (51 cm.) in length whereas the others seldom exceed 10 inches (25 cm.).

The Mackerel, *Scomber scombrus*, p. 334, well known to many holiday-makers, is easily caught and delicious to eat if cooked when really fresh. The brilliant greens and blues on the back, with curved stripes, and a white belly with a metallic sheen, make this one of our most beautiful fish. Mackerel are mid-water feeders on krill, small fish and plankton. Mackerel migrate from the south to our coasts in the summer and the shoals are sometimes enormous. Mackerel grow to about 16 inches (41 cm.).

The John Dory, *Zeus faber*, p. 334, is the most peculiarly shaped of any fish caught by trawlers round our coasts. It is not uncommon round our south-western and western coasts and it is said to be good to eat. It has a high narrow body compressed from side to side, up to $22\frac{1}{2}$ inches (57 cm.) long and 18 lb (8 kg.) weight. The spines of the dorsal fin are continued into long filaments that trail behind and the fish itself is olive or brown with yellow bands. A conspicuous large black spot surrounded by yellow on each side of the body brings the John Dory into that group of fishes, which includes the Haddock, that are said to bear the mark of St Peter's thumb. The name John Dory is said to be from the Italian *Janitore* or door-keeper.

The Bass, *Dicentrarchus labrax*, is another southern marine species which is only rarely

Bass

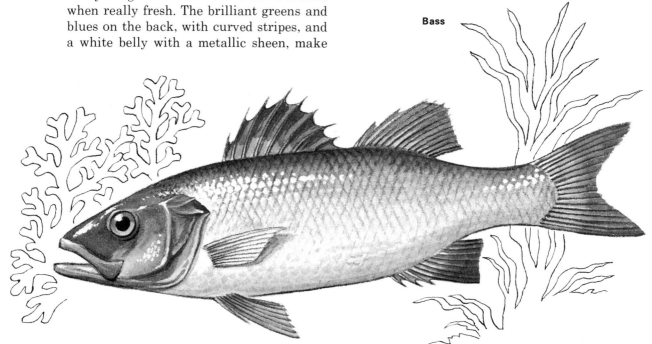

caught as far north as Scotland, but it extends farthest up the west coast. Bass are often found in estuaries, and even in fresh water. Sea anglers think very highly indeed of this species which may weigh up to 18 lb (8 kg.) or more.

The Perch, *Perca fluviatilis*, p. 323, is a handsome freshwater fish, olive-green above, silvery below with a brassy sheen, and a series of black vertical bars on the flanks,

There is, however, a good food supply of crustaceans and bivalves, so when the tide comes in, the fish migrate from below low tide mark. There they can return in due course, when replete.

Apart from small flatfish and the two gobies which are described later, the most typical fish of sandy beaches are the sandeel weever and the dragonet.

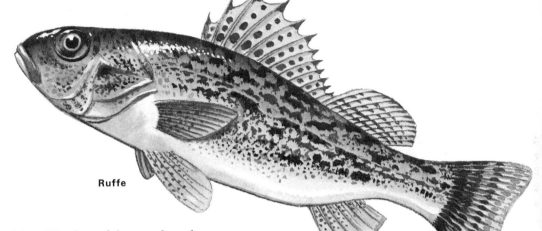

Ruffe

and red paired fins. The first of the two dorsal fins is spiny, and so are the gill covers; Perch must be handled with respect, because the spines draw blood easily.

Perch are common in Britain, apart from the north of Scotland, in pools, lakes, canals and sluggish rivers in the kind of habitat favoured by pike, eels and roach. Spawning takes place from April to June, when sheets of eggs several feet long are laid among weeds.

Perch are caught in enormous numbers by young and old anglers. Some grow to over 5 lb (2·3 kg.) in weight but these are rare and specimens of 1–2 lb (0·45–0·9 kg.) are commoner. Perch live to over 17 years of age.

The Ruffe, *Gymnocephalus cernua*, 10 inches (25 cm.) long, is superficially similar to the Perch, but is less colourful. It is confined to south-east Britain.

When the tide is out there is little shelter for a fish on a sandy or shingle beach and there is little protection from the movement of sand and gravel flung up by the waves.

There are several species of sandeels, but the Lesser sandeel, *Ammodytes tobianus*, p. 333, 7 inches (18 cm.) long, is the commonest on the shore. It is a stiff, long thin fish which burrows into sand at the low tide mark, and can be recognized by its long dorsal and anal fins. Another species sometimes found intertidally is the Greater sandeel, *Hyperoplus lanceolatus*. Larger than the Lesser sandeel it also has a black spot on the side of the snout. The other three species are only found offshore.

The Weever, *Trachinus vipera*, p. 324, 6 inches (15 cm.) long, has a poisonous dorsal spine, and woe betide anyone who steps barefoot on it as it lies buried in the sand. The sting is extremely painful.

The 8-inch (20 cm.) male Dragonet, *Callionymus lyra*, p. 333, is very colourful, but the female is much drabber. During courtship the male displays his blue-striped fins in front of the female. This very marked sexual colour difference is very uncommon among British fish. Dragonets are more often reported from sand in deeper water than near the beach.

Rocky shores provide more cover and food for fish than do sandy beaches, and many more species can be found. They include representatives of offshore fishes as well as those living entirely inshore, among them the rocklings, already mentioned, and sticklebacks.

The wrasses are typical of inshore rocky coasts. They are dumpy colourful fish with a long dorsal fin, the first part of which is spiny. The Rockcook, *Centrolabrus exoletus*, 4–5 inches (10–13 cm.) long, which has five spines on the anal fin, is commonest in Scotland. The Corkwing, *Crenilabrus melops*, and the Goldsinny, *Ctenolabrus rupestris*, both with three anal fin spines, are commonest on western shores. The Goldsinny is an orange-red or brown, and the Corkwing is very variable in colour – both these species tend to be small, up to 6 inches (15 cm.). The Ballan wrasse, *Labrus bergylta*, p. 333, grows to 20 inches (51 cm.), has conspicuous scales,

and is found just offshore, where the much more elongate Cuckoo wrasse, *Labrus mixtus*, is also found.

Many of the fish most commonly found on rocky shores belong to the blenny group. A deep-water representative is the Catfish, *Anarhichas lupus*, which reaches 4 feet (122 cm.) in length. Shore blennies, such as the very common Shanny, *Blennius pholis*, p. 324, are much smaller. The Shanny is usually 4 inches (10 cm.) long, yellow or greenish with dark blotches, and eats barnacles and bivalves which it bites off the rocks with its broad teeth. The Tompot blenny, *Blennius gattorugine*, the largest of our blennies, is found on the west coasts and has a single branched tentacle over each eye, as also has Yarrel's blenny, *Chirolophis ascanii*, $7\frac{1}{2}$ inches (19 cm.) long, but this fish is more elongate. The Butterfish, *Pholis gunnellus*, p. 324, 7 inches (18 cm.) long, is very common, the colour of mustard, with about 12 black spots along the base of the dorsal fin. As with some other blennies, the eggs are guarded by an adult until they hatch. The Viviparous blenny, *Zoarces viviparus*, gives birth to live young which have developed within the body of the female since the eggs were fertilized. This viviparous method of reproduction is rare among fish. The Vivi-

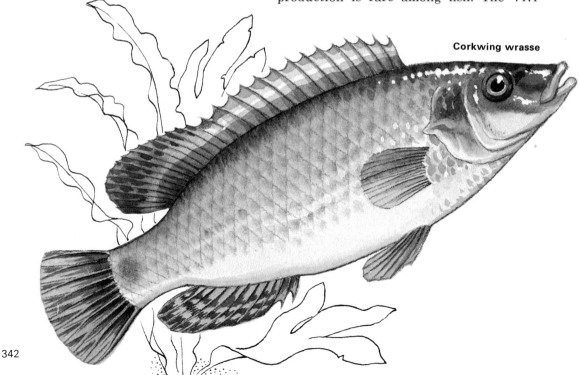

Corkwing wrasse

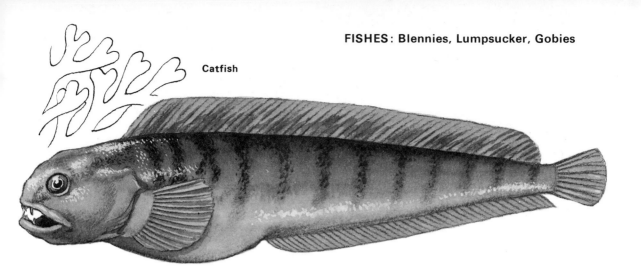

Catfish

parous blenny grows to 2 feet (61 cm.) long and is thin, with a continuous dorsal, tail and anal fin.

It is clearly advantageous to an animal living on a wave-swept shore to be able to cling to the rocks, and in several groups of shore fish the pectoral fins are modified to form suckers.

The Lumpsucker, *Cyclopterus lumpus*, p. 333, has a very powerful sucker indeed. It is a dumpy fish, and has rows of horny plates. Although it grows to 2 feet (61 cm.), usually only 2 to 4 inch (5–10 cm.) specimens are found on the shore. The eggs are laid close inshore and are guarded by the male. The much smaller Montagu's sea-snail, *Liparis liparis*, also has a powerful sucker.

The commonest of the four species of cling-fish is *Lepadogaster lepadogaster*, the Shore cling-fish or Cornish sucker, up to 4 inches (10 cm.). The second is the Two-spotted

sucker, *Diplecogaster bimaculata*, which does not exceed 2 inches (5 cm.) in length. In these fish the relatively large sucker is made up partly of modified bone and partly from fused pelvic fins. It is more complicated, and effective, than the suckers of other shore fish.

In the gobies the sucker is very obviously derived from the pelvic fins, and the fin rays can easily be seen. There are at least 15 British gobies, and some are the most plentiful of our shore fishes. The Sand goby, *Pomatoschistus minutus*, p. 324, and the Common goby, *P. microps*, both up to 3 inches (7.5 cm.) long, are found in shallow pools on sandy and muddy shores. The latter species often penetrates into estuaries with brackish water. The eggs are laid in empty shells and are guarded by the male. The larger Black goby, *Gobius niger*, which grows to 7 inches (18 cm.) is also found in

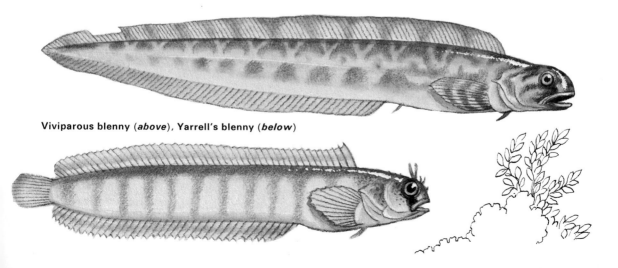

Viviparous blenny (*above*), Yarrell's blenny (*below*)

Montagu's sea-snail

Cornish sucker

estuaries, but the Rock goby, *Gobius paganellus*, is restricted to rocky shores under stones or in rock pools. The Two-spot goby, *Chaparrudo flavescens*, is more often found in shoals off the bottom and swimming among seaweed. The identification of the different gobies is often difficult.

The flatfish are some of the best known and more interesting of British fish. They are well known because of their great economic importance. Not only are large numbers landed at our ports, but also the quality of some, such as the Dover sole and Halibut, is very high indeed.

Much of their interest lies in their remarkable adaptation to a bottom-living existence. Unlike the skates, flatfish have taken to the bottom by lying on their sides. The eye which would otherwise be pressed against the sea floor, moves over when the flatfish first takes to the bottom, so that it comes to be on the same side as the upper eye and some stages

of this migration of the eye in plaice are illustrated. The movement of the eye is brought about by a remarkable twist of the skull, and leads to a twist of the nerves to the eye and an asymmetrical mouth with stronger teeth on one side than on the other. Associated differences between the two sides of the flatfish are found in the size of the fins and skin colour which on the lower side is usually white and only the upper side being pigmented.

Most species of flatfish almost invariably lie on their left sides, but others are nearly always on their right sides. One or two

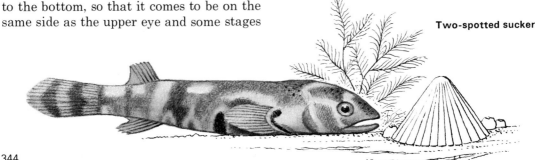

Two-spotted sucker

species, particularly the Flounder, are fairly often found lying on the 'wrong' side, but usually there are very few of these variants.

The twist of the skull which facilitates the bottom-living existence, does not appear to have led to any lack of adaptability. There are numerous species, and they inhabit all kinds of marine and estuarine bottom habitats at a variety of depths and from the Arctic to the tropics. Most species, however, are limited to finding their food on the bottom, though the Halibut does appear to catch some food in mid-water.

The Plaice, *Pleuronectes platessa*, p. 351, is the best known of the flatfish and even if it has not the exceptional flavour of the Turbot, Dover sole or Halibut, it is one of our tastiest sea fish. Large numbers, amounting to over 3,500 tons (3,560 tonnes), are sold annually in Britain; Lowestoft, Grimsby, Fleetwood and Aberdeen are the main ports where this species is landed. The most important Plaice fishery grounds are in the North Sea.

Plaice lie on their left sides and the right (upper) side is a reddish mottled brown, with bright orange or red spots which extend on to the fins, and a few white ones on the body only. The left (under) side is pure white. The scales are smooth, and this means that the body is not rough as in some other flatfish. The lateral line has only a slight curve by the pectoral fin. Plaice grow to a length of over 2 feet (61 cm.), but most areas are so heavily fished that there is little chance of many specimens reaching this size.

Spawning takes place from December to late February and one of the largest areas is in the southern North Sea. The fertilized eggs float in the surface water and hatch after nearly three weeks. The larvae at first subsist on the remains of their yolk, but soon begin to feed on minute planktonic plants and animals. As the larvae grow they remain symmetrical with an eye on each side. However, after about three weeks they begin to metamorphose into the adult form. The shape of the body changes and becomes more oval and the whole skull becomes twisted

so that the left eye appears to move over the top of the head on to the right side. Stages of this metamorphosis are illustrated. Usually when this stage is complete the young have drifted over the nursery grounds and they go to the bottom as little Plaice barely three-quarters of an inch (19 mm.) long. Here they feed on small crustaceans, worms and other bottom invertebrates. These young Plaice are often found very close inshore on sandy beaches and may be trapped in shallow pools by the retreating tide. They stay close inshore for the summer, and migrate to progressively deeper water as they grow older.

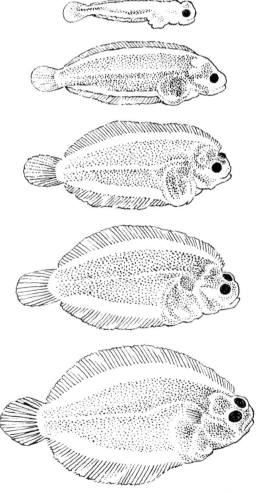

Development of Plaice showing migration of the left eye to the right side

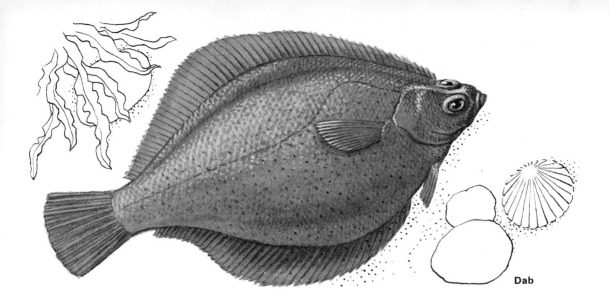

Dab

The age of Plaice can be determined from rings laid down in the otolith, or ear stone. By the time they are four years old, they will have grown to about 10 inches (25 cm.); after eight years they are about 15 inches (38 cm.); and they reach 2 feet (61 cm.) in length at 20 years old, but the growth rate differs in different localities.

Adult Plaice feed to a large extent on mussels, cockles and other bivalves, as well as worms and crustaceans.

Plaice are found all round the British Isles and are most common in the North Sea. They prefer a sandy bottom but are also found on muddy gravel. They do not penetrate far into the fresher water of estuaries.

The life history of the Plaice, as briefly outlined above, is typical of most flatfish, and it is only necessary to emphasize the differences in other species.

The Dab, *Limanda limanda*, is a distinct species from the Plaice and Flounder, though small Plaice are often loosely called dabs. The Dab can be distinguished from the Plaice by rubbing a finger from the tail to the head; Dabs feel very rough owing to each scale being finely toothed, whereas Plaice feel smooth. The lateral line of the Dab has a very pronounced curve by the pectoral fin, whereas it has only a slight bend in Plaice.

Most Dabs are lighter coloured than Plaice and the spots are yellower, smaller and sometimes even absent. Dabs never grow to the large size that Plaice attain and one over 12 inches (30 cm.) is exceptionally long.

The Dab is extremely abundant and often caught on sandy inshore banks, or in a few feet of water in sandy bays. Dabs breed in March and April and the stages of metamorphosis are similar to those of the Plaice. Their food is more varied than that of Plaice and includes more worms and crustaceans, and fewer bivalve molluscs. The rate of growth is slow; Dabs reach about 7 inches (18 cm.) when four years old and 9 inches (23 cm.) after eight years.

The Flounder, *Platichthys flesus*, is also often confused with Plaice and the name Flounder is often loosely used for any flatfish. The character that distinguishes Flounders from Plaice is that they have three rows of sharp spines, at the base of each 'side' fin (which are, of course, the dorsal and anal fins) and another row down the lateral line. The skin in between these rows of spines is smooth and not rough as in the Dab.

The Flounder, up to a foot (30 cm.) long, is much greener than the other two species; the upper side is a marbled olive-green and the underside sometimes has brownish patches, but is most often completely white. Flounders usually lie on their left sides, but specimens on their right sides are much commoner than in the other species.

Spawning takes place offshore in March and April and the eggs are small. The stages of metamorphosis are very similar to those of the Plaice. The young Flounders after they have settled on the bottom, move into estuaries and then penetrate far into fresh water where they may remain throughout adolescence for two or three years, by which time they are 5 inches (13 cm.) long in the case of males and 7 inches (18 cm.) in females. Flounders always migrate back to the sea to spawn. The distance they move inland is remarkable, but they cannot negotiate waterfalls and similar obstructions.

In fresh water they feed on insect larvae, worms and crustaceans, and in the sea they feed on bivalve molluscs, marine worms, crustaceans and small shore crabs.

Flounders are found all round the British coasts, most plentifully in estuaries. Their flesh is not as well flavoured as the Plaice or Dab.

The Lemon sole, *Microstomus kitt*, also lies on its left side, and is more oval than the previous species. It has a small mouth. The body is very smooth and marbled, with brown, orange, yellow and green markings. The Lemon sole is not a true sole but belongs to the plaice family. It is a more northern and offshore species and has a very good flavour. It grows up to 20 inches (51 cm.) long.

The Halibut, *Hippoglossus hippoglossus*, is the largest British flatfish. It grows to about 9 feet (2·7 m.) in length and 700 lb (318 kg.) in weight. It is mainly fished for with long lines on offshore banks in northern waters.

There are several species of true soles, most of which are rare. They live on their left sides and have a very characteristic elongated oval shape. The Dover sole, *Solea solea*, p. 351, the only one we need consider, grows to a little over 18 inches (46 cm.) in length. It is found most commonly round the southern half of England. Its food consists mainly of worms and some crustaceans and bivalves.

The Turbot, *Scophthalmus maximus*, is an example of those flatfish which lie on their right sides, and the eye moves to the upper left side. It is a large round flatfish, reaching 30 inches (76 cm.) in length.

There are three similar species of grey mullets, which, unless they can be compared one with another at the same time, are often difficult for the general naturalist to distinguish. The commonest is the Thick-lipped grey mullet, *Crenimugil labrosus*. When disturbed mullet usually swim powerfully in shoals, but at other times they laze near the surface. The body colour is silvery, with longitudinal grey stripes. The Golden grey mullet, *Liza auratus*, has a golden sheen on the sides. The Thin-lipped grey mullet, *L. ramada*, has a narrower upper lip. All species

Turbot

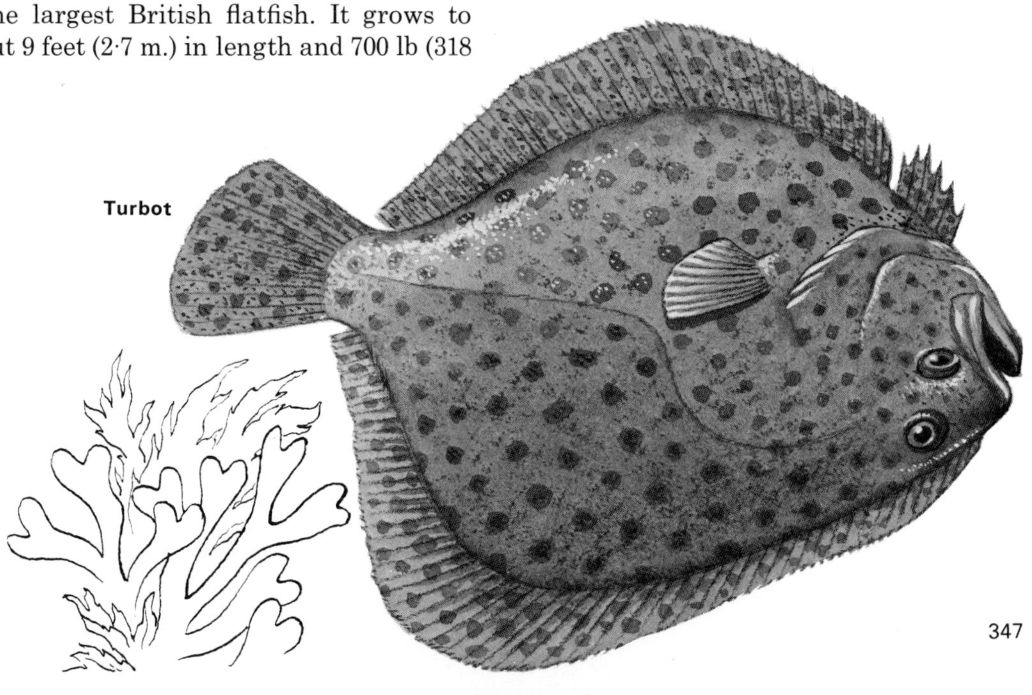

347

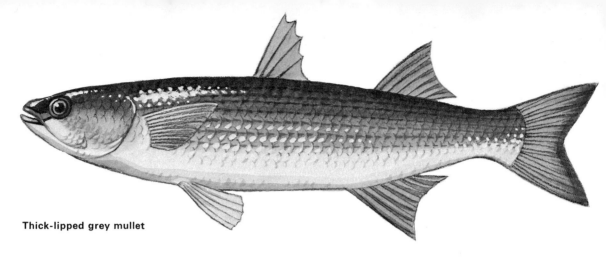

Thick-lipped grey mullet

of grey mullet grow to over 3 feet (91 cm.) in length and come to inshore waters in the spring and then into estuaries and even fresh water in summer. They are mainly herbivorous and eat green algae.

There are two common marine bullheads, the Short-spined sea scorpion, *Myoxocephalus scorpius*, p. 324, and the Long-spined sea scorpion, *Taurulus bubalis*, and one freshwater species, the Bullhead or Miller's Thumb, *Cottus gobio*, p. 323. These species are superficially similar, each having a large mouth, spiny head and obviously bottom-living habit. The eggs, after being laid under a stone or in a shell, are guarded by the male. The Long-spined sea scorpion is 6–9 inches (15–23 cm.) long, the Short-spined slightly larger.

There is also the Armed bullhead or Pogge, *Agonus cataphractus*, which grows to about 4 inches (10 cm.). This a common but very local fish on the east coast which migrates to the shore in winter.

Of the five species of gurnard, the Grey gurnard, *Eutrigla gurnardus*, up to 18 inches (46 cm.) is the commonest. These lethargic fish have three pectoral fin rays modified as 'feelers' which are used for finding food. Bony plates on the large angular head give the gurnards an armour-plated look.

The Three-spined stickleback, *Gasterosteus aculeatus*, p. 323, usually under $2\frac{1}{2}$ inches (63 mm.) long, is extremely familiar and abundant in lowland fresh waters everywhere, and is also found in brackish water and rock pools. The dorsal fin has three separate strong spines. The back is dark and the sides are silvery, and in spring,

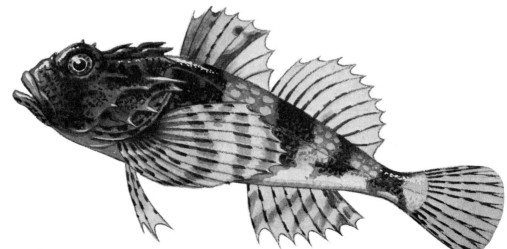

Long-spined sea scorpion

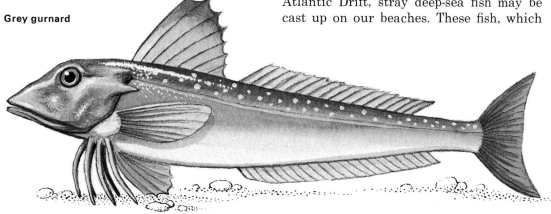

Armed bullhead

at spawning time, the male develops a brilliant red belly and throat. He establishes, and pugnaciously defends, a territory in which he makes a nest out of plant material stuck together with a secretion from his kidneys. The nest is always situated on the bottom, usually in a depression in sand. A female is enticed into the nest to lay her eggs, and several females lay in the same nest. The male guards the nest and aerates the eggs with his pectoral fins until they hatch.

The Ten-spined stickleback, *Pungitius pungitius*, is less common, and is absent from the north and west. It has 7 to 12 (but usually 10) dorsal spines, and the breeding dress of the male is black. The nest is always built off the bottom.

The Fifteen-spined stickleback, *Spinachia spinachia*, p. 324, has a long thin body. It is wholly marine, and is found inshore, particularly where there is plenty of weed. It grows to 6 inches (15 cm.) in length.

The Angler fish, *Lophius piscatorius*, p. 351, is one of the most interesting British fish. It

is a loose-skinned, slightly flattened, bottom-living creature, 3 to 5 feet (91–152 cm.) long, with an enormous head, and broad mouth. There are two rays on the head, the first of which has a fleshy end that is used to lure prey within range of the large mouth and curved teeth – hence the English name for this species. Very many different kinds of fish are eaten.

The body is a mottled and blotchy brown, and has a fringe of skin flaps which break up its outline, so that when it has settled into position on the sea bed it is extremely well camouflaged and almost invisible.

Spawning takes place in very deep water off the edge of the Continental Shelf. The eggs are in the form of a ribbon up to 30 feet (9 m.) long.

In the Introduction, where the origins of the British fish fauna were discussed, it was pointed out that because the coasts of these islands are washed by the North Atlantic Drift, stray deep-sea fish may be cast up on our beaches. These fish, which

Grey gurnard

normally inhabit the great depths, often have a very bizarre appearance. An example of one of them is the Hatchet fish, *Argyropelecus olfersi*, which had been chosen, not because it mouth; many deep-sea fish have huge mouths and some can swallow prey as large as themselves. Most characteristic of all, however, are the 12 pairs of light organs along

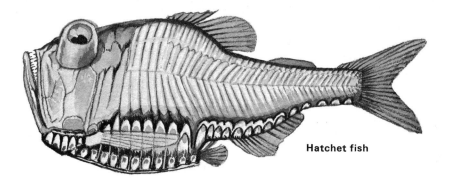

Hatchet fish

is the commonest but because it shows many characteristics of deep-sea fish. Firstly it is small, under 3 inches (7·5 cm.), and few deep-water fish exceed 6 inches (15 cm.). It has a large highly sensitive eye, which one might expect in a creature inhabiting the twilight regions in deep water. It has a very large the belly. These shine very brightly when the fish is alive in its natural habitat. Very many deep-sea fish have luminous organs and they may well help the different species to recognize each other, and may also play an important part in courtship and recognition of the sexes in the inky depths.

**Deep-water marine fish (*from top to bottom*):
Thornback ray; Lesser spotted dogfish; Dover sole;
Plaice (*left*), and Angler (*right*)**

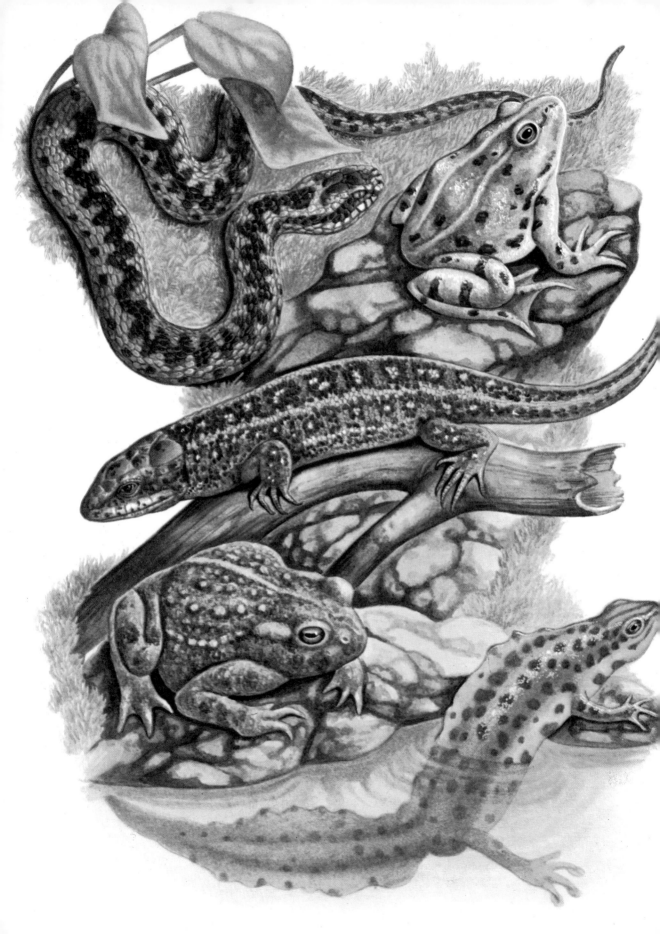

Amphibians and Reptiles

Amphibians and reptiles are two of the five classes of vertebrate or backboned animals which are usually taken together as a single study, called Herpetology (from Greek *herpeton* – a crawling thing). Even so, they have little in common apart from a backbone and a cold-blooded nature.

In the story of Evolution the amphibians came first, and arose from fish ancestors during the Devonian Period, some 300 million years ago. This was achieved by a slow process of change, in which certain types of fishes replaced their paired fins with walking limbs, at the same time developing lungs. With these two aids they were able to emerge on to land and to colonize the Coal Age swamps during the Carboniferous Period which followed.

This transition from water to land is reflected in the life story of today's amphibians, such as our well-known frog. Hatching from an egg laid in water, it grows up as a water baby called a tadpole, which has fish-like qualities such as gills and a swimming tail. Then by a change-over or metamorphosis, it turns into a lung-breathing land creature with limbs, that is, a frog. This is typical of the class Amphibia, a name implying a double existence (Greek *amphi* – both, and *bios* – a life).

Amphibians have soft and unprotected bodies, so tend to lurk in damp and shady places away from sun and dry atmosphere, also numerous enemies. Many are nocturnal. A nearness to water is necessary because the pond or ditch is the nursery for their young. The jelly-like coating to an amphibian's eggs, as in frog-spawn, is protection against damage or attack, and maybe also to hold in

Adder, Edible frog, Sand lizard, Natterjack, all life-size, and a male Smooth newt, twice life-size to show markings

the warmth from the sun's rays. The actual food-supply for the developing tadpole is in the egg itself.

A further step in evolution, an important one, occurred when the first reptiles made their appearance. By covering their eggs with a protective shell they were able to lay them on land. By this means reptiles can ignore the fixed ponds to which the amphibians must resort. Instead, they make their own 'private ponds', so to speak – inside each shell-egg. By the time a baby reptile emerges it is already equipped with lungs and limbs, and resembles its parents. This break-away from water gave reptiles the opportunity to spread over the land surface, in what was one of the greatest invasions the world has known – the conquest of the land. From the Permian to the Cretaceous Periods, spanning some 200 million years, the Age of Reptiles flourished, culminating in those famous giants of the past – the Dinosaurs.

Two of the most striking discoveries of fossil reptiles were made near Lyme Regis, in Dorset, in the early nineteenth century. The cliffs between that town and neighbouring Charmouth are particularly rich in fossils. In 1811, Mary Anning, then a girl of 12, found there the first ichthyosaur, a fish-like reptile. Ten years later she found the first plesiosaur, *Plesiosaurus macrocephalus*, a long-necked marine reptile with paddle-like limbs, may be up to 30 feet (9 m.) long. She finally won the triple crown by finding the first flying reptile, a pterodactyl, to be unearthed in Britain.

Today the cold-blooded amphibians and reptiles have given way to the more active warm-blooded birds and mammals, and their numbers have declined. Because of their changeable body temperature most of them live in the warmer tropics, and numbers fall off as one travels north. It was probably due to the extreme cold of the Ice Age that such

The first plesiosaur found; the fossil skeleton of *Plesiosaurus macrocephalus* and an impression of how this reptile may have looked

animals were driven from Great Britain, at a time when the ice-sheet covered most of the country. With a consequent lowering in sea-level a land connection existed across the North Sea. This slowly narrowed as the ice retreated and the melt-water filled the sea. Finally a break with the Continent occurred, probably at the Straits of Dover, about 8,000 years ago. In the interval only a few amphibians and reptiles managed to return before the sea cut off further arrivals.

The British list is disappointingly low to herpetologists. There are only six native species of reptile, and six amphibians with a further two introductions. All of them occur in the south of England, but drop off in species towards the north, and Ireland has least of all. There are no serpents in Ireland, for which St Patrick cannot be blamed – they just never got there in time.

The Common frog, *Rana temporaria*, is our only indigenous frog. It is a northerly species extending across north Europe and Asia as far as Japan, and occurs in most parts of Britain. In Ireland it is found mainly in coastal areas, and may originally have been introduced there. A date given is 1796. The colouring of this familiar amphibian is most variable and not to be relied on, even in individuals, since it changes with surroundings. The darker spots and stripes, however, are constant, helping to camouflage it in the grass and undergrowth. A useful recognition for the species is the dark band which covers the ear-drum just behind the eye. Albino frogs with pink eyes occasionally turn up.

The Common frog spends much of the summer on land, in shady and damp places in long grass, by lanes and field borders, in water ditches and the vicinity of ponds and streams, often in gardens where there happens to be a pond. Breeding occurs in mid March in the south, as late as June in the mountains of Scotland. It is of the 'explosive' kind, that is, the clumps of spawn are laid together in one corner by the entire colony. There is no finesse in courtship. Each male grabs a female from behind, in an embrace called 'amplexus'. During this brief breeding period the dull throbbing croaking of the males can be heard. As a female lays her spawn containing some 4,000 eggs, the male discharges his sperm to fertilize them in the water. The couple then depart, and the pond is soon deserted save for a large mass of spawn. By autumn the frogs are usually back, and many will spend the winter in hibernation on the pond-floor. Very few tadpoles reach adulthood. They form one of the principal food-sources in a pond, and most are eaten. Those that escape and turn into froglets will suddenly appear on land, usually during a rain shower in June, giving the illusion that it has been 'raining frogs'.

Young tadpoles scrape away at plant material with their larval teeth, then as the legs appear turn scavenger, eating any dead animal they encounter. Once the frog stage has been reached only living prey is eaten, by catching it on the tongue and swallowing it whole. In turn the frog may fall victim to an enemy such as the Grass snake, heron, otter or hedgehog.

The noisy Edible frog, *Rana esculenta*, p. 352, is a familiar species in Europe, ranging from Sweden to Italy. It is largely aquatic, and haunts the numerous dikes and canals, especially in the Low Countries. The loud chorus of croaking may be heard from May

A young tadpole, tadpole with hind legs and froglet with tail

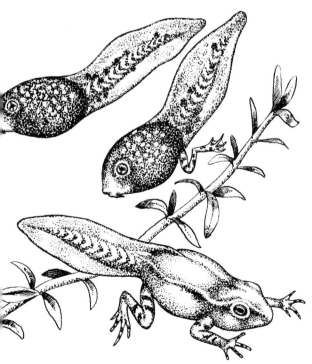

to August, especially in the evening and at night, or after rain. The male blows up vocal sacs at the corners of its jaws, resembling two miniature balloons. General colouring is a bright emerald-green, sometimes brownish or greyish, spotted and striped in black, and a pale stripe running down the back.

Introductions into England started in 1837 when specimens were set free in Foulmire Fen, Cambridgeshire. Later on more were liberated in the Norfolk Broads. Up till the Second World War a flourishing population existed in East Anglia, making the summer nights ring with its cries, so that it earned for itself the name of Cambridgeshire Nightingale. Spawning occurs in May and June, a female laying up to 6,000 straw-coloured eggs in a number of small clumps.

The affectionate name of Froggie which is given to the Frenchman has nothing to do with a continental habit of eating frogs' legs – it was the name which the people of Paris gave to themselves. In the old civic crest of the famous capital are three frogs. The expression 'Qu'en disent les grenouilles?' meaning 'What are the frogs saying?' was directed at themselves. It was a common inquiry when rumours or intrigues were afoot. Apparently the ordinary citizens, i.e. the 'frogs', knew more of what was going on than did the Government circles.

Today the Edible frog of East Anglia has disappeared entirely, but a few may still exist in ponds closer to London, where they were placed some years ago. Even so, the chances of seeing, let alone hearing, this frog are now remote.

More recent, and with better success so far, is the spread of the Marsh frog, *Rana ridibunda*, which arrived in this country to stay in 1935. The late playwright, Percy Smith, set free a few specimens in his pond at his home in Stone-in-Oxney which lies in the middle of the Romney Marsh in Kent. The frogs soon escaped and spread along the ditches and canals of the marsh, a broad and flat expanse of land claimed from the sea. It consists of small fields surrounded by water ditches, and is used in the main for sheep farming. This powerful frog, the largest in Europe, may reach a body length of up to five inches. It prefers larger and more open waters, and ranges from Germany, eastwards to the Urals. Some herpetologists consider it as only a large variation of the Edible frog, rather than a separate species.

Colouring is rather sombre, more of a putty colour marked with black spots and stripes, sometimes suffused with green in the hind parts. The dorsal stripe is missing from the Kent colony. It is much stronger and more aggressive than its cousin, and rival males will fight over the same mate by leaping at one another. A chorus in full blast can be almost deafening, and its popular

movement, poor leapers, there should be little difficulty in telling our frogs and toads apart.

The Common toad, *Bufo bufo*, occurs throughout Europe and north Asia. It is widespread on the British mainland, but absent from Ireland. Toads are less tied to the damper areas, and may turn up far from water outside the mating season. Breeding is explosive, and because colonies usually consist of more males than females there is

A Common frog (*left*) and a Common toad for comparison

name of Laughing frog is well deserved. Spawning is extended from May into July. This British colony appears to be declining in numbers of late, but can still be heard over a wide area of the marshes. All three frogs belong to the typical family Ranidae. Similarly, our two toads belong to the same family Bufonidae. More squat in build, with dry and warty skins, slow and clumsy in

some competition for possession of a mate. Two or three smaller males, seldom more than $2\frac{1}{2}$ inches (6·3 cm.) long, will cling to one female who may be twice as big, a real 'knot of toads'. This kind of gigantism among females is not uncommon in amphibians and reptiles, especially among toads and snakes. During the breeding period the males keep up a lively, high-pitched croaking. Eggs are laid in twin strings, as many as 7,000 by one female.

An interesting feature about Common

toads is their choice of a particular pond in which to spawn. Awaking from hibernation somewhere below ground in a hole or drain, even in cellars in villages, the toads set off on a nightly migration to reach the pond, even ignoring the other ponds on the way. How the particular 'toad pond' is found up to three-quarters of a mile (1·2 km.) away, and why a special pond, is still a puzzle. Some of these migration routes must be very old, existing before some of the roadways even. Where they cross, many toads are run over each spring. In gardens it is noticeable what homely little animals they are, remaining for many weeks, and returning each morning to the same shelter under a stone or inside a flower-pot. Mainly nocturnal, they catch large numbers of insects, etc., of which ants figure highly on the menu. A toad placed on the floor of an infested pantry has been known to clear up the nuisance in no time. This is a real gardener's, and housewife's, ally.

The attractive little Natterjack, p. 352, is now, alas, a rarity. Only a few depleted colonies exist, mainly in sand-dunes and heaths in Norfolk, Hampshire, Dorset and Lancashire. An introduced colony also exists in south-west Ireland. It is very common along the Atlantic coast of Europe. Small and lively, sometimes active by day, it may be recognized by the pale stripe along its back, and the habit of running on its short legs instead of hopping. It tolerates brackish water, and spawning commonly takes place in dune slacks close to the shore. The pleasant trilling of the males on warm summer nights is now seldom heard in the land. Natterjack comes from two Old English words, *nether* for low-lying, and *jack* for a diminutive. This toad is 'a lowly little thing', a rather charming description.

Frogs and toads are members of the Salientia (meaning to leap), and use their webbed hind legs for hopping and swimming. Newts belong to the Caudata, and use their tails for swimming. This word comes from the Old English *eft*. By adding the prefix we get 'an eft'. Running this together, and changing

Common frog

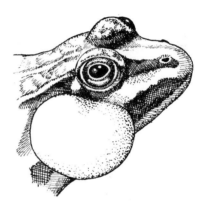

Edible frog

Natterjack

Heads of the Common and Edible frogs and Natterjack showing vocal sacs inflated

A pair of mating toads

the old f to a w, we get a-newt. In other languages these amphibians are called salamanders.

The three British newts are closely related, and have broadly similar habits. Some individuals will hibernate on land, under logs and stones, others remain at the pond-bottom during winter, but in any case they are in the ponds and ditches for the breeding-season, from April until June. Afterwards they may come out on land to spend the summer lurking in undergrowth and catching small animals for food.

The real beauty and grace of a newt is seen in the water as it rises to the surface to gulp down fresh air, or when a male pursues and courts his mate. The males colour up more vividly, and develop a crest along the back and tail. A male will approach a female, probably nudge her with his snout, then suddenly fling himself into a curious stiff pose, the tail curved round and pointing towards the female. Meanwhile the tip vibrates rapidly. One suggested explanation for this is that scent secreted from the excited male is swept in a water current by the vibrating tail towards the female to bring her into a receptive mood. The male then deposits a packet of sperm cells, called a 'spermatophore', on the floor. The female picks this up with the lips of her cloaca, and the sperm cells ascend into her body so as to fertilize the eggs within. Later she will lay them singly on water plants. A leaf is cupped in her hind feet, an egg laid in its sticky capsule on to this and the leaf then folded round the egg to hide it. In time the tiny newt tadpole emerges and goes through a gilled stage, feeding on minute water-life until lungs and limbs are grown, then leaves the water. Occasionally a newt grows in size but fails to develop lungs, remaining in the gilled stage. It is usually coloured white.

The Common or Smooth newt, *Triturus vulgaris*, p. 352, occurs in northern and central Europe as far eastwards as the Urals. In Britain it is found in all counties except for a few mountain areas and parts of the West Country. It is the only newt in Ireland, where

it has been given the curious name of Mankeeper. If you sleep on the ground with your mouth open a Mankeeper is liable to jump inside! This species grows to about four inches. The male has a wavy crest when in the water, is coloured brown to olive with darker spotting, and has an orange belly with black spots. The female is usually more brownish and lacks a crest.

The Great Crested or Warty newt, *Triturus cristatus*, belongs mainly to western Europe, as far as central Russia. In Britain it is widespread but rather local, missing from mountains and from Ireland. This is our largest newt, some females reaching nearly 7 inches (17·8 cm.). The male is a handsome creature, deep olive-brown almost black, with yellow to orange belly spotted in black. It develops a high, serrated crest and a

A male Crested newt (*top*) courting the female

A newt tadpole

have experienced may times. Feeding with earthworms, *Daphnia*, tadpoles, etc., presents no problem. The trouble commences when the newts begin to crawl out!

Of the four living Orders of Reptilia only one is represented in Britain – the Squamata (Latin *squamus* – a scale). This consists of lizards and snakes. The Order Crocodilia (crocodiles, caimans and alligators) and the Testudines (tortoises, turtles and terrapins) are known here only from fossils, and the Rhyncocephalia has but one living example, the Tuatara of New Zealand.

As with the Amphibia, reptiles are much at the mercy of climatic conditions. They are concentrated in the warm latitudes, and fall off towards the north. Even so, there are three British reptiles which can exist well within the Arctic Circle, as we shall see. Although a snake and lizard do not appear

silvery band along the sides of the tail. The old name of Triton, after the water god, is well deserved.

Our smallest species is the Palmated newt, *Triturus helveticus*, 3 inches (7·6 cm.) long. It could be mistaken for a small Smooth newt, which could explain its apparent rarity at one time. It belongs to western Europe, and in Britain is widespread, Ireland excepted. It is the dominant newt on the west side of the country, also in mountains, and seems to prefer ponds and ditches on acid soils. The male has conspicuous black webs between the hind toes, less so in the female, a low, straight-bordered crest, and a curious thread-like extension to its tail. Colouring is brownish with fine spotting, yellowish or faintly orange below. A useful distinction is the clear unspotted throat. In the Smooth newt this is usually spotted.

Newts make delightful aquarium inmates, and the whole breeding cycle can be witnessed at close quarters, something which I

A female newt laying an egg

to be very alike, they have in common a coat of overlapping scales, enabling them to withstand dry surroundings and exposure to the sun. They can bask for hours in conditions which could be fatal to an amphibian. Visible differences are the presence or absence of limbs. There are two lizard families, however, the skinks (Scincidae) and the Slow-worms (Anguidae) which contain species with long and slender bodies, and in some cases no visible signs of limbs. The British Slow-worm has this kind of build, but also retains certain lizard features, such as movable eyelids and a fixed jaw-bone structure similar to ours. Snakes have fixed eyelids which are transparent and cover the eyeball. Also, the jaw-bones work on loose hinges so that the mouth shape can expand to take in large meals which are swallowed whole. A lizard usually has a long tail, which in some cases may easily rupture, whereas a snake's tail is short and fixed.

Britain has three native lizards. The Common or Viviparous lizard, *Lacerta vivipara*, has a wide distribution in Europe, from sea-level to high mountains, spreading well into Asia and up to the Arctic Circle. In Britain it is found in all counties and a number of islands. This is the only reptile found in Ireland. With unbroken tail it grows to about 6 inches (15·2 cm.). Many specimens have a stunted tail which is partly regrown. Colouring varies much and may be a brown, grey, reddish covering with longitudinal rows of clear dots, also a dark dorsal stripe. Below is orange or yellow speckled in black. Males tend to be brighter. Occasionally a black or melanic specimen may be found.

This lively little lizard can be seen sunning itself on some exposed piece of rock, moss, bark, etc., its body flattened against the warm surface. It frequents the drier spots in woodland glades, among heather and bracken, along ditches and country lanes, and on mountain-slopes. Mating in May is followed by the delivery of a family of some eight to ten dark-coloured young in July or August. Generally speaking, reptiles are

egg-laying, or oviparous. In this case there is a 'live-birth', as the name Viviparous implies. What happens here is that the embryos are retained in their egg-sacs inside the mother's body up to the point of hatching, called ovo-viviparity. This has the distinct advantage over egg-laying, in that the embryos enjoy the protection of the mother's body which, so to speak, acts as a living incubator. The basking parent gathers in the warmth of the sun, passing it on to her unborn young. In some situations, during poor summers or at high altitudes, this lizard has been known to give birth prematurely. The young are then delivered in egg-sacs attached to a supply of yolk.

The Sand lizard, *Lacerta agilis*, p. 352, is a west and central European species found in a variety of dry habitats including woodlands. In Britain it lives mostly in dunes and heathland, in very localized colonies in such counties as Hampshire, Dorset, Surrey, Kent and Lancashire.

A good length with tail, is about 8 inches (20·3 cm.). The male is a sandy brown to reddish colour with sides and underparts a bright green, especially during the breeding-season. The female is more greyish brown.

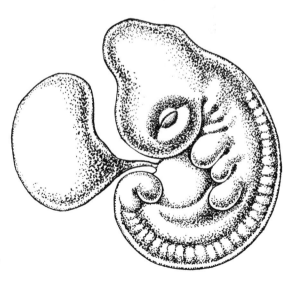

Embryo lizard removed from the egg, with the yolk-sac still attached

Both sexes have 'eye-spots', deep brown rings with white centres along each flank. Breeding starts in May, and by midsummer the female lays about a dozen oval and soft-shelled eggs in a hole dug under some cover such as a stone or grass tussock. From here the young will appear without any assistance from the mother. Today the Sand lizard must be considered a rarity. Its habitat of sand-dunes has been much overrun by the holiday industry. Since a hundred years ago what were small fishing villages have now grown along our coasts to join into large seaside resorts with a sprawl of beach huts eating into the sand-dunes. Heaths in many areas have been planted up by the Forestry Commission, or turned into aerodromes. The Natterjack which has preferences for the same habitat is in the same critical position as the Sand lizard.

The Slow-worm, *Anguis fragilis*, is still fairly common and widespread in mainland Britain. It bears a superficial resemblance to a snake. In Europe it extends from the Arctic Circle to the Mediterranean, and eastwards to Asia Minor. With undamaged tail it can grow 18 inches (45·7 cm.) in the male, longer in the female. The head is lizard-like in appearance, and the eyes open and shut. In the male there is a slight neck region, and the base of the tail is more swollen. Colour is some shade of grey to bronze, occasionally black, sometimes with darker lines along the back, especially in females. Underneath is greyish to putty colour. So-called Blue-spotted Slow-worms occur, usually males, in which there is a scattering of scales coloured a deep azure-blue.

A Slow-worm's build enables it to move in snake-like fashion, and it will burrow a good deal in leaf-litter and loose soil. It frequents the borders of woodland, field and hedgerow, and colonies may be found in such undisturbed places as waste ground, railway embankments and country churchyards. Village rubbish-tips may also contain them. In these situations there is plenty of cover and a good supply of food such as earthworms

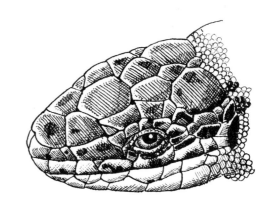

Viviparous lizard

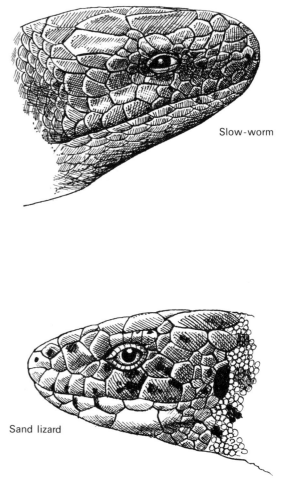

Slow-worm

Sand lizard

Heads of lizards for comparison

and slugs. When feeding a Slow-worm will contemplate its prey, then slowly and deliberately seize it in its jaws. Sometimes a slug will even escape!

A Slow-worm may remain under cover for long periods during dull spells, then quietly emerge to sunbathe. It blends well with its surroundings, and could easily be overlooked. On approach, however, it may quickly retreat at fair speed, belying its name. The alternative of Blindworm is also a misnomer.

Mating takes place from April to June, the female producing ten or so young in August or September. They are pale gold or silver above, with a dark stripe down the middle, and black beneath. The Slow-worm tames readily and makes an interesting little pet.

There are three British snakes. The familiar Grass snake, *Natrix natrix*, has a wide European distribution and comes in a number of varieties. In Britain it is the sub-species *Natrix natrix helvetica*, sometimes called the Barred Grass snake. The sides are marked with vertical black bands. Two crescent-moons of orange or yellow, bordered behind in black, stand out clearly just behind the head, but may be indistinct in old females. This gives the species the alternative name of Ringed snake, now seldom used. The general ground colouring is a grey-brown to olive-brown, with the sides marked in black. Underneath is a chequered black and white. A good-sized male reaches 2 feet (61 cm.), a female 3 feet (91·4 cm.), but occasional giants occur. My largest find was a 4 foot (122 cm.) female. This is not unusual for continental specimens. Those sold in our pet shops are of a different sub-species imported from Italy.

British Grass snakes are found mostly in England and Wales, and are missing from Ireland and most of Scotland. The northern limit is determined by climatic conditions. For the eggs to hatch there must be a guaranteed incubation period of at least ten weeks at about 70 °F. (21 °C.). In July the female seeks out a suitable warm spot in which she can lay her 10–30 eggs. Decaying vegetation,

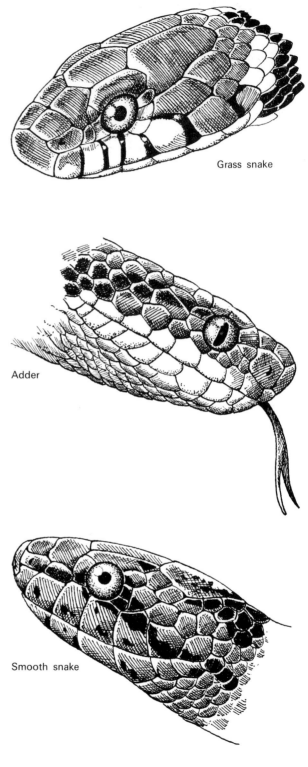

Grass snake

Adder

Smooth snake

Heads of the three British snakes for comparison

A Grass snake swallowing a frog

manure-piles and derelict haystacks where internal combustion takes place provide a warm and moist atmosphere, and many snakes in the same area will make for a similar egg-bed. The result is the discovery of a large gathering of eggs, giving rise to all sorts of curious beliefs about dens of snakes. By September the baby Grass snakes, about the length and thickness of a diary pencil, cut their way to freedom by slicing through the soft egg-shell with a sharp egg-tooth on the end of the nose.

The Grass snake is a slender and graceful creature, especially when swimming, at which it is expert. It feeds mostly on cold-blooded prey such as fish and amphibians, and may be the culprit which steals the goldfish from the garden pond. Food is simply grabbed and swallowed alive. Sight is good, and I remember once watching a Grass snake pursuing a frog through tall grass. The prey was temporarily lost, and

the snake reared its head above the undergrowth, looked around until it spotted movement, then continued the chase. Capture of a Grass snake can be both interesting and disconcerting. It never seems to bite the hand which picks it up, but will hiss loudly and dart its head about in an alarming way. It may also void an evil-smelling fluid which is not easy to remove from one's clothes. If this fails it will go limp in the hand and open its mouth. If placed on the ground it turns over on to its back, as if it had died. Unfortunately this little trick has a flaw in it. If turned right way up it immediately turns on to its back again!

Our rarest serpent is the Smooth snake, *Coronella austriaca*, so named because of the soft texture of the body due to its smooth scales which have no keeled edges. Since the first discovery and identification of a specimen near Ringwood, Hampshire, in 1853, it has only turned up sporadically in a few quiet places on heathland in and around the New Forest area, mainly in Hampshire and Dorset. It grows to about 2 feet (61 cm.). Colour is a grey to reddish brown. Down its back is a series of separate cross-bars. Dark patches on each side of the neck meet on top of the head, and there is a dark band through each eye. The back markings, coupled with the Smooth snake's habit of biting when picked up, may cause alarm at first. However, it is a harmless and non-venomous snake.

Prey consists mainly of lizards and occasional small mammals. Its old name is the Lizard snake. The victim is seized in the jaws, then wrapped up in the snake's coils in constrictor fashion, not to crush but merely to smother the struggles while it is swallowed.

This interesting little serpent is readily tamed. A specimen I once found on a Dorset heath, and later released, fed on a lizard in my lap only a half-hour after capture. It bit me as I picked it up. During its brief confinement it produced a family of eight young. The Smooth snake is ovo-viviparous.

The only native reptile which must be treated with some respect is the Adder or Northern viper, *Vipera berus*, p. 352. Although venomous it is not dangerous, but a shy and nervous creature which will never attack, only biting in self-defence if picked up or molested. It is seldom more than 2 feet (61 cm.) long in England, and is then almost certainly a female. Recognition should not be hard. The build is rather stocky, with a short stubby tail. Colouring in the male Adder is brighter, in greys and yellows, with a dark wavy or zigzag band running down the back. A row of spots along each flank alternates with the dorsal zigzag. The female tends to be more brownish, even a brick-red, with a similar dorsal zigzag band in a deeper colour. Underneath is a greyish brown, or sometimes a beautiful azure-blue. Occasionally one meets a black or melanic Adder. The often-mentioned letter V on the back of the head cannot be relied upon, and is often distorted.

During a ramble there is more likelihood of meeting an Adder than a Grass snake. Whereas the latter usually dives for cover, the Adder will often stay its ground, or move away more leisurely. Sluggish by nature it can nevertheless strike at high speed. On teasing it with a stick it is almost impossible to pull it away before the snake has struck its mark. The mechanism of the bite is one of nature's little marvels, however unpleasant, and is as efficient as the doctor's hypodermic. Each hollow fang is fixed to a rotating jaw-bone, and levered into position as it strikes. Muscular contraction on the two venom glands squeezes the poison along ducts, into the hollow fangs, and so into the victim or enemy. Not a drop is wasted.

Deaths among humans are fortunately rare, the only danger is to young children and animals like dogs. I was bitten myself as a schoolboy, by foolishly picking up a large female, and suffered a very painful period in hospital. Adder venom is haemolytic and affects the nervous system, causing vomiting and nervous prostration.

Adders usually frequent the drier places

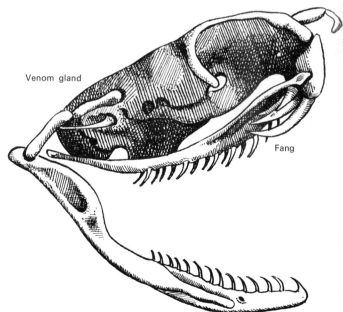

Venom gland

Fang

The skull of an Adder

in woods, heaths, among rocks and ruins, on cliffs and mountain-slopes, even at high altitude. It is called the Northern viper to distinguish it from more southerly species, and occurs widely in central and northern Europe, northern Asia and well up into the Arctic Circle. It is Britain's commonest and most widespread serpent, from Cornwall to north Scotland, but absent from Ireland. Mating takes place in May or June, and an average of ten young are born in midsummer. The advantage of retaining the young to the point of hatching, as with the Viviparous lizard and Slow-worm, makes it possible to live far to the north. At high latitudes it will mate in one short northern summer, then produce its family in the following summer. Finding living young inside an Adder which has been struck down with a stick, or run over, may have given rise to the old belief that she 'swallows her young in times of danger'.

The Adder's prey consists of lizards, small mammals and birds, also eggs. It will come out on warm summer nights to track down prey by scent. Once in the New Forest a gipsy friend took me to an Adder glade deep in the woods and late at night. He lit a camp-fire, and in an hour we had a ring of Adders for company, attracted to the warmth.

Birds

Britain is fortunate in her bird-life. There is probably a greater diversity of species over the country as a whole than in any other land in the North Temperate Zone. This wide dispersion of species is a relatively recent phenomenon, due to the varied mosaic of habitats which today covers the greater part of the British Isles. It has not always been so in the past, nor will be in the future if present-day trends in land-use continue. While we have such variety we should cherish it and seek actively to promote sufficient diversity in town and countryside to retain this rich heritage for our children and grandchildren to enjoy.

More than half of the smaller bird species of the countryside have a forest origin, despite the fact that woodland today covers only 6 per cent of Britain's land area – less than is buried under bricks and concrete. Their present abundance is a triumph of their adaptability to changing circumstances down the centuries. It harks back to the situation at the height of the Atlantic Phase of prehistory, the few centuries either side of 4000 B.C. when Britain became an island, and when the vegetation achieved its climax of a billowing green mantle of oak, elm and other deciduous trees. With perhaps more than half the land under high forest birds must have been far more numerous than at any time before or since, for oak is much the richest source of insect food among our native trees.

In the Highlands of Scotland one can still meet a few birds – Red-throated diver, Ptarmigan, Dotterel and Snow Bunting among them – which may have held on precariously to southern England through the worst of the Würm Glaciation 20,000 years ago. They spread northwards as the tundra, with its dwarf birch and willows, succeeded the retreating snowfields, doubtless picking up such recruits as Golden plover, Grey-lag

goose, Dunlin, Red-necked phalarope, Meadow pipit and a few species of ducks on the way. In Lapland such alpine heath has a pleasantly varied assortment of birds which embraces Purple and Wood sandpipers, Ruff, Long-tailed duck, Velvet and Common scoters. Fieldfare, Redwing, Bluethroat and Lapland bunting, all of which probably bred in England in Late Glacial times but have long since disappeared. Forest birds began to arrive only when the birch trees formed woods on the tundra, perhaps 10,000 years ago; doubtless the Willow warbler filled them with song, and its companions probably numbered Wren, Dunnock, Tree pipit, Great tit and Redpoll among those species which remain as breeders today.

In the warm, dry Boreal Phase of climate from 7000 to 6000 B.C. pine woods appear to have covered much of Britain, bringing Capercaillie, Black grouse, Woodcock, Hooded crow, Long-eared owl, Crested and Coal tits, Redstart, Bullfinch and Crossbill, with perhaps a few other species which are to be found in existing remnants of the old Caledonian Forest around Rothiemurchus and Glenmore. Birch, aspen, hazel and alder attained their greatest extent in the north, taking Wrens, Dunnocks and Song thrushes to the Outer Hebrides, where they live today among the rocks and heather now that the trees have gone.

The deciduous forest of oak, elm, lime and ash, spreading slowly during the Boreal, dominated all England and much of southern Scotland throughout the Atlantic Phase when the climate was warm and humid. Wood warbler, Pied flycatcher and above all the Chaffinch and Great tit must have become widespread and common. There may have been more predatory birds – Buzzard, Sparrowhawk, Tawny owl – and newcomers in the shape of Green woodpecker, Nuthatch, Treecreeper, Long-tailed tit and especially the Jay, whose habit of burying acorns may well have helped the woods along.

Thus long-term climatic changes, altering the dominant vegetation types, determined the nature of Britain's bird-life until man began to play a part in the Neolithic Period around 2500 B.C. For many centuries he practised a shifting cultivation, and pastured his flocks, on clearings made in the beech forest which clothed the Cotswolds, the Chilterns, Salisbury Plain and the North and South Downs. Such cleared areas must have reverted quickly to thorn scrub, a pioneer stage in the succession to new forest, when the fertility of the soil became exhausted and the tribe and its flocks moved on. This downland scrub, together with the ever-increasing open habitats along the woodland edges, must have encouraged many species which had been previously scarce. We may guess that Kestrel, Skylark, Woodlark, Whinchat, Stonechat, Whitethroat and Lesser whitethroat, Garden warbler, Redbacked shrike, Linnet, Goldfinch and Yellowhammer were among them.

It is unlikely that the vast oak forests in the valleys came under serious attack until Roman times or even later, when an increasingly settled populace endowed with iron tools and heavy ploughs made large-scale clearance possible. Skylark-song may have charmed the Neolithic herdsman, but this and many other species such as Lapwing, Partridge, Swift, House martin, Swallow, Rook, Corn bunting and House sparrow must have been uncommon until a lot of the forest had been replaced by an open-field system surrounding the villages. The destruction of forest has gone on relentlessly ever since, limiting the distribution of some characteristic birds like the Wood warbler and Nuthatch, though others such as Blackcap and Chiffchaff have managed to cling to the shreds of copses and spinneys that remain.

An important medieval development was the management of large areas of the forest, mainly in the lowland region, as 'coppice'. Coppicing is a rotational cutting of young growth springing from the stumps or 'stools' of felled trees; it provided firewood, poles for hurdles and fences, bark for tanning, and charcoal for the glass-blowing and iron-smelting industries. Mature trees were often left here and there as 'standards'. More sunlight penetrated among the trees, inducing richer herb and shrub layers. The woods would be more varied, with the growth in different 'coupes' or compartments at different stages of development. Coppicing is an important aspect of the ecology of British birds which has never been studied, and it must have materially affected the numbers and distribution of many species. It is likely that Pheasant, Song thrush, Blackbird, Dunnock, Wren and similar woodland 'edge' species benefited from this widespread practice; indeed, the logical succession of colonization from forest, through coppice, to the more fragmented scrub situations of the farmland environment may go far to explain why these species are so ubiquitous and abundant in England today compared with the Continent.

During later medieval times man modified the landscape in many different ways. The perpetuation of grasslands on the chalk by a sheep-grazing régime, the drainage of fens and marshes, the establishment of orchards and market-gardens, the enclosure of private parks with their new plantations of exotic trees and shrubs, must have shuffled and reshuffled birds that were learning to adapt to new and ever-changing situations. Between 200 and 300 years ago English farmland began to acquire the distinctive panorama of small fields interlaced with quickset hedgerows, often carrying tall timber, that we know so well today. Some hedges have considerable antiquity as parish or other boundaries, but the vast portion of the 600,000 miles said to criss-cross Britain today is not more than a couple of centuries old.

Against this changing background the

(*from left to right and top to bottom*): Golden eagle, Red grouse, Dotterel, Golden plover, Peregrine and Red-necked phalaropes

influence of climate remained, varying from the benign weather of the 'Little Optimum' of Viking and Norman times when vineyards flourished in the west Midlands and south, to the bitter years of the 'Little Ice Age' in the seventeenth and early eighteenth centuries. This period is likely to have affected numbers rather than distribution: recovery from a climatic setback is slow, and the greater frequency of severe winters must have kept the more susceptible species in constant check. During the first 30 or 40 years of the present century a kinder climate prevailed, and some of its profound effects on our bird-life are touched upon in the following chapters.

We shall see that whilst man may have ruined many habitats, he has unwittingly created others, and a profit-and-loss account of his influence on bird-life (if one could be drawn up) might be less damaging than many of us are inclined to believe. Towns and cities, with the extra food and shelter they provide, especially in the winter-time, have encouraged an increasing band of birds to live commensally with man. Improved farmland, which covers some 60 per cent of the land area of Britain, is a mixture of many different habitats offering something of value to a wide spectrum of birds. The old woods may have largely disappeared, or have been exchanged for new forests dominated by western American conifers, and although these provide poor quarters for bird-life when mature, they are richly endowed with a variety of species in their early stages. Industry engulfs great plots of land, but new habitats suspire from its ruins: none would deny the potential value as nature reserves of the scrub surrounding old quarries and mine-workings and flooded sand- and gravel-pits, or of the thousands of miles of country lanes, closed branch railway-lines and disused canals.

The industrial revolution has exploded during the last decade into a technological and chemical revolution, and the consequences for wild-life may be enormous. There are fears that the constant use of toxic pesticides and weed-killers in field, garden and forest will contaminate the whole environment, and deprive birds of vast resources of plant and insect food. Large numbers were killed directly by the chlorinated hydrocarbons used by farmers in the 1950s, and although this danger seems now to have passed, our predator species remain at risk because they accumulate toxic residues from the flesh of their prey. Some have decreased alarmingly, others have shown impaired fertility. Added to this there is the spectre of a prairie countryside devoted to a cereal monoculture, devoid of hedgerows and copses and with only a minimal amount of cover to support wild birds. The fear of a conifer monoculture in forestry is perhaps less real, since present policy seems to favour a wider diversity for amenity's sake, especially in the lowland zone. Water storage barrages in the Wash and our larger estuaries, should they come to pass, will affect hundreds of square miles of coastal feeding-grounds. There will be immense new towns, new airports, new motorways.

Throughout history the background against which birds live their lives has undergone dynamic change, yet with relatively few exceptions they have adapted, survived and flourished. The difference in future will be the greatly accelerating rate of change. Successful accommodation to new habitats takes time; and unless we help with well-planned conservation, time may no longer be on nature's side.

The sea is an immensely rich food source and many groups of birds have learned to exploit it. To some, like the ducks and waders, the sea is merely incidental to a land-based ecology; but to others, such as the petrels and auks, it is the mainstay of their existence, and indeed the land can be a hazard. Fulmars, Shags, Leach's petrels and young shearwaters occasionally meet with disaster when severe cyclonic storms sweep them from the sea and fling them in their hundreds against a lee shore, so that a trail of dead and dying birds is found across the countryside.

In the North Atlantic, because of the relatively homogeneous marine environment, the sea-bird species are few. The vast expanse of ocean south of the Equator has a wealth of 'tubenoses', as the petrels, shearwaters, albatrosses and their allies are called from the possession of a tubular nostril on the top of their beaks. But only four species resort to the British area as breeders, though three

Little auks

others appear regularly as migrants from the south. The poverty of our marine environment is further illustrated by the fact that only six auks (four of them British) breed in the North Atlantic, compared with 16 in the North Pacific.

Notwithstanding the lack of variety, the total number of individuals is very large. Indeed, the distinction of being the commonest bird in the world undoubtedly belongs to one of the sea-birds visiting the North Atlantic – either Wilson's petrel, *Oceanites oceanicus*, which comes on migration from Antarctic islands, or the Little auk, *Plotus alle*, which breeds in immense 'rookeries' on the rocky capes of Arctic coasts. Wilson's is a sooty white-rumped petrel the size of a Swallow, distinguished from the British Storm petrel by its long legs, which protrude beyond the tail, often showing the yellow

webs. The Little auk is not much bigger than a Starling, and is a black and white bird with a short, stubby bill: it is particularly prone to be cast ashore, sometimes many miles inland, by winter storms.

There are two species whose numbers in British seas are fairly accurately known, the Gannet and the Fulmar, and there are believed to be about 100,000 breeding pairs of each. The Gannet, *Sula bassana*, is unquestionably our most spectacular sea-bird, large and so shining white that it is easily recognizable when flying a considerable distance out at sea. The mature bird has a buff head and neck, black wing-tips, and blue-grey bill and feet, and spans nearly 6 feet (1·8 m.) across the wings. The gleaming quality of the plumage may help birds to locate one another and therefore share the best feeding-grounds, for they are highly sociable and live largely on surface-shoaling fish such as herring, mackerel and saithe. Spotting its quarry, the Gannet bends back its slim wings at a sharp angle and power-dives into the water, raising an impressive column of spray. Its immensely thick skull has a honeycomb structure of tiny air-cells to act as a shock absorber when the bird strikes the surface, often from a height of nearly 100 feet (30 m.), and a cellular tissue beneath the skin can be inflated to cushion the body against the impact.

Some of the Gannet's staple food-fish increased in abundance during the warmer years of the first half of this century, and it is one of the species which has shown a positive response to the climatic amelioration. New colonies grew up in Shetland, southern Ireland, the Channel Islands and at Rundø in Norway. The tiny island of Grassholm off Pembrokeshire well illustrates the rapidity of this population growth. First settled about the middle of the last century, there were 200–300 pairs in the 1890s when the amelioration began, ten times as many in the 1920s, 6,000 by 1939, and 15,500 when the colony was last counted in 1964. Here the birds live on the flat top of the island and as you approach they seem to fold back like a living carpet, the birds waddling in procession into the wind, seeking sufficient 'lift' to take off. The historic colony on the steep-sided Bass Rock in the Firth of Forth was reckoned at 4,374 pairs in 1939, and now has about 7,000 pairs. Ailsa Craig in the Clyde showed an increase from 5,419 nests in 1939 to 11,700 in 1963. Little Skellig off County Kerry, Sula Sgeir and Sule Stack off northern Scotland (*Sula* is the Old Norse name of the Gannet), also have colonies; but all these are puny compared with the vast concourse of 44,500 pairs on the cliffs of Boreray and its pinnacles Stac an Armin and Stac Lee at St Kilda.

The regular spacing of the bulky nests each with a single chalky white egg, is dictated by the space each sitting bird can defend with a lunge of her powerful beak – for, gregarious though they are, Gannets are not averse to stealing nest-material from one another. When it leaves the cliff in September, after two months of devoted parental care, the fledgling is extremely fat, and at this period several colonies were formerly raided by island communities – though only Sula Sgeir in Britain is regularly cropped today. The first plumage is dark brown flecked with white, but a juvenile Gannet is

Fulmar, *left*; Gannet, *right*

easily recognizable from the similarly clad young of Great Black-backed and Herring gulls because the long bill and long, stiff tail protrude to give the body a characteristic cigar-like shape. It takes on more and more white plumage with successive moults and becomes mature when four or five years old. Youngsters from British gannetries migrate south to the Mediterranean and the Senegal coast, but they travel less far with advancing years, and few of the adults leave home waters at any season.

The Fulmar, *Fulmarus glacialis*, is very like a medium-sized gull in appearance, except that head and body are 'old ivory' rather than white and the bill appears shorter and stubbier because of the tube-nostril above. The wings are held straight, not angled like a gull's, and much of the time on the wing is spent in gliding. A century ago its only British breeding-station was St Kilda, where the people subsisted mainly on the fat young of this bird and the Gannet, and on Puffins snared in horsehair nooses. About 40,000 pairs of Fulmars inhabit St Kilda today. Early in the nineteenth century the Icelandic population seems to have 'exploded', the birds pouring southwards and colonizing first the Faeroe Islands, then Shetland, and eventually almost every stretch of suitable cliff along the British coastline. Its history in British seas has been dealt with fully in a monograph *The Fulmar* by James Fisher. This violent range-expansion, which has slowed down but does not yet seem to have stopped, is thought to have been set in motion because a new food-source became available in the offal from the whaling and deep-sea trawling in northern waters.

Fulmars have a habit of prospecting a bit of coast for several seasons before they settle down; the pairs will sit in little grassy alcoves, waving their heads and bills at one another, cackling loudly the while; birds gliding about the cliffs often attempt to land alongside the pairs, so that sometimes one may see groups of half a dozen displaying together. The sitting bird looks quiet and demure, but her behaviour belies her appear-

Storm petrel, *left*;
Manx shearwater, *centre*;
Leach's petrel, *right*

ance when she is approached, for she will retch and spit an evil-smelling stomach oil to ward off intrusion – a secure enough defence against avian predators. They are birds of the open ocean and even at the height of the breeding-season may range hundreds of miles from base, so that it is quite usual for the partners to take turns at incubating the large white egg for five or six days (up to nine has been recorded) at a time. As with the young Gannet the young Fulmar grows into a large ball of fat and when fully grown may weigh a third as much again as the adult bird or over 2 lb (1 kg.). Towards the end of August parental visits become very intermittent and may even cease, and the young one makes its own way to sea.

The Fulmar excepted, the 'tubenoses' are difficult to observe because they spend the day seeking plankton well out at sea and make their landings only under the friendly cover of night. There is a splendid talus slope called Carn Mor on distant St Kilda where one can pass the night surrounded by the strange activities of all the British species, a spectator intruding into an utterly bizarre world. The crazed yodelling screams of Manx shearwaters echo and re-echo among the massive boulders as birds fly in from the sea to change places with their mates on subterranean nests; and soon these seagoing mates sweep overhead with the speed of projectiles, with a menacing 'whoosh' of wings that is often too close for comfort. The small Storm petrels come in unobtrusively,

almost without sound, and flit like tiny shadows among the rocks; but the Leach's petrels add to the cacophany of noise with their demoniacal laughing cries as they twist and turn and tumble in rapid flight. When underground in their nesting-burrows the pairs of both petrels croon to one another with a vibrant dynamo-like song. All night long the sinister shapes of the gulls patrol the boulder-field – it is because of this menace that the smaller birds come ashore under the protective cloak of night.

The Manx shearwater, *Procellaria puffinus*, is a black and white bird about the size of a pigeon, with legs set far back in the body so that, while it can swim powerfully, it can only slither along on the full length of its legs when ashore. Its classic home was the Calf Island at the southern extremity of the Isle of Man, where thousands of fat young ones were drawn from their burrows every August to provide a table delicacy for the Lords of Mann and their households. The vast colony, first mentioned in an Icelandic saga, was extirpated by rats which got ashore from a Russian ship wrecked on the island. The Irish Sea continues to be one of the main breeding-areas of this bird, and there are very large colonies under the dense growth of bracken on Skomer and Skokholm. It is

also abundant in the Scilly Isles. These southern islands provide a very different setting for shearwater music than the steep boulder-slopes of St Kilda, but an even more curious nesting-place is the Isle of Rhum in the Hebrides, where many thousands of pairs burrow in the soft strata at about 2,000 feet (610 m.) below the cloud-capped summits of the mountains. At all these breeding-places vast flocks or 'rafts' can often be seen at sea, waiting for the darkness to fall.

The small, sooty Storm petrels, *Hydrobates pelagicus*, oftener to be seen following in the wake of ships (which Leach's petrels seldom do) than ashore, are frequently associated with Manx shearwaters at their colonies; in addition to burrowing, they often nest in old buildings and drystone walls. Their white rumps, small size and manner of flight are reminiscent of the House

Puffin

(*top*): Razorbill, *left*; Great Black-backed gull, *right*
(*bottom*): Herring gull, *left*; Kittiwake, *right*

martin. Leach's petrel, *Oceanodroma leucorhoa*, is larger and longer-winged, not unlike a Swift; it is dark brown with a pale area in mid-wing, and a whitish rump divided by a dark band down the middle. It chooses grassy places on cliff-slopes for its nesting-burrows, which may twist and turn for 3 feet (91 cm.) or more beneath the surface. It is the most remote of the petrels, known to breed only at St Kilda (where there are several large colonies), the Flannan Islands, Sula Sgeir and North Rona.

The auks are more accommodating than the remote and nocturnal petrels, and along a suitable stretch of coast or on islands like the Northumberland Farnes or Handa off Sutherland, the watcher can sit quietly on the cliff-top and enjoy their intense social activity. It is not often that the four British species can be found in one place, since each has marked preferences in its nesting-site requirements. At St Kilda, the Shiant Islands and other places, the Puffins, *Fratercula arctica*, fly in their thousands round and round the huge boulder-slopes, or walk with mincing steps in little groups on the tops of the rocks; when darkness descends they disappear into the labyrinth of passages and caverns beneath the boulders, where they talk to one another with almost human groans. Elsewhere they burrow in the soft soil of the higher brows. Alone of the black and white auks they have white faces, and throughout the summer their high conical bills wear an extra horny layer coloured in bright blue, red and yellow, which has value in courtship and falls away after the breeding-season. Guillemot, *Uria aalge*, and Razorbill, *Alca torda*, have the whole head dark, and while the former has a slender bill as long as its head, the latter has a much deeper conical one neatly decorated with white lines. Guillemots like open ledges, especially on cliffs with nearly horizontal strata where the softer layers have worn away, leaving tier upon tier of ledges along which the birds stand as upright as tiny penguins, growling incessantly. Between its webbed feet and brood-patch each bird clutches a single,

Lesser Black-backed gull

Guillemot

Tystie

long pear-shaped egg – a shape wonderfully designed for open-plan nesting in exposed positions, for if the sitting bird is suddenly disturbed the egg spins on its larger end and seldom rolls over the edge. The variety of colour and marking is quite remarkable, and this also is an adaptation, enabling each bird in the crowded colony to recognize her own. The Razorbill's egg is a less extreme pyriform shape – it is not at risk to the same extent, since Razorbills like to lay in some kind of hollow or cavity in the rock or among fallen stones. In many places one can find the two together, the Guillemots crowding the cliff-face, and the Razorbills filling in where the rock has become weathered and broken.

Perhaps the most delightful of the auks is the Tystie, *Cepphus grylle*, as he is known in Nordic and Celtic languages, though all the bird-lists and books unimaginatively label him 'Black guillemot'. He is wholly black in summer except for contrasting white wing-patches, but in winter the black is exchanged for a dappled grey-brown and white. The feet are scarlet, and so is the inside of the mouth when the bird opens it to emit his high-pitched whistling cry. Tysties too are sociable but the colonies are small and the pairs may be scattered along a suitable length of shore. Nests are usually under fallen rocks at the foot of the cliffs, but sometimes in the shelter of a cave, while in some places they have taken quite happily to holes in harbour walls. Their courtship displays are complicated 'water dances' often involving a num-

ber of pairs, and are beautiful to watch from the cliff-top; birds often 'leap-frog' one another as they swim along in follow-my-leader fashion, and in their underwater pursuits the regular flash of the white wing-patches gives them the appearance of big marine butterflies. Unlike the other auks, Tysties lay two eggs and remain close inshore throughout the year.

A close associate of the auks at their breeding-cliffs is the most pelagic of all our gulls, the demure Kittiwake, *Rissa tridactyla*, so called from the perpetual plaint which rises from the crowded colony. This is the smallest of the seagoing gulls and does not have the white spots or 'mirrors' on the black wing-tips; the bill is greenish yellow and the legs are black. Young birds, called 'tarrocks', have a distinctive black collar, tail-tip and triangular band across the spread wings. Kittiwakes seem able to attach their nests of grass and seaweed quite firmly to the slightest and most insecure-looking knobs and projections; the colonies are customarily low down and often in the entrances and roofs of caves. Like the Puffin, their wanderings are ocean-wide, and birds ringed at British colonies have been found in winter from the Murmansk coast of Russia across the Atlantic to the Newfoundland Banks.

As rapacious as the Kittiwake is gentle is the Great Black-backed gull, *Larus marinus*,

Terns, *left to right*: Common; Sandwich; Little

as big as a goose and with black wings and mantle and flesh-coloured legs. Although, like other gulls, it will eat fish and marine invertebrates, it is a carrion-eater and also a killer of other birds. Rogue pairs often settle in puffinries and prey upon the inhabitants, grasping them by the neck as they emerge from their burrows. Occasionally, they nest colonially along with the medium-sized gulls, but more typically round much of the coast the pairs will nest on the tops of big rocks or isolated stacks. The Lesser Black-backed gull, *Larus fuscus*, is smaller, has bright yellow legs, and the dark plumage of the upper parts differs in the contrast between the black wing-tips and the dark sooty-grey of the rest of the wings and mantle. Like the more commonly observed Herring gull, *Larus argentatus*, which has a grey back and wings and flesh-coloured legs, it is a sociable species, and sometimes the two are found in mixed colonies. Herring gulls are more widely distributed round the coast on the rocks and cliff-brows; they congregate to scavenge in seaside towns, and are more commonly seen inland than the other gulls.

The climatic amelioration of the first half of this century resulted in a great increase in gulls in general, and the Herring gull in particular. This increase also owes much to man, for the birds have learned to find food behind plough and tractor, to use reservoirs for roosting, and to exploit rubbish-tips and sewage outfalls. This abundance poses some problems, not least from the pressure the

Shag

bird is now exerting on the elegant black-capped terns. Arctic and Common terns are much alike and often nest in the same colony; the Arctic, *Sterna paradisaea*, has a uniformly blood-red bill and legs when mature, whereas the Common, *Sterna hirundo*, has a black tip to its paler red bill; but, as the birds swirl over their nesting-ground in a shimmer of shrill, harsh sound, a better guide is the darker grey breast of the Arctic and the translucency of its wings. The Sandwich tern, *Sterna sandvicensis*, is a size bigger, almost as large as a gull, and has a black beak tipped with yellow, and a rakish crest. Similar in size to the two first-mentioned is the scarcer Roseate tern, *Sterna dougallii*, but it is whiter looking and has longer tail-streamers, while often a beautiful pink flush shows on the underparts. Apart from the islands in the Forth and Clyde estuaries, the best Roseate tern colonies are in Ireland.

Once-flourishing colonies of one or more of these delightful 'sea-swallows' have disappeared as increasing hordes of Herring gulls have taken over their traditional sites on small offshore islands. Those terns which elect to nest among sand-dunes or on shingle-beaches are relatively safe from take-over by the gulls, but with more and more humans flocking to the seaside the main deterrent to successful breeding is disturbance. The beau-

Oystercatcher

Cormorant

breeding-season, features which are absent from the green-glossed Shag. Their nests are untidy affairs built among fallen rocks and talus, and of all sea-bird colonies theirs are perhaps the most offensive to human nostrils! There is a primeval air about the emerald-eyed Shag as she sits on her half-dozen chalky white eggs, sinuously weaving her long neck to and fro in an effort to

tiful Little tern, *Sterna albifrons*, not much larger than a Swallow and with a white forehead and yellow bill, is greatly at risk from such interference, and a census of its colonies in 1967 showed that not more than 1,600 pairs remain in Britain and Ireland.

Two other cliff-nesters which are common enough in inshore waters are the Cormorant, *Phalacrocorax carbo*, and Shag, *P. aristotelis*: they have all four toes webbed, like their close relatives the pelicans and Gannet, and are long-necked crested birds. Adults look black at a short distance, but young birds of both species are dark brown with whitish underparts. The bluish-glossed Cormorant is the larger, as big as a goose, and sports a white throat and thighs during the

Eider

intimidate the intruder. Both birds can be told from other diving-birds when quite a distance out at sea by their habit of leaping clear of the water before diving round-backed beneath the waves. Cormorants have a proverbially large appetite and are said to consume more than their own weight of fish in a day, a fact which has incurred the enmity of fishermen; they often visit inland waters but Shags do so only when storm-driven.

Finally, we must look at a few birds which, though not in any sense sea-birds, are most often to be seen on the coast. The Ringed plover, *Charadrius hiaticula*, Shelduck, *Tadorna tadorna*, and Oystercatcher, *Haematopus ostralegus*, are characteristic of shingle beaches and dune systems, the first often nesting in and near terneries, and the second raising surprisingly large families in disused rabbit-burrows. The combination of green head and neck and rusty band across the forepart of the white body make this a strikingly handsome duck. The Oyster-catcher is largely a bird of rocky headlands and islands in the north and west, and in recent decades increasing numbers have penetrated far inland from Yorkshire north-wards along river-valleys and straths. There is an engaging gaiety about this handsome pied wader with its bright red beak and eye-rim and pink legs. They delight to get together in small groups, and pipe excitedly at one another with downcast heads as they trip along in a quaint procession. The shrill piping is also a feature of the nuptial 'butterfly-flight' on slowly beating wings, and is one of the evocative sounds of the estuarine mud-flats in winter as the birds mass to feed at the tide's edge.

Often a close associate of the Oyster-catcher in the north is the roman-nosed Eider, *Somateria mollissima*. The drakes, a picturesque contrast in white upper parts and black wing-tips, tail, belly and cap, swim offshore with their undistinguished brown ducks, throwing back their heads to utter a faintly surprised *aw-oo-oo*. A hollow among the rocks quite close to the sea is the

Raven

Chough

usual nesting-site, but in the northern isles some birds will nest among the heather a mile or more inland. The duck will sit motionless on her half-dozen olive-green eggs, cosseted in a warm bed of grey-brown down plucked from her own breast, and she may be so broody as to suffer herself to be lifted off the nest.

Another cliff-haunting bird of the north is the Rock dove, *Columba livia*, ancestor of the town pigeon and the many varieties of homing and fancy pigeons. Small groups usually nest together in the roofs of caves along parts of the coast where the birds have access to cereal crops. The typical plumage is blue-grey with double black wing-bars and a white rump, but the wild strain is often diluted by admixture with lost homers, and a common variety has a grey rump and heavily blotched wings.

Ravens, *Corvus corax*, big, black and menacing, with harsh guttural voices, often nest on rocky coasts, and there are often colonies of the much smaller, grey-naped Jackdaw, *C. monedula*. Much the most maritime of the crow tribe, however, is the fascinating Chough, *Pyrrhocorax pyrrhocorax*, which was once common enough on English coasts but is now restricted to north and west Ireland, Wales, the Isle of Man and a few localities in the Inner Hebrides. It has the richly glossed black plumage of other crows but can be recognized by its bright scarlet legs and slender downcurved bill. Choughs are gregarious creatures, and even though they build solitarily in caves or large fissures in the cliffs (and sometimes in old mine-buildings and other ruins near the coast) the birds of a particular area maintain a loose flock system throughout the breeding-season. They are wonderful aerial acrobats using the upslope currents off the face of the cliff to spectacular advantage. Their stooping and stunt-flying, and switchback-riding on the wind with wings alternately spread and folded back close to the body, is punctuated with the sharp, high-pitched call *chwee-aw* which has given the species its name – for the old pronunciation, still used in the Isle of Man, is 'cheeow', not 'chuff' as in modern parlance.

Apart from the special races of Wren, *Troglodytes troglodytes*, inhabiting the cliffs of St Kilda and Fair Isle the only small song-bird exclusive to the sea-coast is the Rock pipit, *Anthus spinoletta*. It is slightly larger than the Tree and Meadow pipits and more olivaceous in colour, with dark brown legs and buffish (not white) outer tail-feathers. It has an equally pleasant song-

Rock pipit

flight and nests in cracks and crannies in the rocks, securing the marine invertebrates and insects which form its food on the shingle and wrack and in the grassy fields above the cliffs.

Mountain, moor and loch have some of the most ancient of British birds, which colonized as soon as the Late Glacial ice-fields gave way to tundra and alpine heath. There must have been a time in the warm Boreal Phase of climate when much of this heath was clothed in dwarf birch and juniper and thickets of willows, and throbbed with the songs of Willow warbler, Redwing, Fieldfare, Brambling and Bluethroat, much as the upland areas of Lapland do today. But centuries of relatively cool and sunless summers, with consequent lack of evaporation, encouraged the growth of peat and blanket-bog – a process which was still actively engulfing pine forests as late as the stormy 'Little Ice Age' of the seventeenth century. Repeated muirburn and the constant grazing of too many sheep and red deer have effectively prevented the growth of woody cover among the hills. One has only to look out from the bare margins of the lochs at the richly vegetated islands where no sheep tread to realize what habitats, and what birds, Scotland might hold today.

When all this has been said, however, it is to Scotland that we go for some of our most thrilling and magnificent birds. Pride of place among them goes to the Golden eagle, *Aquila chrysaetos*, p. 369, whose hunting-ground may cover 10 or more square miles (26 sq. km.) of moor-grass and heather, the home of the game-birds and blue hares which form its staple food. This majestic brown bird – females are 3 feet (91 cm.) long and have almost twice the wing-span – is named from the golden mane on head and neck; this is duller in young birds, which show some white in mid-wing and, until their fourth year, have a whitish tail with a black terminal band. The eyrie is usually among hillside crags in a lonely valley, or on a coastal cliff, but a small number nest in pine trees. Most pairs have alternate nesting-sites, used in different years, and a much-used nest of twigs, heather-stalks or bracken may grow to an immense size. Normally one or two eggs are laid, and the combined incubation and fledging period occupies nearly five months. Often only the first-hatched youngster, which may be as much as three days older than the second, survives, especially if food is not abundant.

The bird most likely to be confused with the Golden eagle in Scotland is the Buzzard, *Buteo buteo*, p. 399, since both are brown and broad-winged and frequently soar for long periods. But the Buzzard is hardly 2 feet (51 cm.) long, and the head and tail do not protrude so far from the spread wings as in the eagle, nor are the 'fingered' primary wing-feathers flexed upwards so markedly when soaring. Buzzards often nest on inland and sea-coast cliffs in Scotland, but also – as elsewhere – they haunt wooded country, often drawing attention to themselves by their plaintive, far-carrying *pee-oo* cry.

There have been success stories – and some failures – in recent years among our birds of prey. Not long ago there were few Hen harriers, *Circus cyaneus*, outside Orkney, where they quartered the moors with lazy, flapping flight in search of Orkney voles; elsewhere, they were under suspicion as killers of game-bird chicks, and were given short shrift by keepers. Nowadays a more enlightened view prevails, and there are many districts on the mainland where the grey, white-rumped male and his brown 'ringtail' mate have been allowed to breed. As with most birds of prey, the female is larger than the male, with a body-length of about 20 inches (51 cm.). The Osprey, *Pandion haliaetus*, a splendid white-bellied fishing-hawk as big as a Buzzard but with narrower, angled wings and a whitish head, was hounded out of Scotland by egg-collectors in the last century, but is now back again. A pair has nested annually during the last decade in a tree near Loch Garten, under the care of the Royal Society for the Protection of Birds, and events at this historic eyrie have been glimpsed by thousands of tourists from a near-by 'hide'. In 1969 as many as four pairs may have bred in Scotland. R.S.P.B. wardens have also cherished, for three years past, a pair of Snowy owls, *Nyctea scandiaca*, on the moorland of Fetlar in the Shetland Islands. The difference in size of sexes is very pronounced in this species, the black-speckled male being only two-thirds as big as the immaculate white female, who stands quite 2 feet (51 cm.) tall. Young reared by these handsome birds, mostly on rabbits and young sea-birds, have been seen on other islands, and may soon consolidate the foothold this Arctic predator has gained in Britain.

The Peregrine, *Falco peregrinus*, p. 369, and Merlin, *Falco columbarius*, are swift-winged, dashing creatures which capture smaller birds on the wing; unfortunately,

383

both have suffered a serious collapse in numbers during the past decade. There is a superficial similarity since in both species the tiercel (male) is blue-grey above and marked with brown on a buffish ground below (though only the Peregrine has black moustachial streaks), while the larger falcon (female) is brown above with heavily spotted

falcon), and in defence of its territory will attack and drive off birds much larger than itself.

The magic of moor and loch does not end with the birds of prey. There is no more handsome pair of water-birds in Britain than the two divers, the Black-throated, *Gavia arctica*, of the larger lochs, and the Red-

Common scoters

underparts. The Merlin is our smallest falcon, barely a foot (30 cm.) in length, but the Peregrine is almost as big again – a robust, 'broad-shouldered' bird with sharply pointed wings which are angled steeply backwards towards the long tail when it stoops with devastating speed upon its prey. Pigeons are a favourite food but birds as big as crows, ducks and gulls are frequently struck down. The Merlin hunts closer to the ground with buoyant, agile flight, relying on swift pursuit, and sometimes snatches small birds and mammals from the ground. Since the earliest days of falconry it has been esteemed for its courage (it was the ladies'

throated, *Gavia stellata*, p. 370, of the smaller waters among the hills. Swimming or in flight they look like slim-built, grey-necked geese, and the wild, forlorn wailing of the Black-throat on a remote sea-loch is one of the unforgettable sounds of the north. The Red-throated diver is the only one in Shetland, is the more frequent in the Hebrides, and has a western outpost in County Donegal. Because the blood-red of its throat often seems black at a distance, the best guide to identity is the uniformly greyish-brown rather than boldly patterned back; moreover, the bill always has an uptilted appearance, whereas that of the Black-throated diver is strong and straight, and this is the only really good distinguishing feature in winter when both are brown above and white beneath, and are likely to occur at sea as far south as the English Channel. They have picturesque displays on the water, particularly the 'plesiosaur race' of the Red-throated, when two or three birds speed along with necks held stiffly upright and most of their bodies submerged. Their legs are set so far back, for efficiency in swimming and diving, that the birds move awkwardly on land, so that the nest with its customary clutch of two shiny brown eggs is generally on a small islet, or very close to the margin of the loch.

Other water-birds of the north, less than half as big as the divers, are the Slavonian grebe, *Podiceps auritus*, and Black-necked grebe, *Podiceps nigricollis*, both twentieth-century gains to our British fauna. Of the two, the rufous-necked Slavonian or Horned grebe (the 'horns' are golden tufts above the ears) is restricted to north-eastern Scotland, where it nests semi-colonially on a few favoured lochs. The Black-necked was more widely dispersed over Britain and Ireland but has had a chequered history. Some former breeding-haunts were deserted after a few years' occupation, like the lough in County Roscommon where no fewer than

250 pairs are said to have nested in the 1930s. Today it is confined to a few lochs in central Scotland. Both require waters with a liberal marginal growth of horsetails, sedges and bogbean, among which they moor their floating water-weed nests.

At Loch Druidibeg in South Uist and a few other places, flourishing under protection, there is a remnant of the Grey-lag goose, *Anser anser*, population native to Scotland. In Galloway and the Lake District birds of feral ancestry turned down in the interests of wildfowling are also doing well. The pale grey fore-wing, contrasting noticeably with the brown body and neck in flight, together with an orange bill and pink legs, serve to distinguish this from other wild geese which winter here: its overall length of 36 inches (91 cm.) makes it one of the largest of the geese, and its voice is similar to that of the barnyard variety which was derived from this species in the past.

The two saw-billed ducks – so called from the tooth-like serrations on the cutting-edges of their beaks – are often seen on the rivers and lochs of northern England and Scotland, especially in coastal areas. They are Goosander, *Mergus merganser*, p. 370,

Wagtails (adult males), White, *left*; Pied, *right*

and Red-breasted merganser, *Mergus serrator*, p. 370. The drakes have glossy dark green and the ducks reddish heads, and both show large white wing-patches in flight; the Goosander is whiter beneath, with a lovely pink flush at close quarters, whereas the merganser has a rusty breast-band and grey-brown flanks. The Goosander, with a length of 26 inches (66 cm.), is slightly the larger. Both have increased in this century despite the dislike of the angling fraternity: the damage done to trout and salmon fisheries is minimal, however, and it is a pity such handsome birds do not have full protection.

The Tufted and a number of other ducks have increased in Scotland as elsewhere, and one which is probably confined to the northern lochs is the Wigeon, *Anas penelope*, p. 370, better known in the south as an abundant winter visitor to the estuaries, where the whistled *wee-oo* of the drakes carries far across the tide. Distinguishing features of the male are its rufous head with a creamy-buff band over the crown, and warm cinnamon breast contrasting with grey black and paler grey flanks. The all-black Common scoter, *Melanitta nigra*, and his dark brown, pale-face mate also have a restricted range in the north-west, though a few nest also in Ireland.

The moorland community differs markedly from place to place, but there is always a heart-warming quality in its wild music and exciting personalities. The Craven Uplands of the Pennines provide a refreshing and easily accessible change for those whose leisure is customarily restricted to the semi-rural surroundings of England's cities and towns. The name-cry and liquid bubbling song of the Curlew, *Numenius arquata*, provide the signature tune, and the bird itself is unmistakable – dark brown flecked with buff, paler beneath, standing 20 inches (51 cm.) tall and with blue-grey legs and a slender downcurved bill which may be as much as 6 inches (15 cm.) long. A large triangular white patch on the lower back shows up well in flight. Interspersed with this music are the plaintive cries of the pied, round-winged Lapwings, *Vanellus vanellus*, p. 397, as they tumble in nuptial ecstasy above their grassy territories. Standing rather short of a foot (30 cm.) high, this is one of our most beautiful birds at close quarters, the dark plumage of upper parts glinting with green and purple reflections; a black shield divides the white face and belly, and the head is adorned with a long upturned crest. In the wetter, rush-grown fields the brown Redshank, *Tringa totanus*, similar in size but with lanky red legs and bill, utters noisy and excited protestations. With luck one may see the slightly larger Spotted redshank, *T. erythropus*, p. 426. It is a rare passage migrant in spring and autumn, stopping here on its journey between the Mediterranean and northern Scandinavia.

At dusk the sky hums with the un-bird-like drumming of the Common snipe, *Capella gillinago*, a noise made by the rush of air past the vibrating outer tail-feathers as the bird plunges down, perhaps to settle on a stone wall and give vent to its staccato *cheppa-cheppa* call. On the higher moors the Golden plover, *Charadrius apricarius*, p. 369, stands sentinel on a knoll: he has much the same body-size as Lapwing and Redshank, and like the much smaller Dunlin, *Calidris alpina*, who also haunts the high ground is black-fronted in the breeding-season, with a mottled whitish face and golden-spangled back.

Among the smaller, sparrow-sized birds are the white-rumped Wheatears, *Oenanthe oenanthe*, whose tuneless anxiety call is like two stones being struck together; they go to and from their nests in old rabbit-burrows or cavities in rocks and drystone walls. Male and female are buff-breasted, the former having a clear grey back and black wings and a black patch behind the

(*top*): Bittern, *left*, and Heron, *right*;
(*centre*): Dabchick, *left*, and Marsh harrier, *right*;
(*bottom*): Water rail, *left*, and Great Crested grebe, *right*

eye, the other being uniformly warm brown above. Skylarks, *Alauda arvensis*, p. 397, sing above the rough pastures, and the smaller, slimmer Meadow pipits, *Anthus pratensis*, equally undistinguished in their brown plumage, are scattered far and wide over the uplands. The drystone walls and rocky places along the streams are favoured by the Ring ousel, *Turdus torquatus*, who replaces the Blackbird on the high moors and in size and shape and plumage is almost a twin, except for the prominent white crescent on his chest and a pale patch in the wing. The song is weaker than the Blackbird's, and very disjointed.

Dippers, *Cinclus cinclus*, are frequent along the streams; they look podgy and pied as they hurtle past with rapid wing-beats, and effect due to their disproportionately stout bodies and short tails. A dark red band separates the white breast from the black vent and upper parts, which give way to a dark chocolate-brown on the head. You may find one bobbing on a favourite rock before he drops beneath the surface to walk expertly along the stream-bed: with head down and broad back flattened against the flow he has evolved a way of exploiting a food-source out of reach of other birds. The domed nest is like an outsize Wren's (indeed, the Wren is a surprisingly frequent neighbour along these rocky rills) and is often in the splash-zone behind a waterfall, or underneath a road-bridge or culvert.

Haunting the streams almost throughout Highland Britain is one of the loveliest of our small birds, the Grey wagtail, *Motacilla cinerea*, p. 398, blue-grey above, canary-coloured below, with a black bib and an extraordinarily long and fluent tail that takes up nearly half of the bird's 7 inches (18 cm.) total length. Often it shares the streamside with the Pied wagtail, *Motacilla alba*, though this smart black and white

(*from left to right and top to bottom*): Mallard, Shoveller, Pochard, Bearded reedling, Kingfisher, Sedge warbler and Reed warbler

creature is equally conspicuous around the hamlets and homesteads, and about the drystone walls which often provide it with a nesting-site. The Common sandpiper, *Tringa hypoleucos*, flitting here and there with spasmodic wing-beats and thin whistling song, or bobbing even more emphatically than wagtails or Dipper as he settles on a stone, is also a cheerful feature of upland streams and loch-shores.

The moors of Unst, the northernmost island in Britain, are very different from the Pennines. Ring ousel, Dipper and Grey wagtail have gone, but most other species remain. Curlews call in the rushy fields beside the lochs, but here they encroach on the preserve of their smaller northern cousins the Whimbrels *Numenius phaeopus*, who differ in their shorter bills and brown-striped heads. The Whimbrels occupy the higher slopes, above which they climb on quickly beating wings, a repeated mournful *koo* accelerating towards a fine climactic trill as the song-flight becomes a fast-declining glide. Dunlins are commoner than in the south, and their lovely trilling song can be heard on lower ground. In a few choice haunts in Shetland and the Hebrides the little pools and lochans, especially where bogbean provides good cover, are blessed with those avian jewels the Red-necked phalaropes, *Phalaropus lobatus*, p. 369, engagingly trustful as they swim buoyantly close to the shore, sometimes spinning in tight circles. Their form and the buff stripes on their grey backs, are reminiscent of the Snipe, but they are smaller, about 7 inches (18 cm.) long, and the most striking feature of their plumage is a chestnut patch on the sides of the rather long neck. The female is brighter coloured than the male and more often seen, since the latter is left with the sole responsibility for incubating the eggs.

Much of the moorland character in Shetland is due to two closely related but very dissimilar birds, the Great and Arctic skuas. Both are pirates, chasing gulls, terns and auks at sea and forcing them to disgorge

Arctic skuas,
light and dark forms

their last meals, which the swooping skuas deftly pick out of the air; both nest colonially, though since each pair needs a few acres of territory for its growing chicks, the colonies are spread over wide areas of the peaty moors. The Great skua or Bonxie, *Catharacta skua*, is a rotund bird as big as a Buzzard, generally dark brown mottled with buff, though some individuals are sandy while others incline to a rufous shade. They are powerful birds, and the pair will sometimes team up to rob the much larger Gannet, one grasping the victim's wing-tip and causing it to stall, the other waiting on to catch the food which the Gannet dis-

gorges. The Arctic skua, *Stercoparius parasiticus*, is smaller in body-size and the total length of 18 inches (46 cm.) includes a longer tail which has sharply pointed middle feathers. The wings are long and angled and the flight is as thrilling to watch as a falcon's. Birds love to sport over the nesting-ground, twisting and turning in pursuit of one another with loud yodelling cries, or uniting to harry some passing gull or crow. There are three plumage-types, a wholly dark brown one, a white-bellied one, and an intermediate type with buffish-brown underparts contrasting with a dark brown skullcap and wings. In British colonies the dark

Black grouse,
Greyhen, *left*
Blackcock, *right*

and intermediate types are the commonest, and there is no selection in choice of mates. The young hide among the heather and peaty banks for a month before they are able to fly, after which they are encouraged to chase their parents before they are given food – the first stage of their training for a piratical life.

Rather distant cousins of the skuas are the Common gulls, *Larus canus*, which also nest in scattered colonies on the moors. They are only two-thirds as big as the Herring gull which they closely resemble in plumage, though easily distinguished by their delicate greenish bills and legs. Like the slightly smaller and noisier Black-headed gulls, *Larus ridibundus*, which nest here and there beside the lochs and small tarns, their numbers have increased much in this century. A close view shows that the 'black' head is really sooty brown; this, but not the bright red of the legs and bill, is lost in winter, a dark collar and a few grey marks remaining. A good identification feature is the broad white leading-edge to the wings.

A few species which have already been mentioned as coastal birds are not infrequent moorland *habitués* in the breeding-season; they are the Eider duck, Oystercatcher and Ringed plover. Another interesting wader, who stands over a foot (30 cm.) tall on his long green legs, is the Greenshank, *Tringa nebularia*: it is grey-brown with a white belly, and a white triangle reaching from the barred tail to the middle of the back is very noticeable in flight, as also are the long upturned bill and the feet projecting beyond the tail. The Sutherland flows and the moors of Inverness-shire and Wester Ross are its stronghold, and over much the same area, usually on the wetter ground, the rare Wood sandpiper, *Tringa glareola*, has been found nesting in recent years. This is another white-rumped bird with pale green legs but it is only two-thirds the Greenshank's size, and a darker brown above.

The watcher to whom early rising presents no difficulty may find the Blackcocks, *Lyru-*

rus tetrix, Black grouse males displaying at their meeting-ground or 'lek' on the moorland fringe close to the woods. They stand nearly 2 feet (61 cm.) tall and are glossy black with red wattles and a white wing-bar, and their bizarre posturing makes great play of the long lyre-shaped tail. The Greyhens are smaller, closer to the Red grouse, *Lagopus lagopus*, p. 369, in size, but their richly variegated brown and buff feathering is less rufous than in that species, and the tail is forked. They attend the cocks at the 'lek' but often seem to pay little or no attention to the crowing and formalized fighting of the males, though the 'lek' is the scene of courtship and mating as well as of social activity. The Red grouse, which is much more a bird of the open moor, has a more diffuse social life, neighbouring males sometimes coming together to challenge and scrap with one another; but they are not polygamous like the Blackcock, and generally each male defends a well-defined territory. An oft-heard note is the loud *go-bak, go-bak* as one challenges another, and when flushed the dark red-brown bird goes away with a noisy whirr of wings and an explosive *kowk, kok-ok-ok*.

On the highest tops, generally above 2,500 feet (762 m.), the grouse is replaced by the Ptarmigan, *Lagopus mutus*, a greyer bird of similar size which has white wings and underparts in summer but is almost completely white in winter, except for a black tail. Because of the complexity of its moults, of which it has three each year, it is a variable species. It feeds on the shoots and leaves, and later the fruits, of bilberry, crowberry, cloudberry and other low alpine plants. The Cairngorm chair-lift has brought this interesting but previously remote species within easy reach of the tourist.

Only two other birds regularly go so high as the Ptarmigan, the Dotterel, *Charadrius morinellus*, p. 369, and the Snow bunting, *Plectrophenax nivalis*. The first is a 9 inch (23 cm.) long plover with a dark brown back, white face and eye-stripe, and chestnut belly, which has a well-deserved reputation for extreme tameness, since it will continue to brood its three eggs almost at the feet of the observer. It is also very confiding when with chicks, being as pertinacious as the grouse and Ptarmigan in attempting to lure the watcher away by 'injury-feigning'. It is a summer visitor, migrating to North Africa, and may be seen on low ground during spring and autumn passage. The Snow bunting, like the Dotterel, has suffered a sharp decline in numbers in this century and is now a rare bird of high corries in the Cairngorms, preferring the screes and rocky ground. It is about the size of a Skylark and the nearly white male has a sweet and musical song, sometimes uttered on the wing. Although territorial, it is usual for a small number of pairs to nest in close proximity, while after the breeding-season, when the plumage is a mixture of buffish brown and white, it is highly gregarious, large flocks resorting to the coast.

Man's first concern is to create habitat for himself, and there are certain kinds of environment which are inimical to his interests. Bogs, marshes and natural wetlands of any kind are agriculturally unproductive, and human progress demands that more and more of them shall be drained and rendered fertile. From the middle of the seventeenth century the reclamation of fen country in East Anglia greatly reduced our water-bird population and many species dependent on fens, pools and marshes reached their nadir about 100 years ago. Some of them have only recently become re-established through conservation, while the building of new reservoirs and the flooding of old sand- and gravel-workings has assisted the spread of water-birds in general.

Alongside these developments two other factors have helped to enrich our waterfowl fauna. From about 1870 a gradual amelioration of the climate took place in north-west Europe, culminating in the 1930s. During much the same period many of the marshlands of south-east Europe dried up, and there was an exodus of displaced birds

which found congenial conditions for colonization as they spread across the Continent. It is hard to believe when one walks beside the lakes in London's parks that the impish, yellow-eyed Tufted duck, *Aythya fuligula*, first nested in Britain in 1830, the Gadwall, *Anas strepera*, in 1850, and the Pintail, *Anas acuta*, in 1869. We now 'take them for granted' as though they had always been part and parcel of the British scene.

There are many species of ducks but

Tufted ducks, drake above

fortunately the drakes of all of them wear distinctive plumages, except in the 'eclipse' or moult phase following the breeding-season; the females, however, are nearly all undistinguished brown birds and can cause difficulty. The Tufted is a rather small, boldly pied species 17 inches (43 cm.) long with a purple-glossed head and rakish crest; his mate is dark brown but shares the yellow eye and grey bill and a pale spot on the face. The Pintail is longer-necked and larger, a

grey bird with a brown head, white front and long needle-like tail. The Gadwall is less strikingly coloured than other drakes, having a brown head and neck, grey body and black posterior: the female can be told from the female Pintail by her yellow, not grey, beak and a white 'speculum' or wing-patch in flight. A good deal of the recent increase in this species has stemmed from artificial introduction. The red-headed Pochard, *Aythya ferina*, p. 388, an otherwise grey bird with a black front and tail (and a mate looking like a dull shadow of itself) has increased less spectacularly than the others, and does not yet seem to have gained a permanent footing in Ireland.

One of our most striking ducks, the Shoveler, *Spatula clypeata*, p. 388, also took part in this advance across Europe. It has a glossy green head and dark chestnut sides and white breast, while the wing is variegated with white and pale blue. It has a disproportionately long, coarse bill which renders both sexes immediately recognizable. There is a superficial resemblance, in colour only, between this and the common wild duck or Mallard, *Anas platyrhynchos*, p. 388, which is a bulkier bird 2 feet (61 cm.) in length, has a yellow bill, and the breast (not the sides) chestnut, separated from the dark green head by a white neck-ring. The female Mallard has some orange in the bill-colour and in flight lacks the blue shoulder which both sexes of the Shoveler show. Another colourful duck with a small and restricted population that has arisen from deliberate introduction is the flamboyant Mandarin, *Aix galericulata*; it is restricted to a few waters in wooded haunts in Berkshire and Surrey, where it nests in trees. The female is a grey bird with some white markings, but the male has spectacular chestnut-orange adornments extending from the wings and the sides of his white face. He is only a little bigger than the Teal, *Anas crecca*, at 14 inches (36 cm.) long the smallest of the British ducks, and with his grey body, dappled breast and red head with large green eye-patch one of our handsomest.

Geese, *flying,* **Brent with light form centre** *below,* **Canada,** *left;* **Barnacles,** *right*

The bird which, next to the Tufted duck, has benefited most from flooded sand- and gravel-pits is the Great Crested grebe, *Podiceps cristatus*, p. 387. The fashion in 'grebe fur' had reduced the English stock to fewer than 50 pairs by 1860; but protection, the growth of sand- and gravel-pits, and probably some increment from the European expansion, have all contributed to the current success of this species, which now has probably more than 2,000 breeding pairs in Britain and Ireland. It is a particularly handsome bird, some 20 inches (51 cm.) long, brown above and satin-white beneath, including its slender neck. The nape is bright chestnut in the breeding-season, its lower part expanding to form a dark-tipped frill or ruff, which is nicely balanced by the long ear-tufts projecting behind the black crown. These features are coquettishly displayed during the varied and always delightful ceremonies which accompany mating. In one of these, the 'penguin-dance', the partners approach each other with strands of weed dangling from their bills, and 'stand up' breast to breast, swaying in the water. The striped youngsters (usually three to five in a family) are not infrequently carried on the back of a parent bird.

In 1904 and 1908 two new grebes arrived in Britain, the Black-necked and Slavonian respectively. They are both rather larger and more showy than the Dabchick, *Podiceps ruficollis*, p. 387, the most ubiquitous and least obtrusive member of the family, often haunting quite small ponds if there is sufficient weedy cover. This small bird, only about 10 inches (25 cm.) in length, has glossy black cap and fore-neck, and red cheeks and throat. In courtship the pair face each other and sing a trilling duet, and indeed on many waters this trill and its variants are more often heard than the birds are seen. Like the Great Crested grebe, the courting Dabchicks make presentations of water-weed, and they also suffer their youngsters to ride 'pick-a-back'.

The graceful Mute swan, *Cygnus olor*, is another adaptable and very successful bird.

It has a long history of semi-domestication, for throughout medieval times it was well regarded as a table delicacy. The ownership of swans was licensed by the Crown, and the birds were pinioned and given distinctive ownership-marks by cutting notches in the bill, and sometimes slits in the webs. 'Swan-upping' for the purpose of catching and marking the cygnets still takes place annually on the Thames, whilst at Abbotsbury in Dorset there is a marked herd of several hundred birds. Elsewhere Mute swans have mostly reverted to the wild state, and their confiding nature as they and their grey-brown cygnets wait for food at the water's edge, has made them everybody's favourite. At nesting-time swans are cantankerous towards other birds and also to human intruders, and are best admired from afar. The Mute swan is never more impressive than when flying; it rises with difficulty, thrashing the water with its black feet, but when airborne the wings produce a distinctive and not unmusical throbbing sound.

Artificial introductions on a number of estates have added the splendid Canada goose, *Branta canadensis*, to our avifauna. With a length of over 3 feet (91 cm.) this is much the largest of the 'black geese' which include the winter-visiting Barnacles and Brents described later; it is a browner bird, with a black head and neck interrupted by a white throat-patch. It was first brought to Britain to grace ornamental ponds some 250 years ago, and was described by Latham in 1785 as 'breeding freely in many gentlemen's seats'. It is still based largely on these estates.

(*from left to right and top to bottom, opposite*): Lapwings, Kestrels, Red-legged partridge, Woodpigeon, Cuckoo, Barn owl, Swallow, House martin and Skylark

(*overleaf, left*): Dunnock, Blackbird, Whitethroat Bullfinches, Goldfinch, Linnets, Grey wagtail, Yellowhammers and Yellow wagtails

(*overleaf, right*): Buzzard, Red kite, Greater Spotted woodpecker, Lesser Spotted woodpecker, Jay, Long-eared owl and Woodcock

An equally splendid sight, quite 3 feet (91 cm.) tall, is the gaunt grey Heron, *Ardea cinerea*, p. 387, as he stalks in the shallows with neck stiffly stretched, his spear-shaped beak ready to pounce on some fish, frog or young rat. When relaxed he looks much more compact, with the white neck curved so that the plumed head rests on his back. In flight too the head is retracted, but the long bill and long legs project from the broad-winged silhouette. The nesting-colony or heronry is usually in tall trees, sometimes a few miles from the birds' feeding-area; but occasionally in Scotland birds build in low scrub on islands in lochs, or on the cliffs. Only rarely in Britain, though regularly abroad, do they make their nests among reeds.

Another ubiquitous water-bird is the round-backed, all-black Coot, *Fulica atra*, looking rather like a small duck at a distance, though the head-bobbing as it swims along is diagnostic. It is a poor flyer, and the green feet project well beyond the short tail. The Coot is a somewhat larger, more gregarious and more pugnacious edition of the Moorhen, *Gallinula chloropus*, which has the short bill and its frontal shield red and not white. The Coot prefers large waters but the Moorhen will live happily on the smallest of field and roadside pools, and in the most insignificant ditches. He feeds as much in the fields or on park lawns as in the water, and his white under tail-coverts flash conspicuously when he runs for cover. Both are far more numerous than their close relatives the Water rail, *Rallus aquaticus*, p. 387, and Spotted crake, *Porzana porzana*; indeed, so retiring is the latter that its true status in Britain is imperfectly known. These are birds of marsh and fen rather than open water and are heard more often than they are seen. The Water rail is barely a foot (30 cm.) in length and is brown above and

(*from left to right and top to bottom*): Robins, Great tit, Stonechats, Nuthatch, Chaffinches, Redstarts, Crossbills, Dartford warbler and Willow warbler

slate-blue below: its 'sharming' is a strange sound, part grunt, part squeal, and is often heard at night. Its slender reddish bill seems entirely adequate for collecting earthworms and insects, but it is also known to kill small mammals and birds.

A bird which nests in the artificial habitat of flooded gravel-pits and practically nowhere else is the Little Ringed plover, *Charadrius dubius*. It differs from the common Ringed plover of shingly shores in its slighter build (it is 6 inches (15 cm.) long), greener legs, absence of white wing-bars and shriller call-note. The first to nest in England were found in 1938, and by the end of the 1940s they had spread over much of the south-east. Today perhaps 200 pairs breed regularly, but it has not yet reached the Lake District and Scotland, or the southwest peninsula and Wales. Old sand-pits and even sites where noisy machinery is still at work often attract large colonies of Sand martins, *Riparia riparia*, but this small brown and white relative of the Swallow has a wide habitat choice and often burrows in the bare sandy or peaty soil of river-banks. During migration vast flocks roost nightly in reed- and osier-beds.

The Kingfisher, *Alcedo ispida*, p. 388, is also catholic in its choice of waters, haunting slow-flowing streams and canals as well as lakes, reservoirs and marshes. This most beautiful of waterside birds is a jewel of topaz and jade, with rich ruby under parts and a long, strong beak for its sparrow-like bulk. It is much less common than formerly, the pollution of rivers and streams restricting its feeding-places. Like the Grey wagtail, a neighbour on many streams, it suffers heavy mortality in severe winters, while there is gathering evidence that Kingfishers are more susceptible than most fish-eating birds to the toxicity of the industrial effluents which contaminate their prey. Its halfdozen white eggs are laid in a round chamber at the end of a tunnel excavated by both sexes, and towards the end of the season this often becomes extremely noxious with fish offal and excrement.

**Godwits, Bar-tailed, *above*;
Black-tailed, *below***

was originally bought to encourage the Black-tailed godwit, *Limosa limosa*, an aristocratic red-fronted wader, nearly twice as tall, which has a long upturned bill and a distinctive patterning of black and white in the wing and tail. The first nest was found in 1952, and in springtime nowadays the wild and beautiful song-flight of some 40 male birds enlivens these flat, marshy fields.

Another R.S.P.B. reserve, at Minsmere in Suffolk, provides as good a feast of marsh- and water-birds. Among the great reed-beds several pairs of Bitterns, *Botaurus stellaris*, p. 387, breed, and they can often be seen from the specially constructed watch-towers or 'hides' as they tread stealthily at the edge of the pools. When alarmed the Bittern stands bolt upright, his spear of a bill pointing to the sky, and the long black and buff striations on the brownish breast and flanks cause him to melt into the background of rushes and reeds. He is almost as broad-winged and long-legged as the Heron in flight, and his resounding 'boom' is one of the strangest of bird-sounds.

Here too, among the reeds may be found a few pairs of the rare Marsh harrier, *Circus aeruginosus*, p. 387. The long-winged, long-tailed silhouette is distinctive as the big birds quarter the reed-beds, looking for voles and unsuspecting birds. Their plumage is somewhat variable, but usually a bright brown with buffish head and neck, and black finger-tipped borders to the wings. The male delights in spectacular display-flights in the spring; later, when he hunts for the family, he drops food for the female to catch as she rises from the nest.

At Minsmere lagoons with artificial islands have been excavated among the reed-beds to attract wading birds and nesting terns. Avocets, *Recurvirostra avosetta*, steal the show, especially when accompanied by their young. This is a graceful bird indeed with its beautifully sculptured head and neck and long upturned, awl-like bill. It is of mainly white plumage with long blue legs, a black crown and nape and bold

Britain is fortunate in having an organization, the Royal Society for the Protection of Birds, which believes that the more specialized birds banished from the fens by drainage a century and more ago can be lured back if enough of the right kind of environment can be re-created and properly managed. A newly opened reserve is the monotonous expanse of flat cattle-grazings called the 'Ouse Washes', where deliberate flooding early in the season has already encouraged Black terns, *Chlidonias niger*, p. 425, to stay and nest. They are small but long-winged birds of black and dark grey plumage, with reddish-brown legs. Another new breeder in this area is the Ruff, *Philomachus pugnax*, a foot-high (30 cm.) wader of generally brown plumage which, in the male sex, is almost entirely eclipsed by a large erectile shield of breast-feathers which is individually variable in colour, some black, some white, some chestnut. This land

Bearded reedlings

black bands on back and wings, and stands some 18 inches (46 cm.) tall. It is yet another of the lost fenland birds which R.S.P.B. care has re-established, with over 100 pairs now breeding at Minsmere and Havergate where a mere handful first nested in 1947.

There are all manner of small noises in the forest of tall reeds, and a loud *ping* or plaintive *teeu* may advertise the presence of Bearded reedlings *Panurus biarmicus*, p. 388, among the most handsome of our small birds, with their tawny plumage and long graduated tails. The bird is named from the prominent black moustaches which decorate the grey head of the male. Its alternative common name, Bearded tit, is misleading as

it is not related to the tits. Often they are shy and difficult birds to find, but in some years they gather together in large parties at the end of the breeding-season, and 'explode' out of the reeds to spread far and wide. Here also, and indeed all over England and Wales where suitable reed-beds exist, by lakes or disused canals, one hears the discordant, repetitive chattering of Reed warblers, *Acrocephalus scirpaceus*. The warm brown of back and wings brightens to rufous on the rump, and the underside has a creamy tinge. The Reed warbler attaches its remarkably neat nest to the swaying reed-stems, whereas the other common wetlands songster, the Sedge warbler,

403

Acrocephalus schoenobaenus, p. 388, builds close to the ground in bushes and coarse vegetation. This has a rusty rump also, but its clear whitish eye-stripe and dark streaking on the back distinguish it readily where the two occur together. The Sedge warbler is not restricted to waterside situations, however, and its ebullient song not infrequently enlivens the rank growth of dry ditches and field hedgerows.

The bird-life of farmland has received much attention in recent years, mainly as a result of the large amount of data harvested annually by the British Trust for Ornithology's 'Common Birds Census'. This is a count of the bird territories on about 100 sample 'plots' averaging some 180 acres in extent. Its prime purpose is to establish an index of year-to-year fluctuations among the 30 or so commoner species of agricultural land. It is a monitoring device which seeks to inform naturalists of the effects of hard winters, the large-scale use of toxic chemicals, the destruction of hedgerows and other habitat, and so on. It has taught us much concerning the distribution and densities of the common birds in different regions of the country, and has revealed some interesting points about the adaptation of different species to different features of the agricultural scene.

English farmland embraces many kinds of habitat, but usually in quite small amounts: most birds like an ecotone or 'edge' where one habitat merges with another, and the best farms from a bird-watcher's point of view are those which fill this requirement – farms with rather small fields, a good deal of well-grown hedgerow (most of it with trees), a varied cropping programme, the odd stream and pool and spinney, and of course the homestead with its outbuildings and garden. Such a farm might harbour from 35 to 40 different kinds of birds.

The Blackbird, *Turdus merula*, p. 398, 'ousel cock so black of hue with orange-tawny bill' is much the most abundant farmland bird. The hen is a blackish brown with paler, mottled, underparts, and with a length of 10 inches (25 cm.) this is one of the largest of our song-birds. This species claimed 13 per cent of the 18,000 territories mapped for the C.B.C. in 1968, no other approaching this total. Level-pegging in second place with 8 per cent each were the Dunnock and the Chaffinch, while the Robin was not far behind. All these are birds with a forest origin, and the most typical of the open-country species, the Skylark, came no higher than fifth.

Chaffinch and Robin like well-grown hedges with occasional tall trees, but the Dunnock, *Prunella modularis*, p. 398, does not mind if these are absent and will readily accept well-clipped and even remnant hedges. The alternative name of Hedge-sparrow, for the Dunnock, gives a clue to its size, and because of its dull brown and blue-grey plumage, simple warbling song and unobtrusive habits it is much overlooked. It hops quietly about the hedge-bottoms and has a habit of shivering its wings. Although primarily an insect-eater it will turn to seeds and is sturdy in hard winters. Not so the tiny brown Wren, *Troglodytes troglodytes*, with its jaunty cocked-up tail and pale eye-stripe; this sprightly bird suffered more than any other in the severe winter of 1962–3, its numbers being reduced by 78 per cent. It has since made a remarkable recovery. In recolonizing the farms it settled first of all in copses and spinneys, and along streams with woody cover, and only when these favourite niches were full did the surplus spread to the field hedgerows.

As characteristic of the hedges as the Dunnock, but more noticeable because of its ebullient song-flight, is the Whitethroat, *Sylvia communis*, p. 398. In spring the white breast has a delicate pinkish flush, and the grey head and a rusty patch in the wing aid identification. It is much the commonest summer migrant on English lowland farms, but gives way to the olive-green, yellow-fronted Willow warbler, *Phylloscopus trochilus*, p. 400, in the north and west. Next to the Chaffinch, the Linnet and Greenfinch are the most widespread farm finches, but all are better represented in other types of habitat, such as woods, heaths and gardens.

A brief examination of the farm bird community leads to the rather surprising conclusion that the open-country birds are for the most part doing badly in an area where one would expect them to flourish. Indeed, one of them, the Corncrake, *Crex crex*, has become almost extinct as an English farm-bird, except for a few haunts in the Severn Valley. As in all the terrestrial rails and crakes its body, about 10 inches (25 cm.) long, is very narrow, to facilitate movement through dense vegetation; the brown upper parts and buffish flanks are streaked with black, and a bright chestnut wing-patch and untidily trailing yellow legs show well on the rare occasions when the bird takes flight. In more leisurely days when the grass grew long and hay-making was a late summer activity the Corncrakes had time, and peace, to rear their sooty chicks. The rasping travesty of a song filled the fields day and night, the disembodied voice sometimes appearing to be quite close, at other times far away, such is the ventriloquial skill of the performer. The earlier cutting of grass for silage, with consequent disturbance of the breeding-cycle, has undoubtedly driven it from many parts, but the great decline in grasshoppers and other food-items may also have played a part. Nowadays it finds a safe haven only in the slow-growing rye-grass fields of the Shetland Islands, the Hebrides, and parts of north-west Scotland and Ireland.

The Grey partridge, *Perdix perdix*, has also fallen on evil days and despite the efforts of those who value it as a game-bird it is becoming scarcer everywhere. This dumpy foot-high (30 cm.) bird has a variegated brown back and rounded wings, while a russet head and tail and a brown 'shield' below the grey breast bring colour to its plumage. Cool, wet summers and a scarcity of sawfly larvae have caused high chick mortality in recent years. When they are fortunate Partridges rear large broods from their pale brown, porcelain-textured eggs, and it is a pleasant sight in autumn to see a covey of a dozen birds lift with rapidly whirring wings.

The slightly larger Red-legged partridge, *Alectoris rufa*, p. 397, has a white throat bordered with black, a long white eye-stripe, and pale flanks boldly barred with black and chestnut. Sometimes called 'the Frenchman' from its country of origin, it was introduced to East Anglia 200 years ago, and this remains its stronghold, although it can be found sparingly over much of the Midlands and southern counties. In the eastern counties it now outnumbers the Grey partridge, but this dominance is believed to be fairly recent.

Most partridges like a hedge with good, thick outgrowths at the base for their nests – just the kind of hedge that is becoming scarcer on farmland – but the dun-coloured hen Pheasant, *Phasianus colchicus*, more often resorts to denser cover in copses and spinneys. Some Pheasants live as truly wild birds but in many areas – and particularly in East Anglia – numbers of young are hand-reared and turned down for shooting. This Eastern bird may have been 1,000 years in Britain but introductions of new stock have been made on many occasions, so that the plumage is now rather variable and includes a handsome melanic type. Nevertheless, the reddish-brown cock with his long lanceolate tail and dark green neck and head adorned with bright red wattles is quite unmistakable. The tiny Quail, *Coturnix coturnix*, only 7 inches (18 cm.) long and like a miniature partridge in shape, belongs to the same family. It is now little seen and seldom heard outside a few Thames Valley counties where it appears to be a regular summer visitor, though subject to wide annual fluctuations. It seems to have a preference for grassland and leguminous crops on the lighter soils, and its rhythmic whistle has been written as *wet-my-lips*.

Although generally looked upon as the 'indicator species' of farmland the Skylark, *Alauda arvensis*, p. 397, has a patchy distribution: it is rare in the Cotswolds and seems not to like country with small grass fields and many hedges. It is the farmland bird of the cereal-growing eastern counties and where the fields are large and hedgerows are scarce it outnumbers the Blackbird. It takes well to root-crops in many places, and in Highland Britain from the Pennines northwards is a bird of rough hill-grazings and the moors beyond. Its brown, striated plumage may not commend it to the eye, but what matter with a bird that has so marvellous a song! Where larks are common their clear warbling music as they hang poised above the fields is almost part of the very air we breathe. One compensation of the current trend towards vast cereal-growing prairies is that the Skylark must surely increase.

Another brown bird of more portly build, 7 or so inches (18 cm.) long, is the Corn bunting, *Emberiza calandra*: this too is a brownish bird but lacks the Skylark's crest and white wing-lining. It is also likely to be favoured by present-day trends. The male – who is sometimes polygamous – has a not unpleasant though stereotyped song which has been likened to the jingle of a bunch of keys. It is very much a bird of the eastern lowlands, extending fairly far north into Scotland. Like the two other farmland buntings mentioned below it is a late breeder and its song can be heard in July and August when most other birds, including the Skylark, are silent.

The male Yellowhammer, *Emberiza citrinella*, p. 398, has a golden head and underparts and a russet rump adding colour to its darkly striated brown back; the female is duller, especially on head and breast. It is as characteristic a hedgerow species as Dunnock and Whitethroat, preferring pastoral to corn country, and it likes a fairly lofty stance for its lazy, drawling song *a-little-bit-of-bread-and-no-CHEESE*. Equally stereotyped is the string of staccato notes which stumble from the bill of the Reed bunting, *Emberiza schoeniclus*, which has russet in its wings and a black head and bib contrasting smartly with a white collar and underside.

The hen and young birds are much duller, but have the male's habit of shivering their white-edged tail when perched. Much of the damper, rush-grown ground which is traditionally the habitat of this species is being drained and the ditches piped underground; yet the C.B.C. results show that it is actually increasing on farms, and may well be adapting to a drier environment. It will nest in scrappy, relict hedgerows if there is good ground-cover, and has been found holding territory in the middle of barley-fields. All the buntings seem to have a liking for lucerne and other legumes.

A bird inseparable in the mind from warm sunny days on the farm is the Swallow, *Hirundo rustica*, p. 397, with its ever-cheerful twittering song, shiny blue plumage and red forehead and throat. Few birds are more delicately designed and the sharp wings and long tail-streamers make this an entertainingly acrobatic bird as it darts in and out among the quietly grazing cattle, gathering the flies stirred up by their hooves. Swallows are always most in evidence in pastoral country, and commonest on 'old-fashioned' farms where they can build their mud nests in the shippon and other outbuildings. They are very faithful to a traditional haunt, and ringing has shown that the young return from their African wintering to nest not far from their birthplace. Usually two broods are reared and fledglings from the first will sometimes help to feed the nestlings of the second. They are sociable and several pairs may use the same building, but it is in early autumn when they gather on the telephone-wires that their gregarious nature is most obvious.

Among the grazing cattle in lowland pastures and water-meadows the Yellow wagtail, *Motacilla flava*, p. 398, often runs briskly seeking insect food. A fairly long tail, constantly bobbing up and down, takes up much of the 7 inches (18 cm.) total length, but the tail is noticeably shorter than in the similarly coloured Grey wagtail, *M. cinerea*, p. 398, of rivers and streams. The head and the whole of the underparts are canary-yellow in the male and somewhat duller in the female, the back of both being olive-brown and the tail-edges white. The call-note, a drawn-out and musical *tsweep* often attracts attention as it moves with undulating flight from field to field. The Pied wagtail, *M. alba yarrellii*, is handsome for his contrasts not his colours, and usually occurs in the vicinity of the farmyard. Both are common on the upland grazings of the Pennines. The White wagtail, *M. alba alba*, a continental subspecies with a pale grey back, is a not uncommon spring and autumn visitor which sometimes interbreeds with the Pied wagtail.

Mallard and Moorhen are the only waterfowl which have become in any true sense farmland birds (though the Teal occurs sparsely on northern farms), being attracted to field-pools and tolerant of human activity on the land. It seems hardly likely, in view of the progressive filling in of pools and ditches, that either will adjust successfully to modern agricultural changes. Another species which is similarly at a disadvantage through loss of habitat, and also through the increased disturbance consequent upon farm mechanization, is the Lapwing, *Vanellus vanellus*, p. 397. On some farms where a suitable, undisturbed field remains the species is learning to live colonially. It would be a

great pity if lowland farms were to be without the spring charm of its tumbling, buoyant song-flight.

The satin-breasted Barn owl, *Tyto alba*, p. 397, which stands over a foot (30 cm.) in height and has soft feathers of silver-spangled buff on head and back is also much less common than formerly. Nowadays one most often sees it as a ghostly form flitting through the beam of the car headlights as it clears a roadside hedge in its hunt for bank-voles, field-mice and shrews. Young rats and moles are included in the diet, and the undigested bones and fur thrown up as 'pellets' provide useful nesting-material in an old barn or hollow tree. It is an early nester and may rear two broods, and when young and old are disturbed they intimidate the intruder with a peculiar snoring noise. The yellow-eyed, grey-brown Little owl, *Athene noctua*, barely reaches 9 inches (23 cm.), is more often abroad in daylight since beetles, worms and other invertebrates supply a large part of its food, though it will take small birds and mammals. The species is native to southern Europe but has spread rapidly in England following its introduction towards the end of the last century.

Over the country as a whole the Kestrel, *Falco tinnunculus*, p. 397, is the farmland

Rook

bird of prey, although the Buzzard is perhaps as frequent in the west. Its marionette hovering, with grey head looking down and black-banded grey tail spreading outwards from a darkly mottled russet back, make this an easily recognizable bird. The Kestrel has innocuous habits for a raptor, subsisting almost entirely on small mammals and large insects, and it is the only falcon which has not decreased in recent years. It will rear its young in a hollow tree or on a rock-ledge in a quarry or inland cliff, and will sometimes take over an old crow's-nest.

So far as the small birds are concerned there is more danger to eggs and young from the crow tribe than from owl or Kestrel. Carrion crows, *Corvus corone corone*, nest solitarily on most farms, in hedgerow trees, but they are sociable during much of the year and there is a large non-breeding element always ready to attack the spring corn. The Hooded crow, *Corvus corone cornix*, is the northern counterpart of the Carrion crow. The Rooks, *Corvus frugilegus*, which walk sedately in groups about the fields are a more valuable ally of the farmer, their main diet comprising leather-jackets, wireworms and other noxious insects. They have a bare greyish patch at the base of the bill which serves to distinguish them from the

Carrion crow, and the all-black plumage has a purplish rather than a dark greenish gloss. The 'clanging rookery' is sometimes sited in the trees which shelter the homestead, but the winter roost is often a focal gathering-point for many colonies in the district.

The black and white Magpie, *Pica pica*, a bird of bouncing hops and strident chatter, is perhaps the greatest menace of all to the small birds, stealing their eggs and nestlings. It is rather less common on farms than the Carrion crow and is smaller, most of its 18 inches (46 cm.) belonging to the long green-glossed tail. It builds a substantial spherical nest of sticks, strengthened internally with mud, and with an entrance at the side. Tree sparrows, *Passer montanus*, may use it in a subsequent year. The sexes are alike and in voice and appearance not very dissimilar from the male House sparrow, *Passer domesticus*, but the cap is chocolate and there is a brown spot in the middle of the white cheeks. Tree sparrows are increasing on farmland and should be looked for along hedgerows with mature oak, elm and other trees which will provide nesting-holes.

As a family the pigeons and doves have made remarkable strides during the present century – so much so that the blue-grey Woodpigeon, *Columba palumbus*, p. 397, has

Crows, Hooded, *above*;
Carrion, *below*

Magpie

reached pest proportions, there being an estimated 10 million birds in the country after the breeding-season. It is a fine-looking, sturdy bird 16 inches (41 cm.) in length, with a habit of crashing noisily from the hedge-row trees when disturbed, to fly strongly away on white-barred wings. It is a late nester and many have their 'squabs' sitting on a flimsy saucer of twigs in the hawthorns as late as August. The pleasant, modulated cooing song is superior to that of the other doves, as is the undulating courtship-flight in which the rising bird claps its wings together.

The newly arrived Collared dove, *Streptopelia decaocto*, is in danger of emulating the Woodpigeon's bad name in the south-east counties. This rather lovely vinous-grey bird with its white tail and black half-collar hardly had a foothold in Europe at the turn of the century, but has since swept across the Continent in a feathered avalanche. Reaching the North Sea in the early 1950s it made a double-pronged attack on Britain through bridgeheads in East Anglia and the Moray Basin, and is still spreading rapidly. For much of the nineteenth century the Stock-

dove, *Columba oenas*, was virtually an East Anglian bird, and it still has its highest density on cultivated land in the eastern counties. It is a shade larger than a street pigeon and blue-grey with a paler rump and black wing-bars. There can be little doubt that the climatic change, fostering increased cultivation of legumes and brassicas, especially in the north, has helped this and the Woodpigeon to increase their numbers.

Tree sparrow

In their bird content heaths and commons really form the transition from farmland to woodland; nevertheless, they have several species which are scarce in, or absent from these two environments. In the past the greensands of Surrey and East Anglia have developed large areas of heather, ling and gorse with a scattered tree-cover of Scots pine and birch. Similar sandy soils in Hertfordshire and elsewhere are largely overgrown with bracken, gorse, thorn bushes and birches. Many of these areas, including the famous Dorset heaths, are gradually being whittled away for building or agriculture, while in the New Forest and other places heaths have been planted up by the Forestry Commission. The chalk grassland of the North and South Downs, Chilterns, Berkshire Downs and Salisbury Plain, though not heath in the strict sense, has a somewhat similar bird-life. Much of this land too is threatened by the plough. The story of our heathland birds is very largely a sad one of diminution in numbers and contraction of range, due mainly to the increasing fragmentation of their habitat, but also partly perhaps to recent climatic change.

There was a time – 250 years ago – when the turkey-sized Great bustards roamed Salisbury Plain, but the only 'Bustard' you will find there today is a pub. A smaller relative, the Stone curlew, *Burhinus oedicnemus*, still breeds in a few similar haunts, especially on the chalk. This sociable bird is 16 inches (41 cm.) long and plover-like, with sturdy yellow legs – features responsible for its other names of Norfolk plover, for it is well established on the Brecks, and Thicknee. Its generally sandy plumage is highly cryptic against a background of light stony soil and, except for its staring yellow eye, it is inconspicuous until it flies, when the black and white wing-pattern is distinctive. Its numbers have greatly declined in this century. The reason seems to be mainly the disappearance of traditional haunts, since the turning-point came when much of the downland was ploughed during the Second World War. However, the species has shown an ability to make some adjustment and many now nest in cultivated fields. The birds are most active at dusk, even after dark, communicating with one another across the flinty fields or downland grass with their plaintive *coor-lee* calls.

The Hen harrier and Montagu's harrier, *Circus pygargus*, have given an excellent example of the adoption of a newly created habitat by moving into young Forestry Commission plantations to feed on the short-tailed voles which the forester finds so destructive to young trees. The birds are unable to settle for long in any given place, however, since the vegetation grows rapidly and in a few years is too high and dense. Nevertheless, this adaptation has enabled the Hen harrier to multiply and spread; but the Montagu's has not been so fortunate, and from a peak in the early 1950s has now declined to little more than a score of breeding pairs. The male has clear grey upper parts with black wing-tips like the male Hen harrier, but with a total length of 17–18 inches (43–46 cm.) it is slightly smaller: its dark mid-wing bar and the absence of a white rump distinguish it. Hen harriers are unlikely to occur in the Montagu's remaining haunts in southern England until the winter months, when the other bird has migrated to Africa. In East Anglia a few pairs of Montagu's harrier are found in the same reed-bed setting as the larger Marsh harrier, and occasionally pairs have bred on saltings on the edge of the Wash. Elsewhere it favours gorse-grown heaths, and sometimes sand-dunes. The male is less acrobatic than the Hen harrier in spring display flight, in which he rises and falls steeply and sometimes stoops playfully at his mate.

Another predatory bird of heaths and dunes, though it also ranges over park-like country and cultivated areas where there are plenty of trees, is the Hobby, *Falco subbuteo*, which is 14 inches (36 cm.) long. Like Montagu's harrier it is a summer visitor – as indeed are most of the small birds it takes for food – and whilst the New Forest is its stronghold it can be found sparingly in a

Long-tailed tit at nest

number of southern counties. In its aerial courtship play, and its hunting of Swallows and Swifts, it shows great speed and agility, and is a thrilling master of flight; it might pass for a small Peregrine were it not for the scimitar-outline of its wings when gliding, and the red flanks and under tail-coverts of the male.

The most characteristic owl of open heaths, dunes and saltings is the Short-eared owl, *Asio flammeus*; although it is a few inches smaller it is reminiscent of a harrier as it quarters the ground, often in broad daylight, but its long wings and large round head make it unmistakable. It has been known to form 'larders' of small birds under grass tussocks, the owl returning later when hungry. In years of vole plagues, when food for the young is easy to come by, as many as a dozen round white eggs will be laid in a scrape among the grass or heather, and at such times the birds may be double-brooded. The owlets leave the nest after ten days or so and hide in gorse or similar cover near by until they take wing when nearly a month old.

Nightjar, *Caprimulgas europaeus*, numbers are certainly low today compared with the warmer summers of the 1930s but this 10 inch (25 cm.) long bird of beautifully variegated soft brown plumage remains a widely distributed species. It also has found in young plantations a temporary substitute for the shrinking heathland habitat. It is a crepuscular species feeding mainly on large moths and other insects which fly at dusk and dawn, and rests during the day among the old bracken where the mottled brown and buff feathering provides excellent camouflage. It is little use searching for the Nightjar until towards the end of May, when the loud churring song and wing-clapping display-flight advertise its presence. It often shares the twilight with the larger Wood-cock, *Scolopax rusticola*, p. 399, whose high-pitched *physic* call and hoarse croak can be heard as it makes its 'roding flight' above the breeding territory, its plump round-winged shape and long bill providing an unmistakable silhouette.

Turtle doves, *Streptopelia turtur*, are often an attractive feature of bushy places, with their rufous upper parts and white-rimmed black tails, which are widely spread in the steeply rising display-flight. Usually several pairs of these small doves, less than a foot (30 cm.) in length, nest close together, in high hedgerows or thorn scrub, or in young conifers. The Long-tailed tit, *Aegithalos caudatus*, has similar haunts. It is an extremely pretty combination of dark brown, white and pinkish buff, and quite half of its overall length of 6 inches (15 cm.) is taken by the tail. The nest, the size of a coconut, is made of moss and lichen and lined with numerous feathers (over 2,000 have been counted) collected singly and worked into place by each bird in turn.

Our only resident warbler is the Dartford warbler, *Sylvia undata*, p. 400, similar in size to the last species and named after Dartford in Kent where it cannot have bred for a century or more. Its headquarters today are the Dorset heaths, but after a spell of mild winters the numbers build up and it spreads over most of the south between Devon, Wiltshire, Berkshire and Sussex. Snowy winters are its worst enemy since they completely cover the heather among which it feeds. Prior to 1962, when there was a heavy snowfall in January, it was at a peak of abundance with more than 450 pairs, but this setback, so soon followed by the longer cold spell of early 1963, reduced it to a pathetic remnant. Smaller and darker than the previously described Whitethroat, p. 398 – which is often found on heathland – it is terracotta-coloured with a grey head and long tail; it shows similarities in its notes and song-flight, but is more secretive and keeps much to the gorse and long heather. When it does show itself at the tip of a golden spray, its tail cocked jauntily, it is a pretty sight. Usually it builds close to the ground in heather, and like the Wren the male makes 'cock's nests', whereas the real nest, in which its young are reared, is largely the work of the female.

Nowadays the Woodlark, *Lullula arborea*, regular as far north as Yorkshire 20 years ago, is very much an East Anglian and south coastal species, with scattered pairs on the chalk hills and in Wales. It likes short grass-land and relatively bare, even stony, ground, with some scrub and trees, and in East Anglia is a bird of the sandy heaths. Grassed-over spoil-heaps from coal-mining in the Forest of Dean, warrens before myxomatosis killed the rabbits which kept the vegetation short, thinly timbered parkland, felled wood-land before it became much overgrown, are or were its typical haunts. It resembles the slightly larger Skylark in plumage but has a briefer crest and short tail, and there is a small black and white area on the fore-wing. The song-flight is much less sustained than the Skylark's but has a rich musical quality.

The Red-backed shrike, *Lanius collurio*, may soon be in equally dire straits, for its range has contracted much during the past two decades, and few now remain outside East Anglia, Surrey and the New Forest. The recent deterioration in summer weather, rendering less conspicuous the large insects on which it feeds, has been advanced as an explanation for its decline here and on the

Continent, but there is no doubt that the species has suffered greatly through loss of habitat to building development. Both sexes are reddish brown, about 7 inches (18 cm.) long, the male with a blue-grey head and prominent black eye-stripe, and a warm pinkish flush on the breast. The female has a pale stripe through the eye and crescent-shaped dark markings on the underside. Another name is Butcher-bird, describing its habit of impaling bees and beetles on thorns and even barbed-wire, often forming a 'larder'. Small birds are killed but often only the brain and part of the head are eaten, and it will also take frogs, lizards and small mammals. The male has a surprisingly pleasant warbling song, but the usual call-note, a repeated *chak*, is as tuneless as the not dissimilar anxiety-notes of the three chats described below.

Another bird that poses something of a problem is the Cirl bunting, *Emberiza cirlus*, which like the Dartford warbler has a Mediterranean origin. Both are likely to have first reached England during one of the warm periods of history and to have been extremely scarce – even absent – in periods of hard winter weather like the 'Little Ice Age' of the seventeenth century. They have always been at the periphery of their range in Britain and the withdrawal of the Cirl bunting to the southern counties may be linked with the somewhat colder weather since the 1930s. It is not a true heath species but can be found on the scrub-grown slopes of the chalk downs, also in park-like pastures for it seems to have a liking for tall elms, while more recently it has become increasingly a bird of the transitional zone between farmland and suburbia, often nesting in large gardens. The male is a yellow-fronted bird with a black eye-stripe and bib and a greenish pectoral band, while the female closely resembles the hen Yellowhammer but lacks the latter's reddish-brown rump.

The Whinchat, *Saxicola rubetra*, and the Stonechat, *Saxicola torquata*, p. 400, are frequently found together on gorse-grown moors in Scotland, particularly at the edges of young plantations, but in the south they are less often in company. The Whinchat prefers rough ground near cultivation, and a favourite haunt is a railway-line, whilst the Stonechat is more frequent on coastal brows, though after a period of mild winters small groups appear in inland localities such as the Surrey heaths. The male looks like a miniature in stained glass as he sits in clear view on a sprig of gorse, warmly coloured in brown and reddish buff, and with black head and contrasting white collar. The Whinchat is also a markedly buffish bird and sports a conspicuous pale eye-stripe offset by blackish cheeks. Their close relative the sprightly, white-rumped Wheatear used to be much commoner on heath and down than it is today; it is really a bird of coastal brows, rough hill-pastures and moors.

The gay, carmine-breasted Linnet, *Acanthis cannabina*, p. 398, is one of the regular small birds of heaths and commons, often nesting in loose colonies where there is an ample growth of gorse and hawthorn scrub. The Goldfinch, *Carduelis carduelis*, p. 398, with its red face and flashing yellow wing-patches, and its more varied metallic twittering song, is also found in such areas, especially if there is a good supply of thistles; but equally with the Linnet it is a farmland bird and 'charms' can often be seen too in orchards and large gardens. Another small finch found particularly on birch-clad commons is the Lesser redpoll, *Acanthis flammea*, but this streaky brown bird with its bright red forehead and pink-flushed breast is really a northern species and its numbers in the south fluctuate from year to year. It has a rippling trill which it constantly utters on the wing.

The Meadow pipit, *Anthus pratensis*, is not a meadow-bird; indeed, it is extremely scarce on any kind of farmland except rough hill-pastures, and in the lowlands is associated more often than not with salt-marshes and reclaimed coastal pastures. It attains a high density among the scattered hawthorn and gorse scrub of some of the chalk down country. Its attractive song, which reaches a climax as the bird parachutes from the sky, gives the lark strong opposition. Commons on sandy ground where birch trees grow have Tree pipits, *Anthus trivialis*, instead, a little larger and more brightly coloured and with pink, not yellowish, legs and bill, but with a rather similar but sweeter song uttered when flying from tree to tree.

Whether the scrub is hawthorn or birch, it is likely that the Willow warbler will be found there and Yellowhammer and Whitethroat are also characteristic of both kinds of environment. The chalk scrub is a good area for the loud repetitive song of the Lesser whitethroat, *Sylvia curruca*, saved from mediocrity only if you are close enough to hear the quiet warbling that accompanies it. The two whitethroats are similar in size, but the Lesser is the greyer bird and has no rufous in its wings, while the song is delivered from the heart of a bush and not in flight. The Whinchat is one of the scarcer summer visitors to this chalk scrub and the strange 'reel' of the Grasshopper warbler, *Locustella naevia*, is a prominent feature of bird-song at dusk and dawn. This elusive, striated brown bird is yet another of the heathland fraternity which has successfully invaded young forestry plantings in many parts of the country.

The Cuckoo, *Cuculus canorus*, p. 397, is attracted to any heathland where Meadow pipits breed for they are the chief host of this brood-parasite. This long-tailed bird is over a foot (30 cm.) long, blue-grey above and on the breast, with bold barring on the pale belly. It ranges widely over many kinds of habitat and nowadays is much commoner in Scottish hill-country than in the south. It finds dupes among other species such as Dunnock and Robin on farmland, and Reed warblers in the marshes. The advantages of brood-parasitism, a habit shared by nearly 80 different species in the world, not all of them cuckoos, are that it permits a greater output of eggs during the season, and emancipates the bird from the tiresome duties – to say nothing of the hazards – of the incubation and care of the young. An early student of Cuckoo behaviour, Edgar Chance,

showed that whilst a hen bird normally lays 12–15 eggs in the course of a season, careful 'human' preparation of fosterers' nests could step this production up to 20–25. On alighting at the nest the bird takes one of the pipit's eggs in her bill, lays her own directly into the clutch, and flies off with the stolen egg to a short distance, when she usually eats it.

The egg does not always resemble that of the foster-parent – Cuckoos do not produce pale blue eggs like Dunnocks, for instance – but in the case of the Meadow pipit the likeness is very good. Birds are said to belong to different 'gens' or groups victimizing different species, normally the one which reared them in the first place. For its first few hours of life the nestling Cuckoo has a very sensitive back and instinctively throws everything else with which it makes contact out of the nest; as it grows it fills the whole of the structure and the diminutive 'parents' often stand on its shoulders to cram food into its yellow mouth. The mysterious ability of this young bird, which has no contact with adult birds of its own kind, to migrate to Africa and return in spring is one of the marvels of migration. The Cuckoo's food is made up largely of the caterpillars of moths and butterflies, particularly the hairy ones which other birds seldom touch. In addition to the familiar name-call there is a loud bubbling or chuckling cry used by the female in flight, especially when being chased by one or more of the males on her territory.

What a wood contains in the way of birds is dependent on a number of factors, among which are its geographical situation, the species of trees, the age of the timber, the presence or absence of a shrub-layer, and the kind of management – if any. Basically it is a matter of food-supply, and the existence of a shrub-layer adds substantially to the potential of a wood in this respect, but the availability of nesting-sites, especially natural holes, is also important. From the viewpoint of British birds there is nothing better than oak, which supports a more abundant insect-life than any other tree, but although oak is the climax forest in our climate the tree is so slow-growing as to be quite uneconomic, so that most modern planting uses the rapidly growing but ornithologically less attractive conifers.

The B.T.O. 'Common Birds Census' returns for woodland of all kinds (including some wooded heaths and scrub habitats) show that Robin and Blackbird are the commonest birds, each with 11 per cent of the recorded territories. If pure woodland alone were considered the Robin, *Erithacus rubecula*, p. 400, would certainly have a commanding lead. It is hardly necessary to describe this familiar red-breasted bird, a great favourite because of its engaging tameness, and also because its sweet warbling song brings cheer to dull autumn and winter days. Even on farmland the Robin likes to be near trees, but the typical nesting-place is low down among brambles, thorn-bushes or other secondary growth. It was an excellent choice as Britain's 'national bird', since in no other country does it dominate the woods as it does here, being a rather shy and retiring species on the Continent.

Next in order of abundance, with 9 per cent each of the recorded territories, are Wren and Willow warbler which, like many other forest species, have also colonized farm hedgerows. The Willow warbler, *Phylloscopus trochilus*, p. 400, is under 5 inches (13 cm.) long and olive-green in plumage with some yellow beneath (particularly in young birds in autumn), and is unquestionably the most successful summer visitor to northern latitudes. The hillside birch woods of Scotland are alive with its sweet, descending song, and either this or the Chaffinch, *Fringilla coelebs*, p. 400, must be the most abundant bird in that country. The Chaffinch is a little larger and the male is more brightly coloured with his brick-red or pinkish underparts, slate-blue head and dark chestnut back; both sexes show a striking white wing-bar and white outer tail-feathers when they fly. The song-phrase, like that of the Willow warbler, is short and oft-repeated, but is more vigorous and the final emphatic flour-

ish is subject to more variation. The nest, usually in the fork of a tree, is mainly of mosses and lichens and is a paragon of neatness.

The Song thrush, *Turdus philomelos*, is another woodland bird which has spread far into the agricultural countryside. It has warm brown back and wings and the creamy-buff breast is liberally spotted with black. The well-known song consists of a series of short phrases each repeated three or four times, and the variety is so great and the tonal quality so good that it holds a deservedly high place among our song-birds. The larger Mistle thrush or Stormcock, *Turdus viscivorus*, is famed for singing in wild weather early in the year; its voice has great carrying power and the phrases are more flute-like, resembling more the Blackbird's song. Its length of 11 inches (28 cm,) makes the Mistle thrush a noticeably bigger bird than the Song thrush, and it is a greyer brown above, with larger breast-spots and a white margin to the tail. Usually, it builds high up in a tree-fork, whereas the Song thrush prefers shrubs and other secondary vegetation for its nest, and will even build on the ground.

An equally talented singer is the Nightingale, *Luscinia megarhynchos*, whose russet back, brightest on the tail, and greyish underside give the impression of a large warbler. After its arrival from Africa in May it frequently sings far into the night – a loud, impassioned performance introducing a great variety of rich, liquid notes, and many dramatic pauses and thrilling crescendos. It is extremely rare north and west of a line from the Humber to the Severn, and even within this region has declined in many places in recent years.

One of the larger and more attractive forest-birds is the Jay, *Garrulus glandarius*, p. 399. It is over a foot (30 cm.) long and a lovely vinaceous plumage is offset by black moustaches, a white black-tipped crest, and a startling bright blue patch narrowly barred with black in the wing. When it flies the white rump affords a striking contrast with the black tail. Birds communicate with explosive, shrill, raucous cries as they search the woods for acorns – which they have a habit of burying – beechmast and other fruits which form their main food, but they are not averse to taking the eggs and young of other birds.

Another handsome devourer of hard fruits is the Hawfinch, *Coccothraustes coccothraustes*, which has a very stout conical bill designed for the purpose, and a heavy looking head and thick neck to match. Despite its size, being nearly as big as a Starling, it is difficult to get a good view of the bright browns and greys which adorn its plumage, for it is one of the most secretive of woodland birds, usually keeping to the tops of the trees. The smaller Bullfinch, *Pyrrhula pyrrhula*, p. 398, is also rather elusive but the pair will often give themselves away by their soft, musical piping notes. Few birds are lovelier than the male with his clear grey mantle, black cap and rose-red underparts. The female is a much duller edition, and both show a conspicuous white rump when they take to the wing.

Some birds are particularly associated with the upper canopy of leaves, even though they may nest on or near the ground. Such is the Wood warbler, *Phylloscopus sibilatrix*, a small leaf-green bird with bright yellow throat and white belly. It is one of the delights of the sessile oak woods of the west and north, but not a typical bird of pedunculate oak in the south and east. It is often in beech, sweet chestnut and mixed woods where these satisfy its requirements of a thin shrub-layer and sparse ground-vegetation. Its song is a repetition of a high-pitched *pee* which starts rather slowly but quickly becomes a shivering trill. The nest is on the ground under dead bracken-fronds, bramble or heather.

The Chiffchaff, *Phylloscopus collybita*, is another lover of tall trees, but likes a well-developed shrub-layer beneath them. In Scotland, where it is scarce, it is most often found in woods with an undergrowth of rhododendron. It is slightly smaller than the

Wood warbler and the olive-green upper and buffy-yellow underparts make it a duller bird, and almost the twin of the Willow warbler, which however has pale brown and not black legs. The name Chiffchaff hints at the song, a variation on a two-note theme, and the earliest to be heard from our returning summer visitors in spring.

Most Chiffchaffs, and also Blackcaps, spend the winter in the Mediterranean Basin, but in some years a number of both species stay in England, the latter especially being attracted to bird-tables. The Blackcap, *Sylvia atricapilla*, is primarily a bird of the canopy, and its loud and richly varied song can be heard even in places where the undergrowth is sparse. Apart from the cap (brown in the female and young) the plumage is a combination of grey-brown above and creamy white below. The plain brown and white Garden warbler, *Sylvia borin*, is less interested in tall trees than in a luxuriant secondary layer and often occurs in well-grown scrub on heaths and commons. Its song is mellower and more hurried, the notes less clearly enunciated but equally rich and musical.

The Pied flycatcher, *Ficedula hypoleuca*, is mainly a western bird and its distribution follows pretty faithfully that of the sessile oak woods. The Spotted flycatcher, *Muscicapa striata*, on the other hand, attains its highest density in the ash woods of limestone districts, though it can be found in most open woods and is often a garden-bird. The flycatchers are about 5 inches (13 cm.) long, and the female Pied is olive-brown on the upper parts where her mate is black, and the flash of white in the wing as she flies suggests a hen Chaffinch. This species nests in holes in trees and will take readily to nesting-boxes. The grey-brown Spotted flycatcher likes to sit bolt upright on a favourite, exposed perch, to which it will return following its swift sallies in quest of flying insects. The small, compact nest is frequently built against a tree-trunk or in a creeper against the wall of a house.

A neighbour of the Pied flycatcher in the

sessile oak, and also frequent on the margins of beech and old mixed woods, is the Redstart, *Phoenicurus phoenicurus*, p. 400, another species which will use a nesting-box in default of a natural hole. It is a colourful bird with the breast, flanks, rump and restless tail bright chestnut, the mantle a soft grey, and the lower part of the face and throat black. The female is altogether duller and lacks the black. Also an inhabitant of these woods, though it extends far north into the Scottish birch and is attracted by almost any 'open' woodland, is the Tree pipit. Wood warbler, Pied flycatcher, Redstart and Tree pipit, though so characteristic of the forested parts of Wales and the Lakes, reach Ireland only as scarce migrants.

Four woodpeckers are known in British woods, though one, the Wryneck, *Jynx torquilla*, is aberrant in having a weak bill and soft tail-feathers, and in taking its insect food from leaves and twigs. The others delve into the bark with their strong pointed beaks and use their stiff tails for support as they climb up the tree-trunks. The Wryneck has a beautifully barred and vermiculated sandy-grey plumage and derives its name, and also the name Snake-bird, from the sinuous, almost hypnotic twisting and swaying of head and neck when it is handled or disturbed at its nest. The ringing *quee quee quee* call is alas very seldom heard now in the open woods, parks and orchards which were favoured haunts over much of the English countryside less than a century ago. Only a handful of pairs remain in Kent, though autumn migrants from Scandinavia are common in some years along the east coast.

The Green woodpecker, *Picus viridis*, with a length of over a foot (30 cm.), is twice the Wryneck's size, and has a bright red patch on the crown. It likes open woods, parks and big gardens and will feed on grassland well away from trees, especially if it can get a good supply of ants. The deeply undulating flight and far-carrying laughing cry are good hall-marks of identity. The Barred or Lesser Spotted woodpecker, *Dendrocopos minor*, p. 399, is hardly bigger than a sparrow and has

its black back barred transversely with white. It is absent from Scotland and northeast England but is otherwise a well-distributed if somewhat elusive species. The call is a loud, shrill *pee pee* and its drumming noise is like that of the Great Spotted woodpecker, *Dendrocopos major*, p. 399, though the 'roll' is faster in tempo and a little longer. The bigger bird is 9 inches (23 cm.) long and distinguished by its broad white shoulder-patches and reddish under tail-coverts; the male has a red mark on the hind-crown, lacking in his mate, while in young birds the crimson extends over the whole crown. This species has a more catholic choice of habitat than the others and is the only one found in coniferous woodland: it extends far north in Scotland, where it has advanced markedly like the Green woodpecker, in recent years, but neither this nor any other woodpecker nests in Ireland or the Isle of Man. In addition to a loud, sharp *tchwik* it advertises its presence by drumming with its bill against a bough, seeming to strike rapidly at the chosen spot and produce a throbbing 'roll'. The true woodpeckers bore their own nesting-holes in dead or dying trees but the Wryneck uses natural cavities and will take to nesting-boxes.

The Nuthatch, *Sitta europaea*, p. 400, suggests a small woodpecker with its strong bill and short tail, and its habit of moving jerkily up and down the tree-boles in quest of food, often descending head first, which woodpeckers never do. It nests in natural holes and the pair will reduce the size of the entrance for security's sake by plastering round it with mud. The bird is hardly 6 inches (15 cm.) long and has the head, back and tail blue-grey, with a thin but prominent black eye-stripe, and the underside chestnut. Nuthatches are normally easy to find in the early spring as they have a variety of high-pitched ringing calls, but they become strangely quiet after about mid May. The range of this handsome bird excludes Scotland and Ireland and much of northern England.

A closely related but unlike bird is the unobtrusive Treecreeper, *Certhia familiaris*, brown with black and buff striations above and satin-white below. It is slightly smaller than the Nuthatch and has a slender down-curved bill, a useful tool for prising hidden spiders and insects out of cavities in the bark. It has a variety of sibilant notes, uttered as it searches the boughs or spirals up a trunk before fluttering like a blown leaf to the foot of another tree. The usual nesting-place is behind a piece of peeling bark or in some cavity or fissure in the trunk.

Coal tit, *Parus ater*; it associates more with conifers, especially larch, pine and yew. It is the same size as the Blue tit and has the white cheeks bordered by a black crown and throat. The upper parts are grey-brown and the underparts white, only young birds showing any yellow. A white patch on the nape helps to distinguish it from the two other brown and white, black-capped tits, the Marsh, *Parus palustris*, and Willow, *Parus montanus*. These are so similar that a very

Tits, *left to right*, Coal; Willow; Marsh

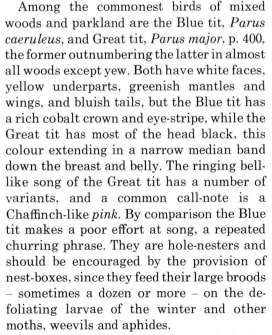

Among the commonest birds of mixed woods and parkland are the Blue tit, *Parus caeruleus*, and Great tit, *Parus major*, p. 400, the former outnumbering the latter in almost all woods except yew. Both have white faces, yellow underparts, greenish mantles and wings, and bluish tails, but the Blue tit has a rich cobalt crown and eye-stripe, while the Great tit has most of the head black, this colour extending in a narrow median band down the breast and belly. The ringing bell-like song of the Great tit has a number of variants, and a common call-note is a Chaffinch-like *pink*. By comparison the Blue tit makes a poor effort at song, a repeated churring phrase. They are hole-nesters and should be encouraged by the provision of nest-boxes, since they feed their large broods – sometimes a dozen or more – on the de-foliating larvae of the winter and other moths, weevils and aphides.

Less common in deciduous woods is the

good view is needed to tell them apart. The crown of the Marsh is glossy, that of the Willow 'matt', and the latter has a more prominent pale patch in the wing. Both have a note rather like the 'engaged' burr of a telephone, more realistic in the Willow, and interspersed with a *pit choo* note in the Marsh which is diagnostic. The songs of these other tits have less of the metallic quality of the Great tit's voice but are all clear repetitions of a basic note.

The Crested tit, *Parus cristatus*, has a black throat and black tips to his jaunty, pointed crest, and a white face; the species has a very restricted range within the old

Caledonian pine forest. The various kinds of tits join into mixed hunting-parties which roam the woods in the winter, often with Treecreepers and Goldcrests, *Regulus regulus*. The latter is our smallest British bird, 3 inches (7·6 cm.) long and quarter of an ounce (7 gm.) in weight: it is green with two white wing-bars, a dusky face and a bright orange-yellow crest. It is fonder of conifers than hardwoods and suspends its small nest from a side-branch, or may build in ivy, gorse or juniper. The song is an extremely high-pitched shivering trill.

The commonest owl in conifers (and the only one in Ireland and Man) is the Long-eared owl, *Asio otus*, p. 399, which stands over a foot (30 cm.) tall and gets its name from the erectile tufts above the staring facial discs with their bright orange-yellow eyes. It appropriates old nests of crows or hawks and its young hatch at intervals of about 48 hours, so that there is always a smallest and weakest member of the family who fails to survive in seasons when food is scarce.

The most magnificent bird of the pine

Capercaillies, cock above

woods is the Capercaillie, *Tetrao urogallus*, huge and dark-plumaged with a splendid rounded tail which the displaying bird raises and spreads almost vertically above his back as he struts to and fro in his chosen glade. The cock stands 3 feet (91 cm.) high and is slate-grey below with brown wings and a green-glossed band across the breast, but the mottled rufous-brown female is only two-thirds the size. The present stock is not native, but was introduced from Sweden in the 1840s, some 70 years after the Scottish Capercaillie had become extinct. Having a taste for the young shoots and buds of conifers it is unpopular among foresters. The Black grouse is also found in the pine woods, and its numbers have increased due to Forest in recent years. The Scottish cross-of Britain.

The same can be said of the Lesser redpoll and the golden and black Siskin, *Carduelis spinus*, an equally small finch which has colonized plantations in North Wales and from Northumberland south to the New Forest in recent years. The Scottish cross-bill, *Loxia pytyopsittacus*, however, has re-mained restricted to the old pine forest of the central Highlands. The Common crossbill, *Loxia curvirostra*, p. 400, makes irregular invasions from the continental spruce forests and following these influxes a number usually nest in conifer woods in England and Ireland, though only in a few places have such colonies become perma-nent. Crossbills are extremely entertaining birds and their loud communication-note, a sharp repeated *chink*, gives away their posi-tion in the trees, where they prodigally scatter the seeds as they cut them from the cones with their strong scissored mandibles. They are fond of descending to puddles and small pools to drink, when the variation in plumage can best be seen – pink males, green females, and heavily streaked brownish youngsters, the older among them showing a little patchy colour of one or other of the adult stages.

Some fine birds of prey are to be found in the woods, but they are scarcer now than formerly: as a group, they have always been persecuted in the interests of game-rearing. Goshawk, *Accipiter gentilis*, and Honey buzzard, *Pernis apivorus*, are extremely rare. Both are about 2 feet (51 cm.) long, though the male Goshawk is smaller than the fe-male, and will inhabit coniferous as well as deciduous woods. The Goshawk is a larger version of the Sparrowhawk, *Accipiter nisus*, and has the same round-winged, long-tailed silhouette. The male Sparrowhawk is greyer above and more rufous on the boldly barred underparts than the darker female, and both have bright yellow legs. Common and wide-spread in all kinds of woods down to the mid 1950s, the species has since vanished from many counties. The Red kite, *Milvus milvus*, p. 399, with its long forked tail and impressive soaring flight is confined to the sessile oak country of mid-Wales, where careful protec-tion over many years has enabled it to maintain a viable population. There and in most parts of the north and west that other broad-winged soarer the Buzzard is the commonest woodland predator, its numbers having recovered well from a temporary setback in the 1950s when myxomatosis removed the rabbits which formed its staple prey.

The Briton's ceaseless activity in the im-mediate vicinity of his home has done much to enrich the bird-life of town and suburb. His garden is really a small area of con-trolled scrub, providing in its hedges, fruit and ornamental trees, lawns, herbaceous plants and turned soil a medley of the ecotones or 'edge' habitats so attractive to birds. Suburbia is only one important aspect of the complex environment with which man has surrounded himself. In this techno-logical age sufficient warmth is generated in towns and cities to prove a real boon to birds in winter, and since man is also prodi-gal in supplying food, either accidentally or deliberately, bird mortality in towns is low. Predation by our $3\frac{1}{2}$ million cats does little to offset this important gain. Black-headed gulls, Mute swans, Mallards, Coots, Moorhens, Tufted and other ducks can find rivers and pools which hardly ever freeze, and where their welfare is assured by people who value their presence as an amenity.

The great boom in the Herring gull population has resulted in birds nesting on buildings, especially the flat roofs of factories, in and near seaside resorts where sewage outflows create a rich food-source. For a longer period those lesser gulls the Kittiwakes have been prone to exchange real cliffs for the window-embrasures of warehouse walls at certain North Sea ports, and only recently one such colony was established nine miles inland on the Tyne. Inland, Herring and Lesser Black-backed gulls live at the rubbish-dumps, jostling the Jackdaws and Carrion crows, and go to roost nightly on the reservoirs. Pied wagtails join the Starlings at the sprinkler-tanks, and like them roost socially on buildings and roadside trees – and even in greenhouses. There are many other situations which birds have learned to exploit in man's manufactured landscape. It is a dynamic process and the end of the story is not nearly in sight.

It would be interesting to know when the House sparrow, *Passer domesticus*, first entered Britain – it is now so dependent on man that its origins are obscure. It is not only much the commonest town-bird, but extends outwards into cultivated country, though relatively few build their untidy domed nests in field hedgerows. Corn forms a big percentage of its food, but it also takes injurious insects, and in urban areas is a great gleaner of scraps and offal. It is highly gregarious and yet often seems quarrelsome, especially in spring when a number of males display aggressively to one another for the benefit of an apparently disinterested female, lifting their tails and drooping their wings. It is indefatigably noisy, and although its varied chirpings can delight only the ear of another sparrow, this small chestnut and brown creature with its blue-grey cap and black bib has a presence which would be sorely missed if it were ever to

vanish from the city scene.

So commensal with man is the sparrow that its fortunes would seem to be well insulated against the adversities of ecological and climatic change. Yet its numbers decreased markedly in many towns earlier in the century when the horse and its nosebag gave way to the internal combustion engine. During the height of the climatic amelioration, however, it was prob-

House sparrows

ably as dynamic as any species, its total range expanding northwards in Europe with the spread of cultivation to northernmost Norway and the Faeroe Islands but not Iceland. In the same period it infiltrated most of the upland and west coast areas where it had previously been scarce or absent; and the demands of our exploding human population for new towns and suburbs, coupled with the current growth in barley production, should ensure it a bright future.

Equally a character of the city, though to many a less pleasant one on account of its truculent and greedy nature, is the Starling, *Sturnus vulgaris*. Probably it was originally an inhabitant of the sea-coast and inland cliffs, for there are well-defined races which have long been settled in this habitat in the Faeroe and Shetland Islands. It is also

Jackdaw

common in old woodland, but resorts there only to nest in holes, going to near-by fields and gardens to feed. The diet is extremely varied and includes much insect matter, as well as grain and fruit and the scraps it can wrangle for in the town streets. The adult is a portly black bird with highly glossed feathers and a noticeable throat-frill, bright yellow beak and short legs, though in the winter the bill loses colour and the underparts are spangled with white. In their first plumage the young are mouse-brown with a paler belly. The song is a curious one made up of low whistles and wheezing noises and liberal borrowings from other birds, with imitations of such unlikely things as cats and bicycle-bells. Vast flocks enter London and many other cities, especially in the winter-time, to form large roosts high on public buildings or bridge-parapets, and the collective noun 'a murmuration' of Starlings is indeed apt in such situations.

There are other town-birds which were originally cliff-nesters and were therefore preadapted to nesting on the brick, stone and concrete precipices of the modern city. The first is the street pigeon, *Columba livia*, whose ancestor is the Rock dove which still haunts many coastal localities in the west and north. The feral bird has changed but little in size and form and omnivorous

tastes, but the plumage is exceedingly variable though generally some shade of grey with black wing-markings and an iridescent throat. Pigeon and sparrow penetrate to the heart of the noisiest centres of human activity such as dockyards and rail-way-stations, where so much food is available that they are able to breed virtually throughout the year.

The Jackdaw, *Corvus monedula*, is a small edition of the crow, with a white eye and pale grey nape; many have moved from the cliffs into seaside resorts where they compete very successfully with the gulls for food, and the bird is also common in many inland villages and small towns. Like the Starling, many resort to old woods where they can find tree-holes for nesting, and almost every big rookery has its Jackdaw associates.

The other cliff-haunting species, the House martin, *Delichon urbica*, p. 397, cannot tolerate too high a human density (though some nested in Inner London in 1966) and prefers the quieter towns and suburbs, where the overhanging eaves of houses are sometimes studded with its spherical mud nests. Their white rumps flash as the little birds sweep like dark blue arrow-heads over streets and gardens, uttering hard twittering calls. Where the suburbs encroach on open fields the Swallow may be found nesting in garages and outbuildings, and even house-porches.

Not in any way related to these two, although its aerial feeding habits are similar, is the somewhat larger dark brown scythe-winged Swift, *Apus apus*. Church-towers and other tall buildings provide good nest-ing-sites for the short time – late April to mid August – that the Swifts are here from their long winter sojourn in Africa. In the evening they caper madly in screaming groups among the houses, often breath-takingly low and fast. They have such a wonderful mastery of flight that they are able to ascend to great heights and roost on the wing. Coition takes place in the air, and indeed when birds come to the ground it is usually through accident, for they are so short-legged and long-winged that they have the utmost difficulty in taking off. A favourite feeding-area is high up among the entrapped insects at the top of the warm column of air immediately ahead of a thunderstorm, and off-duty or non-breeding birds will often travel hundreds of miles with such weather.

The two predatory birds which have taken well to the human scene are the Kestrel and Tawny owl, *Strix aluco*. The russet-backed falcon is not only a frequent sight hovering over motorway verges, or quietly watching for food from the telephone-wires along a railway-track, but is particularly attracted to big marshalling-yards, and has even penetrated to central London and other cities where ledges and window-sills afford nesting-sites and the big sparrow population a reservoir of food. The Tawny or Brown owl, a 15 inch (38 cm.) high round-headed bundle of soft feathers beautifully mottled with buff and narrowly streaked with black, has two plumage phases, some inclining to grey and others to rufous. Its hooting is a common spring sound after dark in town parks and churchyards, and although mice and young rats supply much of its food it will frequently take House sparrows from their communal roosts in evergreen bushes and ivy. The bird also has a penetratingly loud *ke-wik* call.

Two of our recent gains in man-made habitats are the Little Ringed plover on the gravel-pits and the Black redstart, *Phoenicurus ochruros*. The latter first nested on the south coast in the 1920s and has now colonized several seaside towns in the south and east, as well as a number of districts in London. It was first noticed in the City in the late years of the last war, haunting bombed sites on which willow-herb and other rank vegetation grew among the rubble; and although this proved to be an ephemeral habitat, the Black redstart has stayed on in dockland and other industrial places. It is almost the equal of the sparrow in size and like the common Redstart of the woods has a flashing red tail, but the rest of the plumage is either sooty grey with white wing-bars in mature males or dark brown in the females and young.

The well-grown suburban garden is a splendid haunt for a small, select group of song-birds and indeed a few species achieve a higher density there than they do in woodland. Such are the Blackbird and Song thrush, which nest and feed so close together in many gardens that the normal division of the breeding-area into individual territories seems hardly to apply. That two such closely related birds can together dominate this habitat is due to a striking difference in their food spectrum; the Blackbird's diet is largely berries and fruit, whereas the Song thrush takes many more earthworms and slugs, and has evolved a method of attacking snails by hammering their protective shells against a selected 'anvil' stone. Dunnock, Robin and Chaffinch are as common in gardens as in the woods, but the Wren and the commoner tits, Great and Blue, are scarcer. Linnets, Goldfinches and Tree sparrows are found sparingly, especially where there are orchards; the Bullfinch is a less welcome associate because of his attacks on buds in the spring and ripening fruit in autumn.

Parks and larger gardens, especially where poultry are kept, attract the newly arrived Collared dove, and in London especially the Woodpigeon and Jay are now well established. Mistle thrush and Greenfinch, *Carduelis chloris*, are at a higher density in parks than anywhere in the wild. Originally, the latter must have been a woodland edge species and it is unlikely to have become at all common until gardens and shrubberies were planted on a wide scale in the seventeenth and eighteenth centuries. The male is some 6 inches (15 cm.) long and olive-green, with a yellowish rump and bright yellow wing-bars and edges to the tail; he serenades his much duller mate with a drowsy, drawn-out, nasal *dweer*, but also has a simple twittering song.

In many parts of the country the Rook, which has colonies in churchyards and well-timbered grounds in the built-up zone, is becoming a more frequent visitor to the television aerial and the gardens below than was the case a few years ago, though it still shows some timidity when awaiting its chance to take food-scraps off the lawn. The Magpie is equally wary, and usually makes its visits, as do the winter Woodpigeons, in the early morning. Where conifers have been planted the small voices of Coal tits and Goldcrests can be heard, and Treecreepers have learned to fashion cosy beds for themselves in the soft red bark of introduced Californian redwood trees. Indeed, a number of forest species can now be reckoned as fringe birds of suburbia, and one may suppose that more will adapt to the extremely diversified surroundings of human homes within the next few decades. Man can do much to encourage them, by putting up nesting-boxes and planting berry-bearing trees and shrubs, and by offering a well-stocked bird-table with suet, peanuts and half-coconut, to tide the tits and others over the difficult winter months.

Vast numbers of Britain's breeding visitors leave our shores at the end of the summer and migrate to winter quarters in Africa. During August and September, especially along the east coast, innumerable birds of the same species, with the same ultimate destination, touch down on passage from the north European forests. Big 'falls' of Willow warblers, Pied flycatchers, Tree pipits, Whinchats, Redstarts and other small birds take place when the wind is easterly and fine anticyclonic weather prevails on the Continent.

Before this passage has died away the winter visitors are sweeping across the North Sea, for many birds which would find the harsh northern winter insupportable are able to survive in Britain's milder maritime climate. Some of our own Blackbirds, Song thrushes and others make room for them by moving from Scotland and northern England to Ireland and the West Country. This internal movement is strongly intensified when frost and snow threaten to

cut off the birds' food-supplies later on, and a glance at the brooding skies will then reveal a continuous traffic of Lapwings, Starlings, Skylarks, thrushes and finches as they head purposefully towards the south-west.

Many Blackbirds arrive from Scandinavia in October and November to spend the winter here, while hosts of Starlings come from eastern Europe and assemble in vast noisy roosts in woods and spinneys; but Scandinavian Robins, which have paler breasts than English ones, touch briefly on the east coast before passing on to Spain. Flocks of Fieldfares, *Turdus pilaris*, p. 426, and Redwings *Turdus iliacus*, p. 426, gather in the fields throughout the winter; the former are larger than Blackbirds and show a good deal of grey in their brown and chestnut plumage, and they fly with a harsh chattering note. The Redwings, who often feast on the haws, are more like Song thrushes but have a distinctive white eye-stripe and reddish under-wing and flanks. Often at night their thin *see-ip* communication-note can be heard overhead, even in towns above the hum of traffic noise. Sometimes these wintering thrushes form big roosts in evergreen cover, as also do Greenfinches, Chaffinches and Bramblings, *Fringilla montifringilla*, p. 426. The best place to see flocks of Bramblings is in the beech woods, where they search among the leaf litter on the bare floor for mast. The male is a particularly handsome bird in the spring with his inky head and terracotta body-plumage, and the species can be told at once from the Chaffinch by its white rump.

Some species are not true migrants in the sense of moving regularly between a summer and winter home. In some seasons, when conditions are particularly congenial, the population builds up to a level which the resources of the home area cannot support, and flocks move out in quest of new feeding-grounds. The best known of these so-called

(***from top to bottom***): **Long-tailed ducks, Goldeneyes, Smews, Black tern and White-fronted goose**

'irruption' or 'invasion' species are the Crossbill, Waxwing, Siskin, Redpoll and Great Spotted woodpecker. There were four successive Waxwing, *Bombycilla garrulus*, p. 426, invasions in the winters of 1956–60, and a particularly massive one in 1965–6; a few may come in other years, and this decorative creature is always worth looking for along the hedges, where a party will soon strip the rowans and hawthorns of their berries. They are very confiding and enter parks and gardens to feast at the cotoneaster, pyracantha and similar shrubs. They are Starling-size and their plumage is a pleasant blend of grey and pinkish brown, and features to look for are the pointed crest, yellow-banded black tail, black throat, and the curious red waxy tips to the white mid wing-feathers. In the winter of 1968–9 there was an invasion of Slender-billed nutcrackers, *Nucifraga caryocatactes*, from Siberia on a scale unparalleled in ornithological history; it is a Jackdaw-like bird but has a longer bill and white-spotted brown body-feathers. Other species whose numbers fluctuate from year to year are the Rough-legged buzzard, *Buteo lagopus*, distinguished from the common Buzzard by its white rump and the Great Grey shrike, *Lanius excubitor*. The latter, a fine grey and black bird 10 inches (25 cm.) long, with a long tail and conspicuous white bars in the wings, often returns to the same favourite field or heathland haunt in successive winters.

At the coast Skylarks, Meadow pipits, Snow buntings and Twites feed on the seeds of sea-rocket and sea meadow-grass, the buntings looking like big white butterflies at a distance as they change position on the saltings, their rippling twitter and tuneful *tee-oo* filling the air. The shores of both sides of the North Sea are their main haunt, though wintering birds can also be found among the purple moor-grass on the hills.

(**from left to right and top to bottom**): Knots, Bar-tailed godwits, Spotted redshanks, Turnstones, Redwing, Fieldfare, Waxwing and Brambling

Not infrequently the scarcer and more soberly clad Lapland buntings, *Calcarius lapponicus*, accompany them. By springtime, when their wine-coloured bills have changed to bright yellow, the males are resplendent with black heads and chestnut shawls. Small groups of Shorelarks, *Eremophila alpestris*, are a great delight if you can find them on the saltings; they too have tuneful calls, and their yellow and black faces, black gorget and pinkish-brown backs prevent confusion with any other species.

Farther out on the shore, among the muddy pools or at the edge of the sea, are the waders. Whatever their size they are usually some shade of mottled brown or grey above and whitish below. The biggest of all, with long downcurved bills, are betrayed by their voices as Curlews; often, in company with other waders, they feed and cry all night long if the state of the tide is favourable. Flocks of tall, slender Black-tailed godwits winter on the south coast and in Ireland; they are of Icelandic origin and have increased in numbers in recent years. The next in size, with long greenish legs and an upward tilt to their bills, are Bar-tailed godwits, *Limosa lapponica*, p. 426, a little smaller than the Oystercatchers who are often their companions. After them come the Golden and Grey plovers, *Charadrius squatarola*, and the slightly smaller Knots, *Calidris canutus*, p. 426. The two plovers look much alike at this season, round-headed and short-billed, with pale spangled upper parts, and the best distinction is the black patch which shows very clearly under the Grey plover's wings when he flies.

The Knots congregate in enormous flocks in favoured bays and estuaries, and it is a splendid sight to see the thousands of birds weaving like billowing smoke-clouds over the horizon, while close at hand one cannot but admire the incredible discipline which enables so many birds to perform such complicated aerial evolutions as one. Dunlins, which are smaller, flight in this way too where their numbers are large. With them on the mud-flats are usually a few of the

whiter Sanderlings, *Crocethia alba*, whose dabbling is even brisker as they scurry along on twinkling black legs. Stony and rocky shores attract the short-legged Turnstones, *Arenaria interpres*, p. 426, which are as big as Starlings and indeed are sometimes joined by them as they rummage among the seaweed and jetsam for small crustaceans, scattering debris to right and left and exposing food for their companions. Mostly they are brown and white birds of the year, but now and then the beautiful tortoiseshell plumage of an adult catches the eye. In flight they show a distinctive pattern of white on the wings and lower back suggesting a mini version of the Oystercatcher. Purple sandpipers, *Calidris maritima*, dark and portly, are sometimes in company with Turnstones, but are more often a law unto themselves, resting with studied composure on tide-washed rocks whilst the waves shower them with spray.

There are rarer waders to look for. The Curlew sandpiper, *Calidris testacea,* is a little larger than the Dunlin with which it often consorts, but has a more markedly downcurved bill and shows a clear white rump in flight. Like the Knot and the two godwits, late-staying birds in spring put on a most beautiful reddish plumage. The Little stint, *Calidris minuta,* is hardly bigger than a sparrow, and two pale buff stripes down the back make a good identification mark. On the saltings or in the wetter meadows where the alarmist Redshanks feed one can often flush a Jack snipe, *Lymnocryptes minimus,* smaller than his common relative and with a less wayward flight, and at close quarters showing a purple sheen on the back.

Out at sea the black Common scoters fly low above the waves. Long-tailed ducks, *Clangula hyemalis,* p. 425, ride the wave-crests easily, looking rather chubby and showing much white, especially the handsome male with his whip-lash tail. When migratory restlessness brings the birds together in spring and they fly around offshore, their chorus is reminiscent of the distant baying of a pack of hounds. Two dark headed ducks, the Scaup, *Aythya marila,* and Goldeneye, *Bucephala clangula,* p. 425, are often on the sea at this time; the former has a black front and vermiculated grey back, whilst the latter has completely white underparts and a florin-sized white spot behind the bill. One of the largest birds to be seen, over 30 inches (76 cm.) long, is the Great Northern diver, *Gavia immer,* grey-brown above and white beneath; and the smallest is the Little auk, though this is not often seen close inshore unless buffeted by stormy weather.

Farther out at sea the auks and Kittiwakes disperse in autumn and the skuas travel south, harrying them and the flocks of Arctic terns which are bound for Antarctic waters. In addition to the Arctic skuas there are the larger Pomarines, *Stercorarius pomarinus,* with their long, blunt, curiously twisted centre tail-feathers; and also the smallest and daintiest, the white-fronted Long-tailed skua, *Stercorarius longicaudus,* from the fells and tundra. Little gulls cross the North Sea from Denmark and Holland for a brief spell in the autumn, distinguishable from the ubiquitous Black-headed gulls (now without their brown hoods) by their very dark under-wings. Later on Glaucous gulls, *Larus hyperboreus,* and Iceland gulls, *Larus glaucoides,* as big as Great Black-backed and Herring gulls respectively, settle at odd places for a few months' stay. They are commonest in Shetland waters, and occurrences in the south are usually of the oatmeal-coloured young birds rather than adults, which lack the black wing-tips of the resident gulls. From an entirely opposite quarter the Mediterranean Black-headed gull, *Larus melanocephalus,* also without black in the wing, now comes regularly to winter haunts on the English coast.

At dawn and dusk the honking geese fly over the mud-flats and saltings in 'V' or 'W' formation, spilling out of the sky into the potato- and stubble-fields. There are several species – Grey-lags with their pale grey forewings, Pink-footed geese, *Anser brachyrhynchos,* with their dark heads and necks, and White-fronted geese, *Anser albifrons,* p. 425, with a white 'blaze' behind the bill and black bars across the breast. Often one kind greatly outnumbers another, depending on the locality; thus Whitefronts from Greenland are commonest in Ireland, central Wales and Dumfriesshire, while European Whitefronts haunt the Severn Estuary, and the best Pinkfoot haunts are on the east side of Scotland and England. The smaller 'black geese' are either Brents, *Branta bernicla,* or Barnacle geese, *Branta leucopsis*: of all geese the former, of which there are dark and pale breasted forms, is the most addicted to salt-water, feeding largely on eel-grass from the Wash south to the Thames. The Barnacle is slightly larger and darker above and has the black head and neck relieved by a cream-coloured face: its main haunts are in Ireland, southwest Scotland and the Hebrides.

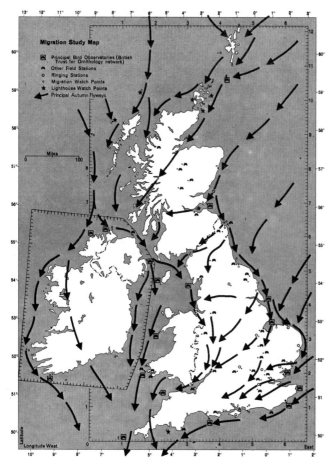

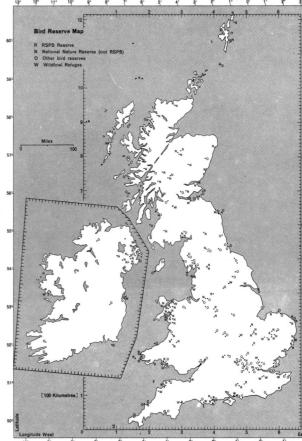

Migration Study Map of Britain and Ireland
As they operated in and around 1964 or 1965, the principal Bird Observatories, Field Study or Research Stations, Ringing Stations and Migration Watch Points are plotted, as are Lighthouses, from which intermittent observations have been made since pioneer times. Inland there is a rapidly developing system of Daily Bird Count Points (formerly known as Inland Observation Points), Radar-Stations from which birds are monitored and Field Study Centres from which DBCs are usually made. Note also that at many of the Bird Reserves in Britain and Ireland (map on right) regular migration logs are made. As the inland system is in the process of rapid change by trial and error, and is unlikely to stabilize for some time, the inland plots are confined here almost solely to the Field Study Centres and inland Research and Ringing Stations of some long standing. Some duck-ringing decoys now inactive are omitted. The map will be quite out of date in a few years, so rapidly does the sport and hobby of migration watching develop under the drive and leadership of the British Trust for Ornithology's Ringing and Migration Section.

Bird Reserve Map of Britain and Ireland
R. Reserves of the Royal Society for the Protection of Birds; a few are also National Nature Reserves.
N. Other National Nature Reserves which have importance as Bird Reserves; and Wild Bird Sanctuaries of the Government of Northern Ireland.
O. Other Reserves of the Society for the Promotion of Nature Reserves, County Naturalists' Trusts, the National Trust and other private charitable bodies, Local Authorities, Forestry Commission and private landowners which are declared to be Bird Reserves or have importance as such. Some such reserves have been deliberately omitted from the map for security reasons.
W. Wildfowl refuges (national, regional and private).

The meres and reservoirs are dotted with ducks from abroad, and although the species are usually the same as our own breeding birds, there are a few welcome additions, in particular the small white Smew, *Mergus albellus*, p. 425, and his red-capped mate. The London reservoirs are a good place to see these, the salmon-tinted Goosanders, the Goldeneye and other winter-visiting waterfowl. Drakes of all species come into full plumage quite early and courtship is a popular winter pastime, with the result that many drakes from northern Europe and Siberia find British-bred mates who 'abmigrate' with them in the spring. The Ouse Washes have their concentration of the slenderly built Bewick's swans, *Cygnus bewickii*, much smaller than either the Mute swan or the Whooper swan, *Cygnus cygnus*, which often occur together on inland waters, the latter looking more streamlined and having bright yellow, not orange, in the bill.

Britain's geographical situation at the edge of the Continent assures us of a wide variety of irregular vagrants, the rarities which so delight the bird-watcher on his visits to coastal bird observatories where migration is studied, and are indeed a potential source of interest on any estuarine mud-flat, marsh or inland reservoir. In addition to birds which breed at no great distance, like the Bluethroat, *Luscinia svecica*, and Barred warbler, *Sylvia nisoria*, there are some rarities which reach Britain annually from Siberia, occasionally in fair strength – like the Yellow-browed warbler, *Phylloscopus inornatus*, and Richard's pipit *Anthus novaeseelandiae*. Before the last war most of the new birds added to the British List had an eastern origin, but since the 1950s the majority of newcomers have originated more than 3,000 miles (4800 km.) in the opposite direction, on the North American continent. There is little doubt that these American vagrants are carried across the ocean by the strong westerly winds of the Atlantic depressions. At least 50 New World species have come to Britain in this period, and of these 27 had no previous record. They include a few gulls and waterfowl, and a score of song-birds, but they are predominantly waders.

In many respects the spring migration is more exciting than the fall; the welcome summer birds are returning for a new season, and they are in their finest dress. The excitements at that time are largely due to 'overshooting' when migrants, flying from Africa in fine clear weather, continue far beyond their normal range. Some, like the small Red-footed falcon, *Falco vespertinus*, and the Subalpine warbler, *Sylvia cantillans*, belong to south-east Europe; others, like the crested brown Hoopoe, *Upupa epops*, with barred wings, the green and yellow Golden oriole, *Oriolus oriolus*, the Jay-sized blue and chestnut Roller, *Coracias garrulus*, and the Swallow-like chestnut and green Bee-eater, *Merops apiaster*, with its striking yellow throat and long tail-streamers, have nesting-grounds as close as France and Germany. Indeed, a few of these strays, especially Hoopoe and Golden oriole, have tried to breed in the southern counties, sometimes successfully, though none has yet managed to establish a permanent footing in England.

Mammals

Mammals are the most advanced and most versatile of the eight classes in the Vertebrata or backboned animals, which is the more advanced of the two divisions of the Phylum Chordata, in turn the most advanced of the 22 phyla or major divisions into which the Animal Kingdom is divided. The other seven classes of vertebrates are the birds, reptiles, amphibians (frogs, toads and newts) and four groups of fishes. The mammals total some 4,500 species scattered all over the world, of which 53 terrestrial forms are established in the British Isles (13 of them introduced aliens) and 29, mostly whales and other cetaceans, have been recorded in British seas. The British Isles thus have one of the most impoverished faunas to be found in an area of comparable size anywhere in the world, even allowing for the handful of species which have become extinct in historic times. This is largely because they lie on the extreme western edge of the world's largest land mass, from which they were cut off by the waters of the Straits of Dover, around the middle of the sixth millennium B.C. only about 4,000–5,000 years after they had once more become inhabitable following the retreat of the ice at the end of the Ice Age.

Because of their terrestrial locomotion most mammals – bats excepted – spread much more slowly than birds, and so comparatively few species had time to colonize the British Isles before Great Britain became an island, as Ireland already had before it. A few of those which did make it, notably the brown bear, the lynx, the wolf, the aurochs or ancient wild ox of the European forests, the reindeer, the giant Irish elk and the beaver, were subsequently eliminated by the rise of man and his 'development', to use the modern euphemism, of the land for his own purposes. For much the most important mammal in Britain in the past 5,000 years or so has been man, and many early men also recolonized Britain as it became warmer after the Ice Age, at first crossing the dry land now beneath the North Sea and English Channel, but later showing their superior brain-power by taking to boats and often bringing other mammals with them. Since the final cutting of the Straits of Dover, man, bats, seals and whales are the only mammals which have been able to reach the British Isles unaided.

The extant British mammal fauna contains representatives of nine of the 19 Orders into which the Class Mammalia has been divided, viz. Insectivora (mole, hedgehog, shrews), Chiroptera (bats), Primates (man), Lagmorpha (rabbit, hares), Rodentia (rats, mice, voles, squirrels), Cetacea (whales, porpoises, dolphins), Carnivora (fox, badger, otter, wild cat, weasel, stoat, pine marten, polecat, mink), Pinnipedia (seals) and Artiodactyla (deer). During the million years of the Ice Age, which included both warm and cold spells that lasted for many thousands of years, two other Orders were represented in the wild British mammal fauna, the Proboscidea (elephants) and the Perissodactyla (horses, rhinoceroses).

Within the vertebrates the mammals are especially characterized by their superior intelligence, the hair on their bodies, and the nourishment of their young on milk secreted by the females in the mammary glands which give them their name. They are also noted for having adapted themselves to a wider range of habitats and so spread themselves over a larger proportion of the globe than any other animal group except the birds and insects. Some mammals have achieved this by a high degree of specialization, as the whales and seals by returning to the sea, the otter to a life in fresh water and the bats to bird-like flight and the use (also like certain groups of birds) of echo-location as a means of finding their way about and detecting their flying prey in the

Hedgehog

dark. Other mammals, notably the insectivores and primates, with man himself as the supreme example, have acquired the capacity to occupy almost any kind of habitat by retaining an unspecialized body. Because his brain has developed rather than his body man has been able to join seals – Eskimos in their kayaks – wild asses – bedouin and Kazakhs on their horses – and recently even bats – aviators – in their chosen habitats. It is his unspecialized body which leaves man in his curiously lowly position in the zoological classification, near the bottom between the bats and the sloths. Zoological classification proceeds from the primitive and unspecialized to the highly specialized. The classification of mammals starts with the very curious spiny anteater (*Echidna*) of Australia and ends with the sheep. This is far from meaning that the sheep is the most advanced or intelligent mammal, only that it belongs to the most physically specialized group, the Artiodactyla or even-toed hoofed mammals.

The eight families of Insectivora contain some 370 species, the great majority of them shrews, of which three families and six species, the hedgehog, mole and four shrews, occur in the British Isles today. The majority of insectivores are small, primitive and unspecialized animals with small brains, weak eyesight and clawed fingers and toes. Unlike the primates, their first digit is not opposable to the other four, so that in the words of Desmond Morris, 'insectivores are incapable of grasping anything awkward, either physically or mentally' and so are living reminders of the sort of animals from which the earliest mammal stocks developed.

The Hedgehog, *Erinaceus europaeus*, is one of the strangest mammals to be found anywhere in the world, and looks just as odd as the Australian spiny anteater or the Old World crested porcupine. Its most notable characteristic is its spiny coat, which enables it when rolled into a ball to defend itself against many of the predators it is likely to encounter, or has been

433

encountering in the million or so years prior to the invention of the internal combustion engine. For it is no defence against an advancing motorist to roll yourself up into a ball, and this is what many Hedgehogs still appear to do, with the result that large numbers of dead ones can be seen on our roads from spring to autumn. In fact they freeze first and most road casualties are first injured in the head. They could move out of the way because although Hedgehogs seem to be slow, almost lethargic, they usually proceed at a trot, they seldom walk, but often run fast even when not being pursued.

Hedgehogs are widely distributed throughout the mainlands of Great Britain and Ireland, and on many of the larger islands, such as Anglesey, Wight, Man, Skye and Shetland. They inhabit open wooded and bushy places, including larger gardens and town parks, and sometimes make an astonishingly loud noise by rubbing themselves against bushes. Many a suburban householder has gone out with a poker to confront a putative burglar advancing through the shrubbery only to find that this commotion among the dead leaves was being kicked up by an animal no more than 8–10 inches (20–25 cm.) long. They hibernate in the colder weather, but not in the full sense, like the Dormouse whose temperature drops right down for the whole winter, for Hedgehogs are sufficiently aware of changes in the weather to emerge sometimes on fine warm nights. For reasons as yet unknown they may also be active in snow and on frosty nights. A curious and not fully explained habit is the way they will anoint themselves with foam which is produced in the mouth after licking the skin of a dead toad, a piece of wood or any one of a wide variety of substances, including cigar stubs. The animal then places gobbets of the foam on its spines with its tongue.

Hedgehogs eat a wide variety of invertebrates, such as earthworms, snails, slugs and beetles, and have for centuries been accused by game-preservers of making a dead set at the eggs of game-birds, especially partridges. From what is known of the diet of the Hedgehog, however, it seems improbable that eggs constitute normally more than a very tiny fraction of it, although individuals can become regular egg-thieves. Nevertheless, the idea is well embedded in the consciousness of the more old-fashioned gamekeepers that all Hedgehogs are guilty, so that pathetic Hedgehog corpses can still be seen swaying on their gibbets.

Young Hedgehogs may be born any time from May to October, with a gestation period of 31–32 days, in a nest at the bottom of a hedge or thicket. Their eyes open at about 14 days and a week later they may leave the nest.

Many mammals are rarely seen because they are nocturnal, but the Mole, *Talpa europaea*, which is only partly nocturnal in its activity, is so for another reason, that it lives underground. But if the Mole itself is rarely seen the evidences of its underground activity, the so-called 'molehills', are the most obvious features of wild mammalian life to be seen on an average country walk. Moles spend their lives in an extensive system of underground burrows, which they excavate themselves, either just below the surface, showing as a ridge – and known as a 'surface run' or 1–2 feet (30·5–61 cm.) down when they push out the surplus earth at the surface, making molehills. Each branching system of burrows belongs to a single Mole, and may extend from the 30–40 yards (27·4–36·8 m.) of the average female to the 50–150 yards (45·7–137·2 m.) of the more adventurous males. They may also use main tunnels or 'highways' and mole-catchers may trap a dozen in a short while at one point. In the spring males often make a long straight tunnel into the burrow system of the nearest female. The tunnels themselves are little more than $1\frac{1}{2}$ inches (3·8 cm.) in diameter. Chambers, oval and about 10 inches (25 cm.) long, provided with a nest of dry grass or leaves, are associated with the network. Sometimes these chambers are beneath the outsize molehills known to naturalists as 'fortresses', a name which is now abandoned because it expresses an erroneous idea.

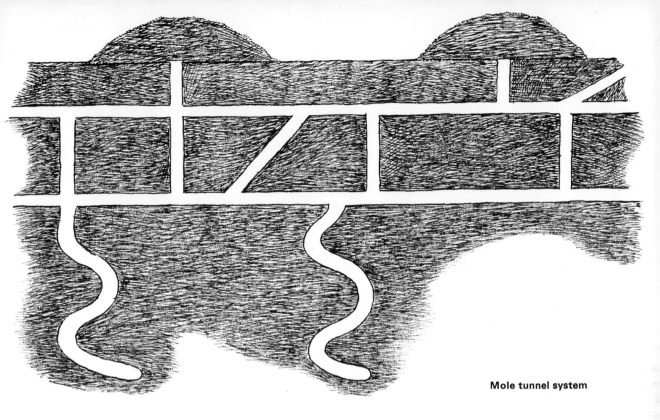

Mole tunnel system

Many are anything up to 2 feet (61 cm.) below the surface.

Moles are very distinctive little animals, rather oblong-looking with their narrow snout, tiny tail and flat hand-like front feet. These feet are highly specialized for the Mole's lifework of excavation. The Mole's soft grey-brown fur was once sufficiently highly prized by the fur trade for country-men to make a large part of their living from trapping Moles, but in recent years the price offered has not been sufficiently tempting, so that a substantial increase in the Mole population has followed the falling off in human predation. Since too many molehills are a great hindrance to the farmer, resort has unfortunately been had to poisoning, using strychnine. The farmer's main objec-tions to them are that they disturb seedlings, of wheat, for example, and throw up stones on their molehills that blunt the cutting-edges of farm implements. Humanitarians wish that some equally effective means of control-ling Moles could be found, because not only is the use of strychnine extremely cruel, but this last loophole enables large quantities of this deadly poison to escape into the countryside for probably illicit use on other so-called 'pests'. It was recently discovered that enough strychnine had been issued for Mole control in one Welsh county to kill every Mole in Wales, and doubtless every crow as well.

Moles are widespread throughout Great Britain and occur on many of the offshore islands, such as Anglesey, Wight, Skye and Mull, having been introduced to the last-named more than 100 years ago. From Ireland, the Isle of Man, and most of the Scottish islands, it is, however, absent. Moles are found especially in farmland, grassland and woodland, though showing a great preference for broad-leaved over coniferous woods. The distribution of Moles is closely linked with that of earthworms and both are found in the greatest numbers in fertile and, especially, damp soil. This is why they are apt to be numerous in gardens. Their food consists almost entirely of earthworms and various insect grubs, together with some slugs, snails, centipedes and millipedes.

Their diet of earthworms leads people, who

Mole

believe earthworms are of the greatest value in the maintenance of the structure and fertility of the soil, to consider that Moles need controlling. However, this is a very short-sighted view, for Moles are no more harmful to worms than any other predator is to its prey, the two having evolved together. Moles are now known to store earthworms when these are very abundant, biting off the head end so that the worm still remains alive but cannot escape readily: as many as 470 worms have been found in a single such store. To do this the Mole bites off the tip of the head end and twists the worm into a knot. Experiments have shown a decapitated worm will not untie itself as long as it is in the dark, and will not seek to escape until it has regrown its head. Should the Mole not come back to its store for several days the worms regenerate the missing part and disperse.

The breeding season is short. Courtship occurs in February and March, the young are born about a month after mating and leave the nest some five weeks later. They are able to breed when they are about a year old.

Shrews (Soricidae) are small and mouse-like yet resemble Moles, with the same tapering snout and dark greyish velvety fur. They are largely insectivorous but may be carnivorous also, readily eating carrion. They inhabit the ground layer, bustling about among the dead leaves and grass stems, and in burrows, including those of Moles and small rodents, just below the surface. Shrews are restlessly active, and have an extremely high rate of metabolism. They must constantly keep finding food to stoke themselves up. It was at one time thought that they died of shock when captured, but it is now realized that they usually die of starvation, from their captors not knowing how much and how often they need to be fed. They alternate feeding and sleeping every three hours throughout the day and night, and die of starvation if left without food for more than two to three hours. Shrews are short-lived, living not much more than a year, and dead shrews are a familiar sight in the countryside in early autumn. They have just dropped dead of old age, and they do so even with plenty of food around. Shrew flesh is distasteful to many mammals, which is one reason why so many dead shrews are seen lying about killed by cats, but owls eat them, so do buzzards.

Four species of shrew inhabit the British Isles, or five if the Channel Islands are included. Three of these belong to the sub-family Soricinae or red-toothed shrews of the genera *Sorex* and *Neomys*, whose teeth are conspicuously tipped red. The other two belong to the genus *Crocidura* in the sub-family Crocidurinae or white-toothed shrews.

The Common shrew, *Sorex araneus*, is the commonest over most of Great Britain, but is absent from Ireland. It inhabits some off-shore islands, such as Anglesey, Arran, Skye and Wight, but not Man, Scilly, Lundy and most of the Scottish islands. Though larger than the Pigmy shrew, about 3 inches (7·6 cm.) long, it can always be identified by its tail being usually half the length of the head and body combined and never more than two-thirds. A proportion of Common shrews have white ear-tufts. Common shrews occur where-ever there is thick ground-cover of grass or other herbage from sea-level to quite high on

mountains. They are sometimes very noisy, uttering repeated very high-pitched squeaks. Their food consists mainly of insects, es-pecially beetles, and other small inverte-brates found in such situations, but also of carrion, such as dead shrews. They also eat seeds, and captive shrews die if not allowed a small amount of cereal.

Common shrews begin to breed in March and April, the gestation period being from two to three weeks, and may have up to four or five litters in a season. The young develop slowly, their eyes not opening till nearly three weeks old, just before they are weaned. Common shrews are among the most short-lived of all mammals, dying between August and October of the year after they are born, with the result that all shrews which survive the winter are young of the previous year.

The Pigmy shrew, *Sorex minutus*, is the smallest British mammal, at 2¼ inches (5·7 cm.), and can readily be distinguished from the Common shrew by its tail, which is always at least two-thirds the length of the head and body combined, and is both relatively and absolutely longer, stouter and hairier than the Common shrew. Unlike the Common shrew, the Pigmy shrew never has white ear-tufts. It is scarcer but more widespread than the Common shrew, occurring in Ireland and on most offshore islands except Scilly and Shetland. Its habitat, however, is very similar, although it appears to ascend about

Common shrew and Pigmy shrew (*right*)

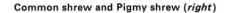

Scilly shrew

found in woodland at some distance from water. In north Berkshire, for instance, Tawny owls, with territories two miles from water, have been found, from the bones contained in their regurgitated pellets, to have eaten the occasional Water shrew. Water shrews not only swim well but have been seen walking along the water-bed like a dipper. Their diet includes land and aquatic insects, freshwater shrimps, earthworms, small fish and frogs as well as carrion. Fishing interests have accused it of eating fish-spawn, and no doubt it does occasionally, but it seems unlikely that this can have any great effect on fish stocks.

The nests of Water shrews are usually made in a burrow in a stream-bank, and the breeding-season lasts from April to the autumn, with two litters. Gestation takes some 24 days, the young leaving the nest after five or six weeks.

The only shrew inhabiting the Scilly

Water shrew

1,000 feet (305 m.) higher up mountains, to the very summit of Ben Nevis, for instance. Food, voice and breeding-season also appear to be substantially like those of the Common shrew.

The Water shrew, *Neomys fodiens*, is the largest shrew found in the British Isles, reaching nearly 4 inches (10·2 cm.) in length. In general appearance it is like that of the other shrews, but with a usually darker, almost black back, and its underside may be anything from white to almost black. A distinctive feature is the keel of hairs on the underside of the tail, which acts as a rudder, and the fringes of hairs on the toes. The Water shrew is virtually confined to the mainland of Great Britain, being absent from Ireland and almost all the offshore islands except Anglesey and some of the larger Inner Hebrides. Although normally seen near water it is especially fond of clear running streams and cress beds, but is not infrequently

Isles, *Crocidura suaveolens*, is known, for good reason, as the Scilly shrew. It is a representative of the sub-family of white-toothed shrews, which is widespread across Europe and Asia as far east as Japan. Three inches (7·6 cm.) in length, it differs from the Common and Pigmy shrews in its white teeth, more conspicuous ears and the white hairs on its tail. Next to nothing is known about its habits in the Scillies, despite its being widespread on all the larger and some of the smaller islands. It also occurs on Jersey and Sark in the Channel Islands, but the three other main islands Guernsey, Alderney and Herm are occupied by the closely related and slightly larger Musk shrew, *Crocidura russula*. A curious habit of both these species is caravanning, in which the young shrews follow their mother in single file, each holding on to the tail or fur of the one in front, the foremost gripping the mother's fur.

The bats (Chiroptera) form one of the most distinctive mammal groups, being the only one adapted to powered flight, though some mammals, in other parts of the world, have become adept at gliding. Bats have achieved this conquest of an unusual element for mammals by a striking development of the forelimb into a membrane-covered wing. Having evolved from the same stock as the insectivores, bats are predominantly – the British species wholly – insectivorous.

Their adaptation to flight has enabled them to exploit a source of food not available to the land-bound insectivores, flying insects. Moths, beetles and other winged insects which fly at dusk or by night are the principal prey of British bats, but spiders and some unwinged insects are also taken, and some winged insects captured at rest. For instance, Michael Blackmore, the leading expert on British bats, has seen Greater Horseshoe bats coming down into the grass to take Dor beetles that were feeding on cow dung, while the Long-eared bat regularly picks insects off leaves and bark. The proverbial blindness of bats is as erroneous as most proverbs which derive from the efforts of medieval moralists at mass communication. Ever since the Italian scientist Spallanzani's experiments in 1794, it has been known that bats have a remarkable ability to avoid obstacles in the dark, due, not to any specially good night vision, but to echo-location. This was not proved until nearly 140 years after Spallanzani, by the Dutch scientist Sven Dijkgraaf.

Bats not only use this technique, as do certain birds, notably the swiftlets of South-East Asia, to avoid obstacles in the dark, but more importantly to home on to their flying prey. They emit immensely high-pitched squeaks (which are of course not the squeaks that younger human beings can hear), each lasting for 1/500 of a second, at rates which vary from ten a second when they are at rest to as many as 200 a second when they are in hot pursuit of prey. When the echo bounces back on to them, aided in the case of the Horseshoe bats by their curious nose-leaves, they are guided in the same way that they would be if the insect had been buzzing.

The most important factor in bat ecology, after the presence of an abundance of winged insect food, is the existence in the neighbourhood of safe roosting-places. Winged insects are largely confined to the months from spring to autumn, and as our bats do not migrate they are obliged to find a safe place to hibernate during the cold weather when food is scarce or non-existent. Bats are found mainly in wooded country, or at any rate in areas with many scattered trees. Natural bat-roosts are in caves which in summer are often forsaken for tree-holes. In Britain there have been for centuries a great many more buildings than caves, and bats have learned to roost in these; not just in the traditional belfry. They are not complete hibernators like the Dormouse, and can sometimes be seen on the wing in winter when the air temperature at night is 50 °F. (10 °C.) or more. The presence of water is another valuable element in a good bat habitat, because this is also the habitat of so many flying insects.

Bats mate in the autumn, the sperm being

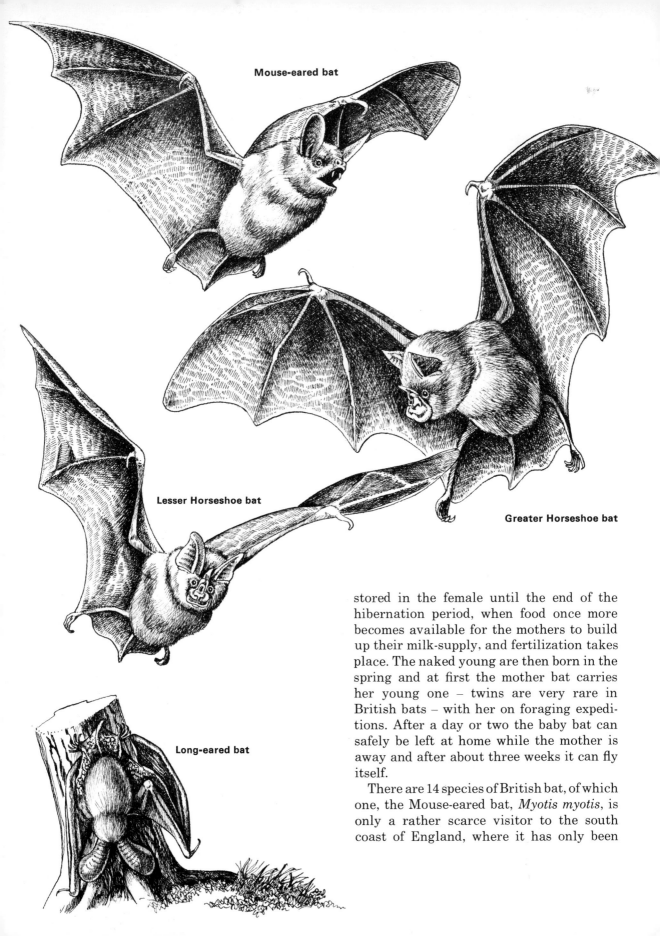

Mouse-eared bat

Greater Horseshoe bat

Lesser Horseshoe bat

Long-eared bat

stored in the female until the end of the hibernation period, when food once more becomes available for the mothers to build up their milk-supply, and fertilization takes place. The naked young are then born in the spring and at first the mother bat carries her young one – twins are very rare in British bats – with her on foraging expeditions. After a day or two the baby bat can safely be left at home while the mother is away and after about three weeks it can fly itself.

There are 14 species of British bat, of which one, the Mouse-eared bat, *Myotis myotis*, is only a rather scarce visitor to the south coast of England, where it has only been

Grey Long-eared bat

spicuously long ears. The largest is the rare Mouse-eared bat previously mentioned. Much the commonest and most widespread is the Long-eared bat, *Plecotus auritus*, with ears around $1\frac{1}{2}$ inches (3·8 cm.) long, which roosts in buildings, caves and trees and is one of the bats most likely to be seen about on a warm winter's day. Only as recently as 1964 did naturalists discover the presence in parts of southern England of a very closely related and similar species, the Grey Long-eared bat, *Plecotus austriacus*, with darker fur on the face, whose identification is a matter for museum experts. The remaining long-eared bat is the fairly large Bechstein's bat, *Myotis bechsteini*, whose ears extend well beyond its nose when they are laid flat forward. It is a very local species, confined to southern and western England from Sussex and Somerset to Shropshire.

Besides the Greater Horseshoe and Mouse-eared bats, two other large British bats have forearms of 2 inches (5·1 cm.) or more, and a wingspan of around 13–15 inches (33–38·1 cm.), the Noctule and the Serotine. The Noctule, *Nyctalus noctula*, has bright golden-brown fur and is one of the earliest bats to emerge, often before sunset; a strong flyer, it often dives steeply after its prey. It is

known regularly since 1956. It is larger than any other British bat, with a wingspan nearly up to $17\frac{3}{4}$ inches (45 cm.). The identification of British bats in the field is an extremely difficult exercise even for experts, and not merely because they are usually only seen in the dusk. In the hand, however, some species are fairly easy, notably the two Horseshoe bats with their extraordinary nose-leaves and no tragus (earlet).

The Greater Horseshoe bat, *Rhinolophus ferrum-equinum*, is one of our three large breeding bats, with a forearm more than 2 inches (5·1 cm.) long, and is confined to the southern half of England and Wales. The Lesser Horseshoe bat, *Rhinolophus hipposideros*, has a forearm not reaching $1\frac{1}{2}$ inches (3·8 cm.) in length. Its habitats extend further north in England and Wales and it is also found in the west of Ireland. Both the Horseshoe bats roost exclusively in caves or buildings. They hang upside down with their wings folded round them, unlike the vesper bats, which crouch against the wall of their roosting-place in a huddled posture.

The four most distinctive of the 12 British vesper bats, which comprise the remainder of the British bat fauna, are those with con-

Noctule

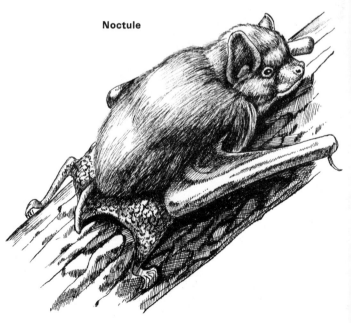

Bechstein's bat and Serotine (*top*)

it is broad. The Serotine also has the last two vertebrae of the tail projecting beyond the membrane which joins the tail to the hind feet.

In the next size group downwards we have already mentioned the Lesser Horseshoe and Bechstein's; there are two more, Leisler's and the Barbastelle. Leisler's bat, *Nyctalus leisleri*, is slightly smaller than the Noctule, readily distinguished in the hand by its broad-tipped tragus; it is locally but widely distributed over England north to Yorkshire,

Barbastelle

common over most of England and Wales, thinning out northwards into Scotland as far as the Moray Firth. The Serotine, *Eptesicus serotinus*, on the other hand, is largely confined to the districts south of the Thames, especially in the east, but extends as far north as Suffolk and Cambridgeshire. In the hand the two can be distinguished by the tragus of the Noctule being broadest at the tip, whereas the Serotine's, like those of most of our other vesper bats, is longer than

and is not uncommon in Ireland, where the Noctule is unknown. The Barbastelle, *Barbastella barbastellus*, with one of those names that make zoological nomenclature a laughing-stock, is best distinguished from all our other vesper bats except the two Long-eared bats by the fact that its ears are joined at the base. A rather local species, it is scattered over England and Wales north to the Lake District.

We now come to a group of three small bats, which are at the lower edge of the size-range of the rather variable Lesser Horse-

Leisler's bat

Hares: Brown, *top*; Blue in winter coat, *left centre*, and in summer coat, *right*; Irish, *bottom*

Daubenton's bat

Natterer's bat

Whiskered bat

shoe, that is, with a wingspan of 10–11 inches (25·4–27·9 cm.), the Whiskered, Natterer's and Daubenton's bats. Natterer's bat, *Myotis nattereri*, is identified by the fringe of hairs along the interfemoral membrane which joins the two hind feet to the tail: it is widespread in the British Isles, though completely absent from the northern half of Scotland. The Whiskered bat, *Myotis mystacinus*, is also widespread, but is rare in both Scotland and East Anglia, whereas Daubenton's bat, *Myotis daubentoni*, is found everywhere except, apparently, South Wales. The two can be separated by the fact that the calcar, a piece of cartilage that extends along the interfemoral membrane from each foot, extends half-way towards the tail in the Whiskered but two-thirds of the way in Daubenton's. Daubenton's bat is especially fond of feeding over water, and has been

called the Water bat, but plenty of other bats also feed over water, so this is an unsafe guide. The smallest British bat, the Pipistrelle, *Pipistrellus pipistrellus*, with its forearm little more than an inch (2·5 cm.) long

Squirrels: Grey in summer coat, *top left*, and winter coat, *right*; Red in summer coat, *bottom left*, and winter coat, *right*

445

Pipistrelle

and a wingspan of 8 inches (20·3 cm.), is also the commonest and most widespread, being found throughout the British Isles.

Until comparatively recently the rabbits and hares were included among the rodents, from which they differ structurally mainly in their teeth, especially in having two pairs of upper incisors, a smaller pair behind the larger pair. However, it has now been decided that they evolved contemporaneously with the rodents, and should be treated as a separate Order, the Lagomorpha. The British species of rabbit and hare are all much larger than any of our native rodents, with long hind legs which they use to put on a great turn of speed in escaping from danger. Though sometimes seen in woods, they are mainly open-country animals, living above ground, and as such have had to develop acute senses of both hearing and smell to enable them to outwit their many enemies. There are two native species of hare and one introduced species of rabbit in the British Isles. All three are exclusively vegetarian, and have a curious habit of sometimes digesting their food twice by eating their own droppings. This is known as 'refection'. Some of the pellets are soft and only partially digested. These are swallowed again to complete the digestion.

The Rabbit, *Oryctolagus cuniculus*, is still, despite the devastating myxomatosis epidemic of the 1950s, one of the most familiar wild mammals of the countryside. Since 1956, when the disease had brought it very low indeed, it has recovered, though for-tunately nowhere to the plague proportions which prevailed in many districts prior to 1954. It comes as a surprise to many people to learn that the Rabbit is not a native British animal. It was in fact introduced from France at the end of the twelfth century – by the Plantagenets not by the Normans as many otherwise authoritative textbooks still state – and was at first kept closely guarded in warrens as a luxury meat for the nobility. The earliest documentary evidence of its presence in Britain relates to the Scilly Isles in 1176 and it was also kept very early on Lundy in the Bristol Channel and Skokholm and Skomer off Pembrokeshire. Just when it broke out into the countryside in general is not known, but the time of the Black Death in the mid fourteenth century, when labour became very scarce, is a plausible guess. Not until about 300 years later do we hear of it being in great abundance anywhere in Britain, and parts of Scotland were not colonized until little more than a century ago.

Rabbits are smaller than hares, with shorter hind legs, shorter ears and greyer fur with no black tips to the ears. They are common in all types of open country, both cultivated and uncultivated, though not very high on mountains, and can also be seen in woods. Unlike hares they sleep and breed mainly underground, constructing for themselves elaborate systems of burrows; on marine islands they have probably substantially affected the distribution of such sea-birds as puffins and shearwaters, which take over their burrows. Rabbits eat many wild plants, and all too many cultivated ones for the peace of mind of the farmer and gardener, but there are certain plants which they will not eat, such as elder, ragwort and hound's-tongue, and these therefore remain the characteristic flora around their warrens. The young especially are a favourite prey of many of our predatory birds and mammals, such as the buzzard, fox, badger and stoat, all of which thus deserve better of the farmer than the persecution which is all too often their lot.

Young rabbits may be born at any time of the year, but the great majority appear in the first half. The does often excavate special short breeding-burrows away from the main warren, which they seal up after their visits to feed the young. The gestation period is 28 days and lactation ceases after about three weeks. Within three or four months the young are sexually mature and as does may become pregnant again within 12 hours of giving birth to a litter of up to seven, it is no wonder that the breeding of rabbits has become proverbial.

Unlike the Rabbit the Brown hare, *Lepus capensis*, p. 443, is a native of Britain, although since zoologists have recently decided that there is no fundamental difference between the hares of Africa and Europe, and the African hare was described first, our hare has recently acquired an African scientific name. Hares, though still widespread on the mainland of Great Britain, are not nearly so common as they appear to have been at the end of the last century, due no doubt largely to changes in farming practice. In Ireland, Man and various Scottish islands the Brown hare is both introduced and uncommon. Hares are even more animals of open country than rabbits, though on mountains the Brown hare does not go so high, being replaced by the smaller, shorter-eared Blue hare. Even so it is not unusual to flush a hare in woodland. Extraordinarily little is known about the diet of the hare, except that it has a regrettable taste for turnips and other farm crops and annoys the forester by gnawing the bark from trees. Brown hares are important sporting animals, being both shot and pursued on foot with beagles or harriers.

The habits of the Brown hare which have brought it into common speech in the phrase 'mad as a March hare', and so into English literature in the pages of *Alice in Wonderland*, are those associated with its spring courtship. Again, it is strange that so little is known about so common an animal, for the 'March hare' behaviour has never been scientifically studied, but many country people are familiar with the sight of two hares standing upright in a boxing posture, and generally gallivanting around. Even the exact breeding-season of hares in Britain is not known. They seem to breed the year round but the majority of young hares appear to be born between May and July. Hares sleep in thick grass or other vegetation in a 'form' and this is where the young hare is

Rabbit

left while its mother is away feeding. Unlike rabbits, young hares are born furred and with their eyes open, but they take eight months to reach sexual maturity and so do not breed in their first year.

The Blue or Mountain hare, *Lepus timidus*, p. 443, replaces the Brown hare on the mountains of the Scottish Highlands and in Ireland, and has been introduced with varying degrees of success on the hills of southern Scotland, northern England and North Wales. The Blue hare is smaller and more rabbit-like than the Brown hare, with shorter ears and blue-grey fur. In winter, especially in Scotland, it turns white, providing a better camouflage against the snow. Scottish Blue hares spend most of their time on mountain-slopes above 1,000 feet (about 300 m.), although they may come lower down in hard weather, but the Irish Blue hares, p. 443, in the absence of Brown hares, also occupy the normal low-ground habitats of the Brown hare in Great Britain. The main food of Scottish Blue hares is heather, but in summer they will also eat mountain grasses, sedges and other plants. On the whole the Blue hare is regarded with disfavour by those who have paid large sums for a share in a grouse-shooting beat, on the ground that it disturbs the expensively reared grouse when they are about to be shot. Breeding arrangements are similar to those of the Brown hare, except that Blue hares make shallow burrows for their greater protection in the harsher climate they have to endure.

There are more species of rodent (Rodentia) in the world than of any other Order of mammals, and probably more actual rodents than members of any other Order. The same applies in the British Isles, which have 15 resident species (of which 6 are aliens): 2 squirrels, 4 voles, 4 mice, 2 rats, 2 dormice and the introduced coypu. Rodents are highly specialized for gnawing grain, nuts, bark and other tough vegetable food, and at the same time, in a different part of their jaws, for grinding up what they have gnawed off. They will, however, also eat some animal food. Except for the squirrels which are diurnal, most rodents are either nocturnal or are active by day and night. Wood mice and Yellow-necks, for example, are mainly nocturnal, although they may sometimes be seen by day. Dormice are almost entirely nocturnal. Water voles have a four-hourly rhythm of activity throughout the 24 hours. Harvest mice and House mice have a three-hourly rhythm. The Common rat is active by day and by night.

At least one important rodent has become extinct in the British Isles in historic times, the Beaver, *Castor fiber*, which died out in England probably in Anglo-Saxon times, in Wales probably in the thirteenth century and in Scotland possibly not till the sixteenth century. Another more welcome extinction was the extermination in the 1930s of the North American Musk-rat, *Ondatra zibethica*, which had escaped from fur farms in the 1920s and threatened to do as much damage to river-banks in Britain as it has done in those parts of central Europe where it is now permanently established.

Squirrels are distinctive diurnal rodents which live mainly in trees. The Red squirrel, *Sciurus vulgaris*, p. 444, our only native species, has had a chequered history, having become virtually extinct in Scotland in the early nineteenth century and in the south-eastern half of England in the early twentieth century. In Scotland it recovered, thanks partly at least to reintroductions, but in southern and midland England it so far shows no sign of reconquering the territory it has lost to the introduced Grey squirrel. The Red squirrel is basically an inhabitant of coniferous woodland, so that it cannot easily compete with the Grey squirrel in the broad-leaved woods of England. There is some reason to suppose that the Red squirrel has entered into a long-term decline in England quite independently of the arrival of the Grey, which has taken the opportunity to occupy its vacated territory rather than actually driving it out. At present, to see a wild Red squirrel it is necessary to go to northern or south-west England, the Isle of Wight, Wales, Scotland or Ireland, though there are still a few in the conifer plantations of East Anglia. Squirrels are easily identified by their long bushy tail, and the Red also has characteristic ear-tufts, which are a better distinction than its chestnut-red fur because at times the Grey squirrel can also have a rather rufous appearance.

Red squirrels eat all kinds of seeds, buds and other vegetable food, enraging foresters by nipping off the leading shoots of their young trees as well as by stripping bark off more advanced ones. They also eat some animal food, including the eggs and young of birds, and are noted for their habit of storing nuts and other food against the winter. Squirrels do not hibernate; they merely lie up in the severest weather, but only for two or three days. Young are born at two peak periods, March and June, in a specially constructed nest, known as a 'drey', fairly high up in a tree. They are blind and hairless at first, and become sexually mature some time in the second half of their first year.

The North American Grey squirrel, *Sciurus carolinensis*, p. 444, has been one of the most successful mammals introduced into the British Isles, having colonized almost the whole of England, large parts of Wales, southern Scotland and Ireland, all from quite small beginnings around London and Woburn (Bedfordshire) in the 1890s, supplemented by equally misguided introductions in various other parts of England. Like other aliens the Grey squirrel has been much hated – by farmers, foresters, gardeners and game-preservers, and it must be admitted that it can be very destructive to their interests, especially those of the forester. Whether the Red squirrel, with its very similar habits, would not be equally hated, if it were still as widespread, is a moot point. Grey squirrels are almost confined to woodland and parkland, and are quite capable of colonizing town parks. They were, for instance, numerous in the Inner London parks until virtually exterminated by the authorities in the interests of the other wild-life. In most of its habits the Grey squirrel is very similar to the Red, which explains how it has been able to fill the vacant niche so successfully. It is, however, a bolder animal in the neighbourhood of human settlements, and is quite capable of entering kitchen windows incautiously left open and of pillaging any food left around, even going to the extent of gnawing away the lid of a plastic refuse bin to get at the contents.

Voles (Cricetidae) are blunt-muzzled mouse-like rodents, distinguished from the sharp-nosed mice and rats by their shorter furry ears and tails and by the triangular pattern on the grinding surfaces of their cheek-teeth. Four species are native to the British Isles, the Short-tailed, Orkney, Bank and Water voles. Much the commonest is the brown-coated Short-tailed vole, *Microtus agrestis*, best identified by the length of its tail, which is from one-third to one-quarter the length of its body. Short-tailed voles, also known as Field voles, are widespread on the mainland of Great Britain, absent from Ireland and the Isle of Man, but found on many Hebridean and other offshore islands. Among the islands from which it is absent are the Orkneys and Guernsey, where it is replaced by forms of the continental *Microtus arvalis*, which is both larger and deeper brown in colour. Breeding takes place more or less continuously from March right through to September or even later in the autumn, the young being born in a grass nest on or just below the ground. Gestation takes three weeks and weaning another fortnight or so. Young females become sexually mature almost immediately and mate when six weeks old. Hence the ability of any given population to mushroom into plague proportions when conditions are favourable.

The Bank vole, *Clethrionomys glareolus*, p. 453, is equally widespread but not so common, and has recently been discovered in Ireland. The Pembrokeshire island of Skomer has a special form of Bank vole which was for long regarded as a separate species. The Bank vole is distinguished from the Short-tailed vole by its more rufous fur and by its

449

long tail, which is about half the length of the head and body combined. It has a slightly different habitat, being more often found in woodland, scrub, hedgerows and other thick vegetation and will occasionally climb up to the tips of twigs after wild fruits. Its diet is much more mixed than that of the Short-tailed vole and includes a good deal of insect and other animal matter. Breeding habits are similar to the Short-tailed vole.

The Water vole, *Arvicola amphibius*, p. 453, sometimes erroneously called the Water rat, is much the largest of our four native voles, ranging up to 8 inches (20·3 cm.) in length with the tail up to 4½ inches (11·4 cm.) long. In the south all Water voles are warm brown, but in the Highlands of Scotland a great many melanic individuals occur. Water voles are most often seen in or near still or slow-moving fresh water, but do sometimes, and probably more often than is generally realized, visit or even live in areas at some distance from water. Their food consists predominantly of the stems and leaves of aquatic grasses, such as reeds, Flote-grass (Floating Sweet Grass) and other plants, but freshwater molluscs and other animal food are sometimes taken. The nest, of grass and rush stems, may be either in a short burrow or above ground in a reed- or sedge-bed and the breeding-season lasts from April to October. Fortunately, there are only a very few districts in Britain where the Water vole has developed the habit of deep-burrowing which in parts of Europe, where it also burrows into clamps of potatoes and root crops, has caused it to be treated as a pest.

Mice (Muridae), and rats which are zoologically only outsize mice, are easily told from voles by their sharp muzzles, their larger ears, longer, almost hairless tails and tuberculate cheek-teeth. There are four British species of mice, the native Wood, Yellow-necked and Harvest mice and the House mouse whose origins in the British Isles are obscure. The two rats, the Black and the Brown are both invaders from Asia during the past 800 years or so.

Commonest and most widespread of our native mice is the Wood mouse, *Apodemus sylvaticus*, p. 453, sometimes still known as the Long-tailed Field mouse, as distinct from what the naturalists used to call the Short-tailed Field mouse, but now known as the Short-tailed vole. The Wood mouse is a little larger than the average House mouse, its brown fur being tinged yellow, especially along the flanks and with a distinct yellowish spot on its chest and a tail as long as head and body combined. It is much the most widespread small rodent of the British Isles, occurring throughout both mainlands and on the majority of the offshore islands. Though pre-eminently a woodland species it extends into scrub, hedgerows and also, where Short-tailed voles happen to be absent, into more open country. The food of Wood mice is more mixed than that of Short-tailed voles and resembles the Bank vole's in containing a good deal of insect and other animal matter besides seeds, fruits and other plant elements. Being woodland animals their chief predator is the woodland owl, the Tawny owl. Wood mice sometimes seriously graze down early wheat and enrage the gardener by digging up his choice bulbs. Young Wood mice are born below ground, in grass nests, from April to October.

Widely scattered over the southern half of England and Wales, but rare in the north and not found in Scotland, are small populations of the Yellow-necked mouse, *Apodemus flavicollis*, p. 453. This mouse is distinctively larger and more brightly coloured than the Wood mouse and differs from it also in having the yellow chest spot enlarged into a broad chest band, although often this is not pronounced. Its tail, too, is usually longer than the head and body combined. In habits and breeding habits it is very similar to the Wood mouse, but it is more robust and active, often coming into houses for the winter, especially where apples or nuts are stored.

The Harvest mouse, *Micromys minutus*, p. 453, at 4½ inches (11·4 cm.), half of which is tail, is our smallest rodent. More rufous than any of our other mice, it used to be widespread and fairly common in the southern half of Great Britain, though always rare in Scotland. In recent years it has become much scarcer and is now rarely reported except in the south and east of England. Usually an animal of open country, especially corn-fields, tall grass and reed-beds, but some-times extending into hedgerows or even allotments on the edge of towns and villages, climbing about the plant stems with the aid of its long almost prehensile tail. In winter Harvest mice may go underground or resort to corn-ricks for shelter. Their diet, like that of other mice, combines animal and vegetable elements, but little or nothing is known about it in the wild. Its sleeping-nests are of shredded grass built at ground-level, but unlike our two other native mice, the Harvest mouse also builds a nest above ground. This is typically slung between cornstalks or stout stems of herbaceous plants, and is shaped like a cricket ball. The young are born in it, probably between April and October, but there has been virtually no observation on this point in Britain.

The House mouse, *Mus musculus*, p. 453, is a widespread, common and all too well known inhabitant of these islands which probably arrived here in the baggage of our Neolithic ancestors some 4,000 or 5,000 years ago. It can be distinguished from the Wood mouse by its greyer-brown fur. The Wood mouse has much whiter feet and under-parts and has no noticeable odour. Every-body knows that the House mouse inhabits houses and other buildings, but it is less well known that they are also common in the countryside, breeding in the banks and hedgerows and taking to the warm abun-dance of corn-ricks in the winter. In corn-ricks, of course, they eat grain, and in build-ings whatever human stores or scraps they can find. Nothing, however, is known of their diet out in the fields, though presumably it consists largely of the seeds of wild plants, especially grasses, probably with an ad-mixture of insect food and whatever comes as grist to the mill of this supreme oppor-tunist among small mammals. One reason for the House mouse's success is its capacity to breed all the year round in suitable sheltered habitats, such as attics or corn-ricks. There a female mouse may have as many as ten litters a year, because the food-

Common rat and Ship rat (*left*)

supply problem is solved for her. In the average town house food is a little harder to come by, so that the number of litters per year is more like five or six.

The Brown or Common rat, *Rattus norvegicus*, is undoubtedly our most disliked wild mammal, as it certainly is our most destructive one. It is also known as the Norway rat, from the belief that it was in timber boats from Norway that it originally invaded Britain in the first half of the eighteenth century. The Common rat is now ubiquitous in industrial and commercial buildings in towns, in sewers, and in and around farms, from which it spreads out into the surrounding countryside in spring and summer. Its rather blunt muzzle, paler brown fur and shorter and stouter tail distinguish it from the now uncommon Ship (Black) rat. It is in fact an altogether coarser looking animal, and one of the few capable of inspiring a feeling of revulsion even in a naturalist. Large sums of money have been spent on official campaigns to reduce the numbers of Common rats, which are especially destructive to grain and other stored products, but unfortunately no rat poison has yet been discovered which is both humane and effective. The widespread destruction of their potential predators, such as stoats and the larger birds of prey, in the supposed interests of game preservation, is probably one of the most important factors in the seemingly ineradicable occupation of the countryside by rats. Occasionally there are mass movements from some unfavourable environment and these can be dangerous to any other animal crossing their path, or even to man. In favourable habitats like corn-ricks Common rats, like House mice, breed almost throughout the year.

The Ship or Black rat, *Rattus rattus*, used to be known, in the eighteenth century when the Common rat was beginning its invasion, as the Old English rat, quite erroneously, for it was just as much an invader, having arrived in Britain in the Middle Ages, traditionally in the baggage of the returning Crusaders. It soon became almost as wide-spread as the Common rat is today, but with the arrival of this larger, tougher, more ruthless competitor, it has been driven back into the ports, the centre of London and a handful of islands (Lundy, the Channel Islands). In appearance it is slenderer than the Common rat, with fur varying from brown to black, a sharper muzzle and a longer tail. It is even more agile than the Common rat and more of a climber, being a tree-dwelling species in some parts of the world. It can be equally destructive to stored grain and other foodstuffs, as well as destroying and fouling materials.

The dormice (Muscardinidae) are intermediate between squirrels and voles in appearance, having blunt muzzles and long furry or bushy tails. There are two British species, the native Dormouse and the introduced and very local Fat dormouse. The Dormouse, *Muscardinus avellanarius*, p. 453, was once fairly common in the south of England, being found also in smaller numbers in the west and north, though not apparently in the Midlands or East Anglia. It has always been absent from Scotland and Ireland, at least in historic times. Nowadays the Dormouse ranks as a scarce and even rare animal even in the formerly favoured south, and it is not at all clear why, like the Harvest mouse, it should have decreased. The Dormouse has bright rufous-brown fur, but is best recognized by its long furry tail. It is a woodland animal, preferring woods with plenty of scrub and understory, especially of hazel, whose nut is one of its favourite foods. It also eats the fruits of other trees as well as bark and shoots. In summer the Dormouse builds itself a nest typically of honeysuckle bark with some grass in a tree, but will also occupy a nesting-box put up for

Dormice, Mice and Voles: Edible dormouse, *top left*, with Dormouse, *below*; Harvest mouse, *top right*, with Yellow-necked, *below*; House mouse, *centre left*, with Wood mouse, *right*; Water vole, *bottom left*, with Bank vole, *right*

Overleaf left page, Deer: Red, *top*; Roe, *centre*; Fallow, *bottom*; *and right page*, Sika, *top*; Muntjac, *centre*; Chinese water, *bottom*

birds. In winter it retires to a nest on or below the ground and enters into a period of true hibernation, being the only British mammal to do so. The animal becomes torpid and its metabolism is greatly slowed down so that its temperature falls to that of the surroundings. This habit of the Dormouse was well known to our ancestors, for its name means 'sleep-mouse', and contributed to making it one of the best-known animals in English literature, as a participant in the Mad Hatter's tea-party in *Alice in Wonderland*. Nothing is known of the breeding habits of the Dormouse in Britain, but on the Continent the breeding-season lasts from June to September or October.

The Edible or Fat dormouse, *Glis glis*, p. 453, so named because it was fattened and eaten by Roman epicures, is much larger than our native Dormouse at 14 inches (35·5 cm.) compared with $5\frac{1}{2}$ inches (14 cm.) total length and is also distinguished by its greyer fur and much bushier, more squirrel-like tail. Indeed, it is much more likely to be taken for a young Grey squirrel than for a Dormouse. It has a very restricted range, being confined to a triangle of country in the Chilterns around Amersham and Wendover, which it colonized after being released at Tring at the beginning of the century. The Fat dormouse has a habit of entering houses in the autumn, and performing antics in the roof which sound to the sufferers below as if 'a herd of small elephants' were capering about. Breeding takes place in holes rather than special nests, and hibernation in holes in the ground, trees or buildings.

The Coypu (*Myocastor coypus*) is an outsize rodent, $2\frac{1}{2}$ feet (76 cm.) long, weighing up to 20 lb (9 kg.), belonging to the South American family Capromyidae. It appears in the list of British mammals only because escapers from fur farms have established themselves so firmly in the Norfolk Broads that it is unlikely they will ever be exterminated. To the fur trade they are known as 'nutrias', and it was a fall in the price of nutria fur, leading to a relaxation of human trapping pressure that had been containing them, which probably led to the explosive outburst of Coypus a few years ago. An official trapping campaign was needed to prevent them from bursting out of East Anglia to occupy the rest of the country. Coypus are found almost exclusively in or near fresh water. When they become numerous they may not only alter the local habitat by severe grazing of marsh plants, but may start to harm farm crops and even, like Musk-rats, undermine river-banks with their burrows.

Even more than the bats the whales (Cetacea) are one of the most specialized groups of mammals, their anatomy, physiology and behaviour being adapted to an entirely aquatic life. Whereas marine birds, and even seals, have to come to land at least to lay their eggs or give birth to their young, whales perform every biological function at sea. They come to land only when driven by storms or for some other exceptional reason,

Carnivores: Pine marten, *top left*; Stoat, *top right*; Weasel, *upper centre*; Polecat, *lower centre*; North American mink, *bottom*

Coypu

when they are quite helpless, being incapable of terrestrial locomotion. Among their many interesting (fascinating to the zoologist) adaptations are the migration of the nostrils (except in the Sperm whale) to the top of the head well away from the snout; the disappearance of external ears and even more strikingly of the hind limbs; and the thick layer of blubber fat that both conserves heat and acts as a food-reserve. Whales are divided into two main groups, the whalebone whales, whose mouths are filled with baleen or whalebone, frayed at the edges which sieve out of the water the plankton on which these giant animals feed; and the toothed whales, which besides having teeth like other mammals differ from the whalebone whales in having one blowhole nostril instead of two. The toothed whales include

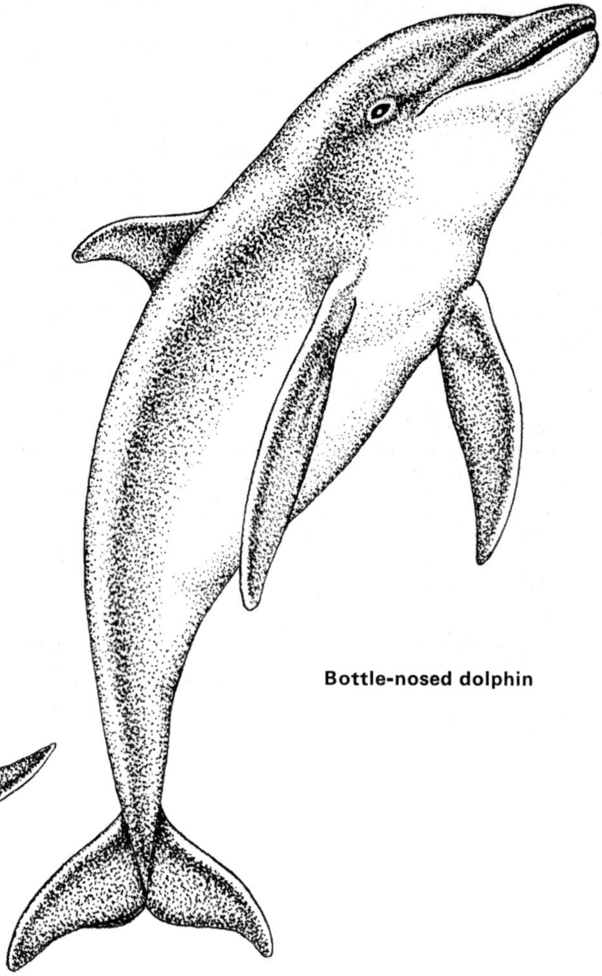

Bottle-nosed dolphin

Common porpoise

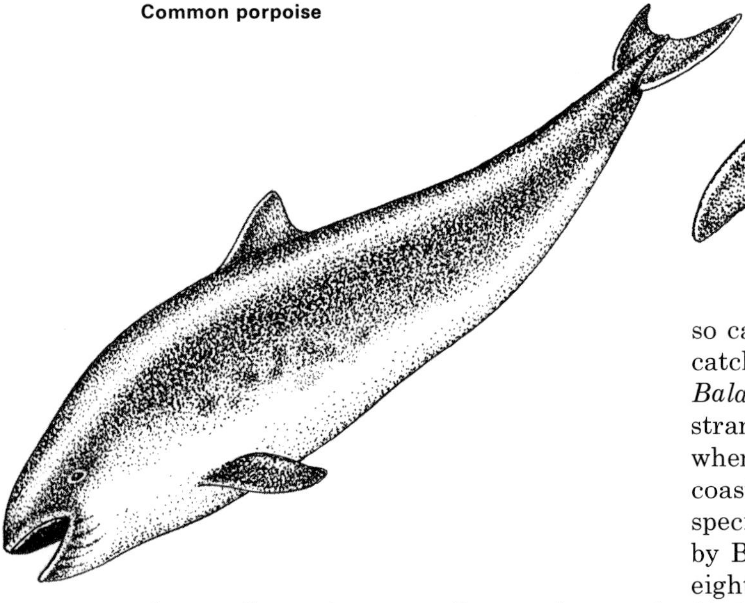

the small species we call porpoises and dolphins. Altogether 23 species of whale have been recorded in British waters, but 11 of these are rare visitors.

Two families of the Mysticeti or whalebone whales are represented in British waters, the one species of Balaenidae or Right whales and the five species of Balaenopteridae or Rorquals. Our only Right whale,

so called because it was the right whale to catch, the North Atlantic Right whale, *Balaena glacialis*, is now very rare, and no strandings have been recorded since 1913, when systematic recording on the British coasts began. It was the first of many whale species to be largely exterminated by man, by British and Basque whalers in the late eighteenth century. The Rorquals can be distinguished from the Right whales, among other characters, by the grooving on their throat and by the presence of a dorsal fin. They include four of the species which have been brought near to extinction by intemperate whaling in Antarctic seas, together with the small Lesser rorqual or Minke whale, *Balaenoptera acutorostrata*, distinguished by a white band across each flipper, which is

Common dolphin

not uncommonly stranded on most British coasts. The almost dumpy Humpback, *Megaptera novaeangliae*, and the giant Blue whale, *Balaenoptera musculus*, both of which are now completely protected from whaling, are now rare in British waters. The Blue whale is the largest animal which has ever existed, and can attain 100 feet (30 m.) in length and 120 tons (122 tonnes) in weight. The only slightly smaller Fin whale or Common rorqual, *Balaenoptera physalis*, of up to 80 feet (24·4 m.), 60 tons (61 tonnes), and the Sei whale, *Balaenoptera borealis*, the principal current subjects of Antarctic whaling, are not uncommonly seen at sea off our western coasts, though not often stranded.

The remaining 17 whales of British seas belong to the Odontoceti or toothed whales, and many of them are quite rare visitors. The most frequently seen offshore is the Common porpoise, *Phocena phocena*, a small whale about 6 feet (1·8 m.) long, feeding on fish, crustaceans and cuttlefish. It is generally black and white or grey, and can be recognized by its triangular dorsal fin and lack of any beak.

The second most frequent is the larger Bottle-nosed dolphin, *Tursiops truncatus*, which grows up to 12 feet (3·6 m.) and has a distinct beak or snout and a backward-curved dorsal fin. It sometimes ascends quite high up rivers, including the Thames as far up as Chiswick. This is one of the species most often trained to show its intelligence at seaquariums. About equal in abundance off our south and west coasts is the rather smaller Common dolphin, *Delphinus delphis*,

distinguishable by the pattern of dark and pale bands on its flanks. This is one of the small whales that play and gambol around the bows of yachts and other vessels. Another common dolphin, especially in the North Sea, is the very gregarious White-beaked dolphin, *Lagenorhynchus albirostris*, with a less prominent beak but coloured white; it is intermediate in size between the Common and Bottle-nosed dolphins. The closely related but less common White-sided dolphin, *Lagenorhynchus acutus*, is whiter on the flanks. Two 20–30 foot (6–9 m.) whales which are fairly common around parts of the British coasts are the 25–30 foot (7·6–9 m.) Bottle-nosed whale, *Hyperoodon ampullatus*, from the Arctic, with a short dorsal fin set well back, and the world-wide Killer whale or Grampus, *Orcinus orca*, with its strikingly tall dorsal fin of up to 6 feet (1·8 m.), which feeds on seals and porpoises. The Pilot whale, *Globicephala melaena*, was once common enough off the Orkneys and Shetlands to be hunted, but has become scarcer in recent years. It is very gregarious, going in schools of several hundreds.

The remainder of the toothed whales of British seas are recorded as stranded from time to time, but are unlikely to be seen, except by great good fortune, by the average

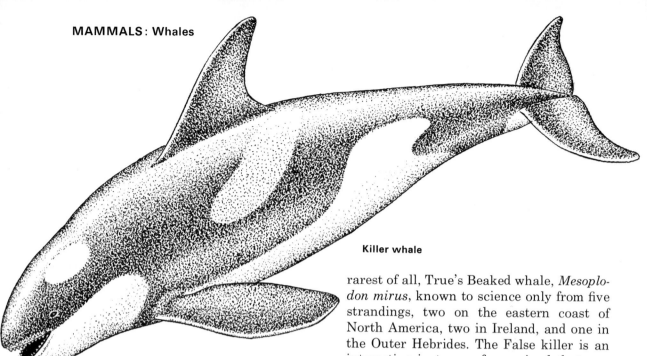

Killer whale

rarest of all, True's Beaked whale, *Mesoplodon mirus*, known to science only from five strandings, two on the eastern coast of North America, two in Ireland, and one in the Outer Hebrides. The False killer is an interesting instance of an animal that was known only from subfossil deposits until a school hurled itself on the shore of the Dornoch Firth in 1927. One of the very few strandings of the Narwhal in Britain took place in the Thames Estuary at Rainham, Essex, in February 1949.

cliff-watcher or sailing holiday-maker. They comprise the Sperm whale or Cachalot, *Physeter catodon*, a wanderer from tropical seas; the little-known Cuvier's and Sowerby's whales, *Ziphius cavirostris* and *Mesoplodon bidens*; two vagrants from the Arctic, the Beluga or White whale, *Delphinapterus leucas*, and the Narwhal, *Monodon monoceros*, with its extraordinary elongated tusk in the male; the gregarious False killer, *Pseudorca crassidens*, schools of which were stranded three times between 1927 and 1935, but not before or since; two little-known dolphins, Risso's *Grampus griseus*, and the Euphrosyne, *Stenella styx*; and,

The carnivores (Carnivora) are a large and successful group of mammals, in many ways the flesh-eating equivalents of the ungulates which are, however, the principal prey of the larger carnivores. Their special adaptations are in speed and agility for running down their prey, and in dentition, for tearing the flesh when caught. Some species specialize in feeding on carrion, while others eat a good deal of insect and even vegetable food. There

Pilot whale

are eight surviving British carnivores – Pine marten, Polecat, Stoat, Weasel (which all belong to the subfamily Mustelinae and are often referred to as mustelids), Fox, Badger, Otter and Wild cat – and one established alien, the North American Wild mink, also a mustelid. Two other carnivores have died out in historic times. The Brown bear, *Ursus arctos*, seems to have become extinct in Great Britain before the Norman Conquest, but the Wolf, *Canis lupus*, survived in England until around 1500, in Scotland until 1743, and in Ireland perhaps as late as the 1760s. The Lynx, too, may well have only narrowly escaped emerging into the historic period in northern Scotland. Many more and larger carnivores inhabited Britain at various times during the million years of the Ice Age and its warmer interglacials, among them species of hyaena, sabre-toothed cats (often wrongly called sabre-toothed tigers), lion and leopard. As long ago as 1823 Dean Buckland was writing about the enormous pile of hyaena bones in Kirkdale Cave in Yorkshire, now dated to about 100,000 years ago. The lion and leopard were probably still here within the last 40,000–50,000 years.

The Fox, *Vulpes vulpes*, which if we were not so insular we should call the Red Fox to distinguish it from the many fox species in other parts of the world, is, since the departure of the Wolf, our only surviving native member of the Dog Family (Canidae). In appearance it is too well known to need description, but it is worth remembering that any animal of the right size seen disappearing into the gloaming with a white tip to its tail is likely to be a fox. It is one of the few British mammals more likely to be heard than seen. Once its characteristic calls have been learned – the high-pitched and often triple bark, usually from the dog and the loud wail or scream, usually from the vixen, the presence of foxes in a district can easily be detected. To hear a fox's scream may be a most alarming experience. Roger Burrows, in his first-class field study of foxes in Gloucestershire, *Wild Fox*, describes one that sounded like a duck being slowly and painfully strangled, while I have myself heard one that suggested a human baby undergoing the same process.

Foxes inhabit all kinds of open and wooded country, both cultivated and uncultivated, including sea-cliffs and sand-dunes, and eat almost anything that moves that they can catch, from young rabbits to Dor beetles and earthworms, as well as carrion and wild fruits. They are of course unpopular with those chicken-farmers who do not shut up their fowls securely at night and with sheep-farmers who do not guard their sickly lambs. As a prime object of sporting activity the Fox has acquired a somewhat spurious popularity with some sections of the community. The number of fox-watchers, with a genuine interest in foxes, is still small but growing. Young foxes are born in an earth in the spring and first emerge from their earth when about three and a half weeks old. They play around it for another month or so before becoming independent. They are sexually mature in their first winter.

Feral domestic dogs are not infrequent in the wooded countryside of the south and there are records of feral bitches with pups.

The Pine marten, *Martes martes*, p. 456, so called to distinguish it from the continental Beech marten, is the second rarest British carnivore, being confined to the north-western parts of the Scottish Highlands, the Lake District, North Wales and parts of Ireland. During the last century it was much sought after for its fine fur, as well as being generally persecuted by gamekeepers, but since the Second World War it has shown a distinct tendency to increase and spread from its northern and western redoubts. The Pine marten is the largest British member of the Mustelinae or weasel-like animals, attaining a length of nearly 30 inches (76·2 cm.) of which a foot (30·5 cm.) is represented by its long bushy tail. In colour it is a warm rufous-brown, with a creamy-white patch on the throat. Although, as its name suggests, basically an inhabitant of northern conifer woods, the widespread destruction of these in Scotland in the eighteenth and nineteenth

461

centuries has driven the Pine marten out into the open rocky hillsides of Sutherland and elsewhere. The young are born in March and April in dens in rock crevices or occasionally in the large old nest of a magpie or other bird, even a squirrel's drey. On the Continent the marten is a great squirrel-eater, but, perhaps due to a shortage of Red squirrels, Scottish Pine martens seem to feed mainly on small rodents and small birds with an admixture of larger insects, carrion, berries and even fish.

Most people have seen a Stoat, *Mustela erminea*, p. 456, if only as a slim form dashing across the road in front of their car at night, since the Stoat is mainly nocturnal, but may not know how to distinguish it from a Weasel. In Ireland there is no confusion for only the Stoat is there, although it happens to be called a Weasel. The Stoat is considerably larger than the Weasel, attaining a length of 17–18 inches (43–45·7 cm.), of which $4\frac{1}{2}$ inches (11·4 cm.) is its tail, whose black tip

is a good point of distinction from the Weasel. Especially in the north – but sporadically elsewhere – the Stoat tends to assume a white coat in winter, like the Ptarmigan and Blue hare. These are the ermines whose skins were so sought after for the adornment of medieval monarchs and other dignitaries. The Stoat is widespread on the mainlands of the British Isles, and is present on many of the offshore islands, having been introduced, for instance, in the Shetlands. The form found on the Hebridean islands of Islay and Jura is classified as a separate sub-species, so it must have been there for a long time. Stoats are found in almost all kinds of both open and wooded countryside. They feed on whatever small animals and birds, from rabbit-size downwards, they can catch, as well as on larger insects and berries. The myxomatosis epidemic was a severe blow to the Stoats of England, for rabbits were their chief prey, and the Stoat has still not recovered its pre-

Fox

1954 numbers in many parts of the country. Stoats are widely and probably unjustifiably persecuted in the supposed interests of game preservation, for the harm they may do to artificially maintained game-bird stocks is surely outweighed by the important part they play in keeping down rats and rabbits in the countryside. Young Stoats are born in underground burrows in the spring.

The Weasel, *Mustela nivalis*, p. 456, is a small edition of the Stoat, distinguished from it by its shorter tail with no black tip; it also much less often turns white in winter. Weasels are confined to the mainland of Great Britain, where they are widespread and generally common, but are absent from all the offshore islands except Skye. In Ireland, as already mentioned, there are no true Weasels, but the Stoats are called weasels. Habitat, food and breeding arrangements are very similar to those of the Stoat, except that Weasels naturally prey on smaller animals. However, the fierce little Weasel is well able to tackle a rat twice its own size if need be, and certainly kills young rabbits. Persecution of the Weasel by game-keepers is even more misguided than the killing of Stoats, for they do a great deal to keep down the mice and voles in farming country.

The Polecat, *Mustela putorius*, p. 456, is the rarest British carnivore, being virtually confined to central Wales. Polecats reported from other parts of Wales and perhaps from Devon, Cornwall and the Lake District may also be genuine wild stock, but reports from any other part of the British Isles are almost certainly of escaped polecat-ferrets, the dark or parti-coloured form of the domestic ferret. The ferret is derived from the closely related Asiatic polecat. On Mull a population exclusively of feral polecat-ferrets may still exist. Polecats are smaller and usually darker than Pine martens, though in Wales reddish Polecats can be seen. They also have shorter and less bushy tails, and are whitish about the cheeks instead of on the throat. Polecats are basically woodland animals, but in Wales also inhabit bare open hillsides and sand-dunes. They are fairly ferocious predators, preying on rabbits, rodents, birds, fish, snakes and frogs, and have a bad reputation as raiders of hen-roosts. This, together with an alleged propensity for

Badger

game-birds and their eggs, brought on the Polecat the severe persecution in the nineteenth century which reduced it from a once widespread range to its present Welsh fastness. At one time Polecats were hunted with hounds in both Wales and the Lake District. Breeding habits are similar to those of other mustelids.

The North American mink, *Mustela vison*, p. 456, is the only alien carnivore which has succeeded in establishing itself in the British countryside in the past 2,000 years, having escaped from fur farms, mainly in the past 20 years. It is a fairly large mustelid, about the size of a Polecat, and since a wide variety of colour forms are found on fur farms may occur in colours strikingly different from the normal wild dark brown, relieved only by a small white spot on the chin. It is always found by fresh water, and feeds voraciously on fish, birds, Water voles, crayfish and insects, though records of food taken by feral mink in Britain are understandably biased towards such misdeeds as the raiding of fowl-houses. Little information is yet available about its adaptation to feral life in Britain, but there seems no doubt that before long it will be found on almost all river systems in the British mainland, and will no doubt have an important impact on both wildfowl and fish stocks.

The Badger, *Meles meles*, is probably the most popular wild animal in Britain today, and Badger-watchers rival deer-watchers as the most numerous group of wild mammal enthusiasts, except for the large number of people who put down bread and milk for the Hedgehog. There is a strong pressure for the Badger to be protected, in view of its generally harmless and beneficial nature. It is not easy for townsfolk to understand the degree of prejudice which still surrounds this attractive animal in the countryside and which is currently blocking any conservation moves. The grey Badger with its striking black and white head pattern, which has been adopted by the county naturalists' trust movement as its emblem, is one of the most easily identified of British mammals.

It is widespread on the mainlands of the British Isles, but absent from all islands except Anglesey and not really common in Scotland, especially the north. The Badger is predominantly a woodland animal, but is sometimes found on sea-cliffs and other open places. It lives underground, and its short but powerfully muscled legs are well adapted for excavating its sets. It is quite omnivorous, eating a wide range of both animal and vegetable food. It tends to be accused of many crimes, such as lamb and poultry killing, which are actually committed by foxes. This is partly due to an irrational wish to exculpate the fox, and all helps to create an unfortunate and quite unjustifiable prejudice against Badgers among many country people. Young Badgers are born in late winter and early spring, and the time of their first emergence from late April to early June is one of the peaks of the badger-watching year. At first the cubs play around the entrance to the set, but as the season advances they go off to forage for themselves.

Fewer non-anglers have probably seen a wild Otter, *Lutra lutra*, in Britain than have seen any of our other wild animals of comparable size. Indeed, most naturalists have to confess to never having seen one in the wild. The shyness of this attractive animal is understandable when its persecution by water-bailiffs and huntsmen is considered. Until the arrival of the mink, the Otter was an unmistakable waterside mammal, but now it needs to be distinguished from the invader by its larger size, paler coat, broader muzzle and longer, stouter tail. Otters live closely associated with water, both fresh and salt; they are found not only by rivers, streams and lakes, but also on the rocky western shores of Great Britain. In recent years many people have feared that Otters were becoming scarcer, and this has been confirmed by a survey undertaken by the Mammal Society and published in the May 1969 issue of *Oryx*, journal of the Fauna Preservation Society. Over a wide area of southern and eastern England Otters have declined in the past 20 years and as a result

Otter

the Masters of Otter-hounds Association has agreed to suspend or curtail hunting in these areas. In the west, however, especially on the west coast of Scotland, they continue to be quite numerous. The diet of the Otter is a contentious question, but it seems clear that they will eat what fish, crayfish or other aquatic animals they can get, and in trout streams and salmon rivers this will be trout or salmon, just as on streams where eels are plentiful it will be eels. However, most anglers are so pleased to have an occasional sight of an Otter that they are prepared to overlook its competition with them, and it is more than likely that Otters take more sick fish than healthy ones. Extraordinarily little is known about the breeding of Otters, except that it apparently goes on all the year round, making a close season impossible.

Since the demise of the Lynx, probably more than 2,000 years ago, the Wild cat, *Felis silvestris*, has been the only native British representative of the Cat Family Felidae. Being very shy and nocturnal, the Wild cat is very rarely seen, but any daylight glimpse of it will reveal a large upstanding tabby cat, and a really close view the fierce glare of its yellow eyes. It is more striped than the typical tabby cat, however, with a bushier blunt-ended tail marked with black rings. The Wild cat, once fairly widespread in Great Britain, was driven back into the Highlands of Scotland, mainly west of the Great Glen, by the same persecution that reduced both the Pine marten and the Polecat to tiny remnants of their former abundance. However, the relaxation of this pressure since the First World War has led to a spread back across the Great Glen, and the Wild cat is now not uncommon, though still very rarely seen by day, in many parts of the Highlands south to Argyll, Perth and Angus. Wild cats inhabit both wooded and open hill country, and are ferocious predators on many small mammals and birds up to the size

Wild cat

of a Blue hare and a Roe fawn. This, of course, is why the Wild cat was, and in many places still is, so unpopular with farmers and game-keepers. Fortunately, the foresters welcome its aid in controlling rodent pests, and this has helped it to re-establish itself. Young Wild cats are born in dens among rocks or old tree-stumps in May.

If a 'wild cat' is seen anywhere outside the Scottish Highlands, it is likely to be a feral domestic cat, populations of which exist, especially in wooded areas, in almost all parts of the British Isles, often quite un-suspected by the human inhabitants. Many feral cats become as ferocious as genuine Wild cats and there is good evidence that they increase considerably in size after going wild.

The Seals (Pinnipedia) are a very distinct group of mammals, which are sometimes regarded as specialized carnivores, but are on the whole better treated as of independent and equal status. They are highly adapted to an aquatic life, their limbs in particular being much reduced, but they have not car-ried their specialization to the same lengths as the whales. They must still come to land, sometimes for considerable periods each year, to give birth to their young. Both our breeding species belong to the Phocidae, the family of the true or hair seals, as distinct from the fur seals and sea-lions on the one hand and the walruses on the other. There are casual records of five northern or Arctic species stranded or hauled out on our shores, but few have been recorded in recent years, probably because these seals have become scarcer in the areas from which they wan-dered to Britain. The species concerned are the Ringed seal, *Pusa hispida*; Harp seal, *Pagophilus groenlandica*; Bearded seal, *Erig-nathus barbatus*; Hooded seal, *Cystophora cristata* and Walrus, *Odobenus rosmarus*. The Harp and Hood seals are the ones which get themselves into the news every spring when the Canadian seal harvest takes place. The Walrus now breeds nowhere nearer to Britain than Novaya Zemlya; formerly it bred on both Spitsbergen and Bear Island. Its rarity, largely due to human persecution, has earned it a place in the IUCN *Red Data Book* of species in danger of extinction.

The larger of our two species of seal is the Grey or Atlantic seal, *Halichoerus grypus*, old bulls attaining more than 7 feet (2·1 m.) in length. It differs from the smaller Common seal in its longer muzzle, flatter head and more widely separated nostril slits. Grey seals breed on our northern and western coasts, from the Scilly Isles northabout to the Farne Islands, and have recently shown signs of colonizing sandbanks off the coast of East Anglia. They are one of the more controversial of British mammals, on the one hand having a special protection Act of their own, and on the other being accused by fishermen of damage to both fish and nets. A recent attempt by the Ministry of Agriculture and Fisheries to control the large and growing colony of Grey seals on the Farnes generated an enormous amount of heat and publicity without achieving any great measure of control, the Ministry having failed to persuade public opinion of the need to take what many people regarded as an inhumane step. There is no doubt that seals eat a great deal of fish; what is in doubt is the degree to which they affect the actual catches of fishermen. Grey seals gather at their breeding-colonies, usually on fairly remote marine islands, late in the summer, when bulls take up their territories and capture as many cows as they can. The young are born mainly from September to the end of the year, after a gestation period of nearly 12 months. They do not become sexually mature until they are five to six years old.

The Common seal, *Phoca vitulina*, sometimes known as the Harbour seal, is generally smaller, rarely attaining more than 6 feet (1·8 m.) and can be distinguished by its shorter muzzle, and more domed head, giving it rather the outline of a puppy, and the fact that its nostril slits converge at their lower end, making a V. Common seals are distributed all round our coasts, on sand- and mudbanks in estuaries in the south as well as on rocky islets in the north. Their breeding arrangements are quite different; the young are born in June or July while their mother is briefly hauled out between tides and take to the water almost immediately. There are no territories, and the social organization is of the loosest. Mating takes place in the water soon after the breeding season, so that the gestation period is nearly as long as that of the Grey seal.

During the Ice Age several species of elephant and rhinoceros (Proboscidea and Perissodactyla) inhabited the British Isles

Grey seal

along with the rest of Europe, the best known being the Mammoth, *Mammuthus primigenius*, which actually survived in Siberia until about 10,000 B.C., the Straight-tusked elephant, *Elephas antiquus*, which stood 13 feet (3·9 m.) at the shoulder, and the Woolly rhinoceros, *Coelodonta antiquitatis*, which also survived in Europe until almost the end of the Ice Age, around· 12,000 years ago. Frozen or otherwise preserved specimens of both the Mammoth and the rhino have been found in Siberia, so that they are among the few fossil animals of whose actual appearance we have some direct knowledge. Wild horses, which non-zoologists always find it odd to be so closely related to the rhinos, survived much later still, and although the Tarpan or Woodland horse became extinct in 1918, the plains form, Przewalski's horse, *Equus przewalskii*, still survives in a remote part of the Mongolian-Chinese border. The horses that still live in semi-wild conditions in the New Forest in Hampshire, and on the hills in various parts of the north and west of the British Isles, including Dartmoor and Exmoor, are almost certainly all reintroductions by man rather than descendants of the original wild stocks.

The even-toed ungulates (Artiodactyla) include the cattle, deer, antelopes, hippos and pigs. They are a large and successful group, which have adapted themselves to grazing and browsing, sometimes going to extreme lengths, as the giraffes have done, to exploit the foliage of trees. At one time all the hoofed animals including the horses, tapirs and rhinos, were grouped together in one Order, the Ungulata. Modern zoologists, however, split them into two Orders, the horses, tapirs and rhinos in the Odd-toed Ungulates or Perissodactyla, with the axis of the limb passing through the middle of the third digit, and the rest in the Even-toed Ungulates or Artiodactyla with the axis passing between the third and fourth digits.

Several interesting extinct artiodactyls flourished in the British Isles during the Ice Age, some surviving down to historic times.

Among them were the Giant Irish elk, *Megaloceros giganteus*, which survived quite late, and has even been tentatively identified with the *schelch* of the *Nibelungenlied*; the Saiga antelope, *Saiga tatarica*, which has been present in the British Isles during the past 70,000 years; the Aurochs, or Forest ox, *Bos primigenius*, which did not become extinct in Europe until 1627; the Reindeer, *Rangifer tarandus*, which survived in Scotland until the twelfth century and has since been reintroduced into the Cairngorms; and the Wild boar, *Sus scrofa*, was being hunted ·in Windsor Great Park as late as 1617.

The wild artiodactyls of the British Isles today are almost all deer, together with the feral goat, *Capra hircus*, which is widespread in the hill districts of northern and western Britain.

Deer (Cervidae) belong to a group of ungulates characterized by the possession of antlers as distinct from the horns of antelopes and cattle. Except in the reindeer, only male deer have antlers, which are bony growths from the skull, shed each year and growing again to a larger size the next year. They are covered with a thin skin called velvet, which dies when the antlers are fully developed, and is frayed off by the deer on trees and bushes, an act which may cause some damage to young saplings.

There are two native species of deer in the British Isles, the Red and the Roe, one long-established alien, the Fallow, and three recent introductions, the Sika, Muntjac and Chinese Water deer, all from Asia.

The Red deer, *Cervus elaphus*, p. 454, our largest wild land mammal, is still widespread and locally common in the Highlands of Scotland, and has scattered outlying moorland populations in the Lake District, Exmoor, the Quantocks, and County Kerry, and woodland ones originating from escaped park deer in a number of English counties. It gets its name from the often rich rufous tint of its coat, and can be distinguished by its large size, $3\frac{1}{2}$ feet (106·7 cm.) at the shoulder in the stags, as the males are called, 3 feet (91·4 cm.) in the hinds or females, and by its large spreading antlers, not flattened or palmated. From September to November, the stags also have a shaggy mane on their neck. Stags are growing their antlers from April to mid July, fraying them until mid September, and then rutting until mid October. In late February and March they shed the old antlers and the cycle begins again. The calves, which are at first white-spotted, are born from mid May to mid June.

The Fallow deer, *Dama dama*, p. 454, is only a little smaller than the Red deer stag, standing 3 feet (91·4 cm.) at the shoulder. They are easily identified in summer both by their white-spotted pelage and by their flattened or palmated antlers, though a dark form which does not acquire spots in summer is also not uncommon. Fallow deer are widespread on the British mainland, but much more frequent in the woods of England than in those of the three other countries. It has been claimed that the Fallow deer is an original native of the British Isles, but this can be neither proved nor disproved. The odds are that it was introduced by the Romans. Certainly Fallow deer were well established in some English forests at the time of the Saxons, who are most unlikely to have introduced them. The great majority of the Fallow deer in our woods today, however, are descendants of escapers from deer-parks during the past century. Fallow bucks cast their antlers in April and May, grow their new ones in June and July, fray in August and early September, and rut mainly in late October. The does drop their fawns in July.

The Roe deer, *Capreolus capreolus*, p. 454, is appreciably smaller than either the Red or Fallow, standing only 2 feet (60·9 cm.) at the shoulder, and having much simpler and shorter antlers. It is bright rufous in colour in summer but much greyer in winter. Roe are widespread and locally frequent in England and Scotland, but absent from Ireland and Wales. In England they became virtually extinct at the end of the eighteenth century, but were reintroduced, and are now not uncommon south of the Thames and in the northern hills. The bucks cast their antlers in November and December, grow new ones in January and February, fray them in April and May, and rut in early August. The does drop their kids from late April to early June.

Most widespread of the three recent alien introductions is the Sika, *Cervus nippon*, p. 455, from east Asia, which looks like a small Red deer standing a little less than 3 feet (91·4 cm.) high at the shoulder, and combining Red-deer-type antlers with white spotting in summer similar to that of the Fallow. Feral herds of Sika, either escaped from deer-parks or deliberately released for hunting, are found in about a dozen English, seven Scottish and five Irish counties; the New Forest in Hampshire and Ribblesdale on the Yorkshire-Lancashire border holding two of the most famous herds. The yearly antler cycle of the Sika is similar to that of the Red, except that the antlers are not usually cast till April. The calves are born in June and July.

The Muntjac or Barking deer, *Muntiacus muntjak*, p. 455, from China is quite different from any of the previous four species, a small dog-like deer less than 2 feet (60·9 cm.) at the shoulder, and with distinct tusks, which originally escaped from Woburn Park in Bedfordshire, and is now spreading widely over southern England within 50–60 miles of its point of origin. It is a shy woodland animal, and may often be quite numerous in a district before anybody realizes its presence. Hardly anything is known of its seasonal cycle in Britain.

The Chinese Water deer, *Hydropotes inermis*, p. 455, is in a much earlier stage of establishing itself after escaping from Woburn and one or two other parks. It is most likely to be seen within 20–30 miles of Woburn or in Hampshire or Shropshire. It differs from the Muntjac in standing more uprightly, and having no antlers, but the male has tusks like the male Muntjac. In its homeland it is a swamp-loving deer and in Britain might be seen in either woods or reed-beds.

Index

Black and white illustration page numbers are in italics, thus *201;* colour picture references in bold, thus **201**

475

476

477

480